THEODORE H. WHITE
AT LARGE

The Making of the President 1956–1980

In Search of History

Breach of Faith: Fall of Richard Nixon

The Making of the President 1972

The Making of the President 1968

Caesar at the Rubicon (play)

The Making of the President 1964

The Making of the President 1960

The View From the Fortieth Floor (novel)

The Mountain Road (novel)

Fire in the Ashes

Stilwell Papers

Thunder Out of China

THEODORE H. WHITE
AT LARGE

The Best of His Magazine Writing, 1939–1986

**Edited and with an Introduction by
Edward T. Thompson**

A CORNELIA & MICHAEL BESSIE BOOK
PANTHEON BOOKS   NEW YORK

Library of Congress Cataloging-in-Publication Data

White, Theodore H. (Theodore Harold)
  Theodore White at large: the best of his magazine writing,
1939–1986/Theodore H. White.
      p.   cm.
  ISBN 0-679-41635-8
  1. United States—Politics and government—1945–   2. World politics—1945–   3. World War, 1939–1945.   I. Title.
E743.W55   1992
909.82—dc20   92-54108

Book design by Chris Welch
Manufactured in the United States of America
First Edition

THIS BOOK IS DEDICATED TO
TEDDY WHITE'S CHILDREN AND GRANDCHILDREN

CONTENTS

PUBLISHER'S NOTE
Why This Book?

When Teddy White died in 1986, I had been a close friend for forty years and his book publisher for the last twenty-five, starting with *The Making of the President, 1960*. That book had changed Teddy's life by turning him into a celebrity and, more seriously, labeling him as having changed the writing of American politics. As Ed Thompson writes in his Introduction to this book, that book effectively changed Teddy from a magazine writer who also produced books to a book writer who also turned out magazine articles.

That book also affected my life by greatly enhancing the existence of our then brand-new, small publishing house, Atheneum. And, since I had edited that very successful book with Teddy, it established a relationship between writer and publisher which carried through the next seven books he wrote.

Those books became the center of Teddy's life, but he continued to produce magazine articles frequently, except when he was concentrating on a book. Even then, he might do an article if it was related to the book or gave him an opportunity to learn more or express himself about something he thought important.

After he died, several of us cast about for a way of memorializing him. One was found in creating the annual Theodore H. White lecture and seminar at the Shorenstein Barone Center for Press and Public Policy in the Kennedy School at Harvard, now in its third year. This book represents another, and has been made possible by the cooperation of his children, Heyden White Rostow and David White, and, especially, the great skill of his good friend Edward T. Thompson, former Editor-In-Chief of *Reader's Digest*. In selecting, from more than a million words, the rich and varied contents of this book and in putting them in illuminating context, he has produced a book fully worthy to stand beside Teddy White's best.

SIMON MICHAEL BESSIE
1992

EDITOR'S INTRODUCTION

By Edward T. Thompson

Theodore H. White will no doubt be best remembered for his series of books on "The Making of the President" from 1960 to 1980. They profoundly affected American political writing, and their effects will be felt for decades.

But before and between books there were magazine articles—nearly two hundred of them from 1939 until White's death in 1986—seen by millions of people who didn't read any of the books. In them he developed and honed the techniques that made his books best-sellers. This volume brings you the best of those articles.

To read them together is to take a remarkable and fascinating—if selective—trip with a unique teacher through a half-century of our history. White's star qualities shine brightly throughout: superb reporting with an extraordinary grasp of history; a brilliant sense of emerging issues and political trends; a rich and graceful writing style that weaves key facts and statistics into fine cloth and engrosses the reader by playing on basic emotions. Yes, the prose might occasionally tend toward the purple; and one certainly wouldn't agree with his every message—he nearly *always* had a message; but virtu-

ally all of us in the business agree with David Maness, who was often his editor at both *Collier's* and *Life*, that in our time he has no peer as a political journalist.

Teddy's family and mine have been close for some forty years. In the 1960s we always spent Christmas Eve together, with Teddy, who was Jewish, leading carol singing after the goose was picked clean. By his rule—Teddy *loved* being at the center of everything—each person had to begin one carol, no exceptions, and never mind if you couldn't carry a tune; he wasn't all that good, either.

In those days I was a junior editor at *Reader's Digest*. As I moved up the ladder, I began to look for ideas that might entice Teddy to write for us. Nothing jelled until 1973, when it seemed obvious to me that Watergate was blowing up into something huge. With permission (if not enthusiasm) from my Editor-in-Chief, I suggested the topic to Teddy for a 15,000-word Special Feature. At first he was cool to the idea. He'd been in France on holiday, and the press there wasn't making much of Watergate. But he agreed to go to Washington for two weeks to investigate—and returned panting to do not a long article but a book. Fitting it in before his expected "Making of the President 1976" (which he ultimately decided not to write) was a problem, but he *had* to do this. Two years later the book was published jointly by Reader's Digest Press and Atheneum as *Breach of Faith: The Fall of Richard Nixon*.

Now Teddy and I were professional as well as social friends. Over the next decade, while I was Editor-in-Chief of the *Digest*, he and I worked on several article assignments for the magazine, and for me it was an altogether satisfying experience; for he was always the consummate, if stubborn, pro.

IN ASSESSING what made Teddy White a master journalist, and in particular a master *magazine* journalist, it is important to note that his magazine career had four main phases: China, 1939–45; Europe, 1948–54; domestic politics, 1954–60; domestic and world politics, 1960–86. The year 1960 was a watershed. Before that he was a magazine writer who also wrote books; after—with publication of *The Making of the President, 1960*—he was an author of books who also wrote magazine pieces. Before 1960 he wrote for many magazines, some of them definitely not prestigious; afterward he wrote almost exclusively for magazines that he felt had "clout," primarily *Life*, *The New York Times Magazine*, and *Reader's Digest*. And we were all eager to have him in our pages, for not only was he a hell of a storyteller, but he had clout of his own.

To help the reader cope with the diversity of White's magazine writing,

I've begun this book with two chapters of articles that span his entire career. After than, each chapter deals with one basic subject (China, Europe, Race Relations, etcetera), arranged chronologically; some subjects require more than one chapter. Notes at the beginning of each chapter will, I hope, put its contents into historical perspective and give some insight into what White was trying to achieve.

One mutual friend who read a large portion of this book worried that "it will be difficult for nonprofessionals reading Teddy's work today (repeat, today) to realize how superb were his instincts for political trends, his ability not only to root out important facts and statistics but to organize them into a coherent, powerful projection of what the future would hold." It seems to me, however, that a reader with an average knowledge of history will be able to see clearly enough the *zeitgeist* of White's articles without gratuitous help from an editor. And he or she will, I'm confident, come to the same conclusion that the above-mentioned friend and I do: Teddy White was both "a sage and a seer."

The Historian-Reporter

White was a dogged, highly intelligent reporter. But he was more than that. Thanks to a classics-based education, he was also an historian.

His public grammar school education in Boston was augmented, from the time he was eight, by two hours a day of Hebrew school where he not only learned the language, but became engrossed in the history of Judaism and the Bible; all his life he could quote extensively from the Bible, in Hebrew and in English. He went to high school at The Boston Public Latin School, perhaps the best public school in the United States at that time, where he thrived on history and acquired a reading knowledge of Latin, German, and French.

When he graduated in 1932, the depression was in full force, his father had recently died, and the family was very poor. He'd been accepted at Harvard, but without a scholarship there was no way he could go. For two years he sold newspapers on the city streets. Finally scholarship funds did appear, and in the fall of 1934 White matriculated at Harvard. There, almost by chance, he learned to speak and read Chinese. More importantly, he continued to develop a deep understanding and appreciation of history, thanks to a group of distinguished professors whom he later called "a colony of storytellers, held together by the belief that in their many stories they might find a truth."*
Thus when, soon after graduation, White turned to journalism, it seemed to him natural to underpin current facts

---

*Included were such notables as Arthur Schlesinger, Sr., and Paul Buck on American History; Crane Binton on the French Revolution; Abbot Payson Usher on Economic History; and John King Fairbank on China.

(which any reporter might have gleaned) with a matrix of history that gave his readers unique perspectives. Throughout his career, this ability more than anything else set him apart. Examples abound throughout this book.

Even as a "conventional" reporter, however, he was a cut above. He was burrowing, persistent, he read widely, went everywhere, tried to interview everyone who could possibly have information. By most measures, he overresearched his subjects. But that was essential to his method—he was, he was fond of saying, like a sieve: Only if you pour more than enough information through can you be certain that all the nuggets of truth will be caught. White was dedicated to the truth.

He had unquenchable curiosity, and an ability to master almost any subject. Consider the arcane world of social and economic statistics. Early on he discovered that under the surface of dreary lists of numbers, usually the unenviable province of business writers, lay a vast trove of *ideas*—not merely illuminating the past but harbingering future social and political trends that were not yet otherwise visible. Over the years he assiduously cultivated the professional keepers of statistics, particularly at the U.S. Bureau of the Census and among political candidates' campaign managers (who live and die by demographics). It was a time-consuming process, to be sure, but by making such an effort White consistently gave his readers material of value that they rarely found elsewhere.

Always, White had to see things for himself. Even after 1960, when he became a celebrity, going to meet the story like a cub reporter remained his style. One example: In the late 1960s he was determined to report firsthand on Vietnam. David Maness, in charge of the Articles Department at *Life*, tried to dissuade him: He was no longer a kid; he'd been involved in enough danger for one life; he didn't need more reportorial credits. "Teddy wouldn't listen," says Maness. "I refused to push his case. So he bypassed me and managed to get accreditation from our Newsfront editors." Another example, related in a eulogy by his very close friend, former Time Inc. Chief of Correspondents Richard Clurman: "Just before he died, he was working on a story about America as a nation of immigrants (see "A Thin Green Line," Chapter 1). I told him, 'this will be a piece of cake for you. You'll never have to move from your chair. You've got it all.' Not Teddy. Next day he flew off to the Mexican border at Tijuana. When he came back, I could hear him forming his lead as he told me about it: 'Twilight. Sad-eyed American border patrolmen shrouded in black coveralls, mounted on black horses'—the drama, the complexity, the anguish of it all. Where did it fit into the Ellis Island of his parents' generation? What was the answer?"

After 1960, White did three basic types of articles: short essays; longish, thoughtful pieces with a high price tag (as much as $10,000 in the mid-1960s—very high indeed); and less-long, less-remunerative assignments that he liked to call his "White Fang" pieces: important, fast-breaking sub-

jects that he could, like a predator, quickly sink his teeth into, tear off the meat, and be off to find his next prey. Many of the latter were done for the weekly *Life*, which had a late-closing section that could be held open (at considerable expense). No other magazine could match it, which of course gave *Life*—and thus White—unparalleled clout.

Perhaps the best remembered of these was an interview with Jackie Kennedy a week after the assassination (see Chapter 1). White had written his emotion-packed piece in forty-five minutes, and at 2:00 A.M. phoned it into *Life* in New York from Hyannis Port. Managing Editor Ralph Graves, Dave Maness, and a high-speed typist were on phones, the magazine was holding the presses. White finished dictating and asked Graves and Maness what they thought of it. Graves suggested that a reference to Mrs. Kennedy's kissing the President's hands and feet might be too intimate. There was a pause and Teddy said, "Okay, take it out." Then Maness told him that four references to Camelot were at least one too many. A much longer pause (clearly Mrs. Kennedy was at his elbow) then Teddy said, "They stay." And they did. Says Maness, "We knew we had a historic story, exclusively. So why carp?"

White slavered to do White Fang articles, perhaps unaware that he was not always admired for them within the profession. As one journalist described it: "White would arrive late at the scene, catch up quickly on all the facts up to that point from the reporters who had preceded him, then use his personal special status to obtain exclusive access to key newsmakers." Not surprisingly, the other reporters resented being milked, particularly when White's story, thanks to *Life*, came out first.

Only twice did White try to collaborate. The first time was in 1945 when he coauthored *Thunder Out of China* with Annalee Jacoby (see introduction to Chapter 5). The other was in 1984. Anxious to continue to chronicle presidential races, but "tired of being the oldest person on the press bus," he suggested to Time Inc. that he write the first and last chapters and one "think piece" for that year's volume on the subject. All the rest would be reported and written by Time Inc. correspondents. Complex, but a good idea, said Ralph Graves, by then the company's Editorial Director; "Let's do it." The primaries began, and soon four chapters were on White's desk. At which point Teddy canceled the whole project—partly because he and a project editor at Time Inc. were at odds, but primarily, says Graves, because "Teddy just couldn't stand being dependent on the work of other reporters."

For all reporters, the name of the game is access to sources. From the first White was fascinated by power, and proved to be adept at getting to see those who had it. More important, his best sources welcomed him back again and again. Partly they were taken by his demeanor: this short, freckled, owlish-looking, nonthreatening writer-cum-historian who was always gentle in his approach, always seeming to under-

stand their point of view, often giving them ideas and information in return for theirs. Moreover, they sensed that White *liked* them personally, which was frequently the case, and that he was trustworthy—he was not about to misquote them, he didn't see hanky-panky or worse around every corner. But mostly he got to see powerful people because his work was widely read and just might be history.

Many of his best articles were possible only because of "access." He became such a pal of Jack Kennedy and his family that he found all doors in the 1960 campaign and in the White House open to him. Again, when White accompanied President Nixon to China in 1972, his subsequent story would have been far less effective if he hadn't, years before, made friends with Chou En-lai.

But his thirst for access gradually led to a problem: he hesitated to offend highly placed contacts. As a minor example, White's first wife, Nancy, tells of a small White House dinner they attended. President Kennedy asked the other seven diners why it was that Adlai Stevenson was considered an "egghead" and he, Kennedy, wasn't. Stepping into an awkward silence, Nancy explained that it was only a matter of perception: while Stevenson's intelligence was the hallmark of his personality, what showed out front for JFK was his good looks, his youth, his family; and that many Americans disapproved of his father. "People just don't know *your* mind yet," she concluded. Kennedy was unperturbed; but at home later Teddy was irritated that Nancy should have presumed to answer or to have risked insulting the President.

But the problem was potentially far more serious than that. These accessible folks had warts, and to write about them inevitably demanded some criticism. And, friends say that the prospect of doing so sometimes put White into such turmoil that he left out "inconvenient" facts, or opted not to cover certain subjects at all. It's possible—sins of omission are hard to document. But as far as I have been able to determine, when he wrote for magazines *1)* he *did* fret about criticizing certain sources and friends (Caspar Weinberger was one, see Chapter 17), and *2)* in the final article he always reported the warts and all. If White had a weakness in this regard, it was far from fatal.

The Writer at Work

How a journalist says something is frequently more important than what he is saying. White, the peerless reporter-historian, was a fine stylist, a great explainer, and—as noted earlier—an unexcelled storyteller who won over his readers and surely did his former Harvard professors proud. Indeed, at heart, he too was a teacher both in person (friends called him Rabbi White) and in print. It is not the purpose of this essay to analyze White's prose style. The

reader can best savor it for himself. But a few observations may be useful.

White had a strict writing regimen: He wrote in the mornings on a typewriter, with a cigarette dangling from his lips, grabbing first one and then another of his myriad reportorial notebooks. (White kept every note he ever took, every memento, every letter. His papers, given posthumously to Harvard, weighed four *tons*). For lunch he invariably had a tunafish sandwich (unless he was going out). And in the afternoon he polished what he'd just written, usually nursing a glass of bourbon.

Like any good writer, knowing that the reader must be grabbed quickly, White agonized over his story leads. Hedy Glickenhaus, his research assistant from 1970 on, recalls frequently seeing him in his office surrounded by balled-up pieces of copy paper, each with a single sentence on it—an unacceptable lead. From the agonizing, however, came memorable results; readers couldn't *help* but be carried along. Consider just two examples (from Chapter 15), written thirteen years apart in articles on Indo-China— very different in style, each powerfully compelling:

On February 19, 1954, General Henri-Eugène Navarre summoned together a group of newspapermen in Saigon and there, as Commander in Chief of the French Expeditionary Forces in Indo-China, permitted himself one of the most fatuously optimistic situation reports ever made by a military leader on the eve of disaster.

SAIGON, 1967.

It is night and the monsoon pours down, pelting and slashing the city, drumming on the iron roofs of the Tan Son Nhut base where Americans sleep, thrashing the mat shacks of the refugees. The lightning stabs, the thunder cracks and in between crumples an occasional softer thud. In the corridor of the hotel, the 3-year-old child of an English diplomat next door runs out barefoot, sobbing in fear. I try to soothe her with a few words of English, her dark-haired Vietnamese *amah* pads out to rock and comfort the child, cradling blond curls against black pajamas.

Who can resist going on to the next paragraph?

Once he had his lead, White was a whirlwind. He wrote almost as quickly as he could talk (another reason he was so successful with his White Fang pieces). He packed every article with emotion. He made heavy use of adjectives and kinetic verbs (e.g., the 1967 lead just cited), particularly after 1960. Some of his editors protested—one says he frequently came very close to being absurd. But White knew this technique was effective in keeping the reader involved.

How did White get on with editors? In his early days, White fought with a number of them over ideology:

With Henry Luce of Time Inc.: In 1944–45 White began writing stories criticizing Chiang Kai-shek, but Luce as a matter of policy was allowing *Time's* Whittaker Chambers to alter White's stories so that they appeared to support Chiang's policies. Eventually Luce and White parted company (see introduction to Chapter 5).

With former Vice-President Henry Agard Wallace, Editor of the *New Republic*: White worked there as an editor in 1946–47, just long enough to realize that Wallace was not only using the magazine primarily to bolster his campaign to be president, but had as his chief advisers a group of American Communists.

With Max Ascoli, owner and editor of *The Reporter*: White wrote for Ascoli's magazine from Europe and after he returned in large part because it was probably the greatest liberal publication of its time. But its liberalism was of a frenzied sort that came to disturb White, himself certainly a liberal. Moreover, though Ascoli was brilliant, he was also an imperious S. O. B. to work for. They broke in 1954 when Ascoli tried to insert *his* solutions into White's coverage of social problems. But for awhile it looked to White as though he might never escape. Ascoli had courageously continued to publish Teddy during the McCarthy years, even when White came perilously close to being declared a subversive and losing his passport. The charges were ludicrous and were ultimately dropped (see also introduction to Chapter 14). Says White in his memoir: this "freed [me] of fealty to Dr. Max Ascoli. Had I not won my passport back, I would have had slim choice: service to Ascoli, or expulsion from the profession. Ascoli was so flamboyantly brave he would have insisted on keeping me on his payroll, as a known subversive, if only to taunt the primitives. I would then have been a pawn to his will."

From then on, however, White and his various magazine editors had no serious ideological quarrels and shared only "normal" tensions. Julian Bach, his literary agent (who Teddy referred to as that "gentlemanly pirate"), says there really weren't any tensions: "Teddy was always amenable to changes." Others of us remember it a little differently. White's most frequent problem was a tendency to write too long, coupled with a tenacious resistance to changing copy that he had finished polishing. "He was consistently guilty of repetition," recalls *Life*'s Dave Maness. "I'd call the duplications to his attention. He'd insist—with some justification— that most of the repetition was necessary for emphasis. I'd disagree. He'd eliminate one or two, just so I'd get off his case. As his reputation grew, he became less inclined to listen." *Life*'s Ralph Graves is more lenient: "His pieces were certainly long, but not *that* long." In my experience at the *Digest*, perhaps because it was understood between us at the outset that we would be condensing his articles to our space, length and resistance to change were rarely a problem.

Maness, it should be noted, believes that White's most objective work was done prior his post-1960 prominence. "He always had ego," says Maness, "but he was less cocky back then."

Most people who knew him agree that the celebrity status he achieved through the 1960s changed him. Outwardly, he seemed to revel in being famous. At political conventions everybody wanted to interview Teddy; candidates wanted his advice. In a way Teddy became a politician himself. Dick Clurman vividly remembers inviting Teddy to go along with him on an interview with British Prime Minister Harold Wilson: "I asked the PM a soft question to open up, and he promptly said he'd be more interested in hearing Mr. White's view of the political situation. And so we did—for my entire allotted hour."

Privately, however, despite fame and success, White evinced considerable insecurity. He never stopped routinely asking his wives (Nancy from 1948 until the late 1960s, Beatrice from 1973) to edit his copy. Their unvarnished comments did not always sit well, and Nancy in particular remembers long arguments with him. Surprisingly often, however, he would finally agree. Friends, too, were often asked to advise before a manuscript went to a publisher. Michael Bessie remembers that his comments were always considered, "especially when they touched on something that Teddy found disturbing, such as race relations or the truthfulness of Richard Nixon; but they were not always followed." Julian Bach has on his office wall a framed 1969 letter: "Dear Julian, Will you please give me your *best* thinking on this. Fondly, Teddy." It was, says Bach, "typically humble Teddy." In all, then, despite public adulation, he remained a sentimental, gentle, caring man, lacking in pretense, naïve in that he simply didn't see evil in people. He cared deeply about friends—and devoted extravagant amounts of time trying to help them and virtually anyone they sent his way.

He was a born Cassandra. One day Beatrice White brought buckets of flowers into town from the country. "Teddy helped carry them in," says Bede, "and clearly liked them. Then he said, 'But why did you go to so much trouble? They won't last.'" He had the same feeling about success—he was sure it couldn't last, that the next project was certain to be a disaster. And when the next project was a hit, he was genuinely relieved.

THE LAST TIME I saw Teddy was, like our Christmas Eves, also a time of singing. With our wives we had decided to try to bring out an album of the original recordings of the most popular songs of World War II. Each of us had independently come up with a list, we'd merged them more or less amicably, and now we met to make final selections. Nothing would do, said Teddy, but that we go somewhere and sing them. And off we went to an unsuspecting East Side New York restaurant—where fortunately we were the only customers for most of the evening, imbibing freely and singing our hearts out (our lungs, too, I fear). I was about to leave on a trip, and we agreed that as soon as I returned we'd get together with Skitch Henderson (unbeknownst to him), and make it all happen. An unforgettable evening, a marvelous album we agreed, and Susie and I watched fondly as Teddy and Bede headed uptown for home.

We were still away two weeks later when Teddy had a stroke and died. He left some things unfinished—at least two articles and, truly a loss, the sequel to his splendid memoir *In Search of History*. The record album, too, died with him. But a magnificent legacy remains. Much of it is in these pages.

Editor's Note: The text of White's articles is verbatim as originally published except for footnotes to identify certain individuals. Headlines and subheads are also as published. A few editorial precedes—those entitled "From the Editors' Prologue"—have been condensed slightly to delete duplication and/or extraneous material. Not all photos, artwork, and sidebars created by the magazines are included.

THEODORE H. WHITE
AT LARGE

Chapter 1

Five Decades of Insight

To begin, some highlights of White's magazine work over the years are useful. The articles in this chapter, from each of his five decades as a journalist, exemplify the great breadth of his interests and insights and his enduring concern for the human condition.

His first national bylined piece, "The Rape of Chin Valley," was for *Time,* the first time the magazine had ever given a byline to one of its own correspondents. It demonstrates a quality of reporting and writing that belies his neophyte status.*

*Earlier, en route to China, he had done a backgrounder on Arab-Jewish conflict from Palestine which was published in the *Boston Globe.*

Reporting from Europe, White covered the great men of the time. One of them, a particular favorite of White's, is portrayed vividly in "The Three Lives of André Malraux."

For White, no politician of the times was more significant than John F. Kennedy. And when JFK was killed, *Life* appropriately assigned White to do its eulogy, published as "One Wished for a Cry, a Sob . . . Any Human Sound." A few days later, the widowed Jackie Kennedy called White to say she had something to say to the country, and asked that he come to see her in Hyannis Port. The resultant "For President Kennedy, An Epilogue" will long haunt everyone who reads it. (See also Introduction, page xvi.)

White's fascination with Asia extended well beyond China (see Chapter 15). In 1975 he wrote "Putting Down, for Good, the White Man's Burden," a pained obituary for failed U.S. foreign policy. As always, he shrewdly positioned current events within the broad sweep of history.

Fittingly, one of White's last published pieces was also in *Time*. The problems of illegal immigration from Mexico had recently absorbed his attention. In "A Thin Green Line," a fragment of an article he was working on at the time of his death, he continues his lifelong penchant for seeing and revealing the people behind the statistics. (See also Introduction, page xvi.)

THE RAPE OF CHIN VALLEY

From the Editor's Prologue: *Some day Shansi Province in the north may be China's Pennsylvania. Its rough mountains are heavy with anthracite and iron, and Japan wants it more than any other province. Most coveted area is the Chin River Valley, a valley once bright with wheat, cotton, corn, yellow rice, persimmons, pears; surrounding hills dotted with grazing sheep and goats; and folded into the hills untold treasures of coal and iron. When the Japanese began a drive into that valley late last summer, White decided that was the part of Shansi he most wanted to see.*

To get there, he flew from Chungking to Sian (400 miles) in five hours. Thence it took him five days by train to get to the Yellow River (70 miles)—his train jumped the track once, a bridge washed out from under it once. He was given a horse and for three solid weeks (rising at five, riding ten hours a day, sleeping wherever night caught him) he followed precarious mountain passes until he came to the Chin Valley.

What he found was no longer a land of rice and persimmons. It was a battle-ground, a mud-soaked, blood-soaked Hell. The severest rains in years and a Japanese Army crazed with hunger and lust had simultaneously descended on it. By the time he arrived the Japanese had been pushed back, but he was told and could see what had happened. Writes White:

"The physical impact [was] tremendous. Village after village completely destroyed. Houses shattered and burned, wells fouled, bridges destroyed, roads torn up. Houses were burned by the soldiery both out of boredom and deviltry, and because they were cold and needed fire and warmth.

"The Japanese looted indiscriminately and efficiently. Everything of value was stripped and taken away. Telephones, wires, clocks, soaps, bedding, objects of art were collected by the Japanese for transfer to their own supply department. On their own, the soldiers went in for simpler forms of looting. Clothes and food were what they wanted, and they were not very discriminate in their tastes: women's silk garments, peasant cotton trousers, shoes, underwear, were all stripped off the backs of their possessors whenever Chinese were unfortunate enough to fall into the hands of Japanese detachments.

"The Japanese soldiers were caked in mud, chest high; their beards were bristling with two weeks' growth; and they were ravenously hungry. The peasants, in fleeing before the approach of the Japanese, had taken their pigs, cows, grain and other food with them into the hills where the Japanese could not follow. All through the valley, tiny Japanese garrisons were mired in mud, unable to communicate with one another, and slowly starving. When off duty, simple soldiers would sneak out of their garrison posts in twos and threes and rove the countryside looking for abandoned chickens and eggs—many were caught and killed by the Chinese.

"The names of the villages (Liushe, Wangchiachuang, etc.) are meaningless 100 miles away, but in some, every single woman, without exception, was raped by the soldiers in occupation. In villages whose occupants had not fled quickly enough, the first action of the Japanese was to rout out the women and have at them; women who fled to grain-fields for hiding were forced out by cavalry who rode their horses through the grain fields to trample them and frighten them into appearance.

"Male villagers were stripped naked, lashed to carts, and driven forward by the Imperial Army as beasts of burden. Japanese horses and mules were beaten to death in the mud; and on any road and all the hills of the valley, one can see the carcasses of their animals rotting and the bones of their horses whitening in the sun. The Chinese peasants who were impressed to take their places were driven forward with the same pitiless fury until they collapsed, died, or were driven mad."

The Chinese counter-attacked and fought so furiously that Generalissimo Chiang Kai-shek gave them a bonus of $20,000, a lot of money in North China.

Sick Men. Behavior of their maddened troops is a source of great shame to responsible men in the Japanese Army and Government. Along his way, White learned some good reasons for that behavior. He was told that most of the Japanese soldiers in Shansi have been there over two years. They have had no furlough, no home leave, not even a Peking week-end.

"The fighting," White wrote, "is nerve-tearing. A Japanese soldier sits in a muddy garrison post exposed to guerrilla sniping; he camps in a muddy town hated by its people; he goes out guerrilla chasing and is probably wounded, perhaps killed. Frequently supplies fail to come through and the unit goes on short mess—or starves.

"The men are sick of a war which is never won, eaten with worry for home and family. If they try to desert, Chinese fall on them and kill them. Missionaries in Shansi report that Japanese often steal inside mission compounds to cry, or come to the gates to whimper and beg for little comforts. Superstitions are epidemic. Nearly every dead Japanese soldier has on him a charm, worn in life to ward off death. Often a man draws about himself a magic circle (the round of his life is full; no escape) and puts a bullet in his head. Instead of cremating bodies to be returned home for proper Shinto burial, Army officers cut off heads, cremate them for home burial, and bury the bodies in China, or drop them in rivers or wells. All these things prey on the Japanese will to fight."

Progress. "The Chinese," White concluded, "have advanced during the war from a fourth rate Army to a second rate Army. This is progress. Before the war the Chinese Armies were notorious for the fact that they could run faster and retreat in worse disorder than any known national group of armed men. This was understandable because of the world in which they lived, and the causes for which they were asked to die. Cowardice was common—'*kai pa*' (I'm afraid') was heard on every hand. But the present Chinese Army has spirit. It glows. The men are willing to die. They mix and tangle with the Japanese with a burning hate that is good."

TIME December 18, 1939

THE THREE LIVES OF ANDRÉ MALRAUX

As literary revolutionist, as de Gaulle's leading propagandist and as philosopher of art, the author of 'Man's Fate' has deeply influenced the French scene.

PARIS

Unless one examines the hole in the green shutters carefully, the mark looks like a rust spot. Closer up, however, it is easy to see—the torn edges of the hole, furling back like petals of iron, mark the passage of a bullet fired too low to hit its mark, but aimed from the street to pass directly over the writer's desk.

In the story of any other writer, such an attempt might have marked the man's promotion to momentary celebrity. In the story of André Malraux, already gory with bullets and blood, the shot of the unknown assassin was no more than a punctuation mark. It would have been noteworthy only if it had struck home, and then only in retrospect. For, had it done so on that winter night of 1947, it would have ended a career that has enthralled France for a generation—at precisely the moment when that career split in a baffling, schizoid divergence of purpose.

In a country that reserves for its great writers a special measure of passionate interest and devotion. André Malraux is crowded by only two contemporaries—the aging Nobel laureate, François

Mauriac, and the owl philosopher, Jean-Paul Sartre. But André Malraux has been able to call from his countrymen something more—a quality of excited, almost animal, fascination which neither of his two great rivals can evoke to match. And it is this that infuses the French as they look with bafflement on their new Malraux.

THE DARK-EYED, glossy-haired young man, taut and resonant as a violin string, who, twenty years ago, remade the French literary scene by projecting the heroes of his writing into the violence of contemporary politics, torturing and brutalizing them in the convulsions of history—that Malraux has vanished. The new, middle-aged Malraux—his dark hair still thick but receding, his eyes sunken in great hollows of darkness—is someone else. He is, in fact, two men, both new.

One is a politician, involved and tangled in the brambles of French party strife. The other is a philosopher of art—serene, remote, aloof from all matters unmeasured by eternity. This divergence, moreover, has taken place

8

in the past five years—since, roughly, that winter season when the bullet designed for the politician passed over the desk where the philosopher was preparing that treatise on art and humanism, "Les Voix de Silence," which has become, in the first year since its publication, one of the monuments of this literary century in France.

Malraux, the politician, is a Gaullist. As such, he sits on the twenty-four-man National Council of General Charles de Gaulle's R.P.F. (Rally of the French People), in its gray, soot-smeared headquarters on the Rue Solferino on Paris' Left Bank. Within this party, Malraux has two sources of strength. One is his influence over the personality of General de Gaulle, sole commander of the party, in whose entourage of ambitious captains Malraux, the unambitious, ranks first. His second is his influence over masses of Frenchmen by his skill with words. Whoever has seen Malraux on a platform, his hands suddenly transformed into claws that tear at the air as his voice winds up with a fantastic, hypnotic eloquence to sweep an audience of thousands into a frenzy, knows that in naming this man as director of his national propaganda, General de Gaulle has chosen the most effective rabble-rouser in France.

MALRAUX, THE philosopher of art, lives in a high-roofed, white-walled studio on a tree-lined street in suburban Boulogne. Between the nervous, twitching philosopher of enormous eloquence and stupendous learning of the studio and the self-intoxicated man of the platform there seems no kinship whatsoever—until, suddenly, the studio conversation wanders off into art. Then, as Malraux talks of what men can see with their eyes, make with their fingers, grasp with their imaginations, an ecstasy grips him. He is up, almost dancing from his chair, showing the line of a painting that hangs on his wall, his hand following the curve of a Gandhara head on his piano, his fingers flickering over the strange Hopi heads his friends have brought from America, as if a current jumped the gap between the inanimate object and his own quivering consciousness.

THE LEGEND of Malraux, as it is strained out of the shreds of Paris gossip, is of a life that squirms with restless activity. Trained as an archaeologist, a student of Sanskrit, he set out for Asia at the age of 21 to search for Cambodian antiquities. There the wild, revolutionary politics of Asia sucked him in, drawing him to participation in an Annamite revolutionary movement (for which he was arrested on trumped-up charges of theft of art objects by French authorities).

From Indo-China, after his release, the turmoil of Asia carried him to China, in its days of great revolution, where he sat in the inner sanctums of Chiang Kai-Shek's Nationalist party, in the days when that party was Stalin's chief ally in the Orient. From China, after the collapse of that revolution, he made his way back to Europe as a member of an archaeological expedition through Afghanistan and Persia.

SUCCESS CAME to Malraux with the publication of his third book, at the age of 32—the savage, magnificent and hopeless story of the Chinese Revolution, "Man's Fate." In awe, the sedate and polished literary stylists of France saw his arrival in their midst, in the words of François Mauriac, "advancing like a man with a dagger in his hand" determined to kill—and recognized him as an authentic, towering man of genius.

Malraux's literary success coincided with the decade of fascism and for the next decade his life was submerged in that struggle. He received the German and Jewish refugees who fled from Hitler in the name of France; he joined the French committee for the defense of Thaelmann, the German Communist leader; he helped found the World League Against Anti-Semitism; he flew to Berlin to protest the trial of Dimitrov under Hitler's nose; he fought in Spain as commander of the Republican aviation in the first weeks of the war.

When France herself was caught in 1939, Malraux followed the colors—he was captured as a tank commander in the campaign of 1940, escaped, joined the Resistance, was captured again, escaped again and ended by commanding a brigade of French troops in the advance across the Rhine. Out of each of his adventures, from Indo-China to the German prison camp, Malraux refined a novel—novels drenched in blood, obsessed with the savagery of men, mes-

merized by the spectacle of men in the presence of death, novels all of them imbued with the mystique of revolution.

When, thus, in the chaos of post-war France, André Malraux emerged first as a Minister (of Information) in General de Gaulle's government and later as chief ornament of the general's party (which most Frenchmen set at the extreme right of the political spectrum), the shock to France was immeasurable.

THE SHOCK of France's intellectuals at Malraux's association with the Gaullists still irritates Malraux. For Malraux holds he is not of that legion of innocents betrayed by communism, the roster of the Silones, Spenders and Koestlers. Malraux makes no attempt to deny that he worked with the Communists. "But no one was fooled," says Malraux, for he was neither a member of the party nor a fellow-traveler.

He has not, insists Malraux, changed since—it is the world, and most of all the Russians, who have changed. "It happened," said Malraux several years ago, "that André Gide and myself were asked to protest to Hitler the condemnation of Dimitrov who was innocent of the Reichstag fire. And now—when Dimitrov in power hangs Petkov who is innocent—who has changed? Myself or Gide? Or Dimitrov?"

It was the Russo-German pact that widened the cleavage between Malraux and the Communists (which had begun in the Spanish civil war) into an open breach. "For I could understand the pact," says Malraux, "it was perfectly comprehensible from a Russian point of view." There was a logic, a Russian logic, to the pact to turn Germany against the Western world—"but I could not agree that Stalin had the right to pay for this logic with the blood of millions of ordinary Frenchmen whom he had doomed." It was in defeat then, and in the Resistance, that in his own words "I married France."

BETWEEN MARRYING France and espousing Gaullism another episode intervened. As Minister of Information in the early post-war French Cabinets, Malraux saw, from the inside, the ramshackle machinery of French politics slowly mincing down the triumph of French Liberation to the shabby despair and frustration of present French life. Men talk of how stupid and inefficient government is in France "but to know how foul it really is, one must be in it," says Malraux, "one must be married to it, and be frustrated as a man is by a wife with whom he is hopelessly coupled."

France had to be changed, therefore. And, since the only party organized technically to change France was the Communists, who wished to destroy her, another party had to be formed. This was the R.P.F., General dé Gaulle's party. The R.P.F. was not conceived by Malraux, but its appeal to the nation was swollen with Malraux's ideas.

THE R.P.F., says Malraux is not a party with a philosophy of history, like the Communists or the Fascists or the Hitlerites; it is a group of men seeking a pragmatic, workable way out of France's dead-end. There are only two planks to the R.P.F.'s program. The first is that France must become great again; this is a need foreigners have difficulty in understanding, for, says Malraux, it is impossible to explain the gigantic emotional effect of a simple fact: "We were a great power—and then we simply stopped being so." The second is that France cannot become great until its present constitutional anarchy is reformed to give it a strong working executive that can attack the social misery in which millions of underprivileged Frenchmen are permanently frozen.

The R.P.F. went up over France in 1947 like the swift burst of a skyrocket—and has ever since, slowly, steadily, been falling. Its very success was its own undoing. For not only were millions of patriotic Frenchmen of the old Resistance lured to the general's banners, but after them trooped millions of the most abominable Vichyites, who had betrayed France in the war, seeking in the general a new guardian against communism. So swift was the ascent of the party, so enthusiastically did former collaborators and old-fashioned reactionaries clamber aboard its bandwagon that all the forces of France's democratic core rallied against it.

"GAULLISM MIGHT have succeeded," said a Paris wit, "without General de Gaulle." Almost every Deputy of the National Assembly agreed in 1947 (and still agrees) that France's parliamentary chaos must be replaced with the firm kind of executive leadership Americans have. But the general's party seemed to offer more than a presidential executive—its radically reactionary fringe made it sound like a would-be dictatorship.

If the years since then have proved this fear false, it has brought little yield of good fortune to the Gaullists. In 1947, when they polled 40 per cent of all French votes, the Gaullists might have seized power by force. But they would not—they waited. And waiting year by year, all the while meticulously abiding by the rules of the French democracy that they denounced they have ebbed in strength.

The ebbing of Gaullist fortunes has come as a not unrelieved sorrow to Malraux who helped give the movement birth. For what has been lost is the far-right wing of the party and what remains under the general's standard is basically the left, or social revolutionary wing. This heightening of his own influence within what may be a fading party might oppress another man with the irony of politics or stimulate him to great exertions. But with Malraux the development has had contrary effect.

More convinced than ever that France must either accept the Gaullist solution or decay, Malraux himself is far less active than formerly in the technical machinery of his party's politics. The explanation is simple: in the past few years, Malraux, the philosopher, all the while acknowledging and believing in his bowels that France must be remade, believes that it is more important now,

in this generation, to begin the elaboration of that new humanism, the new and universal culture of man which this age has been first enabled to approach. Moreover, he believes that this new culture must be founded not on words, which have been demonetized and failed, but on the images of art, which are the only permanence.

Malraux, an adventurer of ideas as well as of experience, is peculiarly fortunate to live in France. For France is a nation whose marketplace of ideas is crossed and recrossed by wandering men seeking truths—not little facts, but the large, all-embracing Sole Truth.

In this marketplace, Malraux has in the last year offered, as a prophet, Art. The package of his wares is the single book, "Les Voix de Silence," which in the year since its publication has sold more copies than any other book ever published on the plastic arts in France.

EVEN ON the lips of his political enemies, Malraux's book is treated not as a book, but as an event. A reworking and rewriting of the thoughts and essays of fifteen years' reflection, all written in typical close-textured Malrauvian prose, the book's greatness rests on its illustrations and their binding thought. The 500-odd illustrations are, very simply, perhaps the greatest collection of reproductions of man's art ever put together in the covers of one work. This greatness rests not on the individual glory of each artifact of genius, but on the breadth and spread of the world from which they were assembled.

Drawing on his wanderings around the world, Malraux has summoned from memory and knowledge illustration after illustration to set side by side—an Asian bust of the fourth century set against a French Gothic bust of the thirteenth, an early American primitive of buffalo shooting set against an impressionist masterpiece of Rousseau—to show the underlying unity of genius, the quality of kinship of man that spurts only in the contact of genius with the world and results in beauty.

The success of the book is no surprise to Malraux. For he believes he is the first to note a development that has already altered all modern life, the first stirring of what he calls the age of "universal culture." This development rests on a device as simple and prosaic as was the invention of printing—the development of new techniques of reproduction.

In our times, the reproduction by modern photography of the world's plastic master-works, by modern recording of the world's music, by the cinema of the world's drama, has made us the first heirs to all the world's visions of genius. We are no longer limited as Frenchmen to the cathedrals and the Louvre, as Italians to the statues of Michelangelo, as Chinese to rare glimpses of the Sung paintings. We are the first generation to inherit all.

This revolution, which has escaped the attention of journalists, has not escaped the attention of ordinary people themselves, for the phenomenon is world-wide. Malraux notes that in France, the cradle of the modern arts,

the Louvre reports that admissions to its galleries last year multiplied by six times the record of the last pre-war year.

THE WORLD thus sits in audience on a prodigious contrast. On the one hand, the arts of the world, stirring the roots of civilization, are bringing men to the knowledge that wood-and-stone, line-and-color seen through Chinese, American, French or Persian eyes promote a kinship that languages cannot approximate. Yet, at the same time, the politics of the world force men farther and farther from this kinship.

There was a time, says Malraux—from Michelet to Jaures—when Frenchmen believed that the more deliberately they abandoned love of country the closer they came to humanity. Yet, today, Russia weighs upon the world, sweeping away these dreams, making men know that in abandoning their French-ness, their British-ness, their American-ness they weaken, not strengthen, their common culture. For Malraux the task of this generation, and for himself most of all, is somehow to lay the foundation for tomorrow's universal culture, which has just become possible in the teeth of world politics which threaten to destroy it.

BETWEEN THESE two concepts—of the art that unites and inspires, and of politics that divide and sterilize—Malraux, like all other men, is trapped.

He apportions his time between the two judiciously, but art seems to be gaining ever more on politics. Though his high faith in the need for remolding France under the Gaullist banner has not wavered, he now limits himself to attendance at weekly meetings of the R.P.F. executive council and to less frequent visits with the general—to whom his personal devotion is unshaken.

His role as R.P.F. Director of National Propaganda is difficult to define as he pays only perfunctory attention to daily routine but can sweep the movement with a new idea whenever he wants. By far the greater part of his time is now devoted to finishing his studies on art and completing a great trilogy novel to be entitled "La Lutte Avec L'Ange" ("The Struggle With the Angel").

In his own estimate there is no doubt at all how Malraux sees himself. "Write it down," he says, "the art excites me five hundred times more than the politics."

NEW YORK TIMES MAGAZINE February 15, 1953

ONE WISHED FOR A CRY, A SOB ... ANY HUMAN SOUND

No bugler sounded taps, no drum beat its ruffle, no band pealed *Hail to the Chief* as John F. Kennedy, 35th President of the United States, returned for the last time to Washington, the city where he practiced the magic art of leadership.

It was 17 years ago he came here from Boston; and, in the years since, his arrivals and departures came to punctuate the telling of American history. When he arrived, the door would open and the lithe figure would come out to give that graceful wave of the arm which became the most familiar flourish in American politics. There would follow then the burst of applause, the shouts and yells, the oohs and ahs as he tripped down the stairs with that light, graceful step which was his style.

But he came this time in silence.

The faint shrill of distant jets, the sputter and cough of belly-lighted helicopters carrying the men of power from Washington to the field, the subdued conversation, all made the silence larger. It was moist and chilly and the twilight bars of pink had just given way to a quarter moon hung with mists when Air Force No. 1, the presidential

jet, silently rolled up the runway from the south. The pilot in his cockpit must have sensed the hush—so skillfully had he stilled the motors, so surprisingly did the plane appear in the total glare of the lights and soundlessly come to a stop. It was 6:03 p.m.

One wished for a cry, a sob, a wail, any human sound. But the plane, white with long blue flashings, rested under the punishment of the light—sealed and silent. A great cargo lift—glistening yellow on the outside, dazzling white on the inside, framed with lights of red and white—rolled as far as the plane, and paused. A door opened in the rear of the plane; a man appeared and, for a moment, it was as it always had been: Larry O'Brien's round face peered out first. But O'Brien stooped down and, as he moved, lifted something. For the first time the ugly glint of the dark, red-bronze box showed. Behind O'Brien was Dave Powers; and then Kenny O'Donnell. These men had followed him from Boston to Washington and across the land, carrying his papers, his coats, his briefcase. This time, in last service, they carried the President himself.

They set the coffin down gently on the floor of the roomsized lift. It jounced, then steadied, then began to settle to the ground quietly with its burden and those from the plane who accompanied it. An honor guard of six reached out their hands to receive the coffin. The bearers bent to hand it down to them; it shook in the passing over and O'Brien's hand, almost caressing, reached out as if to steady a fragile thing or a tumbling child; then, not being needed any more, the hand fluttered uselessly in the air.

There was, still, no voice audible except those of the broadcasters pattering as quietly as possible into their microphones. The silhouettes at the edge of the lift, cut sharp by the light, parted; and a slender woman in a rose-colored suit with dark facing appeared, then hovered at the lip of the low platform. Bobby Kennedy was there, lifting up his arms to help her down, then guiding her into the gray service ambulance with the red dome light—steady, not winking. Mrs. Kennedy's hand tried to open the ambulance door and fell limply as Bobby leaned forward, opened the door, guided her in. Then, silently, the ambulance rolled on to the north and was gone.

One watched and knew the nation was watching; and behind the lights watched the true government of the United States. There they stood, the young and old—McNamara of Defense, his jaw tight, his jaw muscles flexing; Harriman of State, tall and grim and gaunt, the last man in Washington to carry his greatness vigorously

on from the New Deal through the wars to the New Frontier; George Ball of State, Postmaster John Gronouski, Anthony Celebrezze of the Cabinet, Franklin Roosevelt Jr. of Commerce. There were the grizzled leaders of Congress—Hubert Humphrey, eyes red with weeping; Mike Mansfield and Everett Dirksen, looking worn and weighted by years. And apart, on the apron, the others—the younger men: Ted Sorensen, white of face and unapproachably solitary; Ralph Dungan and Arthur Schlesinger, bleak and somber; McGeorge Bundy, pale and contained as usual; Fred Holborn; others.

Heads bowed, the shock covering them all, they watched the gray ambulance go. Lyndon Baines Johnson and his wife emerged and quietly, with a minimum of words, selected three among the many men who gathered around him: McNamara of Defense, Ball of State, Bundy of the White House staff. The three joined the new President and his lady, and the waiting helicopter lifted them all from the field, its red lights at the rotor staff winking as it lurched its way through the sky toward the White House.

JOHN F. Kennedy loved the noble art of politics, which is the government of men; and he would have understood that now, while his body still lay in the Bethesda Naval Hospital, where his wife and brother sat vigil, the men of Washington could not help but talk of the government of the country, of those who would carry on—which ones would the new President use, which dismiss. For there are two parts to government: the machinery, and the individuals who sit at the levers of machinery.

The machinery in Washington functioned with marvelous efficiency. By noon Saturday, less than 24 hours from the assassination of John F. Kennedy, the White House had begun to change. On Thursday, the White House staff had seized Kennedy's absence to do over again the curtains, rugs and decorations of his office; by early afternoon Friday they had finished and, even as news of his assassination came, the staff was moving furniture back where it belonged.

Saturday morning, starting at 9 a.m., all the furniture of John F. Kennedy was moved out—the desk, the paintings, the decorations, his rocking chair—leaving it as bare as when he entered, except for the two white opposing sofas by the fireplace.

THREE YEARS ago this very month, John F. Kennedy gathered his band of Bostonians in his brother's home at the compound in Hyannis Port to make a government. On the night of the assassination, at his tapestried French chateau in Spring Valley, Washington, President Lyndon Johnson gathered the Southerners and Texans of his own inner circle. And by morning it was clear that Johnson meant as certainly to govern with his own men in the White House as had John Kennedy. Johnson's personal staff has always been far smaller,

never so emotionally fused to an incandescent chief as Kennedy's staff was. But by Saturday morning George Reedy, Johnson's spokesman, and Walter Jenkins, his chief administrative officer, and Bill Moyers, a bright young man from the Peace Corps, were installed as the first element of a new palace guard.

Meanwhile, in the outer White House lobby, grim men came and departed. Some wept openly. Beyond, in an inner office, one who had followed John F. Kennedy from the beginning looked out over great windows which showed Washington in the rain and said: "I'm here because I loved John F. Kennedy, not because I'm a Democrat. We served this man, we talked his language, we thought his thoughts. It was his magnetism, his ability, his brain that drew this remarkable group of men together. Lyndon is a man of different background, different abilities, and it's damned hard to shift. But I didn't spend 10 years of my life trying to do what's been done and let it all be wiped out with one shot by some nut in Dallas. Whether it's five weeks or five years, I'm going to go on here trying as hard as I can to help."

In the crowded lobby of the White House, moist with damp raincoats and crowded with sleepless men and women, the talk is mostly of people. But beyond the lobby, in the red brick homes of Georgetown, there is other, more considered talk—talk of the future, near and far.

Yesterday's unhappy Vice President, whose first love was Congress, is now

President. The area of Kennedy's greatest problem—the deadlock over domestic policy—is the area of Johnson's greatest strength. In the minute chronicling of the new President's every move, the city noticed at once that Johnson called together first, in the early hours of his Administration, the leaders of Congress—not the executive branch. It is with these men that Johnson will seek to accomplish his own vision of the nation's future.

The most consistent theme of talk was of Johnson in relation to the outer world. Said one man who has sat with Johnson: "At Cabinet meetings he was silent, cautious, always taking notes. In foreign affairs, when he speaks, he speaks usually on the hard-nosed side." Said another: "Johnson was one of only two men who sat with the President on every single decision-making session of this government—Cabinet meetings, Security Council meetings, executive committee meetings, congressional meetings, press conference meetings. He is the most prepared President we have ever had."

Johnson certainly was in a position to share Kennedy's vision of the American future. Yet the two were men who differed in pace, in timing, in taste, in attitude. On the night of Kennedy's death, Averell Harriman sat in his study and reminisced, out of that enormous memory which reaches back to the earliest days of Franklin Roosevelt. He remembered Roosevelt as a supple man, a man who enjoyed guiding his purposes and programs through the labyrinth of Congress, playing the game of persuasion. But Kennedy was different, thought Harriman. He met his Congress head on; he locked with it; he pointed to the purposes of requested legislation and his fights with Congress were, as a consequence, clear.

Harriman's thought catches better than any other the true legacy of the Kennedy administration—the realization that this is a changing country in a changing world, and the job of the President is to force the country to recognize and face these changes. Historians will argue for a generation about the seminal legislation and proposals of the Kennedy administration; but no man in Washington who knew John Fitzgerald Kennedy well thinks that his style soon will be matched.

ON SATURDAY afternoon the gushing fall skies outside the East Room of the White House made the light inside this greatest chamber of the mansion gray. The tiny golden bulbs of the great chandeliers had been dimmed to faintest candlepower; and there, in the half-darkness, rose the immense hulk of a sarcophagus draped with the American flag. One filed by and, for a long moment, one lingered—grief all but overpowered by the rage of frustration for all that had been only begun, and for all that was now unfulfilled promise.

One mourned for the remarkable, astringent candor so rare in public men. One thought of the night in the airplane over the skies of Montana when Kennedy, about to challenge the Democratic convention in Los Angeles for its nomination, was asked: who would the Democrats' best presidential candidate be if it could not be he himself—and he said, flatly: Lyndon B. Johnson—the man with whom he was about to duel.

One mourned for the gaiety, the elegance, the graces he and his lady had brought into this house.

One mourned for a man about whom historians may long debate, arguing whether the courage shown in the confrontations with Russia was less or more memorable than the compassion shown in introducing to the American Congress its first legislation to care for the ills of age, the troubles of youth, the hopelessness of the unskilled, the humiliation of its darker citizens.

One mourned because it was so still in this room. For this was a man of gallantry and of action, of motion and of the trumpet.

For, of all the many miles that this reporter followed John F. Kennedy on his long marches back and forth across this country, remembered best is the sound of the voice—that wonderfully clear voice so often tinged at once with sadness and the glee of combat, the voice which one night described best, for his time and his successor, the office and function of the presidency.

It was Election eve, the night before the first Tuesday after the first Monday in November of 1960, and he had come home to Boston and was speaking at the Boston Garden when suddenly, he extended his hand, pointed the long forefinger in summons and said, "I run for the presidency of the United States because it is the center of action and, in a free society, the chief responsibility of the President is to set before the American people the unfinished business of our country."

This was the essence of his presidency.

LIFE November 29, 1963

FOR PRESIDENT KENNEDY, AN EPILOGUE

She remembers how hot the sun was in Dallas, and the crowds—greater and wilder than the crowds in Mexico or in Vienna. The sun was blinding, streaming down; yet she could not put on sunglasses for she had to wave to the crowd.

And up ahead she remembers seeing a tunnel around a turn and thinking that there would be a moment of coolness under the tunnel. There was the sound of the motorcycles, as always in a parade, and the occasional backfire of a motorcycle. The sound of the shot came, at that moment, like the sound of a backfire and she remembers Connally saying, "No, no, no, no, no. . . ."

She remembers the roses. Three times that day in Texas they had been greeted with the bouquets of yellow roses of Texas. Only, in Dallas they had given her *red* roses. She remembers thinking, how funny—red roses for me; and then the car was full of blood and red roses.

Much later, accompanying the body from the Dallas hospital to the airport, she was alone with Clint Hill—the first Secret Service man to come to their rescue—and with Dr. Burkley, the White House physician. Burkley gave her two roses that had slipped under the President's shirt when he fell, his head in her lap.

All through the night they tried to separate him from her, to sedate her, and take care of her—and she would not let them. She wanted to be with him. She remembered that Jack had said of his father, when his father suffered the stroke, that he could not live like that. Don't let that happen to me, he had said, when I have to go.

Now, in her hand she was holding a gold St. Christopher's medal.

She had given him a St. Christopher's medal when they were married; but when Patrick died this summer, they had wanted to put something in the coffin with Patrick that was from them both; and so he had put in the St. Christopher's medal.

Then he had asked her to give him a new one to mark their 10th wedding anniversary, a month after Patrick's death.

He was carrying it when he died and she had found it. But it belonged to him—so she could not put *that* in the coffin with him. She wanted to give him

20

something that was hers, something that she loved. So she had slipped off her wedding ring and put it on his finger. When she came out of the room in the hospital in Dallas, she asked: "Do you think it was right? Now I have nothing left." And Kenny O'Donnell said, "You leave it where it is."

That was at 1:30 p.m. in Texas.

But then, at Bethesda Hospital in Maryland, at 3 a.m. the next morning, Kenny slipped into the chamber where the body lay and brought her back the ring, which, as she talked now, she twisted.

On her little finger was the other ring: a slim, gold circlet with green emerald chips—the one he had given her in memory of Patrick.

THERE was a thought, too, that was always with her. "When Jack quoted something, it was usually classical," she said, "but I'm so ashamed of myself—all I keep thinking of is this line from a musical comedy.

"At night, before we'd go to sleep, Jack liked to play some records; and the song he loved most came at the very end of this record. The lines he loved to hear were: *Don't let it be forgot, that once there was a spot, for one brief shining moment that was known as Camelot.*"

She wanted to make sure that the point came clear and went on: "There'll be great Presidents again—and the Johnsons are wonderful, they've been wonderful to me—but there'll never be another Camelot again.

"Once, the more I read of history the more bitter I got. For a while I thought

history was something that bitter old men wrote. But then I realized history made Jack what he was. You must think of him as this little boy, sick so much of the time, reading in bed, reading history, reading the Knights of the Round Table, reading Marlborough. For Jack, history was full of heroes. And if it made him this way—if it made him see the heroes—maybe other little boys will see. Men are such a combination of good and bad. Jack had this hero idea of history, the idealistic view."

But she came back to the idea that transfixed her: "*Don't let it be forgot, that once there was a spot, for one brief shining moment that was known as Camelot*—and it will never be that way again."

As for herself? She was horrified by the stories that she might live abroad. "I'm *never* going to live in Europe. I'm not going to 'travel extensively abroad.' That's a desecration. I'm going to live in the places I lived with Jack. In Georgetown, and with the Kennedys at the Cape. They're my family. I'm going to bring up my children. I want John to grow up to be a good boy."

As for the President's memorial, at first she remembered that, in every speech in their last days in Texas, he had spoken of how in December this nation would loft the largest rocket booster yet into the sky, making us first in space. So she had wanted something of his there when it went up—perhaps only his initials painted on a tiny corner of the great Saturn, where no one need even notice it. But now Americans will seek the moon from Cape Kennedy. The new

name, born of her frail hope, came as a
surprise.

The only thing she knew she must
have for him was the eternal flame over
his grave at Arlington.

"Whenever you drive across the
bridge from Washington into Virginia,"
she said, "you see the Lee Mansion on
the side of the hill in the distance.
When Caroline was very little, the
mansion was one of the first things she
learned to recognize. Now, at night you
can see his flame beneath the mansion
for miles away."

She said it is time people paid attention to the new President and the new
First Lady. But she does not want them
to forget John F. Kennedy or read of
him only in dusty or bitter histories:

For one brief shining moment there
was Camelot.

LIFE December 6, 1963

PUTTING DOWN, FOR GOOD, THE WHITE MAN'S BURDEN

It was time for us to go.

Our air force can still land in Thailand; and we maintain a beachhead in South Korea. But the Asia we dominated, from the Yalu to the Indus rivers, 30 years ago, has thrown us out. It is an event of such immense historic scale that we will be generations trying to understand it. Yet it is vital that we look at it now, for on this first reading depends the immediate future and whether we compound tragedy into disaster.

The proof of the matter is that we are hated there—and the roots of this hatred are so difficult for millions of good-willed Americans to understand that further blind good will can only make matters worse. I was watching television a few nights before the end, watching the on-loading and off-loading of orphans. It was an act of that characteristic humanitarian impulse that makes Americans proud, and makes American foreign policy so difficult for others to grasp. But I could not keep from translating what I saw on screen to my past in Asia, and imagining how, if I were on the other side, I could use this act of good will to inflame, prolong, and add

legend to the hatreds already rooted there. By such acts, the Vietnamese could be made, ultimately, to see us as the Balkan peoples saw the Turks—strangers who kidnapped their orphans, or stole their young, and carried them off to the Janizaries.

Groping to explain to myself why I was sickened, the word "iatrogenic" came to mind—that condition where the act of the physician to cure or heal an ailment intensifies and makes worse the disease he means to cure. Whatever we have tried to do to help Asians in the convulsion of their civilization has hurt them.

We were good-willed but stupid from the day I first set foot in Asia as a young reporter 35 years ago. What I left out of my reporting in all the years there was the simple dynamics of race hatred. Our presence there was self-defeating because they hated all of us, with historic good reason—and our efforts to aid always produced the effect of a drug for which a sick system has a built-in intolerance. We gave our first Asian aid to Chiang Kai-shek in the thirties to help him fight the Japanese. We increased our aid in the late forties to help him fight Communists. If we were to go the same road, he pleaded, we must help with guns. But he, too, hated white men, not because they were white but because of what Europeans had done to his country. For a century, the century of imperialism, Westerners had brutalized his people. Western civilization had pumped opium into them, policed their cities, overridden their laws, kicked them, beaten them, humiliated them. He took our aid shortsightedly, because he needed it, and became dependent on it as a narcotic, which he loathed but craved, and thus lost touch with reality and was ruined.

Perhaps only black Americans can sense that wild and helpless fury which the Asians felt at the presence of the white men. I saw it vividly for the first time in Hanoi, in 1940, where I discovered how much their life in the colonies had transformed the French I had known only in Paris. I remember watching appalled as Frenchmen, when annoyed, slapped or cuffed their native rickshaw drivers like children. I had never seen grown men cringe before. And I only clumsily recognized the connection between such brutality and the politics of the "rebels" whom the French had been trying to put down since the 1930's. But I remember a night spent with a lovely Annamite, who came of that beautiful stock that marries the robust Malay body with the delicate features of the Chinese. When I talked of permanent friendship with her later, however, she would have none of that. We both spoke broken French, but I gathered that she hated all white men,

and the conversation ended with her spitting on me.

Two and a half years later, early in 1943, I flew with the lead plane of the Eleventh Bomb Squadron, the most gung-ho bomb squadron of memory. It specialized in surprise strikes, and we made the first hit on Hanoi, the first American planes ever to strike that target—and a few days later we made the first hit on Haiphong. We were doing that more than 30 years ago to help free the Vietnamese and French from the Japanese. We were trying to do good. But given our crude bomb-sights of the time, and the jitters we always had on first strikes, I am sure we killed 100 Vietnamese innocents for every miserable Japanese installation we managed to splinter.

Through 40 years of war in Asia, we tried to help our friends by helping them kill other Asians, without understanding the political consequences of our actions. It went that way for years. I remember the long trail of retreat up from the lowlands of Kwangsi to the heights of Kweichow in the fall of 1944. We desolated the Chinese countryside, devastating every installation that might be useful to the Japanese advance, while the Chinese watched us, not understanding why we had to blow up their roads, bridges, villages in order to save them from the Japanese who were hard on our heels. The act was comprehensible to us, and justifiable in terms of war. But by 1967, when I last visited Vietnam, the practice had escalated into "free-fire zones." I was kept awake all one night by the boom of artillery around the headquarters of the I Corps where I was sleeping. It was supposedly safe country. When I asked in the morning what we were shooting at, I was told we were shooting at nothing—just putting out shells over the countryside to keep the guerrillas from moving around in the dark. War is politics—and the politics we left behind by years of such warfare is what incubated the end result in Vietnam.

The postwar Europeans were wiser than we because, I think, they bore the guilt of a century of imperialism, and they were less pious than we when it came to sacrificing their young men to do the dirty work of an empire once the profit was gone. The Europeans got out—out of China, of Indochina, of Indonesia, of India, of all their imperial dominions. But they needed some great power to help them on their way out. We did. We moved into Vietnam to get the French off the hook. And we hung ourselves instead, for, as we moved in, we inherited from the French the Vietnamese hatred of the white men left behind.

The unrecognized stupidity of the action did not come to me until years later. It was a compound stupidity. The lesser stupidity was the injection of our technology, which we should have known to be useless from our experience with Chaing Kai-shek in 1945–1948. We knew how to fight only one kind of war—the massing of machines and metal against the enemy to get maximum impact at a fixed contact point. We flew the divisions of Chiang Kai-shek from his real base of strength in the

Yangtze valley up to Peking, Tientsin, Manchuria, and the Yellow River valley for the redemption of China from Japanese occupation. They were dependent on our technology, our airlifts, our logistics for resupply—and when we decided to pull out our logistical resupply, we left his divisions artificially pocketed in cities that the Communists had already surrounded in the countryside. Once we decided to get out of the Chinese civil war, Chiang was doomed because he had become dependent on external aid and support. His forces were rigid and brittle.

The same thing, of course, happened in Vietnam. We built a defense force for the Republic of South Vietnam on the Fort Benning model—infantry taught to keep to the roads, supported by tanks, heavy artillery, sophisticated air cover. Once the American Congress decided not to support it any longer, it was doomed.

But the larger stupidity was political—truly iatrogenic. Our presence, in and of itself, spread political disease. Whomever we openly supported—that man, that premier, that general—could be tagged as the puppet of the white man. Against the white man's puppet, one could mobilize the emotions of everyone from rickshaw puller to peasant to student-intellectual. The critical thrust in a war comes from the simple ideas that move a man to lie in a ditch with only a shaped charge to hit the tank coming at him; the emotion that makes him go out at night to seek the enemy and kill; the purpose that makes him keep coming and coming still ready to die. If you can persuade a man that something is more important than his own life, he will gamble his life against odds that the staff and command school at Fort Leavenworth would consider suicidal.

I recall being in Vietnam in 1961 and discovering that the Communists had a popular tag on Ngo Dinh Diem. They called him simply "Mei-Diem," which meant "America's Diem." And being tagged as our puppet, he became, politically, a figure of futility. So, too, were all the other replacements we sought after he was assassinated in 1963. The politics of the war baffled us because they were so simple.

The corollary to the grand political stupidity was our ignorance of the culture, the history, the tradition of those we were trying to save. Millions of Vietnamese hated the Communists. One eighth of the population of North Vietnam had fled from the Communists after the settlement of 1954. In proportionate terms, it was as if 25 million Americans had fled this country after a change of regime. For ten years of battle the South resisted the North, because there was a real fabric of resistance to Communism. But we never learned to deal with the politics of the many anti-Communist groups we clustered under the leadership of Saigon. Of the 16 million people in South Vietnam, there were 2 million Cao Dai, and their rose-red cathedral made of their provincial capital in Tay Ninh one of the most stubborn centers of resistance to Communist assault. But we did not know who they were, what their strange cult-

religion held, why they were so anti-Communist. There were 2 million Catholics, a million Hoa Hao, half a million mercantile, ethnic, anti-Communist Chinese; another million Montagnards; plus Buddhists. We ignored them all, let the Saigon regime ignore them too, and rested our policy, uncomprehendingly, on the shifting military leaders of Saigon, who became ever more rigidly dependent on us, divorced from their own people, and political cartoons of white man's puppets.

IT IS what comes next that counts. The most natural instinct politically would be for Americans to recoil, to retract into isolation, and stuff away into forgetfulness the great blunder in Asia along with the triumphs of American policy elsewhere abroad.

If so, nothing can redeem the tragedy, for the only gain we can possibly carry away from the long war is by contrasting what we have learned there in Asia against what we have learned elsewhere in the world. If we do not draw the lessons correctly, then the defeat in Vietnam could be remembered as the defeat of the Spanish Armada is remembered—the end of Spanish greatness, the shrinking of the greatest empire of the sixteenth century into a province-state locked in an enclave protected by the Pyrenees. The Spaniards learned nothing from their defeat, neither of the new arts of war nor of the new politics of nationalism in northern Europe that underlay such arts. They, too, confused their faith with their interests, and did not understand the faith or politics of other peoples.

What we should have learned in Vietnam can, perhaps, be very simply stated: we can offer no aid that will advance the cause of our friends in Asia or Africa if that aid is accompanied by our presence. Wherever, in the old colonial world, the virus of race hatred remains, as it does, it will be stimulated by the returning presence of the white man. Such aid will always be iatrogenic.

But if we contrast the American record elsewhere than on the Asian continent, there still remains a huge and viable arena of American action. If our greatest postwar triumph of diplomacy came with the Marshall Plan in Western Europe, it came because that massive aid program was delivered to peoples who shared our culture, values, and understanding of the past. That aid worked because it could be understood both by European leaders and Europeans in the street. But it was not our only triumph. Japan has been treated by American statecraft with enormous skill and success—and remains the greatest

legacy of Douglas MacArthur, who had lived years in the Orient and come to understand it. South Korea remains viable because there the remembered conquerors are other Asians, Chinese, and Japanese, not white men. And in the Middle East, Israel, sharing its politics and traditions with Western culture, remains not only viable, but essential as an ally of American policy—the sole beachhead we can think of retaining as leverage in the oil-rich center of contemporary energy.

In short, therefore, the episode in Vietnam can be allowed to become unmitigated disaster or it can be reduced to a tragedy that we must mourn but can live with, depending on what we have learned. What we should have learned is clear: the reach of American power is not the reach of our bombers, our helicopters, our fleet, our logistics. The reach of American power extends only as far as the reach of American political understanding.

NEW YORK May 12, 1975

A THIN GREEN LINE

Three miles to the west is the legal gateway where 24 lanes fan out from the two main highways leaving Mexico. There the border control sorts out returning tourists, cross-border transients and legal immigrants from the illegals. Beyond, to the north, the lanes join again in Interstate 5, 16 miles from San Diego. But the legal gateway, though the largest immigrant inlet in the U.S., is not the real gateway.

One comes on that on the ridge, just south of Highway 117, where the border patrol is posted. One jounces over the rutted dirt roads and passes a watchtower, where three black horses mounted by three dark-uniformed men are waiting for nightfall. Bad casting—good guys ride white horses. It is explained: here good guys ride dark horses because they patrol at night and white horses show.

On the ridge, one looks out over the basin they call the "soccer field," a darkening patch beyond which the hills of Mexico are cutouts against the fading sun, and the twinkling lights of Tijuana define the line that divides Mexico from the U.S. Between those lights and this ridge is the bowl of contention. Where

we stand is American land: the people gathering in clumps below are determined to enter it.

The eye takes in the scene casually, picking out antlike figures here and there. Then the mind focuses: these are people exploring a word-of-mouth folk gateway. Law does not bind them. One scans: mostly men, some in white shirts, most in black pants and jackets. One picks out women too—in red skirts, flowered blouses. Little fires show where supper is being cooked and eaten. A dozen here, 40 there, and suddenly one is aware that there must be several thousand down there preparing to push across the border.

Along the rim of the basin are 30, perhaps 40, green-uniformed men of the border patrol—a thin green line. They must be young and vigorous for they must run on foot to catch the invaders in the night: many of them are Mexican Americans whose parents once waited in line to get visas to enter this country legally. Now down below are those who are driven by hunger to enter without permission. The thin green line has been deployed to catch a wave of thousands. Most of those below will get through because the protection net cannot possibly shield this corner of America from the pressures that force these migrants to the dash. Shooting would stop them. But our men are forbidden to shoot unless fired on. This is a cops-and-raiders game conducted under humane rules.

At dusk, the figures down below begin their surge up the slopes below Highway 117, over the sandy paths and foot-trodden trails, up the sage-and-mesquite-covered hills. It is dark now. An American helicopter hovers over them, its belly light picking out those closest to the border. We hear the crackle of the radio giving coordinates; we see the men on black horses rounding up the clumps of those who have already crossed; one horse has thrown its rider. The more timid migrants pull back to the lee of Tijuana's airport on the mesa below. A boy pushes his bicycle up a hill; if he can get through, he will speed off to safety. We are too busy to chase a singleton. The women are fading into the dark; they are few but occasionally troublesome. One woman gave birth a few months ago in the back of one of the vans that bus illegals back to Mexico. But the baby was born on American soil and is thus an American citizen, entitled to all the privileges and support systems of the American nation—and so are her father and mother once the child reaches the age of 21.

The guards that perform the roundup do not even bother to herd the night's catch into razor-coil pens; they take them immediately to the Mexican gates. Of course, the Mexicans can and will make another try another night. Illegal immigrants can be tried in federal courts and receive six months in jail and a $500 fine. But even one night's catch if held for trial would clog all the federal courts in Southern California for months on end. The border patrol holds the Nicaraguans, Salvadorans and Asians who slip into the flow; they cannot merely be bused back to the borders of their countries.

And the flow mounts. The pressure back there beyond the Mexican rim is overwhelming. The border patrol picked up 4,000 lawless migrants back in 1965; in 1985 the number was 421,000. In one month alone last year, on the 18-mile stretch of the San Diego sector, the patrol shipped 49,900 back. This year, in April, the number rose to 72,000, an average of over 2,300 arrests a day. The farmers, wanderers, smugglers, pregnant mothers, drug peddlers do not seem like the stuff of crisis, but they are. The immigration service estimates that in 1986 they will catch 1.8 million illegals crossing our borders; but more will get through and change our cities and our lives.

Up the hills from the soccer field, chances for slipping through are fifty-fifty. There is the highway to traverse with blazing headlights and American speed to contend with; some get killed crossing that way. Once across though, it is only a few miles into San Diego and the America whose streets are paved with gold—or at least with $4-an-hour jobs. A young man pressed by hope and hunger can make it to the city in a good night's hike.

What makes them come? Alan Eliason, chief patrol agent of the troubled
sector, answers. Eliason is a tall, husky,
thoughtful man, well read: "We've been
sending out the signals too long. The
signal says: come. There are jobs for you
here, schools for your children, hospitals for your sick, and the whole security
net we've built is waiting for you."

One drives back to San Diego in the
night, and one passes the base of America's Pacific Fleet in San Diego Bay. In
the dim lights, one can make out flattops, missile cruisers, Aegis cruisers,
destroyers, perhaps $50 billion or $100
billion worth of hardware to guard our
shores. But the U.S. Navy cannot guard
the hills and gullies a few miles inland
from the invasion not of an enemy but
of the poor, the hungry, the persistently
determined to find a way in.

TIME August 25, 1986

Chapter 2

Three Who Made a Difference

White was ever fascinated by the world's movers and shakers, and profiles of them became a trademark. Here are three, quintessentially Teddy White:

Chiang Kai-shek, peasant, soldier, leader of wartime China: "[We may be at] the beginning of an era in which China will emerge as one of the world's top powers and Chiang as Asia's greatest man since Genghis Khan." [It must be noted that this was written well before White became disenchanted with Chiang, a change of heart that ultimately precipitated a total break with Time Inc. founder Henry R. Luce. (See also introduction to Chapter 5.)]

W. Averell Harriman, patrician, dedicated troubleshooter for presidents: "No American in public affairs today can match his knowledge of the people and pressures who, all around the world, shape the decisions and posture of America in this age of torment."

Dean Rusk, son of a Georgia preacher, secretary of state under John F. Kennedy: "That Dean Rusk should be a cause of controversy has come to Washington as a surprise, for in any quick poll at the beginning of the Kennedy administration, solid Dean Rusk would certainly have been voted that member of the President's Cabinet least likely to arouse controversy."

CHIANG KAI-SHEK

The leader of fighting China plays a commanding role in the Allied war effort and the destiny of all Asia.

On Feb. 10 China's Generalissimo Chiang Kai-shek, accompanied by his wife and 15 military aides, having crossed the border of his native land for the first time since 1931, arrived at New Delhi, India. There, that evening, he attended a large formal banquet given by the Marquess of Linlithgow, India's Viceroy, who in his address of welcome quoted Confucius to the effect that it is "delightful to have men of kindred spirit come to one from afar." Always practical, Chiang replied with an even more appropriate Chinese proverb: "To have one look at things is a hundred times more satisfactory than hearsay."

The day after the banquet, Chiang and General Sir Alan Fleming Hartley, Commander in Chief in India, reviewed Indian troops from a Rolls-Royce on which a Union Jack fluttered from the radiator cap like a raccoon tail on a college boy's Ford. After the review Chiang mounted a dais to be cheered by a large crowd. At New Delhi, Chiang and his party stayed in villas specially provided for them, within view of the lofty blue dome of the Viceroy's palace. In contrast to Chungking, where conveniences are makeshift, they were waited on by servants in red coats and gold braid. During his stay Chiang got word from London that His Majesty's Government had seen fit to make him an Honorary Knight of the Bath, Military Division, in honor of "outstanding achievements in the Allied cause."

Chiang Kai-shek's visit to India was not, despite its pleasant appurtenances, a vacation. Its true purposes were: 1) to see how munitions factories, from which arms have been moving to China across the Burma Road were functioning and how they were being defended; 2) to talk of the new ersatz Burma Road, from Assam into China and find out what the Indian Government had done to make the new road function; and 3) to investigate India's general military potential, including relations between his British friends and the Indian Congress under the leadership of Mahatma Gandhi and Pandit Jawaharlal Nehru.

Chiang Covers Ground Rapidly

Between formalities, Chiang attended to business. This took the form of an air

33

inspection of border fortifications and a series of momentous conferences with both British authorities and Pandit Jawaharlal Nehru, whose Party believes that India must be guaranteed full independence as a reward for a full war effort. Starting his trip back to Chungking, Chiang, accompanied now by Nehru as well as his own party, stopped off at Calcutta to see the shriveled old Mahatma himself. The conference with Gandhi resulted in nothing so grand as a "people's alliance," but it seemed extremely possible that Chiang had at least made his point that passive resistance might prove to be a hopelessly feeble weapon against Jap aggression. That the more immediate objectives of his visit had been accomplished at least in part was indicated by an announcement while he was staying at Calcutta that Rangoon harbor had been mined and that henceforth his armies would be supplied by rail and river over the route from Assam.

Alternatives to sound co-operation between India and China are fairly obvious. If the Japs can persuade India to feel that India fighting for England would be like a fish fighting for the frying pan, Asia will be taken over by the Axis in short order. On the other hand, if India's 390,000,000 souls become convinced that their interests, like those of China's 450,000,000 will be served best by defeating Japan, Chiang's excursion last week may be as far-reaching in its consequences as Winston Churchill's recent one to Washington. It might mark the beginning of an era in which China will emerge as one of the

world's top powers and Chiang as Asia's greatest man since Genghis Khan.

Five years ago Chiang Kai-shek was practically unknown outside China. He first emerged on the world stage in December 1936, while lying sick and captive in a war lord's lair at Sian. Announcers at American radio stations, which issued frequent bulletins on his kidnaping, were puzzled by the name of China's leader. They referred to him consistently as "Kai-shek," unaware that, since Chinese surnames come first, this was as inappropriate as calling Stalin "Joseph." Many young Americans, twisting the dials in search of swing music, must have twirled the misused name into hearing and then flicked it out. They might have lingered to hear more if they had known Chiang was the man who, five years later almost to the week, would be placed in complete command of their lives and personal destinies, as Supreme Commander of Allied land and air forces in the Chinese theater of war.

By the end of the first month of America's war, Chiang had turned up in American headlines with the only Allied land victory in the campaign against Japan: the smashing of the Changsha thrust which cost the enemy up to 50,000 men. Even more significantly Chiang Kai-shek sent into action over Burma a handful of American volunteer pilots recruited from every walk of American life. In continuous swift battles Chiang's Americans shot down more than 120 Japanese planes, lost only about ten of their own and proved that man for man, plane for plane,

Americans could shoot Japanese out of the sky at will. Last week, Chiang's land forces were successful pushing the Japs across the Siam border to Chiengmai.

These operations were carried out efficiently, with a minimum of waste motion. If U.S. soldiers in training at home gave thought to the possibilities of later service under Chiang, it must have encouraged them to reflect that he was a military technician of surpassing skill. Chiang Kai-shek led his first unit into fire in 1911. Of the past 17 years of Chiang Kai-shek's life, not one has failed to include some war, great or small. He wrung the title Generalissimo out of Chinese history by winning over or destroying completely, over the course of 20 years, a group of generals, marshals, comrades and variously designated free-booting adventurers who were tearing China to bits. All his mature life Chiang Kai-shek has been using force as habitually as some other leaders have used words. The habit has made him cold, relentless, slow to give confidence. It has also made him a first-class fighting man, and the men who serve under him or with him are content with that.

The most important single fact about Chiang Kai-shek is, of course, that he is a soldier. This obscures the fact that he is also the shrewdest politician in China. Chiang's talents for both war and politics were developed in the violence of the Chinese civil wars. Now, as his greatest war rises to climax with new allies, new problems and new frictions pressing for attention, Chiang is probably serene in one of the basic convictions the Chinese civil wars made clear to him: a good common hate can be the strongest bond between two allies. Chiang Kai-shek has been hating the Japs early and late for a good five years. Sometimes his tenacity in this direction has puzzled not only the outside world but some of his own weaker-willed associates as well.

"Ni Men Ta Suan Pan!"

In the summer of 1940 the spirit of the Chinese reached one of its all-war lows. The Japanese had taken the Yangtze port of Ichang, putting their bombers within 300 miles of Chungking. Raids went on day and night. The same clear sky that brought the raiders burned rice in the stalk and famine was in prospect. The French Army had blown up, the Japanese were in Indo-China, America was in a state of nervous hysteria. To top things, the British, alarmed by Japanese threats, announced that they were closing the Burma Road for three months. With the Burma Road closed, the sole remaining link of China with America and the West was gone.

During this period of unrelieved gloom Chiang Kai-shek called a meeting of his councilors. The Japanese—unofficially—had made known what they required for a settlement. Peace was in the air. What would Chiang say to his dispirited advisers?

Chiang's speech was characteristic. "Ni men ta suan pan (You people are counting beads on a counting board)," he burst out, going on to explain. "You count how many troops we have, how many rounds of ammunition, how many gallons of gasoline are left. But I don't count. I don't care. When I started 15 years ago I had only 2,000 cadets in a military school. And America was against me, and France, and England, and Japan. And the Communists were more powerful than they are today. And I had no money. And I marched north and I licked the war lords. I united the country. Today I have 3,000,000 men and half of China and the friendship of America and England. Let them come, let them drive me back into Sikong [part of Tibet]. In five years I will be back here and I will conquer all China again."

That was the end of peace talk for that summer.

Chiang has only one emotion: China. He looks at the war map with a sense of dispassionate detachment, moves his armies and men about like pawns on a continental chessboard. In 1938, Japanese armies were wheeling down out of the plains of Shantung on what was then the most strategic rail junction in the country, Chengchow. There was only one way to stop them—blow up the dikes on the south bank of the Yellow River so that the turbulent muddy current would cut across their path. To give the order meant that thousands of Chinese peasants would drown along with the enemy, that thousands more would be driven into the interior on a mad, disease-cursed trek. But it was the only way. Orders were given—with Chiang Kai-shek's consent—and the

dikes blew up. The map was changed, but the Japanese were stopped.

The stubbornness of Chiang is reflected in the map of China today: the battle fronts, soggy with blood, stretch almost exactly along lines held for three full years. Chiang Kai-shek has simply refused to retreat farther.

Chiang's Stubbornness Is Military Virtue

It is unlikely that American officers and men who serve with Chiang will find his stubbornness unpleasant. Friction, however, is sure to develop when tough Chinese Burma Road truckies find that American standards of road practice differ from theirs and that the American standard must prevail, and when Chinese mechanics find that American aviators will curse and complain until they learn to handle delicate machinery with American care. It will go on too until Americans learn that barefoot Chinese soldiers know more about fighting Japanese than the best infantry divisions in the U.S.A. Tough Chinese top sergeants will show scant courtesy to spick-and-span American officers as they explain how Japanese machine-gun posts are laid out, how a Japanese charge can best be met, how a depth-defense position can be embroidered in 48 hours to mousetrap an overwhelming enemy. Both Chiang Kai-shek and the American command probably discount such difficulties in advance. Chiang is an astute horse trader and a first-class swap is possible: American technical and administrative standards for China's practical five-year-old skill in Jap killing. Chiang will make his subordinates see that the deal works.

For more than 20 years it has been almost impossible for Chinese journalists, even when they wanted to, to write honestly of Chiang. In enemy territory it was unhealthy to praise; in Kuomintang territory, unhealthy to detract. In any case, the facts were little known, partly because Chiang's origins were obscure and partly because his activities have been complex. Chiang was born in 1887 to a farming family in the village of Chikow, near Fenghua, in the province of Chekiang. He still speaks with a crisp Chekiang accent that irritates Chinese intellectuals who affect the liquid syllables of North China Mandarin. Chiang still loves his native village. In peacetime he retires there as often as he can for vacation and lavishes money on its beautification. It is mountain country, incised with the crescent slivers of rice paddy fields, the slopes of the hills bamboo-covered, and the streams clear, thin and fast. Chiang's father was a man of dignity and standing who had, successively, three wives. Chiang was born of the third mating and the love he bears his mother is sincere and deep. On his 50th birthday he said:

". . . Now that the trees by her grave have grown tall and thick, I cannot but realize how little I have accomplished and how I have failed to live up to the hopes that she had placed in me. . . . My father died when I was 9 years old. . . . My family, solitary and without influence, became at once the target of insults and maltreatment. . . . It was entirely due to my mother and her kindness and perseverance that the family was saved from utter ruin. For a period of 16 years—from the age of 9 till I was 25 years old, my mother never spent a day free of domestic difficulties. . . ."

Chiang was born at a moment when powerful neighbors were trampling on China. China's humiliation was based on one thing—she was simply unable to organize men and machines into military and industrial patterns as efficient as those the Western nations had taught themselves. Out of China's weakness came Chiang Kai-shek's determination to become a soldier. He placed high in his provincial examinations for admission to the first Chinese military academy at Paoting. He was an outstanding member of its first class and chosen to go on to Tokyo for further instruction.

In Japan, Chiang first met Sun Yatsen, China's George Washington, who won him to the cause of revolution. The first military action in which Chiang took part was an insurrection against the Manchu Empire in 1911. When this putsch was finally betrayed by its own Dictator-President Yuan Shih-ai, Chiang slipped back into obscurity. For a while he was connected with the sinister Green Gang of Shanghai—a semimystic, violent society that flourished in the underworld of the mud-flat metropolis of northern China. Chinese are careful to point out that the revolutionary movement in China was so persecuted that it had to draw support from any and all groups who wanted to overthrow the Manchu regime. Chiang during this period lived on a limited budget except for a brief interval when he was a prosperous stockbroker on the Shanghai exchange.

China's Civil Wars Were Complex

The period that followed the revolution against the Manchus was one of confusion for China. For people outside China, the confusion indeed was such that it seemed impossible to understand at all and most intelligent newsreaders wisely made no effort to do so. What actually happened was that by 1921 China had been carved up into a patchwork of satrapies run by war lords who were usually both colorful and vicious. Each war lord had an army, each army its district. Pock-marked, syphilitic soldiers, often wolfish with hunger, often looting for sustenance, marched back and forth over the map of China, establishing chaos as the normal state of civil affairs.

China's multiple civil wars had little in common with properly organized civil wars—like those for instance of the U.S., Russia or Spain. Since the Chinese had a profound contempt for soldiering in general—which it took Chiang years to uproot—no more than a minute percentage of the population was ever engaged in all the wars put together at any given moment. Inured to accidental disasters like floods and famine, which were far more inclusive in their effects, the majority of the population seemed to go about its business as if the struggle for power between the war lords did not concern it at all. Consequently this period of the civil wars also included a surprising amount of progress in civil affairs like roadbuilding, transportation, education and industry. Out of the wars themselves, moreover, there eventually evolved the Kuomintang, or Chinese Nationalist Party, fathered by Sun Yat-sen and staffed with such men as Chiang Kai-shek, which has run China ever since.

Sun Yat-sen, wanting as much as any human could to establish democracy in China, knew that words alone were not enough. There was only one man whom Sun Yat-sen knew to have both ability in the field and a fidelity to China that transcended his fidelity to force. That was Chiang Kai-shek. From 1921 on, Chiang was always by the side of Sun, fighting to whip together an army for the revolution. The Chinese Nationalists in 1923 were offered the political and military support of the Soviet Union. In 1923 Chiang went to Moscow to visit and came away unfavorably impressed. His antipathy to Communism as an influence in Chinese governments has lasted ever since.

Chiang came back to Canton in the spring of 1924 to perform a profoundly important act—the organization of the Whampoa Military Academy. This academy became the West Point of new China. To Chiang the young officers gave the personal devotion that exists only between a Chinese student and his teacher. The Whampoa Academy differed from its predecessors in that it had a political motif: the lives of its students were important only to make China strong and united. As they graduated from their hurried courses, Chiang made his students officers in the new armies of Nationalist China. Chiang's generals were drawn from every stratum of Chinese war lordism; but the brave young captains and lieutenants were his own Whampoa boys. As the boys grew to maturity in days of later civil war, they fought their way to the command of regiments, brigades, divisions and army corps. Always, ever since, no matter who has ruled the Government of China nominally, the young officers of the Chinese Army have been Chiang's own men.

Chiang's Agents Organized Revolution

While Chiang organized the academy—getting up at 5 in the morning, making up his own room, drilling students, inspecting equipment and planning—his agents were sneaking off to the north, organizing peasants and workers for the great day of insurrection. By July of 1926 the revolutionists were ready. Chiang gave the signal to the troops he had assembled. As they marched north, the ground seemed to heave in welcome to them. Moving swiftly, Chiang cut down one war lord after another. In three months his armies had occupied Hankow. Five months later they were in Nanking. By the middle of 1928 North China had been entirely conquered.

But Chiang was not yet through with war. In 1929 began a second series of civil wars which Chiang undertook to establish the authority of his Government. Two campaigns in 1929, two more in 1930, brought further victories. Gradually war lords learned that the "Central Government" meant to govern. Chiang ruled with an iron hand. When his autocratic conduct of the government and arrest of political opponents brought cries of "dictator" from every part of the country, Chiang simply resigned again and returned with Madame Chiang to his native village. It was the Japanese who underlined how ill China could spare Chiang on this occasion. They had seized Manchuria in the fall of 1931, three months before Chiang was forced out of the Government. As the conflict spread, Shanghai erupted in the first Shanghai war of 1932. The Chinese realized that only Chiang Kai-shek could supply the necessary leadership during crisis. They made haste to call him back.

The years from 1931 to 1937 were, for Chiang, mostly years of preparation and domestic progress. He pushed his anti-Communist campaigns but he knew that the civil wars were only preliminaries and that eventually, in the main event, he would have to fight Japan. As Chiang's Central Government grew in strength, the currency system throughout the country was unified, railroads were pushed through, the Army modernized and a stable basis of commerce and industry laid down. By the spring of 1937, Chiang had made of China one nation for the first time in a generation.

The Japanese could not wait to see China become powerful—and so, in July 1937, they struck. Chiang's armies could not match the mechanized Japanese. Slowly he retreated, trading space for time. A year and a half after the war's outbreak he had finally reached a stable line—and that line he has held almost changeless for the past three and a half years. From his rocky, uncomfortable mountain capital Chungking, Chiang today looks out on 2,800 miles of battle front, guarded by three million and more soldiers and the war goes on.

Lean and shaven-pated, Chiang is, by Chinese standards, a handsome man. He stands always as if there were a ramrod of steel in his back. When seated, he sits bolt upright in his great chair, always listening, rarely talking, frequently stroking his smooth chin with a nervous gesture. Chiang has a terrific temper. In anger, his naturally high-pitched voice shoots up till it is almost falsetto and the blunt harsh words come tumbling out, sparing no one. In such fury he has been known to demote the highest-placed generals without a second thought.

Chiang's favorite form of assent is the single one-word grunt, "hao" (good), or "ko ye" (can do). With such a grunt he may set in motion half a million men. Chiang rarely composes the smoothly eloquent declarations that appear over his name. They are the products, usually, of his old secretary, Ch'en Pu-lei, a former journalist who joined Chiang's staff many years ago. Chiang's widely published diary of the Sian kidnaping consists of Chiang's original curt, staccato jottings, polished up to a bright gloss for popular consumption.

Chiang declaims his speeches in a high falsetto that is quickly absorbed and lost in great mass meetings. He finishes his speeches with an abrupt gesture, a flat sweeping motion of the hand, a short bark, "wan le" (finished). In off-the-record conversations with his ministers, he is pithy, picturesque or profound but his public pronouncements rarely reveal his personality. His niggardly, grudging use of the spoken word is the despair of visiting journalists who may be granted an audience of ten or 15 minutes with the great man. They usually spend two or three minutes outlining long involved questions to which Chiang listens in quiet patience. When the question is over and translated Chiang usually murmurs softly, "yes" or "no" or "very difficult."

Chiang is Generalissimo of the Armed Forces, Chairman of the National Military Council, Chairman of the Supreme National Defense Council, President of the Executive Yuan (Premier), Chairman of the Presidium of the People's Political Council, Chairman of the Joint Board of the four Government banks, Director-General of the Kuomintang, President of the National New Life Movement, Director General of the San Min Chu I Youth Corps, Principal of the Central Military Academy, of the Central Political Institute and the Central Aviation Academy—in addition to his United Nations job as Supreme Commander. His favorite job is the Army. Most distasteful to him is probably the premiership. He appeared at meetings of the cabinet, it is said, only four times in the first 18 months after he assumed the post. Chinese usually refer to Chiang as *"Wei Yuan Chang"*— a title meaning "The Committee Head" (National Military Council). When his old comrades, the buccaneering, colorful, roistering crew of old soldiers who have fought with and against Chiang for the past 20 years, speak of him they say simply *"lao chiang"*—"old chiang"— with a reminiscent affection.

Chiang today is an ascetic—he neither smokes, drinks, plays cards nor gambles. The turbulence of his youth, the gay parties and long nights in Suchow for which he was famous, are over. He is rather humorless—which is odd in a nation noted for its highly developed sense of humor. Chiang's only personal relaxation now is picnicking. He likes long walks in the country with Madame Chiang and a few personal friends. While the children of many lesser Government ministers are safe in America or in soft jobs, Chiang's own children—two sons—are working hard in unimportant posts far from their father. His younger, Ching-kuo, is a lieutenant at the northern front. The elder, Wei-kuo, is a prefectural superintendent in South Central China.

Chiang lives in a ten-room house in a Chungking suburb, surrounded by a 40-ft. stone wall, whose driveway is guarded by two fully armed soldiers. Within the compound, the grounds are most carefully patrolled by plain clothesmen and uniformed guards. Chiang rises at 5 in the morning, does Chinese physical exercises in his own

room, prays in silence. At 7 he eats a light meal of fruit, toast, coffee. Madame and the Generalissimo used to have specially selected foods (including Sunkist oranges, Knox's gelatin, apples), flown up to them from Hong Kong. After breakfast he reads reports, petitions, mail sifted to him through the army, the Party and the civilian Government, marking the documents with one simple Chinese character in blue ink "yes" or "no."

He and Madame Chiang usually lunch alone, except on Fridays. On Fridays, Chiang has about 20 important people in to discuss problems of state. After lunch he has a short rest, then more reports and conferences. In the afternoons he is likely to drive downtown, in one of his enormous American-built limousines, to the National Military Council for a conference. On such drives Chiang is preceded and followed by cars of bodyguards dressed in gray or black. Chiang's bodyguard, organized by Germans and highly efficient, is with him constantly. Chiang has lived in constant danger of death since the first assassination attempt against him in 1914. Many attempts have been made to kill him since, but during the war years in Chungking all such incidents have been immediately shushed. Chiang's personal courage is unquestioned. During air raids he is the constant worry of his subordinates who urge him to shelter long before he himself is ready to go. Occasionally, after the alarm is sounded, he will decide to sit the air raid out across the river in his mountain cottage. With all the streets deathly still, Chiang will race through the empty, dusty roads in his limousine, shoot across the swiftly swirling Yangtze in his private launch and then unhurriedly stroll into the waiting car on the other side.

The Chiangs dine at 7:30, usually in private, although there may be entertainment for important visiting foreigners or generals later in the evening. When Chiang spreads himself on a banquet, the food is superlative, but normally the table is quite simple for a Chungking official. After dinner Chiang reads, wearing simple rimless reading glasses. He has a fondness for history and almost never reads fiction. Before going to bed he writes in his diary—briefly, simply. The last thing he does before turning in is to plug a phone call through to the National Military Council asking for the latest reports from the front. These being all right, he goes to sleep.

Chiang has aged greatly during the war. His mustache has begun to show flecks of gray. His back was injured during the Sian kidnaping and he has never fully recovered since. He used to suffer badly from toothaches, but is now quite satisfied with his new false teeth made by a Canadian dentist at the mission-supported West China Union University School of Dentistry. Chiang is always immaculately dressed. He usually appears on public occasions in a simple khaki uniform, trussed in a Sam Browne belt. For pictures he sometimes appears in his epaulets. At other times he likes to wear simple Sun Yat-sen suits—a popular pajama-like garment, buttoning high at the neck. At home,

he often wears his long Chinese gown and a dark jacket over it.

Chiang's chief joy and delight in life is his wife, Mei-ling, whose career and accomplishments are probably better known to most U.S. newsreaders than her husband's. Chiang first met Mei-ling Soong in Canton during the early days of the revolution. As the outstanding military figure of the Nationalists, Chiang had as associates such leaders as Sun Yat-sen and H. H. Kung, both of them married to Soong sisters, daughters of the celebrated Bible salesman Charles Soong. Promptly, and conveniently, the handsome young general and the beautiful daughter of what was to become the most distinguished family in the nation fell genuinely in love. Chiang was already married to an old fashioned Chinese girl from whom he had separated. His divorce, courtship and conversion to Methodist Christianity took place over a period of eight years.

Romance with Mei-ling Was Dramatic

He and Mei-ling were married in 1927. Chiang Mei-ling is almost more American then Chinese. She came to the States at the age of 9 and lived here till she was 21, rounding off her education at Wellesley. Madame Chiang's almost legendary charm overwhelms even the most sophisticated Westerners. She is not, however, as some Americans believe, the power behind the throne but rather Chiang's confidante and close companion.

Although the Generalissimo speaks

no English, he has learned one word from his Americanized wife: "darling." During their honeymoon, he called her "darling" so often that the chair bearers thought it was her official title and addressed her as Mrs. Darling themselves. She fondly calls him *"Chieh-hsiung"*—an untranslatable term of respectful affection. During the United China Relief Campaign in America, certain Americans wanted her to come to the U.S. to help in the drive. Madame wanted to go, but Chiang was firm. "But she will be worth a division of troops to you in America," one American expostulated. "Ah," said the Generalissimo, "she is worth ten divisions of troops to me in Chungking."

Chiang's Christianity is something foreigners find very difficult to understand. Madame Chiang's mother did not wish her daughter to marry a heathen. Chiang replied that he would be a poor Christian if he adopted the faith only because he wanted to marry Mei-ling, but he promised to reflect on the matter after they were married. His conversion occurred three years later. A man of Chiang's iron will does not easily doff or don a creed; nor does he adopt a religion for the sake of publicity. And yet Chiang's life of violence, his ruthless treatment of Communist students dur-

ing the white reaction of 1931–34, seems to cut directly across the rather gentle faith which he professes. Missionaries in China explain the contradiction by saying that Chiang is an "Old Testament Christian."

Chiang's is a life that spans two worlds—the ancient world of feudalism in China, the revolution that broke it, the new world of force and machines into which he is leading his country via the war. Military prospects, despite the current threat to the Burma Road, last week seemed reasonably bright, in the light of his new alliance with the U.S. and England and with the aid of India in prospect. Chiang's thoughts, as he flew back to Chungking must have been in part somewhat also on the role China will have to play in the post-war world, a role that will be totally different from that of her past. An Allied victory would make China one of the four great powers of the world. Hers then will be the leadership of the restless masses of the world's greatest continent. In the fashioning of that leadership Chiang Kai-shek may have greater influence than any other single human being of our age.

LIFE March 2, 1942

"WISE MAN" IN QUEST OF SECURITY

Averell Harriman, America's global agent and consultant to NATO, is at his best in creating a right climate for important actions.

Of all the practitioners in the art of giving away money none, since the records of history began, can match William Averell Harriman. In the course of the past twelve years, Mr. Harriman has supervised the giving away of some 25 to 30 billion dollars worth of American goods and money to a score of past Allies, current Allies and potential Allies not to mention three of four ex-enemies and enemies-to-be.

No possible description of Mr. Harriman's great contribution to American foreign policy could irritate him more than this. The words "giving" and "aid," especially when modified in such a phrase as "foreign aid," act on him like an emetic. In his own personal estimate, he "gives" nothing. What he does, and has been doing, ever since Harry Hopkins chose him to boss Lend-Lease distribution in wartime England is a purchasing agent's job—the purchasing for America of a vital commodity called Mutual Security. This is a favorite phrase of Mr. Harriman and makes him all the more pleased with his new job whose august title is Director for Mutual Security.

As Director for Mutual Security, Mr. Harriman will in the next few weeks ask Congress for almost eight billion dollars more to give (or buy security) over the next year. And this will be only a down payment on the purchase of a system of global security which may, by 1955, cost the United States yet another ten to twenty billion dollars.

To many people, giving a billion dollars away seems as easy as making water flow downhill. Actually, it is an intricate and highly specialized craft. When the giving is bungled it can buy not security, but disaster. In China, where America gave an estimated two to three billion dollars worth of aid after the war, it purchased tragedy. Mr. Harriman, it should be noted, had nothing to do with the giving in Asia, although, in his new job he is charged with the supervision of Asia too.

Skill in the art of giving requires, in the first instance, a cold appreciation of what money is and what the true meaning of a "million" or a "billion" is. In the days when Pitt was bracing England's continental alliance against Napoleon, a million meant simply a given weight in gold sovereigns, sealed in lead coffers and smuggled by agents into the hands of England's continental

Allies. An American billion is something else again. It is a kinetic, creative force which, to be useful, needs cold but imaginative direction.

In modern American diplomacy, as practiced, say, by Mr. Harriman under the Marshall Plan, it has meant among other things, the decision and tools to clean malaria off the island of Sardinia, to create a modern steel industry in France, to open a railway through the African jungle to bring out raw materials for the Western world. Mr. Harriman must now convert the billions that Congress gives him to buy security not only into several score European divisions, several hundred squadrons of combat-ready planes in Europe and a stable economy; he must also, in his spare moments, see that the wand waves alive new fisheries in Indonesia, irrigation dams in India, and rice cooperatives in Formosa.

MR HARRIMAN'S apprenticeship in the interrelation of money and power began at an early age. The glamour of a single mil lion was rubbed off in a home presided over by a father much less interested in the numerous millions he had amassed than in the mileage and power of the railways with which he attempted to girdle the globe. The elder Harriman, who never quite succeeded in extending his empire to China as once he hoped, left his sons, W. Averell and E. Roland, with a rail domain that stretched from Illinois to the Pacific coast.

Averell Harriman learned how to operate this heritage literally from the ground up, racing swiftly up the ladder held for the boss' son from track-layer and fireman to the eminence of vice president of the Union Pacific Railroad at the age of 24. Despite the handicap of being an enormously wealthy young man, Harriman displayed an energy and lust for work that made him, by the time he was 35, one of the most seasoned and respected investment bankers in Wall Street, in an era when Wall Street boiled with successful investment bankers. It was as an investment banker that Harriman learned Europe first; he helped finance the first major resumption of Soviet trade with America (a fur deal); and also displayed considerable skill in dodging the disastrous collapse that brought sorrow to other American enterprises of that period in central Europe.

THE SOCIAL turbulence of the Nineteen Thirties diverted the Harriman energies, always prodigious, from banking and business into public affairs. "Ave has an instinct for power," said a friend recently. "He gravitates to it like a bee to a honey pot." Averell Harriman of the Long Island polo-playing set, with an up-country estate in New York, a winter place in Florida (Hobe Sound) and several lesser establishments scattered around the world, including a hunting lodge in Austria, seemed an unlikely candidate for eminence in the New Deal. Under the patronage of Harry Hopkins, the saddler's son from Iowa, however, he became one of its prize millionaires and an almost permanent decoration of the Democratic party.

Harriman's devotion to Roosevelt, to Hopkins and to Truman is deep and sincere; he considers these three men great Americans. But he is in no sense a parochially partisan man.

One of the stories his friends like to tell most is about the visit of Wendell Willkie to Franklin Roosevelt just before Willkie set out on his "One-World" trip. Roosevelt, unable to resist the pleasure of needling his unsuccessful rival, said: "When you stop in London, Mr. Willkie; you must be sure to call on Averell Harriman, who directs Lend-Lease there. I am giving you a letter to him. Mr. Harriman is a very smart man, you know—he contributed $5,000 to my campaign fund."

"Oh yes," said Willkie, "Harriman is a very smart man, indeed. He contributed $5,000 to my fund, too."

WHETHER APOCRYPHAL or not, the story underlines a truth. Harriman is as willing to serve a Republican as a Democrat provided he is convinced that the chief is pursuing the great and historic interests of America. This definition, in Harriman's opinion, most definitely leaves out Senator Robert A. Taft of Ohio, a man whose election prospects Harriman views with unmitigated gloom. It does include, conspicuously, Gen. Dwight D. Eisenhower. A bipartisan Eisenhower foreign policy would have no difficulty enlisting the aid of Averell Harriman, for, by now, the Harriman ambition has burned away to a simple desire to be known for the next decade as America's Elder Statesman.

Harriman's claim to that title rests upon gilt-edged credentials. No other American has, over the past twelve years, been so intimately and continuously involved in so many major decisions and turnings in American foreign policy; no one else in the world has sat in on so many of the first history-making conferences of our times. This career began with his stewardship of Lend-Lease to Britain in 1941, continued through supervision of Lend-Lease in Russia (where he was Ambassador) was interrupted briefly with a tour of duty as Secretary of Commerce (in 1946), continued through the Marshall Plan (he was its European chief) to his present assignment. No American in public affairs today can match his knowledge of the people and pressures who, all around the world, shape the decisions and posture of America in this age of torment.

The amazing energies and record of Averell Harriman contrast sharply with the personal impression the man makes. Tall, thin, long-jawed, his features cut as classically as a senior Arrow Collar man, he is, at 60, a handsome man. But when he moves, he moves slowly, sometimes awkwardly. There is no visible, galvanic throwing-off of energy, such as usually emanates from the human-dynamo type of operator. On occasion, indeed, his exhaustion will be almost transparent, his cheeks sallow and yellow, his every movement aching with fatigue. But then, when newspaper men who have just seen him say "that guy won't last another week" he mysteriously snaps back resilient, his face unlined, his gestures smooth and coordinated, his thought precise, clear and illuminating.

THE EXHAUSTION that he invites, say his friends, comes from a curiously deep-rooted passion for travel and an obsession with work itself. Harriman-in-motion probably runs up more mileage than a State Department courier. In his last six months in Paris as director of the Marshall Plan his travel-routing for the period January 13-June 14, 1950, read, unbelievably, thus:

Paris, Brussels, Paris, Geneva, Paris, London, Washington, Paris, London, Paris, Rome, The Hague, London, Washington, London, Paris, London, Paris, London, Paris, London, Frankfurt, London, Paris, London, Paris, London, Paris, London, Paris, London, Paris, London, Geneva, Paris, London, Washington, Paris, Washington and, one hopes, a brief rest. Each of these trips meant a major international conference or a major international decision, almost always on a Chief of State or Ministerial level.

In the past ten years, Mr. Harriman, say his staff, has racked up between 150 and 160 Atlantic crossings. No one seems to have kept a calendar of his travels in 1951, the year he served as President Truman's international troubleshooter. His trips seemed to be less numerous but broader-ranging, with his mission to General MacArthur spanning the Pacific, and his mission to Mossadegh spanning the Mediterra-

nean. Mr. Harriman found these gentlemen equally difficult to handle.

Harriman's obsession with work has deepened with the years. Although he was once an 8-goal polo player, is occasionally a skier, and amuses himself now and then with croquet, canasta, and modern art (as E.C.A. chief in Paris he collected some of the finest of French moderns on the market) none of these pleasures in recent years matches the excitement he finds in his work. Each hour is crowded with every appointment possible in sixty minutes and his dinners and cocktail parties are usually seminars in the state of world affairs.

HE HAS a banker's gift for finding able men, and the men he has discovered and thrust forward to high position and prominence now include such independently notable names as David K. E. Bruce, William Foster, Charles Bohlen and Milton Katz. From men such as these, and from a host of devoted and tireless subordinate experts, Harriman is constantly sucking with a vacuum-cleaner technique the results of their own lesser conferences, experience, wisdom and research.

As a master of experts, Harriman has the super-statesman's craft of ignoring figures, details and specifics and getting to what he thinks is the core of a problem. Occasionally his thought processes are described as "intuitive." But they are no more intuitive than those of a doctor who has been treating an old patient for a long time and does not need to make a blood test or remember the blood pressure on every visit. All his experience has been digested down to huge, broad truths that now permit him to think simply.

"We used to figure," said Harriman once, "that to add a million tons of new steel capacity during the war it took about a billion dollars for the whole capital investment, figuring in the cost of extra coal capacity, extra rolling stock, extra mill and rolling equipment." Give or take a couple of hundred million, the figure was probably correct. Thus while lesser men worry about the drain on sterling, the flight from the franc, the number of German divisions Germany will contribute to the European army, Harriman takes a less statistical view.

ENGLAND IS Churchill, Attlee, Cripps and people like Bevan. France is Jean Monnet, General DeGaulle, that funny parliamentary situation and, of course, the Communists. Germany is Adenauer and Schumacher—a tricky situation, he thinks, one with a rapidly moving time quality to it. Russia is Stalin, Molotov and the Politburo—Mr. Harriman was among the first to loathe them because he was among the first to know them well. The problems of American foreign policy, like old patients, have chronic syndromes. In moving into a fast-breaking situation Harriman needs no ABC's—he can sense the limit of a deal or a need without precise measurement.

The description usually applied to Harriman is that of global "trouble shooter." This is one of those inevitable misnomers chosen because it covers a function too delicate to be defined. Harriman is neither a policy-maker nor a decision-maker. What he does best is to absorb, clarify and create the climate in which decisions are made.

HARRIMAN'S MOST recent job of "trouble-shooting" is as good an example of the Harriman function as any. When, at the Ottawa Conference of the North Atlantic Treaty Organization in September, the European powers declared their original military commitments to NATO unachievable and NATO's military goals too ambitious, the Council of Ministers set up the Committee of "Three Wise Men" to examine their plaints. Harriman was the American member of the trio. For six weeks he and France's Jean Monnet and Britain's Sir Edwin Plowden examined both generals and financiers as if they were auditing the books of a concern wobbling in a depression. Harriman did not decide on, or commit America to, a scaling-down of the arms target. But the climate and understanding he helped create did result in just that, because the inevitable was made clear.

It is not that Harriman simply follows a trend—when a trend starts jelling, Harriman is usually found to be among the leading jelly-makers. Foreign chiefs of state find him extraordinarily quick in grasping the sense of their problems, while usually they themselves are still plowing through wordage and figures to explain it. From his trips Harriman brings back to Washington a sample of local climate, a rounded summation of a situation that lets other people make the critical action decisions. Although no authentic report on the Harriman-MacArthur meeting has been made public, it is a safe bet that Harriman's report on the atmosphere at the MacArthur court was large and weighty in the Truman decision to relieve the general.

THE HARRIMAN technique in creating climate is a curious one. In public appearances or in formal addresses he is a painfully shy man, with little eloquence and no glamour. He operates best on his own ground, in small, intimate gatherings over a drink or at the dinner table with the few people who count, whether they be of high or low station. His formal on-the-record press conferences are barren and dreary. But his informal press briefings in both Paris and Washington, usually held in front of his fireplace, with good liquor, and moderately good food, are among the most useful any public officer has ever given.

Harriman realizes his strength and weakness and is quite frank about it. Thus, when describing his appointment to the National Security Council in 1951, he said, "It's not exactly in the Cabinet, but it's a Cabinet rank job. I know all those fellows anyway and call them by their first name. That's important, you know; you have to meet them on a level." Or, in dealing with Congress, Harriman reserves his major efforts not for formal committee presentation but, he said once, "I have them over to the house for dinner. I talk to them in little groups and try to explain things to them."

It is only by looking back over the last ten years, that the strength of the Harriman record becomes fully apparent. In ten errant years of American foreign policy while one great reputation after another has been shattered, Harriman's has grown more firm and sound. He was one of the first to grasp the depth and drive of Soviet emnity to the American world, a fact certified in most of the great memoirs from Hopkins through Forrestal. His record on civil liberties in his term as Secretary of Commerce was bold and virtuous.

He did the intricate preliminary spadework on the Marshall Plan and, as its field director, captained it through its two most successful years. He was the first to force the Office of European Economic Cooperation to act and make sounds like a living thing by forcing European nations to allocate among themselves the Marshall aid he was offering. He was among the first, likewise, to conceive of the need of NATO and see how it could be worked.

THIS RECORD, to be sure, is not one of unbroken success and among his associates are several who are less-than-enthusiastic. One of them put it this way: "Harriman's got all the shyness of a rich man's son, and all the abnormal admiration such men have for generals, intellectuals and self-made men. He wants to know the right people all the time—not the 'right people' socially, but the 'right people' to get things done. He thinks if you sit down and talk things over sensibly you can get almost anything worked out."

Among the errors with which Harriman's name is sometimes associated, two particularly, are singled out in Europe. The first is the original 1948 estimate that America would be able to arm Europe out of its surplus war stocks, a gross miscalculation which has resulted in the present winter crisis. It was Harriman, incidentally, who was the first to recognize the crisis and, as one of the Three Wise Men, the chief searcher for a solution. The second error charged up is the failure of the Marshall Plan, under his leadership, to get to grips with the social inequities in France and Italy. This failure has left from a quarter to a third of those populations firmly wedded to Communist leadership and thus a permanent threat to Western liberties.

————

"SURE, YOU can make all these charges about Harriman," said an aide who had been with him since his tenure at the Commerce Department, "but he's got something no one else has, and you can't define it. When he was Secretary of Commerce we were flying out West one day, and he asked me to come up into the cockpit. We were way up there above a mountain range and there was the Union Pacific going through a pass underneath. Then he pointed to another pass off in the distance and explained why the railroad had not taken that one. We were way up high and he made it all seem very clear. I always think of that trip. He's way up high and can see a long way. That's why he's useful."

THE NEW YORK TIMES MAGAZINE March 16,
1952

DOES HE DRIVE OR IS HE DRIVEN?

Theodore H. White first met Dean Rusk 19 years ago in the Far East. To research this article, White spent many weeks in Washington, interviewed 60 officials.

At 5 in the morning, the shapeless hulk of the State Department Building squats black beyond Washington's Mall—stilled by the same dawn hush that washes the red brick Georgian home where, six miles away, the Secretary of State sleeps.

But the sun, as it races around the globe to bring day to Washington, is already leaving Asia to the night—and in Formosa the telegraphers of the American Embassy are beginning to feed the net. In minutes now the Signals Center of the State Building will catch Formosa's message. With a subdued clatter, one of 19 gray teletype receivers, double-racked against the oyster-white wall, will begin to tap, in five-letter groups of coded, incomprehensible gibberish, the close-of-day report on the mysteries of China.

It is unlikely that the duty officer will wake the Secretary for this report; only half-a-dozen times in a year and a half has his rest been broken by emergency. But if the Secretary stirs uneasily in sleep, it is natural—the message flood is rising, as the sun moves west around his world.

An hour after Formosa, the embassy in Saigon will begin to close its day with the tally of killing, intrigue and hope in Vietnam's jungle war. So will our outposts in Laos and Thailand. An hour later, from the elegant sun-flooded embassy in New Delhi, will come the peak of message traffic from India. Shortly thereafter, the Middle Eastern embassies will begin to close their dispatches on the Moslem world.

By this time—7:30—the Secretary will have risen to scan, over breakfast, the public report on the world's doings in the New York *Times* and the Washington *Post*. But by then it is high noon in Europe, and the tide of messages from the Atlantic rim *is* reaching full: deep in the 10,000 messages it cables each day; Paris, reporting at 100 words a minute on each of two machines.

Now, in the great building, other offices have begun to stir. The Bureau of Intelligence and Research has almost completed its overnight task of summarizing the secret reports of the "intelligence community" (CIA, Army, Air, Navy and others) for the Secretary's first briefing of the morning. Simultaneously the Bureau of Public Affairs is digesting the world's many-tongued press opinions to make its own morning summary.

An entire world, wakened or put to bed by the circling sun, waits upon the coming of America's Secretary of State: Communist thrust in Laos, Riot in Caracas, Coup in the Middle East, Uprising in Africa, Grumbling in Bonn, Conference in the Kremlin, Clash in the Indies. Which report signals alarm, which flashes opportunity? Which report will make the Secretary pause, which can he dismiss to others? Which will make him stretch from his chair to the white phone, on the window ledge behind him, that reaches the President's desk directly?

No one has ever measured the flood of words from all sources that arrives overnight for consideration by the Department of State and its Secretary. Nor is it worthwhile measuring it. For it is not the volume that moves across his desk that is meaningful but how—by instinct, philosophy and experience— the Secretary finds his way through it. He, more than any other individual, is deputized to develop from this information a picture clear enough to let the President of the United States act and the people respond. This is the task that waits for him at his desk, the task that follows him by telephone when he drives by car, that follows him by radio when he golfs. This is what he must face each day, every day.

It is about a quarter to 9 when the Secretary's black Cadillac arrives at the basement entry of the building and de-

posits him underground before the private elevator that opens to his key. When the Secretary steps in, the doors close and the elevator automatically shoots up, with no other stops, to the seventh floor; there it opens within the glass-walled, green-planted inner sanctum where he keeps his private office— and out he steps.

"Out he steps," growled one bitter capital official, "onto a treadmill. And from then on, until he gets home at night, he walks the treadmill. And the treadmill is driven by everyone else's engine but his own."

And with this hard statement, one enters immediately into the simmering Washington controversy on the personality and performance of Dean Rusk, 54th Secretary of State of the United States, steward and guardian of its foreign policy in this time of trouble and hope: Does he drive—or is he driven? Does America act—or is it acted upon?

That Dean Rusk should be a cause of controversy has come to Washington as a surprise, for in any quick poll at the beginning of the Kennedy administration, solid Dean Rusk would certainly have been voted that member of the President's Cabinet least likely to arouse controversy.

Yet here is the sound of debate as it rustles in a reporter's notes:

"This is a man of absolutely fabulous ability—he is the best-informed man in Washington, in the country, in the world. He has the most impressive capacity for absorbing, retaining and retrieving information I have ever met"—from the chief of an American intelligence network, versus:

"Yes, I suppose I'd agree he's finally doing better—but that's because our expectations have shrunk to the limit of the man's capacity"—a senior State Department appointee, versus:

"From beginning to end this man is a moderate; a master of the briefing; absolute intelligence; complete mastery of the technical detail of every problem; articulate in the most impressive way; a superb negotiator. But for that reason he's a poor administrator—his motives obscure, his words flat, all the things that make him a great negotiator are what make it difficult for him to imbue his staff with drive"—the liaison officer of an independent executive agency, versus:

"He's always away from Washington. He comes to the committee, makes the most beautiful presentations you ever heard of. Perfect. Then, when he's all through, we ask, 'What the hell did he say?' His eye is always on the clock as if he had to catch a plane. He understands them all right—but he ought to try to understand us a little too"—from a distinguished U.S. senator.

But, finally:

"He's got guts. And his judgment is good. And in final analysis those are the qualities a Secretary of State needs. I wouldn't want to make a final decision on a vital matter involving our security until I'd heard his view. He sits on my right"—John F. Kennedy, the President, in private conversation.

Praise more extravagant, criticism more caustic can be heard by any political eavesdropper in Washington. Yet, as one listens, recognition slowly comes: this debate has a familiar ring. Since World War II every major Secretary of State has been the most controversial member of the Cabinet. What is significant about the present chapter of the debate is that not even the particular personality of Dean Rusk has been able to still it.

For Dean Rusk is a man designed for friendship. His voice is low and even, his manners courtly, his speech humorous; he combines, with natural warmth, qualities of gentleness and manliness. Attentive in conversation, he leans his bald, Daniel Webster-like head forward, his brown eyes alert to each nuance or suggestion in a visitor's remarks. And when, as so often he must, he firmly administers the rebuff, it usually comes with a broad smile, crinkling the eyes into a friendly outdoorsman's squint, as if to indicate that disagreement holds no malice or bitterness.

Beyond that, physically, the man throws off an impression of power. Burly, still at the age of 53 muscled like a fullback, he has the serenity so often found in physically large people, along with an almost extravagant capacity for work. With the impression of power goes eloquence—for Rusk is a master of words, who uses them with precision for clarification, for insistence, for inspiration, or for deliberate opacity.

Finally, the man's training for this job has been no less than superb. A Rhodes scholar at Oxford (where he won the Cecil Peace Prize), a summer student in Germany, a professor of political science in California, Dean Rusk came from these to enter the big war as captain and rise to colonel and deputy chief of staff in General Joseph Stilwell's China-Burma-India theater. There, in the searing heat of New Delhi from 1943 to 1945, in a baking office at the Imperial Hotel he deftly guided the diplomacy of a command which required Americans, Britons, Indians, Burmese and Chinese, plus assorted hill-tribesmen, all to pull together to defeat Japan. So well did he perform that in 1945 he was returned to Washington as a Pentagon expert in international relations. From the Pentagon, George Marshall brought him to the State Department where, under Dean Acheson, he rose to Assistant Secretary of State for Far Eastern Affairs. This post he left in 1952 to become president of the internationally minded Rockefeller Foundation, where he was author of some of the most lucid civilian contributions to American diplomacy in the last 10 years.

Yet, with all this, Dean Rusk remains a figure of controversy—just as those very different men, George Marshall, Dean Acheson and John Foster Dulles, were before him.

Thus the controversy over Rusk must be examined in terms of job and performance—not personality. Any Secretary of State is, in the popular imagination, the bearer of ill tidings; he is the man who stands sentinel for America over an uneasy globe. What is required of such a sentinel? Is he to be

an executive or a philosopher? How, under a President like John F. Kennedy, at a revolutionary moment in world affairs, does a Secretary of State make clear the nature of his leadership—and America's leadership—in world affairs?

TO ASK such questions is to plunge into the knottiest constitutional problems of the American republic. No one has ever defined all the jobs locked up under the title of Secretary of State, or made precise the Secretary's responsibilities in the escalator of problems which run from Hong Kong's garment exports to the possible annihilation of the human race. Yet the jobs must be seen clearly.

First, and above all, the Secretary of State is servant to the President, as *his* Minister of Foreign Affairs. The personality of each President and the season of history thus determine what each President wants of his minister. And if this President, John F. Kennedy, gives roughly 80% of his time to decisions on foreign policy, the burden on the Secretary of State increases proportionately. Dean Rusk must be at Kennedy's side with personal counsel whenever required. On a slow day this means three or four telephone calls; on a bad day it means three or four visits to the White House as crisis or ceremony may require.

Next comes the burden of representation and negotiation with foreign powers, friendly and hostile, in which the Secretary of State must speak for America. Critical as Dean Rusk once may have been of the globe-wandering diplomacy of John Foster Dulles, no sooner did he sit at Dulles' desk than the same world clamored for his attendance too. In Rusk's first six months of office, with trips to Bangkok, Ankara, Oslo, Geneva and Vienna, he racked up 53,000 miles to 30,000 miles in Dulles' first half year. Nor has Rusk's pace slackened in the year since as his mileage has run up to 145,000 in 17 foreign countries.

Whether any man can handle these first two jobs without total exhaustion is questionable (Rusk has already lost 10 pounds this year). Yet both jobs are less in demand of his energies than the third that history assigns to the nation's Secretary of State. The United States is the leader of the free world. Like it or not, the United States directs a revolution in an age when old and new, decay and rebirth, traditions and technologies challenge each other the globe over. And the Secretary of State, through his Department of State, must be executive chief of this revolution.

Time was, just before the big war, when the State Department presided calmly over its affairs behind the slatted swing doors of the old baroque State Building located next to the White House. In those days, the Secretary directed 920 employees in Washington, 4,000 overseas. Today, State employs 6,500 in Washington and 16,500 overseas, for a total of 23,000. In those happier days this nation's interest in the world was so low that State's press room was comfortable with just four desks; now it has 50 desks for 150 accredited American and 50 foreign correspon-

dents. In those days, so innocently free of "entangling alliances," the Secretary could regard with distant objectivity the political squirmings of other nations; today the United States is linked by treaty with 43 emotional allies, and each one requires executive attention or assurance of affection on a daily basis.

But this is only the beginning; for the turbulent world of today has explosively magnified the Secretary's instrumentation of responsibility. He must direct the 11,000 employees of the United States Information Agency in the war of ideas. He must guide the economic war through the 15,000 employees of AID, the Agency for International Development. He must watch the Peace Corps, the Disarmament Agency, and all the other agencies that Congress has spun off from his control but committed by statute to his guidance.

Yet his executive burden is not limited to wrestling with the bureaucracy of his own State Department. Theoretically his voice is second only to that of the President in shaping foreign policy, but in the Cabinet and the National Security Council he meets mighty challengers for the President's ear from vast rival apparatuses of power led by other dedicated men.

There is the hidden bureaucracy of the CIA, over which, in theory, the Secretary has responsibility for "political guidance," a task which successive Secretaries have not so much bungled as shirked out of simple lack of adequate executive channels to link the two agencies. (In many countries the CIA has more agents than, and 10 times the spending money of, State.) Then there is the Pentagon, with vast global installations and policies of its own. There is the Atomic Energy Commission, whose deadly rivalry with the armorers of the Soviet Union projects it directly into foreign affairs. There is Agriculture, with the swollen farm surpluses for export. There is Commerce, involved in every foreign trade problem; and other agencies—all clashing, all exerting pressure on decisions by fair means or foul.

The pressure of these bureaucracies on high policy sometimes takes on a juggernaut effect; once set in motion by high policy, the bureaucracies seem to acquire a momentum of their own, as if fueled by interior wellsprings of power. No Secretary of State approved the specific U-2 overflight across Russia two weeks before Eisenhower's doomed meeting with Khrushchev in Paris. This was a decision ground out as routine by the mills of the CIA. Nor was it a decision of the Secretary of State, President Eisenhower or President-elect Kennedy to send, a week after the election of 1960, the submarine *George Washington*, armed with 16 Polaris missiles, on a mission to patrol off the Soviet Union— a dagger at the Russian throat. This decision was ground out automatically by the defense agencies.

But perhaps no episode in recent U.S. history highlights more dramatically how bureaucratic momentum, unless thoroughly controlled, can lead policy to disaster than the decision to invade Cuba last spring. The CIA had

been training forces for the invasion fully a year before. Neither Rusk nor Kennedy on coming to power positively initiated the plan to invade; they both were asked whether they wanted to liquidate preparations under way, thus stopping an invasion already plotted or go through with it. When they reluctantly assented, bureaucracy had won; leadership had failed.

The supreme task in modern democracies is for elected political leadership to control such bureaucracies, to goad them without destroying their morale, to refresh them with new faces and new blood, to resist them when the public good requires that they be resisted. ("You know," said Dean Rusk recently, "even Khrushchev has that problem. At times, when we met in Vienna, he talked about the pressures of his military men and scientists just like a plaintive Western politician.")

It is on this third task, control of America's instruments of foreign policy, that Dean Rusk and John F. Kennedy have been laboring hardest in the past year and a half. In their difficulties the two men have provided not only a new perspective on American power but a fascinating study in two personalities of contrasting experience and background.

JOHN F. KENNEDY is an "action" man. He was born to the most prominent of the families of the New Boston, totally unawed by the aristocracy of the Old Boston, and his own wealth and family power have permitted him to regard other established forms of power with cold and calculating detachment. Secure in spirit, he has been able to indulge himself, in a swift upward career, by seeking as lieutenants some of the earthiest and most colorful characters in American politics and thought. He has been able to gamble on his choices, demanding of them, above all, performance in action.

Dean Rusk is an "issues" man, a thoughtful person. Born to the neat and threadworn gentility of a Georgia preacher's family, he could indulge himself in few luxuries of chance. To make *his* way up, he could offer to those who could use them only his enormous capacities for lucidity, work and devotion. Thus Rusk's career is marked not by public triumphs like Kennedy's but by the names of successive great patrons who first recognized his values, then moved him forward. From General Joseph Stilwell, through George Marshall, Dean Acheson, John Foster Dulles and Robert Lovett, an entire generation of older, established men saw in Rusk one of the outstanding talents of the generation following them.

Where life bred in Kennedy a delight in risk and action verging on the impetuous, it developed in Rusk an instinct for wary deliberation. The two balancing qualities buttress and strengthen their present union—for the attraction of opposites, a governing rule in romance, frequently rules also in politics.

YET CERTAINLY there was more to Kennedy's selection of Rusk than the simple attraction of opposites. Ken-

nedy, who affects a disdain for many traditions, is exquisitely sensitive to the traditions of American government. For his Secretary of State he consciously sought a man in the majestic tradition of 20th Century American diplomacy, the distinguished line that begins with the great John Hay and runs to our own day. Thus he turned to the elder statesmen for advice; and it was Dean Acheson who first proposed the name of Rusk, a man Kennedy had never met. Wherever Kennedy turned for advice in the next few days, to men like Robert Lovett, David Bruce and Adlai Stevenson, he found Dean Rusk's name either enthusiastically thrust forward or pleasantly acceptable. Kennedy's scouts traced every lead on Rusk; only two men in all the vast investigation offered demurrers (a distinguished Washington correspondent and a man now high among Rusk's deputies).

On a plane trip to New York from Washington, one of President-elect Kennedy's aides delivered to him Rusk's now famous article on foreign policy, published in *Foreign Affairs* in the spring of 1960. There Kennedy read Rusk's thesis that only a President can make the nation's foreign policy (". . . in a unique sense," wrote Rusk, "the President is the custodian of the national interest. . ."). Rusk's eloquent insistence on the predominant role of the President suited Kennedy completely. He met Rusk for the first time on Thursday, Dec. 8, for an hour at his Georgetown home. On the following Sunday, after a second meeting in Palm Beach, Kennedy appointed him.

In politics, normally, strong men move with strong teams, carrying their favorites and lieutenants with them from post to post. But Rusk was a "loner" and commanded no such team of intimates. When he entered his office, he found his chief executives had largely been chosen for him by others. Only a newcomer to politics with no team of his own would have tolerated such unorthodoxy of procedure.

One can best imagine Rusk's dilemma by imagining the little scene when Rusk first confronted his star-studded new staff. The Secretary himself had been a good citizen in politics—but his sturdy good-citizenship had carried him only as high as the post of campaign chairman of the Kennedy-Johnson Volunteers in the suburb of Scarsdale, N.Y. (population 18,000). When Rusk sat down with his senior deputies, he found they included ex-Governor Adlai E. Stevenson of Illinois, ex-Governor W. Averell Harriman of New York, ex-Governor G. Mennen Williams of Michigan, ex-Governor Chester Bowles of Connecticut—a crew of some of the most robust and forceful characters raised in American politics since the war. It was up to Rusk to govern them. No longer was he the gifted deputy of such famous men; his was the authority *over* them, second only to the President's.

Under Rusk lay the huge bureaucracy of the State Department and its agencies, locked in inertia, its morale riddled by years of Dulles' distaste for administration and by prior McCarthyite attack. Above Rusk was the White House and the President's inner team of action men, fresh from political victory at home, demanding a blueprint for seizing the initiative abroad. And the world sizzled all about: Communists advancing in Laos, Berlin under threat, Vietnam in civil war, the Congo in chaos, new cables of crisis arriving in cascades each morning.

There was no doubt that a clash between the impatient White House staffers and the State Department's complicated bureaucracy would soon develop—nor was there any doubt that a thoughtful man who perferred to concentrate on issues rather than crack heads would soon be caught in the middle.

The low point of relations between White House and State was reached in three months—with Cuba. The State Department's Latin American experts were against a Cuban invasion. Inwardly Rusk was against it too. He so stated *before* the invasion to at least one member of the White House staff. But in final counsel, as the Joint Chiefs and the CIA pressed forward, Rusk, when asked his ultimate yea or nay, said "yes." After which the President also voted "yes," and the disaster of the Bay of Pigs was ordained.

What followed was a summer chaos in the mechanisms of American foreign policy, in which it seemed that the Department of State's authority was dissolving. Presidential task forces with diplomatic functions were established outside of State—on Cuba (first under Paul Nitze of the Pentagon, later under Richard Goodwin of the White House), on Southeast Asia (under Roswell Gilpatric of the Pentagon), on Berlin (under Dean Acheson). A special Crisis Center was set up at State, to which the President assigned a trusted brother-in-law, Stephen Smith. Letters to foreign chiefs of state drafted by the State Department were torn up and rewritten completely at the White House. On one occasion, while Rusk was out of the country, a high State Department official presented the National Security Council with State's new position papers on Cuba, and one of those present snapped, "I wouldn't have turned in a paper like that in Gov 1 [the freshman course] at Harvard." Foreign ambassadors set out to contact one or another of the President's inner staff at the White House, seeking direct access to American power.

CRITICISM OF the department and its Secretary bubbled wherever New Frontiersmen gathered: "Ideas, ideas, why can't they come up with any new ideas over at State?" Or: "You toss a request in there at State and it's three weeks before you hear the echo when it hits bottom." Or: "Rusk has got to learn to shake the department up, he's got to learn to fire people. It isn't enough to say [of a known incompetent, since removed] that we can't fire him because we just brought the man back from his post, that he's bought a house in Washington and brought his family here."

A more fragile, more nervous man than Rusk might well have panicked. But never once did he allow himself to lose his composure and lash back in headlines at his critics. Never in the months of torment, beginning with the Cuban fiasco in April, did Rusk's devotion to the President flag. ("I've seen Rusk get emotional only once," said a fellow member of the National Security Council. "That was right after Cuba. When the President left the room, I remember Rusk pounding the arm of his chair and saying, 'What matters now is this man, we have to save this man.'")

Nor, above all, did Rusk forget his priorities—and in July and August what mattered was not Washington gossip but the renewed threat of war in Berlin. Here Rusk concentrated. Exerting his authority, he rejected the action proposals of his great patron, Dean Acheson, for handling the Berlin crisis. Slowly, through the tense July-August weeks, the State Department re-established itself as leader in recommendation on policy. The Pentagon's original suggestion for full-scale mobilization was turned down, and Rusk and the President joined in an approach of graduated build-up to meet the measure of the threat. Step by step, from the first dispatch of our military task force to Berlin over the autobahn, through the exercise of Allied rights in East Berlin, through the sending of Lyndon Johnson (Rusk's idea) and of Lucius Clay, the delicate Berlin confrontation was steered back from the edge of war. Meanwhile, at home, Rusk was gently but firmly liquidating the chaos and duplication of functions created by the presidential task forces. Quietly one by one, the Cuban, Berlin and Vietnam task forces were drawn back under Rusk's direction at State.

By late fall the crisis in Berlin had shrunk from its summer dimension of immediate cataclysm to its normal state of ever-present danger. In the process, in the long discussions, councils and emergency sessions, the President and his Secretary of State had come to know each other. Both men are pragmatists, both men like facts, both men look out on the world in the same manner. What bound them together was a philosophy of confidence, and they shared in common the problem of executive direction of State's bureaucracy.

In November there came the first of what may be several reorganizations of State: George Ball, the department's ablest administrator, was named Undersecretary and alter ego to Rusk as chief operational officer. George McGhee and Chester Bowles were transferred to new functions. Averell Harriman was elevated to Assistant Secretary, and three vigorous White House staff members were transferred to State to add vitality to bureaucracy—Walt Rostow, Richard Goodwin and Fred Dutton.

These moves freed Rusk to operate in areas where his talents shine most: policy-framing and negotiation. With the negotiations in January at the Punta del Este conference (a 14-to-one victory, with six abstentions, for an American proposal to expel Cuba from American partnership), Rusk scored his first positive public success. And with his long March session on Berlin and disarmament at Geneva, he demonstrated clearly the style of his diplomacy in fin-

ished form: When the negotiations at Geneva began, America was still faced with a Russian ultimatum on Berlin. At no time did the Russians formally back down. Nonetheless, the ultimatum has dissolved and apparently it no longer exists. This is a victory without a triumph, a victory for the quiet diplomacy in which Rusk believes.

FOUR YEARS ago he wrote, "Might there not be an advantage to quiet and 'pointless' talks over a period of time about the common imperative to avoid a holocaust? . . . Lesser questions might become more manageable and a few peepholes might open up through veils of misunderstanding and distortion. At least such talks might clarify the real nature of the issues which divide us and thus give us a better base for future action." Last month in Washington the Berlin crisis was dead-ended into just such talks between Dean Rusk and the Russian Ambassador Anatoly Dobrynin. Similarly, last month's NATO meeting in Athens, heralded as the revolt against American strategy of our European allies, was firmly and quietly steered by Rusk into a blur of public agreement, under cover of which our differences can be more reasonably and privately discussed.

This same quiet style colors all of Rusk's behavior in Washington. It was he who from the very first insisted, in the President's inner circle, that American nuclear testing must follow immediately upon Russian nuclear testing. It was Rusk who, within the State Department, insisted that the sweeping new foreign trade bill be brought to debate in Congress this session rather than wait for a more favorable Congress next year—and Rusk won the point.

The flavor of Dean Rusk's developing leadership within the State Department is still elusive of definition. Mostly it is to be found in his Socratic method of provoking aides to think more deeply by guiding them with his questions. Last month, for example, a small departmental task force brought in a proposal to soothe the claustrophobia of Afghanistan, a country landlocked by an aggressive Soviet Union, a hostile Pakistan and an unstable Persia. The task force proposed to build a road from the sea across Persia to Afghanistan at a foreign-aid cost to us of scores of millions of dollars. Rusk listened, then offered this observation: during the war he had watched from New Delhi the building of the Burma-Ledo Road; by the time that fantastically expensive road had been build, the Army's Air Transport Command had learned to fly more tonnage more cheaply over the Hump to China by air than the road could ever hope to do. Rusk pointed out that the advent of jet aircraft in the United States was making obsolete thousands of old propeller-pulled airline planes, which could be bought at fire-sale prices and shipped to Persia to provide an air-transport link to Afghanistan, thus encouraging development in both countries. When the department task force rose to leave Rusk, an entirely new avenue of exploration was open to it.

As Rusk has grown in authority, criticism has muted. Administrative direction of the Department is now largely in the hands of George Ball. Enormous initiative is enjoyed by such deputies as Walt Rostow (Policy Planning), Roger Hilsman (Bureau of Intelligence and Research), Averell Harriman (Far East) and Adlai Stevenson (United Nations). White House support in the delicate matter of personnel and recruitment has been consolidated in the hands of the able Ralph Dungan. Yet many in the Department complain that the Secretary fails to bind them together in a team responsive to his own intuitions. Only with such young men as Assistant Secretaries of State Philips Talbot and Harlan Cleveland has Rusk apparently kindled the glow of personal enthusiasm such as unites the White House team. Complaint persists that Rusk spends too much time abroad—but no critic has a pat solution to this demand on the Secretary's time. (Rusk has toyed with the idea of appointing an American Foreign Minister for representation abroad and for conference negotiations, but no action has been taken.)

Chief among the criticisms still leveled at Rusk concerns the operation and reorganization of the Foreign Service. The Foreign Service is the officer corps of American diplomacy and its senior officers are probably the ablest such corps in the world—but at old-fashioned diplomacy. Trained before World War II, these older men are able, polished, articulate and vigorous. Yet these men, though not exactly without convictions, matured in an age of

American detachment, in a tradition of clinical noninvolvement. What is needed now, many in Washington argue, are aggressive men who can, in the diplomacy of revolutions, commit themselves not only to involvement but to action in the affairs of other people. Such officers do exist in the department, but they are the younger men, roughly 40 years old, who entered the Foreign Service from the hot, combat action of World War II. How to dismiss the older generation, how to promote swiftly the younger activists is one of the most intensely debated problems in the inner circle of State—and Rusk, above all a kindly man, is caught in the crossfire. He is criticized by senior career officers as being too anxious to please the White House, and by New Frontiersmen for shrinking from the purge necessary to rid the department of deadwood.

ALL SUCH criticism, it is obvious, must reach a state of balance at some given level of judgment. And where it counts most—that is to say, in the judgment of the President of the United States—the verdict is unmistakably favorable. The Secretary of State pleases this President. In every modern state, foreign affairs have become the chief domain of the Chief of State—of Khrushchev and De Gaulle, of Adenauer and Chiang Kai-shek. The complexity of modern government is such that only the Chief of State can command and bring together all the vast machinery needed to direct matters of war and peace. Abroad, as at home, a modern

Chief of State must be the unquestioned captain of his ship. In Washington, John F. Kennedy is captain of the ship. But the captain needs a pilot—and the pilot Kennedy has chosen is Rusk.

Further, it has been decided that the pilot's place cannot be in the engine room of the Department of State, but must be at the captain's side on the bridge. It is the pilot's chart of the drifts, shoals and channels that guides the captain's course. And if, today, after many years of uncertain adventure, the course is one of optimism and cheer, then the chart that sets that course must be found in the world as Dean Rusk sees it.

DEAN RUSK dislikes criticizing the foreign policy of the Republican administration that he succeeded. A new Washington administration, he says, can change no more than 10% or 15% of foreign policy because we remain fundamentally the same country no matter what our administration.

Those changes that do occur in our conduct of foreign affairs are rarely a matter of partisan decision. President Truman's course was wholly different from that of either Eisenhower or Kennedy, Rusk feels, because Truman enjoyed an atomic monopoly. By the end of the Eisenhower administration, and now in the Kennedy administration, the problem has become simply, as Rusk puts it, "that if war should break out, then the Northern Hemisphere will simply be burned up. That means that Kennedy and Khrushchev both live with the first question of the Westminster Catechism always in mind: 'What is the Chief End of Man?'"

"This injects a new element into policy," says Rusk, as he attempts to define how his administration departs from that of John Foster Dulles. "It doesn't mean you give anything away. But you separate the essentials from the nonessentials. It means you seek the smallest way to improve relations. You don't, for example, use phrases like 'massive retaliation' or 'agonizing reappraisal.' Phrases like that are traps. I don't use them.

"We don't regard neutrals as enemies, or allies as satellites. We don't deal with great issues as drama. We deal with them by quiet, persistent, repetitive effort. If we can make a quiet contribution to the settlement of disputes, O.K. And if we don't get any credit for it, O.K., too."

In Rusk's mind the sources of American power, whether recognized or unrecognized, are both constant and diverse. "I remember when I was in New Delhi during the war, on the day F.D.R. died," Rusk recalls, "the upper-class Indians gave me their traditional salute [their hands cupped under their chins]. But the ragged, dirty, lower-class Indians simply came up and touched my hand in sympathy because they were sad. That's understanding of what the United States is all about. Among other things, that's power, too."

The drags on American policy remain constant, also. "One of our chief difficulties is our own influence," says Rusk. "You have to realize that influence on American policy is a Number One target for every foreign office in the world. Whenever differences arise—France and Algeria, Afghanistan and Pakistan, Guatemala and the United Kingdom, Togo and Ghana, the Arabs and the Israelis, the Dutch and the Indonesians— they all try to enlist our understanding and support of the problem as they see it. We could live without this burden, but it arrives on our doorstep with every days' flow of cables. A nation as big, as powerful, as influential as the United States can't escape this role. As a result we can't have 100% perfect relations with any nation in the world."

Fully aware that he is successor to such vivid figures as George Marshall, Dean Acheson and John Foster Dulles, Dean Rusk decisively refuses to match their style. People must recognize, insists Rusk, that tedium has an immeasurably important role to play in diplomacy. Peace is to be sought by continuing, quiet, apparently pointless but enduring conversation. There is nothing Rusk deplores more than what he calls the "football stadium psychology of diplomacy," the hunger of people to know after each day's negotiations who won, who lost. "How the story comes out is more important than what people say about it," says Rusk.

OF HOW the story will come out, Rusk seems to have no doubt. Underlying much of the mood of confidence—as well as caution—in Washington today is a new Western analysis of Soviet strength. Western analysts have recently made what has been described as an information breakthrough of major proportions in estimates of Soviet missile strength. They believe that Khrushchev's belligerence of several years ago was a bluff based on the first Soviet ICBM, with little to back it. We now know that the Soviet Union has weaknesses far graver than was supposed two years ago. The Soviets know the West knows, and when the Russians started testing again they tested for military reasons.

But Rusk's optimism about the future goes far beyond any such technical reassurance. It rises from a political estimate of the world today that reaches back generations into the American past and stretches from there to a reading of human experience in general.

In the mind of Dean Rusk, the American experience since the end of World War II has been moved by currents so simple (yet profound) as to be hidden from both ourselves and the world. These currents rise "from what kind of people we are and what kind of geography we occupy," and they need redefining.

"There are three threads," says Rusk, "to American foreign policy—and if you look, you can see them expressed everywhere in the world."

The first of these is as simple as a high school civics lesson: we believe governments derive their just powers from the consent of the governed.

"If a new ambassador from a foreign country came in to me and asked how he could predict the probable American reaction to any foreseeable new situation, I would tell him to keep in mind this one simple notion," says Dean Rusk. "It is a scarlet thread through all policy that makes a certain order out of most of our reactions. We *actually* believe in it. It explains our attitude to Eastern Europe, to totalitarian governments, to colonial areas, to our own failures to live up to our highest commitments. It's hard to get the new Afro-Asian countries to realize just how simple this attitude is, or that our attitude towards freedom in their areas and in Eastern Europe comes from the same roots: What kind of governments are they; do they speak for their people?"

Thread one, in Rusk's mind, interweaves with thread two: America insists that the shape of the world community be the shape envisioned in the charter of the United Nations—an organization of *independent* states, settling their disputes by peaceful means and cooperating voluntarily in common interests.

This is not the shape of the world community envisioned by the Marxist-Leninist society. But once our insistence on national independence for others is grasped, our confrontation with the Marxists becomes clear. Over the long run it ranges the Soviet Union not only against NATO but against the neutrals, the emerging nations, even against its own allies. Rusk believes that Americans have grown more sophisticated in their attitude toward the neutrals, and some of the neutrals, in turn, are growing more aware of the nature of the world conflict. "The issue that faces neutrals," he says, "is the same as ours—the independence of their countries." Even within the Communist bloc this guideline of independence shapes American policy. Thus we have one policy for Communist-yet-independent Yugoslavia, another for the Soviet Union, and various shades of policy for other Communist countries which tug towards but have not reached independence within Communism.

Yet is is the third thread that Rusk insists is the dynamic one: the impact of the American social and economic experience in this century, the interaction between this and what men call "the revolution of rising expectations." For the impact of American life, achievements and dreams is more explosive than any other force of modern times—and Rusk believes we have underplayed it.

"Sometimes," says the American Secretary of State, "I think that the greatest cost of the big depression of the early 1930s was not economic but ideological. It came along just in time to convince many people that the Marxist analysis of capitalism, as adopted by some fashionable economists in the West, was right, that our system was washed up. And just at a time when so many leaders of the new colonial nations were being educated here and in Europe. It's taken a full generation for this impression to wear off. As a matter of fact, the contrast between the Communist world and ours is just beginning to take hold. And this contrast itself creates tensions—the contrast between East Germany and West Germany, between South Vietnam and North Vietnam. As a matter of fact, they [the

Communists] launched the war in South Vietnam in 1958 just when the contrast became visible there, too.

"Some people say, quite wrongly, that it will take 200 to 300 years to bring the social and technological development of the West to the new Asian-African countries. But what we in the West have failed to point out is that these developments can be transferred in our system more quickly than anyone thinks, more quickly than the Marxists imagine.

"In 1920, when I was a boy, only 1% of the farms in America had electricity, now 98% have it. Since 1920 the increase in our national product—the *increase* itself—has been greater than the *total* national product of the Soviet Union today.

"We've lived through it all ourselves. Take Americans like Mr. Speaker Raybun, like Lyndon Johnson, born on backward farms in a prescientific, pretechnological, preeducational, premedical-care, prepublic-health society. They lived in what we'd call today an underdeveloped society. I did myself. I was born in an area where babies were delivered by an old veterinarian who had one year's training in the Civil War. We've seen with our own eyes what can happen in one lifetime, but in our rush forward we've forgotten what American life used to be.

"And I feel this: I feel that the American experience is the most powerful revolutionary force in the world today, this demonstration that such things aren't just acts of Providence alone. President Kennedy and I have a deep conviction that the story of freedom is our strength. It's a long story—it goes to the root of human nature and human aspirations. Its victory is inevitable. This revolution going on around the world is a part of our own.

"And we're convinced that in these revolutions freedom can't lose. No country freed from colonialism for independence since 1945 has gone Communist on its own, not even the ones we sometimes worried about. Guinea sent a Soviet ambassador home. Nasser pulled students out of Russia and put Communists in jail.

"If you put these things together—our insistence that governments be based on consent, our seeking to provide security and independence for other countries, our own dynamic of social progress—then this is *our* revolution. It can't lose."

LIFE June 8, 1962

Chapter 3

China I: War Correspondent

Every journalist's first major assignment has a special place in memory. White's was China, and it became his enduring journalistic love. He traveled there on a Harvard fellowship, not as a journalist but to see what war was like (a "sightseer," he later called himself). After three months, with his money nearly gone, his Chinese studies at Harvard proved to be enough to get him a job as a Chinese government translator-writer in Chungking. There, almost by accident, *Time*'s John Hersey found him and took him on as a stringer. Eager to be more than that, and frustrated by the bounds of being a government employee, he went off to Shansi Province and reported "The Rape of Chin Valley" (see page 5). It was such a success that he was hired full-time by Time Inc.

From 1939 to 1945 he covered China from end to end: short pieces, mostly for *Time,* longer, more analytical articles for *Life* and *Fortune*—including a tour de force for the latter in which he wrote three of the four articles for a 1941 Special Section, "China the Ally"; two are included in this chapter—"The Unbelievable Burma Road" and "Japan-in-China."

Other selections herewith from White's war correspondent days include a rather bizarre interview with a Japanese naval officer; two *Time* dispatches on the devastating famine of 1942–43 in Honan Province—virtually unreported elsewhere; the first uncensored comprehensive account of mid-war China to be published in the United States (*Life*); and the Chinese reporting he was most proud of, "Inside Red China" (also *Life*), which he achieved by wangling his way to the caves of Yenan, headquarters for Mao Tse-tung and his guerrilla forces. White was the first foreign journalist of stature to go to Yenan, and his views of U.S. policy in China would never be the same.

Like most of White's magazine writing, these articles are models of the genre.

MEET CAPTAIN CHUDO

BANGKOK, THAILAND

Although he has spent only one year at sea in the course of his career, well-mannered Captain Kando Chudo was head of the Japanese naval delegation which recently wrested military privileges for Japan from French Indo-China. At a recent interview in Hanoi, Indo-China, I found him very willing to talk to American journalists.

The world, he said, was going to be divided into four parts. One part for Germany—Europe. One part for Russia—Russia. One part for Japan—Asia. One part for the U.S.—America. England was going to be defeated and that was a great danger for America. I asked why. Because, he said, the English Government and Navy would then come to Canada and they would fight with the U.S. in America. In his Nipponesque view there is no room for two strong nations in one continent. (I could feel his "sympathy" for us.)

He touched on the negotiations in Indo-China very briefly. Here too it seemed there was a misunderstanding. Japan had wanted co-operation and the French had been unwilling to cooperate. That was all. What did the Japanese Navy want? Only a few Indo-Chinese naval bases. (I made a mental note of that one—it was the first time any Japanese naval officer had admitted point-blank that they were asking for naval bases.) And how would the negotiations end? Everything would be all right, Captain Chudo assured us. The French would not fight, but were only mobilized. Japan would wait a little while and the French would give in.

Then Captain Chudo suddenly shifted the conversation. He wanted to ask us some questions. He had heard that we had just come from Chiang Kai-shek's capital at Chungking (. . . so that was why he had consented to see us . . .). Was Chungking being badly bombed? Very badly indeed, we said. And I added that his planes had hit my house once and destroyed all my clothes. He was very sorry and smiled. I went on to flatter him—Japanese Navy planes were much better than the Army planes. The Navy planes do more damage and are more accurate. Oh, said Captain Chudo quite modestly, we do not try to be accurate, we just drop bombs anywhere over Chungking. (I checked that one too. The Japanese Foreign Office spokesman had always insisted that only military objectives were sought. Evidently these Japanese gentlemen disagreed, but Captain Chudo certainly knew more about Navy policy than the Foreign Office.)

He set off on another conversational tact. Had I left Chungking by road? Yes, I had. Had I seen any Chinese airplane factories on the way? (Very eagerly put.) No, I had not. Where were the Chinese airplane factories then? In the southeast, I replied vaguely. Captain Chudo was disappointed in me, but he continued.

Where did I live in Chungking? In the Press Hotel. Where was that in Chungking? With my finger I traced an imaginary diagram of Chungking on the table and said: "There." Immediately Captain Chudo handed me a piece of paper and pencil. "Draw it, show me," he implored. I drew a vague, triangular wedge on the paper and made a cross on it. Now Captain Chudo felt he was getting somewhere. He leaned for-

ward and said confidentially, "And where does Chiang Kai-shek live?" (I am sure the Japanese Navy knows the whereabouts of Chiang Kai-shek at any moment better than any correspondent, but still the captain wanted to know.) I put my full forefinger down on a spot that covered two-thirds of the very tiny wedge that I had drawn and said: "There." Captain Chudo sighed.

Captain Chudo began seeking information again—this time a bit more circumspectly. American journalists, he said, were always taking pictures of countries they passed through. He was very interested in pictures of China. Maybe I had some pictures of nice scenery, of interesting planes, of Chungking? Regretfully, I shook my head. I had no pictures with me. So sorry. Captain Chudo paused, sucked his breath. He was very sorry too, The interview was over.

LIFE November 11, 1940

THE UNBELIEVABLE BURMA ROAD

The life of Free China literally hangs on the most dangerous (and beautiful) road in the world—"scratched out of the mountains with fingernails."

Next month the rains will stop in Burma. The sticky red gumbo that coats the valleys and mountains through which the Burma Road winds its tortuous way will begin to dry out. The ruts will cake, then crumble into dust, then go smooth and flat as thousands of new American trucks begin to pound into China with the cargoes of war.

During the five months of the rainy season the Burma Road operated at only half capacity, barely sustaining with a thin trickle of supplies the armies of Chiang Kai-shek. For the Burma Road is literally Free China's life line: except for the overland route from the U.S.S.R. through Turkestan, which never furnished more than a mere 2,000 tons a month, it is the *only* inlet for the matériel Chiang vitally needs. Today, with supplies from the U.S.S.R. via Turkestan cut off by the Soviet-German war, Chiang's three million regular soldiers are more than ever dependent on this single, hair-thin thread for every essential of war except food, bullets, and rifles. The tonnage figures of traffic over the Burma Road mean as much for China as the figures on shipping losses, airplane production, and food supply mean in combination for Britain.

Thus today, with the U.S. and China engaged in common cause against the Axis, the Burma Road is a more vital factor in U.S. defenses than any single road or railway in the continental U.S. itself. For the defense of this road a hundred American pursuit planes are to be poised on the airfields of southwest China. Hundreds of American pilots and mechanics are to fly and service them. Thousands of American trucks are rolling off production lines in Detroit; and heavy-laden tankers and freighters, hull down in Pacific brine, are butting their way through the seas westward to Rangoon.

What Is This Road?

From Lashio at one end of the Burma Road to Kunming, its other end, a crow would make of it 360 miles. The glistening silver-winged Douglas transports of China National Aviation Corp. can make the flight in two hours—the merest incident on the long run across the face of China from Hong Kong to Rangoon. But the toughies who pilot the grinding trucks of the Chinese Government know that from Burma to

71

China the Burma Road runs through 726 miles of the foulest driving country in the world, twisting and contorting through some of the deepest gashes on the wrinkled face of the earth. To them the road is a long week and a half of nerve-sapping concentration, of nightmare by day and mosquitoes by night; of rain to blind the windshield half the year around and dust to choke the carburetor the other half; and chills and fevers and high prices in the inns.

Long ago the merchants of Asia realized that the shortest route from China to India and Europe was not by the long waterway of the Strait of Malacca (a 3,000-mile detour) but over the parallel mountain fingers of Yünnan. The present route of the Burma Road follows with romantic fidelity the old silk route by which the trade of the Middle Ages made its way. But its cargoes of death little resemble the silk and jade, gold leaf, amber, and ivory it carried in the days of Marco Polo. When missionaries now living arrived in Yünnan province some forty years ago, there were aged Chinese who remembered seeing tribute elephants bearing gifts up from Burma to the dragon throne at Peking.

The old silk route, however, had long since fallen into disuse when China entered upon her war with Japan. A few pack trains of mules made the mountain trip in the dry season carrying native produce. But the traders of the modern world came to China's front door, regarding the 3,000-mile Malayan detour as an unavoidable necessity. The Chinese Bureau of Roads, in a bulletin published on its work and plans in August,

1937, during the week the Shanghai fighting broke out, made not the slightest reference to any projected road building between Burma and China's back door.

And understandably so. The building of such a road would have been immensely difficult for any nation; and with China's lack of equipment and experience it seemed impossible. The province of Yünnan, over which the road would have to be slashed, lies on an inclined plane tipped from northwest to southeast, from the Tibetan plateau to the coastal plains of Indo-China. From the plateau in the north, like fingers of a giant hand, a number of ranges cut the province on north-south lines. Between these ranges run some of the deepest canyons in the world—the canyons of the jungle-fringed Mekong and the emerald-green Salween rivers. On the slopes of the mountains and on the plateaus the trees had been cut down by generations of Chinese, so that the waters rushed down torrentially in summer and the slopes baked in dust in the dry winter season. Finally, manpower was a problem. The province of Yünnan was underpopulated and sapped by malaria. Moreover, its people could see no immediate benefit from having such a highway: in all of Yünnan, when the war broke out, automobiles, busses, and trucks together totaled only 180.

In spite of all this the Chinese Government decided, following the outbreak of the war in eastern China in July, 1937, that a road to Burma must be driven through. At the time China was in possession of all the south China coastline, half a dozen supply routes inland from the Pacific, and two routes to the interior that ran through Indo-China under the protection of the French flag itself. Yet the Chinese felt instinctively that one anchor line to safety in the rear must be secured.

THERE WERE two routes available for the road. One was shorter than the other; but the longer route could make use of some 263 miles of provincial road to a town called Hsiakwan that had already been laid down by Lung Yun, the one-eyed provincial Governor. The sensible thing was to link the new route to this stump, which ran due west from Kunming across the central provincial plateau to Hsiakwan. The new route would then turn southwest, dip dizzily down into the bed of the Mekong, cross it and run south alongside it for several miles. It would strike west across the Salween, dipping from 7,200 feet to 2,500 feet and soaring again to 7,500 feet, all within the space of forty miles, cross a few more assorted mountain ranges, and finally coast down into the lush fields of Burma. It would end at Lashio, the rail head of the Burma system, with an alternate terminus at Bhamo, the head of navigation on the Irrawaddy. Construction would be in the hands of the provincial government, working with a subsidy from the central government of less than $2 million.

By October, 1937, two months after the decision to build, the job was well under way. Out to every village and hamlet eight days' journey on either side of the road went the summons for workers. Every county was assigned its stretch of road to build, its quota of workmen to provide. The mountaineers grouched and complained. They said that only the people who lived by the roadside would get any benefit of it— but they came, bringing with them their own food and their own adzes and baskets. It was Chinese construction of the classical sort: the lavish application of the toil of human beings. Thus the Great Wall had been built 2,100 years before. An American engineer, studying the construction of the road said: "My God, they scratched these roads out of the mountains with their fingernails." And they did. The stone rollers for smoothing the road were chipped out of rock by hand and drawn by bullocks. The grades were filled with earth chiseled from the cliffsides and carried in baskets. The only modern machinery used on the entire job were a few compressed-air drills for planting the charges that blasted the shoulders of stubborn mountains. The simple mountaineers of Yünnan liked the dynamite and blasting charges, the noise and the fire and the shower of rocks. They worked hard. From the Burma end the British were working hard too, extending their own roads up to the Chinese border. Just which dusty truck had the honor of first rolling through the sleepy terminus at Lashio is unrecorded. But in December of 1938 Ambassador Nelson T. Johnson and Major James M. McHugh of the U.S. Marine Corps drove into the town in a dust-gray sedan to complete the first recorded passenger trip over the Burma Road.

In sixteen months some 200,000 men had built a strip of relatively smooth and graded surface across the roof of the Malayan promontory of Asia. They had dug some 2,000 culverts and built almost 300 bridges, including two suspension bridges that swayed hundreds of feet above the gorges. They had lost to malaria, truck wheels, and blasting powder hundreds, perhaps thousands of lives. For 726 miles a strip of land from nine to sixteen feet wide was draped over stark unterraced mountains, coiled about ridges, notched into passes, snuggled into the contours of the land masses of Asia.

It was the most malarious road in the world. For fear of disease-bearing mosquitoes, which are worst at night, men drove certain stretches only by day. Incidentally, it was the most beautiful road in the world. From the rich green fields of Burma through the unrelenting mountains, over the gorges of the great rivers, it ran through the sky and beauty. It was to become eventually the most dangerous and most confused and most important road in the world; but all that was to come. By the end of 1938 the Burma Road was a fact. Trucks were rolling through sleepy villages, and goiterous, torpid-eyed, suspicious mountaineers were learning the meaning of motor horns. In mud-walled villages, dreary with poverty and brute ignorance, wallowing pigs, cackling chickens, and barebottomed babies scrambled and bawled before the furious clamor of the gas-stinking trucks.

———

THE BURMA ROAD entered the world a legend. Every one in China who could read knew of the Mien-Tien Lu (literally, the Burma-Yünnan road), and the outside world soon filled with tales of it. Men wrote about it, embroidered it with so rich a collection of adjectives that people almost forgot that, like any road, it was supposed to serve a useful purpose. The Chinese, so responsive to praise from the U.S., glowed pink with the flattery showered on them. For they, the Chinese, had built the Burma Road when the world had said it couldn't be done.

It was pleasant to have the world believe that the Burma Road was important. But in China men knew that it really wasn't—yet. The Southwest Transportation Company and other government agencies put several thousand trucks on the road. Despite rain and avalanches that closed the road for weeks at a time, these trucks did haul quite a sizable quantity of munitions into China from Burma. But all through 1939 and the first months of 1940 the bulk of China's imports still entered from the Pacific coast, as they had done for over a century. The Burma Road simply wasn't needed. In good months the railway and road from Indo-China were carrying close to 40,000 tons of goods into China a month. Passengers could fly out via Hong Kong. And the fantastically effective coastal smuggling ring was silently sneaking huge quantities of vital material past the penny-blinded eyes of the Japanese Navy.

Then, in November, 1939, Nanning was taken by the Japanese, and the most important route for gasoline imports was cut off. The result of this was increasing traffic on the Indo-China railway, which in the spring of 1940 reached a peak of 23,000 tons a month. In June, 1940, however, the Germans destroyed the French Republic. Shorn of the motherland's protection, French Indo-China trembled before Japanese threats like a virgin about to be ravished; and with only a protest for the record shut her territories to the passage of Chinese goods.

Suddenly the Burma Road was the only route of any consequence into all China from the outside world. The Chinese blinked as they realized the fact. Quickly they set about shipping to Rangoon and prepared for heavy trucking on the road. And then came the bitter climax. On July 18 Britain, herself in mortal danger, yielded to the Japanese, and closed the Burma-China border. For three despairing months China was blockaded, thoroughly and completely. In Chungking morale cracked badly. Furious with Britain, sick with industrial malnutrition, uncertain as to American policy, China reached its all-war low in spirit. The Japanese, to make matters worse, quietly and efficiently began to plug the leaks in the coastal blockade through which the Chinese smugglers had been nursing supplies.

By October of 1940, however, the world situation had changed completely. Britain had withstood the blitzkrieg over London. American policy

had stiffened. And on October 18 the Burma Road was thrown open again to traffic. The opening was a hilarious event. Goods estimated at 100,000 tons or more were piled up in Burma waiting for transport, and 2,000 trucks were assembled at border points. The Vice-Minister of Foreign Affairs himself came down from Chungking to see the first convoy off. After being dined, and toasted, at midnight on a starlit night, the drivers took the first fleet off the northern hills.

During the long hunger of the summer of 1940 want had burned itself into the subconscious of every government agency in Chungking. "If the Burma Road reopens . . ." they would say and figure out on paper just what was to come in on their first trucks. The army and all its divisions, the Ordnance Department and all its arsenals, the Red Cross and its hospitals, the Ministry of Communications and its repair shops, the Ministry of Economic Affairs and its factories—all wanted something *vitally* and *immediately* over the Burma Road. It took them only a few weeks after the reopening to realize that they were due for disappointment. The tonnage figures told the story. The official count said that from November through January an average monthly tonnage of 4,000 to 6,000 was entering Kunming, the China terminus. And this was the major supply line of an army of three million regulars, a nation of more than 400 million. From every bureau and department anguished howls went up. It was true that the Japanese naval air force from its new French bases was bombing all out. The Japanese slashed at the bridges, hit the Mekong bridge at least twice and the Salween bridge at least once. But in much-bombed Chungking bombing is no excuse for failure.

First Aid

First of all, the Burma Road was functioning as a peacetime commercial highway when it was essentially something else: a military supply line from coastal depot to advance base. Commercial truckers on the road were operating fancy free. Secondly the Chinese government's equipment, about three-quarters of all the rolling stock on the road, was ill-chosen. It consisted of between 2,000 and 3,000 American light trucks—mainly Fords, Chevrolets, Dodges—designed for duty on American roads. What the Chinese needed were heavy-duty, large-cylinder trucks such as Macks and Whites. Almost half of the stock was usually under repair; and there was a shortage of spare parts. As lately as last May, American technical advisers found that of 2,887 trucks of the Southwest Transportation Company 1,407 were laid up with mechanical troubles.

Also there was confusion of administration. The Ministry of Communications, the provincial government, the Ministry of Military Affairs and the Southwest Transportation Company (chief government trucking agency) each had a voice in questions of road maintenance and repair. Other smaller bureaus and agencies arrogated to themselves tiny shares of authority. It was impossible to pin down responsibility on any single agency.

Most important of all, the individual truck drivers had got out of hand. Truck drivers in China are like machine-tool makers in America in that they are comparatively scarce and belong to the working-class elite. Most government drivers were Chinese from Shanghai and Singapore who had originally volunteered from a sincere patriotic urge. But they had immediately found themselves underpaid in an area of high living costs and subject to administration in which graft was a matter of constant rumor. They reacted by proceeding to siphon off gas to sell to private truckers. Soon they had learned to save gas for bootlegging by hurtling down the steep inclines of the road with motor cut, one foot on the brake, one foot on the clutch, one finger on the ignition. They began to carry passengers and cargo on their own. They produced the most vivid wartime slang in China. A private passenger was a "yellow fish"; bootleg gas was "white wine"; private freight was "pidgin cargo"; and any other graft was generically called "sugar." Most drivers were paid at a rate of approximately Ch. $80 a month (about U.S. $4 at current rates) but they managed to pick up Ch. $1,000 to Ch. $1,500 in extras—more than a government minister receives. The money they earned so easily they spent just as easily. Drivers would sit up half the night wining, wenching, feasting, playing mahjongg or checkers, then spin their cars over the road the next morning with foggy eyes and trembling hands. Since the road was opened, 1,300 trucks have hurtled over the gorges to damage or destruction.

Trucking over the Burma Road, as 1941 opened, was expensive at best. Western firms estimated that it cost them Ch. $2,754 (about U.S. $137) to ship a ton of goods from Lashio to Kunming. This is the equivalent of about U.S. 19 cents per ton-mile. The government estimated the costs of its own shipping at 13 cents a ton-mile. In addition, cargoes were subject to the normal hazard of the road itself and the menace of marauding Japanese raiders. When to this was added red tape, confusion, incompetence, and undisciplined truck drivers, it was obvious that drastic steps would have to be taken.

IT WAS the visit of Lauchlin Currie to Chungking last February that marked the turning point in the road's career. Before Currie were spread all the facts of China's wartime life in as complete a confessional as the Chinese had ever made. From the welter of confusing statistics emerged the one root fact—that it was essential that the road be taken over by some single individual agency. Currie urged that the road be made a military road, under military discipline. Behind his words was all the weight of the pending Lend-Lease Bill. The Chinese tentatively suggested the name of John Earl Baker, American relief administrator in China with considerable transportation experience. Currie approved; and in the presence of Currie

and Chiang Kai-shek, Baker was ordered to take charge of the road.

With Currie gone, Baker was left alone to assume his new assignment. Now to many Chinese administrators the appointment of a foreigner to control over their vital life line seemed a loss of face beyond compare, and these gentlemen set to work to whittle down Baker's mandate. In the give and take of Chinese politics during the next few months Baker's status was finally worked out as that of Inspector General of the road. There was to be a five-man board of a new Burma Highway Commission, with representatives of the Ministry of War, Communications, the Southwest Transportation Company, and the Burmese Government. Chairman of the Board was to be General Yu Fei-peng, head of the Military Transportation Department; but Baker was to be established in Kunming with sweeping powers and a second title—that of Acting Chairman under General Yu. By the time Baker left for Kunming to take over the road in May, however, pressure and urgency had already begun to force traffic up. Almost 10,000 tons were reported as arriving in April; and with Baker on the job, optimistic Chinese claimed that traffic in June, despite the rains, reached the 15,000-ton mark.

Baker and Yu have established cordial relations, and with the help of American trucking experts who arrived in July Baker should be able to lick some of the administrative problems. Among the most important being the truck drivers themselves. The drivers are basically good men. They volunteered for the toughest job in Asia out of high spirit. Through malaria, through danger, under bombs and machine-gun strafing over roads that would reduce other men to nervous jellies in a few weeks, they pilot their trucks through to Kunming. With proper treatment they can be kept in line.

In converting the road from a public highway to a military supply line much remains to be done. Truck drivers' pay must be raised and rigid military discipline enforced over their personal lives. Dispatching and checking must function with the unbending efficiency of a modern railroad. The roadbed must be improved. Some 10,000 tons of asphalt is now enroute from the U.S. and should speed traffic over the entire road immeasurably. The defenses of the road must be made air-tight. With the Japanese military occupation of Indo-China, their air bases can be strung out on a line of 500 miles paralleling the Burma ad; and they can bomb and strafe it end to end from the border to Kunming. Unfortunately, the 100 Curtiss P-40's sent out to China are not sufficient for the job—bombers must be sent to pound the Japanese air bases in Indo-China; and more anti-aircraft guns are necessary to guard the suspension bridges.

THE CHINESE hope that by fall the road can carry 20,000 tons a month and that ultimately, with adequate trucks, it should be able to carry 30,000 tons. But even these figures are pitifully small in the light of informed estimates that China must have at least one million tons of military supplies to mount a successful counteroffensive. The Burma Road, fully used, can preserve China's present function in the world front— that of the anvil upon which someone else's hammer will beat the Japanese to submission. But to give China sting and killing power new lanes of communication must be forced open—freight airline service, the new railway now under construction south of the road, the India-Sikang highway now being surveyed north of the road. (See map on pages 52 and 53.)

For better or for worse during the coming months the Burma Road may determine the fate of Asia; and thereby, also, perhaps the eventual fate of America.

FORTUNE September 1941

JAPAN-IN-CHINA

Although her soldiers have kept their foothold on Chinese soil, Japan's economic offensive has failed colossally. She had nothing to sell but slavery.

In the caverns of the great North Station in Shanghai the clock points the noon hour. But it is not noon. The passengers who hurry through, the coolies who sweep the floors, the few foreigners who still make the trip to Nanking read it and mentally turn the clock back. For time in the station is Japan's time; and in Shanghai it is China's time. Wherever the conquerors go they carry with them the standard time of Tokyo city, one hour in advance of the time standard of China's coastline. Only the sun itself, lagging behind the clock, dares openly to challenge the Japanese sentries' right to do this. And in the contradiction of sun and clock is the story of a war, the fiction of Japanese conquest versus the reality of Asia.

The war in Asia, like all the wars of our time, springs from want, the collective and contradictory wants of the Japanese people for a variety of things that they believe can be found in the conquest of China. Basically it stems from what men please to call the "world revolution" of our times, the impact of the machine and the ideas that spring from the machine upon the ordered society of men as it has existed for centuries.

JAPAN'S WANTS are endless. She is the poorest of the world powers. Little coal, almost no iron, an inhospitable climate, few strategic minerals, and a rapidly growing population on a land 85 per cent nonarable breed a powerful urge to action. Unable to support her people, Japan exploded on the modern world from internal pressure. Her economic life since then has run briefly thus: she exported enough silk to the western world and borrowed from the U.S., France, and England enough funds to build up a small stake of capital. This capital came to exist primarily in a group of some fifteen families. With it they created the Japanese industries that, in the forcing bed of World War I demand, achieved imposing production. During this period Japan added to her chief export, silk, the export of cotton tissues, overhauling and then in the postwar period passing Great Britain, the world's chief exporter for over a century. In the 1930's she developed her heavy industry.

Japan's exports were made possible chiefly because she could operate her economic system on a Dr. Jekyll and

Mr. Hyde basis. Her great industries produced western goods either with western techniques or with depressed household labor; but the bulk of her domestic goods and all her food were produced under feudal conditions. Her workers could get along at an unbelievably low wage because their daily life was one of oriental poverty and consumption and because their food was produced by an incredibly industrious and undernourished peasantry. The acceptance of their lot by the people of Japan was rigidly seen to by effective police supervision of provocative ideas and a general system of indoctrination that the Japanese bluntly call "thought control." Within Japan from time to time dissatisfaction would make itself felt both at the polls and in labor and rice disputes. But in 1937, by the process of muffling any open expression of want on the part of the masses and by diverting these wants and thoughts into "patriotic" channels, Japanese leaders had achieved that national state of mind which permitted the great adventure in China.

Japan to be a great state sought resources. She needed iron, coal, cotton, oil, and rubber—most of all, iron. China has iron (1,302,600,000 tons); little by western standards, little per capita, but much compared with Japan's minuscule deposits. China has coal deposits that are rich by any standards, estimated at 240 billion tons. China has cotton: nearly two billion pounds of it were produced in 1936. These were the chief things China had to offer Japan. There was also an extra handful of blue chips: China's near world control of the markets in tungsten, antimony, and tung oil, plus furs and wools, plus tin, plus salt. China lacked only oil and rubber.

THE JAPANESE in 1937 had reached a point where they began to view the geographic expression called China with alarm, for the Chinese were beginning to show a most irritating ability to organize their own economic resources. The textile factories of Shanghai, turning out cotton cloth in appreciable quantities, were beginning to worry the Japan Cotton Spinners' Association almost as much as the Japanese two decades before had worried the mill-owners of Lancashire. A banking system, a communications system, a stable government had all been set up by China in the thirties.

To share the resources of China with the Chinese meant for Japan in terms of trade just what it means in any international trade situation—to exchange for China's products the products of Japan. Now the products of Japan that are sold on the markets of the world are divided mainly into three great categories: raw silk, textiles, and industrial machinery. China needed no silk and she was almost self-sufficient in textiles. And by 1937 it was obvious to Japan that only under extremely bitter competition could she offer heavy equipment to match products of the highly mechanized western nations. There were two important things that Japan could offer China: she could offer China shipping services, for

Japan has a natural aptitude for the sea. And she could offer her educational services, for Japan, having already absorbed western technique into Oriental setting, could teach it to China and, in fact, had been doing so for a generation. But these were not enough to promise Japan a sufficient share of China's produce. Thus, reduced to its essence, Japan could offer China fewer and fewer light products (because China was producing her own); and not much heavy production (because the western nations could match or outsell her).

FOR ALL the foregoing reasons, if Japan wanted to profit by the resources of China, it was necessary for her to move quickly. There was still another reason for speed. Japanese internal equilibrium rested upon "thought control." But should China, that quivering jelly of unrest, come to firmness, there would be another thought form established in the Far East that would inescapably force the Japanese people to examine the basis of their own society. Moreover this reorganization of the Chinese state spelled strength—the strength of more than 400 million people with eventually more coal, more steel, and more soldiers than Japan. It was an ominous enough development for all the nations that had transgressed against China in the course of the past hundred years; but for Japan who had transgressed most, and who was closest to the gathering wrath, it was a galloping nightmare.

It took from 1854 (when Commodore Perry opened Japan) to 1915 for Japanese expansion to develop to a point where its demands might be formulated in economic terms. By 1915, however, the Japanese understood their own inner urges and desires thoroughly enough to present to the Chinese one of the most significant diplomatic documents of the twentieth century, the Twenty-one Demands. In these demands, presented when Europe was at war, Japan insisted that China in effect yield all its rights to Manchurian mineral resources and railways, give up the most important iron and coal deposits in the Yangtze Valley, yield up all German rights in Shantung and enter into political commitments for all the rest of China that would have made her a puppet state. The Chinese, supported by the U.S., refused most of the demands. But for a decade or more the demands stood as the most complete Japanese expression of Sino-Japanese relations.

The next Japanese formulation of Japan's mission in Asia was both more ambitious and more eloquent. It was the famous Tanaka Memorial, a document supposedly presented by the Premier Baron Tanaka, to the Japanese Emperor upon his retirement from office in 1927. Its authorship has been denied by the Japanese, but whether or not it was penned by the Baron, many students of the Far East consider it a valid expression of Japanese purpose. "In order to conquer China," it says, "we must conquer first Manchuria and Mongolia. In order to conquer the world we must first conquer China. If we succeed in conquering China, the rest of the Asiatic countries and the South Sea countries will fear us and surrender to us. Then the world will realize that eastern Asia is ours and will not dare to violate our rights."

Japanese expansion on the mainland proceeded not so much with logic and excuse as with a certain biological vitality. They took Manchuria in 1931, invaded Chahar and Jehol in 1935. Like a vegetable growth, slowly but inexorably, the Japanese entwined themselves about China's future. But in the thirties, south of the Great Wall, Chiang Kai-shek had at last succeeded in erecting the framework of a unified government; and the ground swell of China's overdue renaissance was making itself felt in every production figure, newspaper, and cocky shrug of Chinese coolie. The present war in Asia was the inevitable clashing of the ground swell of Chinese unity and the Japanese expansion on the mainland. The Japanese Army on July 7, 1937, at a sleepy village west of Peiping clashed with the ragged provincial soldiery of north China. A shot was fired, and for better or worse the Japanese were off on their great adventure.

China's Quisling

The task of the Japanese Army was the simplest of all. They had merely to go to the war office, haul out the plans for the conquest of north China, and press the buttons. It went well. "Without cessation," wrote an American correspondent from Tokyo at the war's outbreak, "from 5:00 A.M. till noon . . .

departing troops rode to military barracks in trucks, busses, streetcars, and taxicabs, completely blocking traffic along the main highways. The truckloads of cheering soldiers, waving flags and banners and singing war songs, followed each other so closely that they extended in a line as far as the eye could see . . . Children in streets waved flags and joined in the war songs."

The military tasks of conquest of China were seemingly easy. The armies were soon far inland. But the real task was not conquest but organization; for the Japanese, fundamentally, meant what they said when they declared that they wanted a New Order in east Asia. They wanted an Asia in which China should not only be subordinate to Japan, but in which China should willingly and understandingly accept that role. For the tasks of military organization—the defeat of armies in line of battle, the occupation of towns, the seizure of railroads—the Japanese in Japan could well generate enough energy—at least until the fall of Hankow. But for the proper organization of China, Japan herself could not hope to supply either the manpower or the political talents. The Japanese had no sooner defeated the armies of north China than they set up the apparatus of a civil government, outwardly manned by Chinese. The conquest of Peiping was finished by September; in December the "Provisional Government of China" was established there. Nanking and central China were conquered by the spring of 1938, and in March the "Reformed Government of China" was organized.

Let us examine the thinking by

which their acts were guided. Japan believed that both socially and economically the nerve system of China life was composed of the Yangtze Kiang, the railway lines, their towns, and the great terminals. These were the centers of westernization in China, the hot beds of nationalism and hatred of Japan. The Japanese felt that once these ganglia of sensitivity were anesthetized, the great backward mass of the Chinese peasantry would groove naturally into somnolence and submission. The Chinese traitors to man their puppet governments were readily available—they were old men most of them, some of whose careers dated back to the Manchu dynasty. All had in common a deep and smug distaste for westernization and the new experiments of Chiang's China. These men would not be brilliant or energetic or imaginative—but this added up to virtue in Japanese eyes.

No sooner had the Japanese occupied the railways and large towns, however, than they found that they had precipitated a social revolution. The villages reoriented their entire life away from the railways and towns and withdrew completely first into a shell of sullen, silent noncooperation, then into enflamed resistance. There were several factors that brought about this development. There was the studied brutality of the Japanese soldiery wherever they went. There was the plodding dullness of the men set up to rule. In north China there was the establishment of the "Border Government" by the Chinese, operating almost entirely behind the formal lines of Japanese conquest. Students moved by simple and

ardent patriotism walked about among the villagers binding them together with a oneness that had never before existed in China. This activity provided the basis for the guerrilla organizations that were later to filter with marvelous efficiency all through the Yellow River areas. In north China resistance to the Japanese was linked with an economic reorganization of the countryside that gave it permanent strength. In central China the countryside was not reorganized economically; but being close to the Central Government armies, it was swept along in the tide of hate and felt itself strengthened by the resistance that those armies were making. In central China, moreover, the Japanese had wantonly devastated the factories of the Shanghai area. Thereby they alienated the business class, the only element in China that might have cooperated in setting up an efficient puppet government.

Unwittingly the Japanese had been midwives to a revolution in Chinese life. By wiping out the cities, they forced the peasantry to accept the very same revolutionary and nationalistic ideas they had sought to exterminate. With the peasants against them and the urban classes hostile, the puppet governments found themselves sitting atop a Japanese bayonet; there was no cushion. They lacked completely the support of any group of Chinese from whom they might draw strength.

IN SUCH a situation Wang Ching-wei's defection from Chungking in December of 1938 seemed to the Japanese a godsend. Here was one of the flaming characters of the Chinese revolution, for a generation one of the outstanding figures in the Chinese Government. Suave, handsome, a brilliant speaker, highly emotional, Wang was a man of words rather than of deeds. Wang had deserted Chungking partly out of jealousy of Chiang Kai-shek, more out of weariness of war. Whatever it was that had so twisted him to treachery, here was a man of unquestioned standing and ability in China, a focus about which all the elements of compromise in Chinese society could gather.

The first year of Wang's regime must have marked the Japanese awakening. Not a single man of importance, not a single group of any standing came over to his banners; there were no elements of compromise in China. For Wang too this was a year of bitterness. While he sought unsuccessfully to fashion a government, his name became a mocking word among his own people.

On March 30, 1940, finally shouldering the unpleasant task after three postponements, the Japanese inaugurated Wang Ching-Wei as Premier of a "legitimate" Central Government of China in Nanking. The ceremony was a farce. The building in which it took place was ringed round with Japanese sentries, while within a brass band played and the nondescript carpetbaggers who made up Wang's official family were shown to their places on numbered chalk circles in the hall. In an hour and a half the pompous and shabby rites were over and in the afternoon thousands of Chinese were forced to march in a "deliverance" parade, supposedly "spontaneous," to be filmed by Japanese photographers for home consumption.

Ever since, the Japanese and Wang Ching-wei have been forced to work together. It is not easy. On the one hand the Japanese have a boundless contempt for Wang, even refusing to give him full jurisdiction over the puppet government in north China. On the other hand, in order to infuse some vigor in the regime they have had to accede to Wang's demands for money (they lent him 300 million yen last June) and have even permitted him to meet the heaven-born Emperor.

That all is not well with Japan and Wang Ching-wei is seen in the thinly veiled bill of criticism that Ambassador Honda, Japanese emissary to Wang's government, brought back with him to Tokyo in June. He said frankly that Wang's government had to be powerfully assisted militarily, economically, politically, and culturally and admitted the conflict between Japanese military policy and the need of strengthening Wang. He said, moreover: "Monopolization of profits by a certain portion of Japanese people under the name of Sino-Japanese joint capital should be shunned. National policy companies have been established in accordance with the governing law, and I wish to refrain from commenting on them, but at least the minds of the people who are running them should undergo a change. One should fully realize that a little movement of the Japanese officers, officials, and the people has effects on the Chinese people that cannot be ignored."

The fine words of Wang and his Japanese friends create no illusions for the little Chinese who must live under their banners. The system of communal responsibility for all actions even of individuals, the constant police surveillance, the torture chambers in the big cities of occupation, the unbridled opium trade fostered by the Japanese, all spell out for the most illiterate peasant the word *slavery*. No group of Chinese has yet been found ready to accept this system of life. And failing of popular acceptance, Wang and his court of marionettes cannot deliver to the Japanese the civil stability that alone makes economic enterprise possible and profitable.

The Pay-Off

The economic organization of conquered China, however, is even more important to Japan than its political organization. For the only hope of Japanese success, as of German success, is to make the conquered pay the price of their own conquest.

Japanese have had their chief recent experience in the organization of conquered countries in Manchukuo. In the ten years since their invasion in 1931 the Japanese have lifted the production of coal, iron, and other industrial goods. Plans and programs have been under revision constantly in Mauchukuo, but it is difficult to assess them since Japanese capital has been drained off for the fruitless Chinese war in the past four years. But even in Manchukuo certain phenomena are worth marking out. First is the dangerous inflation that is now bringing about a flurry of small business that, in turn, is necessitating increasingly intricate governmental control. Second, heavy industrial construction and mining has siphoned labor from the villages making an acute shortage in the fields. Further, arbitrary methods of land administration in Manchukuo have so shaken peasant confidence in the future that an alarming decrease in commercial food production has set in. In 1938 and 1939 there were partial food shortages in what once was called "the granary of Eastern Asia"; food production had actually fallen in yield per acre. Another recent phenomenon is the refusal of north China coolies to continue their seasonal migration to Manchukuo in the volume required by Manchukuoan mining, construction, and industry. Japan has on paper a favorable balance of trade with Manchukuo. But this favorable balance represents not an increment of strength but a heavy drain on Japan's home economy of vitally needed heavy industrial goods. Its principal yield is paper claims to future profits, the reality of which is growing ever more dubious.

WHEN JAPAN invaded China in 1937 and 1938 the army set up economic agents in its own image. These were the North China Development Co., the Central China Development Co., both subordinate to the China Affairs Board in Tokyo, which has as its President the Prime Minister and for Vice Presidents the Army and Navy, Foreign, and Finance Ministers of the Japanese Cabinet. Capital is supposedly half governmental, half private. On paper these enterprises seem to be as smooth and rounded as cushioned silk. They are equipped with subsidiary companies for the development of tobacco, furs, cotton, coal, and other essential commodities. In essence, the subsidiary corporations are merely feeders of key raw materials for the gigantic hopper of Japanese industry and distributors of the product of Japanese factories. It is difficult to appraise them, for no figures are available in the U.S. But that they have failed up to now seems to become increasingly evident with each fragmentary statistic revealed.

Cotton, for example, was one of the key commodities the Japanese hoped to take from China. In 1937 their imports had been 53 million pounds; in 1938, swelled with the original loot of accumulated warehouse cotton, the import figure jumped to 191 million pounds; in 1939 their imports were 8,500,000 pounds. By the end of 1938 the guerrillas, aided by stupidly fixed Japanese prices, had convinced the peasants that the growing of cotton was a betrayal of the country. From a north China cotton production of 853 million pounds in 1937 the figure had fallen to 173 million pounds in 1939. By the beginning of this year the Japanese were forced to pay 1.5 yen a pound—more than the world price—for their north China cotton, and Japanese cotton textile factories were working at 40 per cent of capacity.

Other raw materials told an equally sad story. Japan produced in 1940 about 7,100,000 short tons of steel—a record. One-third was derived from American scrap iron and at least half of the rest came from overseas ore, chiefly from the Philippines and British Malaya. But whereas China might have been supplying the bulk of the foreign ore imports (the North China Development Co. originally planned on producing three million tons of ore annually by 1942), imports of ore from that country were less than prewar totals. An import total of 1,300,000 tons of iron ore from China was recorded in 1936; in 1940 estimates of iron-ore shipments ranged from 800,000 tons all the way down to 200,000.

In coal, especially coking coal, another critical shortage affected the war industries of Japan last year. But although Japan substantially increased her coal imports from China last year, it is believed that the best part of this coal comes from mines in China operated by the British, such as the Kaiping field. Chinese mines seized and operated by the Japanese were producing well below their prewar levels with a reduced export surplus. Reliable figures on the production of the four leading seized Chinese mines in north China indicated that daily coal production in tons had fallen from 17,500 in 1936 to 10,100 in 1940. If coal exports from these mines were up, it was because Japan was diverting to herself fuel that had formerly been consumed in China.

THE FOOD picture in Japan's New Order last year was completely chaotic. In Japan there was rice rationing and though at least 500,000 tons of rice were seized from the Chinese peasantry in central China in 1940, rice is still rationed in Japan itself. Moreover, Japan politically could not let the devastated Chinese countryside starve although morally she might willingly have done so. Therefore, while forced to cut down on her wheat imports for home consumption, she was also forced to raise wheat exports to China to feed the helotry. As a final irony, Japan's seizure of rice in China made the situation so critical there that large quantities had to be shipped to that country from Indo-China, thus increasing shipping expenses all around. Simply stated, all the Far East was starving because Japan had diverted so many men in China and Japan from food production for war and for construction of war materials.

The general-trade picture was one of cold comfort. Japanese exports to China had increased but Japan was still sending more goods to China than she was getting in return, and Japan was actually restricting the shipment of goods from Japan to north China because north China could only pay in worthless Japanese-issued paper money.

THE REASONS for the failure of this battery of corporations to produce wealth in China were many. First was the studious cultivation by the Chinese Central Government and the guerrillas of a policy of complete noncooperation and blockade of the railway districts. Next was the fact that Japan, strained to the breaking point, had little skilled manpower and less capital to spare for the administration of such a vast sphere.

More than anything else, however, the hopes of the Japanese had been un-dermined by their own stupidity and avarice. Perhaps the starkest anecdote of Japanese business suicide is the tale of the fur and wool trade of Paotow. The furs and wool of the central Asiatic wastes were usually collected in Mongolia and brought to the railhead at Paotow, whence they were shipped to Tientsin and the waiting world market. Occupying Paotow within a few months of the outbreak of the war, the Japanese held Asia's fur trade in their palm. At the same time the Chinese Government was entering into an agreement with the Russians whereby they would gather Chinese furs and wool at Lanchow on the Yellow River to pay in part for Russian munitions arriving there. It would have been impossible to divert this trade from Paotow to Lanchow normally. But fur merchants coming to Paotow were offered prices by the Japanese that shaved the profit margin to transparent ruin. Thereupon Paotow's fur and wool trade declined while the new Chinese entrepôt for Russian trade at Lanchow boomed.

Four years of war have sadly altered the neat structural perfection of prewar Japanese industry. In the 1930's the accent in Japanese industry had gradually shifted from light to heavy products. Under war strain it was to be expected that all heavy industry would boom even more. Not so, however. In 1939 Japanese industry had passed its peak production.* Shipbuilding by 1941 had fallen off not only in absolute tonnage

*The production index (1929-100) of the *Oriental Economist* read: July, 1937: 172.1; December, 1939: 187.9; September, 1940: 178.2.

but in productive efficiency, and Japan desperately needs ships. Steel and coal production in the homeland hit their plateau in 1939. Productivity in the coal mines has since dropped because of lack of manpower. And in the spring of 1941 steel production in Japan was running 15 percent less than last year for lack of raw materials, even when Malayan and Philippine iron ores were still available. Furthermore, the demands of the steel industry for coal aggravate the coal shortage for many other industries. For example, cement production (January to November, 1940), for lack of coal, was about 25 percent below that of 1939's like period; in 1941 cement mills were operating at 60 percent of capacity. Fishing, which supplies so large a portion of Japanese foodstuffs, fell off in catch for lack of gasoline, fishermen, and cotton fishing nets. Light industrial production is even harder hit. Here almost all the indexes are now showing declines.

Now in midsummer of 1941, ringed around with hostility north, south, east, and west, the Japanese people can comfort themselves only with the knowledge that their troops hold a battle front 2,000 to 3,000 miles long (see page 48), have inflicted millions of casualties on their enemies, the Chinese, and have suffered probably more than a million casualties themselves. Within China the state they planned to build exists only on paper. Economically the great corporative skeletons still stand bony and naked to the wind.

They operate mostly, if at all, through the medium of agencies previously set up by the Chinese, over communication systems previously laid down by the Chinese.

When the Japanese entered China they had an even chance of success. That success depended on their ability to make the Chinese people agree to cooperation. The armies did their part quickly—won the foothold and fought their way inland. Behind them it was the duty of their civilians to create such a system as would generate new power and energy to feed their forward thrust. It was essential, once the railways were conquered, that the Chinese peasant be won to compliance. But conquest, the Japanese showed, meant secret police and constant surveillance, heavier taxes, forced labor at the docks and factories, high prices at the counter, and low wages in the field. Conquest, the Chinese found, meant slavery.

The Japanese political and economic agencies have not only failed; but they have failed so spectacularly and resoundingly that now it is realized that not only do they not help the armies to victory, but they make that victory almost unattainable. And although the Japanese flag may wave victoriously on every front in China today, it is probable that historians will write that the Japanese in China defeated themselves.

Unfortunately, this is a thesis that the Japanese cannot accept. They began this war possessed of an inner conviction of the divinity of their empire, and the corollary conviction of their own invincibility. To them, such round Gilbert and Sullivan phrases as the "Co-prosperity Sphere in Greater East Asia" are symbols of destiny, sanctified now with the best blood of Japan. To them it is not only intolerable that they should be beaten by what they consider a rabble in arms, but more than that—unthinkable. Thus in their casting around for the reasons of their apparent failure they fix upon England, the U.S., or communism, as the case may be. In their sense of history the feeling grows that victory or defeat is no longer to be had in China, but must be had in the world arena, in mortal combat with the Great Powers of the earth. It is this, perhaps most of all, that causes the failure of Japan in China to cut so directly across the course of the future of the United States of America.

FORTUNE September 1941

THE DESPERATE URGENCY OF FLIGHT

Time's Correspondent Theodore H. White *last week cabled from Chungking this dispatch on starvation in China:*

Twenty or more thousand square miles in northern Honan Province are clutched in the grip of hunger. Men and women are eating the bark of trees and grass roots; swollen-bellied children are being sold for grain. Thousands have already died, hundreds of thousands are failing, ten millions face the slow winter-long agony of starvation. Causes: 1) the Japanese, who destroyed the rice before they retreated; 2) the gods, who sent no rain for the wheat.

Honan Province is shaped like a sloppy rectangle and is bounded on the northeast by the Japanese army, which also occupies one-third of its area. Seventy counties are left free in Honan. The 35 counties crowded close against the Japanese in the northeast pocket are being withered by the worst civilian disaster in China since the outbreak of war. Refugees crossing the Chinese lines from Shantung report worse conditions there than in Honan. The refugees drift along in a stupor of hunger and despair, having no destination, but only the desperate urgency of flight.

Missionary E. P. Ashcraft wrote from Chengchow in September: "At the mission a few days ago six children were tied to a tree by their parents so they would not follow them as they went in search of food. One mother with a baby and two older children, tired from the long search for food, sat down to rest under the tree. She sent the two older children to the village ahead to beg a little food. When they returned the mother had died of starvation and the baby was still trying to nurse at her breast. These are just a few authentic reports which come to us. Children are being sold, I mean larger ones, both boys and girls, for less than ten dollars."

Catholic Bishop Paul Yu-pin returned to Chungking last week from a tour of the stricken areas. In Loyang he saw bundles of leaves being sold to refugees for food, a dollar a bunch. Children's bellies were bloated and distended with such foodstuffs. Sometimes starving families collect all remnants of food in their homes, eat their last meal and then commit suicide. While the Bishop was visiting one village, a farmer gathered his family round him, fed them their last full meal and then told them he had poisoned the food they had just eaten.

At nighttime missionaries rove the

roads picking up waifs. They are afraid to collect children publicly for fear of increasing the abandonment of children on mission doorsteps. Other missionaries report an alarming increase of armed assaults on roads as hunger-mad peasants seek food. Farmers are starting to kill farm animals for meat.

From the 20,000-sq.-mile blighted area, refugees are streaming in hundreds of thousands along two main routes: the Lunghai railway and the trail of the old Peking-Hankow railway. The Government has placed a free train daily for refugee disposal along the Lunghai railway, which is carrying out 1,500 people every 24 hours. But the jammed cars, stuffed with clinging, clambering people, are evacuating only a portion of the stricken hordes. Four or five thousand people daily are setting out on the westward march along the line.

The flat and usually fertile plains of Honan are periodically visited by famine, but the last great famine, in 1927, was alleviated by rushing food supplies down railways from Manchuria. The railways and Manchuria are both in Japanese hands now, and all other roads within Honan have been cut in ribbons by the Chinese to prevent a Japanese advance.

Unless farmers get seed grain within the next two weeks, it will be too late to plant the winter wheat and next spring there will be no harvest either. The Chinese Government is rushing 1,000,000 piculs of seed grain from Shensi Province and the same amount from Anhwei. It is also urging farmers not to eat seed grain, but to plant it, assuring them that supplies for their relief are being rushed.

The Government has appropriated $10,000,000 Chinese for direct relief and ordered the Food Ministry to rush seed grain to the threatened areas. United China Relief appropriated $400,000 Chinese in August, $1,200,000 in September and $3,000,000 so far in October. The main relief agency is the Farmer's Bank, which has appropriated $40,000,000 for relief projects such as well-digging and irrigation.

However swift the decision in Chungking, all relief measures are bound by the slowness of the ancient Chinese countryside. The bone-piercing cold of the Honan winter is approaching. Already cholera is reported. The gaunt, hungering peasants cannot understand the administrative difficulties of their relief. For them this is only anger-heaviness which, according to folklore, is visited on earth for the misdoings of people.

TIME October 26, 1942

UNTIL THE HARVEST IS REAPED

How ageless are China's problems and how bitterly Chinese history repeats itself in cycles of wars, floods and famines, Time *Correspondent Teddy White could tell last week from firsthand knowledge. He was just back from a two-week trip through starving Honan Province. His report:*

My notes tell me that I am reporting only what I saw or verified; yet even to me it seems unreal: dogs eating human bodies by the roads, peasants seeking dead human flesh under the cover of darkness, endless deserted villages, beggars swarming at every city gate, babies abandoned to cry and die on every highway. Nothing can transmit the horror of the entire great famine in Honan Province, or the irony of the green spring wheat with a promise of a bumper crop which is not ripe for harvesting for two more months. Most terrible of all is the knowledge that the famine might have been averted.

Those Who Run Away. With Harrison Forman of the London *Times* I arrived in a town called Tunghsientien, a funnel through which refugees pour out of Honan. The refugees are stuffed into boxcars, flatcars, old coaches, layer upon layer deep. They are crowded on the roofs, children, old men & women clinging to any possible fingergrip as the trains hurtle along. Sometimes their fingers get so numb from the cold they fall off. The trains never halt.

In ten minutes we saw the first casu-alty—a peasant lying bleeding near the roadbed. He had fallen from a refugee train some hours before. The train wheels had cut his foot off. He was all alone, crying, and his flesh was mangled on the rail. The bones of his foot were sticking out like a thin white cornstalk. I broke open my medicine kit and gave him some sulfanilamide and we raced on to tell someone to send water and a doctor. But there was no doctor within a day's journey.

Nobody knows or cares how many refugees die on this road. They say two million people have moved out along this route since fall, by now probably 10,000 a day are drifting along westward. Of Honan's 34 millions we estimated that there have been three million refugees. In addition, five million will have died by the time the new harvest is gathered.

Those Who Stay and Beg. In Loyang we went to call on Bishop Thomas Megan of Eldora, Iowa, a greathearted Irish padre. When we came out of his relief dispensary, which is supported by American funds, the refugees tried to mob us. Men fell on their knees, surrounded us, folding hands in supplication.

The next day we went east, riding in an Army truck accompanied by Father Megan. Trees on the road had been peeled of their bark. Peasants dry and powder the elm bark and then cook it. They also eat leaves, straw roots, cottonseed and water reed.

The Army gave us horses to ride on farther east. In the cold first hour after dawn we passed the first corpse—a woman dead on the road. She must have been there at least overnight.

Those Who Die. When we arrived in Chengchow the snow-covered, rubble-ruined streets seemed full of ghosts in fluttering grey-blue rags. They darted from every alley to screech at us with their hands tucked in their gowns to keep warm. When they die they just lie down in the slush or gutters and give up. We prodded one or two of them gently to see whether they were still alive. The relief committee here is supported almost entirely with American funds from United China Relief and tries to keep some women & children alive in a relief camp. The next day we saw the relief committee distributing grain. There were only six sacks of flaked bran.

That afternoon we heard of a cannibalism trial. A Mrs. Ma was being tried for eating her little girl. Parts of the baby's flesh were brought in as evidence. The state charged she killed the child and ate it. Her plea was that the baby had died from hunger first and then was eaten.

Those Who Eat. When we left Chengchow we had a fairly good idea of what had happened in Honan. Crops had failed since 1940. The normal surplus had disappeared. The Army in this vital war area is supported entirely by local foods collected as grain taxes. Civilian officials also each get a monthly quota of grain. The Government people hoped the fall crops of millet corn would meet the needs of the peasantry. But no rain fell and the autumn harvest was almost a total loss.

By a tremendous miscalculation no grain was sent to the famine land in autumn when it might have arrived in time. Now, aside from American relief money and energy, there seems little hope of getting enough grain over the war-smitten routes of interior China before it is too late.

Before we left Chengchow the officials gave us a banquet. We had two soups. We had spiced lotus, peppered chicken, beef and water chestnuts. We had spring rolls, hot wheat buns, rice, bean-curd, chicken and fish. We had three cakes with sugar frosting.

TIME March 22, 1943

VICTORY ON THE YANGTZE

From Chungking, Time *Correspondent Theodore H. White cabled this week:*

The Japanese Army has been whipped. All last week, through villages and towns they devastated in the past month, raked by Chinese and American airmen, elements of five Japanese divisions, plus straggling traitors in their pay, were marching back to the north bank of the Yangtze and the protective river barriers.

No one knows, even now, what the Japanese objectives were in this campaign. It was probably the artless pessimism broadcast from Chungking during the original drive through the lowlands south of the Yangtze that stimulated the Japanese to the blunder of overextension. Without consolidating their rear, without digging in, they drove headfirst into a trap that the Central Chinese Command had prepared for just such a campaign.

Tea Trucks & Jeeps. On a concave line some 60 miles south of the Yangtze, General Chen Cheng, one of China's top field commanders, met the frontal thrust. South of the Japanese, in the rear, burly General Sun Lien-chung held a secondary force for a counterblow. In Chungking the Government commandeered a motley fleet of private and public motor vehicles—from tea trucks to jeeps—and rushed to the front all the reserve supplies it could mobilize.

To counter the Japanese air force, which had cleared the way for the first advance, Generalissimo Chiang Kai-shek decided to throw in a new Chinese air force never before risked in battle. Elements of the Fourteenth Air Force of the U.S. Army moved up from South China bases almost overnight. In three days they erected a new communications system through Central China and flung heavy and medium bombers and pursuit planes into the battle.

By the Rock of Shihpai. Ten miles up the river from Ichang stands a mammoth slab of rock called Shihpai (stone tablet). Here was one key to the fortifications of Central China, and against it the Japanese threw two full divisions. To the defenders of Shihpai the Generalissimo sent a personal message exhorting them to hold firm. This was the crisis—and they held.

The Chinese pursuit force swooped down on the Japanese positions and, unopposed, raked them from end to end. The Chinese pursuits flew so low that at times the Japanese on the hilltops could shoot at them from above. At the Japanese rear Chinese bombers, lumbering Russian SBs and U.S. Lockheed Hudson A-29s, B-24s and B-25s were smashing bases and devastating the railhead at Yochow, smashing ferry points at Ichang, sinking river shipping, laying waste the Ichang airdrome and artillery emplacements.

The Retreat Begins. By Memorial Day the Jap retreat from Shihpai to Ichang had begun. Simultaneously Sun Lienchung struck north from Changteh against the Japanese rear with a mighty blow. The Japanese decided to withdraw entirely from the flatlands to positions on the north bank of the Yangtze.

But the decision had been too long delayed. As their pedestrian columns, slowed by pack-animal transport, strung out across the native roads, American P-40s caught six columns and strafed them viciously and unmercifully. The columns broke and ran. The P-40s went on to blitz all river craft being assembled in the Yangtze for retreat.

By week's end Sun Lien-chung's drive from the south had taken Kungan, the main Japanese forward base, recovered Nanhsien and Nanhsian on the northern shore of Tungting Lake and was forging on to the river. Chen Cheng had driven to the south bank within sight of Ichang, and eliminated the last Japanese ferry head at Itu.

A New Confidence Born. The Chinese had defeated the largest single striking force the Japanese had put together since Burma in 1942. The Japanese were back almost to their starting point, had lost most of the rice bowl, had yielded control of the river from Ichang to Shasi to mine-laying squadrons of the Chinese Navy.

In the perspective of global war the victory was small. The Japanese struck with probably no more than 60,000 men. They lost perhaps no more than 10,000. The entire arena of combat was only 70 by 60 miles. There was little likelihood of a further change in the lines, as the Chinese Army lacked supplies to surge onward in a full offensive.

But in the Battle for Asia it was a most important victory. It emphasized once again the importance of air power in a limited arena, underlined Japanese weakness under attack. It brought priceless harmony and understanding between the U.S. and Chinese air forces. And it gave the Chinese new confidence in themselves. Ultimately this was more important than anything else.

TIME June 14, 1943

LIFE LOOKS AT CHINA

Editor's Note: *Theodore H. ("Teddy") White, 28, became* Time *and* Life *correspondent in the Far East five years ago. In that time he has traveled the provinces of Free China more extensively than any other journalist and has observed, both in Chungking and afield, the winding course of Chinese war and politics. Last month Teddy White returned to America from China and India after spending two years overseas as a war correspondent. Because in that period no really comprehensive picture of what goes on in isolated China has been passed by overseas censors for publication in America, White has tried to sum up the total impact of war on Chinese life in this article.*

Now is the time to talk about China. Last year in Chungking a book was published by Generalissimo Chiang K'ai-shek detailing to all China the nature of her destiny. In this book the Generalissimo flayed the foreign powers and their role in Chinese history. Upon them he heaped the blame for warlordism, prostitution, gunrunning, opium smoking, gangsterism and all the bloody chaos that accompanied and followed the

birth of the Chinese Republic. He bewailed the influence on Chinese thought of foreign universities and culture. The foreigner, he said, had made China weak and despised. This book sold a reported half-million copies before it was withdrawn from circulation for "revision." Not a single foreign correspondent was allowed to cable out a direct quotation from this book until last month. No American or any other foreign publisher has been allowed to make a translation.

The suppression of this book for foreign consumption is only a symbol of the tendency of the Chinese government to prevent the public of the Western world from acquiring a full and accurate idea of what goes on behind the great blockade. It is this and other things that make it so important for Americans to try to fit all the fragmentary shreds of gossip and the butchered news dispatches emanating from that country into a true and fair appraisal upon which we can base our future policy.

The popular American conception of China today is compounded of three powerful modern myths.

The first is the Treaty Port legend. This legend was born at the bars of

Shanghai, Tientsin and Hong Kong and stems directly from the traders who went to the China coast to make a profit. The legend holds that all Chinese are sly, stealthy characters, untrustworthy, cowardly, dirty. They must be treated as an inferior race, beaten and cowed by gunboats and arms. According to this legend, East is East and West is West and thank God for it.

The second legend is the Madame Chiang K'ai-shek legend. Perhaps nothing attests more eloquently the genius of this brilliant woman than the skill with which she has clothed all China in the radiant glamor of her personality. According to this legend all Chinese are noble in spirit, governed by courtly statesmen who like herself are inspired by a philosophical blend of Confucianism and Christianity which is altogether beautiful. There is no corruption, no disunity. The Chinese armies, according to this legend, frustrate the Japanese in attack after attack upon the heart of China with nothing but skill, daring and superior moral courage. China bleeds, and there are none to bind her wounds.

The third legend, more difficult to define, is stained with the sour breath of the folklore of cynicism. It is shared alike by such widely differing groups as the Communist Party and disillusioned foreign officials. According to this legend the government "gang" in Chungking is out-and-out fascist. Democracy is only a "gag." We are being played for suckers by the administration in power which seeks to accumulate stores and supplies against the day of inevitable civil war. The Nationalists in Chungking are rotten from skin to soul, beyond hope of redemption or reform, unwilling to fight even if they could, while only the Communists in the north keep the wicked Japanese at bay.

None of these legends is true. And by the time a correspondent comes to know China well enough to discard the legends, he realizes that whatever he writes will be understood against the background of one or another of these myths. Every correspondent as he sits down to his typewriter realizes that without a scholarly and myth-dispelling preface almost any serious dispatch he writes will be born dead.

The most important fact about China is that it is a land of peasants—of hard-palmed, nut-brown men and women who work each day from dawn to dusk in the fields, who hunger for the land and need the land and love the land. What binds all these people together is not only their common language and their cultural tradition but also their common subjection to a poverty and ignorance that knows no counterpart in the Western world. It is out of this searing crucible of want that comes the desperate struggle of all Chinese to live. And out of this struggle of the miserable to be less miserable come the most pressing of China's problems—for when the miserable struggle against nature, they usually struggle against each other.

Until 30 years ago this fabric was bound together by one of the most curious instruments of government ever created by man, the Imperial Civil Service directed from Peking. Weakened by the flux of time and shattered by the impact of the West, it vanished almost tracelessly, bequeathing nothing but a memory to the governmental forms that followed it. Before this Civil Service vanished, however, it had produced and standardized a civilization which with several significant breaks had hung together for almost 2,000 years. It produced a code of manners and thought that reached from the coolie to the mandarin a pattern of human decency and tolerance that the West has rarely approached. The Chinese have a profound pride in their way of life; and though the archaic machinery of government which that way of life produced was shattered by collision with the modern world, there is still left a vivid emotional conviction of China's greatness. This conviction carried through all the chaos of bloodshed, treachery and disunity in which China weltered for almost three decades. This conviction is in itself no legend; it is a fact in Oriental politics. The brutality of the West to China was as much psychological as physical, and it was the psychological brutality which most outraged Chinese scholars and administrators.

If you could take apart the tangled skein of Chinese history in the past 30 years and unwind it, you would find three continuing strands. First, in point of emergence, after the collapse of the Manchus was the rise of the warlords— the brutal, wolfish soldiers who ravaged the land, trailing pestilence and disaster in their wake. These warlords were queer, mad people who in themselves personified the entire break with the past. Their weapons were shoddy, their leadership atrocious and their allegiance bought with silver dollars. They mor-

seled China into a crazy patchwork of fiefs and subfiefs in each of which the warlord ruled as an absolute despot.

Second in emergence were the Nationalists. They were in the direct line of Chinese tradition; after each great collapse of Chinese government there has come a force to reintegrate the nation. The Nationalists, however, were not only a unifying and historical force but also a product of the general impact of Western culture. As schools grew, railways were laid, factories were built, scholars agitated and mighty cities arose where were bred large groups of men different from any that had appeared in China before. They were workers, clerks, compradores, bankers, intellectuals, teachers, social workers and middle-class citizens. They not only wished to make their country whole again but they realized it had to be done with Western tools.

Though they were Western in their thinking and technique, it would be a mistake to assume they had accepted the West wholeheartedly and without reservation. No one can understand China today nor the mentality of Chiang K'ai-shek who does not understand the hatred and bitterness of the intelligent Chinese for the foreign businessmen who treated him like a coolie in his own land. In some cities this foreigner closed the public parks to Chinese; in some boats Chinese were not allowed to ride first-class. Much of this foreign sentiment focused in the great metropoles of Shanghai and Hong Kong where Chinese were wealthiest and most advanced. I have seen my Chinese friends quiver with shame as they recalled foreign brutality toward the Chinese in China 15 or 20 years ago. This emotion is a healthy and normal reaction to an intolerable record of shame and humiliation. And it is this humiliation set against the whole background of disunion, bloodshed, decay and warlordism that explains why, in so many Chinese minds of the first order, unity takes precedence over all else.

The third great force in China was the Communist Party. It was the latest to arrive on the scene and the extent of its influence is difficult to assess. Like the Nationalist Party, it analyzed the situation and decided China needed unification, modernization and power. But it went further and, in effect, asked: Who will organize China and for whose benefit? The basic Communist answer is clear: China is to be organized as Russia was, not by the rich, the well-born and the educated, but by the peasantry and the working class. With these theses sharply etched into its program, conflict with the Nationalists could not be resolved except by recourse to arms.

On occasion the two parties could and did cooperate. They cooperated in 1925–27 in the first great counterattack against imperialism and warlord anarchy; their agents jointly marshaled the great mass movement that surged from the south and overwhelmed all central China and the bastions of foreign influence.

Three Against Japan

In China today, in 1944, we have a loose association of three forces against the Japanese invasion. Central government,

Communists and warlords alike are all more or less committed to the war against the enemy. This war has gone on for seven years. But whereas it started in the closest and most inspiring alliance of all three groups against the invaders, today this association for a common end has sadly changed.

In the long process of Chinese deterioration, America's responsibility has been great and inescapable. We have made promises to the Chinese government but kept them only halfway. Individual American soldiers have sacrificed their lives and their sanity in a gallant attempt to keep China at war and supplied, but as a nation we have considered the cracking of the blockade about China a secondary concern—hardly even that. And so long as the blockade blankets politics and thinking it is difficult for Americans to point any finger of scorn at the whole dark pageant of Chinese life.

It is paradoxical that the Chinese government, rather than attempting to proclaim to the American people its troubles, should have sought to conceal them and cling to the outworn phrases of 1938 and 1939. To prevent the American and English public from learning of the true state of affairs a shameless censorship is imposed on all foreign newspapermen in China. This censorship is stupid because all the embassies of the great powers in Chungking have full access to the facts and file voluminous reports to their governments.

The over-all picture of China today is compounded of three interwoven problems: blockade, inflation, political deadlock.

No country in modern times has ever been blockaded as China is now. Since the Burma Road closed in the spring of 1942 the Chinese have lived almost on their own. When the road closed it was estimated that there were perhaps 15,000 trucks operating on China's roads. Now, two years later, there are perhaps 5,000 trucks that can operate regularly in the country. The others have worn out. The difference between these two figures spells tragedy. It means that when there is a famine such as has taken place in Honan or Kwangtung no trucks are available to move food in or people out; and people die on the roads and dogs eat them and villages are abandoned. It means that there is no facile way of getting raw materials to factories. It means that centralized control over the provinces dwindles from day to day and the various generals at the front conduct themselves more and more like independent satraps. It means that decisions and orders of the central government are denatured and vitiated with every mile and every hour's distance from the capital.

It means that the whole system of internal economic interchange slowly succumbs to paralysis. The busiest highway in China, clocked last summer over a period of a month, averaged a daily count of 125 vehicles. This figure was for traffic going both ways (jeeps, trucks, buses, commercial vehicles) and this was a road carrying a very heavy load of strictly military traffic. One of the three main arterial highways leading into Chungking clocked in the same way showed a daily average of only 60

vehicles—again for traffic going both ways.

The Chinese armies march on foot. They move divisions 1,500 miles on foot, and only one who has seen the barefoot, undernourished and underclothed soldiers slog the rocky roads over the mountains and through the rice-paddies knows what misery means. There are no food supplies along some of the routes of march and sometimes the soldiers may not eat all day. In some cases the soldiers sell their blankets to buy food from villagers and at night in the mountains they sleep rolled up all together, huddled to each other's bodies against the cold. They die on these marches and no one can help them. I know of one unit making a 500-mile march from a front- to a rear-zone concentration point in which 30% of the troops died on the way. They were examined by an American doctor at their arrival point and 15% of those arriving had tuberculosis. This of course was an exceptionally poor unit but tuberculosis in the Chinese Army as a whole runs between 5 and 10%.

The transportation situation means that even if the government could organize an efficient quartermaster corps in the rear there would be no way of getting meats, fresh foods and beans to the front in quantity to feed the soldiers. The glory of the Chinese armies lies not in their battles, for they have fought few battles in the past three years, but in the fact that they exist at all. The soldiers of China are hungry. They get 24 ounces of rice a day, some salt, some oil and some vegetables. They rarely eat meat. These soldiers suffer from malnutrition, disease and starvation.

The Forges Are Hungry

The breakdown of transportation is the first and primary incidence of blockade on Chinese life, but it is only a transmission belt spreading the evil through the entire national system. Blockade has other effects more direct and just as pernicious. China lacks copper, lacks alloy steels, lacks electrogenerative equipment. All figures on production are rightfully secret but it is impossible for any man who has not suffered under the naked impact of the figures themselves to conceive of the difficulty of fighting a war in China. The figures on small-arms ammunition production—bullets for rifles and machine guns—are so pitifully small that no sane Western staff could conceive of sending troops into battle with so small a national reserve. The result of these shortages is seen in a desire, that has now become almost a habit, to avoid battle under any circumstances. Arms and ammunition are more important than territory and each general stores up his bullets and shells behind his lines sometimes for years against the day of crisis.

Under such circumstances a Westerner might rightly ask how China stays in the war at all. China has been kept in this war as a united nation by the leadership of Chiang K'ai-shek. Up to now, whatever its other faults, this leadership has been unswervingly, unflinchingly and heroically anti-Japanese. It is Chiang K'ai-shek who, at the darkest

moments of China's loneliness, has held his government and his people to their destined task. In this sense he, more than any other man, represents the entire corps of unnumbered and nameless devoted men in every branch of the national life subordinating all their personal future to victory and offering leadership, however limited, to the masses beneath them.

This leadership, however, would be a sterile and sickly thing were it not based on the enormous stability given Chinese society by her peasantry. The equations the budgeteers and statesmen make with paper figures are phantom equations. The real equation of Chinese resistance is simple enough. The peasant produces two things: he produces food and he produces sons. The government takes food from him by its voracious grain tax and with the food it feeds the civil servants, the factory workers, the army. The government takes sons from him and keeps the weak cadres at the front replenished. The peasant is the great raw material of war in China. Even nitrates for the explosive that fill shells and bullets are processed from human excreta. If the rains fall and the sun shines the peasants eat. No blockade can interpose itself between him and the land he cares for.

The second great problem of China is inflation. There are no real sources of revenue left in the country—no great taxable incomes, no industry to produce profit. China finances her war by the printing of paper currency. Last year approximately $40,000,000,000 of Chinese currency were dumped into the circulatory stream of the nation. This year the figure will be greater.

This inflation is a serious menace to national resistance—not because of purely economic reasons but because of its moral consequences. Corruption, official and private, monetary and moral, exists throughout the length and breadth of the land. Since money means so little, people come to have little respect for it or the methods by which it may be accumulated. You get your cut where and how you can. In the counties where the peasant meets the government, there is corruption in the collection of his grain tax and corruption in the recruitment of his sons. If you know the right people you can buy your way out of the army. The weighing-in of the grain tax, the storing of the grain and its distribution, are all filthied with extortion. In one case an American relief representative was attempting to transport a large quantity of grain over the Hunan-Kwangsi R. R. for the relief of the famine sufferers in Kwangtung. He found it impossible to get freight cars on the railway until he had found the right official and paid the "tea money" which ran to thousands of Chinese dollars.

Corruption stems directly from inflation. It is unavoidable. If a general at the front in command of a division is paid, let us say, $4,000 a month in salary, and his family expenses in Chungking or Chengtu come to $5,000 a month ($50, U.S.) he has a deficit. He has to make up his deficit where he can—and he does it usually by diverting public funds or stores in his possession. Or if a general is allotted a certain sum of money for purchase of supplemental food for a division he soon finds that rising food prices have halved the amount of food he can buy. He then has a choice of keeping on his rolls soldiers suffering from grosser and grosser malnutrition or cutting down the number of soldiers he has, to feed the fewer number with better food. No one knows to what extent the names and figures of Chinese divisions are padded. The difference between the actual and nominal figures represents, in part, supplies of rice the general can sell or can distribute among his favorite officers. There are some divisions listed in the Chinese armies with as few as two or three thousand actual combatants.

The most terrible effect of inflation is the cynicism engendered among the honest and decent elements of Chinese life. Civil servants who try to live on their salaries suffer more bitterly than white-collar workers of any other nation at war. Thousands upon thousands of Chinese civil servants are honest and decent and refuse to cut the easy corners. They sell their clothes and valuables, live in unheated houses and work in unheated offices, borrow money from friends and try desperately to keep themselves abreast of the rising tide. The government supplies them with official rice, with official cloth, salt and oil. On this they must get along, hungrily, envying the profiteers and their more practical friends.

Business As Usual

Out of this situation has arisen the most curious front that ever existed between two warring nations. Across the semi-static battle lines a flourishing trade moves both ways. This trade is fundamentally sound—it serves to bring in medicines, cloth, utensils and other necessities. What is bad about the trade is its effect upon army officers who profit by it and are frequently unhappy to see good trade contacts broken up. At one point on the Indo-China frontier, a Chinese troop unit was actually buying its rice from the Japanese side of the lines and feeding itself on supplies procured from enemy sources.

The war is responsible for blockade and inflation—with their mentally evil consequences. No change of government, no legislative sleight of hand can acquire for China more trucks, more copper, more electric power, more medicines until the blockade is broken. Any government in China would have to resort to inflation because there is no real source of revenue in the country except grain; and more cannot be taken from the people without thoroughgoing social revolution of cataclysmic nature.

Deadlock in Chungking

The war is not responsible, however, for the flat, black deadlock of politics in Chungking. There were alternate solutions facing the Chinese government when the blockade forced a reorientation of all its thinking; it could have appealed to the people and liberal intellectuals in dynamic and revolutionary terms demanding even greater sacrifices in return for greater freedom and hope. Instead it chose to defend itself and the nation by regimenting conduct and

freezing thought under the control of some of the hardest characters in national life.

To understand the politics of China one must understand that the machinery of government is in the hands of a single party. According to the theory on which the Chinese government is founded, the masses of people are insufficiently educated and experienced to handle their own destiny. Until education and modern life lift them nearer to the economic and literacy level of the Western democracies their sovereignty is held in trust for them by the Nationalist Party. The period during which this party holds trust is known as the "period of political tutelage."

You have to live in Chungking to feel the weight of the party in men's personal lives. Censorship hangs over authors, playwrights, movie makers and all participants in public expression. The press lives in a shadow world of gossip, handouts and agency dispatches. None of the great problems of China—famine, inflation, blockade, foreign relations or public personalities—can be honestly discussed in public. The greatest paper in China is the *Ta Kung Pao*—staffed with some of the ablest and most liberal journalists of the nation. In the early winter of 1943 the *Ta Kung Pao* published a powerful description of the Honan famine. It did not delve into the corruption, extortion and inefficiency that accompanied it. The *Ta Kung Pao* was promptly suppressed for three days.

The gray atmosphere of Chungking eats into the lives of all who live there. There are not one, but two, secret police outfits in China. One secret police operates for the National Military Council, another for the party itself. Their spies and agents are everywhere. Men can be arrested in China and thrown into jail or concentration camps for any fancied offense. There has been, it is true, little widespread arrest of individuals; physical brutality of the type in which the Nazis and other totalitarians indulge has been slight. But the fact that the secret police has this power and that its agents are sharp-eyed and omnipresent acts as a restraint upon all intellectuals.

In the American mind the government of China is a hazy organism presided over by Chiang K'ai-shek and his wife, its finances controlled by the skilful fingers of Dr. H. H. Kung, its foreign policy expressed by its eloquent and dynamic foreign minister, Dr. T. V. Soong. Across the platform of its public life move such figures as General Ho Ying-chin, chief of its armies; Dr. Sun Fo, its most outspoken liberal; Madame Sun Yat-sen, widow of the founder of the Republic. The most serious omission in this picture are the men of the party, for the party is woven through and through the fabric of government from the humblest functionary's bureau to the highest chambers of council. In Chungking itself, the frame of reference of all public questions is the attitude of the party and more particularly the attitude of the small tight group of men who control the party.

Today the Nationalist Party is dominated by a corrupt political clique that combines some of the worst features of Tammany Hall and the Spanish Inquisition. Two silent and mysterious brothers, Ch'en Li-fu and Ch'en Kuo-fu, known to all the foreigners of Chungking as the "CC clique" (from the initial of their family name) practically control the thought of the nation through a combination of patronage, secret police, espionage and administrative authority. Ch'en Kuo-fu, the elder, is a shy and seldom seen little man who suffers from tuberculosis. As chief of the personnel bureau of Chiang K'ai-shek's headquarters he controls almost all entrance to the Great Presence. Paper work and memoranda to the Generalissimo also filter through this man.

His younger brother, Ch'en Li-fu, a frail and handsome man, is even more important. He is an indefatigable worker, an ascetic, and fiscally honest. His mystic, Olympian and pseudophilosophic writing almost defy understanding except to give the reader the sensation that here he really stands in the presence of some Oriental school of thought beyond Western ken. Ch'en Li-fu trained in America, holds now the vitally important post of minister of education. He is distinguished from the average Chinese intellectual by his ability to roll up his sleeves and get along with the toughest characters of Chinese society.

The Generalissimo is personally attached to both of these men. Their uncle, Ch'en Ch'i-mei, a Shanghai revolutionist, was Chiang's first patron, and in the great northern expedition of 1927, which capped the revolution against the warlords, Ch'en Li-fu was

Chiang's personal secretary. It is important to notice, however, that the character of these two reactionaries differs from that of the "Bourbons" and Colonel Blimps of the West. Less than 20 years ago these men were themselves part of a flaming revolutionary movement in which their lives were at stake. They are not mere members of a *status quo ante* school, but energetic graduates of a school of forceful political action.

CC Cracks the Whip

The CC clique maintains its control over the party by a series of devices. The ruling group in the Kuomintang is the Central Executive Committee which is the closest approach in China to a decision-making body. This committee is chosen from the delegates elected by all the party cells to the Party Congress. There has been no election to a Party Congress since 1935. Hence, for the past nine years the Central Executive Committee has been the creation of a group of men elected in the most reactionary period of modern Chinese history. Some of the delegates elected then have since gone over to the Japs with Wang Ching-wei.

Since the elections of 1935, the Kuomintang has multiplied its membership approximately four times. Many of the best and most vigorous men in China have been forced into the party for political protection or out of patriotism. None of these men can vote or has any voice in the party's decisions. Within the Nationalist Party itself

there is a seething hate of the rule of the CC clique, its dispensal of patronage, its stupid refusal to treat any of China's major problems realistically. The liberals insist that by a policy of freedom within the party and the state, the intellectuals can be brought back and fresh energy brought into the withering cadres of the party. The unity and strength of China come first, they agree, but this unity and strength can be most quickly secured by winning the loyalty of the thinking groups and the landless masses.

In the long range, the most disquieting feature of the dominance of this clique in Chinese life resides in its control over the thought of the land. Through his control over the Ministry of Education, Ch'en Li-fu has inaugurated a state of intellectual terrorism that exists only in the other great dictatorships.

Educational standards have declined precipitously all through the war, partly due to the physical impact of the disaster, but also to the perversion of all standards of academic freedom. Teachers cannot discuss the problems of the nation in class; they are expected to mouth over and repeat the maxims handed down from on high. Ch'en Li-fu controls appointments, salaries, textbook publishing, promotions and careers. Dependent on fixed salaries in a period of skyrocketing prices, weakened by privation and malnutrition, cowed by the thought control of the minister, the great universities of China are now only dull and pallid reflections of what once they were.

The control of education by the CC clique is not simply a matter of expediency. It is based on a deeply bred theory of China's (and Asia's) relation to the West. In the eyes of men like Ch'en Li-fu, Western industry is an interesting trick in the hands of savage men; he regards our industrial techniques much as Westerners regard the poison arrows and bushman craftsmanship of savages in Australia and Africa—interesting, sometimes useful, but unimportant. Ch'en Li-fu is one of the most eloquent proponents of the doctrine that all China can learn from the West are our industrial and scientific techniques, that the basis for future Chinese life is to be found in the old codes of Confucius and the Chinese sages. Any nation has the right to march into the future under its own banners—but an attempt to graft the whole economic-scientific civilization of the West onto the ethics of the medieval Orient was precisely the course sought out by the Japanese with such disastrous results.

At dinner table in conversation with a foreigner, Ch'en Li-fu once explained how much better Chinese oranges were than Western oranges. The famous Sunkist orange of California came originally from China, he said, and was called Sunkist in honor of the district of Sun-ki in China whence it originated.

It is acutely difficult in the Orient at the present moment to point out virtues in the West other than those mechanical skills of which the Orient is already sadly aware. The constantly recurring wars in Europe, the crises both in livelihood and morals in which we found ourselves before the war, the abiding philosophic doubts in our own standards have influenced Oriental thinkers more than we imagine. Each generation, the civilization of the West seems to be shaken by a cataclysm so vast and so terrible that we ourselves question the meaning of society. To the thinking Oriental with a philosophical background old and full of pride, there appears to be little in the West except mechanical contrivances from which he can add to the goodness or beauty of life. To talk to an Oriental of Roman law, Greek thought, Anglo-Saxon democracy, Christian-Hebraic morality or even the "classless state" seems a mockery when the Oriental is confronted with the day-to-day news reports from Europe and America.

The Specter of Civil War

Given the present political texture and leadership of the Nationalist Party, a civil war between Communists and Nationalists seems almost inevitable. If, by some historic necromancy, Japan were defeated tomorrow and the troops of Chiang K'ai-shek marched into Nanking victorious it is quite possible that they might crush the Communist armies in a six-month campaign or so overawe them by show of force as to exact submission. But the war in Asia is a long one, and throughout its course the Communists have been gaining in influence and power much as Marshal Tito has been gaining in the Balkans. Concurrently within the Nationalist Party a progressive deterioration has set in which makes the ultimate test of strength difficult to determine. The shrewdest observers believe and hope that there will be no outbreak of civil war between Communists and Nationalists until the Japanese are defeated. The leadership of both parties realizes that if civil war breaks out, the enemy marches in.

The Nationalists who control most of free China desire above all else to present to the world the aspect of United China. This makes their voice strong in international councils. Therefore their censorship policy on all outgoing dispatches has been to suppress any reference to the activities of the Communist armies in the north or any impression of serious internal opposition to their rule.

As a matter of fact, however, the Chinese Communists rule independently over vast and populous territories in north China. Between themselves and the government there exists so complete and wide a cleavage that their representative in Chungking is almost an ambassador of a foreign power. The Nationalists have done everything in their power to minimize the achievements of the Communist armies. These armies, several hundred thousand strong, are fighting the Japanese all through the vital provinces of Shantung, Hopei, Shansi and North Kiangsu. Completely cut off from supplies by the central government of China, they have woven a net of popular resistance about the Japanese garrisons and railways. Their arms are seized from the Japanese or home-manufactured.

They fight by night, move like formless wraiths through the hills, flicker about the Japanese garrisons and lines of communication like dancing tongues of flame.

In underlining the existence and importance of these Communist armies at this point it is necessary to re-emphasize the fact that the great burden of the war has been borne by the armies of the central government itself. These armies were responsible for the great victories about Taierchwang and Changsha, for the heroic defenses of Shanghai and Hankow and in recent years the gorges and the rice-bowl area.

Because the Nationalist Party has steadfastly refused for the last five years to permit any observers past their blockade of the Red Area it is impossible to judge the veracity of the Communist claims. It is impossible to know how far their control extends or what precisely is their method of political organization of the masses. According to the best information available, the Communist army numbers today between 200,000 and 300,000 men. The guerrilla territories which the Communists dominate—all of them interpenetrated with Japanese garrisons—contain a population of between 30- and 60,000,000 Chinese. The Chinese Communist armies hold down perhaps 200,000 or more Japanese troops.

In their rear the Communists are sealed off from all aid by the central government armies. Perhaps 10 divisions of the best troops which might be employed against the Japanese are employed in the border guard in mid-Shensi. Through this blockade only the most daring smugglers can pass. Even medical supplies destined for the Communist armies have been seized by the central government cordon.

Conditions of health are as bitter in the Eighth Route Army area as in central government areas and there are far less supplies and tools to work with. At the central hospital of their army there was this winter only one set of surgical tools and this incomplete. Amputations are done with butcher knives and carpenter's saws, surgical needles are adapted from those housewives use, scissors, knives, artery forceps are manufactured locally. When there is no anesthetic, operations are performed raw.

Point Counterpoint

The case of the Nationalists against the Communists is explicit. They claim that unity comes before all else, that the nation cannot be strong nor its army powerful if there are two governments independent of each other; two armies under independent command, if the Communists make their own laws, print their own currency and give no obedience to central authority. They claim further that the Communist Party of China, like Communist parties everywhere, is the agent of a third power and that within any state no group can be tolerated whose policy is alien to its own flag.

The Communists on the other hand

claim that so long as they receive no supplies from the central government they need give it no allegiance. They claim that they cannot yield up their independence of action for a share in the Nationalist state unless it is a democratic state in which they have freedom of speech, assembly and press. Were they to give up their armies and their independent areas and submit themselves to the present governing group they would be wiped out as a political entity and many would lose their lives.

The claims and counterclaims on both sides are so complex and detailed that this simplification distorts both sides. But both claims are overlaid with emotional invocations of "democracy." It is still unclear to what degree the Chinese Communist Party follows the pattern laid down in Moscow, and whether their conception of freedom of speech, press and assembly is the same as that of the Soviet Union. It is equally unclear as to what the Kuomintang means by democracy, and whether the present closet-like atmosphere of Chungking is what they offer the Communists in return for surrender of their armies. These, however, are matters of words, and the two parties are locked not over words but over the basic principles on which postwar China is to be reorganized.

The Communist problem is without doubt the thorniest of China's internal political questions and it is complicated by a great and unknown factor: what is the relationship of the Chinese Communist Party to the Soviet Union? It is impossible for Chiang K'ai-shek to decide, or for an outsider to assess his final decision, until it is known how intimately linked this party is to the foreign policy of Russia. It is impossible, furthermore, to assess the democratic protestations of the Chinese Communist Party until it is clear how closely they plan to follow the tactics and methods of the Russian Communist Party.

So much for the Communist problem.

Over all the picture of China looms the brooding figure of Chiang K'ai-shek. Chiang—for all his tempers, moods and shortcomings—is the symbol of China at war, the man whom even the Communists recognize as the only possible leader. Although he is surrounded by a sycophantic court interested in poisoning his mind and feeding his prejudices, he is a man of great intelligence. In his understanding of China he is unsurpassed. Today everyone in Chungking knows that Chiang K'ai-shek is very worried by the condition of his army, by the negligence of his allies in their treatment of him, by recurring famines, by the Communists, above all by inflation and its moral effect on the civil service.

At the grass-roots there is a crumbling away of loyalty to the regime. In the spring of 1943 violent but brief peasant revolts broke out in Kansu. In the summer of 1943 there was a revolt in Fukien. There have been sporadic outbursts in Szechuan and Hupeh. The peasant discontent springs in part from the administration of the grain tax, in part from the corruption and inefficiency of the conscription of manpower.

All these revolts were quelled and none was linked to any national group or party. They were simply expressions of grievance in a system with no democratic outlets for discontent or public discussion.

Chiang bears on his shoulders an enormous burden of personal work. Increasingly he feels that he is the only one he can trust in the entire nation and his energy is more and more channelized into minor administrative matters. He feels, in a sense, that he is not only China's leader but a great teacher of ethics; and that by ethical precepts he can control his hard-bitten political underlings. Chiang's decision in February to invite the Communists to Chungking was sound and realistic; but unless he follows through with an equally realistic overhauling of all the rest of the political apparatus there can come no real change in the present tension-charged situation.

Yet there are solid and profound forces working for good in China today, for the people of China are greater than any man or any government. I once spoke to a famous Chinese who in the early days of the revolution had sat at the bedside of Sun Yat-sen, the night he died. "It was stormy and windy all that night," the teller said, "and we cried ourselves out. In the morning when we woke the storm had passed and it was a clear, blue Peking day in the spring. I remember how I walked in the streets and said to myself it does no good for the sun to shine or the storm to go— the revolution is dead now, Sun Yat-sen is gone and we are lost. I felt we were all through. Then I went south to join the revolution again and found it was still going on with new leaders and new people and stronger than ever, and we won. I suppose I learned then that China is greater than any man or any group. It's the country that is great and nothing can stop it."

Deep within China the great revolution of Asia is working itself up to a climax. Both within the Nationalist Party and out of it are distinguished liberals, scholars and statesmen who are still battling for the creation of a free and freedom-loving China.

The impression Asia made on America on Dec. 7, 1941 was shattering. Curiously enough, in the eyes of history, it was the Japanese rather than the Chinese who thus forced themselves on our national policy. But the Japanese in Oriental history are insignificant. Penned up in their rocky islands with little culture or standards of their own, their present brief and terrifying role on the record of history is a fleeting phenomenon. The real power of the Orient resides in China; she is the nation that has given the East its civilization for over 2,000 years and will do so again. The Chinese people as a group are possessed of an affection for America which is one of our greatest assets in foreign affairs. To keep the permanent friendship of this great nation almost any price is small. We have a real obligation, as allies in arms, to assist the Chinese with force at the present moment on a scale far greater than we have done for the past two years. And if this obligation is not too long denied we shall find on reaching China vital forces eager to join us in pursuing the ends we consider the true ideals of America.

LIFE May 1, 1944

ALL WE HAD TO TELL . . .

Around besieged Hengyang the Jap lay fat and well-fed. Toward him plodded the patient, pauper soldiers of China. Time *Correspondent Theodore H. White went on one such expedition that tried to reach Hengyang's defenders, reported it in this dispatch:*

We waited in our stuffy compartment—a middle-aged U.S. captain, a clean-cut colonel, Graham Barrow of Reuters and I—and were thoroughly miserable. Peddlers were hawking cucumbers, wheat cakes and tea to the Chinese soldiers jammed on flatcars and boxcars. Up front the tired locomotive leaked steam at the joints while soldiers loaded the train with supplies—chickens, pigs, a couple of fresh red and white slabs of meat crusted with flies. Finally the train lurched sorrowfully out in the heat up the line to the railhead.

The colonel, who was an American liaison officer with the Chinese Army, peeled off his gun, unbuttoned his shirt, let the sweat pour down his dusty face in tired rivulets. I peeled down to bare middle and the heat slowly settled in to choke us. The train was making about six miles an hour and the colonel was telling us about the evacuation of Hengyang.

"I was lying asleep by the railway station one night in the rain, then I woke up because there was a train going by. They were stuffed on roofs and in boxcars. They had lashed themselves to couplings between cars. There were refugees on the cowcatcher in front; underneath the trains they had laid some boards across the rods between the wheels. They stretched their mattresses on the boards and there they were, lying one on top of the other between the rods and trains."

The captain began to tell how he sold cosmetics for Max Factor all through the Orient before the war. Then, as if something clicked in his mind, he reverted to the story of the evacuation of Hengyang:

On Top of the Car. "I was riding on the roof of a boxcar that night. It was raining. Refugees were so thick you couldn't move. You know, one of those women refugees, she had a baby that night, right there on top of the car. About an hour after it was born she had a fever of 101 degrees, the baby had 103. There was a Chinese Red Cross man with us. So we broke open my army first-aid kit and I took out my sulfanilamide. The Red Cross man broke one of the tablets into six little pieces and fed them to the baby one at a time. You know, they both lived, too."

It took the train two hours to do twelve miles and we came to the railhead. Thirty miles up ahead were Japs.

It was six o'clock by the time we found billets in an old factory dormitory that smelled like an abandoned pigsty—the kind whose odors are latent but deep, and revive each time you kick over a stale pile of dirt. We lay sleepless through the night.

It was dawn when Barrow and I joined the troop movement; the cruelty of the heat and cloudless skies was already unbearable. The whole Sixty-Second Army was on foot. As far as you could see, strung over the horizon through rice paddies, in single file along the ruined rail bed, crawling through ditches on the devastated highway, were single files of Chinese troops. For every man who carried a rifle there seemed to be two carrying supplies and other impediments. Larded between the plodding, unsmiling, heat-burdened soldiers were blue-gowned peasant coolies, pressed for carrier duty.

One Day Farther. The army was quiet—the Chinese quiet of men who are not suffering acutely but merely bearing the bitterness of decades one day farther up the road. The soldiers were wiry and brown with the sun. Their rifles were old, their clothes threadbare. Each of them carried two grenades tucked in a belt about his neck and a long blue stocking inflated like an enormous bologna roll. The blue stocking was stuffed with dry rice kernels, the only iron rations the Chinese soldier gets. The soldiers wore straw sandals, yellow and green shorts and shirts, and their heads were covered by crowns of leaves that gave shade from the sun.

At muddy brooks some soldiers would break discipline, stoop and guzzle the water—nothing else could be had en route. The fields were barren and deserted, the houses shuttered and hollow. Once we saw a hunchbacked cripple spading his garden. In one village a blind peasant sat on his doorstep amidst the empty houses of his neighbors and listened to the plodding shuffle of passing troops.

As dusk fell, the army fell out along the road. We slept. Next day about noon we arrived at divisional headquarters, four miles behind the lines. We had been assigned to the famed 151st Division, whose chief of staff 25 years ago was Chiang K'ai-shek. The 151st, like all Chinese divisions, was under strength. The entire division had two pieces of artillery—two antique French 75's—several mortars, some machine guns and rifles. It also had guts. What it had to do was to move up the hills in the daylight, ignoring Jap artillery, and dig live Japs out of holes they had had prepared for three weeks.

Hope in the Morning. The division had struck at 3:30 that morning, creeping up the hills in the dawn. By midmorning it had taken seven of the ten hills that guarded the town. Divisional headquarters was certain that by next day the division would break through the Japs and the road to relieve Hengyang would be open. We set out for the front to see the fighting.

We climbed to a regimental command post at the very top of the Chinese positions. From the loopholes you could see out over the field of battle. The nearest hill recaptured was a wooded one and Chinese troops were already sheltered there. But three Jap hills beyond were the highest of the cluster and on these the Japs had concentrated their guns and men. Two white farmhouses in the slopes of the hills held invisible Japs, and Chinese guns were trying to reach them unsuccessfully. Mortars of the Chinese belched from behind us, but nothing happened.

It was the heat of afternoon and in the giddy shimmering waves that rose from the hills there was finally silence. The regimental commander said the Chinese would start attacking again in the evening. By morning, he promised us, we could go through the notch in the hills—the Japs would be cleaned out.

Morning found us at divisional headquarters waiting to move up. But the attack was bogging down. I trudged over to the hospital to see the wounded. Casualties had been heavy and hospital orderlies were working fitfully among the bloody, uncomplaining bodies. The smell of the old barn and the fetid, heavy odor of sickness was crushing. I asked the director where he got his medical training. He said, "I am self-taught. I joined the army medical service four years ago."

Despair in the Dark. The second evening of the attack we could not sleep. From over the ridge came the steady crash of mortar shells, the rumbling, ugly sound of artillery, the rippling of Japanese machine-gun fire. Now and again enormous flashes—whether of artillery or ground lightning from summer heat I could not tell—silhouetted the area in red and black.

By evening of the third day the attack had stalled. The divisional commander, in short, unhappy grunts, gave the old, sad diagnosis—the Japs were dug in; the Chinese could not clean out the enemy with rifle, bayonet and machine gun alone. What could be done, I asked the commander. He said his decision had been made by higher headquarters—he was to shift attacking forces from the railroad into the hills, try to bypass the Jap garrison, close with the enemy positions at some point nearer Hengyang high in the roadless hills. We could go with him or return. We thanked him, said we would go back and write what his men had tried to do.

In the morning we set out once more in the heat on the long road back. Chungking radio was telling of victories on Saipan, at Minsk, in Italy, in France. All we had to tell about was an obscure campaign in an unknown valley and the suffering of a sick, ragged, dauntless army.

TIME July 31, 1944

INSIDE RED CHINA

Editors' Note: Time *and* Life *Far East Correspondent Teddy White recently flew from Chungking to Yenan, the mountain-shrouded capital of Communist North China. There he talked with the Party leaders, peasants and guerrillas who for seven years have been waging their own independent war against the Japanese. In this article Mr. White tells of their long struggle and recounts some of the atrocities committed against them (as against all China) by the Japs.*

In the current crisis of the Asiatic war the Chinese Communists hold a crucial position. In recent months the Japs have scored a great land victory, splitting Free China in two and threatening to knock it out of the war. To meet this threat the U.S. government has been urging Generalissimo Chiang K'ai-shek to accept the Communists' help in a united campaign to stop the Jap invaders. Last week the news hinted that some such political truce might be in the making. Chiang appointed the able and modern-minded T. V. Soong as premier of the Chungking government. A high Communist leader, Chou En-lai, flew to Chungking from Yenan in a U.S. Army plane. There was hope that the dire adversity might at least temporarily solve the deep-rooted ideological differences.

You come down on Yenan from the air, over the wastelands of North China and over loess hills with their tops sliced off. You feel that you are going into a bandits' lair—remote, inaccessible, awe-inspiring, surmounted with an incongruously lovely T'ang pagoda yellow against the China-blue sky.

But once on the ground and with dust swirling over you, whipped by a cold and brazen wind, the familiar smells and sounds are those of old North China. There are mules and horsemen, yellow loess and foot-deep dust, tufted camels from the deserts, the people themselves in shaggy woolens and thick yellow paddings.

This is as it always has been, except that now there is something else—a gloss, a bustle, a driving, vigorous energy that is new. The people are younger, sturdier; bugles shrill and echo and rebound from hill to hill in fine silver tones at dawn. There is an undercurrent of movement, confusion and excitement.

Soon, however, this impression resolves itself into a feeling that this is not a capital and not an experimental Shangri-La—but that this is a camp, an active field headquarters, or a provisional command post that has been pitched at a particular moment in history and that the camp itself can be struck and dissolved and moved on tomorrow if it need be.

There are 40,000-odd citizens in the township. Twelve thousand of them are natives of north Shensi Province—here since before the records of history began. The rest are the brains and hearts, the everlasting core of the Chinese Communist Party with its arteries of bureaus and other organs of operation.

Everything revolves about two separate clusters of buildings which house the headquarters of the army and the headquarters of the Party. Army headquarters are tucked away beneath hills in a compound of mud and gray brick buildings in a garden of limpid loveliness. Party headquarters are three miles up the river in two large buildings of brick.

Out of these two separate headquarters go the orders and directives to all agents and units of Communist movements throughout the length and breadth of the land—to the guerrillas in the hills, to the underground in Japanese-occupied cities and to the radio network that links the Party together.

Yenan itself is unimportant. It is a window, a great, open peephole into the vast areas that the Japanese have conquered. The people within this tiny gobbet of loess are the eyes, ears, nerves and tentacles of the Communist war against Japan. Through them the Party decides what shall be done for the guerrillas ceaselessly fighting the armies of Japan and her puppets, for the Communist army and for the armed militia. When you listen to the people talk it is as if someone had thrown open the grate of a furnace and inside you could see the terrible cruelty of the flames.

Here, behind and flanking the advance lines of Japanese conquest, war has gone on without letup since 1937. The Communist armies can marshal as many as 20,000 to 30,000 trained fighters for a single operation in one area. And beneath this striking power there is a base of peasant popular support spreading out behind and around the routes of Japanese circulation throughout all of North Central China. There are some areas measuring 200 by 100 miles in which no enemy dares set foot.

The organization is not like that of an armed conspiracy of raiding huntsmen nor is it led by a band of Chinese Robin Hoods. It is a vital, integrated military and political movement that has, provisionally at least, solved the most vexing problems of Chinese peasant society. Eight years ago North China was a backward, unhappy political vacuum. The new nationhood of China was confined to cities and railway zones. The peasants in hill villages and roadless plains were still boxed in semifeudal ignorance, superstitious slaves to neverending labor, captives of the land and of the landlords.

The Communists, wise and shrewd with 15 years of merciless class warfare, knew how great were the social tensions in the villages and how much power was locked up in the immobile struggle between the landlords and landless, between the rich and poor. As their army expanded it carried with it as a packaged unit its political organizers. These were to reorganize the social structure. The peasants were told to elect their own governments and officials. They were urged to cut rents and reduce interest rates from 40% a year to 20%. The landlords were given guarantees that rent would be paid and interest accounted for. Patriotic intellectuals and students who left routine careers at the start of war were called in to staff the government and act as administrators. They have succeeded in resolving these tremendous internal tensions into an all-consuming, external war against the enemy: the Jap.

It is their war against the Japs that has made the Communists popular among the people. The Communists offered the peasants protection. And they offered resistance, the only possible outlet for the terrible, quenchless hatred of the Chinese peasants for the Japanese soldier.

"Kill All! Burn All! Loot All!"

What the Japanese have done to occupied China is one of the most monstrous historic crimes ever perpetrated against one people by another. In a sense it is so great that the Japanese themselves have been trapped, for as each succeeding barbarity failed of success it called forth some new device and doctrine of savagery. In seven years the baffled Japanese have arrived at a total political

bankruptcy in North China that is summed up in a new Japanese army slogan: "Kill all, burn all, loot all."

From one end of North China to another the hills and valleys are dotted with the blackened, empty shells of villages which the Japanese have razed. But because of the relentless opposition to them, the invaders have had to dig protective trenches and ditches parallel with their railway lines for hundreds of miles. Blockhouses are strung out along the highways and the hillcrests are crowned with strongpoints. Every bridge is guarded by blockhouses. Telephone poles are sometimes set in concrete to protect them against guerrilla destruction. Yet none of these Japanese devices has been able to halt the organization of popular peasant resistance.

The motive and impulse of war comes from hate. The atrocity lists here in Yenan couldn't even be published in America. Rape in every ingenious variation is commonplace. Murder is a low form of crime. Massacres follow one another with degraded monotony. There were a series of massacres at Pingyang on Oct. 18 last year which became famous. The Japanese gathered the villagers together and cut the head off one girl. Then they impaled it on a chair and forced the people to kneel and contemplate it. This was part of a softening-up process to make them talk. They made the girl's mother fondle the head, then beheaded the mother too. They picked out five pretty women for their pleasure, then herded the rest of the villagers into a cave and burned them to death. They moved on to neighboring villages, burning 16 peasants alive in one spot, eight alive else-where. They got tired of simple burning and at the next spot, Shantsuitou, they blindfolded 15 villagers and kicked them alive from the mountaintops.

Up and down the Pingyang area the Japanese roved. Rarely did they waste bullets. In one village the Japanese took a pregnant young woman and sum-moned 20 other village women to watch as they placed the woman in a coffin and cut her at her breasts. A Japanese sol-dier inserted his hand and tore the tissue away till he reached her heart. She had died before he reached her heart, but he ripped it out. All this was done as a public demonstration to strengthen army authority. The unit was com-manded by a Colonel Arai. The Chinese have recorded many such cases.

So deep is the hatred of the peasantry that it often cuts directly across the Communist Party's efforts to capture Japanese soldiers alive. When Japanese are captured alive they are brought usu-ally to Yenan or some other center for classification. The most radical ele-ments are normally turned over to a Japanese-personnel school for instruc-tion under the direction of a Japanese Communist leader. Incorrigible ele-ments are usually turned over to the central government. The politically ad-vanced elements form the nucleus of the "Japanese People's Emancipation League," which now numbers more than 300 active members engaged in anti-Japanese propaganda and intelli-gence work.

Three Conditions that Cause a Fight

The regular army of the Communists operates usually in companies and de-tachments of little more than 400 men. Their basic arms come from supplies captured from the Japs and the troops fight only under special circumstances. They go into action, first, when there is a good opportunity to capture enough rifles and ammunition to make up for what they expend; second, to protect the countryside during the period of the grain harvest when stores are being con-centrated; and third, when a major Jap-anese offensive against one of their own primary administrative centers must be stopped.

The peasants themselves have raised mine warfare to a high level. The Com-munists began to teach mine warfare to the peasants two years ago. Now local newspapers report the exploits of "mine heroes" the way American sports pages report home-run kings. Old temple bells or scrap are brought to the army arsenal department which gives the peasants the equivalent in mine shells. These the peasants fill with black native powder and smokeless powder produced by the guerrilla governments. There are also mines made of porcelain, logs and rocks. Bridges are mined. Stepstones in brooks are mined. Mines are rigged around Jap blockhouses so that an un-wary Jap garrison will blow itself up when it moves about. Some of the vil-lagers mine all approaches to their resi-dences, leaving a different approach clear each night. When Jap raids are threatened, mines can be scattered everywhere—in the village squares, by the gate, by hitching posts.

The peasants love hand grenades, too, which they make themselves out of black powder and native fuses. You can go into a country home and see a housewife doing her wash or cooking a meal and on on a shelf over her head she has two "potato masher" hand grenades ready for use. It is all a part of the peasantry's preoccupation with war and resistance which also makes it the most perfect intelligence net ever conceived. No Jap moves, no truck passes but what the peasants watch and report. On the hills are long poles, tufted at the top so that from far off they look like brooms. These are alarm signals. When the hilltop sentries see Japs moving on the paths below the tufts are knocked down. Each village is mobilized so that every citizen knows what to do the moment the alarm is given. Women and children disappear into tunnels in the hills.

On the plains, where there is no hill cover, the war has gone underground in the literal sense. The peasants began by building tunnels under the individual villages for hiding, then village was linked up to village. Now there are places where the underground network runs for miles, complete with ventilation chambers to thwart the use of poison gas. The Jap who crawls into such a rabbit warren with a rifle is at the mercy of the peasants.

The Party schools and conferences at Yenan exist as a laboratory and symposium where the experiences and experi-

ments of outlying areas are discussed, analyzed, debated and raised to the theoretical status of Party policy. The Party and the army are constantly sucking in the alert, energetic elite of mass organizations in the forward areas, training them in schools and pumping them out again. One of the leaders of the Party estimated that between 30,000 and 40,000 such cadres have already been indoctrinated in Yenan.

Hardheaded Pragmatists Run the Party

The Party leadership remains in the hands of the same body of men who have directed the movement since it was driven underground almost 17 years ago. They are men in their late 30s or middle 40s, recruited mostly from the ranks of youthful intellectuals who were set ablaze by the great revolution in China in the 1920s. The long, tough years have weeded out the frail in body, the vacillating in conviction, the sterile in ideas. The leaders thus developed into a group of grim, hardheaded pragmatists who cast away tenet after tenet of early Marxist theory. They are hard men and can be rough. So many of their families have been butchered in civil wars that almost all of them live now for their Party and convictions. They are proud of their achievements, have an assurance in their work and above all they have the patience and trust in one another that come only from common suffering jointly endured and jointly surmounted.

The top leaders of the Political Council are divorced from actual administration and have leisure for long discussions and extended theoretical reflection. An interview with any member of the council can last five or six hours. Their knowledge of the outside world is primitive, sometimes wrong—but it is combined with an amazing sophistication as to the motives that impel states and masses to action. They preach and revere Marxist shibboleths; and as they abandon one after another they justify each abandonment by historical dialectics. Their policies are now based on an empirical wisdom that comes after years of civil war and war against the Japanese. Within themselves they are trying to weed out the sins of intellectual dogmatism that their younger cadres learn from classics based on Western revolutionary experience and theory. Party leadership is trying to turn the younger theorists back to the study of Chinese society and history for a new program of action.

Said Mao Tse-tung, Communist Party Chairman, stressing the new Party line: "No one has begun in a really serious manner to study political, economic, military and cultural history during the past century, the period of real significance. . . . Many of our comrades regard this ignorance or partial knowledge of our own history not as a shame but, on the contrary, as something to be proud of. . . . Since they know nothing about their own country they turn to foreign lands. . . . During recent decades many foreign-returned students have made this mistake. They have merely been phonographs, forgetting that their duty is to make something useful to China out of the imported stuff they have learned. The Communist Party has not escaped this infection."

At present the basic foreign policy of the Party is directed at the U.S. in recognition of the fact that we will be the strongest power in the Pacific and that we are a great ally now against the hated Japanese. In pursuing that policy the Party in all its declarations is now trying to sell three ideas to the U.S. The first is that their party disposes terrific power in the battle against Japan, a power that can be coordinated directly with the U.S. efforts. The second is that the Party itself, its government and its armies, is based upon a functioning, democratic system. The third is that the Party is willing to go to any length to be friends with the U.S.

There is no question about the military power that the Communist Party disposes. Its extent is reflected in the disposition of Jap and satellite troops.

There can be just as little question at present about democratic methods. The Communist Party is for democracy currently because democracy pays. You take a peasant who has been kicked, swindled and beaten and whose fathers have transmitted to him the memory of oppression reaching back for centuries; then you treat him like a man, ask his opinion, let him vote for his local government and police, let him vote himself a reduction in rents, let him vote himself an army and militia—if you do all that you have given him a stake in society and he will be willing to fight both for society and the Party that has given him this stake. Behind the Japanese lines the peasant follows the Party because the Party has given him a stake in his society. To follow or vote for anyone else or any other party would seem ridiculous to him.

Whether or not such blanket Communist leadership in democracy can be maintained after the war in larger cities where political corruption is possible and where the urban middle class fears and hates Communism—and where there is a well-organized, well-moneyed, eloquent opposition party—remains for the future to decide. The Communists feel that if all adults of all classes are given a vote the Party can retain control of the masses and that, therefore, democracy is precisely the best medium for the three-fold development of China itself, of the Communist Party and of the masses.

In proclaiming their friendship with the U.S. the Communists at present are sincere and if their friendship is reciprocated it can become a lasting thing. The war against Japan has been so bitter and soul-consuming that the Communists have become out-and-out nationalist while at the same time any enemy of the Japanese becomes a sworn friend of theirs. The U.S., as the chief enemy of Japan, is their friend and they feel, in addition, that the U.S. can be the greatest aid in producing peace and the future orderly development of China. They say that China has had too much war, and it is true that since 1911 the country has run with blood, destruction and pestilence. The people are surfeited.

The Chinese Communist Party, deriving its theory out of experience, has come a long way since its early politics of land confiscation and indiscriminate hostility toward all Western powers. Presently it wants American friendship more than any other single conditioning force for the future China. It wants this friendship, however, not as a beggar seeks charity but as a friend seeks aid in furthering a joint cause. With or without this friendship, however, their war against Japan will go on till victory or death. In victory they will remember who were friends and who stood coldly aloof.

LIFE December 18, 1944

PEACE COMES TO SHANGHAI

Chinese city goes on a fortnight's bender:

Shanghai is an eruption of volcanic gaiety which burst loose when the Japs surrendered and still continues unabated. It is a thousand Mardi Gras rolled in one, decked out with noise, color, music, happiness and all the arts of the Orient.

Nature itself has conspired to clothe the city in carnival spirit. The air is crisp and the sky blue. A high breeze whips around the corners of the great buildings, lifting the skirts of pretty girls and fluttering every scarlet banner atop the towers of the city. U.S., British and Russian flags snap in the wind from store windows which are filled with huge photographs of Chiang Kai-shek. Automobiles, bicycles and trucks all fly the national colors right in the faces of the stolid Japanese still guarding the buildings and bridges. On the sidewalk of the pompous Custom House building on the Bund a stern Jap soldier stands guard. Before him little hucksters are selling stinking dried fish and bright little buttons bearing Chiang Kai-shek's picture. Other vendors are hawking oversize flags quartered so as to include the U.S., British, Chinese and Russian colors on the same pennant.

There are only a few hundred Americans in the city but their presence seems to dominate the entire Bund and International Settlement. They have commandeered transportation from municipal authorities and moved in to occupy Shanghai's fabled hotels. Every truck loaded with Americans that passes to and from the airfield touches off a celebration. Crowds cheer and dance with glee. They swarm around the few jeeps that arrive by air and almost crush them with joy. Overhead in the clear skies B-29s flying errands of mercy are dropping food and relief supplies on internment camps that hold so many thousands of our people still within the walls. Parachute packs of goods drift down through the skies and the people, yelling and cheering, chase after the mannalike food. Less than half the supplies seem to fall within the internment compounds and hungry Chinese retrieve the remainder. They consider the food as victory gifts, given and accepted in the spirit of carnival.

The Americans who led the way into Shanghai are a fascinating study in rapid adjustment. They are men of the China-Burma-India Command, orphans of the war effort. They are the men of the squalor, misery and hunger of the Central China Command. They have come from the feudal mountain bivouacs of the Chinese hinterland into fairyland. This is what they always dreamed of—only it is better than dreams. Every man is a millionaire. They find themselves in hotels with exquisite service, spring mattresses, clean white sheets and carpets a half-inch thick. T-bone steaks are four times thicker than the carpets and every hotel can serve them. Unlimited Scotch pours across the tables. For men who have lived in central China on K rations and Army fare for 12 months, the mastery of Shanghai's famous chefs is overwhelming. No one needs money at the big hotels, they just sign their names.

WHERE WOMEN are, Americans gather. There are White Russians, Hungarians, German refugees, and their enthusiasm surpasses even the legendary welcome of the Melbourne girls in the spring of 1942. Women cluster about Americans in honest glee, in happiness, to touch them to see if they are real. "Darling," said one elephantine Russian wench to me when I first spoke to her, "Everywhere American soldiers go, people laugh. Everywhere Japanese soldiers go, people cry." No one is lonesome in the city for more than an hour. The tinkling laughter of women resounds through the corridors of the most respectable hotels.

Refugees and internees add a grotesque note to the gaiety. They are permitted to leave Jap concentration camps now during the day. But there is no food for them and no beds in the swank hotels. They inundate the U.S. Army offices asking for transportation home, for rooms, for money. There can be no real help for them beyond the dropping of food parcels until water-borne transportation arrives in a few days.

Shanghai itself is unscathed; the Japanese destruction of 1937 has been completely rebuilt. The business enterprises of the city—heart of China's commercial life—are carrying on as they always did, despite the lack of all normal communications by air, sea, mail and telegraph. The currency situation is, however, anarchic. Exchange rates these days have no relation to financial reality. You can double or triple your money or lose it all by rapidly changing from U.S. dollars to Chungking dollars to puppet money to the Japanese yen. I carry all four currencies about with me, using the ones which seem fitting to the occasion. I spent 2,800,000 Shanghai dollars on drinks for four people at a bar. I hired a car for one day for $3,600,000. This is all in terms of puppet currency and even in terms of puppet currency nothing makes sense. Some things like car-hire and cigarets are exorbitant. Other articles like food and silk are unbelievably cheap when translated back to U.S. currency. A $50,000 T-bone steak really costs 50¢ U.S. money. The most delicately embroidered sheer silken nightgowns cost $3 U.S. money. From basements and storehouses Shanghai black-marketeers are digging up all the goods they hid from the Japanese in the course of the war. Anything can be had at the proper price—the finest soaps, all brands of U.S. cigarets, Scotch, beer, champagne, silks, clothes, curios, automobiles, refrigerators and typewriters. Rolleiflexes, Leicas and Contax cameras, dumped here by German refugees, sell cheaper now in Shanghai than anywhere else in the world.

FOR 15 DAYS now Shanghai has lived in a world that belonged to no one. The ATC had been flying in Nationalist troops of the Chinese 94th Army. As each silver C-54 taxied onto the Shanghai airfield, surging crowds surrounded it, waving Chinese flags of paper. A blue-clad band blared out the *Admiral's March*. Newsreel cameras ground and thousands cheered as each tired, dirty soldier, dressed in his faded yellow combat uniform, climbed sheepishly down the plane's ladder. Everybody in the crowd had leather shoes but the soldiers coming to take over the city wore straw sandals.

Most incongruous of all was the Japanese garrison. Doomed to disarmament and humiliation, the stranded Japs had proudly tried to occupy and hold Shanghai stable and orderly while all about them swirled in joyous confusion. Jap sentries were stationed all along the Bund. Jap trucks bearing soldiers armed to the teeth careened madly about the city. A Jap guard patrolled the key bridges and enforced the curfew.

The Japanese also systematically looted all the houses and buildings they occupied.

The problem of re-establishing order is a delicate and complicated one. Beneath the sparkling surface of Shanghai there is a mercurial element of instability. The people of Shanghai have been waiting for two weeks now for leadership. The circus has been magnificent. Victory arches for the triumphal parade are nearing completion. But soon the evergreen boughs on the arches will begin to wither. The disruption of the financial system by peace and the closing of factories working on Jap war orders have thrown thousands out of work. Joy has sustained the people so far—but more than joy is needed to sustain them indefinitely.

THE PRESENT ecstatic countenance of Shanghai is an evanescent thing. It will pass in a few weeks, leaving only a hangover. Yet underneath that countenance there is joy of a more sober and less striking sort. Our plane flew the first flight from Tokyo to Shanghai since the ending of the war. With us on the plane was a Chinese war photographer who had been designated by Chungking to shoot the surrender scene in Tokyo Bay. I sat beside him and talked as we came in. Eight years ago when he was 19 years old he had marched out of Shanghai with the retreating troops. His home is still in Shanghai. He had marched on every front in China since. Somewhere in the evening mists of the city were his father and mother. He turned to me and said, *"Chin ten kan baba mama"* ("Today I will see my father and mother."). He was the first of a horde. There were hundreds of thousands of Shanghai exiles in the hinterlands slowly making their way back to the great city. There will be no banners, no flag-waving at their return, but the joy they bring will be lasting and real.

LIFE September 24, 1945

Chapter 4

China II:
The Return

It was to be nearly thirty years before White would go back
to China. He went as part of the press entourage covering President Richard M. Nixon's historic visit in 1972. It was, of
course, a far different place than he had left. "Jovial goodwill"
between Mao and a U.S. emissary in 1944 had turn to coldness,
then to mutual hatred; now a wary reopening of relations between the two countries was at hand. White's observations, his
memories, his assessments (for *Life*) make fascinating reading.

Though subsequently he often talked with friends about
spending more time in China, still another decade would pass
before he did return. By then the Cultural Revolution had run

its ghastly course, Mao was long dead, a new leadership was in place, and life had improved for most Chinese. But the future was still anything but clear. Reporting jointly for *Time* and *Reader's Digest,* White illuminated the scene as only he could do.

JOURNEY BACK TO ANOTHER CHINA

A famous journalist returns to see the world Mao made.

China again—and one wonders where to begin, how to thread the memory from past to present.

Perhaps at the Peking airport, as one waits for Richard Nixon's arrival—the airport color-flecked with Mao's white-on-scarlet slogans, its long runway immaculately swept, its terminal building glistening with a Swiss glossiness, Chinese planes poised at the far end of the field, its honor guard and ceremonial band stony-faced, husky, splendidly tailored, waiting.

Twenty-seven years ago, in 1944, I had arrived in Yenan, the hill capital of the revolution, the day America first recognized Chinese Communism by sending an official emissary. The pilot sighted Yenan by the old yellow pagoda that was its landmark, swooped through gullies cut by dark ovals of caves, bounced down a rutted dirt runway and lurched to a stop. Out stepped Major General Patrick J. Hurley, his chest glistening with medals. He perceived a ragamuffin honor guard in padded quilting and then—to their absolute bafflement—warwhooped. Mao and Chou were a few minutes late. They jounced down from the hills in an ambulance, tumbled out, then trotted unceremoniously across the runway to greet the American envoy. We climbed into the ambulance. Passing a flock of sheep, Hurley volunteered he'd once been a cowboy; Mao responded he had once been a shepherd; and, trading jokes, they began their first negotiations in jovial goodwill. The mood changed two days later when the negotiations stuck. The negotiations grew colder in 1945 in Chungking, yet colder at Nanking in 1946. By 1952, in Korea, again in 1954 in Geneva, the dialogue had frozen to the hate and paranoia that has separated us since. We could not understand each other.

It is at Yenan, though, that one *must* begin, for it is the romance of Yenan that still holds in thrall the minds of China's present leaders. Yenan was an idea, and the idea was simple: that people are plastic, human putty, raw material of incredible and explosive and creative power if only properly energized, inspirited, led. In Yenan and for years thereafter, the Communist leadership molded the minds of illiterate peasants, calling them to dignity, writing sharp new ideas on minds erased of thought by centuries of oppression and servility. On these blank minds they wrote the idea of the collective, the common will, the nobility of work, sacrifice and death for the common cause. Out of this they made their revolution.

IT IS best for a returning wanderer today to sort out two things: first, the simple evidence his eye, or ear, or touch picks up—and then those surmises by which imagination tries to build a bridge from the past to what he guesses present reality to be.

Vision of China comes in fragments:

Peking: There is the hush. Chinese towns once rang with sound: the bubble of laughter, the clack and chanting of peddlers, the shriek of street argument, the wailing of beggars made a street symphony particular to China. Now, except for the occasional tinkle of a bicycle bell, the rarer sound of a motor horn, there is only silence on the ears. Through the streets the people stroll—warmly dressed, healthy, unsmiling, subdued yet self-possessed. Down the roads roll the bicycles—thousands of them, glistening with carefully polished chrome rims, all pedaling at the same sedate speed as if some unseen hand had set the pace, never speeding, rarely passing one another. The unvarying pace hypnotizes the eye. Then one notices a policeman calling down, chiding a cyclist who has broken pace.

One ambles through T'ien-an Men Square, the Place de la Concorde of Chinese history. Face north: and there is the great gate—in old memory so shabby,

paint-flecked, yet awesome, now, in restoration, it glistens with ancient patterns of yellow, green, blue tiles, rising above fresh-painted red walls. Then pivot and turn south: the ancient monuments shrivel to an enameled miniature as the eye sweeps the immense plaza overpowered by the bulk of the colossal new halls of government. Old Peking has become a museum. Around and around for miles are rectangular buildings, which overwhelm it, and endless acres of gray five-story apartments and factories.

Shanghai: Clean is the first word that comes to mind. Then, drab. At dawn the sweeping women are up and out, whisk-brooming gutters, pavings, sidewalks. The waterfront Bund, once threshold to a city that throbbed with depravity, offering every pleasure of food and flesh, is moribund. The stone buildings the British Empire left behind now brood above the Bund, signless and lifeless, as if recently unearthed by archaeologists. Gray everywhere, and in the gray scream billboards in all variations of portrayed violence: soldiers crouched behind ridges pointing guns; massed peasants, idealized, all tramping with guns; a bearded Karl Marx, symbolically leading a following column of workers to the revolution, their guns at the ready; a platoon of embattled peasants carrying bayonets, scythes, knives. The city quietly goes about its business; the posters call to kill.

When I first came here 30-odd years ago, the routine lift of abandoned dead in the streets was estimated at 500 a day. These new Chinese are husky, cleanly dressed, their shops well stocked, trade brisk. No beggars. In the old days ricksha men would tout the stranger for prostitutes of every color, race, nationality, any sex. Ricksha men are gone now, even pedicabs are rare; we hired three pedicabs to pedal us about and anticipated arguing the price as once was custom. But when our ride ended, the three pedalers gathered, consulted, then announced the price was 80¢. No argument. I handed over a dollar, insisted my man keep the change. No, he argued back, no tipping in China. We argued more, smiling— but he won. No tips accepted.

The villages: In those that I saw or passed, Crumbledown is gone. Prewar Chinese villages were always in a state of crumbling: holes in the roofs, tiles gone from the rafters, gaps in the adobe walls, pigs, chickens, oxen in the family courtyards. One sees no more Crumbledown about Peking and Shanghai. Paved roads link village to highway; along the road, saplings and young trees are beginning to break the barren endless sweep of Chinese flatlands; little stands of evergreen, clumps of bamboo show at corner crossroads. And the houses, increasingly, are solid gray brick, no longer huts, but homes.

The food: Unchanged and superb. At the best restaurant in Peking—spiced livers, roast duck, bamboo shoots, candied bananas, a soup, vegetables; a new-styled grape wine that tastes like Manischewitz, and as many thimble cups of fiery *kaoliang* as you can hold—all for $3. In an ordinary restaurant in Shang-hai—a soup, cabbage rolls, three platters of meat dumplings, tea—40¢. Best of all: food is clean. The sickening liquid bowels that Westerners remember after Chinese banquets is only a memory. Tap water is safe to drink; so are vegetables to eat.

The language: That, too, is changed as one finds his tongue picking through time-rusted phrases. The waiter is no longer the waiter (*ch'a fang*); he is to be called "*t'ung-chih*" (comrade). One no longer seeks the bureau chief or director. One must ask for the "*ling-tao jen*" (the leading personality). Some phrases are antique. When I use the old phrase "*mei-yu pan-fa*" (no can do), the most familiar phrase in old-time China, someone chuckles and says he has not heard the phrase for years. It is out of fashion, swept out by the revolutionary jargon. And the revolutionary jargon is incomprehensible. The language, like the mind of the people, has been rewired.

How does one measure a revolution?

For Chinese, statistics are the poetry of politics. Every meeting, at school, farm, village, bureau, factory, begins with statistics. Twenty-one million metric tons of steel this year, 246 million metric tons of grain, nine billion yards of cotton cloth (largest cotton-cloth production of any country in the world). And on and on, down to the pounds of cabbages raised per *mou,* the number of barefoot doctors in any commune, the tonnage of any mine.

But statistics are dreary. They add up to a simple fact: power. The 40-mile drive from Peking to the Great Wall shows it visually, factories spotting the road all the way to the hills, smokestacks fouling the sky with soot. There is muscle here, a thrust, a rhythm of growth, a complex of a strength which is by now one of the world's primordial facts. And we must deal with it before the hate freezes irrevocably. This, after all, was the purpose of the Nixon trip.

There are other ways of measuring revolutions, however. For example, who wins, who loses.

THE PEOPLE of Loukouchiao Commune, close by the Marco Polo Bridge where the great Japanese war broke out in 1937, have won. My eyes tell me so. How many showcases like the Loukouchiao Commune there may be in China, I have no idea. Westerners have visited at least a dozen in all parts of China; and from the air between Shanghai and Peking one sees the panorama of land cut by new irrigation ditches, laced by new roads, pocked with new water reservoirs, fields reassorted from the little two- and three-acre garden plots of Chinese peasants into collective farms of hundreds of acres, scored by long, stretching furrows.

On the ground, Loukouchiao Commune tells a straightforward story. "Commune" is, of course, a poor translation, evoking echoes of little Israeli kibbutzim. Loukouchiao calls itself a "*kung shih*" (a public enterprise), a collective of 46,000 people living in 143 villages. We can ignore the statistics of tomatoes, spinach, radishes, cucumbers, wheat, pigs, fruit raised here—all of them rising. What is visible, say in the Meishihk'ao village, totally different from what one remembers of Chinese villages is a main road direct to the village; clean-swept earthen paths; a clinic; a shopping center—and the houses. I pick one at random, solidly built, no pigs, chickens or animals in the courtyard; it has windows, *real* windows with *glass* where once windows were greased paper. It boasts a naked electric light bulb—electricity came here only in 1958. The mother is illiterate; but she has seven children who are going, or have gone, to school; and she shows, with pride, that there are nine separate quilts, one for each member of the family. There is a radio—bought in 1961. Where the ancestral shrine used to be, there is a polychrome of Chairman Mao—and as an offsetting touch of humanity, a color poster from China's current new hit ballet, *The Red Detachment of Women.*

The vice-chairman takes me to the shopping center, and never, in all my years in China, have I seen such a store. Granted this may be a showcase commune, but I have come unannounced—and the slabs of beef and pork in the butcher shop must have been here before my arrival. The shelves stocked with sweaters, shirts, wool jackets, cookies and candy, cans, washbasins are decisively more abundant than in country stores in rural France or southern Italy. Outdoors, people wear drab blues and grays; but women here are buying gay cotton cloth in every flower pattern and color. Granted again that all I see may be a stage set. Yet the adolescents drilling in the high school yard cannot be a stage set. I remember Chinese youngsters as shriveled, scabridden, trachomatous. But these are beefy, outdoor, muscular youngsters, the high red rose of winter in their cheeks. They have been well nourished for years.

The village has had two decades of progress, and Mao, they say, produced it. His name ripples through every conversation, at every fourth phrase. He is as much a presence as the spirit of God once was in Puritan New England villages.

If Loukouchiao has won—and peasants like those of Loukouchiao are 80% of China—then Peking University has lost.

Peking University has been, all through this century, a key to Chinese politics. Peking University's students led the demonstrations at T'ien-an Men on May 4, 1919 to make that day's name a chapter heading in every modern history of China. They led the riots against the Japanese penetration in the '30s. In the Great Cultural Revolution of 1965, they were the first to post wallboard polemics, first to brawl, take to the streets, then roam the country in that three-year savagery of which we have, as yet, no complete account. Protest has been as much Peking University's tradition as great scholarship. But no longer.

We are received on the pine-studded campus and get the statistics; and a drenching, self-humiliating introduction from the vice-chairman, a dignified American-educated professor who all

but abases himself before the Mao-thought which has changed his university.

Five years ago, when the university closed down during the Cultural Revolution, it taught 9,000 students. It was reopened a year and a half ago. Today there are only 3,000 students. No admissions committee chooses entrants; factories, collective farms, government bureaus, party teams decide which of their young members they will send to the university. Nor does the university flunk them out. The "people" decide who studies, who hauls grain.

One tries to pick up conversations with professors, but finds it difficult. It is as if they had been lobotomized, as if China's past were erased. Before the Cultural Revolution, scholars here taught no less than ten courses in history to cover China's chronicle of 3,000 years. Now only three courses are given. One covers the span from primitive past to the Opium War of 1840; another covers the years of humiliation by the West between that date and the May 4th movement of 1919; the third is simply the history of the Communist Party to date. History, sociology and social sciences are unnecessary in China any longer. Indeed, there are more courses in Chinese history, art and culture taught at Harvard University than at China's greatest university. Science is, apparently, well taught. But what there is to know of man and his problems—all this is encompassed in the thinking of Mao; and the university, as all China, vibrates to it, tries to act on it.

IT IS Mao's presence that is so difficult to adjust to. There is no easy way of describing it—this is no classic tyranny or dictatorship but a presence that overpowers and smothers. From it there is no escape, no crevice, for private thought.

He is there: his picture hanging ten feet high at every airport. On every street, above factory, apartment block, government hall, in red and white by day, in flaring light by night, the same five characters: *"Mao Chu Hsi Wan Sui"* (Long Live Mao Tse-tung). The children start the day (and the school day runs 8 to 5) by hymning to Mao, and they close with a ringing, swinging, lusty chorus, "Sailing the Seas Depends on the Helmsman."

I spent three days seeking an old friend, who once many years ago worked with me for LIFE in our China Bureau. On my insistence, it was arranged she sit beside me at a public banquet. I asked her if this insistence had been dangerous to her. She replied that the question showed my prejudice. We have liberty in China, she insisted, what you hear is propaganda, we can read what we want, talk about what we want, the masses debate and participate in all decisions. She is an editor of the monthly *China Reconstructs,* a handsome glossy publication. Even in her office, where she is a "leading personality," the workers are free to criticize her. She has just come back from a year of reindoctrination, living with the masses, learning to understand life in a peasant village doing peasant tasks; the peasants

too, she says, are free. Her English is, as it always was, flawless, easy, gracious, but there is a separation between us, so I stab: "If you are free to talk about anything, why can no one debate the differences between Chairman Mao and Lin Piao?" She retreats as if I were uttering profanity. "But Comrade Mao is everything," she says; then, correcting, "Comrade Mao has given us everything. How can the people judge him?" Only as we part do I realize that she has not asked me a single question about life in America, to which, once, she was so close. Nor does anyone else on the entire trip ask, or care to hear, anything about our life.

When one breaks through to talk seriously to serious Chinese, there is this cleavage of mind, our half-truths and self-doubts against their inflexible rectitude. I talk frankly with a leading Chinese journalist. Journalism, he says, is shaped by social systems. Our system, he continues, is the government of the workers and the people whose vanguard is the Communist party. We follow the party line, he says, and if the party line is not correct, it will change by deep criticism among the people—not necessarily in the open press. I write about politics in my country, I say, I can print what any candidate tells me; what do you print about Lin Piao's struggle with Chairman Mao? I do not want to discuss that, he says. I try to unfreeze the conversation by talking of Vietnam. He says Vietnam is a civil war, America has no business there. I agree and suggest that if China withdraws aid from the North, we could withdraw aid from the South. No, he says, our duty is to help oppressed people everywhere liberate themselves, when you give aid you do wrong. We go on perilously to the Taiwan question. Now comes a flash of anger in his dark eyes, no smiles left. Taiwan is occupied by American imperialism, America must leave at once, there can be no discussion. The anger is so transparent I tingle, draw back, make small talk.

SO ONE moves from things observed or heard to surmises that flow from them.

The first: that the impact of this trip on internal Chinese politics and the stakes for those involved in Peking are infinitely greater than those for Richard Nixon, whose voyage we called "The Peking Primary."

All revolutions, it is said, devour their children. But this one is in the process of devouring its fathers. No one yet quite understands the Cultural Revolution; but the generally accepted theory is that sometime in the 1960s, the old romantics of Yenan found their own achievements too difficult to master by the old thinking. By 1965, the growth of Chinese industry and state had developed machinery, administration, bureaucracy, officialdom—in short, an elite, abhorrent to the egalitarianism of Yenan. Thus the struggle over China's future course, with Mao finally triumphant in imposing his concept of man as a particle of the mass. How brutal the struggle, we cannot guess. Seven years ago, the Standing Committee of the Chinese Politburo

counted seven men. After the Cultural Revolution, in 1969, two had been tracelessly eliminated, leaving, officially, five. In the past three years, three more have been erased, and now only two remain: Mao Tse-tung and Chou En-lai. The figures and names of the full Politburo tell a similar story: of the 21 who safely survived the Cultural Revolution to be officially renamed in April 1969, the last three years have seen the disappearance of nine; and three of those remaining are senile. What has happened to the missing, no one knows.

One can ask many questions in China, about production, archaeology, farming, medicine, urban planning. But political questions are transgressions.

Thus, to a second surmise: that the lives of Chinese leaders have been at stake the past six years. Whatever ignited the Cultural Revolution, one spark certainly must have been the fact that in 1965 Mao himself found the bureaucracy refusing to publish him in Peking. Another fact we know is that Chou En-lai, our host and the premier, was himself held prisoner in his office for two days in 1967. The man who then saved and buttressed both with the Red Army, Lin Piao, has disappeared. The structure of this revolution is solid. But perhaps at the summit of no other state in the world does a narrower or shakier leadership exist than in China today, all signs, slogans, pageants to the contrary.

A third surmise concerns us more: based on the few facts we know, it is clear that foreign policy split China's leaders almost as much as domestic policy. Both former President Liu Shao-ch'i and former Defense Minister Lin Piao sought reactivation of China's link with Russia; their opponents felt an approach to America might be more useful as counterweight to both Japan and Russia. Those who sought the latter have, for the time being, won out.

There is no doubt that President Nixon yielded on the matter of Taiwan to the men who now govern China—not all the way, not even half-way, and by a yielding hedged in language from which any skillful diplomat, if necessary, can wriggle away. The Chinese, on their side, yielded not an inch or phrase. In terms of American politics and the reaffirmation of *his* leadership, this cost Nixon little—indeed, he scored a plus for reelection. In terms of Chinese politics, his yielding may have given the Chinese an even greater plus internally, strengthening leaders who may turn China back from the hate they so long incubated for our country. And this is in our interest.

A LAST fragment remains.

These men who share the leadership of China are old. In dealing with them now we caught a passing moment before mass man hardens in the mold.

No Americans but Messrs. Nixon and Kissinger saw Mao Tse-tung, now 79. All of us saw Marshal Yeh Chien-ying, the burly insurrectionary of other days, the punster, waltzer, cheerful Eighth Route Army Chief of Staff of Yenan, restored to power this year as acting commander of China's Red Army. But his bluff has softened now, at 73, to the whitened round of a grandfather. We saw Li Hsien-nien, who has survived—his eyes pouched and bagged with weariness, tense, pale, the outdoor bronze of the guerrilla commander that once he was vanished. His duties are now desk duties as chief planner of China's industry, more difficult than attacking enemies in the open field.

And all of us saw Chou En-lai, the premier—that entrancing man. At 73, age has overtaken him, too. The old injury to his right arm he once concealed has stiffened; he carried it at half cock. The sleek black hair is now iron-gray, close-cropped, almost crew-cut. The bushy eyebrows, too, grow gray. His dimple has set, by now, in a deep furrow that creases his cheek and thrusts the cheekbone high. In conversation, as one watched him at banquets, his animation was the same as ever. But when Richard Nixon left the table at the great banquet hall to wander among Chinese dignitaries offering toasts, one could see a wondering cast, almost of melancholy, fall upon Chou's face as he sat alone beneath the Chinese and American flags.

We were friends many years ago—or so I thought. I knew I could now no longer have a casual conversation with Chou En-lai as in the days when he was a youthful Robin Hood of revolution. But, as he sat alone, his eye caught mine, the melancholy dissolved to a smile. He summoned me over, poured a glass and said, "*Kan pei*" (bottoms up). We paused and then he said, "Old friend, old friend," and then the party closed in to separate us.

Again, days later in Hangchow, as all

my frustrations with new China were about to burst, he caught my eye once more. Turning, he said to Mr. Nixon, "There's Teddy White, he hasn't been back to China since the liberation." I shot back, "But that's not my fault." The Chinese around me were upset by my effrontery. Not Chou, the premier, however. He turned and made a smiling riposte in Chinese to the translator. Several people tried at once to translate the phrase back, and thought he'd said, "Perhaps it's both our faults." I hope the translation was correct.

LIFE July 17, 1972

CHINA AFTER THE TERROR*

From the Editors' Prologue: In the spring of 1983, Reader's Digest *and* Time Inc. *asked White to return to China to examine what has been happening since the death of Mao Zedong in 1976. Here, in a special report, is his first-hand account of the fate of the old revolutionary leaders he knew in his youth, the extraordinary turmoil of the Cultural Revolution, and the path China's new rulers are taking to the future.*

On my first night back in China, my old friend Wang Bingnan drove me out to visit Fragrant Hill. From the hill you can almost see Beijing (Peking), 25 miles away. In the evening, when the sun purples the range, the mountain passes show the way ancient conquerors cut their entry into the capital. And this

*This article appeared in the October 1983 issue of *Reader's Digest*. Substantially the same article appeared in the September 26, 1983 issue of *Time*. Each magazine worked from White's original manuscript, and their published versions differ slightly. The *Digest's* is slightly shorter, but it is not a condensation from *Time*.

was the way Mao Zedong, the last conqueror, came to Beijing in March 1949. Mao still haunts Fragrant Hill, as he haunts Beijing, haunts all China, haunts its politics, dreams, nightmares.

It was the spring of 1983, but Wang Bingnan was telling me of his first night on the hill back in 1949. He had arrived with Mao and the Zhongyang, the central committee that rules the Communist Party. They came that evening as a nomad encampment, several thousand men and women who promised to give new government to the China they had conquered. [Like Moses and the Israelites, they had been wandering the arid northlands,] pursued by Chiang Kaishek's Nationalist divisions. But in the end Mao had triumphed, and now, in March 1949, it was over—or just beginning.

With relish Wang Bingnan told the story of the encampment. The Zhongyang was all there on Fragrant Hill—Mao, his wife Jiang Qing, Zhou Enlai, Zhu De, Peng Dehuai, Liu Shaoqi—the band of comrades who had shaken not only China but the world, warriors sealed by endless struggle into a brotherhood. Wang Bingnan remembered how Mao, coming in from the march that first evening, had been offered a bed, after having spent the previous 15 years sleeping on a hard board, with only a thin peasant's pad between the board and his body. Wang remembered meeting Mao's wife the next morning. The chairman had slept badly the night before, she scolded. He had finally decided to sleep on the floor, where he was more comfortable. After that Mao always slept on boards as peasants do, even when he occupied the old imperial grounds of Beijing.

The years had toughened Mao. First the years of the Long March, then the hard years after, when he lived in the caves above the north China town of Yan'an.

For ten years this cleft in the hills was the cradle of China's revolution. Today its few visitors come like pilgrims to Jerusalem to see where it all began. Their route is almost as well marked as the Stations of the Cross and, following it, one traces the explosions that overturned China.

First station: the original home of Mao Zedong, where he made his headquarters in January 1937, preparing to fight the Japanese as an ally of Chiang Kai-shek. The shrine sits in a dusty courtyard. Here was his bed, says the guide, this was his table, here are the two blue enamel boxes in which he carried his records on the Long March. Next door is another little house, once shared by Zhu De, Zhou Enlai and their wives. Here Mao lived until 1938, when the Japanese began to bomb Yan'an, and he moved himself and his

party three miles north to the cave encampment at Yangjialing.

Ah, Yangjialing—this I remember from my years as a war correspondent with I first came to hunt out the source of the revolution that was disturbing Japanese, Americans, Nationalists, all alike. By 1938 Mao had two whitewashed rooms and a private air-raid shelter; he had a kerosene lamp; his bed had mosquito netting. Next door, on either side, Zhu De and Zhou Enlai each had separate caves, whitewashed also. These three men were the power, were to remain the power for almost 40 years.

The next stage of the pilgrimage comes another mile or two away, the famous Zao Yuan, or Date Garden, to which the leaders moved in 1942. By then they had broken with Chiang. There are the caves of the same three men. But by late 1944 the caves reflected the growing dignity of the reigning triumvirate. Mao's cave boasted a complex of five rooms; he slept now in a handsome dark-wood bed. (I felt it; the same board with only a thin pad on top.)

On then to the last stop of the pilgrimage: the army headquarters at Wangzhaling a mile or two away. When I had last seen it in 1944, it was a place of excitement, where one could meet famous generals in from the far-flung, ever-victorious fronts. Mao slept here for several weeks in his last days in Yan'an, preparing to pack, flee and reorganize his armies for the final assault on the Nationalists; he and the entire central committee were to be on the march for the next two years, coming at last to Fragrant Hill, above Beijing.

The story of China today—the story I had come to get—begins with what happened when the old Zhongyang came down from the slope of Fragrant Hill to try to make a government.

Mao, of course, was the greatest name; he went on into Beijing and became God—but also, with almost no doubt, insane. His wife, Jiang Qing, one of the great dragon ladies of Chinese history, now languishes under life sentence in jail. Peng Dehuai, who had fought side by side with Mao for 20 years, went on to command the front against the Americans in the Korean War. Later named minister of defense, he was the first to openly criticize Mao in 1958. That cost him dearly. He was placed under house arrest, then jailed, then left to die of cancer in a Beijing hospital ward. Another of those on the hill that night was Liu Shaoqi, once chief organization man in Yan'an, later named by Mao as president of China. Dismissed, he died in solitary confinement in Luoyang in 1969. They, and scores of others, had come as brothers to the long adventure of revolution, brothers in the faith of Marx and Lenin. But history held truths that overrode Marxism-Leninism—for example, that while the brotherhood of suffering is a bond, power is a drug. Once the power was in their hands, the drug addled their minds, and together, when they came down from Fragrant Hill, they brought China to the threshold of ruin.

"Mao Thought"

A ditty of some forgotten Englishman mocks all Western reporters who try to write about China:

Foreign correspondents
Endeavoring to find
Occidental explanations
For the Oriental mind.

And so I must enter a disclaimer of limitations as I write of the China I observed this spring.

My caution has roots that run back to my last visit to China with President Nixon in 1972. We arrived in February, marveled at spots of beauty, visited model farms. When we toured antiquities, little children in bright clothes were strewn like flower petals along our path. But we knew nothing of what was going on. I tried to telephone an old friend and was told, *"Ta bu zai"* ("He's not home"). I asked when he would be back and was told, "not certain." In 1983 when I called, I found him instantly; we visited, and he told me where he had been 11 years earlier—in solitary confinement in a Beijing jail from 1968 to 1973. His wife, too, had been in solitary in the same jail. No charge had been brought against either of them, only that they were "under investigation."

Greater horrors were taking place in China at the time of the Nixon visit. Hero leaders had been killed or forced to suicide; tens of thousands of China's best were in jail or enduring savage punishment; scores of thousands had already been killed by fanatics; the army had been called in to restore order to dozens of cities where youthful Red Guards had bloodied the streets in civil war. But of all this we knew nothing.

We had only the testimony of our eyes. Beijing glittered with garish neon signs, each proclaiming "Chairman Mao—Long Life!" The streets were silent, bicycles were streaming in soundless procession through the avenues, the blare of a horn rare and disturbing. We felt something was wrong but could not tell what. Something called the Cultural Revolution was in full swing. But it was then, as it is now, as if we were feeling for something through a membrane—we could sense shapes, forms and fears, almost touch them. But we could not see through the membrane, or define or measure what it was we really wanted to know.

Beijing in 1983 is, to the eye, a far better place to visit or to live. The city, with its long avenues of young trees, its handsome new architecture, is becoming beautiful. People are well dressed. Men and women are healthy; children are cherubs. Stores are well-stocked, from peanuts to popsicles, from dumplings to ducks. Bookstores are crowded, movie houses and theaters jammed. Color television has arrived, and with it commercials.

Most of all, Mao is gone, his neon signs and banners removed. It is as if the city had been sponged of him and his "personality cult." He rests in the colonnaded mausoleum that dominates the great central square. On visiting day the silent pilgrims are mobilized by the busload and permitted to shuffle by

the body. They pause long enough to look at the face of the man who brought the revolution to them. The face is a mummified leather-brown, quite different from the pale-faced Mao of real life, and as serene and enigmatic in death as in life.

Yet people talk about him endlessly. It is as if he died only yesterday, rather than seven years ago. Those close to him differ about what caused the devilish change in him, as well as when the change took place. He was, some say, suffering for years from Alzheimer's disease, a nerve disorder of the brain that brings on dementia. Others say that Mao began to experience repeated tiny strokes in 1959.

More and more isolated in the imperial quarters, Mao would receive visitors in the 1960s in his bedroom—a sloven's lair, the bed strewn with books, leaflets, reports. Occasionally, as for a Nixon, he would lift himself from bed and let himself be dressed. Cordoned off from the world, he became the prisoner of his palace entourage—of his wife, and of the group who, with her, formed the Gang of Four.

"In the old days of Yan'an," said one friend, "he would listen first, then talk. Now he talked but would not listen." All agree that what remained constant in Mao was his iron will. That will, that invincible conviction of his own righteousness, had driven China from an era of despair to the triumph of the revolution. The momentum of this triumph of will climaxed in two words: "struggle" and "speed."

He had acquired the lust for speed in the last year of the revolution. Exercising his military authority, he overruled his cautious commanders. Strike for the escape ports of Manchuria, he said, *now.* Cut the Nationalists off. Field success vindicated him. Cut off Beijing next, he ordered. And he was right. What he wanted done, he wanted done *now.*

To this impulse was added the driving force of struggle. In Yan'an struggle had become doctrine. Nothing was impossible if his will could drive his people to "struggle against the mountains."

But the flatlands of central China and the paddy fields of south China were not mountains. They could not be climbed; they had to be governed and remade by changing the minds of the peasants who tilled them in the old ways.

The key to changing minds was the thinking of Mao Zedong—"Mao thought." Mao thought was not simply a dogma, or a slogan, least of all a coherent doctrine. It should be thought of as a spike driven by the will of one man into the minds of his people, to nail them to his purpose. But in the next 25 years the spike was driven through the living flesh of people until they bled, or hungered, or died at random.

Thus, what followed first after the revolution was the Great Leap Forward, which collectivized agriculture. Only once before in the 20th century had any major power tried to collectivize agriculture—Russia under Stalin. Millions had died then, and millions more died of starvation as China collectivized.

But the problem of governing China, of reshaping the thinking of millions of peasants, remained. The real China, where peasants sow and reap by season

and by sweat, could not be remade with Mao thought. Yet struggle and speed remained the motor drives of the old man as he slowly became detached from reality. And if there was resistance to his will, it had to be "struggled" against.

If China was not moving with the speed he required toward the socialist millennium he sought, there had to be a conspiracy somewhere. And where else but in his own party, where "class enemies" lurked? So in August 1966 was launched the Cultural Revolution with Mao's slogan, "Bombard the Headquarters." Mao was calling on all his people to overthrow the party that he himself had created. If China seemed no longer subordinate to his will, his enemies had to be purged.

Yet it was not Mao's enemies who resisted; it was China itself. "It was as if the law of inertia took over," said Hu Qiao Mu, once Mao's private secretary. "A body in motion tends to continue in motion. He was speeding the train down the track, the train came to a bend because the terrain of China is different from what Mao thought it was. The train could not take the turn. It went on and derailed."

The derailing of China is what is called the Cultural Revolution. No more ironic title has ever been given to savagery and chaos, or to a dogma that tried to erase all culture.

The Great Terror

The theory of the Cultural Revolution was summed up by the word "egalitarianism." All people—bureaucrats, scientists, engineers, scholars—had to be re-educated to the peasant way of life. Enemies, said Mao, were buried in every Party cell, every government office, every university. The "capitalist roaders," "stinking intellectuals," "rightists," "revisionists" had to be burned out. "The more knowledge you give the people," said Mao, "the more you hold back revolutionary thought." Or: "The more books people read, the more foolish they become." Across China the youth, first the Red Guards, then the careerists and thugs, responded to the call to join in the crusade against the hidden enemies.

They tell the stories in China now, some shamefacedly, some still burning with indignation, of how the country was driven to chaos. A former Red Guard was awakened one night at a Beijing high school by the sound of martial music. A struggle meeting was going on in the courtyard, the Red Guards "struggling" against two teachers and beating them. He waited until 5 a.m. and then crept down to the courtyard where their bodies lay dead. Today, 15 years later, he is still horrified by the memory.

I spoke to a brigade leader in a rural commune who felt he had escaped lightly. He had been strung up from a stable rafter for days, suspended by his arms tied behind his back, while Red Guards beat him with fists, sticks, irons. Finally, the peasants in his brigade rescued him.

In Chongqing (Chungking) I spoke to the vice mayor, old beyond his years. The Red Guards had stormed into his office one day to arrest him. He was "re-

educated" in an iron mine, where he worked underground for three years before being recalled.

Being "sent down," or *hsia-fang* as the Chinese call it, was the simplest punishment. "Stinking intellectuals" were to learn from the peasants what life is like when one must stoop for hours transplanting rice seedlings in the muck, as Mao had done in his youth. A common element of many high-level "re-educations" was round-the-clock interrogation by teams of Red Guards, electric lights glaring in the victim's eyes. "No one beat me," said an eminent editor of a Beijing newspaper. "What was worse was being questioned all day and all night about something that happened thirty years ago."

High and low alike, anyone with an education, anyone suspected of murmuring protest, could be sent down. Universities, except for military research centers, were closed, some for three years, some for five, some for ten. As dogma drove the spike into the flesh of the country, even the revered ancients of their revolution were pushed to death.

The Red Guard tyranny ended in anarchy so sweeping that the army was called in to seize the cities and re-establish food supplies. The army was commanded by Lin Biao, who could see that Mao was dying and that power would go to those who struck quickly. Lin miscalculated; his plot to kill Mao was exposed, and the old man turned on him.

All power then fell into the hands of the palace court that surrounded Mao, controlled access to him, interpreted his wishes. Jiang Qing herself named as minister of health Liu Xiang-ping, one of those ruthless ladies who abound in Chinese history. Liu was not only ignorant of medicine but devoid of decency. She made the hospitals of the capital hostels of despair, as are the psychiatric clinics of the Soviet Union. Few could escape her clutch when she reached for them—not even He Long, a Robin Hood peasant bandit who had joined the Communists in the 1920s, a Long Marcher who had risen to become Marshal of the Red Army. He Long was suffering from diabetes, but in the hospital he was injected with glucose instead of insulin. He died. Old veterans and ranking bureaucrats pleaded not to be sent to the hospitals, from which they feared they would never emerge alive. They were told it was the will of the Party and off they went.

As the terror spread, Red Guard bands began to fight one another in the city streets, in Chengdu (the capital of Sichuan), in Chongqing, in Beijing—all rivaling one another to show loyalty to "Mao thought."

Chongqing had become an arsenal center after 1949, and the workers fought one another there with machine guns, artillery, armored cars and tanks. In Harbin the factions used airplanes to bomb one another. In Wuhan, the center of a great iron-and-steel complex, and the home of several important universities, the steel workers formed three rival "steel bands," while three universities formed "student bands." All fought one another in the name of Mao until work ground to a halt.

There is no real count of those who died. The official record states that 34,800 innocent people were put to death and 729,511 were subject to "unwarranted persecution." This takes no account of how many others died—bystanders at riots; civilians hit by bombs or artillery; individuals stoned, beaten or stabbed to death. Nor does the official record tally those who lost their jobs or were subjected to starvation diets, brutal interrogation or other forms of humiliation. Counting these people as victims of the Cultural Revolution, one Chinese scholar has put the figure as high as 40 million.

The New Old Men

Common sense itself revolted. The new dogma had not worked and it could not work. So, the old army, the aging Red generals of the revolution, had to move in, as they did on the night of October 6, 1976.

Zhou Enlai, the last effective, rational member of the inner circle, had died in January. Zhu De, commander in chief of the revolution's armies, died six months later. And then came the Dangshan earthquake—in Chinese lore great earthquakes foretell the fall of a dynasty. Beijing's water mains burst, citizens had to evacuate buildings and for weeks lived in street shacks. Finally, on September 9, Mao himself died, and it was time for someone to move. Either the Gang of Four would wipe out the last resistance to their rule, and Jiang Qing would reign, or the old veterans of the revolutionary wars would wipe out the Gang of Four.

There is, as yet, no trustworthy story of the night of the coup. There may never be. I rest my knowledge only on the slim phrases I squeezed out of Gen. Wu Xiuqan, vice chief of staff of the army at the time. "We controlled the garrison," he said. "Ye Jainying and Li Xiannian [both old Red Army marshals] made the decision. We moved into Zhongnanhai [the imperial quarters]. No bloodshed, no resistance. We arrested the four, one by one, in their homes."

It was over in one night. The people of China heard the news six days later from the BBC, reporting what British intelligence had gathered of events in the capital. Those who had enough money went out and bought crabs. The crab had been the symbol for the old lady, Jiang Qing. So they ate crabs to celebrate.

It was two years before the old generals could purge and remold the Party. By 1978 they had brought back to Beijing, from exile, Deng Xiaoping, the deftest politician among them. By the end of 1978 their new central committee, under Deng, had repudiated the economics of the Cultural Revolution and ordered reforms. Two more years passed before they felt strong enough to bring to trial and convict the Gang of Four. In 1981, the central committee adopted a resolution admitting Communist error. Another year passed before they could manage to elect an entirely new Zhongyang and adopt a new constitution, the fourth since liberation.

Although Chinese politics is forever a mystery to Westerners, one can discern the outlines of the new ruling regime. Supreme power lies in the six-man standing committee of the Politburo, which itself is composed of 25 men. Below the Politburo is the 210-member central committee where younger people—engineers, technicians, provincial Party leaders—voice the pressures that come from the countryside. Outside them all is the army, wary, suspicious, slowly being subordinated by the old generals to the government. All decisions come to final judgment in the six-man standing committee dominated by Deng Xiaoping, the "paramount leader."

Deng is a tiny man (approximately five feet tall), half-elf, half-gunman. At 79 he is China's foremost pragmatist. A brilliant youngster, graduating from high school at 15, he went off to France during World War I as a student. There he met Zhou Enlai, joined the Communist movement, returned to China, led peasant insurrections in Guangxi Province and joined Mao Zedong for the Long March. With victory, he rose to the highest levels of the Politburo. But in the Cultural Revolution, he was accused of arrogance, gluttony and dissolute habits (addiction to playing bridge and mah-jongg). He was purged and paraded through the streets of Beijing wearing a dunce cap. Reportedly, he was sent down, forced to serve meals at the mess of a Party training camp outside the city. But he bears larger scars on his memory. During the Great Terror, one of his sons was forced to jump—or was pushed—from the fourth story of his school dormitory. That son is now paralyzed from the waist down. Deng is a reasonable man, but hard. He does not forget.

The oldest member of the six-man group is Marshal Ye Jainying, 85. From the Communist uprising in Guangzhou (Canton) in 1927 to the coup against the Gang of Four, Ye was central. He, too, bears wounds. His son, an aviator, was forced into stoop labor during the Terror. Overworked, exhausted, beaten, the son put his hand into the gears of a threshing machine. He will never fly again. Ye does not forget either. But he is ailing, and almost sure to be replaced soon.

Next comes Chen Yun, 80-odd, who was elected to the Politburo in 1934. He has since become China's leading economic thinker, a man who insists that China's people need consumer goods and that the state must loosen its controls to provide them.

Then comes Li Xiannian, 76, also a great marshal of the war. Also a hero. During the Great Terror he was mobbed by Red Guards, and was saved only by Zhou Enlai's intercession. He is today president of China.

Most important for the future is probably Hu Yaobang, 68, secretary of the Party. A peppery personality, Hu ran away from home at age 14 to join the Communists; trooped with them on the Long March; fought against Japanese and Nationalists, rising to political commissar of an army group by the end of the Liberation War.

Lastly comes Zhao Ziyang, baby of the ruling group at 64. He is a favorite of Deng Xiaoping and made his mark, after the downfall of the Gang of Four,

by reorganizing the province of Sichuan. Today he is prime minister. But he, too, must be considered one of the Old Guard, having fought both Japanese and Nationalists.

Together, this ruling group shapes up as the oldest in the world. They are all men of Yan'an, the Valley Forge of China, all but one of them veterans of the Long March. It is as if the United States were, today, governed by a six-man committee consisting of generals Marshall, MacArthur, Patton, Eisenhower and Clay and Admiral Nimitz.

Their problem is the same as it was when they came out of the hills to occupy Beijing: How to give China government? What kind of government? And how, once that government is established, to transfer it to younger hands?

A Countryside Reborn

Lia Qili, deputy secretary general of the State Commission on Restructure of the Economy, is 68 years old. A man of Yan'an, he came over the western range to Fragrant Hill with the Zhongyang in 1949. Sent down from 1968 to 1978, he was named by the new premier, Zhao Ziyang, to the commission in 1980. Still vigorous, his hair iron-gray, Lia dresses in the gray tailored suit that is the fashion of China's ruling elite. But his eyes, behind horn-rimmed glasses, sparkle with a raconteur's delight as he tells of the China that was left after the Cultural Revolution.

"It was," he says, "madness. They

had two systems for the economy—call them line authority and bloc authority. Line authority ran from the central-government ministries down to the smallest factories and mines. We found one factory with four thousand workers—but only one toilet. The workers would line up for hours to get to the toilet. But the factory had no authority to build a toilet on its own; any building of more than two hundred square feet had to be approved by line authority at the top in Beijing; and that decision would go to the Central Planning Commission. Should Central Planning have to decide about toilets?

"We had a woolen factory in Hebei—they produced good worsteds that people wanted for suits. But the plan called for the mill to produce *coarse* woolens. So the mill met its quotas in coarse woolens and the woolens piled up in the warehouses. All over China, Beijing set quotas, factories met quotas and they ignored what the people, the market, demanded.

"Bloc authority meant that provincial governments did the trading and marketing. Villages in north Jiangsu, for example, raised tomatoes, so they needed bamboo staves to make the tepees that hold tomatoes up. Anhui [just across the border from Jiangsu Province] raised surplus bamboo. But tomato farmers in Jiangsu couldn't get bamboo from Anhui because that crossed a provincial border."

On he went with mordant amusement as he described how they were slowly untangling what "egalitarianism" had wrought. There was so much

to do, and so much resistance left from the old bureaucracy, that it would be years before all was straightened out. But much had already been accomplished, particularly in the countryside.

THE COUNTRYSIDE means almost anywhere in China, for 80 percent of China's people still work in the fields. I chose to go to places I had known before and during World War II, to Shaanxi, to Sichuan, which had been my home base for six years, and to Hubei.

Sichuan is so large (100 million people) and so fertile ("Anything that grows in China," ran the old phrase, "grows better in Sichuan") that one cannot ignore it. Sichuan used to feed itself. But then, from the czars of the Cultural Revolution, came the order that all communes and brigades grow *two* rice crops a year. Rice, however, is a tricky crop, its culture unfamiliar to the bureaucrats of Beijing. Beijing did not know when rains fall in Sichuan or when the fields dry up. Sichuan had evolved its own two-crop culture—rice in summer and wheat or rape in winter. But Beijing had ordered *two* rice crops. So the communes and brigades obeyed. Sichuan tried to meet its quotas; when it could not, the government sent into this one-time surplus-crop province grain from outside; and the peasants hungered.

I found Sichuan enjoying change, as a man does when handcuffs and leg irons are removed. The new reforms were quite simple: the peasants could decide what and when to plant; if they met their state quotas, the surplus was theirs to eat or to sell. The commune system is all but gone; most of the land has been turned over to families or individuals to farm as they will. The margin is still precariously thin. The peasants can now keep their chins above water, which is better than five years ago when only their nostrils were visible.

A quick, six-day tour of the province, for an old-timer, is a delight. The small towns throb again, their booths full of sweets, cookies, housewares, clothes, textiles, flowers. In big cities like Chengdu and Chongqing, the huge food markets overwhelm the eye with produce that can be brought without coupons. Hogs come to market in wheelbarrows, on garden tractors, even lashed to bicycles. Peasants bring in chickens, squawking, eight to a basket. Down the lanes peasants sell their geese and ducks; fish from their ponds; fresh vegetables; caged birds are for sale, and cricket boxes delight the children. Shoemakers ply their trade; itinerant dentists, with pedal-operated drills, have reappeared.

The markets are real. So is the astonishing good health, the ruddy vitality of the people who, thronging the streets on market day, are so different from the scrawny peasants I remember from 40 years ago. The gurgling babies please the eye, dressed in scarlet or yellow or pink—no trachoma, no scabies, no rickety limbs, no potbellies of famine.

But the scanning eye can deceive. This has been a good year in China, with a prospective record harvest, record incomes. But if the rains fall at the wrong time, the wheat will be beaten to the ground and lost; and the rains *must* fall at the right time, for if by May the rice seedlings are not planted in the flooded paddies after the wheat is reaped, there will be a slim fall rice crop. Translate this into statistics, and this huge province, as populous as England and France combined, still lives on the edge of hunger. Yet the net impression, after weeks in the countryside, is unshakable. The agony of the Cultural Revolution ended, China's farms are on the mend.

It is in the swollen cities that the observer senses the true dimensions of China's problem, for China still cannot feed them. Fifteen million tons of imported grain (eight million from America) were needed last year. And the cities will continue to grow, for industry is booming.

Surging Cities

Industry is the romance of China's planners. It is their measure of their ability to enter the modern world—and Chinese industry is the ultimate challenge to tomorrow's system of world trade in which the United States, sooner or later, must adjust its economy to China as it has to the industry of Japan.

Chinese leaders love to talk of industry, rippling statistics over their stories as merchants used to ripple silks over their hands. Probe at a Chinese official and figures spurt: they boast of the largest cotton industry in the world today (15 billion square yards annually); steel production up from nearly zero 40 years ago to a projected 40 million tons this year. TV sets, washing machines, refrigerators are pouring out of new factories. None of these is yet good enough for export, but soon, the leaders promise, they will be exporting TV sets of a quality to match the best. Already in Shanghai there is a watch factory making timepieces good enough to export as far away as Singapore.

The theory of the new "responsibility system" blankets the industrial cities too. Industry must make what people need, and make a profit to split with the government. It is responsible, except in the case of military or national need, to the balance sheet of profit and loss.

In Chongqing, that city of rivers, hills and mists, one can find an industrial revolution that has taken place not in centuries but in decades. In 1939 I had first come to this city, a peasant market at the junction of two great rivers—the Chang Jiang (Yangtze) and the Jialing—which had grown to hold 250,000 people as the Nationalists' wartime capital.

That city no longer exists. Chongqing is now the hub of one of the world's largest metropolitan centers, numbering 14 million people.

My plane had landed in 1939 on a sand bar in the Chang Jiang; I had been carried up the cliffs by sedan chair; the sights and sounds enchanted me—the old wall around the city, peddlers at the gates, hawkers chanting in the streets; night soil collected in slop buckets to be shipped up-river to the peasants.

Nothing remains: no city wall, no night-soil collectors, no Press Hotel where I had stayed. The industrial rev-

olution has overrun the old town. Hills have been leveled, gullies filled in, streets paved over, landmarks wiped out.

A new railway brings trains in regularly, disgorges its passengers into a tunnel. When you emerge from it, a new city comes into view: apartment houses as far as the eye can see; a skyline spiked with smokestacks, and then the gaudy, red-and-yellow spectacle of the huge Ren Min Hotel. You cross the river to what were once paddy fields. An iron-and-steel complex there now employs 45,000 people; behind it sprawl arms plants; behind them stretch the electronic and textile plants of new Chongqing. The old Chongqing, with its smell of opium, orange gin, open urine channels, with its blind, blinking beggars, is gone forever.

But for an American, or a German, or an Englishman, or a Japanese, questions arise. What do these people get paid? On the average a steel worker in China earns 15 Chinese *yuan* a week, or about $8. With fringe benefits like medical care, housing, schools, call it $20 a week. How can an American steel company, whose workers' average earnings plus benefits are more than $20 an hour, compete with a Chinese plant whose workers earn $20 a week?

Follow the industrial boom to textiles and garments. The largest cotton mill in China sits in Chengdu. Its cloth is currently absorbed by the China market, but factory management, under pressure to increase sales, is looking to the Western market. The workers in the Chengdu factory take home $6 a week, against a North Carolina or New York wage of about $200 a week. It is inevitable that sometime in the next ten years China will be one of the world's largest textile exporters. Our own government has already begun to wrangle with the Chinese about the market share to which they feel entitled; the wrangle can only get worse as Chinese design improves.

One looks at booming Chinese industry and one knows, by reflex reaction, that this kind of industry is better than that which Mao envisioned. It is better certainly for the Chinese. Is it better, though, in the long run, for Western workers and Western industry? How shall we handle this conflict between our principles and our national interest?

Simmering Unrest

No group could be more sensitive to the changes required by the transition to an enterprise system than the six old veterans of the standing committee. Age presses them. They need new, younger men in the Party, in the provinces, to captain industry. They must choose their replacements now—managers, engineers, scientists.

But how? Transfer of power is dangerous in China. Traditionally, power lay with palace tyrants and the scholar-bureaucrats they appointed. To this Mao added a third element—Party dictatorship. Under all Chinese systems, transfer of power went hand in hand with humiliations and killing.

What haunts thoughtful Chinese and foreign diplomats alike is the question of the stability of the new regime. Can Deng Xiaoping successfully and peacefully transfer power to other hands? How strong or fragile is the control exercised by the standing committee? How many old hatreds and old scores sputter in opposition to the new course?

To discuss this simmering unrest in China it is best to discard the clichés of "left" and "right" that the Chinese mechanically use to describe their politics. There comes first, when one looks for opposition, the old Red Army. Trained in combat, promoted by victory, its leaders were men of capacity and command who recognized only the Party structure as authority. They regarded government simply as a supportive system of logistics. The army was, in its beginning, the people in arms; and then the army became a state within a state, building its own railways, dams, factories, submitting its own budget each year, while the official planning authority scrutinized its demands but always approved them. Under the new constitution, the "government" theoretically must approve that budget. Slowly, then, so as not to disturb a slumbering volcano, the old commanders are being eased out. But the army, most observers in Beijing agree, is restless.

So, too, is the Party. Buried deep in the Chinese Communist Party of some 40 million members are old careerists who grabbed office during the Cultural Revolution. Very few have been punished, though many have been forced down. But millions remain, jealous of their perquisites; they must, somehow, be ousted. A purge is scheduled for late this year. But it will be difficult. Many Party members of prefectural rank refuse to realize that their useless offices, with their privileges, must be abolished. Many still believe in Mao. A threat lurks; and if Deng cannot force the transfer to a new generation before he passes on, then explosion may come again.

There is also a threat that the Chinese say "comes from the right." This is a serious threat because it rises not from loss of power but from envy. For example, I find myself riding along the road in a limousine. There is a livestock fair by the road; I want to look. My escorts clamber out with me and there, along the wall of a cotton mill, is livestock: goats, mules, cows, horses, sheep and pigs. I am pleased that peasants can now raise animals and sell them for their own account. But the Foreign Office diplomat with me purses his lips. His monthly salary is only $200; this peasant lives better than he. I have come to cherish the diplomat; his devotion to his government is total. But how long can such devotion last?

In slightly different terms, this feeling is a massive, subversive danger. It floats sometimes on the sound of music. I walk by the Tiananmen Gate on a spring evening. People are gathered there; a loudspeaker plays melodies— from Taiwan! It means entering the "Hotel of Overseas Chinese," the most privileged visitors in China. The bulletin board announces in English, "Disco Dancing Tonight." And then one learns that young Chinese "radicals" sneak secretly to apartments, don blue jeans and

slit skirts and dance to the disco beat. The puritan China of Mao Zedong frowned on sex. But Mao would erupt from his mausoleum if he could see what Beijing offers now (and, even more vividly, Shanghai and Guangzhou).

The last time I had seen a theatrical performance in China was when I trailed Nixon to a performance of "The Red Brigade of Women." That had been a sterile drama of women storming a reactionary bastion. Beautiful ballet, but no legs showing. This time I went to see the top-billed vaudeville troupe of China, visiting from Shanghai—ventriloquists, magicians, tightrope acrobats, weight lifters. But, above all, I noticed women's thighs in public. Except for concubines, women once showed their thighs in China only to their husbands. Now here were twirlers, dancers, women in tutus. Jiang Qing would have condemned them all to stoop labor.

The immediate shaft of the rightist threat is, however, not permissiveness but greed. The government's chief strength remains the dedication of its civil servants, who work for almost nothing, live in tiny apartments, sleep on bamboo mats. Yet even the most dedicated can be tempted by creature comforts. So one hears of corruption surfacing in the Party—corruption for paid favors (which is small) but, more significantly, corruption of the official structure. One government unit bargains with another for privileges or supplies, or living space for its bureaucrats; there is always a "back door" to the official front.

Some Chinese are getting rich, which means a growing few now live well above the level of poverty. In Shanghai and Guangzhou particularly, which are Special Zones, capitalism has been permitted tiny openings to start up enterprises. Wealthy overseas Chinese come to China and peel off bills with abandon; the amounts are huge sums to government officials; and the undermining of their purity is a silent threat to the regime.

Money is corrosive; on the coast, in China's big cities, the corrosion is rampant, perhaps most so in Guangzhou. There the regime has set up a special, 126-square-mile economic zone, Shenzhen, directly adjacent to Hong Kong, and Hong Kong's merchants and capitalists are now colonizing it. Skyscrapers and hotels rise, factories surge as Hong Kong capital moves to exploit the cheap labor, cheap land and poverty. Anything is for sale in Shenzhen so long as it returns a profit, shared by the exploiters and the regime—even apartments, condominiums, living space that Hong Kong entrepreneurs buy for themselves, or for their relatives in China. Shenzhen is a spectacle of prosperity—but one that mocks the peasants of Sichuan, where to prosper means there is enough to eat.

Too Many People

Of all the budding, or dying, centers of left or right opposition, none is more explosive than the unshaped discontent that pulses from human nature itself.

That threat rises from what is China's overwhelming, perhaps insoluble, problem—population.

China has doubled its population in 36 years, from 455 million people in 1947 to over one billion today. Such figures are too large to grasp.

They can be felt, however: at the Great Wall on a holiday Sunday morning when, at the gate closest to Beijing (70 miles away), the crowds push their way through the opening in a crush of bodies that is worse than the Tokyo subway at rush hour; or on a Saturday night a thousand miles away from Beijing, in Chengdu, when the streets of the city become a half-lit carnival—wanderers, bystanders, families, youngsters, bicycles, carts, trucks, all yelling or ringing or honking to push their way through the throng; or at any village fair as hawkers, peddlers, barbers, peasants, customers clog the lanes in bedlam.

There are simply too many people. Everywhere, the faint rice-tainted breath of the individual Chinese becomes an omnipresent odor, as in a closed and fetid bus.

It is bad in the city, bad in the country. One village I entered had doubled its people in 25 years. When the share-out of land came with reform three years ago, there was so little to share that the land had to be divided into strips. Each peasant picked by lot from the bundle of slips that defined his share. A large family might draw as many as four *mu*, two-thirds of an acre, to live on. In another village I met a single man, perhaps 25 years old; he had drawn one *mu*, one-sixth of an acre, on which to live. He planted and reaped his sixth of an acre at appropriate times, but was looking for work in the construction projects of the big city nearby.

In the cities, housing is an obsession. Since there is no private housing, the Party unit decides, according to rank, influence and the number of people in the family, who gets how many feet of living space. Money is no factor. Rents average less than $2 a month in Beijing. The Chinese are building housing everywhere. But no city can build enough to meet its swelling needs. Each Party unit of a factory or office builds the housing for its people. A poor factory, or a weak government office, can do far less. Beijing offers most—an average of 45 square feet per individual; Hankou averages 40 square feet. Shanghai averages less, a cramping 30 square feet per person (apart from kitchen and community toilet). The figures are grim, inexorable, inescapable.

The Party and government have a policy now: to each family only one baby, no more! In the large cities, this policy is barely enforceable. If by mischance a family has more than two babies, some government offices cut the father's salary by 10 or 20 percent. A third child is declared ineligible for entrance into the quality schools.

In the countryside, the government is reduced to persuasion, propaganda, occasionally coercion. Wall slogans chant the virtues of family planning. But the new "responsibility system," with each peasant gardening his little plot, makes children useful again; they grow up to weed, plant, harvest. If the first baby is a girl, the matter is serious indeed—girls go off and get married. Thus, there has developed a horror that the Chinese themselves find appalling—the killing of infant girls. The government is shocked enough to report such cases in order to denounce them. Girls must not be killed at birth, exhorts the government. Girls will grow up to be citizens too! Stop! Yet the practice goes on.

The government hopes education can slow population growth; Party units meet with a family expecting a second child and "persuade" the family to end the pregnancy. But some will not be persuaded. In some villages the Party requires all women of childbearing age to appear every two months for a pregnancy test. Some women run away from home until the sixth or seventh month, when it is too late for an abortion.

Logic lies on the side of the government; the numbers permit no appeal. But babies continue to come because love lies on the side of babies. Chinese babies, with their sleek black hair, their little snub noses, their bright and shining eyes, are beautiful. The one-baby families cuddle them, caress them, spoil them. What political dynamite lies in family love of babies when second babies are declared sinful? How will the casual cruelties Chinese inflict on one another, as they writhe under the pressure of numbers, translate into politics? What distortion of ambition will result as students ruthlessly compete in entrance exams to colleges that will give them some escape from the mass-pack?

If the population increases, even at its present reduced rate, China must starve or explode.

Clearly, then, there is no internal solution except that which the government proposes—population control. And no external solution except that which it simultaneously pursues—an industrialization effort that will flood the world's markets. The axis of this second thrust is also simple: to employ enough of the surplus population at low enough wages to export China's manufactures (which are constantly improving in quality) to earn back from the rest of the world—above all, from the United States—the food, timber, cotton, edible oils, meat to keep their people above the starvation line. Must our standard of living go down if theirs is to go up? Is that inevitable?

The Three T's

The American Embassy in Beijing sums up Chinese-American relations as the three T's: Taiwan, Technology, Trade. In each of the T's, a different family of problems interlock, but it is only over Taiwan that they could reach gunpoint.

Taiwan involves pride, the nation's sense of itself. In China, after 150 years of foreign humiliations, pride has ulcerated. Chinese are taught a modern history that starts in 1840, when British gunboats defeated them in the Opium War. It runs on from humiliation to humiliation—by the Japanese who tore Taiwan away, by the Russians who tried to make Manchuria a province, by the

Germans who tried to seize Shandong, by the foreign concessions in big cities in which English, French, Americans, Russians, Japanese claimed sovereign rights.

This abused pride exploded in the Japanese war of the 1930s and 1940s, which ravaged the land for eight years. The present government has warred with every one of its neighbors: Japan, India, South Korea, Vietnam. It continually exchanges gunfire with the Russians in border skirmishes. For the old soldiers who lead the government only one thing is lacking to fulfill their dream of liberating all China—Taiwan. And over Taiwan, Chinese passion is quick to boil.

I went to call on one of the old soldiers I had met in Yan'an days—Peng Zhen, who since my spring visit has been elected president of the National People's Congress. Burly, bald, still vigorous at 81, his life is a microcosm of Chinese history: a student insurrectionary in the 1930s, imprisoned for years in his youth, a guerrilla commander; political commissar of the Communist forces that conquered Manchuria, he had more recently been abused by the Cultural Revolution, confined to house arrest, sent down. Now, restored to honor, he is a member of the Politburo again. I had thought, and still think, of him as one of the key figures in modern Chinese history. I could not have been more surprised when he received me in the Great Hall of the People in Beijing and, after a smiling welcome, burst out almost with a roar in an opening statement:

"This United States Administration says it wants China and the United States to be friends, but, as a matter of fact, we are hostile to each other! It says China and Taiwan are both part of the sole legitimate government of China, but they treat us like equal states. How would you feel if we supported California against you? Reagan invited both Taiwan and the government to his inauguration. He says Taiwan is an old friend. Does he mean that we are an old enemy? He thinks Taiwan is an unsinkable aircraft carrier, but we are one hundred times as large as Taiwan. If it comes to war, which aircraft carrier will sink first?"

I had expected a jovial reunion. But, perhaps because he thought he could speak frankly to an old friend, he was lecturing me. He had just been lectured by a U.S. Congressional delegation headed by House Speaker Thomas "Tip" O'Neill, Jr., and he was resentful. The senior men of the Foreign Office were seated around us, and Peng, hammering out the Party line, was laying it on.

"Taiwan is a burden to you," he thundered. "For a century and a half all the foreign powers except the United States invaded China. But now you alone are carrying the burden of hate of our people for that century and a half. Last year you sold Taiwan $600 million in arms; this year it will be $800 million.

"We want to negotiate a peaceful reunion with Taiwan, but whatever we do, you encourage Taiwan to say no. We offer to let Taiwan keep its own troops, maintain its own social and cultural contact abroad, make its own economic arrangements with other countries, but still you encourage them to say no. If Taiwan does not settle with us peacefully, we will settle the problem any way we think necessary.

"And there is technology. I want to emphasize this point: even if you won't help us, it will be impossible to obstruct the flow of technology to China."

By this time, Peng Zhen was working himself into a healthy anger. On technology, the muddle of American policy baffles the Chinese. The United States sends, for example, sophisticated computers to India's air force, because the U.S. considers India a "friendly" state, although its air force is largely equipped with Russian MiGs and is advised by Russian technicians. China is denied such shipments because China falls into the official category of "communist state." The classification of India as "friendly" and China as "hostile" defies logic. Peng Zhen closed his lecture with another threat: "We Chinese have a saying, 'If the East is dark, the West will be bright. If the South is dark, the North will be bright.' If you don't sell technology to us, we will get it from Europe—or Japan."

The Chinese have a good case on Taiwan, and an intricate but reasonable case on the transfer of technology. But it is on the third T—Trade—that the future may most sharply divide the two countries.

Since the resumption of normal relations, Chinese-American trade has boomed—to a total of $5 billion in 1982—and the balance has been running (until this year) in favor of the

United States. This adverse balance has angered the Chinese; and the aggravation has been rubbed raw by recent American regulations limiting textile and garment imports into the United States.

I talked to the Trade Ministry's spokesman. He gave a superlative overview of China's long-range plan and its need to export manufactured goods. Then he fixed on one figure—of all America's imports, only 0.65 percent comes from China. I pointed out that in world trade, surpluses do not balance country by country; the United States has had a slight surplus of exports over imports with China, a monstrous deficit in trade with Japan. Answer: you import only 0.65 percent from China.

I tried to explain that it is the growth of Oriental imports that disturbs America. The United States cannot let the Chinese do to its textile and garment workers what the Koreans and Japanese did to its steel and automobile workers. Answer: you import only 0.65 percent from China.

I pointed out that the United States allots a share of the textile market to four Asian exporters—Korea, Taiwan, Hong Kong and China. Last year exports of cheap Chinese garments to the United States jumped 29 percent over 1981. Answer: you give Taiwan more of your market than you give us. I mentioned that an American Academy of Engineering study has just concluded that of the United States' 2 million textile and garment workers, 1.2 million may be put out of work in the next decade by Oriental imports. Answer: you import only 0.65 percent from China.

Last month the United States finally yielded to Chinese anger over textile exports. An agreement was initialed that lets China increase its exports of cloth to us by two to three percent annually. Whether embittered American textile-industry officials can persuade Congress to reverse the agreement remains to be seen.

Behind the persistent Chinese push lies a possibility one cannot dodge: the Chinese, under their new regime, may finally have straightened out their economy. And, if the new regime can make flourish in China itself the ingenuity and genius of transplanted Chinese-Americans in the United States, then the Japanese challenge to American jobs will be seen as only an opening flare of warning.

Paradoxes

A journey through China today is a journey through paradox. An American judging it by Western standards can find in it what he wishes—progress and cruelty, beauty and filth, pride and shame.

In the first three months of this year, TV production in China doubled over 1982. Consumer goods are advertised on TV; people want them. Distant provinces and their natural beauties are shown on educational TV; people want to travel and see the sights. A rock 'n' roll show is aired, live, from Beijing. The viewers see an audience of youngsters go wild, stomping, throwing, yelling. This upsets old puritanical Communists, so the government must issue new regulations for audience be-havior. Soap opera has arrived; women watch; they go to the new department stores and demand dresses that *fit*.

Beauty is a craving of Chinese cul-ture, and the leadership has been restor-ing it. Each major city, each minor county seat, cherishes its own local beauties—gardens with green, gnarled trees, ancient pavilions with reflecting pools, refurbished monuments with po-etry scrolls. But then one must set against them an ineradicable sloppiness of behavior and custom: spittoons in provincial offices, street people who blow their noses with their fingers and wipe them off on their shirts; babies with their slit pants taught to crouch and let go wherever the urge takes them.

All of China's paradoxes can be found stretched out as in panorama during a two-day trip down the Chang Jiang from Chongqing to Wuhan. In Chongqing I visited an electronics plant that makes oscilloscopes and instru-ments for testing television equipment. Dust-free, climate-controlled, the plant requires visitors to doff their shoes for clean slippers before entering. Inside are young women dipping soldering irons in amber lumps of rosin, touching the melted rosin to connectors, deftly threading together the colored wires, sealing all in circuit panels. They are only three or four years out of the rice paddies, but their product is superior.

Down the Chang Jiang one sails from Chongqing to see stone-hackers, with mallet and chisel, carving building blocks out of riverbed reefs—labor so uselessly expended when concrete is available that it can be economical only if recognized as forced labor. Farther down the river on the same voyage is the town of Wanxian. I lean over the rail of the steamer and see a waiting file of young women stevedores. The first one stoops, and all her muscles quiver as she heaves and finally lifts two huge buckets of pig livers for the third-class passen-gers. She struggles up the gang-plank, followed by other young women, beasts of burden, loading and unloading the ship, staggering under the bamboo staves that carry the bales, the cartons, the loadings of the vessel.

The next morning I come to the pride of Chinese technology, the Gezhouba Dam. It is the first dam to harness the Chang Jiang since nature melted the snows of the Tibetan highlands to carve a passage to the ocean. The Chinese are proud of Gezhouba. All its machinery, its turbines, its locks and spillways, its transformers, are of Chinese design and manufacture. Down below, the first 3 of the 11 planned turbines already spin with the flow, the only noise the hiss of rushing water, muffled deep beneath.

So, all in 48 hours: peasant girls trained to stitch together oscilloscopes and circuit boards; forced labor cutting hard rock with mallet and chisel; young women, treated as beasts; spectacular technology.

The journey raises more questions than answers; and the questions plague the Chinese themselves. Who decides that China needs oscilloscopes? Who decides who chisels stone from a riv-erbed? Why are some young women working in dust-free plants while others slave at menial work? How much relief from suffering can the Zhongyang give its people now, without stealing time and resources from the China of tomorrow? How can China protect itself from the cruelties of its revolution, as well as from the creeping greed that made old China a horror of selfish landlords, loan sharks and warlords?

Step by Step

A final observation: When I came to China more than 40 years ago, I came believing it was a land of much history, whose pride had been erased. These people celebrated as national holidays what they called National Humiliation Days. But, watching the Chinese fight the Japanese, I learned that personal and national pride still smoldered underneath and could be brought to flame. Mao brought them to flame. I saw him change their thinking from humiliation to one of eternal "struggle"; better to die than to submit. The song of the guerrillas ran, "Rise all of you who will not be slave people!"

The Chinese are still a "struggle" people. They have struggled against the Japanese and hate them yet. They have struggled against Russian ideas and repudiated them. They have struggled against the barbarities of their own government and leaders, and erased many. Their current struggle is, certainly, against the realities of their own immense dimensions, the limits of their backwardness. Yet, as they debate this struggle, some may find it easier to

struggle against an outer enemy to restore the national pride.

The United States and China are locked in a narrow, dangerous passage of history. The transition regime in Beijing is "struggling" to recapture control of events. But it chooses to go its own way, trying to re-establish some system of law, rather than foster the graces of a liberty China has never known. To impose Western standards on this internal struggle is irrelevant.

So one returns from China, as one first arrived there long ago, fearful, yet hopeful. Memory recalls most sharply not the old China of 1939 but the first night of this spring visit of 1983.

That first night, when Wang Bingnan took me to Fragrant Hill, another old friend had joined us—Chiao Guan Hua. Chiao and I had been friends in our youth, when he was a fiery left-wing journalist. He had later become foreign minister; he and Henry Kissinger had worked out the landmark "Shanghai Communiqué" of 1972, in which the United States recognized that Taiwan was part of China, but insisted on a "peaceful" solution to the problem. Chiao had gone on with Mao to the end; he had only last year been released from house arrest by the new regime; his wife, suspect because she had been close to Jiang Qing, was with him.

This night Chiao would not let himself be cornered on any subject that touched on his stewardship of Chinese foreign policy under Mao; or on his own arrest after Mao's death; or on the Cultural Revolution. He was witty and tart, as he always had been, and discussed both the personality of Kissinger and the ambition of Lin Biao. He was fascinating on such subjects.

I pressed him on what had gone wrong in China since our youth and his triumphant career; he dodged. He retreated to citing Tang Dynasty poetry, 12 centuries old, to illuminate life under China's millennial tyrannies. His wife added colorful anecdotes about the fashions and whimsies of Jiang Qing. It was a warming evening, with fine food and even better conversation. But, when I finally pressed him, deeply and hard, on China's future, he elegantly replied, "You must remember what Hegel said, that a man reaches an understanding of the history of his own time step by step—only step by step."

Chiao Guan Hua was ill when I met him, a scarf wrapped around his throat. He was in the hospital when I left this spring. I do not think I will ever see him again. But I remember his words, "step by step." Which is the way that both the West and China must go through this passage of history. No ultimate solutions are possible, either for the Chinese or ourselves. But, "step by step," we may get there.

READER'S DIGEST October 1983

Chapter 5

Europe on the Mend

On coming home from China in 1945, and on leave from Time Inc., White teamed with Annalee Jacoby (who had joined him in China for *Time* in 1944) to write "Thunder Out of China (see Introduction, page xvii)." The authors predicted the "inevitable" collapse of Chiang Kai-shek, a thesis that resulted in a complete rupture with Henry Luce. White was out of a job— only to learn later that very day in 1946 that *Thunder* had been named a Book-of-the-Month selection. Best-sellerdom followed.

Financially solvent for a change, White tried his hand briefly at freelancing (see "The Battle of Athens, Tennessee," page 317), then even more briefly as an editor of the *New Republic* (see Introduction, page xix). But Asia kept calling, and in 1948 he headed back to China—he thought. He traveled via Europe, and quickly found himself caught up in the drama of the Marshall Plan and Europe's recovery from war. White stayed on for nearly six years.

After a stint as Paris Correspondent for the short-lived Overseas News Agency, White switched back to magazine freelancing. His subject matter was wide-ranging, his production prolific. The first three articles that follow are from that period: "From the Rubble" is a deft blend of economics, politics, and people in a style that he was continuing to hone. "New Force in Europe: The Catholic Left" traces a ferment that few American reporters had noticed. "France and Germany—Fear and Hatred"—will the two countries unite? asks White; can they afford not to? From his European reporting came his second best-seller, *Fire in the Ashes,* published in 1953.

The concluding article, "Germany—Friend or Foe," written for *Collier's* after White returned to the United States, is a probing and detailed analysis of the German-American postwar honeymoon.

FROM THE RUBBLE

The most solid fact in Eastern Europe today is Polish recovery. Yet it will take twelve years, the Poles guess, to erase the ravages of war.

For four years now, horse carts, bulldozers and trucks have been pushing in from the fringes of Warsaw, drawing a circle of fresh healing tissue over the scar that is the ruins of the city. But what remains of the ruins, the heart of the city, is still among the wonders of the modern world. One sits on a chunk of concrete and from the south the vagrant wind brings the echo of the living city and the traffic grinding its gears on Marszalkowska Street. In the silent square, before the old City Hall, the echoes are very soft, and only the tinkling bells of the old farm carts that haul away the rubble are close. And no sound, near or far, brings any answer to the sharp questions with which one came, or tells him how close or distant war is, only that these ruins and the people who live in them speak a need for peace, and a testament of hate.

Berlin boasts more ruins and more acres of broken masonry than Warsaw. But the windowless shells of Berlin were eaten out by combat destruction. Warsaw's ruins are different: here destruction was planned scientifically and executed methodically, at the leisure of the German army. The stumps of the steel girders are sheared off clean, where Wehrmacht engineers bound dynamite against the steel to make it come down neatly.

To a quick visitor, Warsaw still looks like the cratered face of the moon—tumbling fields of brick, mounds of mortar dust and powdered concrete on which a fuzz of grass and weed has begun to make a green film; walls that stand like wafers against the sky, an empty smokestack pinned on the edge of one, an iron balcony hanging on the side of another, an open door which opens onto nothing, six stories above the ground. But if one speaks to a resident of several years, whether he is an American newspaperman, an Italian diplomat, or just a digger in the rubble heaps, he says, "Why, this is nothing— you should have seen it in the snow and slush when the Germans left; you should have smelled it when they were still digging dead bodies out of the sewers. This is wonderful—the buses are running, you can get a taxi, and there's food in the stores."

In a country where planning dominates the whole horizon of human life the Plan is master of Warsaw. The war reduced its population from 1,250,000 to almost zero by the time the Germans left. For the first six months the Poles concentrated on restoring electric and water systems. The next two years were spent in cleaning the streets and repairing whatever buildings could be more easily roofed than torn down. This is the year they finish repairing anything repairable, and the year they begin on the first of their six-year plans. It will take twelve years, they guess, to erase the destruction of the war from their midst. There are 600,000 people living in Warsaw now and 40,000 of them— the largest industrial concentration— are working on repair and construction. When they are finished, sometime about 1960, the old City Hall square will have precisely the same archaic façade it had before the war, and the wind will have stopped blowing rubble dust through the yards where housewives hang their wash to dry. Warsaw will then be back to normal for the first time in twenty years. Normal, except for the ancient Ghetto where once lived 300,000 Jews. This vast 200-acre stretch will be flat by then, but not flat with the ground. The engineers have decided there is too much rubble to clear away; instead, they will leave it as a plateau six feet higher than the rest of Warsaw. Beneath its surface will lie the unrecovered bodies of 10,000 Jews, along with pots, pans and silverware, hand grenades and rifles, for future archaeologists to tap as the richest lode of 20th Century civilization.

There are secret police in Poland, who arrest men, hold them without trial and lock them in concentration camps; and there are an estimated 100,000 Russian troops still in Western Poland guarding the railroad lines to Russia's occupation zone in Germany. But the Polish government draws its support not so much from these, as from the recovery it has captained and its people's abiding fear of the Teutons to the west.

If one listens for even a minute, Polish government spokesmen will spout a barrage of statistics on recovery. One set of figures is enough to reveal what Poland was like the day the war ended.

There were 35,000,000 Poles in prewar Poland. More than one out of six died during the war—a total of 6,000,000 people. Of these 6,000,000, the overwhelming majority perished not of hunger or disease or by clean death in battle. They were scientifically butchered and cremated.

The Nazis were selective, they chose all the Jews they could find— 3,000,000 of them; they killed 2,500,000 Catholics, picking specifically engineers, lawyers, teachers, intellectuals, priests and local resistance leaders—those who threatened the German aim of reducing all Poland to slave labor.

They left a demoralized nation with hundreds of thousands of homeless children roaming the streets like animals; a problem of alcoholism that still persists; and a moral fabric eroded by years of espionage, treachery and corruption.

Also, they almost succeeded in wiping out Polish learning. After the war, the first medical students had to study from German texts because every medical book in the Polish language had been burned by the enemy.

Human destruction was not all. The Nazis wrecked 516,000 houses, destroyed 14,000 factories and 200,000 shops, tore up roads, blew up bridges, looted the country of more than half of its livestock, and half its machines and trucks.

Since the war the Poles have almost doubled their prewar production of electric power; they have more than doubled their annual production of coal (from 27,000,000 tons to 70,000,000 tons), becoming in the process Europe's most important coal exporter; they have passed their prewar production of steel, and have brought textile and sugar production back to normal levels. They began their first production of tractors last year, turning out 1500 of the farm machines, and plan to produce 10,000 during 1949. This year, too, the first Polish-made automobiles will come off their assembly lines.

Many of these figures may be explained by cynically consulting a map. Prewar Poland lay between Germany and Russia, a flat slab of land which was squeezed each century into a new and different shape by the pressures of its powerful neighbors. World War II changed Polish geography once more. The whole eastern tier of Polish provinces was stripped from Poland and added to Russia. To compensate the Poles the Russians took a somewhat similar strip away from Eastern Germany and added it to Poland's frontier in the west. Some 2,000,000 Germans

were moved out of this area and 5,000,000 displaced Poles moved in.

In Europe, anything can be proved by a history book, and the Poles can prove that hundreds of years ago this eastern strip of Germany was inhabited by Slavs who were chased out later by Teutons. That Poland should now possess territory that was German ten years ago seems to the Poles only historic justice.

The effect of this shift in territory is much more important than appears on the map. In the east, Poland gave up marshland and farmland; in the west, she received a much smaller area, but it included German Silesia—rich in coal mines, factories and heavy industry.

The Poles react hotly when it is suggested that this inheritance of German industry has loaded their statistics on recovery. They argue that industrial recovery is general throughout all of Poland. Even in old Poland, they tell you, electricity production is almost double what it was before the war. Besides, they say, the mines they took over were wrecked, the factories deserted, the heavy industry shattered. They have rebuilt and reorganized all these industries, which are being operated today by workmen who four years ago were farmer peasants in Eastern Poland. "There are six million fewer of us than there were ten years ago," they say, "and we are turning out twenty or thirty per cent more goods than all of old Poland produced."

They hammer home this point by showing visitors the great Pa-Fa-Wag works in Wroclaw. The city of Wroclaw

was formerly the German city of Bres-
lau, and the Pa-Fa-Wag works is the
former German Hoffman-Linke rolling-
stock plant. Before the war, under the
Germans, it was the greatest boxcar
works in Europe, turning out 6000
units a year. The war converted the
plant first into an aircraft factory, which
produced Stukas, then into an assembly
plant for the V-2's which bombarded
England. At the end of the war the
plant was a waste of ruins.

The Poles rebuilt the wreckage, and
now, with raw peasant labor, they are
turning out 10,000 boxcars a year, half
as much again as the Germans did.

The Lean Years

If the recovery of Polish farming has not
been as dramatic as that of Polish industry, it has been far more important. The
food that comes from Polish farms is the
dinner that goes on the table in Polish
cities, and the dinner table is the most
important political influence in any
country. The first two years after the
war were hungry years. During 1946
American food, coming via UNRRA,
saved the country from starvation. In
1947, the Polish government had to
buy 200,000 tons of wheat from Russia
to keep its people eating. Last year, Poland turned the corner; the harvest came
through, the meat animals began to
come back, and the Poles exported not
only 50,000 tons of grain but started
shipping bacon to England. They
opened 1949 with two demonstrations
of farm recovery—they wrote a stagger-

ing five-year pact with England for the
export of thousands of tons of eggs and
bacon; and on January first, they abolished food rationing.

No one traveling through Poland today can say that here is a happy country.
The production of Polish industry is
being poured into the almost bottomless demand of reconstruction. There
are so many bridges to be repaired, so
many houses to be rebuilt, that no one
can guess how soon the average Pole
will begin to approach the level of well-
being of the American worker of fifty
years ago. The Poles have been pushed
around for so many centuries that it has
left an almost permanent scowl on their
faces. The women seem tired and
frowzy, the men thin lipped and harsh.
Their shoes and clothes are patched,
their eyes lusterless with permanent
weariness.

If the loyalty of man could be bought
with bread alone, the trend of improvement would make the communist government of Poland secure beyond
challenge. But men are curious crea-
tures, whose loyalty springs from many
sources. In a Silesian mine I talked with
a miner who had just come home after a
twenty-year stay in France. We chatted
in French and I asked him how he liked
coming home after his life in the western world. He thought for a moment
and said: "I don't know yet. We are eating twice as well here as we ate in
France—but there's twice as much government to deal with." The perplexity
of the miner, written large over his millions of fellow citizens, is a thing that
confounds western observers trying to

decide how successfully the Polish government is winning the support of its common people.

The formula of politics in Poland is the same as in every Eastern European communist land: to keep the loyalty of the working class, to win over the peasantry, and to cause the middle class to wither away and disappear. The job of the party is to keep the people enthusiastic, acquiescent or cowed, as the case may be, but under any circumstances to keep them under control while the technicians of the great plans strive to carry out the programs which they hope will bring socialist wealth to erase the memory of the past.

This means that freedom as we know it does not exist. The press is vetted of every thought that might seduce the people from the Spartan tasks set for them; police ferret out and imprison every disturbing element. There is peril in disagreeing.

In Poland, the formula of communist politics is applied by a tight cluster of tested revolutionaries whose iron spirit was forged in the hunted underground life of prewar Eastern Europe.

Until last summer an unofficial triumvirate ran the party. First was Jacob Berman, the theoretician and political boss of the party, a quiet man with an almost professorial appearance. The second was Hilary Minc (pronounced Mintz), an economist who has won the postwar reputation of being the most brilliant production man in Eastern Europe. The third was Wladislaw Gomulka, a folklore character. Born of the working class, Gomulka had been

beaten by police and jailed for his part in demonstrations. When the Nazis came, he remained to organize resistance and counterterror to oppose the conquerors. Gomulka, with intimate peasant associations, was probably the most popular of the triumvirate.

In the background was Boleslaw Bierut, a man of peasant parentage whose early career had led him to the underground revolutionary movement and prewar Polish prisons. He had resigned his membership in the Communist Party when he was named president in 1944 and his "Polish Provisional Government" had jolted across the ravaged battlegrounds to Warsaw in a Red Army lorry in 1945.

Political Tug-of-War

Last summer the triumvirate disagreed as to how the formula should be carried out, and in disagreeing they rocked the party to its foundations.

At a Cominform meeting in June, 1948, it had been decided that all member states of the Soviet bloc begin immediately on a program to collectivize the farms of their predominantly peasant lands. Tito violently disagreed and his disagreement split the Cominform wide open.

In Poland, Tito's friend, Gomulka, insisted first that Poland should not join in the chorus of denunciation against Tito, and secondly that it was too early to begin collectivization. The peasants had been through two hard years, Gomulka said. They were just beginning to come back; talk of collectivization would terrify them.

For two days the Central Committee of the Communist Party argued the question with Gomulka in a closed meeting that ended in tears, repentance, forgiveness and pledges of mutual faith. But when the meeting was over Gomulka was finished, at least temporarily, as a major political factor in the party. The rift caused by the Gomulka defection was so critical Bierut was called from his nominal nonpartisan political Olympia to take the job of reuniting the party as its general secretary.

The program that Bierut, Minc and Berman applied after the split last summer was mild enough. They set as a target not collectives but co-operatives, and very modest goals were set for the program. Co-operatives would be formed for not more than one per cent of the land under cultivation, and this same goal would apply for each of the next two years. The government hoped to make co-operatives attractive to the farmers by offering them new farm machinery and the best of Poland's consumer goods. But the word that went whispering through the village was not "co-operative" but "collective." Two years previously the Communists had given them the new land of Silesia and Pomerania, and had divided up the landlords' estates into peasant farms; now all this, according to rumor, was to be taken back. The idea of collectives brought a typical peasant reaction. Last fall they began to slaughter their cattle, just as Russia's peasants had done eigh-

teen years ago when the Soviets launched collectivization. How deep or how widespread this peasant action may be, no one can judge. On a mass scale, it could not only torpedo Poland's new meat treaty with Great Britain but also, by cutting supplies, it could force the reimposition of rationing.

The Polish government carries itself today with an air of confidence and solid self-assurance that no other Communist government except Russia's can match. Within its own borders, the underground that fought the Communist regime is dead; new buildings are going up; the beat of life is beginning again after ten years of horror and hunger. On this horizon there lies only one cloud: war.

Whatever may be on the mind of other capitals, in the thinking of Warsaw's leaders, peace is the cold political prerequisite for all they plan to do. All their planning, all their efforts to cultivate loyalty among their people rest on the hope that they will be given a chance to show how much better they can make life than the old oligarchy that ruled Poland before the Nazi invasion. War would steal the chance.

The Poles and War

Their fear of war is compounded by another certainty: war today can only mean war between the Soviet Union and the United States. The Polish government knows, and wants the rest of the world to know, too, that in any such war it is on the side of the Soviet Union. But the government also realizes that its people still remember centuries of fearing and hating the Russians; and while vast suspicion of Russia persists in millions of Polish minds, there exists, side by side, an immeasurable, but great, affection for the United States. War, this year or the next, would be a testing of loyalties that the present regime might not survive.

In attempting to lead their people away from this old affection for the United States, the present Polish government uses two themes. The first is calculated digesting of world news into propaganda capsules so that America is unscrupulously presented to the Polish people as a nation directed by the most amoral, money-hungry, ruthlessly imperialist leadership in the world.

The second is by identifying America with Germany. However much Poles differ among themselves on Russia and America, and they do so deeply, they are united in their hatred of Germany. When they think of the past decade, they think of it across the mist of dread the Nazis left. When the Polish government presents to its people Germany and America as allies, it is reawakening the sharpest emotion that the Poles know.

In this campaign of ideas, the Poles are aided by American policy. When the Voice of America tells of German recovery under the Marshall Plan, the Poles consider it confirmation of their government's thesis that America is rebuilding Germany. America's subsidy to the German zone of occupation and America's desire to see Germany get back her east-

ern strip that was given to Poland, buttress a growing number of Poles in their feeling that America is a potential enemy.

The night we left Poland, I stood at one end of a wet, gloomy railroad station waiting for a train to Czechoslovakia. There was a woman standing near me and we fell to talking. The government, she said, was hard, and no one enjoyed life; the once rich were poor now and the poor hadn't become rich. Russians, she volunteered, were savages; they really ran the government, she was certain.

I asked her what she thought about America. "You Americans," she said. "What choice do *you* leave us? Every day we hear over your radio about the airlift to Berlin. Do you expect us to love you because you feed the Germans? They let us starve; now you will fight in order to feed them. They killed my father at Auschwitz and my brother in a labor camp. What do you leave us to hope for?"

Lukewarm Welcome

The bitterness mobilized by the government against Americans is a rather impersonal one. If you come as a visitor you will be welcomed as a dollar-bearing animal and the Poles need dollars to buy machinery, cotton and oil. Visas are more easily granted for Poland than for any other European country. You will not be welcomed in Warsaw, but this is because Warsaw lacks rooms to accommodate you. The Hotel Polonia and Hotel Bristol are reserved only for journalists, diplomats and dignitaries. But the Poles will entertain you in Wroclaw at good hotels and show you the Exhibition of the Recovered Territories, as handsome and artistic a fair as was ever put together in Europe. They will be glad to have you visit Cracow, the Polish "Vatican," their only major city undamaged by the war, or the spas and skiing resorts of the Tatra and Giant Mountains. Trains are efficient, but far from pleasant; Minc has the Poles working on boxcars to haul coal and has not yet given the word to put in service first-class passenger cars or sleepers. Wherever you go, however, you will find food—mounds of bread and butter, stuffed carp, borsch, meat, whipped sour cream and rich pastries.

One thing the returning visitor will find missing in postwar Poland are the Jews who formed one tenth of its population ten years ago. They are gone now, and with them has disappeared that ancient community which for almost a thousand years cradled the custom and convention of rabbinical learning. Of the 3,500,000 Jews who once lived in Poland only 100,000 remain. Perhaps 150,000 managed to flee safely, but the others are ghosts in the night winds or white ash strewn over the fields about Tremblinka, Majdanek, Belzec and Auschwitz.

The 100,000 still living in Poland move and live among other Poles as full citizens. Some are coal miners, some are workers in leather and other crafts. Some are government leaders. But they are separate individuals. They are no longer a community with a community's tradition.

Macabre Monument

In their passing, they have left a last awful monument. Their monument is Auschwitz, tucked away in the dark moorlands of Southern Poland, beneath the rim of mountains where the Tatras stretch out to touch the Carpathians. Auschwitz is now a national museum and it has been cleaned up as befits a national museum. The paths are neat, the guide has a set speech, the human hair is stacked in bins, the endless dumps of spectacles, toothbrushes, shoes, suitcases stripped from the 4,500,000 victims murdered there are neatly cased.

If you ask the director of Auschwitz, he will tell you how to get down the muddy road to Brzezinka only a mile away. At Brzezinka, nothing has been cleared and the gray shacks are huddled in endless monotony along the spur line that brought living people to the crematoria. Here the Nazi technicians gave mass murder top-production efficiency; here, in August, 1944, they hit peak capacity of an estimated 24,000 murders a day. At that rate, they believed, it might be possible to destroy the entire people of the Polish nation.

Many of the guides are former inmates and they do not like to go to Brzezinka. But if you can persuade one to come with you he will explain that toward the end the Nazi efficiency experts decided that although gas chambers killed fastest, the accompanying crematoria were too expensive and slow to handle the bodies. The Nazis found that it was cheapest to sandwich the bodies of the people they killed between wooden logs in the open air or in sunken pits, and then burn them. The guide will show you how to recognize the filled-in pits by the wild, lush, yellow color of the grass that grows from the enriched soil, contrasting with the green of the normal grass.

One or two of the pits were left open, in the German rush to get out at the end. These have since filled with rain water, but the half-burned bodies are still there and the water still bubbles, four years later, with slow fermentation. If you bend down close to the water's edge, the guide says, you can hear it.

HOLIDAY June, 1949

NEW FORCE IN EUROPE: THE CATHOLIC LEFT

The scene was Paris, the time evening, the occasion the Communist riots protesting the arrival of General Ridgway.* As the rain drizzled down on the milling mob, the police—their white truncheons flailing against the spike-studded clubs of the demonstrators—charged one particularly firm knot of demonstrators and swept them off to the station house. There, smarting from their wounds, the police, true to the code of vengeance that rules every station house in the world, proceeded to beat the most conspicuous troublemakers to a pulp in retaliation for the two hundred cops who had been wounded and the twenty-three who had been hospitalized.

Such a roughhouse would have passed unnoticed in the violence of the day's events had it not, during the next week, set off a controversy in which the Archbishop of Paris, Monsignor Feltin, was ranged against the Prefect of Paris Police, M. Baylot. For two of the rioters beaten by the police were priests of the Catholic Church—Fathers Louis

Bouyer and Bernard Cagne. Dressed in the rough working clothes of Paris's toiling citizens and thus stripped of the protection of the cloth, they had been beaten along with the Communists they accompanied. Furthermore, Paris learned, the priests had been practicing no deception in casting off frock for working clothes and had been trapped by no accident. They had rioted with the Communists against the police. Furthermore, the Church, instead of repudiating them, was defending them.

To morning newspaper readers, Catholic and non-Catholic alike, the report brought surprise and consternation. If, however, they had been alert to the slow but profound ferment simmering in the bosom of the oldest of churches, the report would have brought neither surprise nor consternation but a quiver of recognition. They would have known that the arrested priests were true priests, not Communists, submissive not to the party but to the discipline of the Church, which had given them a mission that ultimately had ranged them against the authority of the state by the side of the Church's worst enemy.

*Matthew B. Ridgway, the new commander of NATO.

What were they doing there?

The answer is not to be found in a minute analysis of the events of that day, nor of the individual decisions of the two priests. The answer is to be found only in tracing the vast restlessness of faith which today has touched every Catholic land in Europe, not even excepting Spain, and has reached its most vivid expression in France, the traditional center of Catholic ferment.

The Paris Mission

The two priests—who were released the morning after their arrest—were members of the Mission de Paris, whose headquarters are on a hushed street behind a leafy cemetery on the slope of Montmartre. The quiet, gray upstairs offices of the Mission de Paris do not seem like the headquarters of a movement with revolutionary implications; but there, with the cold precision of laboratory analysts, the spokesmen of the mission will tell not only how the two priests came to participate in a political riot, but also why, in the deep tide of change in French souls, it was necessary for them to be there.

They start by telling of the slow decline of the authority of the Church in France all through the last century, describing how, by the turn of the century, it had been rejected and repudiated in a country ninety-five per cent of whose citizens had been brought up as nominally Catholic. By opposing, at every step, each of France's fumbling efforts toward republican liberty, the Church had gradually lost the trust of a vast majority of middle-class French citizens who loved and supported their republic. What had happened to the Church among the working class was even worse. The Industrial Revolution had drawn peasant Frenchmen away from their villages, and from the village curés, to the ugly slums of the new industrial centers where they worked in a savagery of twelve-hour days and seven-day weeks, living a life not so much hostile to the Church as absolutely divorced from it. In the vacuum of the workers' dreary bitterness, the faith of Marxist revolution had replaced the faith of Catholicism.

Whither Thou Goest . . .

The Mission de Paris itself was not founded until the recent Liberation. Its inspiration came from an obscure chaplain, the Abbé Godin, whose experience in organizing Catholic working-class groups had convinced him that French workers should be appealed to not as if they were strayed sinners but as if they were pagans who had never heard of the Church. In 1944 he persuaded the Diocese of Paris to open a new mission whose sole purpose was to re-establish the Church in the slums. Today the mission counts twenty-odd priests who are at once priests, missionaries, and workers. They wear no frocks, for in certain parts of Paris the frock is hated; they work in factories on the regular eight-to-four shifts of Paris workmen. They wear overalls and working blues and live on their earnings. They dwell wherever they can rent a room in the slums, as other bachelor workers do. Only one thing sets them apart from the others—at night, when they come home, they don their vestments and offer Mass in their rooms in the presence of any fellow workers who wish to attend.

'Neither for Nor Against'

They join the dominant union in their plants—usually the Communist-controlled CGT. They do so not because they are for or against the Communists, but because whatever the experience of any worker may be—in hunger, in unemployment, in sickness, in strike, or even in riot—they must be part of it. When the Communists called for a demonstration against Ridgway, the two priests went with them—neither for nor against Ridgway, says the mission, but simply because the men they worked with at their automobile plants were going. Their presence was commanded by a strategy which has a longer range than Communist tactics. The strategy is to convince the workers that wherever they struggle, the Church is there too.

The adventure of the mission in Paris's industrial agglomeration is duplicated by 420 other worker-missionary-priests in other parts of France. Specially trained at a seminary in Lisieux for assignment to the "pagan" strata of French life, they have gone out to all of France's major industrial De-partments. They fish with the fishermen on the Channel coast; they hack coal in dark mines of the Nord; stripped to the waist and bronzed by the sun, they unload cargo as stevedores at the Marseilles wharves among the Senegalese, Algerians, and Italian immigrants whom the Communists now dominate.

Faith in Action

It is a hard, lonesome life—toil by day and devotions by night. Occasionally the Church fathers worry about their young priests, isolated from monastery or parish, hungry for human warmth and affection in the squalor all about them. Boarding in family homes, as some of them do, or drinking in the evening at cafés with other men, they are exposed to temptations that test them severely. One of the worker-priests, indeed, has recently married and left the Church—but continues to spread the gospel and faith among the workers in his own way.

The worker-priests have no politics. They have no blueprints of the Christian City to come. Their sole purpose is to win back souls to the sacraments in an adventure that, as the Mission de Paris says, will take fifty years before a first judgment can be made. Yet their work, whether the Church fathers recognize it or not, would lead to no larger a change than the opening of a few more churches in a country already equipped with hundreds of empty ones unless it were framed and sustained by a broader movement rising from the same restlessness of faith that has inspired their work.

This movement and this restlessness, for want of a better term, is called the Rise of the Catholic Left. The phrase is an artificial one, for the Catholic Left is a twofold minority—a leftist minority among Catholics and a Catholic minority among the Left. Yet in its persistence since the war, by its vigor, by its impact upon the groping minds of Europe in disillusion, the Catholic Left has now become one of the most important elements in European politics.

It is difficult to give a coherent account of what the Catholic Left is, for it is not an organized movement. In every country of western Europe except Spain, it shows the same clinical signs—a faction of left-wingers organized in a larger Catholic political party; millions of Catholic trade-unionists organized in Christian trade unions or led by acknowledged Catholics in secular trade unions; study groups of intellectuals weaving new theories; small groups of activists trying to press theory swiftly into practice.

In an age of disillusion, when to millions Marxism has become arid and the old political attitudes of Christianity and nineteenth-century liberalism no longer bring hope, the Catholic Left is trying to combine what best it can salvage in Christian doctrine and tradition and blend it with what best it can discern in new urgencies of reform and justice. It is set apart from previous Catholic experiences in politics in Europe by one great binding dynamic: Whereas Catholic movements have usu-

ally sought to brace and buttress authority brought down from the past, the Catholic Left seeks to change, to alter, to reweave the whole social fabric of Europe today.

Fighting Fascism

The morphology of the Catholic Left is seen best in France, for it is there that the Church in this century has been most rejected and thus compelled by the repudiation, to forge new ideas.

The historians of the French Catholic Left rightfully, of course, trace their roots far back into the past—as far back as the Gospels themselves, with their revolutionary content and their compassion for the poor. In more modern times, their story begins immediately after the turn of the century. It was then, in a France that prided itself on being republican and anti-clerical that a handful of chaplains began to organize small groups among the few workers who wished to remain Christian but believed in trade-unionism. It was then also that a few Catholic intellectuals began to sketch the outlines of a doctrine that would accept republicanism and imbue it with Christian faith.

The movement grew slowly. Not until after the First World War, indeed, did the Church send forth chaplains to organize a nation-wide net of Catholic workers youth groups, the Jeunesse Ouvrière Chrétienne. For the first time Catholic thinkers began to reach out politically and affect masses of agnostic Frenchmen. Some, like Jacques Maritain and Emmanuel Mounier, tried to work out a new philosophy marrying democracy inseparably to Christianity. Others, like Georges Bidault—who was to become Foreign Minister and Prime Minister of France after the Second World War—focused sharply on current events. *L'Aube,* Bidault's paper, insisted, as a Catholic journal, that the Spanish Republic was not the enemy and Franco not the friend of the Church.

Emergence of the M.R.P.

The little groups that formed and dissolved on this questioning fringe of the faith were, however, almost without importance in French life until the war brought defeat and the defeat brought the Resistance. For over a year, from the collapse of France until Hitler's attack on Russia, the Catholic Leftists were the best organized and most vigorous force in the Resistance. Their underground journals—like *Témoignage Chrétien*—their youth organizations, their intellectuals' study groups, their skeleton national structure of Catholic trade unions were able, in the underground, to channel behind their leadership all manner of fresh spirits and patriots who had previously been hostile or apathetic to anything tinged with Catholicism. When, belatedly, in 1941, Hitler's attack on Russia brought the Communists into the Resistance too, the Communists tried but were never able to erase the lead or wipe out the positions the Catholic Left had already established. When, in 1943, the underground

Council of National Resistance chose a new chief to replace the one the Gestapo had just captured, it chose Georges Bidault—a member of the Catholic Left.

The prominence of so many individual devout Catholics in the Resistance saved the Church in France. For Marshal Pétain, the senile dictator of Vichy, had so wrapped himself in the sanctity of the Church and had received such fervid support from so many imposing members of the hierarchy that the entire Church might have been stained with his record had it not been for the prodigious heroism and courage of the Catholics of the underground. When Liberation came, these Catholics of the underground had a new party called the M.R.P. (Mouvement Républicain Populaire) already prepared for the people of France, one unlike any they had known before. It was consecrated to a vast program of social reform midway between New Dealism and pure socialism, yet devoutly Catholic in spirit and purpose.

The Catholic Unions

The support of the Church and its influence over the millions of woman voters enfranchised for the first time after the Liberation combined with the M.R.P.'s own fine record of achievement to make it the largest party in France. If today the M.R.P. has lost this primacy as millions of Catholic voters have returned to more traditional parties of the Right, it remains still the main prop of the present Cabinet coalition, the equal of any of the other five big parties in the Assembly, and it controls the Ministry of Foreign Affairs as it has ever since the war.

Just as the M.R.P. emerged from the war as the chief rival of the Communists for the new and questioning voters of liberated France, the CFTC (Confédération Française des Travailleurs Chrétiens) emerged as the chief rival of the Communist-controlled CGT at the organized working-class level. What had been a skeleton national organization before the war had been fleshed out in the Resistance.

Like all trade-union groups in France, the CFTC has since lost strength in the slow erosion of working-class vitality since the war. But whereas the Communist CGT has fallen from an estimated six million adherents to an estimated two million, the Catholic unions have fallen from two million to one million. They hold their ground more firmly than the Communists, and in recent months have even been gaining in union elections.

The leftism of both the CFTC and the M.R.P., the chief creations of the wartime Catholic Left, has now been diluted by years of responsibility and power. The M.R.P. has seen much of its program written into the law of the land: A segment of industry has been nationalized, and the vast social-security system it demanded has been enacted. Its main unfinished business, which it still pursues with vigor, is the restoration of state subsidies to Catholic schools and the creation of a European union into which France will fit.

The leaders of the CFTC have likewise been tempered by the years; today they operate more like American trade-unionists than any other union leaders in France. They dig in and fight on bread-and-butter issues, pressuring the Deputies of the M.R.P. (whom they support) not for revolution but for higher wages and lower prices, more housing and paid vacations. The Church has lost its grip over the CFTC. Though its younger leaders still come from the Church-directed Jeunesse Ouvrière Chrétienne, they become in the CFTC as pragmatic as any other union leaders. If, in a local strike, the local priest sides with the boss, the CFTC will haul off and let him have it just as hard as any godless union would.

If the CFTC and the M.R.P. have thus settled down, it is not that the tug and moving rhythm of the movement to the Left has quieted. Within the M.R.P. a left-wing faction of at least fifteen to twenty Deputies is still fervid with the vision of the Christian-socialist France they hoped to build; they force the M.R.P. to remain the farthest left of the Cabinet elements within the working coalition of M. Pinay. Within the CFTC, another factional group of thinkers, publishing a magazine called *Reconstruction,* still keeps a doctrinal ferment simmering.

Rubbing Shoulders

Some of the newer postwar groups go so far left as to rub shoulders with the Communists. Such a one is the M.L.P.—Mouvement de Libération des Peuples. The M.L.P. is staffed and led by graduates of the Church's own Jeunesse Ouvrière Chrétienne, but it has gradually thrown off all Church control. Shortly after the war its members began as simple humanists to cultivate those areas of homely, stagnant misery that Socialist and Communist politicians had overlooked.

In the slums of factory districts they organized co-operatives of working-class girls and wives to provide nursing and housekeeping help for tired mothers who fell sick and could not care for home and children. They organized and now operate more than forty co-operative vacation camps in the mountains and by the shore for working-class families who cannot afford expensive holidays. Their members have formed co-operatives to buy and market potatoes and coal for families who want to shave a few francs off the necessities. Their weekly newspaper has a circulation of fifty thousand copies.

A certain naïveté, however, has led them, bit by bit, to comradeship with the Communists. Insisting politically on more money for social reforms and aid to the poor of France's shabby cities, they first began to oppose all appropriations for the war in Indo-China, then all defense expenditures. Next they fell into step with the Communists, chanting the clichés of the Stockholm "Peace" Appeal and the canards of American aggression and bacteriological warfare in Korea. In their bare and primitive little headquarters on the Left Bank they shed an equal amount of the same pure enthusiasm on visiting the sick and helping mothers and children as on denouncing their own government and that of the United States.

The Catholic Parties

The renascence of Catholicism in politics in Europe is, of course, a phenomenon that transcends terms of Right and Left. No working observer in Europe can overlook the fact that the governments of every one of America's allies on the continent of Europe has chosen its Foreign Minister, and usually its Prime Minister too, from frankly religious parties of Catholic inspiration. Only the Netherlands, where in this summer's election the Catholic Party lost control of the government to the Socialists, is currently an exception to this rule. No American statesman can be ignorant of the fact that the strongest working ally of American diplomacy on the continent is the Catholic urge to European union. When Robert Schuman of France, Konrad Adenauer of Germany, and Alcide De Gasperi of Italy gather to write treaties and discuss the future, they act instinctively out of a common religious inspiration that sees Europe reunited in a common faith and culture as it was before the days of the Reformation and the rise of nationalism.

But if these conservative Catholic spokesmen seem more supple, more enlightened, more socially conscious than their counterparts of other centuries, it is because each of them depends, in larger or smaller measure, on support from groups that only ten years ago were bitterly hostile to the Church—support mobilized for them by the Catholic Left.

In Italy, as in France, the most vigorous opposition to the Communist trade-union net is the Catholic trade-union net, the CISL; in Italy, too, the factional left-wingers within the dominant Christian Democrats keep the party's preponderant conservative majority from slipping too violently to the right. In Belgium, the Catholic trade unions oppose the dominant Socialist trade unions, and there too the Church is experimenting with worker-missionaries. In Germany, pressure exercised on the Government by the Catholic Left is no less constant than in France, but it is less strong and lacks the flair of France's movement. This is partly because of Germany's Protestant-Catholic cleavage, and partly because Germany's war had no Resistance movement and Left Catholics have no such rallying experience to pull them together. *Mitbestimmungsrecht,* the chief social reform of postwar Germany, the code whereby German workers are given a share in the control of their plants, was of Catholic inspiration and guidance, although adopted and claimed by the Socialists as their victory.

The Intellectuals

Even more than the working class and the politicians, the intellectuals of Europe are hungry for new ideas. Thus the most important magazine of opinion in Germany—the *Frankfurter Hefte*—is the citadel of the Catholic Left. And of France's two most influential monthlies of opinion, one is Jean-Paul Sartre's rationalist *Temps Modernes,* but the other is the profoundly Christian *Esprit.*

Esprit and the *Frankfurter Hefte* are more than magazines. They are springboards for study and discussion groups all across their countries. The *Frankfurter Hefte,* whose monthly circulation is the largest in all West Germany, boasts of at least 464 *Kreise* independently organized by the readers of the magazine. *Esprit* offers no count of the numbers of *cercles* which are organized by its subscribers, but they exist and are active in every university town and intellectual center of France.

For *Esprit* and its readers, the evil in modern civilization is money. Money and the measures of money, they feel, have resulted in that type of capitalism and bourgeois civilization which in France had reduced the worker to primitive savagery and paralyzed the middle class with hopeless cynicism. History is only an advance of men to the understanding of Christ, and men shackled by the measures of money cannot know Christ. The new society, the true Christian society, must have other measures and values.

In a recent issue of *Esprit* is a leading article by Professor Henri Bartoli of the University of Grenoble, one of the leading luminaries in the constellation of *Esprit.* Bartoli finds the civilization of the Soviet union a higher one than that of the United States, for the Soviets have freed men from the reign of money. Where the Soviets go wrong, he holds, is that for the reign of money they have substituted the reign of the technician with its inevitable tendency to edge off into police rule. The error in Soviet society springs from its Marxist philosophy, which sees all men related to one another only as they are related to the process of production; this rigid status strips men of the "mystery of personality." Though the Soviet world, according to Bartoli, has freed men of the grip of money measures, it has not given them the Christian freedoms.

The doctrines of the *Frankfurter Hefte* are much more pragmatic, less "advanced" in the theoretical sense, more closely linked to practical issues of the day than those of *Esprit*. Consequently they exert a greater influence in German trade unions, over the German radio, through radio commentators and columnists, in the main stream of German life, than those of *Esprit* do in France. For the *Frankfurter Hefte* the abstract evil is not money but what it chooses to call the Restoration.

The Restoration is the old order of authority and relationships in pre-Hitler Germany, and the *Frankfurter Hefte* sees Konrad Adenauer and the Allied occupation swiftly pressing Germany back into the old authoritarian molds. The German Catholic Left attack on the Restoration is more practical, more specific than the French Catholic Left attack on the evils of French civilization. The first draft law of *Mitbestimmungsrecht* was written in the offices of the *Frankfurter Hefte*. Its men have plugged for European union as the vessel of their revolution more fervently and more persistently than the men of *Esprit*. Though more friendly to American civilization than *Esprit*, the *Frankfurter Hefte* also questions U.S. policies. For example, it does not wish to see Germany rearmed. It would prefer to make Germany part of the neutral belt of Central Europe that runs from Sweden to Switzerland, while merging socially and culturally with other countries of the West.

It is thus a quest in common for new answers rather than a common doctrine that pulls the men of *Esprit*, the men of the *Frankfurter Hefte*, and Catholic Left intellectuals everywhere in western Europe together. All of them feel that Europe's old ideas are no longer valid in the twentieth century—neither Marxist ideas, liberal ideas, nor dogma. Somewhere in the future, they say, is a point where that which is valid in Christianity meets and shapes again the marching forces of the twentieth century.

The Church Militant

What the Church fathers think of this rustling in the cathedral is difficult to discern. Rome has been very cautious in imposing discipline within the national churches or within those orders, like the Dominicans in France or the Jesuits in Germany, which seem most affected intellectually by the ferment of their lay brethren. The French Church, protected by its tradition of Gallican autonomy, seems the most benevolent of the churches to the new movement and its spokesmen, but even in Germany the bishops seem unwilling to check or cramp its development.

Perplexed themselves, the spokesmen of the Catholic Left know that they perplex their Church even more. "Rome doesn't know what to make of us," one of them told me. "Rome believes it lives in an age of persecution, and so it is on the defensive; everywhere it is rigid and unyielding before the changes. But we—we believe the Christian must go out and meet the changes, and possess them. Today it is we who are the Church Militant, not Rome."

THE REPORTER September 16, 1952

France and Germany—Fear and Hatred

The fate of a united Europe hinges on both nations' ability to overcome a thousand years of bloody memories.

PARIS

Georges Heuillard is dead now.

But no one who sat in the crowded gallery of the National Assembly of France during the great debate on the European Army a year ago this month—when Georges Heuillard was carried, frail and trembling, to the rostrum—will ever forget that day. Pleading the indulgence of the Assembly for the condition in which he had come before it, M. Heuillard explained that he had come to make his last speech. He had come to talk about the dream of a European Army, which summons Frenchmen and Germans to abandon nationhood and unite in a new community—and he had come to fulfill a vow.

At the concentration camp of Flossenburg in Germany, where every one of his Resistance comrades had been butchered, he had sworn with them a common oath—that if any one of them emerged from the hell alive he would dedicate himself to see that Germany should never be permitted an army again. He alone had come back from Flossenburg alive, crippled and incurably ill.

"I am going to die, Sir," he said turning to the Minister of Foreign Affairs, "I am condemned to death. My election to office found me in a hospital. I am dying because of the German Army. I do not want my sons or my grandsons to be incorporated as comrades-in-arms with the tyrants and butchers of their father, that my son should serve side by side with the son of von Stulpnagel." The interests of Germany, he continued, are eternal—to thrive, to rearm, to reunite, to turn again on France and sack her. Then, his short speech having visibly drained his strength, he concluded: "I have done my duty. I promised my comrades that I would. I am happy that destiny today has let me replace the strength which is now gone from me with this energy that lets me come before you and cry: 'Beware the Germans! Beware the Germans!'"

As M. Heuillard finished and limped down from the rostrum in the arms of friends, the entire Assembly of France rose to its feet—Gaullists on the right, Communists on the left, Socialists, Radicals, Conservatives, Catholics in the center, all of them united on the

180

floor for the first time since Liberation—cheering him in a frenzy that made the hall an animal pit. And six months later M. Heuillard, as he predicted himself, was dead.

Though Georges Heuillard is now dead, the emotion out of which he spoke persists today with almost undiminished force deep in the bowels of France. For M. Heuillard, a relatively inconspicuous Deputy from central France, had not created that emotion. His sense of death had merely freed him from the restraint which rests on other Deputies who know they must continue to live in a world of unescapable fact. Only death had licensed him to voice that deep, instinctive emotion on which all Frenchmen have been nursed to manhood.

THE FEELING of Frenchmen for Germans—and of Germans for Frenchmen, which is just as deep and bitter—is probably the most ancient force in the politics of Western Europe. It goes back 1,100 years to the first documented treaty in history, the Treaty of Verdun, by which three barbarian princes quarreling over the domain and tribes of their father formally separated the people on one side of the Rhine from the people on the other and launched them in rivalry.

It echoes vaguely but powerful even further back than that—to the time of Julius Caesar, who, with his magic political intuition, conquered the savage Gauls on the pretext of protecting them from the yet more savage Teutons. And,

were records available, it could probably be traced even further back than that to the days of the Druids, of Oden and of Leki.

THIS FEELING has, for almost a millennium, prevented Europe from becoming Europe. And today, when the making of a European Community is the first order of business of the civilized world, an adventure on which all Atlantic and American diplomacy is based, the feeling of Frenchmen about Germans and Germans about Frenchmen is the greatest burden on the new world struggling to be born.

The "why" of this feeling is one of those mysteries that perplex all observers of political life—to answer the "why" seriously is as difficult as to say why cats hate dogs, or why the Black Lolos and White Lolos of the Tibetan foothills murder each other on sight. The attitudes of Germans and Frenchmen to each other change in the swinging cycle of the centuries, as now one, now the other power gains the upper hand. A century goes by in which French armies march across Germany, blasting, burning, sacking and looting the country; and then follows another century in which the Germans do the same.

Clash and counter-clash follow one another endlessly, the narrative monotonously recounted by German and French historians as variations on two central themes. For the French historian, the theme is Invasion—the German wars are an endless attempt by the

French to hold back the Teutons who come surging from over the Rhine. For the German historian the theme is Germany's struggle to become one single nation in the teeth of France's everlasting diplomatic effort to keep her weak, divided and separated into tiny meaningless states and compartments.

IN THE cycle of this century it is the Germans who have had the upper hand. Having achieved national unity only eighty years ago, they have terrorized the French and ravaged them as never before in the history of the two feuding countries. And the current emotions of politics all reflect the present phase of the cycle in which the upper hand is Germany's.

IN ANY other domain of political analysis it is dangerous or deceitful to write that a nation "feels" this or a nation "feels" that. But when one writes of France and Germany popular emotion is so clear that generalization becomes a worthy substitute for fact.

Outside the narrow arena of technical politics, where the Deputies of the Assembly must face France's future in sober consideration of the facts of the world, French popular feeling about the Germans can be summarized in two easy words: fear and hate.

These are not contrived emotions, as emotions of the Soviet world are contrived by Government indoctrination and purpose. They spring from French life in this century. France has been in-

vaded and looted by the Germans in 1870, in 1914 and 1940. Every generation of Frenchmen has called the Germans by a different name—"les Prusses," "les Boches," or "les Fritz," and each name marks an invasion.

THE MEMORIES that spring from these invasions are preserved, moreover, not simply by words and anecdotes; they are imbedded in the soil and face of the country. One goes picnicking in the suburbs of Paris and stretches on the grass under the apple tree in the meadow—and there, when one stretches out relaxed, one finds half covered by the grass an angry stone epitaph: "Ici fut sauvagement assassiné par les Allemands, Robert Martelleau, le 19 Aout 1944—âgé de 17 ans."

School children visit the National Assembly, and as they pass the gray walls they peer at the four white marble plaques that record the names of four simple Parisians shot dead at this point by the Germans in the summer of 1944.

In the public square before the *mairie* of every village in the land is the monument to the dead of 1914–18 where the wastage and sometimes the total obliteration of the village's ancient families are recorded. It is in these squares, in the shadow of sorrow, that little children play, old men doze and young men court their girls.

These ordinary French people do not think in terms of statistics, dates, or great decision. They know only that Germany is strong, and growing stronger. The statistics say that truncated Western Germany counts only 48,000,000 Germans as against 42,000,000 Frenchmen. But there are 17,000,000 more Germans in East Germany, 7,000,000 in Austria, several million elsewhere. Without counting, the Frenchman knows that there are twice as many Germans in Europe as Frenchmen.

Without reading the details of trade and industry, Frenchmen know that Germany is booming while France is frustrated by inflation at home and bleeding to disaster abroad with war in Asia. Vaguely they remember that Germany was to have been punished, bound, purged, rendered impotent; yet, somehow, Germany today is the prime source of energy on the Continent. Germany weighs on them.

ONE FRESHER emotion finally complicates the primordial French instincts of fear and hate. It is an emotion linked with treason. In every town, in every village of France, the German occupiers seduced individual Frenchmen to collaboration during the war. The collaborators were unquestioned traitors—but in those days they covered their treason by mouthing big words about Franco-German friendship, the need of a European community and the ending of the age-old irrational feud. Now that the shape of world politics forces France to partnership with Germany, the collaborators lift their voices again and preen themselves as being simply "premature Europeans." The enthusiasm of former traitors for the new partnership with

Germany operates in the mind of millions of their countrymen to make them question the true virtues of the new alliance.

SINCE FEAR and hate are the dominant emotions of the French in this cycle of the old rivalry, then probably the dominant German emotions are envy and contempt.

The Germans' envy of the golden sun and fair fields of France is as timeless as the clash itself. The classic expression of this envy was coined by the greatest of German monarchs, Frederick the Great, who defined happiness by saying: "*Froehlich wie der leber Gott in Frankreich*" (Happy as dear God in France). But the essential nostalgia of Germans for what they know of French life is even more vivid on the lips of this generation's Wehrmacht veterans than in the phrase of the great king.

Whenever one stops on the smooth, ribboning autobahns of Germany to give a hitchhiker veteran a lift on his way, wherever one falls into conversation with a man who is willing to talk of the war, the memory of France seems to glow golden in his mind. The campaigns in Russia, in the Balkans, in Central Europe, in Africa seem to have left the German veteran with no emotion except bitterness. But France—ah, France, they say, that was different.

France was where they found perfumes and stockings for their ladies, where they bought butter for their families, where they lived fat, easy and happy until company by company they were sucked off to the distant bloody fronts. France is where the German student, the German middle-class family, the ex-officer all want to go back to spend their vacation, to see Paris again, to know Burgundy once more, to sun on the Riviera sands.

With this emotion of desire goes a complementary emotion of contempt. And it is the contempt, rather than the envy, which translates most easily into politics. German contempt for the French, in this phase of the cycle, has its roots in the swift and unbelievable collapse of the vaunted French Army before a handful of German panzer divisions in the spring of 1940. Nothing can erase the German memory of that superlatively easy victory.

AND THUS, when the Germans talk of the French their contempt and their envy blend imperceptibly—France is a beautiful country, they seem to say, its wines, its foods, its soil, its sun, its monuments all so magnificent. But the French! What a mess the French have made of France; how wonderfully France would thrive under German management!

German parliamentarians, comparing their own stable Bundestag with the French Assembly constantly in crisis, consider France unreliable: "If you force us to join the French," said one, "we'll have to do it. But if France proves a swamp that can't be drained, then we must insist on dealing with America directly."

German industrialists, unaware of France's great technical achievements since the war, still claim (erroneously) that the two best steel plants of France were those built in Lorraine before 1914, when Germany ruled Lorraine.

There are, to be sure, contrary points of view, but these are usually in the world of culture. In letters, in the plastic arts, in philosophy and science, in periodical journalism, French achievement still wrings respect from the Germans. But real Francophiles of importance in Germany are few.

IT IS against this tradition of enmity and this immeasurable gulf of suspicion that the events of this winter season take their seeming majesty. For, despite all the encumbrance of past passion and blood, France and Germany today stand closer together than ever before and their sovereign but unhappy parliaments have been wrestled to the point where, in the next few months, they must decide whether to submit their sons to a common uniform, common flag and a common command.

This revolutionary event has been produced by a number of forces which the statesmen of neither France nor Germany have been able to escape.

The first of these forces is the menace of the Russians. Neither the Germans nor the French can ever hope to defend themselves in the very near future with their own resources alone. They are in peril. To hold the Russians at bay in Central Europe, Germany and France must combine their efforts. The reading of the map, the reports of intelligence, the addition of divisions which ordinary people cannot weigh, press the statesmen inexorably forward in their course to union.

The second force is the United States. Over and over since 1948, with each portion of aid, with every shipment of arms, Americans in Europe have told Europeans that all American aid to their chaotic society, along with Europe's own hope of survival, depend on their coming together in a unity. Some Europeans insist that without America, France and Germany would still be making faces at each other across the Rhine. Others insist that had it not been for rash and reckless American pressure, France and Germany would have made their own union, more certainly and successfully, even if more slowly. But both schools agree that at this moment in the cycle it is America which has pressed the Governments of the two countries to their present positions.

A third force, perhaps the most difficult to define, is also perhaps the most important. It is the influence of the Catholic Church. Both in France and in Germany, the Catholic Church has reconquered a political influence it has not known for centuries.

The Soviets, cutting East Germany from Western Germany, sheared off the most important Protestant centers of the nation. Protestants in Western Germany today are reduced to a bare numerical equality with Catholics. Their Government is captained by the Christian Democratic party, led by Konrad Adenauer, one of the most devoutly Catholic statesmen of modern times.

IN FRANCE, similarly, the post-war years have been a revitalization of Catholicism both in spirit and influence. The Catholic M. R. P. party has insisted on, and received, direction of the French Foreign Office since 1945.

From 1948 until last month the French Foreign Minister was Robert Schuman of the M. R. P., a man whose piety is unexcelled even by Konrad Adenauer. It was these two men, knowing each other, trusting each other, inspired by a common religious political faith, who step by step led the parties and the Cabinets they dominated to accept the knowledge of the Russian challenge and to entertain the vision that has never died in the church's mind—of a Europe reunited in the Christian faith. One of the most striking measures of the vitality of this vision was the fact that when Schuman was removed from office during the last reshuffle of the French Cabinet his replacement was chosen from within his own Catholic party— Georges Bidault. Bidault himself could well serve as a symbol of the torture of spirit with which Frenchmen have been brought to acknowledge the need for alliance.

For it was Georges Bidault who flirted with death dodging the German Gestapo in the days when he was underground president of the French Council for National Liberation during the Nazi occupation, and it was Georges Bidault who declared only seven years ago, when France was thirsting for vengeance, "many things change with time—but Germany is something that never changes." Yet today the same Georges Bidault is Foreign Minister in a Cabinet in which he has promised to lead the fight on the floor of the French Assembly for conclusion of the European Army Treaty binding Germany and France into one community.

BOTH FRENCH and German Governments realize that now, in this last-ditch battle for acceptance of union, they are talking not so much to their people as a whole but to their parliaments. The people cannot be wooed from their old emotions until the new world proves a better one; but the parliaments must decide whether it is reasonable to give the new world a chance.

French Deputies rise and insist that union is a snare and delusion, that the Germans will turn and betray as they always did. Asks one: Did not Napoleon and his European army come to disaster when his Prussians and Saxons went over to the Russians at the Battle of Leipzig? Who will guarantee, asks another, that the new German divisions can be made into a one-way army—one that marches only East, never West? Have we not gone far enough in merging our heavy industry with the Germans in the Schuman Plan, ask others? Must we now merge our sons, too?

In the German Bundestag members raise other questions. Say the Nationalists: If the West needs German arms, let the West deal with Germany directly, give her a national army in NATO, not this monstrous half-beast, half-machine organization called Europe. Will not a merger with the French doom Germany to eternal division from her Eastern territories, asks the Socialist opposition to Adenauer? Is not the Adenauer-Schuman plan of union a scheme of the "Black International" ask the Protestants?

THESE ARE the questions on the floor of Assembly and Bundestag. And to all these questions the Adenauers and the Schumans reply over and over again: What other way is there? How else can we build the future? How else can we defend ourselves? How else can we retain American support?

What alternative is there to union but resumption of the feud? No one offers any answer to these questions—no answer but the echoes of a thousand years of bloody history and memories of countless millions of silent dead.

THE NEW YORK TIMES MAGAZINE
February 1, 1953

Germany—Friend or Foe?

Germany is now one of West Europe's strongest nations—potentially a mighty ally or a powerful enemy. On her future may rest the fate of the world . . . and no one knows which way she'll go. Here's an expert's special report?

It is two in the morning, and I wake to the sound of singing. I get up, throw open the window, and lean out. I see only the black streets of Düsseldorf, wet with rain, shimmering in the street lights—deserted. But from around the corner, I can hear young, strong voices in a marching song. I try to make out the words and tune. It is no song I recognize, and the voices fade in the distance.

I go back to bed and think of how often, on my visits to West Germany since the war, I have listened for voices, always trying to catch the echo of remembered cadences. Song in Germany is different from song in other countries. In Germany, when they sing, strangers in the beer halls lock arms and sway in tribal brotherhood, keeping time to the music; or friends singing on their way home from a party find they are no longer strolling, but tramping to the undertread, the beat in the music. Song in Germany can be dangerous.

So always, in Germany, I listen to the singing. Other people will tell you they have heard it. An intelligence report comes in of the German Border Guard singing the Nazi Horst Wessel Lied in its barracks in one town. In another town, someone confides, he has heard people singing Wir Fahren Gegen England—We Are Driving Against England. But I myself, in all these years, have never heard the Germans singing any of the old songs, not even Lili Marlene.

Indeed, I have never felt more at home or at peace on any postwar visit to Germany than I have this winter. Yet I have been listening more sharply than ever, for the Atlantic world has summoned the Germans to put together a new army. Only 35 years ago, the Treaty of Versailles permitted the Germans an army rigidly limited to 100,000 men; out of that cramped *Reichswehr* Hitler succeeded in six years in building the army which drenched this same Atlantic world in blood. Now a new German army of 500,000 men is to be brought into being. In three years it will furnish 12 divisions to man the line against the Russians in central Europe, more than twice the divisions we Americans maintain there, three times as many as either the British or French.

This army will swing the balance of power decisively, perhaps permanently,

187

to the Atlantic nations. But it will also make the Germans once more masters in their own house. It will restore to German hands the tools of destruction and force so desperately wrenched from them less than ten years ago.

I have too often traveled the roads of Europe, pausing at the fields of white crosses which mark the American dead of two wars with these people, to forget what happened the last time German soldiers held such force and power in their grasp.

How will it go this time? Is it dangerous? If so, to whom? To the Russians? To us? To the fresh and fragile German democracy we have so carefully nursed to life?

So I have been listening.

THE ANSWERS, if there are any, begin in Bonn, the capital of postwar Western Germany.

Only yesterday Bonn was a sleepy university town, snuggling along a curve of the Rhine just across the river from the murky hills where Siegfried slew his dragon. Tree-shaded, its old buildings throwing antique shadows over the narrow cobblestoned streets, Bonn became capital of Germany quite by accident—because in 1948 the handful of men who were writing Germany's new constitution found there an empty normal school where they could work conveniently. When they had finished in 1949, they simply decided to stay.

Like a chrysalis bursting, the town has changed since. The old normal school has added on a parliamentary chamber and two wings for offices. The school lawn, once kept cropped by several dirty yellow sheep, is now a manicured bed of velvet grass. The Gold-Red-Black banner snapping overhead proclaims that this is now the capital, seat of Germany's freely elected *Bundestag;* in summer, vacationing children from all over Germany serpentine through its chambers. The little white Palais Schaumberg of the Schaumberg-Lippe princelings has been transformed into the offices of Chancellor Adenauer; several old barracks have been converted to ministries.

Beyond this, the Germans have built huge new blocks of yellow stucco, of gray stone, of white facings, austere and crisp, rising out of the huddle of mellowed buildings of the past generation. This is a capital where a henhouse operator keeps his chicken-run and advertises his eggs across the street from the palace where Konrad Adenauer governs the nation. It is a capital where children sell raffle tickets on fat geese for St. Martin's feast at the front door of Germany's new Pentagon while, at its rear, an old woman grinds her hurdy-gurdy.

The contrast between Bonn and Berlin, the true and ancient capital of the Germans, speaks more eloquently than a volume on politics. Berlin, even in its blackened ruins, retains the somber magnificence of bygone glory. The Brandenburg Gate calls back every memory of Teutonic majesty. An air of greatness still lingers over the broad avenues of the Charlottenburger Chaussee, Unter den Linden or the Tiergarten, echoing yet of trumpeting parades of state. But nothing fits more naturally into Bonn's streets than the wheezing yellow Toonerville Trolleys which provide its daily transport.

Berlin once was a city constantly sputtering with the romantic excitement and repressed violence which is the essence of German history. Nazis and Communists vomiting up from the slums could hack one another to bits in the street or terrify cowering legislators into submission. The colossal buildings of the city amplified every little man's megalomania.

Bonn, by contrast, is soothing; its tranquillity and folksiness cap Germany's history most strangely. I have seen only one demonstration there in all my visits, and that was three years ago—a Communist protest meeting which in 15 minutes fizzled into nothing, absorbed by the drowsiness of the town.

Bonn's question is simple: Is this placid place the genuine capital of excitable Germany? Or is it a mirage? Are the men who govern here permanent or transient?

There are certain important points to note about Bonn. Here, in the *Bundestag*, sit 487 representatives of the people, put there by an election in which 86 per cent of all Germans eligible to vote went freely to the polls. (In our own 1952 elections, only 63 per cent of eligible Americans bothered to vote.) Yet among all these elected representatives of Germany there is not one latter-day Nazi, not one Communist. These men of the *Bundestag*, together,

have given Germans the freest, most decent government in their history. Together, they have captained a recovery from the ruins which is one of the wonders of the postwar world. In foreign policy they have, so far, proved themselves, even though clumsy, the most restrained and co-operative member of the Atlantic community. With the assistance of the Atlantic world, they have met each test more than adequately. German history and world events now hang, simply, on whether these men of Bonn can continue—on whether they have the strength to meet tomorrow's trials on their own.

For nearly ten years Western Germany has submitted itself, restless yet willing, to occupation by alien troops. These troops have provided the most important element of all government— order, discipline and the force to back it. No bloodshed has stained West Germany's streets, because Allied armies forbade it. No plots have hatched in Germany, because spies and intelligence agents of three nations have punctured them. Relieved of the cruel task of applying or threatening force against their own people in the starvation days when no people would voluntarily accept the stern measures necessary to cure their misery, the men of Bonn have also been spared the unpleasant duty of disciplining men and women who could vote them in or out of power. They have been able to focus on the wise and simple tasks of housekeeping.

Theoretically the occupation forces have had the legal right to move troops in or out of any town at will; to requisition homes and fields; to try Germans in their courts; to summon the chancellor like a servile chief before the Allied High Commission and veto any of the laws of his parliament. But the Allies have applied these rights with infinite caution—and diminishing need. It is now almost four years since proud Konrad Adenauer came, brief case in hand, to explain his conduct before the High Commission. It has been more than eight months since any law of the *Bundestag* has been vetoed by Allied action. But the occupation has been there nonetheless. The Germans have never forgotten the ultimate power of its intrusion in their daily lives.

On the day the Treaties of Paris are finally ratified, our occupation troops will change from conquerors to guests and allies of the Germans. The Bonn government will be on its own, alone with its own people, under the scrutiny of a world waiting to see if it can pass a new set of tests—tests which have crumpled German governments one by one, like peanut shells, all through this century.

It is not too difficult to define these tests, for they have natural or olden origins: the desire of a long-divided people (now dismembered into unnatural Western and Eastern halves) to recapture their unity by any means, fair or foul; schisms among themselves as to how the rewards and burdens of recovery shall be shared; a taste for glory; a curious tribal fascination with arms and violence. This last, more than any other, has meaning for us, the ex-enemies-newly-turned-allies,   because

no government of free German choice has ever been able to stop this martial lust short of those lunatic outbursts which have wet the world with tears and blood.

Against these trials of tomorrow the new Bonn government can probably marshal more internal support than any German government in the past. Above all, it can truthfully boast to its people that under its captaincy they have gone from starvation and squalor to good health and prosperity swifter than under any previous government in their history. All manner of sinister or unhealthy memories may lie dormant under the surface of the German mind. But present prosperity and hope blanket them all. Prosperity is the biggest positive fact in German politics today. It is a success story which millions of individual Germans share with the Bonn government—and they do not wish to risk it.

YOU CAN read the German success story in statistics. The statistics of today, sprayed over the Germany of yesterday, are dazzling.

The Germany of 1945 was a nation broken. Its cities were deserts of rubble. Its rivers were choked with sunken barges, its bridges were down. In the American zone alone, of 12,000 factories only 1,200 still worked—when they could find the raw materials. As rations dwindled to their low, in 1947, of 1,040 calories a day, Germany starved. Around the corners of garrison blocks and post exchanges, German girls offered themselves to the foreign troops for candy bars, soap or cigarettes.

The Allied powers, fearing lest their occupation be remembered as a savagery almost as dreadful as that which Germans had visited on the rest of Europe, poured in aid by the billions of dollars. Yet even as late as 1948, when, after currency reform, the early Marshall Planners felt they had finally straightened things out, they dared only hope that someday, when Marshall aid trickled off, the West Germans might be able to sustain themselves on a standard of living at most about three quarters as high as that Hitler had given them. This estimate also assumed that Germany, at that standard, would still have a billion-dollar deficit in foreign trade.

Against this background, the figures of Germany today tell a miracle. In recent months, steel production, auto production, foreign trade have hit all-time highs. Taking the index of 1936 under Hitler as 100, the index of industrial production in Western Germany last fall reached 185! Germans who only five years ago pushed wheelbarrows through desolate streets now complain of the traffic jams in their cities. In 1953, Germany's exports hit a solid $4,400,000,000, a postwar peak, and economists figured they had ceilinged off. But exports for 1954 will probably even out at around $5,000,000,000, and the Germans are preparing to up the figure again with trade missions selling steel in California and Canada, mills in Egypt and India, machinery and automobiles in Europe, South

America and Asia. The new German mark, in 1948 backed by nothing more than hope, is now, except for the Swiss franc, the hardest currency in Europe.

Germans Like Germany Better Now

Only a few short years ago, every American consulate in Germany was twined around with lines of putty-faced, bedraggled men and women prayerfully waiting for a visa to the United States. Last spring they began to disappear. By midsummer U.S. officials discovered that many were letting their applications drop. By last October, the number of lapsed applications had climbed to 50 per cent. Germany looked good to Germans again.

These are statistics. But even more telling is the face of German recovery.

When, after the war, I first came to Frankfurt, the capital of the American occupation, it had only two poles of activity. One lay around the railway station, dominated by the American-occupied hotels and PX; the other, far larger, was the massive yellow I.G. Farben Building, our military headquarters. In between spread a wasteland of gray mounded ruins where ragged people trudged about their leaden tasks.

Today the I.G. Farben Building seems like a prosaic office center; the railway station is a dingy traffic point; between, out of the ruins, have risen some of the handsomest new buildings in Europe, airy, clean-lined, buildings that blaze at night in a lavish burst of neon. There are still as many Americans as before, but Frankfurt has shrugged them off. This twinkling, bustling city of merchants is German again.

When I visited Düsseldorf in 1949, it took a full day's wandering through half-empty shops to find a souvenir for my wife. Today the luxury stores on Koenigsallee compare with those on the Rue de la Paix or Fifth Avenue; caviar sells at five dollars a spoon in its night clubs; the tobacco shops, as if to recompense for Germany's earlier nicotine craving, offer more fat cigars of all shapes and forms, more novel brands of cigarettes than any other mart in Europe.

Behind the radiant face of Germany's new prosperity are myriad individual success stories which give this national prosperity its transcendentally important political impact. For at the root of the national success story lies an individual "busyness" of the German with his own affairs, a healthy, unabashed preoccupation with the getting and making of things. And behind this lies an all-pervasive, almost psychopathic desire to have nobody rock the boat. In every conversation Germans voice the explicit wish—half prayer, half hope—that, above all, another war will not be allowed to happen, a war which, in this age of absolute weapons, might reduce their freshly rebuilt homes, shops, factories to radioactive wilderness overnight. This political fruit is the most solid nourishment of the little government at Bonn.

There is, for example, Willy Schlieker. I have known Willy ever since the day, six years ago, when he was "delivered" to me, a correspondent of

the conquerors, by British political officers in his small, shabby flat on Breite Strasse in Düsseldorf. I had wanted to see Willy because once, at the age of twenty-eight, he had been the boy genius of Hitler's war effort, the mastermind who controlled the iron-and-steel industry not only of the Ruhr but of all the Continent. When I first saw him, Willy had already been purged, denazified and shoved around; he had settled into a hovel where he traded in junk and scrap iron. But from his tongue still fell trippingly all the figures and facts of Germany's titanic war exertions. "Memory," Willy said once, "is my only capital," and his prodigious memory of Germany's war capacity and techniques made him one of the chief targets of any Allied inquiry into Germany's military past.

In the years since, I have seen Willy flourish, like a parched flower soaked with rain. I have watched him build his scrap-iron business into one of the largest metal-trading concerns in Western Germany; I have watched him reach out to buy a little rolling mill and reconvert it; buy another, buy a shipping line, then buy a shipyard in Hamburg and expand it. I followed his move from the dingy flat to an elegant, modern home in Meererbusch, the suburb of Ruhr industrialists.

On this visit, being interested in Germany's rearmament, I prodded Willy with questions; on arms, he is one of the world's great experts, and his eloquence on the mysteries and crafts of arms-making had in the past held me enthralled. This time my questions evoked only brief, flat replies. Willy was bored with arms. He wanted instead to tell me of his new mill in the Ruhr, with a process that lets him make electrosheet cheaper and better than anyone else in the country.

His spanking-new plant, when I visited him, was rolling out one third of all Germany's electroplate production that month. We went out to the clanging, warm rolling mill. Willy pulled the spotless white handkerchief from his breast pocket, smeared it over the steel sheets coming from the line and said, "Look. Perfect. Not a trace of oxidation. No one can make better than this." Willy wanted to tell me of his new coup in building tankers to export liquefied gas to northern Italy; of his new hunting lodge in Bavaria. But the new army and arms program both bored and frightened him. Somehow, it threatened his new plants, house, shipyard, hunting lodge. "But, Willy," I finally asked, "doesn't anybody here want to make guns?" Willy smiled: "Well, planes maybe, but not guns. That's because you didn't try any of the plane makers at Nuremberg, or put any of them in jail."

Millions of Germans have similar success stories to tell. There is Victor-Emanuel Preusker, who is Minister of Housing, and justly proud. Ten years ago the cities of West Germany showed a leper's face to the world, abscessed with the eyeless sockets of 2,250,000 totally destroyed homes and another 2,500,000 heavily damaged. Now 600,000 of these homes have been rebuilt; another 2,500,000 have been built anew. In 1954, the Germans built more dwellings per capita than America has achieved in any year of its postwar building boom. This year, the figure will be even higher.

One hears this success story told by a minister of government across his desk and glances down at his hands, white and clean now, neatly manicured. Yet not long ago Preusker's hands were rough and red from cutting lumber, fixing doors, windows, frames, repairing children's toys and furniture. For when Preusker was finally cleared and returned to civilian life from the *Lutfwaffe* (he had been a lieutenant), he and his brother began life again as carpenters, opening a woodworking shop in Frankfurt. The success of Preusker's ministry blends with his personal triumph, and one senses his fear of whatever might menace it.

Or there is Rolf Horn in Berlin. Tall, blond and handsome, Rolf Horn looks the model of a German infantry officer, which is what he once was. Today he is Berlin's leading fashion designer. While Rolf was at war his shop was bombed out four times; when he came back there was nothing. To decorate his shop windows he made his wife strip her wardrobe, and hung her dresses in the window. Each employee had to bring needles, thread and flatiron from home; the shop had none.

Fifth-Avenue Figures for Fraüleins

Rolf's success since the war has come by his skillful adaptation to German taste of American fashions. German women, he says, have seen American women of the occupation. They want to dress like them—the same décolleté, the separates, more color. Rolf likes to think of himself as molding the sturdy bodies of German women into something slimmer, more sporty, more Fifth Avenue. He is a very happy man—and he talks of war, past and future, with a barely repressed shudder.

What the Germans have now is a lot more than they had any reason to expect ten years ago, and they know it—the clerks, the shopkeepers, the workers who are saving up for the motor bike, the Volkswagen, the down payment on the house. What is past was exciting—perhaps, in their dreams, even glorious. But this is good now, in many ways better—and they are proud.

All too often Americans and other ex-enemies of the Germans are irked by this German pride in the work of their hands. The irritation is in many ways justified. Among all the Germans I spoke to, only one (a Cabinet minister closely connected with the Marshall Plan) mentioned the vast sums of aid, the enormous efforts America had lavished to make Germany prosperous again. Not one German in a thousand is conscious of the fact that West Germany, having sacked and ravaged Europe, has paid back only $500,000,000 in reparation to the Western World, and has received some $4,000,000,000 in help from this Western World it sought to destroy. No German who denounces the French for backwardness ever recalls that Germany looted France of 80,000 machine tools during the war and retained all but 8,000 after defeat.

Yet, in history's long perspective,

gratitude among nations is nonexistent; to expect gratitude is naïve. German prosperity was something the West actively sought, purchased by its blood transfusions and skillful regulations. It sought this prosperity only to lay the base for a new kind of German government, a democratic one whose successes would guarantee the world against the recurring threat of German greed and violence. If this guarantee has been bought by the success of Germany, then postwar Germany, with or without gratitude, has been our success.

BY ALL normal portents of politics the present prosperous, contented, peaceful bustle in Germany should assure any government that fosters it a long life. Yet, always, with every statement of satisfaction, comes a blurred expression of unease, a murmured postscript: ". . . so long as it lasts" or ". . . if no war comes." Germans talk like people living in a brief interlude between nightmares past and nightmares future, haunted by the sense that most of these nightmares have been of their own making. They are uneasy not only because of the Russians stacked up in menacing divisions just behind the glowering Thuringian ridges, but also because of what is in themselves. Talk of war and armies fascinates Germans still—yet they shrink from it, by reflex. They resemble nothing more in all the world than reformed alcoholics talking of binges, watching the bottle opened by the host, the drink being poured, thrusting it away, saying, "No, thanks—not this time, I'm off it now." As they say it, one knows that their fear of the bottle is sincere, yet that their mouths water for the taste. After the first few weeks of this visit I realized as so often before that here in Germany, what lay beneath the surface—the unuttered attitudes, the twists of soul and personality—was more important in terms of gross politics than parties, personalities, treaties or stipulated divisions.

In Frankfurt, therefore, I went to call on a psychiatrist, Wolfgang Bredtschneider. It seemed hardly possible, I began, that in Adenauer's Cabinet you could seat 19 men at a table, four of whom had been at least nominal Nazis, two of whom had been humiliated in Nazi concentration camps (in addition to the chancellor himself, who had been imprisoned by Hitler), and expect them to arrive at reasoned, co-operative, trusting decisions. It seemed even more difficult to expect co-operation and trust in government from more ordinary men and women who had witnessed the collapse of three forms of government in one generation, who had endured two wars and two defeats, bombings, flight, alien invasion, hunger, denazification. There must be scars on people's minds as well as bodies, I said, but where did it show?

Germany must be viewed, Bredtschneider replied, not just as before and after Hitler, but as a continuous parade throughout this century. The first war came after the golden age, the sunny decades of Kaiser Wilhelm II, at the beginning of what promised to be a glorious century full of beer and happiness.

When it all blew up after Versailles, said Bredtschneider, there was a conscious desire in the minds of Germans to get it back. The image of Germany before World War I was too sweet to let die; they could not admit it collapsed of itself. So there came the legend of the *Dolchstoss* (the stab in the back): there came the *Freikorps,* freebooting soldiers revolving around the skeleton army of the *Reichswehr;* there were monarchists calling for a return to the crown. It was only a question of time before this desire to recapture yesterday's authority, this remembered image, became a real-life projection onto somebody who could talk and look like authority—Hitler.

But after World War II, continued Bredtschneider, things were quite, quite different. Now, instead of projection and identification, what have you? Denial. "'To hell with it,' our people say." He went on, "'Maybe we killed all those Jews, maybe we didn't, but we don't want to hear about it; stop talking!' This may not sound nice to you Americans, but remember—it is the projection that was dangerous, the denial that is healthy."

I pressed on. Just how did this show up in mental disturbances? Could you trace it? Yes, said Bredtschneider; since the war, German medical journals have been full of papers on a condition German doctors find new and disturbing. They call it "vegetative dystonia"—a malfunctioning of the autonomic nervous system, quite clearly linked to emotional disturbances, like ulcers in an American businessman. Pathologically, there is nothing to see. But for the patient it is torturing—a varied combination of headaches, stabbing chest pains, dizziness, sweating palms, sleeplessness, instability, a constant feeling of impending doom. Since the war tens of thousands of Germans have shown up with it as a chronic condition.

Psychiatrists like Bredtschneider do not use the medical term "vegetative dystonia." They use a simpler, old-fashioned term: "anxiety neurosis." Its causes reach back a long way, not only to the war, although the war, with its long nights of bombing ("I still get the shakes myself when I hear airplanes," said Bredtschneider) must have helped. It goes further back, to the days between the wars, when governments came and went, when riots turned cities topsy-turvy. All these have left an emotional aftereffect not only on the people who lived through them, but on their children, emotionally weakened by parents too busy or harassed to give them love and affection. This is one of the amazing theoretical perplexities of mental illness, said Bredtschneider, how so many people can stand the actual danger without cracking, then, years later, break into this chronic anxiety pattern.

Somehow, somewhere it is linked to the problem of being an individual, Bredtschneider concluded. If people lack anything in Germany, he said, it is civil courage, to stand up and be alone. "Who is brave enough here to risk his job just to express an opinion, who can afford it? Now, with the golden dream of Wilhelm dead, and Hitler dead and denied, we have a new kind of government. Under it, every man is forced to be an individual. But we Germans have not been conditioned to be individuals and it is a great effort. The struggle to be an individual brings the anxiety to the surface—they are worried. It gives me, personally, as a German, a very unpleasant feeling to see you here in occupation. But I think you Americans should stay perhaps for fifty years. It is better that you should stay until we are used to this conditioning."

THE GREATEST test of the Germans' conditioning since the war, of their political strength and civil courage, is the new army which world events and the Russian challenge have made necessary.

The army, in Germany, is an expression of national tradition and unstilled atavisms, quite different from armies anywhere else in the world except Japan. It is the army and the warrior who had dominated the pattern of German life ever since the Roman chronicler, Tacitus, first described them in their dark forests—as a people of friendliness, honor and sentimentality, yet given to the most awesome outbursts of violence imaginable.

If the world has suffered from these outbursts it must be remembered that Germans have suffered too, having lacerated one another in civil wars down to the weird bestiality of cannibalism in the Thirty Years' War. Moreover, most Germans now recognize this, as patients do who recognize their own weakness. "Put a German in civilian clothes," a newspaperman told me, "and he is just like anybody else. Put us in uniform and a chemical change happens—we are different." So that when Germans contemplate the coming years, the new army, they talk of it in contradictions and fear. They repeat with pride the old aphorism: "A man without arms is a man without honor." But they also repeat other phrases like *"Schaden macht klug"*—"Misery makes wise."

The one question I tried to put to every German I spoke to was: "How do you feel about the new army?" Of some 70 people I questioned, only 20 felt, either happily or reluctantly, that the army was a good thing. The others, at every level—workers at the blast furnaces, apprentices in school, journalists, union leaders, businessmen, even some of the peasants (the only group I found preponderantly in favor of the army) were against it. It was only partly because they felt that armies inevitably mean war. Even more, it was because they do not like the kind of armies Germany has had in the past, yet are not quite sure whether they can, politically and individually, restrain their patriotic excitement long enough to make this new army different.

I went to see the most popular movie in Germany since the war, based on a novel called "08/15," about the training of prewar draftees. The picture looses on the army and its officers every vulgar ridicule, savagery and contempt the film makers can dream up; almost everybody who wears stripes or officers' pips in the picture is a sot, lecher, sadist or fool. The newly revived and successful Simplicissimus, Germany's famous

humor magazine, has been sharpening its arrow of satire on the new army—to the applause of its growing readership.

Yet with all the ridicule and contempt, the Germans know, fatalistically, that the army is unavoidable. They wonder desperately whether they can take one little sip from the bottle without going off on a tear. One of Germany's finest combat officers, trying devotedly to make the new army a democratic one, said to me: "But it depends not so much on us, as on them, the people. Nobody knows what will happen the day the first battalion in German uniform, with the flag flying, goes marching down the first little village street with the band playing. How much will it excite them? What will it do? This no one can predict."

At present, what there is of the embryonic German army gives barely a hint of what the future may hold. The headquarters of its planning group, the Dienstelle Blank (the Blank Office, so-called for its director Theodor Blank) is neither imposing nor sinister-looking. It is a red-brick building in Bonn that has expanded into several large clapboard annexes, housing 300 officials, all dressed—despite their taut military bearing—in civilian clothes.

Militarily Brilliant, Politically Stupid

Since 1871, the last year in which the German army won any kind of war, almost a century of defeat and disaster has rolled by. During that time German generals have proved themselves simultaneously the most astonishingly brilliant and astonishingly stupid soldiers of modern times. Terrifyingly proficient at the mechanics of combat, they have displayed the political intelligence of oxen. Their stock is nowhere at lower ebb than in their own country. If the German people distrust their army it is because of the generals and officers who have commanded it in the past.

The root trouble of German officers has always been their idea of themselves. They have always thought of themselves as being not the servants, but the partners and occasionally the masters of the state. Unlike the American or English military tradition of an instinctive and enormously wise submission to the civilians of public life, the German officer tradition holds that military and civilian leaders equally guard the destiny of the nation.

The monocled, rigidly correct men of the great German general staff saw themselves as a state within a state. It was these men who lost the first World War for Germany, deciding (against the best civilian advice) to launch the submarine campaign which brought America in; who regarded the Republic of Weimar as a flabby, feckless partner in statesmanship, to be supported when it suited, torpedoed when it displeased; who used their army funds to dabble in politics. In the end it was the army's top politico—Von Schleicher—who, by his intrigues at Berlin, paved the way for Hitler's entry into power. Then the army found itself trapped. Within twelve years Hitler had disgraced, defiled and destroyed both the army and

its officer corps in the *Götterdämmerung* that ended in 1945.

In Bonn, therefore, it is a matter of dogma that the rebuilding of the German army must proceed upon two simultaneous lines: to try to recapture its old field-combat efficiency, and to couple it with political guidance less perilous than heretofore to the whole world and the German people themselves.

There seems little doubt that Dienstelle Blank is well along in the first half of its task—the planning of a combat army. No one quite knows how its 500,000 men and 12 divisions will be meshed with the others of the free world, but, however, deployed, this much is certain: as fighting units they will be good.

One cannot talk with a man like Lieutenant General Adolf Heusinger, chief of the military element at Dienstelle Blank, without instantly realizing how little skill he has lost since, as operations officer of the *Wehrmacht's* general staff, he directed troops all across the map of Europe. Provided America delivers on time the guns, tanks, planes it has promised, and provided Heusinger can find young non-coms and junior officers to volunteer for platoon and company leadership, he plans to have all 12 divisions ready to roll three years from the word go. Like all German officers with experience against Russia, General Heusinger is hipped on mobility. His divisions—whether armored, mechanized or infantry—must be on wheels, complete with organic transport.

As the general's eloquent fingers dart across the table on an imaginary map, they make profiles of European geography, tracing passes and defense points back to the Pyrenees, probing weaknesses and opportunities all the way forward to the Vistula and beyond. One knows, talking to him, that this new army will be deft, quick, able to feint and counterpunch, able to think in broadest strategic terms; it is being built as a mercenary army, but in divisions guided by men who think in terms of supreme national interest.

There is little doubt that Dienstelle Blank can build a fighting army again, once the manpower, equipment, barracks and money are delivered to it by civilian politics. But of the ability of German officers to subdue their will permanently to civilians, one is less sure.

Top Officers of High Caliber

It should be said at once that the men who now staff the top positions at Dienstelle Blank are the best the German officer corps can offer up to world examination, and some are very fine indeed. Young Count Baudissin, for example, who is in charge of officer structure and indoctrination, is a man of glowing conscience who truly wants to make a new democratic army that belongs to its people and is loved, not feared by it. Hans Speidel, its senior military negotiator, Rommel's chief of staff in France who wound up the war tortured in Hitler's prisons, is deter-

mined to fit this new army into the Western defense forces, subordinate to the supreme command of the Atlantic democracies. So are Heusinger and others.

These men have been laboring with the most meticulous care to recast German military thinking. They have elaborated in detail new codes for the ordinary soldier, permitting him to wear civilian clothes off duty, promising him an American system of courts-martial, even extending the hope (so reads one quaint planning proposal) that field drill will "be given in quiet and shady places." They have been debating for months how the new army's senior command (which they refuse even to name "general staff") shall be linked to the *Bundestag,* by what means it shall be kept open to parliamentary inspection and control, subordinate to civilian ministers responsible to the elected spokesmen of the people.

Yet these paper plans, however perfect or imperfect, whatever their disposition when submitted for *Bundestag* approval, do not constitute the real problem of the new army. That problem lies in human beings, in the ungaugeable ability of the present directors of Dienstelle Blank to maintain their authority and leadership in the army when its 500,000 men and officers become the largest enterprise, the biggest business of the fragile Bonn government. For, although the army can find the necessary handful of purified generals to occupy the top spots, it needs hundreds of colonels, thousands of junior field officers, tens of thousands of tough non-coms—and these can be found quickly only by capitalizing on Germany's legacy from yesterday's war. The best, the least war-guilty, of German officers have long since found jobs in prosperous civilian life. Thus those most likely to volunteer for the new army are those who were late in finding civilian jobs—chiefly because they were the most difficult to denazify and clear. These are also the men most apt to cherish an affection for the past.

Again and again, both in Dienstelle Blank and the *Bundestag,* an American inquirer is told: "A great deal depends on you. If you give us time, say five or 10 years, we can make a whole new officer corps and a good one; but if you rush us we'll have to take whatever men we can get—and that can be dangerous."

The gossip swirling about Dienstelle Blank does not encourage any belief that the civilized men who now front for it can retain control without a struggle. Already it is roiled by feuds and factions.

There is a faction called the "idealists," to which Count Baudissin's name is usually attached, which believes that an army should be a living instrument of democracy.

Another loose grouping, called the "progressives," believes that although the German army was the best fighting force in the world, it was imperfect—the chief imperfection being its political stupidity and its craven co-operation with Hitler, the blunderer.

Another group, already installed and growing within the office and usually called the "traditionalists," believes that all other armies are naturally inferior to German armies, that neither foreign nor domestic policy can, or should, be made without consulting the wishes of the army.

Finally, outside Dienstelle Blank are yet other officers who see the army as the supreme expression of national purpose and honor, who refuse to admit that this honor has ever been besmirched. Despite the efforts of Dienstelle Blank to maintain friendly liaison with this prospective manpower, many of these outsiders still see the leaders of Dienstelle Blank as traitors (because most were involved in the wartime attempt to assassinate Hitler) and hate them.

Theodor Blank, the man in whom control of this motley planning staff now rests, is a highly respected Catholic trade-union leader and war veteran. Yet Blank's behavior in Bonn has been upsetting. Blunt and straightforward, he swings from moods of confidence, when he boasts how he has bullied the officers under him (*"Meine Jungens"* he calls them—"my boys"), to moods of unhappiness, when, in emotional, tearful sessions, he moans to intimates that he knows "they are working behind my back." On balance, Blank is a weak man.

Even more important is the attitude of Adenauer himself, who reiterates to visitors: "It was not we who wanted this army. The French Assembly forced it on us when they rejected the European Army." The aged patriarch recently announced that he would give up his post as foreign minister to devote himself mainly to the army.

Fear of the new army is, at once, the most distressing and the healthiest political attitude in Germany. For if the Germans fear this army, it is well that the rest of the world fear it, too. Yet the German fear is the beginning of hope, an indication that the Germans have learned from experience.

An Army under Allied Control

All the necessary plans exist in the desks of the German government to democratize, reorganize, subordinate and direct the army. All the necessary plans have been made by the Western Allies to control it, yet to leave it with enough pride to fight effectively. The army is to be denied atomic, bacteriological and chemical weapons of war. Its arms production will be inspected and controlled along with that of all other European powers; its supply system will be tied to the Allies and most of its financing will depend on them; its divisions are required to take orders from the commander in chief at SHAPE.

Yet the fact remains that by 1958 or 1959, when Germany musters the biggest single chunk of armed manpower in central Europe, ultimate control of the army will be primarily that exercised by the German people expressing themselves politically. By then the catalysis of arms, banners, drums and music will have begun to work, the first sip will have been taken of the old cup, and only the restraint and experience of the Germans themselves will shape the army's role and use. The moral and political climate of German life of that not-too-distant day will determine whether the West has been wise in its choice of new allies.

WHAT THE moral and political climate of Germany may be five years hence can only, of course, be conjectured.

Most Americans who have known Germany only through the years of war and hatred visit postwar Germany with fear of Nazism and the continuing appeal of that idiot faith uppermost in their mind. A good reporter can easily assemble enough evidence to demonstrate that a Nazi movement still smolders underground:

▶ A certified war criminal, SS General Kurt Meyer, is released from jail, returns to his village in the Rhineland, is received back not with loathing but with a torchlight parade organized by SS veterans.

▶ Someone hangs a plaster-cast bust of Hitler on the walls of the Auto-Union Werke in Düsseldorf. The workers scowl at it uncertainly, half frightened, yet let it hang until the management can call the nonpolitical police who alone dare remove it.

▶ In the Ruhr, a magazine called the Ring appears, its logotype surrounded by the barbed-wire symbol of the concentration camp—and one finds it is dedicated to the proposition that those ex-Nazis who were imprisoned by Americans and Britons after the war were not perpetrators but victims of injustice.

Yet when one assembles all these shreds, one finds the evidence of living, waiting Nazism in Germany conspicuously less than in 1953 or 1949. The best intelligence now reports between 200 and 500 groups, ranging in membership from 10 to a maximum of about 2,000, that might be called Nazi-oriented; and these are mostly what, in America, we call crackpot groups. They make alliances and leagues, squabble among themselves; their leaders hate one another, betray one another, break and re-form. Some are linked with the truly dangerous hardcore Nazi groups in exile in Egypt, Argentina or Spain. But they lack a single figurehead leadership; more important, they lack bounce and resonance at the polls.

Although the Nazi ideology remains a potential seed of infection it is not the Nazis but three other groups which one must examine to attempt a reasonable guess of Germany's moral and political climate five years hence. These three forces, each badly organized, dominate German politics today. They can be crudely described as a governing force, an open opposition, and a concealed opposition.

The concealed opposition reflects the existence of an artificial gap in German life. German politics today lack their traditional right-wing, nationalist-reactionary party, the group that powered, supplied and financed Hitler on his way up. Such a group is missing largely because of the history of the occupation and American policy. We who entered Germany as conquerors and reformers took it upon ourselves to license or forbid postwar political parties. We were so bitter at the evils and accomplices of Nazism that we refused to li-

cense any party of the old radical right, any collecting point for the self-intoxicated peddlers of German glory. Many moderate and liberal German politicians now believe this policy was a mistake—for had the German right been grouped in its own party it might have been isolated, sealed off, kept impotent.

Since there is no such open grouping, the many Germans who cherish the illusion that Germany is the senior power of Europe have done their best to infiltrate the moderate governing parties which make up Adenauer's coalition, notably the Free Democratic party. A minor but substantial element of the coalition, this party is a loose, undisciplined organization which in many areas (such as Hamburg or south Germany) is, as its name indicates, a free and democratic party, liberal-conservative, honest in nature and intent. But in at least two provinces of Germany—the Ruhr and Hesse—two of the most critical, the party is honeycombed with ex-Nazis. If they are not more powerful today, credit British Intelligence, which early in 1953 nipped a Nazi conspiracy in the bud and forced FDP leaders to repudiate and purge the most sinister.

Appealing to Patriotic Emotion

These nationalists in the FDP—and their covert allies within other parties and the governing coalition—have enormous emotional resources to draw on. These resources are the German past. Most Germans have brought themselves to repudiate Hitler and his war as evil. But no German can bring himself to say that all who fought for their country were evil, that the war they fought was not without its heroes, its sacrifices for the commonweal. The nationalists, in their insistence on honoring not only those who, in German eyes, cannot be denied honor, but also the truly guilty, have established a flank position which all other German politicians must respect.

The nationalists and their allies grow apoplectic when one refers to the East zone of Germany as "Eastern Germany." They consider the Soviet-occupied East zone as "Middle Germany." To them "Eastern Germany" is an area that runs deep into Poland. Theirs are the most aggressively anti-Russian voices in Germany. Yet paradoxically they are the people who speak most often and openly of a deal with the Russians, a private and separate bargain with Eastern Communism, restoring Germany's rights in the East at whatever expense to the West. These, too, are the men most happy about the new army. For the moment, they are a minority within a party which in turn is a minority fraction within the government. Yet they are constantly growing in strength and influence. It seems inescapable that in the federal elections of 1957, with Germany once again sovereign and free, this group will form some open nationalist political grouping.

The next of the three political forces dominating Germany today, the open opposition to the Bonn government,

comes from the other direction, the left. The Socialists, who count 151, or nearly a third of the members of the *Bundestag,* are in many ways one of the truly democratic forces in the new Germany. The trade-unions, which they lead, are, after years of postwar ossification, finally feeling the pressure of their younger, more vigorous members. The Socialists' opposition to both Nazis and Communists is fervid and sincere. They maintain the best anti-Communist intelligence service in East Germany, and perhaps the best organized anti-Communist underground there. Though they are the most vocal opponents of the new army and most ardent advocates of stringent democratic controls, most of their leaders privately accept the need of an army as a guarantee or bargaining counter against the Russians.

The weakness of the Socialists is simply that they are stagnant—in party structure, ideas, leadership. Since the deaths of Ernst Reuter, the hero of the Berlin blockade, and Kurt Schumacher, their flamboyant, dedicated postwar leader, the Socialist party has had no direction. Bureaucratized, its machinery almost inflexible, it has, like all the Socialist parties of Europe, reached an intellectual dead end. Still wedded to Marxism, most of its thinkers know that Marxism as a system of ideas is as dead as Queen Victoria. Although they have the solid vote of the working class, the Socialists seem doomed to remain an ineffectual, though strong, minority unless they discard Marxism for a modern set of ideas or find allies to join them in a new coalition. The Socialists believe these allies may someday soon be found in the wreckage of the great Christian Democratic Union which now governs Germany.

In this hope, the open and the concealed opposition unite. Both Socialists and nationalists believe that the CDU, the third force in present German life, is too large, unwieldy, disparate to hold together much longer. They are buoyed up by the mystery that perplexes Americans and other foreigners: are the governing Christian Democrats held together only by the personality of Konrad Adenauer—or will the common cement of the Christian faith be strong enough to hold them together even after Adenauer is gone?

Each year that I have visited Germany, I have participated in one of Bonn's favorite guessing games: Who will replace the chancellor? This time I heard the game played again, but with a new note of futility, for, as exertion, excitement and long voyages succeed one another, the stately old man, now seventy-nine, shows no sign of weariness, his antique face no mark of softening.

It is a massive face, this countenance of the man whom the West sees when it looks at Germany. The wrinkles of age crisscross the soft old skin—fine tiny wrinkles about the eyes, long smooth wrinkles under the chin. But these are not the wrinkles of senility. His rivals and enemies (and they are many, even within his own party) admit he shows no signs of age. One said to me: "Adenauer grow old? This man cannot grow old, for he has no heart or soul to grow old with: he governs with ice and stone." Yet even these enemies know that someday soon he must pass on, and they are uneasy at the prospect, for all German politics have been shaped by his personality.

Konrad Adenauer governs his people like a patriarch, like a Moses or Abraham out of the Old Testament. There are no heirs apparent in Bonn: he will permit none.

When he goes off on a trip or vacation, no political deputy is allowed to replace him, or to read foreign office dispatches even for a day. When press criticism irks Adenauer he has been known to summon editors from as far off as Hamburg or Frankfurt, gaze at them sternly and say reprovingly, "Gentlemen, this won't do."

In Fear of German Nationalism

Implicit in his entire attitude (and sometimes explicit in his conversation) is distrust—chiefly of his own people. His personal political bogey is German nationalism, from which he has suffered so much personally. He was imprisoned by Hitler after the Nazis' rise to power, released to live on the Gestapo's permanent "suspect" list, arrested again in 1944 at the age of sixty-eight, to emerge finally with an enduring bitterness for the men who brought his country to ruin.

Adenauer operates as if he must, before he dies, personally attend to every detail of the interment of German nationalism—or, perhaps, as if he were master of a kindergarten of lovable but mischievous and potentially dangerous children.

Many matters that preoccupy other political chieftains bore him. Thus he leaves the details of economics, trade and commerce to his deft Minister of Economics, Ludwig Erhard, and the even shrewder Minister of Finance, Fritz Schaeffer. So long as houses are built, people work and Germany meets her obligations he worries neither about theory nor practice of economics. But he is fascinated with all the homely trivia of family life, insistent on religious education for children in schools, vastly attentive to all legislation to encourage family life (he himself has sired seven children). He is interested, too, in the new army, the cut of its uniforms, the cock of its helmet, the choice of its new marching songs (for he believe these songs are of flammable emotional stuff).

Above all, Adenauer believes that only by sealing Germany into a union of Western nations can the surges and urges of German nationalism be safely, permanently contained, and that only through this union can Germany's dignity in the outside world be restored.

Adenauer's share in pressing a mold of decency on postwar Germany is greater than anyone else's—greater than that of the American occupation, of Germany's new trade-unions, of its clean and dignified daily press, greater even than luck. It is he who has single-handed made his party great, and this, ironically, is the blemish on his record,

for by refusing his party the right to be more than a personal instrument he has gravely weakened it for the trials it must face when he is gone.

His party, indeed, is one of the major riddles of European politics. Predominantly Catholic, it is based frankly on religion, holding that religion as a code of politics has as much place in public dispute and debate as any secular ideas or programs. Its left wing is solidly based on the vote of Catholic trade-unionists, its right wing on peasants and businessmen. The CDU pleases the poor with an inspired system of baby-subsidies and government housing, the rich with laws that now put a ceiling of 55 per cent on income taxes (the Ruhr industrialists poured an estimated $12,000,000 into the 1953 election to support Adenauer's policy and party). On domestic policy the CDU has been frequently split, held to cohesion by Adenauer alone; on foreign policy it has needed no such patriarchal admonition, for the party, as its chief, believes in Western Union almost as divine revelation.

It is the earnest, anonymous men of this party, dependent on the father-Adenauer, who must sort out the problems of the future. And of all the problems that they must sort out—the control of the army, the replacement of Adenauer, the maintenance of prosperity—none so swiftly and inevitably approaches as the unification of their country. And no problem of Germany, not even the army, engages the interests of America more directly.

———

BEFORE THE year 1955 is out, the problem of Germany's unity will be the major diplomatic business of the world.

Once the sovereignty of West Germany is restored, its 50,000,000 people will not be able to rest without seeking to extend freedom and independence to their 17,000,000 countrymen who live under the tyranny of Soviet rule and Communist terror in East Germany. To free their brethren is as compelling an instinct among the Germans as it would be among Americans west of the Mississippi if all our land east of it lay cowering under enemy lash.

The West German government does not plan to celebrate the new independence granted it with parades, banners or public holiday—because in the eyes of its people Germany is neither free nor independent while it remains half slave and half free.

On the contrary, as West Germany grows healthier, stronger and more prosperous, the misery of East Germany becomes a greater offense to West Germany's pride and sense of decency. It is pointless to argue that West Germany, once united with East Germany, must suffer a sharp decline in prosperity as it tries to pump wealth and health into the gutted eastern part. The Germans are not content with a shrunken West Germany, whose 95,000 square miles make it smaller than Oregon.

Without East Germany (41,000 square miles) West Germany is merely a crowded buffer state along the Rhine, a Switzerland writ large.

Thus, as sovereignty draws nigh for West Germany, the problem of freeing

and reunifying with East Germany has come to dominate all German politics. With increasing frequency, in press and parliament, Germans rise to demand when, how, by what means their government proposes to go about the task. Each year another quarter of a million refugees filter into West Germany from the East to add to the 10,000,000 refugees already there. And the 10,000,000 there—one fifth of the population—vote, speak, demand and infect other voters with their discontent.

It would be impossible for the moderate Christian Democrats or the Socialists to leave these pressures to be exploited by the nationalists, even if they could ignore the feeling in their own breasts.

Thus, month by month, they must compete with nationalists in showing themselves champions for the unity and freedom of all Germany.

Already Adenauer has informed his Western Allies, his press and his *Bundestag* that once Germany is a free agent diplomatically, his first order of the day is negotiation with the Russians to end the dismemberment of his country.

It is primarily this pressure for negotiation which makes it impossible to analyze Germany's future logically. I repeatedly asked Cabinet members, ex-officers, students, workers, how they proposed to negotiate with Russia. Over and over they responded with two reactions: that Germany could not afford and would not go to war for unification—but that unification must be won at any price, at the cost of any deal.

Effects of Stalin Diplomacy

This is the disturbing aspect. The Russians cannot be unaware of sentiment so deep and widespread. The surly and stupid diplomacy of Joseph Stalin, which for many years blocked any humanity or compromise on East Germany, forced the West Germans into our arms by convincing them that East Germany could be freed only if West Germany braced itself by closest association with a powerful Western Alliance. But far shrewder men, more skillful in seduction and blandishment, now rule in Stalin's place. Their main goal is to drive the Americans out of Europe and rip apart the Western Alliance. The freedom of East Germany might not be too great a prize for the Russians to yield, provided the Germans were willing to pay for this unity at the price of rupture with the West, or neutralism.

Here, for the Russians, is a true opportunity. And here, for America and the West, lurks true danger.

American diplomacy has nursed and cherished the Germans over the last nine years not so much out of love as out of need. The one dread event that American diplomacy must at all costs avoid is the possible union of Germany's stupendous technical skills with the evil empire of Communism.

Up to now, the interests of America and Germany have coincided as if in patterned precision. America sought Germany's prosperity to quench the infections of Communism and Nazism—and the Germans sought this prosperity with equal ardor. America sought the union of Western Europe as a cornerstone in the grand Atlantic Alliance—and the Germans, led by their Catholic Christian party, sought it even more. America sought to recruit German troops to aid in the military defenses of the West, and the German government, aware of the Red Army's menace, sought this new army also. In all these projects the Germans have needed us even more than we have needed them.

Now, however, the Germans have had all the grants and gifts our policy is capable of bestowing, and we enter a new era. In this era, the sovereign state of West Germany will have one overriding goal—to free East Germany. Whoever stands in the way is already considered an enemy. America, Germany's enemy in the past, can, by the alchemy of German passions, be redrawn as an enemy if our policy lags, or if its justified caution in dealing with Russia seems to postpone what the Germans consider essential.

So long as Adenauer survives and keeps control, it is unlikely that Germany can quickly withdraw from our embrace; so long as Germany is unarmed, it is unlikely that Germans will dare challenge our power or our diplomacy; so long as the present high level of German prosperity continues, it is unlikely that either right or left can mobilize Germans to demonstration or violence in favor of unity. But sometime in the near future the Germans must insist on settling the major problem of their national politics.

In Germany, until now, our diplomacy has been built on a wise combination of force and trust. Having now voluntarily limited our force, we are thrown back on trust—in a people whose history has never merited great trust from any of its neighbors.

Thus one returns to the original questions: Is Germany dangerous? If so, how? Is she permanently friend, foe or neutral?

The answers, after long inquiry, seem to run like this:

First, that any nation can be dangerous to any other when it puts its mind to it, but that the German mind is today less dangerous, less martial, more peacefully inclined than at any other time in modern history.

Second, that if any single factor can upset this present frame of thinking, it will be the new army—which, unless closely watched, may excite the German mind with old emotional symbols and martial chants. This watching must be done by the Germans themselves, above all by Bonn—because, if this army does become dangerous, its first threat will be internal, to the new freedoms and decencies that Bonn has sponsored.

Third, that if this German army does become dangerous, it is unlikely to become dangerous on field of battle. If the Germans are rigidly denied absolute weapons, the atomic and hydrogen weapons—as the treaties insist—our troops can sit back and lob nuclear and fusion rockets across Germany in an instant.

Fourth, Germany can become dangerous politically if she decides to make her own deal on unity with the Rus-

sians. She may do this if a downturn in world prosperity makes the industry of the Ruhr seek the markets of Communist Russia and China as avidly as it did in the depression or in 1949. She may do so if the new army decides it can bargain its way out of the Atlantic Alliance and win honor from its citizens by forcing the government to make the kind of friendship pact with the Russians that the army approved in 1922 and again in 1939.

THERE IS no complete insurance against any of these dangers. But what insurance there is must come chiefly from the American people, to whom history would suggest two courses of action.

The first is simply to maintain the American presence in Germany. Our 250,000 soldiers there not only guarantee a preponderance of military power against possible turbulence in the early transitional years of sovereignty. They are also one of the great educational forces in German life. The flesh-and-blood example of our democratic Army—the privileges and duties of its men and officers, one to another, its subordination to the civilian control of Washington—sets a standard of conduct from which the German army will find it difficult to deviate. The most routine behavior of our Americans excites admiration in Germans unused to such conduct. When several Germans during our maneuvers last fall noticed three of our officers trying to help a GI push his stuck jeep out of the mud, the local newspaper editorially commented that General Heusinger (a guest observer at the maneuvers) would be well advised to pay more attention to such incidents in modeling his new army that to actual American combat techniques. At whatever expense and strain, the continued presence of the American Army in Germany is necessary.

The decision to maintain our troops in Germany is a necessary precaution. Yet great results are not achieved by caution, and the dynamic, complementary course of action must be found in our diplomacy.

Technically, our diplomats have their hands full at the moment. Under the sensitive leadership of our High Commissioner in Germany, James B. Conant, the entire structure of our 10-year occupation is being readied for dismantling, while simultaneously the Germans are being hastened toward ratification of the treaties that will make them sovereign.

In the Chess Game of Nations

Yet, even while it is so engaged, our diplomacy must swiftly and imaginatively prepare for the next move—the use of the new German army as a diplomatic centerpiece in the great chess game of world politics. In American eyes, the new army was not called into being either to make war or to make possible a separate deal between the Russians and Germans. It was called into being to add enough strength to the Atlantic Alliance to force the Russians, finally,

into realistic bargaining on a worldwide basis. For the Germans the freedom of Eastern Germany is the most important item in this bargaining, but for Americans it can be only one item of many. The German army adds strength to the Western World; it is up to our diplomacy to make the most of that strength for a general settlement before Adenauer's successors try to use it for Germany's profit alone.

One last point remains to be made but it is the most important. We Americans have gone through enormous cycles of naïve, almost adolescent, enthusiasm for foreign potentates and princes only to be betrayed and let down later. None of us should or can forget how our wartime honeymoon with Stalin was succeeded by the betrayal we invited by our naïveté.

Our most enduring and fruitful alliances have been with the French and the British, two powers whom we have constantly criticized, called to account, subjected to every form of debate and discussion—yet with whom we have always ended by making common cause.

We have for the past nine years enjoyed a honeymoon with the German people and with Adenauer even more complete than our honeymoon with the Russians and Chinese during the war and, in the individual case of Adenauer, with much better cause.

The last 20 years have proved such honeymoons dangerous. Our friendship with Germany will be solid only if it rests on the same base that sustains our friendship with France and Britain. That friendship rests on no illusion that sovereign nations make alliances and commit their destinies because of honeyed words alone. It rests rather on the belief that in even the strongest alliances each partner must examine each common goal first in the light of its own national self-interest. We are the allies of the Germans today because we need them. Yet they need us more, and it would be best for both peoples to keep this hard, cold fact always in mind.

COLLIER'S *February 4, 1955*

Chapter 6

One Shot: The Dark Continent

Over his career, White stuck mostly to a few, albeit wide-ranging, beats. A few of his best articles, however, were forays into fresh territory. Some of these have been put into one-article chapters of their own: One Shots.

Here he writes of America's partnership with French colonialism in Africa. It is somber—but illuminating—reading.

AFRICA IS NEXT

Will America's blind partnership with French colonialism involve us in an explosion of twenty million Moslems and thirty million Negroes seeking independence and equality? What are the goals of American policy today in Africa? Here is an informed answer by an experienced observer.

In the great tides of struggle that wash around our globe, the Atlantic world has been so deafened by those crests rolling in and breaking from Asia, that few of us have noticed a prodigious fact: Africa is next.

Africa, the last great colonial continent of the world, the richest untapped storehouse of materials for its hungry and expanding industry, is 200 million people sputtering from end to end with ideas, violence, and growing challenge. To lose Africa, as Asia has been lost, means for the Atlantic community a retreat from the great globe into the basin it occupied at the end of the eighteenth century.

In tracing the perspectives on Africa, any future historian of our times will almost certainly describe how two great patterns of conflict intersected beneath the crowded detail of daily life and were confused. The first, of course, will be the civil war within Western civilization so crudely labeled the clash of communism and democracy. The second, perhaps more important, will be the liquidation of a century of conquest.

By the end of the nineteenth century, the Atlantic powers had written climax to an adventure in expansion that had made all other cultures and civilizations of the globe tributary to them. This dominance persisted for a full generation after China's Boxer Rebellion and then, in our mid-century decades, began swiftly to ebb. Given the nature of men and geography, the future historian will note, first, that this withdrawal of Atlantic power was inevitable. He will inquire then only whether the withdrawal was made wisely or whether it was bungled to leave behind bitterness and enmity. So far, the record shows one moderate success—the withdrawal from India—and one perilous failure— the expulsion from China. What we cannot yet judge with the future historian's priceless advantage of perspective is his verdict on Africa.

It is ironically appropriate that the problems of withdrawal from Africa are posed first and above all at France, the weakest of the Atlantic powers. Now that the British have dismantled half their Empire, the French stand forth as the greatest colonial power in the world. They govern eighty million subject people, girdling the globe, inhabiting an area roughly one and a half times the size of the United States. These people thrust at the French the three archetypes of challenge the colonial world offers in this century to the men who conquered them in the last: Asian communism, Moslem nationalism, and the first stirring of the Negro peoples.

Anyone in Paris will tell you that France's war with Asian Communists in Indochina is an almost hopeless conflict in which victory can be won only by utter exhaustion of homeland France or with the massive aid of American men and material. But Africa, they insist, is something else again. And they are right. In Africa, with wisdom, the French still have time to prepare the structure of cooperation to replace the structure of dominion for the inevitable withdrawal. In this, they act as trustees of the whole Atlantic world.

II

French Africa is 4,300,000 square miles of mountain, desert, and jungle. It is, next, fifty million people in various states of restlessness or discontent, stirring in a diversity that reaches from barbarian nomads trailing black slaves after their caravans to the most eloquent and aesthetic Negro leaders familiar in the most fashionable homes of Paris.

What complicates the politics of French Africa is the historic fact that it has only recently—and simultaneously—been rediscovered by three groups of people.

The French were the first. The French, before the war, were perhaps the least enterprising of any of the major colonial powers. But the war, forc-

ing the Free French to base on Africa, suddenly roused their interest in a world they had up to then drowsily claimed only in the clichés of glory and prestige. Africa suddenly was a troop reserve, a storehouse of wealth, a wilderness of unlimited opportunity. The war incubated a revolution in French colonial thinking.

The Africans themselves were the next discoverers. So insistently were the words liberty and democracy used by our propagandists during the war, that they became a yeast in the mind of the Africans, and the ferment created or invigorated all the great movements of African independence which the French now face.

Africa was discovered last by the Americans in the declining years of the Marshall Plan. When it became obvious in 1950 and 1951 that the growth of world demand was outrunning, biologically, the materials and resources we need to keep our delicate civilization healthy, Africa suddenly became important to American policy, too. Africa was iron ore, coal, lead, diamonds, paper pulp, cocoa, copper, which somehow had to remain pooled in the Atlantic community. One American statesman in Paris one afternoon seized a map of Europe and Africa and twisted it around. "Look," he said, "put Europe here as the East and see—Africa is the frontier, Africa is Europe's Far West, the way she must expand."

THE RESPONSIBILITY for executing the political withdrawal from French Africa and replacing it by a partnership that will not dash the hopes aroused by these simultaneous discoveries lies precisely nowhere.

The French Empire was put together in bits and pieces of spasmodic nineteenth-century conquest and then tucked away in odd corners of the Parisian bureaucracy in utter administrative confusion. The French Ministries of the Interior, of Foreign Affairs, of Overseas France, of National Defense, Finance, and Commerce all share various layers and areas of control (Indochina is governed by yet another ministry—that of the Associated States). And all of these ministries change hands several times a year in the reshufflings of cabinets that mark every rustling of French domestic politics.

In practice, this means that no single man or body of men except the Premier and his Cabinet (harassed with a hundred other domestic and international problems) has the right or duty to survey the Empire as a whole and plan or conceive the strategy of the great withdrawal. In practice, too, this means that France's Empire is governed by a corps of colonial civil servants of parochial training who after many years of overseas service become men of prodigious importance and power. The French government can, when greatly provoked, remove these professional Empire-governors—as Truman removed MacArthur—but it cannot direct them. This is part of the tragedy of the French Empire, for again and again since the war the politicians in Paris, sensitive to the climate of the century, have proven wiser than their civil servants in the field.

This ramshackle administrative edifice is overlaid with a glittering high-minded theory, the fruit of France's wartime rediscovery of Africa. By this theory, the French Empire has become the French Union. The theory holds that all men are kin, no matter what their race or skin-color, and that French civilization is elastic enough to absorb in brotherhood all the races French arms conquered in the past. Today, France's overseas territories (except Morocco and Tunis, which are protectorates) contribute one-tenth of the deputies of the National Assembly to vote and debate the laws of France. As the education and ability of these distant people grow, it is promised that they will gain ever greater autonomy in their own affairs until finally at some far off date the French Union will be a real grouping of states. Homeland France with its forty million people will be only one. There will be a Black France in Africa, directing its affairs, and possibly a Moslem France in North Africa directing its affairs. All these Frances will send men to a great Assembly which will provide for common defense, diplomacy, and economic union.

All this is theory. On the ground, in Africa, the Frenchman rules, imprisons, censors, lays taxes, helps or oppresses as he sees fit. On the ground, in Africa, France's Empire is cleft into two separate, geographically-marked problems. Along the rim of the Mediterranean and the North Atlantic are the twenty million Moslems of North Africa who insist upon immediate and total independence from France. Then come the grim emptiness of the Sahara, a belt of insulation between two colonial worlds, and south of the Sahara, Black Africa. Black Africa is thirty million Negro people chopped into fifteen enclaves, who by some happy twist of fortune seek not independence from France but inclusion within a France that offers them the equality and dignity promised in the theory of French Union. Let us look at these Africas.

III

In French North Africa, the tactics and problems of withdrawal are urgent and immediate. They rise from the clash of two intertwined developments—the first a postwar spasm of industrial progress and economic expansion captained by the French, the second a groundswell of native nationalism quickened by this progress and impatient to dismiss the French who have brought it.

French North Africa is a crescent of once fertile, now barren land that stretches 1,400 miles—as far as from San Diego to Seattle—around the rim of the Atlantic and Mediterranean. For a millennium this has been Moslem country. An inland mountain range, heavily forested in Roman days, has been shaved through the centuries to the grim, yellow, eroded hills over which American GIs fought their way to victory in 1943. On the seaward slope of the mountains, a generation of French colonization has here and there restored the fruitfulness of the land. Further inland, peasants scrabble the stony hillsides in poverty, and ignorant nomads march their flocks to devour and wipe out every shrub and protective greenery the eroded soils thrust out. Beyond the hills and mountains are the desert tribes, still savage.

The French have accepted the divisions of North African Moslems as they found them on arrival as conquerors: Morocco, Algeria, and Tunisia, sprawling across the map, west to east, in that order. The folklore of the French Empire divides them with the phrase: "The Tunisian is a woman, the Algerian a man, the Moroccan a lion." All of them, however, are today kindled by the same political slogan: Independence. If the three North African colonies are seen as a chain of sizzling firecrackers, the first of which to pop will set off the other two, then the fuses burn closest in Morocco and Tunisia.

Recently Morocco has been sputtering the loudest. Morocco is the jewel of the French Empire, the fastest developing, richest, most mineral-laden of the North African trio. Morocco is held by "protectorate," recognized internationally forty-two years ago; but an almost explosive population burst (the Moroccans have jumped from 3.4 million to 8.2 million since 1921), a rapid urbanization, and the spread of education have now finally presented the French with a problem for which their theoretical protectorate no longer offers a solution. A Moroccan *alem* put it this way to an American newspaperman: "The protectorate is like a child's nightshirt. As the child grows, the nightshirt shrinks. It gets too tight and tears. Right now it's as tight as a straitjacket and ripping all apart."

Three colorful men have faced each

other from the three corners of Moroccan politics during the postwar years. The first has been the Sultan of Morocco, Sidi Mohammed ben Youssef, a plump, brown, rather venal princeling whose father was chosen by the occupying French army to be their puppet ruler of the land forty-one years ago. Sidi Mohammed ben Youssef, who inherited this fictitious sovereignty twenty-four years ago, now insists on using it as if it belonged to him.

The Sultan, who lives in the seaboard capital of Rabat, is the mouthpiece of the city Arabs, the people clustered about the industries and commerce the French have created. It is among these people that the Istiqlal, the clandestine national independence movement, is rooted. The Sultan, despite all French pressure, has refused to repudiate it by name.

The second man has been El Glaoui, Pasha of Marrakech, the hill city, a grizzled old tribesman of primeval instincts, contemptuous of the Sultan and the city Arabs. In his youth, the Glaoui fought the French with ferocity; now, in his age, he is the staunchest of French allies among the feudal chieftains. If the Sultan speaks for the city Arabs, El Glaoui speaks for the hill tribes and mountain Berbers from whom are recruited the savage Moroccan Goums, the best fighting troops under the French flag. El Glaoui and the Sultan between them represent the cleavage between hill people and seaboard people which the French seek to perpetuate.

The man who directs the balancing act is the third and most powerful figure of Moroccan politics. He is the French Resident General. For four years, until last fall, the post was occupied by General Alphonse Juin, greatest of postwar French consuls, a brilliant soldier with the political instincts of a gendarme. Juin ruled Morocco with a rough hand, forbidding political meetings, subjecting Moroccans to imprisonment without trial, on one occasion in a fury driving the nominal Moroccan ministers of government out of his council chamber because they questioned him too closely; on another occasion, Juin threatened the Sultan with military confinement in his palace. Supposedly, the Resident General is responsible to the French Ministry of Foreign Affairs, which directs the protectorate. But in 1950, when Foreign Minister Robert Schuman made a speech in France admitting that reforms were long overdue in Morocco, Juin censored the reports from the Moroccan press. Juin ended his stewardship in a final tussle for power with the Sultan, forcing the Sultan to sign his name to a basketful of acts and reforms which he had resisted for months and which Juin felt necessary to cap his colonial career.

Having reduced the Sultan to a state of simmering submission, Juin handed over his post to another general—Augustin Guillaume—in October. Guillaume, a chunky, ruddy soldier of bounding energy, is altogether more supple and graceful than Juin. Though he rules with firmness and carries on a running feud with American officials who give ear to Nationalist plaints, Guillaume has succeeded in abolishing the police atmosphere from his immediate court and censorship of the Moroccan press has ended. Between cycles of unrest the French breathe easier in Morocco.

IN THE INTERLUDE, Tunisia seems very troublesome, for a very simple reason. It is next door to Libya and Libya will become free and independent in 1952 if the United Nations honors the promise made at the 1949 General Assembly. Now Libya, even by Arab standards, is a backward country; while Tunisia, its neighbor, is one of the most civilized Moslem states of the Mediterranean. Do you think, say the Tunisians, that it is possible to keep us in colonial guiding strings while the Libyans across the border are free?

The man about whom Tunisian discontent coagulates is Habib Bourguiba. Bourguiba has the blue eyes of a mountain Berber, the eloquence of a burning fanatic, and the suave polish of a French lawyer. He and his neo-Destour party want to drive the French out of Tunisia root-and-branch. With a grace and intolerance frighteningly reminiscent of Pakistan's fanatic Mohammed Ali Jinnah, Bourguiba makes open threat. He says that once Libya is free he can get all the arms and supplies he wants from over the border if he decides a Tunisian uprising is necessary. He also says that if the West is uninterested in what he demands, the Soviet Union is not. Bourguiba has already sent "observers" from his labor movement to "labor" conferences behind the Iron Curtain.

Although the French pooh-pooh Habib Bourguiba, it is only in Tunisia that they have moved to any major reform in the past year. France has now created a cabinet of Tunisians subject to the French governor-general and thrown open thousands of civil service posts to Tunisian candidacy. Although the handful of French colonists in Tunisia (100,000 out of three million population) have protested these Paris-decreed reforms as craven cowardice, the reforms have temporarily appeased the Tunisians. Tunisian leaders now clamor for legislative powers of their own, but this fresh demand will become important or decay depending on events over the border in Libya.

THE FRENCH profess not to be worried by Algeria, the last of the North Africa trio. It is not a protectorate like Tunisia and Morocco, they say, but a part of France as domestic as Burgundy or Provence, controlled by the Ministry of Interior. This means only that of all the problems of Africa, that of Algeria is the one they wish least to talk about.

The trouble in Algeria is that French colonization has been too successful and no one knows how withdrawal can be staged without plunging the country in horror. There are nine million native Algerians and one million Frenchmen living among them. In Algeria, French colonization is not a surface layer of civil servants, bureaucrats, business men, and adventurers as it is elsewhere but a colonization of ordinary Frenchmen—farmers who till the soil, mechanics who work with their hands, doctors, lawyers, storekeepers. This success presents the future with a witches' broth of racial problems as tragic as those of South Africa. To the ordinary problems of racial friction—language, custom, religion—Algeria adds the age-long hatred of class. The French are the rich. In the past forty years they have bought up the best farmlands, the best vineland, the best groves, the best urban real estate. The Moslems work for the French as hired hands or pick at the tired soils they own on the hillsides with ancient hand tools, nursing the envies of the dispossessed for the well-established.

The ultimate goal of native Algerian politicians is independence, complete and unconditional. But if ever this independence is given Algeria, then its French colonists become a wealthy, defenseless minority, ripe for plunder by a semi-literate, fanatic majority. It is unthinkable for most Frenchmen that they should ever turn one million fellow-citizens over to the untender mercies of the Moslems for spoliation; and yet it is unthinkable for most Frenchmen, with their tradition of liberty and justice, that France should ever establish an "apartheid" of racial fascism as South Africa has done.

TAKEN ONE by one, the demands of the North African states offer many contrasts. Actually, all of them are ripples in the single great wave of challenge which is the Moslem renaissance. The heart of the Moslem movement is the formless, palsied Arab League centered in Cairo, but its impulses reach from the Straits of Gibraltar to the Persian Gulf, wherever old controls or privileges persist.

Moslem nationalism is one of the more grotesque phenomena of the modern world, for its leaders almost everywhere are the floating froth on a sea of misery, volatile and temperamental intellectuals, extortionate rackrenting landlords, as cruel and ruthless to their own people as imagination can conceive, yet voicing for them their irrefutable demand for independence from all Western control.

Somehow, by some anachronism, the demand of masters and landlords for national independence translates itself down to the hot village squares, to the Casbahs and oases, and there, when the imam and the mullah chant and jitter and shriek, the mob howls in sympathy and all its itching, scratching poverty is translated into hatred of the infidel.

The standard French reaction to the Arab impulse mixes truth and delusion in as baffling a mixture as the challenge that calls it forth.

The French case in North Africa starts with the fact that the people are still largely too illiterate to master their own affairs. Hospitals and laboratories, hygiene and agricultural research, engineering and industry—the keys to well-being in this century—have not yet been mastered by an Arab middle class which has mastered the techniques of political agitation and the phraseology of revolt. The French have made their North African dominions the healthiest and most promising of all the lands of Islam. They have the best roads, best schools, best health record, most promising future. Pull the French out, and the system would collapse into the squalor of Iraq, or the unspeakable corruption of Egypt.

But the French have exacted a price for civilization. They have staffed their colonial Empire not only with the technicians without whom modern life cannot proceed, but with bureaucrats, time-servers, deskmen, and artisans who occupy jobs and posts that the natives themselves could ably and profitably fill. The British govern ten million Sudanese with less than 1,500 Englishmen; France, until this year's reforms, needed 9,800 Frenchmen to govern three million Tunisians. Not only that. The French govern harshly, with a vengeful discipline that rarely if ever makes the papers in Paris or overseas.

IV

The French call it L'Afrique Noir—Black Africa—because no one has found a better word to describe the strange lost civilization of Central Africa than the color of its people. Black Africa is a great crescent warped around the South Atlantic, larger than the United States of America, where finally, thousands of years ago in prehistory, the Negroes were pushed by more warlike races to the dead end of culture where they have ever since remained. The heart of this Africa is the dark, rustling rain forests. About these jungle masses stretch the encompassing folds of the savannah for thousands of miles: the flat, dreary river basins, the brush, the veld where the millions live supplicant to the rain and

bent to the leached soils in a routine of life that is common to all dark people no matter what the flag of their masters.

Of the hundred million Negroes divided among the four major European powers in Africa, the French rule thirty million. The amazing thing about these thirty million French Negroes is that almost alone among the emergent colonial peoples they face the white world with hope.

While the *mystique* of North African politics is the word "independence," the *mystique* of the Black Africans is the word *"égalité"*—equality of promised rights. Thus, in the politics of withdrawal, Black Africa is perhaps the happiest prospect to study. What complicates the prospect is that perhaps nowhere in the world is the spread between the extremes of culture so unbelievably great as among the Negro people of French Africa.

Over the course of a century, French education and French culture have drawn thousands of Negroes from the upland bush, imbued them with the spirit of freedom and equality, taught them to write verse, make music, feel at home in the twentieth century. These men, for several decades, have drifted down to the port cities and administrative capitals—Dakar, Brazzaville, Saint-Louis, Conakry—where, clustered together, they feel themselves equal in ability and skill to many of the white Frenchmen about them, which they are. But they are uprooted and unrepresentative men, for what they have learned and what they now know cuts them off forever from the parent civilizations of the jungle and bush village.

There in the remote interior men still hold each other as slaves; the rain-maker, the witch-doctor, the elders meet in voodoo huts and babble the rituals of fetishism; the Arab trader makes his infrequent rounds bearing mirrors and gay cloths; and the peasant lives humbly in his prehistoric poverty. Nor are these people homogeneous even in their barbarism; they are not a nation as the Arabs, however illiterate, are. They are split into dozens of distinct, hostile tribes with dozens of diverse dialects and myths.

It is not the backwoods peasant who exerts the pressure for change but the tiny though growing number of educated Negroes drawn from their midst and suddenly aware of what their people must do and have if they are to belong to the modern world. Happily, all of them, from Communist Negroes on the left to the Gaullist Negroes on the right, realize that what must be done cannot be done without the aid of the French and the wealth of the Atlantic world. What they seek are terms of a new partnership. From their slogans comes the profile of the three great problems that define the sodden misery of the backland Negro.

THE FIRST problem is education. For all of French Africa's thirty million Negroes there are only eighty-eight secondary schools. Haute-Volta is a French territory of three million people that counts only seven college students. Primary education is correspondingly thin—one Negro boy in twenty-five learns to read and write, not even one Negro girl in a hundred gets the same opportunity. It is not the reading-and-writing kind of education, however, that is most important—it is the education in farming, in hygiene, in baby care that counts most. And none of these can be pushed until the leaven of those who read and write is spread across the savannahs.

Where once Negroes mistrusted education and the white man's books, now thousands seek and demand them. Schools are rare and widely scattered, but French colonial officials report that families now pack bag and baggage and move dozens of miles to live near schools where their children can learn.

Water is the next problem. The life of the African Negro as well as his entire culture is gripped by thirst for water. He waits all through the summer and the long winter under the milky blue sky while the dust rolls and the sun burns, while the cassava and millet and corn run low, thinking of water. Then, in a monsoon clap of the night, rain bursts on him with spring, the savannah turns green, and for a few months life smiles. Then the sun comes again, the springs turn muddy, the brooks dry out, the land bakes, and he waits. Water can also mean disaster, for when the jungle is cleared for farming, the soft brown gumbo erodes swiftly. The more intensely the Negro cultivates, the quicker he extends the desert until in some areas newly cleared jungle and bush have in a single generation been turned into a new Sahara.

The last problem is roads and communications. Here the problems of Black Africa mesh directly with those of the Atlantic world, for the Negro sits and scratches with ancient tools the surface of one of the great treasure houses of the world. He sits astride mountains of coal and uranium, vast deposits of copper and iron, outcroppings of diamonds and precious metals which are useless to him and to the outer world because the wealth cannot be moved to seaboard and exchanged for the products of the Atlantic civilizations which he needs. He cannot even contribute those things which he is already prepared to give—cotton, meats, rice—because the machines he needs for them cannot be shipped to him, and the products moved out. Before the dams and power plants can be built, or the machinery shipped in, the roads to carry them must be hacked out.

Nor are roads of economic importance alone. They are arteries of life and culture, for only easily traveled roads can open the horizon of the village beyond voodoo-land; only roads and communications can transform the departure of the native son to school from an adventure that cuts him off from family for years to a commonplace journey over which he can retrace his steps.

THESE PROBLEMS and the heterogeneous, almost schizophrenic, people of the Negro world make the politics of Black Africa. Political groups form, break, and fade away. During the early postwar years the most powerful force among French Negroes was the Communist-controlled and manipulated Rassemblement Démocratique Africain—RDA. The RDA was the first political movement to span the gap between Negro intellectual and backwoods villager, demanding full equality in the cities for the intellectuals and better wages, better marketing facilities for the peasant and laborer. In last summer's elections in Black Africa, the RDA was beaten at the polls—partly by the coarsest manipulation of ballots by French colonial officials, partly by what seems a genuine desire of the Negro voters to repudiate all Negro candidates who stood affiliated with parties directed from France itself. Since the elections, Communist influence in the RDA has perceptibly weakened, and some French leftists hope it can be ripped from their control entirely.

The present dominant bloc of Negro deputies in Paris calls itself the Bloc of Independents. They will vote, they insist, on all measures in the French Assembly strictly from an African viewpoint: how many more schools, how many more roads, how much more equality their votes will buy for Africans in Africa.

What surprises any observer of colonial affairs is how insistent French Negroes are on their French patrimony. These men feel at home in France. They throng Parisian cafés, theaters, and public places, intermarry with French girls, are received at every level and in every home and are fully citizens, not on sufferance or charity, but naturally. The pattern of their grievances and politics is very simple: they insist that the equality they enjoy in Paris be equally theirs in their homeland. French officials get better pay in Black Africa than Negro officials. A wounded French war veteran gets a pension six times that of the wounded Negro veteran in Africa. French unions are allowed to bargain over wages, Negro unions are not.

The Negroes thus seek, not revolt, not expulsion of the white man, but partnership, the substance of all the rights promised them by the French Union. This should make Black Africa an easy problem for the French to deal with. But it does not—it makes it a situation which cannot be kept hopeful or promising without calling in a third party, namely the United States. Whatever the Negro wants—schools, roads, irrigation, hospitals—requires stupendous amounts of capital which France, strained on domestic reconstruction and rearmament, cannot afford to spare. The only possible source of funds not only for French Africa, but for the British, Belgian, and Portuguese Negroes too, is the United States—which means that the keys of the African future are in our hands.

V

The United States is already more deeply involved in France's African Empire than any ordinary American dreams of. We have been drawn in, irresistibly, because of the way the world hangs together and because of our own expanding needs.

We slipped in first some time in 1947

and 1948 because it was impossible for American statecraft to heal Europe without tackling Africa. Europe's single greatest need, for example, is food. But the greatest and closest arable potential lies in North Africa, once the granary of Rome. If these lands can be brought under cultivation again—and they can—Europe's single greatest problem is solved and a major burden lifted off America.

In the past two years Africa has entered American policy more directly because of the bottomless hunger of a booming industrial world for more supplies. Both the United States and its partners are running short of the critical materials of production—iron ore, lead, non-ferrous metals, sulfur, phosphates. Since 1949, Marshall Plan survey teams have been conducting across Africa the greatest treasure hunt in history, looking for such supplies. The Marshall Plan has not only helped expand African uranium, lead, diamond, and copper production, but has uncovered outcroppings of yet unsurveyed resources that lead us to believe that we are only on the threshold of African riches.

More recently Africa has entered our military strategy, for Africa is not only a reservoir of fighting manpower but a platform for air bases that we may sorely need.

Already the Marshall Plan has invested over a quarter of a billion dollars in projects in French Africa. Roughly two-thirds of this sum has gone to Moslem North Africa, the other third chiefly to Black Africa.

This huge investment has gone to

mix itself with French investment, both public and private, to touch off one of the world's most spectacular booms. All around the rim of Africa old ports are being modernized, new ones built, sandbars pierced for navigation; untracked wilderness is being pierced by first roads, and old roads are being paved as the first postwar plans of the French, awakened to slumbering Africa, are being transferred from paper to reality. Marshall Plan equipment and financing has followed these plans. Among other projects, our money has helped the French modernize the Congo railroad, supplied earth-moving equipment for the Niger irrigation scheme, dieselized the coal-burning locomotives of Morocco, and is financing a new electricity distribution system for Casablanca.

The most interesting by-product of the boom has been its psychological effect on the French. North Africa has suddenly become a little Texas where the frozen timidity of the French capitalists seems to thaw under the sun, where little business men can gamble with sardine factories (over 150 have opened in Morocco since the war) and big business men gamble in mines. North Africa is a land of opportunity for thousands of ambitious young men and, for the patriots, the dream base on which France will again rise as a great world power.

The statistical fireworks attendant on the boom seems to lend solid strength to French ambition. Morocco has made the most dazzling progress. A tattoo of construction goes on in Casablanca, which has swollen from 82,000 inhabitants in 1917 to 600,000 inhabitants today. With Marshall Plan help, lead production in Morocco has tripled, ending France's import requirements; phosphate production for Europe's fertilizers has doubled since the war; fishing and fruit-canning show unbelievable curves of ascent. Algeria has become self-sufficient in cement production, tripling its prewar rate of 300,000 tons to 900,000 annually. Algeria's wine exports likewise triple prewar figures. Similar figures of development roll on down around the cape into Black Africa.

ON THE SURFACE, it looks good. But politics unfortunately are made not by statistics but by people. And the people who live in the little shacks tacked together out of old plate, the "*bidonvilles*" crusted about the new French towns, have little if any gratitude for what is being done about them or for them. There has been no political net gain for either the French or the Americans. On the contrary, political agitation in Africa has grown, stimulated everywhere by the progress made.

A careful analysis of the Marshall Plan offers several explanatory clues to this paradox. Only a small portion of American aid has gone to help private enterprise in Africa, but this small portion tells a tale. Almost without exception American grants-in-aid to factories, mines, and mills have gone to French individuals or French corporations; the rare exceptions have usually gone to enterprises of British or American capital. To the Moslems in Africa, we have supplied directly only some tractors for agricultural co-operatives. The result has been that American aid has taken the aspect of a prop underpinning the structure of the French Empire. In the politics of withdrawal we have done nothing that can strengthen or sweeten the spirit of those native leaders who must fill the gap when French dominion ends.

In the past year, darker shadows have fallen across the picture. American interest in Africa has become more and more one of bases and strategic materials. So naked has been our hunger for scarce raw materials that we are lucky that the Communists have not twisted our actions to their propaganda use. Nothing so closely resembles the Marxist myth of "imperialist" exploitation as the simple, technical search for and development of African materials unaccompanied by any program of social betterment that brings schools, hospitals, and housing with the engineers.

Each area the Marshall Plan opens upsets a delicately balanced native society, creating new groups and new discontents along with new opportunity. In Guinea, where the Communist-controlled RDA is so strong, the Marshall Plan has been trying to develop the iron-ore resources near the port of Conakry for European blast furnaces. The first strike there two years ago brought an offer of settlement from the Anglo-French entrepreneurs of 104 colonial francs a day; the French government ruled the wage too high and fixed the rate at 96 colonial francs a day—about fifty cents in U.S. money.

To anyone familiar with the earnest-

ness and diligence of the Marshall Plan's African experts, criticism may sound unfair. Their defense is that a snare of prejudices, both French and African, trap their efforts. They cite, first, the inordinate suspicion among Frenchmen that the Marshall Plan in Africa is a thinly disguised attempt to rape the French of their holdings. For the first two years of the Marshall Plan none of our officials was allowed to travel anywhere in French North Africa without a shepherding French official to guide him. Every barrier of direct contact between American officials and Arabs was thrown up. Only in the past year has this French suspicion begun to abate enough to let French officials discuss Africa in detail with American officials deeply concerned.

The restraints on American policy in Africa are not only French-imposed. Some of them rise from the quality of African civilization itself. The educated African Negro now has an image of the United States refracted through the worst prism of our national life: our racial prejudice. The tales of lynching and the whole body of "Jim Crow" custom make Africans who know little else about America tingle to our name as Jews still tingle to the memory of Hitler. One of the most eloquent anti-Communist African deputies in the French Assembly was invited to the United States last year and turned down the invitation saying: "How can I go? What will they do to me there? What hotels can I stay at? What trains will I ride on?" Black Africans are not too anxious for American penetration.

In North Africa, say the American

experts, the restraints imposed on us by the French are braced by the peculiar characteristics of the underlying Moslem society. It is true that none of our industrial aid to equip North Africa has gone to any native group. But the Moslem rich are not interested in industry and lack the engineering or commercial enterprise to master modern productive investment. The Moslem rich, on the Oriental pattern, prefer to invest in lands they can rack-rent, in real estate they can understand, or in gold they can hoard. The kind of aid that we can give best to them is blocked at their end of the approach by their inability to receive it.

THESE ARE the kinds of excuses, however, that administrators make when they feel themselves hobbled by policy, or leaderless for lack of policy. What has happened is that we have been drawn in Africa into a blind partnership not so much with France as with French colonial officialdom, to the exclusion of the Africans themselves. This partnership needs to be re-organized.

We have learned much from the first chapter of Marshall Plan operations in Africa. We have learned, for example, that no other avenue of approach to the French Empire is open except through the French. The United States lacks the staff of Arab specialists to operate directly in North Africa; we cannot operate directly in Black Africa because the Negroes who are most advanced hate us most. Scattered about Africa are hundreds of brilliant French engineers, scientists, public health experts, schol-

ars, and business men whom we could not hope to replace in decades. The Atlantic Community needs the French.

But if we need the French to make the bridge between ourselves and Africa, we have learned that the French need us in no less measure. Their withdrawal can be made orderly, or be replaced by friendly co-operation, only if the United States pays for the necessary capital investment and development to make contentment possible. If we do not help the French, they will be exploded out of Africa as they have been exploded out of Syria and Lebanon, and are being exploded out of Indochina.

By and large, we have learned, too, that high-minded talk and indefinite promises embitter the Africans rather than cheer them. What the Africans need and want are a series of definite programs, cut off into chapters with clear terminal dates, at the end of which they may have autonomy, independence, or partnership on whatever terms seem fair. To such dates must be hitched equally specific programs for the training, education, and promotion of African personnel lest, when withdrawal comes, it results in such stately irresponsibility as in Egypt. This, indeed, has been the substance of the U.S. State Department's diffident pressure, gently urged on the French but to no avail.

In short, the partnership in which we have so quietly trailed behind the French up to now has to be transformed into a clear understanding, whose goals we can help to achieve only if we have helped choose the goals.

American policies are usually made

by crises punctuated by bloodshed. Thus we inherited Greece and the Mediterranean from the British in 1947 and are now being invited to take over French Indochina in Asia. French Africa is quiet today and just possibly may remain so for several more years to come. But violence lies not too far beneath the surface—the last outbreak in Algeria in 1945 cost hundreds of lives; a more se-rious outbreak in Madagascar in 1947 cost tens of thousands of lives. The most solid reason for American insistence on open partnership is very simple: if the next uprising in North or Black Africa proves too much for the over-burdened French to quench, it is we who will pay the bill. We always do.

HARPER'S February 1952

Chapter 7

Politics USA I: The Fifties

Until 1954, White had only briefly reported on the United States. Now, back from Europe, he knew the long-term story he wanted to pursue: where was America going, and how was it going to get there? In a word, politics. National politics, local politics, racial politics, global politics, the politics of science, of poverty, of security, of oil. It became his permanent beat.

Initially he was a staffer for Max Ascoli's *The Reporter,* for which he had written frequently from Europe. This didn't work out (see Introduction, page xix), and White moved to *Collier's* as national political correspondent.

As it turned out, the magazine had just two years more to

live. In that period, though, White did some of his most intriguing political reporting. Two of these articles comprise this chapter. One, "The Democrats, They're Off and Running for '56," was his first broad look at an upcoming presidential election, analyzing the issues, the candidates, the voters, the finances. It was a prototype of most of his future political articles and books.

The second article, "Where Are Those New Roads?" examines the highway lobby in fascinating depth. "I was no more than days into this story," writes White in *In Search of History*, "when I realized that these proposed new highways meant not only life or death for scores of small cities and towns which would be zoned in or out of the mainstream by the planning, but that the plan as a whole was going to change America."

THE DEMOCRATS, THEY'RE OFF AND RUNNING FOR '56

Here's a special report on how the Democratic party hopes to recapture the White House from the Republicans:

When, in the small, darkling hours of November 5, 1952, the mournful chieftains of the Democratic party switched off their radio and TV sets all across the nation they felt that they were switching off not so much the tale of one evening's defeat as an entire era in history.

The American voters—or so it seemed to the Democrats—had cast into outer darkness the party that had led them to triumph in war, and to prosperity in time of crisis. North of the Mason-Dixon line only three Democratic governors remained to survey the ruins of battle from the majestic cupolas of American Statehouse architecture. Though the Republicans had won Congress by only a narrow margin, the irresistible pull of the Eisenhower personality promised him unchallenged power over legislative policy. When, that same night, one unquenchable reporter asked Adlai E. Stevenson whether he would run again in 1956, Stevenson wearily replied: "Have that man's head examined."

Now, three years later, as the fall season rustles with the political whisperings that presage the return of our quadrennial Presidential drama, the mood of the Democratic party—and of Adlai Stevenson—has almost totally changed. What in late 1952 seemed a cataclysmic tide has now, in Democratic minds, shrunk to the limited dimensions of a flash flood. Not since the springtime of the New Deal, in 1934, have the Democrats won so high a percentage of the voters in an off-year election as in 1954. Not since 1938 have they been so strong at the grass roots where politics begin. With 27 of the 48 governors hoisting the Democratic flag; with an unprecedented roster of Democratic mayors, village councils, sheriffs, court clerks and state legislators (the party has added 500 seats in state legislatures since 1952 and lost only 5); with both houses of Congress under firm control, the Democrats see themselves once more as America's natural majority party. Some, in an optimistic sort of numbers game, add up the electoral vote of the states that have gone Democratic (either for governor or senator) since 1952 and argue that if these victories hold in 1956 the party will have 367½ electoral votes, the Republicans only 163½.

Until the end of September, these hypothetical figures had seemed little more than mathematical pleasantries of Democrats whistling in the wind—for the Presidency of the United States is much more than an addition of local political totals. It is a man-to-man contest inviting the nation to the most profound examination of the personalities of two men, and the man whom the Democrats seemed doomed to face, up until the weekend of September 24th, was Dwight D. Eisenhower—the man nobody hates. With the blow that struck the President on that fateful Saturday, the entire structure of American politics changed. The Democrats, rather than facing the problem of seeking a sacrificial offering for the campaign of '56, were suddenly presented with the possibility of naming once again a man who in fact might become President of the nation.

For the past two months, this correspondent has been traveling, sounding out the Democratic party on its own chances of winning in '56. Even before the last week of September, he had found the party strong, healthy and cautiously optimistic. Except in some New England states, California and a half-dozen grain-belt states, party politicians were convinced that locally, where they live and operate, they could overmatch whatever opposition the Republicans put up. At that time, however, they were perplexed by a massive problem of political engineering—how to bring these formidable local resources to bear nationally against the most amiable personality to occupy the White House in modern times.

This thorny problem was, further, immensely complicated by the fact that most of the Democratic politicians this correspondent talked to liked Dwight D. Eisenhower. Said one, "The real trouble with this guy is that we spent all these years boosting him, shouting for him, loving him. And then he turns around and runs not as a Democrat but as a Republican." Their early plan to bring Eisenhower to defeat had little or nothing of personal bitterness about it. They needed to pit a strong man against Eisenhower, chiefly because the voting behavior of the American citizen makes it imperative that every regional ticket be headed by a national name that can add to, not subtract from, the margin of local victory.

It was Hymie Shorenstein who best described the importance of the head-of-ticket to practicing politicians. Years ago the colorful Hymie was a local satrap in the Brooklyn empire of Boss John McCooey. In one of the routine sharings-out of nominations by the big machine, it fell to Hymie's lot one year to name "his" man for a local municipal justice. As Election Day approached, the uneasy nominee—a newcomer to politics—fidgeted at Hymie's inaction in his behalf. No speeches, no posters, no street-corner meetings—in short, no campaign at all. Finally, he took his complaints to the office of McCooey himself. There in the anteroom he bumped into Hymie. Hymie surveyed his candidate coldly, then pithily explained the facts of political life. "Look," he is reported to have said, "did you ever go down to the slip and watch the ferryboat from Staten Island? When it comes into the dock, it pulls in all the slop and garbage, too, doesn't it? Stop worrying! Franklin D. Roosevelt is your ferryboat."

The Democratic leaders are still looking for Hymie Shorenstein's ferryboat; of what size, capacity and pulling-power it must be to out-draw the Republicans' they cannot, at the moment, judge. But in the uncertain weeks that have followed the Eisenhower heart attack, Democratic ambitions and aspirations have flared for its captaincy in a manner unmatched since the wide-open convention of 1932.

As of October, 1955, three candidates dwarf all others on the Democratic horizon—Adlai E. Stevenson, Averell Harriman and Estes Kefauver. All three nurse a deep yearning to be President. All three, despite a warm, personal affection for the President, have believed that he has been used as a front for the scheming of self-interested men. Each, now, has the opportunity of driving his conviction home to the voters without violating the affections the soldier-President has so solidly won from his fellow-citizens.

They are oddly different types, these three Americans of varied origins.

Averell Harriman, governor of New York, is the oldest. He is sixty-three— a tall, handsome patrician. Imperious yet poised in his public personality, he is in private a shy, almost awkward man—dogged to the point of insensitivity in whatever task or conversational subject occupies him. Now, late in his career, he has found in political life the

emotion for which , as a multimillionaire, he hungered for many years. Previously separated from ordinary men and friendships by the extent of his fortune (his father's estate was estimated at $100,000,000), always previously appointed to public posts rather than elected, Harriman in his 1954 gubernatorial victory tasted the pure, unalloyed joy of self-discovery. It has made him a warmer, more gregarious person. He loves the party which has thrust him to eminence with a devotion which, in late night talks with friends, can become incandescent to the point of zealotry. He is the most intensely partisan of the three Democratic contenders.

Estes Kefauver, at fifty-two, is a striking, husky man, touched with the same vivid animal magnetism that shines through Dwight Eisenhower. Like Eisenhower, he comes straight out of the commonality of American citizens. Kefauver seems mighty natural wearing his campaign coonskin cap, calling his wife "sweetie-pie," pumping hands at village or city street corner. But beneath this deceptively homespun cloak, the senator from Davy Crockett's state harbors an incisive mind and a sense of the jugular which, as his investigations show, can make either racketeers or utility executives squirm. Kefauver is a loner; his senatorial friends are few. Yet even those who derisively call him "Old Cowfever" respect him.

Adlai Stevenson, the chief contender of the three, is by all odds the most complex personality to vie for the Presidency since Abraham Lincoln. However often one meets Stevenson, now fifty-five, one goes away thinking of him as a lithe, slim youth. It is always a shock to return and find him plump and middle-aged. Yet within minutes, by the peculiar conversational magic he can weave, he is disembodied again—a mixture of quips and eloquence, with a persistent underlay of Lincolnian melancholy. Stevenson is of the country gentry of America (as Roosevelt was), of those people born comfortably but without great wealth. No Presidential aspirant since Woodrow Wilson has been more freighted with knowledge of the American past or with intellectual perception of the workings of the American system. Contrary to general opinion, there is little of the indecisive Hamlet about him. He worries a problem considerably before solving it, but having solved it, acts with a firm hand, and sleeps easily. Once given to self-deprecation, he has now—as we shall see—grown far more pugnacious and self-confident. (See Adlai Stevenson Speaks His Mind, page 245.)

Each of these three men professes a high respect for the others. Constantly, each tells visitors how much he likes "Estes," or "Adlai," or "Averell." Yet each—because he is the gathering place of other men's ambitions—cannot help but hurt the inner hopes of the other two.

AT THE MOMENT, Stevenson is, beyond doubt, the front runner in the contest for the Democratic nomination. That he should have remained so, de-

spite his crushing 1952 defeat and the subtle efforts of his party rivals to undermine him, is testimonial to his transformation from the Democrats' most graceful political ornament to their most accomplished tactician and organizer.

This transformation started the day after defeat. That afternoon a long-distance call came through from Washington, D.C., to the governor's mansion in Springfield, Illinois. It was Democratic National Chairman Steve Mitchell, who had been Stevenson's personal choice for the job. The conversation went something like this:

MITCHELL: Let's not waste any time talking about what happened yesterday.

STEVENSON: (a bouncy laugh, then a pause.)

MITCHELL: But what do we do now? Do we walk away from the wreck or do we go to work and rebuild it?

STEVENSON: (pause) We rebuild it. We strip the whole organization to the water line and start all over again.

MITCHELL: Okay. Here we go.

The rebuilding of the party that Eisenhower seemed to have wrecked was then a matter of concern primarily to the professional Democratic politicians. But to Stevenson, a man of deep moral concern, it seemed a personal obligation. The party was divided North against South; and burdened with an $800,000 debt, incurred chiefly on his behalf.

Stevenson, after a rest and a trip around the world, pledged his services and time for a full year to lift the mortgage. Month after month, he barnstormed the country, rousing the party faithful at $100-a-plate dinners, backing the local candidates. A single night's work in Harrisburg would net $270,000 to be shared by the national and local parties—and he would move on. He spoke not only in the great centers like New York, Los Angeles, Philadelphia and Chicago, but wherever the party craved help—in Coeur d'Alene, Idaho; Anchorage, Alaska; Albuquerque, New Mexico; Trenton, New Jersey; Sioux Falls, South Dakota.

Now the professional American politician, Democratic or Republican, is one of the most sensitive—and most maligned—folk characters in our national life. It is he who sticks around at headquarters after the amateurs have walked off on election night, who raises the money to pay the bills, who tends the skeleton machinery of our free system of politics in the long dry season between campaigns. Among professional pols, in the past, there has been a lurid proportion of men who extorted a fat personal fee from society for their services. Most of these are dying out— but their lingering repute has given an occupational inferiority complex to the honest practitioners of the profession. As a result, they respond with affection and devotion when men of honor treat them with respect.

Thus, in traveling around the country raising money for the party, showing concern for politicians' problems, talking with them at leisure as he had been unable to do in the fury of the 1952 campaign, Stevenson found—long before he decided to run again—that he

had a corps of zealous men who were, in embryo, his machine if he wanted them. All this, moreover, was done without losing that gloss of wit and earnestness which had endeared him to so many independents and amateurs. To these he spoke on national hookups with continuing eloquence and skillful timing. Instead of fading into oblivion, as many had predicted, he found himself by late 1955 more powerful across the nation than ever before.

Exactly when Stevenson himself decided to run again is difficult to determine precisely. None of his intimates professes to know. Said one: "At the end of 1954 he was just sticking around to lift the mortgage on the party. He still hadn't made up his mind when he went off to Jamaica early this year. Then he went to Africa. When he came back, he'd changed. He was willing. By July he was running. What made him do it? There's just no one thing you can put your finger on."

Even after many conversations with his associates, this correspondent can only crudely reconstruct the reasons for the Stevenson decision. By 1955 his original respect for Eisenhower—an emotional burden all through the 1952 campaign—had diminished. Moreover, his respect—never very high—for John Foster Dulles had fallen even lower. What Stevenson had seen on his 1953 world trip—his first since the war— had deeply disturbed him. As titular head of his party he had had to ponder and orate on national problems as if he bore their responsibility. Gradually, as with every professional critic, his fingers began to itch for the throttle of power.

No formal Stevenson headquarters has yet been established. What substitutes for it lies in two private law offices, cater-cornered across busy LaSalle Street in Chicago. In one operates Steve Mitchell and his law partner, Hyman Raskin, a portly Iowan and walking tabulating machine of votes and delegates. The other is Stevenson's own modest but handsomely furnished office, where his partner and aide, the able William McCormick Blair, Jr., channels all problems that come to Stevenson personally.

The four most prominent professional politicians on the Stevenson active list are Dick Daley, Chicago's mayor; Jake Arvey, its boss-emeritus; Jim Finnegan of Philadelphia; and that philosophic veteran of the political wars, Mayor David Lawrence of Pittsburgh. These men know Stevenson will have to fight for the nomination; they realize it will cost more than the token $1,366 he spent on the nomination last time (chiefly for keeping the press at the convention well lubricated and reasonably content). But they profess to be unworried about financing; and their campaign is already under way.

On paper, at least, one can now make out a pattern of country-wide Stevenson strength:

The Midwest: Illinois Democrats, led by the Cook County machine, are solid for their ex-governor. Indiana is Stevenson's. Minnesota Democrats will follow Senator Hubert Humphrey's lead, and he has declared for Stevenson (although he may take a first-ballot bow

as a favorite son). Michigan delegates will probably vote for Governor G. Mennen Williams on the first ballot and then follow Williams and the controlling CIO power in the delegation and vote for Stevenson.

East of the Alleghenies, a region where the polyglot big city is the Democratic base of power, Pennsylvania Democrats will be for Stevenson because both their political chief David Lawrence and Governor George M. Leader are. But Lawrence's influence extends far beyond Pennsylvania. It may prove decisive for John Bailey, Democratic National Committeeman, who holds Connecticut's convention votes in his pocket; it may even extend as far as Boston, where the conservative Mayor John B. Hynes will probably—but reluctantly—go Stevenson too. New Jersey's Governor Robert Meyner will be for Stevenson, but will probably have to split his own delegation with the pro-Harriman north Jersey bosses. Delaware seems solid for Stevenson, and substantial strength for him exists in Maryland outside of Baltimore.

In the Border States, Stevenson planners count on Missouri because of Harry Truman. They hope to split the Tennessee delegation with Kefauver, basing this hope on Governor Frank Clement's friendship.

The Far West is unpredictable, being, as one professional politician put it, "loused up with these primaries." Even so, Stevenson can count on support from Washington's Senator Henry M. Jackson, New Mexico's Governor John Simms, Jr., and Oregon's Senator Richard Neuberger.

The South offers by far the most interesting change on the party scene. The alchemy of time has transformed several Dixie states from bitter Stevenson enemies to a potent bloc of support. In removing the desegregation and tidelands issues from political controversy, the Eisenhower administration has blunted the worst differences between Northern and Southern Democrats. Southern Democrats can now contemplate their party's candidates with more calm. In the new view, Stevenson seems much more palatable than Harriman, whom they think of as a Tammany-controlled radical, or Kefauver, whom they regard as a renegade. Party revolt may yet flicker in the South if a combination of Allan Shivers, Albert (Happy) Chandler, James Byrnes and other unreconstructed rebels decides to give the Yankees a tussle in 1956. It may still flare if Truman takes an active preconvention role. But so far there is no sign of it. Senator Richard Russell of Georgia, who led the Southern forces at Chicago in 1952, has promised to support Stevenson, whose strategists also count as solid Mississippi, Louisiana, Georgia, North Carolina and most of Alabama (Senator Lister Hill will support Stevenson).

One last note should be added about the Stevenson campaign—the change in the man himself since 1952. He is sharper, sterner, less apologetic, more ready to do battle. When Governor Shivers of Texas verbally machine-gunned him at a Chicago press conference, some Stevenson lieutenants urged him to lash back immediately, on his home grounds. Stevenson instead accepted a convenient speaking invitation from students at the University of Texas for September, to hold forth publicly in the shadow of Shivers' own podium in Austin.

WITH APPROXIMATELY 450 delegates apparently lined up out of probably 600 needed for a majority, Stevenson might be considered almost a shoo-in. The fact that he is not results from the nature of his present support, which lies with the pros, who, however much they may admire him personally, are generically cagey people. As John Bailey of Connecticut, one of the most astute of the younger Democratic bosses, said: "We pros name the candidates. But it's the people who make the elections. When they go in and close the voting booth, they're kings, and they're alone with the candidate. We can't win for him then. He's got to win for us. Our job is to find the man they'll vote for." The pros are with Stevenson now chiefly because they think he is the best vote getter they have. But over and over, Kefauver and Harriman strategists chant a line that can be summarized thus: "He's lost once, he'll do it again. You don't go to the starting line twice with a losing horse." And the misfortune of the President, rather than weakening this kind of talk, has strengthened it. If the race for the Presidency is really wide-open, argue the supporters of Stevenson's rivals, why take a chance with a loser?

This undermining tactic is pursued most persistently by the Harriman camp. For, although the Stevenson forces fear Kefauver as a rival more than Harriman, the whole weight of American history makes Harriman the more formidable threat.

Any governor who presides successfully over the explosive tangle of interests in New York State is automatically a candidate for President. In addition, the geography of Democratic voting supports this candidacy. Since 1864, all but four Democratic Presidential choices have been residents either of New York or New Jersey. This gravitational force was described somewhat inelegantly last December by two Southern politicians who had strayed to a nearby bar from the proceedings of the Democratic National Committee in New Orleans. A Northern colleague overheard them. "Say," said one in a dawning awareness, "do you think this fellow Harriman is a serious candidate?" The other replied: "Can you tell me a white Protestant governor of New York who ain't?"

Harriman not only starts off with the stupendous prestige of the New York governorship; he also offers the experience of a remarkably successful career of service to the nation. He has been Lend-Lease expediter, Ambassador to Russia, Ambassador to England, Secretary of Commerce, Marshall Plan Administrator and Director of Mutual Security. Since his election as governor his personality has been repackaged into the pattern of the "People's Ave." At Albany he now offers New York State champagne or Genesee beer to astonished visitors of his old international set who remember with nostalgia the days when Averell served only the best vintage wines of France. He has won the affection even of Statehouse chauffeurs by ordering them to doff uniform jackets in midsummer heat, in which formerly they had to keep buttoned up.

At the moment, the Harriman campaign is marked by a single, great and bewildering ambiguity. Repeatedly and vigorously, Harriman insists that he is supporting Stevenson. But, just as vigorously, he has refused to say the few words that would withdraw his own name flatly from the contest and thus make Stevenson's nomination sure.

Two men in particular give the Harriman drive its depth. One is George Backer, a sophisticated New Yorker and former deputy director of the OWI in Europe, sometimes described as Harriman's Colonel House. Backer and the men with whom he deals feel that Harriman and Stevenson are not really rivals, but reinsurance one for the other; if Stevenson stumbles in his candidacy, Harriman can move in, pick up the debris of a Stevenson collapse, and guarantee liberal control over Democratic party machinery.

The other major Harriman strategist is Carmine DeSapio. Tammany Hall's first real boss in a generation and a master political mechanic. DeSapio is the "hard" operator in the Harriman camp; his contacts and methods differ sharply from those of Backer. He has seen and met many of the key political figures of the nation in the past few months— Paul Ziffren of California (a Stevensonian), John Bailey of Connecticut (uncommitted), Jake Arvey of Chicago,

Dave Lawrence of Pittsburgh, Earle Clements of Kentucky (who was boosting a Harriman-Lyndon Johnson ticket until Johnson's heart attack laid him low in July). But he has not tried to line up any cold-cut deal. Rather, he has simply been making friends. In so doing, DeSapio has not only been keeping Harriman's availability right up in the frontal lobes of the country's key delegate-brokers, but he has been practicing a tactic at which he is past master, that of keeping a situation fluid until the last minute, of giving himself maneuverability to bargain and deal down to zero hour.

Nothing better describes the Harriman-DeSapio partnership than the old Chinese maxim that "two people who share the same bed may dream different dreams." In Harriman's mind, his rivalry with Adlai Stevenson is a gentlemanly affair to be settled, perhaps, someday next spring after a man-to-man talk as to which of the two can put up the better fight in the campaign. (They have had two private talks so far this year—luncheon in New York in June and a 45-minute tête-à-tête at Stevenson's home in Libertyville, Illinois, in August. No one knows what they talked about; apparently they have settled nothing between them.) But in DeSapio's mind, the Harriman candidacy is a power potential which he cannot, as Tammany's chief, fail to exploit. For Carmine to follow Harriman's public protestation of support for Stevenson would bring him to Chicago with nothing left for trading purposes. By keeping Stevenson and his forces off balance,

yet in the lead (as he did to Franklin D. Roosevelt, Jr., in the 1954 governor's race in New York), DeSapio retains something to trade.

If the Harriman drive collapses, DeSapio has lost nothing—he may be able even to bargain out his strength against a Vice-Presidency for Robert Wagner of New York or some other prize.

Even at this early stage of the race, Harriman's strength is already substantially greater than on convention eve in Chicago in 1952. He can now count on all the 90-odd votes of his native state, with the possible exception of Senator Herbert Lehman, who is flatly for Stevenson. A cluster of Harriman strength—estimated to total as many as 10 to 14 delegates—has shown up in Massachusetts, stemming from John McCormack, majority leader of the House. The heavily Negro population of the District of Columbia will probably go for Harriman because of his excellent civil rights record in New York. Utah and Idaho offer more Harriman votes. There is also Harriman strength in North Dakota, among Baltimore politicians, and also in northern New Jersey, where DeSapio has working contacts with the Democratic bosses of Hudson County. Thus, Harriman backers currently see an easy 150 convention votes available with minimum exertion.

Were this all, however, or were Harriman in the race alone against Stevenson, he might be accused of absurd naïveté. But the Democratic contest is a three-sided show. And it is on the intentions and potential of Estes Kefauver, as much as on their own strength, that Harriman lieutenants rest their chances. If Kefauver successfully challenges Stevenson's hold on the independents and amateurs in Democratic primaries next spring, Stevenson's campaign will collapse. If it does, Harriman's lieutenants believe that the New York governor will benefit far more than Kefauver himself. So anxious are some New Yorkers to see this test that there is talk of raising a kitty to bank-roll the Tennessee senator through the spring primaries against Stevenson.

THE UNCERTAINTIES that surround Kefauver's intentions are not at all complicated. What lies on Kefauver's mind now, as he toys with his decision, is the still-aching memory of his 1952 try. The nation has largely forgotten to what extent Kefauver, *not* Stevenson, was the favorite of the amateurs, the gallery hero, at Chicago in 1952. Stevenson became the Pied Piper of the independents and amateurs only after nomination, when his eloquence began to warm up their blood. As Senator Paul Douglas of Illinois (once a Kefauverite, now pledged to Stevenson) put it: "Estes played John the Baptist for the Stevenson faithful. He called them to the church and they stayed to pray for Adlai."

Kefauver's 1952 drive was perhaps the most exhausting ordeal of any in recent U.S. politics. Flying from one primary to the next, sleeping three to four hours a night, he nearly destroyed his own prodigious stamina. He not only spent his health but his resources.

When the campaign was over, Kefauver was personally in debt to the tune of $36,000. Such considerations, plus the unhappiness of his wife at the prospect of a second ordeal for her husband, still weigh heavily on his mind.

If, however, the indecision in Kefauver's mind is now a 51-49 imbalance, it is this correspondent's opinion that the 51 per cent weighs on the side of declaring himself in. A shadow headquarters exists in the one-man office of Kefauver's former administrative aide, Charlie Neese, in Nashville. In Kefauver's senatorial offices in Washington, folders are arranged state-by-state, cataloguing the mail that comes in. Card files are indexed by name. The long-distance telephone rings constantly.

In the past year Kefauver has visited 22 states. He takes a rather detached view of his candidacy and his merits vis-à-vis those of Stevenson, whom he likes personally. Kefauver, the candidate, believes that he can harness in his own favor all sorts of emotional resources— from the complicated intricacies of public power and Dixon-Yates to coonskin caps and Davy Crockett. "Davy Crockett won't hurt at all," he said recently.

It remains now only for Kefauver to decide he has the strength and can find the indispensable financing to project him openly into the fight.

This decision, however, is singularly different from those confronting the other two candidates. Both Harriman and Stevenson will be able to maneuver their field forces like staff generals. But Kefauver will have to be a line general, personally leading his troops to battle. And he has powerful enemies. Harry

Truman has hitherto disliked him. Many big-city bosses are still bitter about his underworld probe of 1951, which struck so close to home. Kefauver will have to recruit delegates in the only area free to yield them to him—the 17 states which offer direct Presidential primaries. To mobilize this strength he must campaign in person, starting in February (the New Hampshire primary kicks off on March 13th) and not resting until the primary polls close in California (June 5th).

Kefauver strength today reflects, almost like a silhouette, the map of these primary states—New Hampshire, Wisconsin, Ohio, Nebraska, Florida, West Virginia, Oregon, Montana, Arizona and California. If he sits still, he will get nowhere—harvesting only 70 or 80 votes. If he goes out and fights in the primaries, he may show up at the convention with a remarkable 350 to 400 votes—provided, and this is a critically important proviso, that his natural reservoir of amateur support has not by then permanently drained away to Stevenson.

The tough and tricky decision which Kefauver forces on Stevenson—show strength at the primary polls or quit—is the same decision that Thomas Dewey forced on Wendell Willkie in 1944. When Dewey crushed Willkie in the Wisconsin Republican primary that year, the Willkie campaign was dead. If Kefauver can do the same to Stevenson in any major primary in 1956, the Stevenson campaign, too, will be dead.

Stevenson—who wants to do battle with Republicans, not fellow Democrats—is extremely reluctant to fight a country-wide war for the nomination against Kefauver. Most Democratic professionals agree that such a contest would do the party little good. But they point out to Stevenson that he cannot dodge all the primaries; that one or two will have to be contested, no matter what, just to prove to them and the bandwagon jumpers that he is still the nation's No. 1 Democratic vote getter.

Although some Stevenson lieutenants still insist he keep out of the primaries, most now tend to favor a test of strength in either or both Wisconsin and California. Both have advantages and disadvantages. Wisconsin is a close neighbor state to Illinois, only 15 miles from Stevenson's home; he has powerful friends there plus support from the Milwaukee Journal. On the other hand, Wisconsin is still McCarthy territory, and the Democrats there, traditionally in the minority, are unpredictable.

California, packing the electoral vote of the second largest state in the nation, is a much bigger prize. A gladiatorial battle there between Kefauver and Stevenson might not only be quite a spectacle but might also energize the flabby state Democratic party enough to add real strength for the greater contest next November. The main trouble with California, in Stevenson's eyes, is that the June primary comes so close to the nominating convention as to be useless in influencing other states.

CALIFORNIA EPITOMIZES the real problem confronting the Democrats next year because California mirrors the whole of America in a time of change.

Its 12,000,000 citizens are people on the move, good-natured yet prejudiced, erratic yet choosy. For 20 years, registered Democrats have outnumbered registered Republicans by almost a million. But even with this enormous margin they have carried scarcely a *single* major state-wide office in a decade. This is not because of a peculiar orneriness in California. It is simply because the independent voter—no matter what his nominal party ties—is more numerous in that burgeoning state, with its outsize infusion of newcomers, than anywhere else in the Union. And it is this independent vote, not only in California, but all across our restless country, that troubles the political planners.

For we are entering a new age of American politics. Up to now our great parties have rested on solid blocs of voters bound to them by a memory or kinship of great emotional experience. Until almost yesterday, the Republicans could count solidly on that great bloc of North Central States settled by homesteading Union veterans of the Civil War. Similarly, the Democrats could count on a South held even more solidly by the emotions and memories of defeat in that war. In the populous Northeast the Democrats could count on the devotion of a dozen different minorities born of immigrant or second-generation-immigrant stock—while the Republicans could count just as solidly on the upstate votes of these states whose old-stock citizens drew away from the inrush of strangers in the crowded cities of industry.

All this is changing today. The last great partisan political emotion of Americans stirred with the depression, which made America a country in which the Democrats were a majority party. But that emotion has faded. A whole new generation of voters has grown up since the war years which has no real memories of joblessness or hopelessness. Their family political loyalties have weakened.

The problem this creates for the Democratic captains is a difficult one. Over the years, they deliberately built their party on an assemblage of minorities, on platforms and programs aimed at the heart of masses of underprivileged. Today, however, there are very few grossly underprivileged left; and millions of Americans with alien names now think of themselves not as minorities but as common garden-variety citizens with the same problems of schools, old age, taxes, traffic, draft, homes and careers as other Americans. These are the new independents. If they are to win, the Democrats must find a way to get through to them.

The strategy this had forced on the Democrats in their early fall planning was obvious. It was, simply, to compel Eisenhower to run, not as a national hero, but as the active, partisan leader of their traditional antagonists. This, however, was a tricky operation and, in the instant reshuffling of party positions after Eisenhower's sudden heart attack, the Democrats were relieved of the task of handcuffing the President to his party (which might have backfired on them), and presented with the opportunity of going after the Republican party directly.

Kefauver had always approached the

problem of Eisenhower from a domestic angle. He had described Eisenhower, again and again, as a simple soldier who had permitted special interests to direct affairs which he did not completely understand. Kefauver's inclination is to hammer away at Dixon-Yates, at Hell's Canyon, at the school and highway programs, as examples of an incurable Republican tendency to do things "the bankers' way." His approach to the campaign, presumably, will be little changed whether or not Eisenhower is a factor. "The Democratic attitude," says Kefauver, "has always been to consider the need as the paramount thing and then find means of meeting the need. The Republican attitude is that need is a thing to be relieved only if important private enterprises can do it at a profit."

Stevenson's reaction to the Eisenhower news was completely typical. He briskly refused any comment as to what effect the aftermath of the sad weekend might have on his own chances for the Democratic nomination that was now, suddenly, a prize may men would seek. His main concern, he said, was whether the President, however incapacitated, would retain control of his Presidency or whether he would feel morally obliged to turn it over to Vice-President Richard Nixon, regarded by Stevenson as a narrow partisan. This, in Stevenson's mind, though good for Democrats, would be disastrous for a nation entering a period of portentous diplomatic problems. In Stevenson's book, it is not personal vindication he has sought in a rerun against Eisenhower but a chance to lash back at a Republican philosophy which he vigorously opposes. To this

correspondent he described this philosophy as "in many ways admirable—a respect for order, for production, for people who get things done." But, on the other hand, "completely devoid of the faith that government exists only for the benefit of the people—and that means *all* of the people—or that government exists only to improve their lot—and that means *all* of them, not just some of them."

Harriman, whose skill at electoral tactics, although recently acquired, is noteworthy, has little doubt that the Eisenhower mishap will make it easier to force the Republicans into a tight, unmaneuverable position. The day after Eisenhower's attack, Harriman told this correspondent: "I have consistently said that the 1956 campaign must be fought on the great issues of national and foreign policy and not on personalities, and that a vigorous Democratic candidate, willing and able to conduct a fighting campaign on the issues, can win whether or not Eisenhower runs. That still goes.

"Obviously, the Democratic problem would be a different one if Eisenhower were the candidate because of his personal popularity, in spite of the disillusionment with the Republican party shown by the majority of the voters in the elections of the past two years. When it seemed probable that he would run for re-election, we faced the unusual necessity of establishing clearly his identity with and responsibility for the errors and failures of his administration. If as a result of his present illness he decides not to seek another term, then I would expect to see his influence in the

Republican party rapidly decline and the influence of his right-wing opposition increase. That would make it even more vital to elect a Democratic president, to save the country from reaction at home and 'go-it-alone' abroad."

DESPITE THEIR efforts to get over to the independents, none of the Democrats will ignore by any means the mechanical and tactical maneuvers calculated to energize the still-faithful or galvanize the uncommitted. Already at every level, the Democratic campaign is beginning to shape up.

Tactically, the first problem is to measure the temper of the South. Most Democratic leaders believe that the South, with the exception of Texas and Virginia, is already safely back in the fold. "Virginia," said one ruminative Southerner, "is lost. The young folks there have gone just plumb Republican." Texas depends on the outcome of the boiling internal fight against Governor Shivers. Should the Loyalist-Rayburn-Johnson faction prevail, Texas is certainly home safely with the Democrats and with Stevenson. And even if Shivers should win, it is doubtful whether he could deliver Texas to any other Republican but Ike.

To make sure of the Southern base is the first order of strategy among Democrats. If, at Chicago, Southern delegates should prove restive, they will be placated probably by a Border State choice for Vice-President who can appeal not only to the South but to the Northwest, similarly bedeviled by the

public-power issue. The two most prominent Vice-Presidential nominees under discussion if this should be the decision on strategy are both youthful Tennesseans—Senator Albert Gore and Governor Frank Clement.

If, however, the South continues in its present apparent indifference, Democratic strategists will be able to make a bolder move. In the Stevenson camp particularly one hears speculation on the possible effect of a Catholic Vice-Presidential nominee. The Democrats are acutely aware of the disaffection of the traditionally Democratic Catholic vote in the large Northeastern industrial centers. Two exceptionally able young Catholic figures stand out in speculation—Mayor Robert Wagner of New York and Senator John Kennedy of Massachusetts. In this talk, Kennedy is given the edge. Either the Gore-Clement choice or the Wagner-Kennedy choice will show the Democratic strategy clearly.

Vice-Presidential strategy will probably not be settled until the last minute at Chicago, and then, as usual, by the personal decision of the Presidential nominee. Campaign issues are more clear-cut, at least at present. They will be tailored to make maximum use of local and regional strength amassed by the Democrats since 1952. The Dixon-Yates and Hell's Canyon controversies will be employed to rouse both the TVA area and the Northwest, where public power is a primordial issue of political emotion.

In the farm states, the Democrats will keep pounding the farmer with the fact that he is falling behind the rest of the nation in general prosperity; Ezra Benson will be fried in oil, butter and margarine.

In the Northeast, the Democrats will concentrate on unemployment in Pennsylvania, West Virginia and New England; here, despite general prosperity, disconcerting pockets of joblessness fester. The recent New England floods will give Democrats an opportunity to trot out their old proposal for a TVA to control its floods and make cheap power.

Over all, Democrats will hammer at the conduct of former Air Secretary Talbott; at the polio "snafu" and Mrs. Hobby's role in it; at John Foster Dulles; and at Big Business, generally and specifically. Senate Democrats have been quietly accumulating material for investigation for months. They will probably start breaking this in early 1956; one or two senators claim they are on the trail of inside deals, particularly in agriculture, juicier even than Dixon-Yates or the Talbott affair.

Many of the Democrats rub their hands as they look forward to this campaign. Having run campaigns for 20 years from the White House, they have envied the Republicans, who could exhort, expose and denounce with the carefree air of men unburdened by office. Said Steve Mitchell to this correspondent: "This could even be fun. This time we'll be able to concentrate on nothing but running a campaign without worrying about running a war, making taxes, directing an Air Force, conducting a foreign policy at the same time."

All these tactics are, of course, assault material, ammunition for attack. But the party plans also to offer wares of a more positive nature.

Very quietly, in the past two years, top Democrats have brought into being a group whose impact on the party may be almost revolutionary and whose existence has until now been kept among the party's most private secrets. This is the so-called Finletter Group, after Thomas Finletter, former Secretary of the Air Force, who directs its cogitations.

The Finletter Group is an unofficial policy-planning group which meets irregularly and assembles the Democrats' best brain power to prepare not only campaign material for 1956 but policy material for use if victory is achieved. It was born partly out of Finletter's observations in England (he was Marshall Plan Administrator there in 1949) of the way in which the out-of-power Conservatives planned their way back to victory over Labor; partly out of the desire of the Stevenson campaign-train veterans of 1952 to continue their work on national problems.

Convinced that most of the old issues on which the Democrats won and held power for 20 years are now dead—chiefly because they have been successfully solved—the Finletter Group is actively exploring new ideas and new issues. In an age when the national economy seems finally controllable and controlled, when the personal problems of prosperous citizens become ever more pressing in political emotions, the Finletter Group is examining just what the role of the federal government in these problems should be. Its members have studied the problems of the aged and possible federal assistance to them; the school problem; the problem of the mentally ill; national-defense policy; the farm problem; the tricky issue of due process of law in security cases; the reorganization of our tax structure. They have examined the proper priorities in public spending—as, for instance, whether the nation needs roads more than schools, or schools more than health measures.

The group is a loose and challenging assembly of former high New Deal officials, businessmen, lawyers, specialists and professors. They meet usually in New York (either at Finletter's apartment or at the august literary club, the Century). A topic is pre-selected and assigned to a task force, then discussed at sessions that start in early afternoon and run through dinner almost to midnight. Both Stevenson and Harriman have attended these sessions on a more or less regular basis, sometimes both of them at once. Twice the group has met in Chicago for Stevenson's convenience. Kefauver has not yet been included, but he may be invited in shortly. By campaign time, whoever the Democratic candidate is will have a vivid policy program to expound.

———

IT IS HERE, in the explorations of the Finletter Group, that the Democrats are probing most deeply at the questions that underlie U.S. politics today. For America today is fat, smiling and happy as never before—while the Democratic party prides itself on being the party of adventure, excitement and change. The Finletter Group reflects a Democratic recognition that new issues, new programs are needed not only to meet the new perplexities of a prosperous citizenry, but to cajole it out of its current political placidity.

No Democratic leader today, in private, will guarantee that either assault tactics or promissory blueprints can lay the Republicans low in 1956. Regardless of Eisenhower's role in the campaign, Americans will judge Republicans and Democrats in terms of the nation's contentment, an intangible thing at best. If Americans are content with things the way they are (so go the general prognosticians), no scholarly exploration of the future is likely to lure them from the administration that presides over them, no matter who its real or symbolic leader may be. But if they wish to venture out once more on new expeditions, history will witness one of the most dramatic campaigns in the chronicle of human politics—with the result unknown until the votes are counted in November, 1956.

Adlai Stevenson Speaks His Mind

Adlai Stevenson's house in Libertyville sits white and quiet on the rolling plains of northern Illinois, little different or more imposing than any of the other white farmhouses that speckle this green and fertile corner of our Midwest. We wandered about the little farm a bit, wondering whether the stacked hay would last the winter, watching the black-faced English Suffolk sheep ramble about the pastures.

When we came back to the screened-in veranda of the farmhouse, Stevenson sprawled out on the sofa, infinitely comfortable in the heat, in his navy-blue shorts and open-necked blue work-shirt. He began slowly to talk about the campaign. It had been a busy week. Some twenty governors had stolen time from the Governors' Conference in Chicago to come and pay their respects. He'd been listening to the country through them as he has listened to the country and the world in that same house during the past two years. He talked a bit about his mail, about the many well-wishers who kept urging him to run. Then, easily, he began to talk about the Presidency.

"Why, I think of the Presidency as something that should be almost beyond ordinary ambition. I don't think you run for the Presidency as you would for coroner—because you like politics and would like the job. The Presidency—the actual and symbolic leader of the most powerful and influential de-mocracy in history—is something elevated beyond ordinary human experience or desire. And I don't think a man should consider or be considered for that position unless he has deep convictions about public questions, unless he understands the historical mission and principles of his party, and unless he honestly believes that it is the best political instrument to govern the nation and realize its hopes.

"But when you do have convictions, when you feel that there are things that must be said to inform the people, then you don't withhold your body from the battle merely because you might be defeated. The important thing in our system is to continue and improve the dialogue between the two great parties, in order to give our sovereign, the people, educated, understanding choices."

We talked on a bit about his concept of the institution of the Presidency, and then I got him back to the current political scene.

"I have many anxieties about this administration and its combination of demonstrative piety and moral duplicity, its curious contradictions. For example, it seemed to me a little incongruous to fire a Talbott for his conduct in office and also congratulate him by letter—and even give him a decoration of honor for his services, a decoration which serves as an example for our young people to try and do likewise. There seems to be nothing morally wrong to them with promising to tell the nation the whole story of Dixon-Yates—and then withholding significant and embarrassing details. Nor, indeed, was there any audible Republican protest when the chairman of the Republican National Committee sent McCarthy across the country on Lincoln's birthday to denounce the work of fellow Americans as 'twenty years of treason.'"

Stevenson paused, reflected, and went on:

"Then you can go on to the bigger things. I am thankful that after all the abuse of the New Deal the Republican party has not attempted to jettison all the Democratic reforms outright. But I am uncomfortable just now about the similarity between 1928 and 1956 and the undertone of trouble in the midst of apparent prosperity. And, of course, I've been appalled by the erratic swings from one extreme to another in the conduct of our foreign policy, although basically the same foreign policy as the Democrats'. Then there's this flow of domestic proposals, which always say the right things—but little or nothing is done to implement them. There's a national education program put forth in all the right language—yet entirely inadequate for the problems it's advertised to solve. So with the health program, agriculture, polio vaccination and so on. There was all this talk about a higher concept of politics and the proper use of political machinery.

"And it keeps going on—this tendency always to sacrifice the people's credulity, even the nation's welfare, to the greater glory of the Republican party; to appease a McCarthy, a Cohn, a Schine.

"Just think of the grandiloquent foolishness of those phrases—'unleashing Chiang Kai-shek,' 'massive retaliation,' 'agonizing reappraisals,' 'liberation' and so forth. Then think of the total reversal in the past few months. Bluff and backdown; optimism and pessimism; tough talk and love feasts in bewildering succession. Small wonder that many thoughtful people have seriously suspected that calculating men have deliberately conspired to get this country in trouble so they could call in the President to put out the fire at the last moment—amid reverberating applause, but no criticism for letting us get into such predicaments in the first place."

At this moment a new train of thought struck him and he chuckled and began to talk about Republican history. Democrats could never lick the Republicans back in the old days, said Stevenson—not when they were freeing the slaves, giving out free homestead land to the settlers, protecting the infant industries and the full dinner pail. They began to lick the Republicans, he said, only after the people caught on to the fact that the Republican party had deserted them and special interests had taken over the party. Teddy Roosevelt, a radical Republican, interrupted the process for a while, then it began again. I asked Stevenson just what he meant by special interests and he began to choose his words with care.

"I'm not one of those who believe that big business or wealth is bad, per se. A lot of the epithets used in the past have been misleading and unfair. We live in a time when large movements are inevitable and selfish human nature does not change much. It's not the government's duty to hold the clock back to meet some set of doctrinaire principles left over from the last century. But it *is* the duty of the government, I think, to govern for the benefit of all the people, not just some of them—especially those best able to look after themselves.

"Now the men of this administration have been preoccupied with a particular kind of people. Some label it 'big business,' some 'the rich and the well-born,' to use Hamilton's phrase. But there is always this feeling in the Republicans that there are several kinds of people, 'bird dogs' and 'kennel dogs' if you wish, and in every Republican administration going away back the same thing emerges, a special tenderness and care for special groups.

"And I'm worried by these times. This is one of those intervals in our history when the press, money, business and government have coalesced. These are imponderable forces in our national life, and as the tendency to concentration of power and influence grows, the power of coercion grows, too. We see it growing all the time, in the direction of greater control. We see dissent and criticism diminishing. And conformity is always the easiest way! But self-criticism is indispensable to successful democratic government. We have an old American tradition that there are no sacred cows in our public life; and it seems to be going by the board.

"It's this coalescence of force in the country that worries me. Criticism is neither dead nor moribund, but it seems to be at a new low both in fact and fashion. I don't like to see the separations going on between these forces that dominate us and the rest of the people as a whole. I think it's a dangerous trend. And it can get worse."

COLLIER'S October 28, 1955

WHERE ARE THOSE NEW ROADS?

Here is a special report that's of vital and immediate concern to every motorist in the U.S.A.

One year ago—in January, 1955—the American people were invited by the President to embark on an adventure for which nothing in the history of man offered any precedent. It was, in name, a road-building program—but a road program of such stupendous engineering magnitude as to make the works of man in any other age seem almost aimless scratchings of the ground. It was a proposal to build such a system of roads in the United States as would make the Great Wall of China seem no more than a welt on the earth's surface and the Pyramids of Egypt no more than warts. Calling for combined state-and-federal road outlays of $101 billion over 10 years, President Eisenhower's highway program dwarfed any other enterprise ever undertaken or projected by our government, with the sole exception of World War II.

Whatever became of it?

The great highway program of 1955 expired in the Congress of the United States. It died in an extraordinary convulsion of contending interests which paralyzed Congressional action. Hardly a murmur, however, was heard from the ordinary motorist behind the wheel, although his interests are just as intimately—and far more tragically—involved in the inadequacy of our present road net as the big battalions of open pressure.

In January, 1956, the second session of the 84th Congress must again begin grappling with the problem of the nation's highways—the slaughter and waste forced on us by a road system no longer able to match the needs of a growing country. Who will be heard from in 1956?

The highway battle will almost certainly explode in Congress in the same clash of interests (all, curiously enough, recorded *in favor* of better roads). Equally certain, it will end again in paralysis—unless the public bestirs itself as it did not during the Great Roadblock of 1955.

Deep somewhere in the origins of this new national highway program lurk the strains and nightmare fears of the average American motorist. Though historians of the future may someday write that the Americans were a race of killers who slaughtered one another in public places with the casual indifference of a tribe of rubber-wheeled Huns, the everyday carnage does not leave ordinary Americans unmoved.

248

Daily, we mangle one another—ripping limb from limb, hurling two-ton missiles against the frail bodies of unprotected citizens, lacerating our nerves with instantaneous gambles on what may be approaching at the hidden corner or speeding down the other lane beyond the masking truck.

The current Christmas—New Year's holidays, for example, will suddenly terminate the lives of more than 1,000 Americans journeying happily by car. Last year we killed 36,000 citizens on our public roads and wounded or crippled 1,000,000 more. Since 1945, we have killed off as many Americans on our streets and highways as did Nazis, Japs and Communists on every field of battle of World War II and Korea combined. All this, moreover, will go on and on until we get highways of modern design. These, say the experts, can reduce our annual death toll by 25 to 35 per cent, or save a staggering 10,000 American lives each year by engineering alone.

The great highway program of 1955, however, was proposed not so much out of pity and compassion as out of simple need.

We in America are strangling on our own prosperity. Our country is approaching an age and level of development where the problems that face us are of a kind no other civilization has ever known before. We confront an entirely new order of anxieties—and among the foremost of these is the problem of the automobile on our streets and highways.

For it is the automobile, as much as any other single phenomenon, that sets our way of life apart from the rest of the world. Everywhere else, common people have always been separated from their betters by the simple distinction of whether they walked or rode. In times past, people who rode were "cavaliers," hence aristocrats. In America today, every man is a cavalier.

Seventy million Americans—so says the American Automobile Association—take their annual vacation in the family car. Every year their appetite and their range of travel broadens so that, today, it is difficult to remember or recognize how fresh and novel even in our own country this revolutionary impulse is.

It was only yesterday—in 1911, the year that Dwight D. Eisenhower entered West Point—that a commercial automobile first managed the road trip from Coast to Coast. The expedition from Denver to Los Angeles alone took 66 days; tomorrow, if Dwight D. Eisenhower's road program becomes fact, that same trip will be little more than a weekend run.

TODAY, EVERY perspective of our country and times leads us to believe that we are only at the beginning of the automobile age, the era of complete mobility. Today, we have an automobile industry that turns out 8,000,000 new vehicles a year. This industry has already equipped our highways with 61,000,000 cars and trucks; in 10 years there will be some 81,000,000 in use, and in another decade the total will be almost 100,000,000.

What makes these figures ache is

their relationship to our roads. At the outbreak of the second World War, we had about 3,300,000 miles of road in this country; since then we have added about 1 per cent in new road mileage. The present length of our roads is almost permanently frozen. As we add new automobiles, the existing lanes must, therefore, be broadened continuously. Since the war, we have worked energetically but sporadically on bits of superhighway; but in the same period the number of vehicle-miles driven in this country has doubled, and even with the new roads our traffic lanes are totally inadequate. If, at present, every registered automobile in the country took the road at the same time, we would have one car spotted every 700 feet on every street, every country road, every lane of every highway. And in 20 years their numbers may nearly double. Now, to any American who has let his throttle out as he turned off the cloverleaf onto one of our great new superhighways, denunciation of these great lanes must seem like nonsense. We Americans are people who thrill to road building and engineering; each new overpass, each great split-lane seems to have added dimension to our power and imagination as individuals.

Our newest state highways—the majestic Ohio Turnpike, the crowded New Jersey turnpike, the imperial New York Thruway—are superb thoroughfares, the best of all time. But they are only stumps and pieces of a highway net. They are not a *system*. They are built only in and through limited areas where the engineers gamble that the toll fees of normal driving will repay in

precisely calculated and collectible sums the enormous investment of private bondholders. They are not enough, and they dump the traffic they collect on the outskirts of our big cities in chaos and confusion.

The real problem of road building in America is new, and peculiar to our kind of democracy. In a country where every man is equally privileged and equally mobile, no citizen can be prevented from using the roads when and how he wants—even if everyone wants to use them at the same time. And, just as the arteries of our blood must be prepared to handle the emergencies of physical exertion or let us die, so the arteries of our public communication must be able to handle the convulsions of seasonal or weekly peaks in traffic or let anarchy prevail.

This is why our engineers figure that every highway must be designed to carry all normally predictable congestion (except for those 30 busiest hours of the year—the summer weekends and Labor Day and Fourth of July hegiras—whose peaks cannot be handled except by astronomic expenditures.) This is why, too, our highways must be designed to handle any legitimate truck load.

Our roads today, fine as they may feel under the tread of normal weekday traffic, no longer meet these standards. Certain sections of our nation's choking road net are already killer belts—the Boston Post Road between New England and New York, the old Suicide Alley out of Baltimore to Washington which engineers call "Bloody One," the southern leg of the same U.S. 1 as it stretches down Florida from Jacksonville to Miami, the "Grapevine" along U.S. 99 dropping into California's San Joaquin Valley . . . these are already notorious murder lanes.

As fast as we build, we create traffic jams. The New Jersey Turnpike, opened in 1952, is already carrying a traffic load not predicted until the early 1980s. Already, even with its new avenues of access, New York City's approaches are so congested that on a summer Monday morning when returning weekenders mingle with the truck peak, the traffic backs up so fast at the mouth of the Holland Tunnel that an athlete, running as fast as he can, could not keep up with the tail of the jam once it begins to clot backward.

All this is costing incalculable sums of money. It costs us, in addition to the cold valuation of $4.3 billion annually in accidents, another $5 billion in wastage of labor time, gasoline, rubber and equipment. It literally costs less to ship a crate of apples all the way from Oregon to the Hudson River than to get it across the Hudson to New York's East Side.

This road shortage may finally, if war comes, cost us our national life. For none of the great metropolitan areas possesses anywhere near adequate road facilities to evacuate swiftly the more than 70,000,000 people our Civil Defense authorities estimate will have to flee.

The crisis has been swelling for a long time. But up to now our highways and roads have been in the domain of state and local governments, with the federal government appropriating a modest annual sum to subsidize them in their work. Last year, finally, we arrived at a stage when it was obvious that the local resources and local programs could no longer meet what is now a national emergency. Which is why, one year and three months ago, Dwight D. Eisenhower asked a group of five distinguished citizens, headed by General Lucius D. Clay, retired, to devise a program for meeting the crisis head on.

The Clay report that issued from their labors was hailed editorially almost unanimously, and in a few weeks, now renamed the President's Highway Program, was delivered to Congress for action. Whereupon nothing further happened except debate. For suddenly our lawmakers found themselves engaged, at the supreme level of national politics, with those forces and groups which have always, in every Statehouse, made highway politics synonymous with bitterest controversy.

THE CLAY PROPOSALS were not, of course, born simply out of the amateur ruminations of a number of civic-minded gentlemen enthusiastically exploring our needs over a period of a few weeks. They were, as a matter of fact, only the polished form of a dream that had slowly been maturing in Washington for 20 years.

For Washington, among other things, is a city of dreamers. Among the boldest of these dreamers have always been the engineers of our Bureau of Public Roads. And the dreams that emerged in finished form in the Clay report were born at the bureau in the darkness of the depression. At that time, some now unremembered congressman pushed through Congress a resolution calling on the bureau to scheme up a major road-building program to soak up depression unemployment. What the congressman wanted, however, was a geometrical grid across the nation—three multilane highways running east to west, three more running north to south, all of them darting up hill and down dale, straight as an arrow, with little or no relationship to the needs of the country.

The engineers of the Bureau of Public Roads soon pointed out how phenomenally uneconomic and expensive such a grid would be. But they suggested an alternate plan, called the National System of Interstate Highways, which would be something entirely different. Through the years, the dream system gradually won official recognition. Franklin D. Roosevelt blessed it as a measure to pick up postwar economic slack; Congress, in 1947, formally made its map tracings official as the outline of our future in public communications.

The Interstate System will be based on existing roads. In its improved form, as it lies on the planning boards of the engineers, it is still a dream—a spectacular in concrete, asphalt and steel. Forty thousand miles of multiple-lane highway, running between major cities, will stretch across the nation in a road net distinguished from any previous conception of engineers in capacity, durability, grandeur and sweep.

Men will be able to drive from New York to San Francisco, scarcely, if ever, slowing at a traffic light. Truckmen will grind on hour after hour, without shifting gear or slowing to the agony crawl of the upgrade. Passenger cars will sweep by them in other lanes without ever once having to poke their noses out into the perilous stream of opposing traffic. Hills will melt away and distances will evaporate.

Not only that. The Interstate recognizes the tragic plight of our strangling big cities. It is the first serious plan to cleave through the tangled approaches of our great metropolitan areas and clear broad avenues of entrance and exit through the choking metropolitan jungle and its sprawling suburban fringes. Where our present new highways stop at city limits, the Interstate will slice directly through the urban jungle of streets in spectacular expressways that will take people through the heart of metropolis and out to the open road on the other side. It will be a *system*.

The Clay program—the President's Highway Program—made the Interstate System the crownpiece of a simple three-point program.

First, it proposed that the federal government raise some $25 billion to spend on the great Interstate to finish it in 10 years—this sum to represent 90 per cent of the total cost, the balance to be raised in the states. Thirteen billion of this would be spent on urban approaches alone. Where modern toll roads were up to the dream standards of the Interstate—some 2,500 miles of such roads exist, mainly in the North—

the states which had built them would be reimbursed.

Second, it proposed that current routine federal appropriations for highway aid to secondary and feeder roads of the great Interstate be continued at $600,000,000 a year, or slightly less than their present total.

Third, it proposed a way for paying for the great new Interstate—that the federal government would set up a Federal Highway Corporation which would sell $20 billion worth of bonds, the bonds to be paid for out of current gasoline taxes, which would bring in ever more income as the new roads were built. The bonds, it was estimated, would take 30 years to pay off.

It was this third proposal that triggered off the fight. For the politics of American highways has always been dominated by one overwhelming truth: everyone loves roads, but no one wants to pay for them.

ONCE THE great highway program reached Congress last February, all the complications of this truth began to unfold. The 1955 Battle of the Highways, as fought in Congress, proceeded in three main stages, each illuminating a separate area of uncompromising conflict.

Both of the first two stages of battle unrolled in the Senate—and each had a partisan champion. One was the freshman senator from Connecticut, Prescott Bush, an able and distinguished man making his mark for the first time upon the Senate and nation in an issue of na-tional significance. In the absence of senior Republican leadership, he emerged as the captain of the administration's road program to raise 20 billion federal dollars immediately by bond issue, as proposed in the Clay program. The other was the freshman senator from Tennessee, the shrewd and eloquent Albert Gore, who questioned not only the wisdom of so huge and inflexible a national commitment to roads, but, even more, the sweeping powers the federal government would arrogate under the Clay proposals over a domain that had always hitherto been under the states.

The first of the two Senate struggles raged over the bond-financing provisions of the administration's highway bill.

FOR TWENTY years, the Senate had listened to Republicans denouncing Democrats as borrowers and spenders, recklessly saddling the nation with debt and burden down through all the unborn generations of time. And the Democrats had always replied that this was a healthy, growing country whose children could well afford to pay for the benefits we, their fathers, were so wisely preparing for them.

Now the sides switched. The Republican bond corporation proposal, said the Democrats, was trickery, fraudulent evasion of the legal debt limit of the nation. The bonds would eat up $11 billion of interest in addition to their principal; only bankers would profit.

It was as if, they implied, the huge

$280 billion official national debt were about to spin off a satellite "corporate" debt into space, perhaps followed by others, until we had a whole constellation of satellite debts whirling about the economy, all exerting an irresistible inflationary pull.

"I for one," summed up Senator Gore, "think that the need for highways must be considered along with, and balanced with, the need for other programs, such as schools and hospitals. It doesn't make sense to me to segregate the highway problem by excluding highway expenditures from the budget and from the public debt. It doesn't make it any easier to pay for them. In my opinion, no financial legerdemain can isolate the highway expenditures or eliminate their impact upon our economy and upon the Treasury of the United States."

To all of which arguments, the Republicans replied as if the mantle of Franklin D. Roosevelt and all the ghosts of the New Deal had descended on them. Nothing great or creative is ever done, they said, unless one reasonably finances the present out of the future. This is what a homeowner does when he raises a mortgage on a new home, what a corporation does when it issues debentures for a new plant, what the nation must do to finance expansion in time of need.

They argued that if money were available immediately, through the bonds, to build the system now, highway use would increase so rapidly that gasoline taxes would rise enough to pay off the entire debt burden within 30 years without a single extra tax. Roads would be built, said the Republicans—and it would be painless.

"The importance of the Interstate Highway System is so great that it has to be provided for now," said Senator Bush, who led the Republican defense. "It must be completed within 10 years and must be put in effect as a whole, and not piecemeal. . . . The plan contained in . . . the Clay bill . . . is a pay-as-you-use plan. Nobody who has been in business would say that it is not good business to borrow money to build productive assets. That is the only purpose of borrowing money in the field of commerce and industry. It should be likewise in government."

The Senate gravely listened to both sides, then by a resounding two-to-one vote rejected the President's bond plan. It then turned to phase two of the fight—the argument over the alternative plan brought in by Senator Gore for the Democrats. The Gore bill was quite different from the President's original proposal. It carefully omitted any financing provision at all, thus dodging that fight; the money for the highways it proposed would be found, said its proponents, by the House—where, constitutionally, all bills taxing American citizens must arise.

Deep and basic to the thinking of the Gore bill were several convictions—that the secondary and country roads would be shortchanged if the Clay proposals for pouring money into the Interstate went through; that the nation had too many other needs to commit itself irrevocably to so large a program at once; that control of the money it appropriated must rest with Congress, not with any centralized federal agency.

Instead of biting off a 10-year chunk of the future, therefore, it limited its commitments to $7.7 billion over a five-year period, after which Congress could take another look at the problem. Another $4.5 billion would go to the lesser local roads that would feed the Interstate.

The Gore bill represented the best thinking of Senate Democratic leadership. And the Republicans, led by Bush again, denounced this thinking as pitifully inadequate. It was a horse-and-buggy bill, they said, as they went on to open up another continuous area of American highway debate—the everlasting struggle between metropolitan and rural Americans about where and how roads should be built.

What the Republicans objected to most was the way the Gore bill shared the enormous funds for the Interstate among the individual states. The Clay proposal had advocated that $25 billion be spent by the Highway Corporation where needed—largely in the congested population centers of the North and East. But the Gore bill instead insisted that at least half the money be divided among the states by the traditional formula of highway aid.

THIS CONGRESSIONAL formula, first invented in the Road Act of 1916, still quaintly reflects the era of the Model T Ford and the Stanley Steamer. By this old formula, all federal highway aid is divided in thirds. One third is shared by states according to their population; another third is divided among states according to area; the final third is distributed in proportion to their mileage of Rural Free Delivery routes. This, of course, penalizes the heavily congested states of the Midwest and the Northeast and favors the wide-open range and farming states.

Senator Gore said he did not want money appropriated by Congress to be cut up by anybody except Congress. "I just do not believe," he said later, "it would be consistent with the public interest to place this much authority in the hands of any one person . . . As Governor Hugh White of Mississippi has said, 'Those people in Washington might wake up with indigestion some morning and decide not to give my state any money.' I am confident that Congress . . . will never agree to make a permanent appropriation of such huge sums, with the money to go into a 'kitty' to be doled out on the basis of what the Secretary of Commerce considers to be the needs of the various states."

The Republicans called the Gore bill a "blunderbuss bill." Said Bush, "After he has read the analysis of the distribution of the fund, I will leave it to every senator to say whether he does not agree that that is a good term to apply to the proposed legislation. The fact is that 30 states are given less than they say they need to complete the Interstate System and 18 states are given far more than they need and more than they can use. I say [it] . . . scatters dollars and does not build roads where the roads are needed."

Once again, as debate rolled on, the Senate sat in witness of a switch. The Democrats, normally as sensitive as sandpapered skin to big-city votes, voted solidly for the bill. Republicans, normally suspicious of big-city needs, voted solidly against it. But the Democrats had the votes and the Gore bill passed. It passed, to be shelved almost immediately. For while the long hearings and debates had dragged on in the Senate through March, April and May, the members of the House had begun to draw up their own plan—the so-called Fallon bill.

NOW THE Fallon bill—named for Democratic Representative George H. Fallon of Baltimore, a long-time road enthusiast—was offered as a work of courage and forethought. Long before the Senate had finished consideration of the bills before it, House Democrats had decided that their road bill would be one of "real statesmanship"—which is to say that since roads have to be paid for, they would undertake to find the money. The Democrats of the Public Works' subcommittee drawing up the road bill conferred with Sam Rayburn, the Speaker, who praised their inclination and then, in a total breach with House tradition, told them to go ahead and write the taxes themselves.

The Fallon bill accepted the dream plan of the Interstate System, and the continuing federal support of lesser roads as embodied in the President's program, altering them chiefly by spreading out the expenditures over 13 years instead of ten. But it flatly re-jected setting up any federal corporation to borrow the money by bonds. Instead, it bracketed the appropriations it demanded with precise tax measures to meet them.

It insisted that the burden of paying for roads must fall most heavily on those who profit most by them. It called for raising the tax on every gallon of gasoline burned in our automobiles by an additional cent (at a cost to the average motorist of about $5.56 a year). Not only that. The architects of the Fallon bill were convinced that the ponderous, pounding heavy rigs of the trucking industry are the villains that beat our roads to bits. Consequently, they proposed that heavy trucks should pay a sort of supertax—a 50-cents-a-pound tax on every truck tire over 8.5 by 18, a special four-cent tax on each gallon of fuel for the extremely heavy diesel trucks, a new and heavier excise tax on a new truck when purchased. Such taxes meant that the normal five-axle heavy rig would be hit by what the truckmen claimed would be an additional tax bill of some $1,031 in the first year.

Well before news of these tax provisions had leaked, however, and as soon as the House Democratic leadership had made known that its Roads subcommittee was writing a pay-as-you-go tax bill, every economic interest in our country with any direct or remote connection with highways girded its loins for battle in a lobbying fray rarely matched in recent history. All of them wanted highways, but all believed their very survival hung on the way Congress chose to pay for them.

Under our system of government,

lobbying is a clearly legitimate and constitutional right of every citizen and group. But it is up to Congress to weigh the legitimate pleas of every group against the common good, balance off their contentions and come up with a judgment. And rarely, if ever, has Congress been under greater pressure in making a judgment between the broad but diffuse needs of a common citizenry and the sharpened needs of men whose livelihood hung on their decisions.

TWO GIANT camps soon developed in the struggle over the bill. One was led by the railways, supported by the American Automobile Association and backed by most of the state highway officials of the country. They supported the Fallon bill. In the other were the truckmen, the tire dealers, the independent oil dealers, the diesel manufacturers—led in the grand strategy of opposition by the truckmen.

It is easiest to begin the story of the fight over the Fallon bill with the story of the railway men. Now, the railways have an acute and continuing interest in highways. In modern America, truckmen and railway men have been as bitter and unforgiving enemies as sheepmen and cattlemen on the open range of Wyoming, 80 years ago. In the past 30 years the trucking industry has grown to be a giant that grosses over $5 billion a year for freight haulage (against the railways' $8 billion).

If the great Interstate System goes through, with its near-level grades, its limited accesses, its numerous and heavy-paved lanes, the truckers—now

engaged principally in short-run transport—will have a chance to gnaw away as successfully at the railways' long-haul freight business as the airlines have at the railways' long-haul passenger business, and the commuters' automobiles at their suburban passenger business.

Any kind of legislation on the Interstate System thus placed the railways in a delicate position. They could not, in a nation that loves highways, simply come out and flatly denounce better roads. Yet they could scarcely watch with blithe unconcern as the nation proposed to build this spectacular roadbed for their competitive rivals. They had to present their views skillfully—by supporting the highways the nation wanted, yet making sure their competitive rivals, the truckers, gained no advantage out of them. Which, in essence, is why the railways threw all the influence they could behind the Fallon bill.

Robert S. Henry, who is a vice-president of the Association of American Railroads in Washington and a cherubic old man with a twinkle in his eye, explained the railways' position to me thus:

"Highways? Why, of course we're in favor of good highways. But we want a *sound* highway program and any sound highway program has to include user charges—people who benefit from it should pay, and that's particularly true of people who use these facilities to carry on commercial business. We railways pay in taxes 11.9 cents of every dollar we take in; we pay 19.7 cents more of every dollar to maintain our roadbeds and tracks. The truckers pay only seven cents of their dollar for taxes and they get their roadbeds free. That makes 31 cents out of our dollar against their seven cents. That's just not fair— and that's why we think the Fallon bill is such a good bill."

Exactly how much influence the railways brought to bear in the drafting of the tax features of the Fallon bill no one knows. The American Trucking Associations, of course, holds the railways directly responsible for the taxing of big trucks. According to John Lawrence, ATA managing director, "They have intervened in the highway program, attempting to promote punitive taxes on big trucks which will cripple truck competition with their own freight operations. . . . Congressmen have evidence of that on their desks in the form of a barrage of letters, wires and calls inspired by railroad interests, and often indeed sent to their offices in railroad envelopes. No such railroad lobby has descended on Washington in the history of the Republic as that which is now operating in support of the soak-the-truck proposals. It is this wrecking crew which is mainly responsible for throwing the highway situation out of perspective."

THIS BITTER statement must be balanced by other facts, for the truckmen, when they finally mobilized, easily matched the railway men in power and skill of influence. Their open bitterness reflects, mostly, the fact that the railways were informed of the tax measures on trucks weeks before the truckmen re-

alized what was happening in committee. And by the time the truckmen had become aware of what was happening they found themselves trapped as if by political jujitsu.

The railways had already taken up the position of virtue; they were supporting the Fallon bill, the boldest highway program ever proposed. But the truckmen were faced with Hobson's choice. They could accept the Fallon bill, giving them the great Interstate System they so desperately wanted— yet if they did so they would have to accept a tax burden on their industry which they claimed added another $375,000,000 a year. Or they could elect to torpedo the Fallon bill and accept the blame for sabotaging the highway program.

The truckmen elected to mobilize against the bill. And their emergency mobilization drastically outweighed anything the railways had previously been able to muster.

"Yes," says Walter Belson of the American Trucking Associations, "we had considerable influence in killing the Fallon bill. But don't confuse the Fallon bill with the highway program. We're not such stupid idiots as to be opposed to a road program we need as much as anyone else. We were about the first group to support the highway program from the beginning. We supported it before both Senate and House, we agreed to accept increased taxes to pay for it—we'll pay our fair share, the same tax rate on fuel, ties and equipment everyone else pays. Don't misunderstand what this means in dollars.

The same rate of tax will make the big truck pay five times as much as the average passenger car in gas tax every mile it runs, 18 times as much in tire tax and 13 times as much in equipment. This is not per company, but on every individual five-axle truck owned as against a passenger vehicle. And our state taxes run up to 40 times as much per truck as per the average passenger car."

Desperately and doggedly, all through the months of June and July, the truckmen and their allies fought to pull the tax teeth from the Fallon bill. The committee members compromised with the truckmen by moderating their original bill until the additional diesel tax was lowered by two cents a gallon and the tax on large truck tires reduced from 50 cents a pound to 15 cents a pound. But the lawmakers could not be moved from their conviction that it was heavy trucks that profited most from the new roads, that heavy trucks required most of the extra-cost features of the roads—the wider lanes, the sturdier bridges, the pavings of 12 inches rather than the six or eight that might handle normal passenger traffic. A principle was involved, they said—a user charge was being imposed for the first time on a federal level and special users had to pay special taxes. The truckmen could not accept this principle.

By the time Congress got around to voting on the revised version of the Fallon bill at the end of July, the final push against the bill was operating in high. An array of eloquent interests had all convened on Capitol Hill to protest its tax features.

The diesel manufacturers implied their industry would be so hobbled that it might die, thereby jeopardizing the entire national-defense program, which requires diesel engines.

The big oil companies and big tire companies protested, in the orthodox tradition, that they could not see why their products should be made into particular and peculiar tax-collecting agencies of governments—as Robert H. Scholl of Esso, speaking for the American Petroleum Institute, pointed out, state and federal governments were already collecting in taxes some 35 per cent of what filling stations received for each gallon of gasoline.

Independent oil companies and independent tire jobbers protested at the taxes because, they said, it would manacle them in competition with the giants of the industry, whose capital structure could more easily afford to bear the amount of additional capital frozen into the inventory of every tire or oil outlet by the new taxes. Their lobbyists painted a somber picture before the Fallon committee of thousands and thousands of little businessmen squeezed out of business because they could not carry the taxes for their customers.

"I feel," said one of their spokesmen, "like I am representing a plucked chicken with two feathers left in his tail, and there is a hand reaching out for the last feathers."

Each of the trade associations joined in battle against the bill had roots in a thousand small towns and neighborhoods of America. Now these too began to be heard from in a lobbying campaign unmatched, say many congressmen, since the days of the Taft-Hartley bill. Telegrams began to snow on Congress— an estimated 100,000 in all, 10,000 on Congressman Fallon's desk alone.

The telegrams were accompanied by letters. They came not only on stiff white paper under the letterheads of great firms or associations but in the grease-stained handwritten letters that worry congressmen much more—under letterheads of "Art's Filling Station," of "Alf's Friendly Service," of "Lone Star Sales and Service."

In the final days of the fray, the AFL Teamsters Union, perhaps the most powerful influence of all, got to work, as Dave Beck decided that his truckers should back up the truckmen who employed them. Dave Beck made a personal call on Sam Rayburn to press the truckmen's point of view as that of the Teamsters Union, whose resources are so important to Democrats in doubtful Congressional districts.

Some congressmen claim they could even trace a trucker's day at the wheel by following the date lines of telegrams that would arrive. A driver might send his first wire from, say, Philadelphia at eight in the morning, his second from Harrisburg two hours later, his third from Pittsburgh that afternoon, his fourth from Toledo in the early morning.

BY THE TIME , on the afternoon of July 27th, that the final roll call on the Fallon bill took place, the House and its members were adrift under impulses and pressures they could not fathom. The drive against the bill was sharp, pointed and overwhelming; but the support for the bill, which should have come from the average motorist, was conspicuously absent.

Even though experts say that modern highways would save him $100 a year in car expenses, the average motorist was silent. Though Andrew Sordoni, the president of the American Automobile Association (himself a commercial truckman), told the House that his members supported the bill and would accept it, he could deliver few votes.

Some congressmen were deeply upset by the breach of tradition which had let a new committee write the taxes that had always previously been the sole prerogative of the august Ways and Means Committee. Even more important, many of them dimly sensed (and some were sharply informed) that the new bill, by increasing gasoline and tire taxes, was extending the taxing power of the federal government into the domain which the individual states had always considered as one of the reserved areas of their authority. Old-line State righters bridled.

And, finally, party discipline and control on both sides collapsed. The Fallon bill was a Democratic bill. Sam Rayburn, the Speaker, convinced of his authority and prestige, felt certain down to the last minute that party discipline would rouse the necessary votes; when, at last, he realized it could not, it was too late to improvise the tactics or counterpressures to whip his errant Democrats into line.

The Republicans erred as badly. The

White House, which had always wanted to pay for the roads by bond borrowing, came at the last minute to the conclusion that the Fallon pay-as-you-go measure was better than none. But by the time Sherman Adams had phoned this eleventh-hour decision to Republican Congressman De Witt Hyde of Maryland, voting had begun. By the time Hyde got the message to Republican floor leaders, a House colleague later recounted, the Republicans were voting almost solidly against the bill and it was too late to switch. By the resounding margin of 292 (mostly Republican) to 123 (mostly Democratic), the House had rejected the Fallon bill, and with it any hope of a start on the new highways in 1955.

WHAT OF the new session of Congress that opens in January? Will it give America any start on a modern highway system?

At this writing, it is certain that every congressman will vie with his neighbor in his love, devotion and dedication to better highways. After all, 1956 is a Presidential year and neither major party wishes to be stuck, in the voter's mind, as the mossback outfit that was blind to this growing country's needs for better roads.

What kind of legislation we will get is, however, an open question—and one dependent more than anything else on the politicians' assessment of the public temper. It was the conspicuous silence of the average motorist in last year's Donnybrook that left Congress without that directional magnetic field by which it normally guides its actions among contending interests.

IT WOULD be naïve to hold the big lobbies of Washington either solely or chiefly responsible for destroying a program the nation needs by pursuing their legitimate, if individual, interests. True responsibility rests with Congress. This changing and dynamic country, in this age of vast physical and social transformation, needs an enormous range of expensive facilities without which it cannot thrive and for which everyone will have to pay.

The price tag on our growth will, when it is presented, be as high as anything else in this age of prosperity and somehow Congress must see to it that it is paid properly and justly.

It is this fundamental obligation of Congressional judgment that—at present writing—the administration hopes to pinpoint in the coming months. A new highway program stands high on the list of administration priorities for 1956; indeed, in the first business visit permitted Sherman Adams at President Eisenhower's bedside in Denver, the highway program was one of the chief concerns of the ailing chief executive. Since then, the Cabinet has passed responsibility for a new approach on to the Department of Commerce. There, administration leaders have been trying to define their attitude toward all the complex problems involved, yet leave it to Congress to come up with a hard bill in terms of specifics.

On phase one of last year's battle (financing), the administration has decided to yield to the Democratic point of view in an effort to get a program passed—it will now accept a pay-as-you-go measure in place of its original bond-financing proposal. But phase one was a partisan struggle that could be compromised, as it appears to have been now, by responsible party leaders. On phase two (the conflict of urban and rural needs) and phase three (the clash of rival transportation lobbies) unbridgeable differences of opinion seem to promise a new Highway Battle of 1956. In these phases, the differences cut through and across both major parties, for here Congress is struggling to decide on the shape of a new America which neither party sees clearly. In this struggle, the decisive voices will be those who understand the complicated issues best. But 1956 is an election year and the voices Congress aches most to hear are those of the voters. Do they understand? Will they make themselves heard? The kind of highways we get in 1956 and the years to follow depends on the answers.

COLLIER'S January 6, 1956

C h a p t e r 8

Politics USA II: Birth of "The Making of The President"

The demise of *Collier's* left White jobless, and with a fierce determination never again to be anybody's employee—which caused him to turn down a completely unexpected offer from Henry Luce to return to Time Inc. What should he do? He spent six months raising a million dollars to help *Collier's* ex-employees. Then, unemployed and "bored," he began writing his first novel, *The Mountain Road,* a saga of the last days of the Japan-China War he had reported a decade earlier. Book-club selection and a movie sale again relieved his immediate financial worries. Now what? He tried, briefly, to mount several ventures, including a publishing house which among other books would publish "quickly and first," a "Making of the President

Series" which White would write. Nothing jelled, and soon he was writing his second novel, *The View from the Fortieth Floor,* a fictionalized account of *Collier's* last days. Again, book-club and movie income made him flush.

Which, in turn, led him to a momentous decision: to write that book about how a president is made. "The idea," as he said later in *In Search of History,* "was to follow a campaign from beginning to end. It would be written as a novel is written, with anticipated surprises as, one by one, early candidates vanish in the primaries until only two final jousters struggle for the prize in November. Moreover, it should be written as a story of a man in trouble, of the leader under the pressures of circumstances." It was a two-year project, and it was promptly turned down by at least three publishing houses that thought it sounded too much like a textbook. Finally, however, he found an enthusiastic publisher (Michael Bessie of Atheneum); and he contracted with *Saturday Review* to produce a series of short articles throughout the 1960 campaign.

This chapter is that series, "Perspectives/1960," in fourteen installments. It has heroes and villains, it has colorful supporting characters (e.g., The Harlem Fox), it approaches issues with a sense of history, it uses statistics in unusual ways, and, most significantly, it puts the reader on the campaign trail with the reporter. In all, an intelligent and highly readable warm-up (White might have said "finger exercise") for the unique book that was to follow.

Perspective 1960 #1

Editor's Note: *The germinal ideas and events that make history, and the men responsible for them, have long been among this magazine's concerns. Indeed, more than two decades ago, Elmer Davis wrote for SR a series of political essays in which current affairs were set against a broad historical and philosophical background. It is in this tradition that SR presents the first instalment of a feature by the well-known author and analyst Theodore H. White. Mr. White, who for a number of years was a correspondent in Europe and Asia before returning to this country to report the American scene for leading newspapers and magazines, has won numerous awards for both his nonfiction and fiction books. While he may give principal attention in this space to the developing Presidential campaign, he will also be free to discuss other subjects that seem to require perspective.*

If, as someone has remarked, Americans choose their political leaders by their style as men rather than by the issues they speak, no greater paradox of style has been offered recently than by Senator John F. Kennedy of Massachusetts.

For the public style and personality of this youngest of Presidential candidates are those of deceptively radiant freshness. The lithe grace of his motion, the handsome face bearing no sag or wrinkle, are those of a man sensitive enough almost to invite mothering. His speeches, which rove through the corridors of American history, quoting Abraham Lincoln, Uncle Joe Cannon, Will Rogers, and Robert Sherwood's poetry, with an occasional fleck of Dante or T. S. Eliot, have the purity of the scholar's touch and the sweetness of books cherished and remembered. And yet the high, clear voice, unthickened yet by the hoarseness of the political veteran, only its soft, semi-liquid "L" flawing otherwise perfect diction, is that of romantic youth.

But the drive of the Kennedy campaign, the style and pace of its direction speak an entirely different personality—of a man who has mastered the cold grammar of power with a toughness of instinct and clarity of analysis that approach remorseless perfection. Kennedy is, of course, extravagantly financed. He can joke disarmingly about his financing—"I received a telegram from my father last night," he quipped at a friendly meeting recently. "It said, 'Don't buy another vote. I'm not going to pay for a landslide.'" But what is remarkable is not the depth of resources this financing has purchased; it is the precision with which they are organized. For the enormous Kennedy operation has not simply grown; it has been engineered as a machine for the application of power. And the style of its organization is, perhaps, worth more examination than the words of its master. Words, in American politics, are processed by many men; it is organization that separates the men from the boys. It was organization as much as personality or words or anything else that produced the stunning Kennedy success in New Hampshire two weeks ago; and Kennedy organization again, as much as resources, has made the desperate struggle of Hubert Humphrey in Wisconsin's primary apparently so uneven a contest.

THE VISIBLE control room of the official Kennedy-for-President machine is a sunlit ten-room suite on the fifth floor of the air-conditioned Esso Building in Washington, occupied by six men and ten girls who there join three members of the Kennedy family (two brothers, one brother-in-law). Some have been with Kennedy from his first Congressional campaign in Boston in 1946, their careers absorbed in his for fourteen years. Others are new, like the ebullient

Pierre Salinger, his press chief, whose exuberant charm contrasts sharply with the dour countenances Kennedy has brought with him from his Boston past. These people do his housekeeping, arrange his press conferences, release his statements, arrange the travels of the candidate and his guests in the candidate's luxurious Convair. Shrewdly, Kennedy has arranged that his vital energies not be consumed by the exhausting detail of preconvention drudgery which so sapped the strength of Stevenson and Kefauver in 1956. The service personnel of the Esso building are a White House staff in embryo. But, apart from Salinger and brother Robert Kennedy, they are functionaries, not policy-makers.

Policy is made elsewhere—a half-mile away in Kennedy's Senate chambers on Capitol Hill. Here ideas and positions on national policy filter up through a net of semi-anonymous researchers who report to Kennedy's alter-ego, Ted Sorenson. And Sorenson is worth pausing at, for Sorenson is quality. A lean, abstemious thinker who combines for Kennedy the functions Louis Howe and Sam Rosenman performed for Roosevelt, Sorenson has for sixteen years had the Kennedy career as his horizon of ambitions. The luster of such campaign masterworks as Kennedy's National Press Club speech on the Presidency came from the pen of Sorenson, a gifted and eloquent writer.

Outside Washington, meticulously organized and command-perfect, a far larger number of people feed smoothly through their appointed channels in each area of American influence and power to these twin capping headquarters. And in each area quality is the mark of service. From New England come ideas coined by the finest minds of academe; at Harvard and MIT a campus elite of brilliant professional talent forms an advisory committee surveying the far horizon of American moods and problems. From Las Vegas and Hollywood comes a jazz touch, Sinatra himself warbling the campaign songs. In New York, from the Empire State Building, one of the vintage firms of American public opinion analysts, Louis Harris Associates, directs the constant and expensive sifting of American mood so necessary for the engineering of consent.

Practical politics are organized with the same efficiency. One full-time regional operative works in each of the six states where Kennedy plans a primary fight, reporting to a specifically deputized, responsible individual in Washington. In the Midwest, a super-regional chief has been appointed—a battle-scarred veteran of the Stevenson wars, the portly Hy Raskin, peerless shepherd of convention delegates. In downtown New York, father Joseph P. Kennedy deals with the delegate brokers of northern New Jersey and New York City's outer boroughs. Like everything else in the Kennedy operation, organization here is book-perfect, peaking to its own chief of staff, John Bailey, the boss of Connecticut. Bailey holds New England's 114 delegates safe in his pocket; and his raiding of upstate New York for more has been a little clas-

sic of hard politics; it already confronts Tammany's confused leaders with the alternates of complete capitulation or leading a ferociously split, hence meaningless, New York delegation to the Los Angeles convention.

ALL THIS organization marches to the style of its leader. Bailey and Salinger, Raskin and the Harvard professors, Lou Harris and the service functionaries, can advise. But decisions are made by Kennedy alone, impaneled with his two inner-circle alter-egos, brother Robert Kennedy and thinker Ted Sorenson; and these decisions set the pace and style of his campaign.

The pace is swift, well-timed, relentless. In almost perpetual motion, Kennedy provides by his travels from coast to coast a never-ending cascade of news stories and headlines that make him seem omnipresent.

And it is the illusion of omnipresence and omnipotence that Kennedy consciously seeks to create. To win as a Catholic, Kennedy must overturn American political tradition—and he intends no less than this.

He can brook no neutrals, leave no weaknesses of uncertainty. When he speaks theoretically of the "strong" Presidency, he talks from the inner personality, not simply from the speechwriter's text. He leads; others must be compelled to follow. It was he who moved his campaign into the Wisconsin primary over the reluctance of most of his staff to challenge Hubert Humphrey so close to home ground. It was he, per-

sonally, who put the iron to Ohio's Governor Mike DiSalle at a private meeting
at the Pittsburgh airport late this winter. No one else was present when Kennedy gave DiSalle the ultimatum to join
him as a friend or be crushed in the open
primary battle which Kennedy's private
polltakers assured him he could win.
Where delegates can be acquired behind
closed doors, from Queens to the Virgin
Islands, Kennedy's deputies perform the
transaction in silence. Where they must
be taken in battle, battle is openly
joined. Wherever power gathers or is
shaped in American politics, there Kennedy seeks it.

"Jack," said one of his aides recently,
"has the FDR instinct; when he gets
into a fight, the instinct is to kill, not
to wound. He wants to be President in
the worst damned way. Being President
is a tough business, not a panty-waist
business." And, if the business of becoming President is akin to the business
of being President, the inner style of
this campaign, not its outer eloquence,
is the perspective Kennedy offers the
voters.

SATURDAY REVIEW March 26, 1960

Perspective 1960 #2

MADISON, WIS.

From Wisconsin to California is some 1,800 miles as the jets fly. But political kinship has bound these states together in an upheaval of American politics so complex that not for months after the April 5 primary will anyone be able to judge who are the chief losers in the voting of this still snow-mantled state.

To measure this upheaval, which the starshells and political rocketry of Messrs. Kennedy and Humphrey illuminate in this week's primary, one must reflect first on the classic geography of the Democratic Party.

In the old party, the United States, like Caesar's Gaul, was divided into three parts—a South, a Northeast, a West. There sat the South, gripped by the frozen violence of race politics. There sat the Northeast, controlled by the barons of the heavily Catholic big-city machines. And then there was the flabby West, silent and unpredictable since the eruption of William Jennings Bryan. The Northeast led, by providing Presidential candidates. The South, with Congressional control, was content with its veto power. And the West trudged docilely after, a sad third. Any combination of two of these three could carry a Democratic convention and, more rarely, an election. When all three were united, as at the Rooseveltian apogee, they could sweep the nation.

This old map is now as dead as the gold dollar. And the nature of the campaign this month in Wisconsin, better than any textbook, demonstrates what has happened. For Wisconsin is the newest domain in a political revolution in the Democratic Party which has transformed the West into a center of independent power indisputably more dynamic and strong-willed than either of its two old partners in the classic trio.

THE ENTIRE revolution is little more than a decade old. Until late in the 1940s, Democratic organization beyond the Mississippi lay fossilized in traditional ethnic enclaves under leaders who nursed their strength from Washington favor and patronage rather than the grassroots. To find this organization, said an amateur who helped lead the insurrection in California, "you needed a detective to hunt it down and a crowbar to force your way in once you found it."

Had the Democrats won in 1952, it

269

is possible that the organization would have remained indefinitely frozen under the closed leadership of men dancing to the will of the Washington power center. But with the defeat of 1952, strange forces began to operate.

There was, first, the exuberant, leaderless energy of the amateurs and zealots recruited by Kefauver in the Spring of 1952 and organized permanently by Stevenson later that Fall. "Kefauver was their John the Baptist," Senator Paul Douglas of Illinois once remarked. "He called them to the church and they remained to pray for Adlai." There was, next, the discovery by these amateurs that politics was fun—a game to be played in season and out with zest and enjoyment. There was, further, after the defeat of 1952, their realization that the antique Democratic leaders of the West, shorn of Washington patronage, were stumble-bums. And, finally, there was the slow discovery by these presentable middle-class amateurs that they could make their own alliances with the best and most vigorous of local labor leaders far more effectively than the old-fashioned bosses ever conceived.

Now, eight years later, these same amateurs of 1952 are everywhere the regular Establishment of Democratic power in the west; from California, Washington, and Oregon to Minnesota, Michigan, and Wisconsin, they control the party. They have become masters of the organization. But their language, appeal, and emotions are quite different from those of Eastern and Southern Democratic leadership. They talk of ideas, images, programs, policy; with no embarrassment, phrases of deep idealism and concern tumble from their lips. In their attitudes, these people are probably the most lasting residue of Stevenson influence in American politics, except that they are tougher and more hard-minded than their patron saint—and more effective. It was their leadership that capped the Democratic triumphs of 1958 with the stupendous California and Wisconsin victories on the day the vaunted Tammany machine was being humiliated by Rockefeller in New York.

Here in Wisconsin, the virility and vigor of this new Democratic Party is seen everywhere. Wisconsin's Democratic governor, Gaylord Nelson, is forty-three; its Democratic Senator, William Proxmire, is forty-four; the two leading mayoralty candidates in Milwaukee, both Democratic, are forty-eight and forty-two. Their strength, and the strength of their party, rests on the new alliance that sweeps from here all the way to the West Coast—the partnership between professional middle-class people in Wisconsin's small towns who provide leadership and ideas while a hard trade-union base provides troops, financing, and votes. The Wisconsin Democratic Party, described by one of the leaders in the transition as once only an "Irish-Polish marching society," has become respectable. It has drawn to itself half a dozen other ethnic groups in this polyglot state; and the broad Scandinavian support of the La Follette progressives in rural areas has begun to accept it as home. As in Michigan, Minnesota, and California, a solid Republican base has vanished;

the homeland of Joe McCarthy may become permanently Democratic.

PRIMARIES IN American politics are traditionally the occasion of throat-cutting and blood-letting. This hard-fought primary may, however, be the departure for a new strength and surge on the part of Wisconsin Democrats, rather than a datemark in dissension and destruction. Astutely, Nelson and Proxmire have until now maintained a fictional neutrality between the two out-of-state rivals for their party's loyalty, neither wanting to see the party riven factionally while its 1958 victories are still unconsolidated. Thus, the Kennedy and Humphrey organizations have both been allowed to import their out-of-state staffs and their out-of-state techniques to free-wheel from Lake Superior to the Illinois border. With notable grace, Wisconsin leaders at every level have done their best to shove the Catholic-Protestant cleavage out of public discussion, ignoring as best they can the dominant political unknown of the primary race.

No one can tell yet where the center of gravity lies in this new alliance of respectable middle-class and labor union votes. With inexhaustible energy, Humphrey stumps the state, his evangelical eloquence finding its greatest resonance among the stolid workers who gather to hear him at union halls or among the dairy farmers gathered in their Sears, Roebuck gray-striped overalls at crossroads. With equal energy and high literary eloquence, Kennedy crisscrosses the state, drawing thousands to his coffee-and-cookie receptions, and through the receptions drawing them across the bridge of middle-class respectability to the new party.

It has been a hard, but clean, fight and its bitternesses concern chiefly the image of the Presidency. "Hubert," said a Kennedy aide, "behaves as if he were running for sheriff. Whoever heard of a guy running for the Presidency getting in a picket line and singing Solidarity Forever—or putting on a druggist's jacket? You don't run for President of the United States in a druggist's jacket."

"This Democratic Party," says Humphrey in reply, "can't win by quoting Robert Frost. Anybody can look up quotations in a book. The farmers don't know who Robert Frost is and they don't like frost—all they know is that Spring is late and milk prices hurt. They want to know when the freight came in."

Together, these two men have added strength, faith, and glamour to a party movement that has gained by their contest. There can, of course, be only one winner in the primary. But there will be many losers as this new party gathers strength. Only time will identify the greatest loser—whether it be the defeated candidate of this week, the Eastern Democratic machines, or the Southern oligarchy. Or, perhaps, the Republican Party most of all.

SATURDAY REVIEW April 9, 1960

PERSPECTIVE 1960 #3
Politics and the Press

Few, if any, out-of-state journalists could have left Milwaukee on the grey and overcast Wednesday morning following the Kennedy-Humphrey primary without concern over their own role in the dramatic last days of the contest.

For when they came to Wisconsin it was a state of easy and decent tolerance; when they left, it was perplexed and divided. The divisions of origin and religion were, of course, always there. But how much we collectively did to exacerbate and amplify them is the heart of a question that may be of central importance to the Presidential politics of 1960.

Wisconsin, like almost all our states except those that lie south of the Mason-Dixon line, has a thoroughly polyglot mixture. The mixture, however, probably contains a lower percentage of Wasps (*White Anglo-Saxon Protestants*) than any other area in the nation except, perhaps, metropolitan New York. Wasps in Wisconsin number perhaps 5 per cent of its total population, only marginally leading such strains as Jews, Negroes, and native Indians. The rest of Wisconsin is so bi-zarre a combination of genetic and ethnic origins that it has fascinated sociologists for years, and magnificent multicolored charts exist in scholarly institutions cross-hatching Wisconsin's seventy-one counties in different colors for Germans, Danes, Norwegians, Irish, Icelanders, Latvians, Poles, and all the other twenty-four fatherhood stocks significant enough to be measured. The pattern of their cooperation in a living community is fascinating— as fascinating as the manner in which the centipede moves its many legs to make progress. But, like the mythical centipede which went into nervous shock when asked to examine the sequence by which it moves its legs, so, too, can the political animal go into nervous shock by overprecise self-analysis.

Which is what happened in Wisconsin. The commingling of American stocks has always been part of the stubborn reality of American politics as well as its silent glory. But when this commingling is picked bare in public the glory is apt to evaporate, and what results is squalor. The divisions of religion and ethnics have been intuitively recognized in Wisconsin, as elsewhere, for years. But when the horde of out-of-state political reporters gathered to report Wisconsin's primary, they fastened upon these long-known and intuitive differences with the fascination of men freshly discovering the obvious.

For two decades an obscure Minnesota publishing house had been pouring archaic anti-Catholic and anti-Semitic tracts into the small towns of the Midwest. Yet when correspondents discovered them for the first time, they were whirled into headline significance. For years the Department of Rural Sociology at the University of Wisconsin had been trying to understand the patterns of the state's origins. But when the correspondents in Wisconsin discovered such scholarly research for the first time, it acquired the impact of new revelation. And as each story received its play and prominence, correspondents tried to outdo each other proving that they too, were journeymen sociologists.

The response to such stories had its predictable effect on the bigots who sputter endemically in Wisconsin as elsewhere. Their paid advertisements and personal mimeographed leaflets quickly flourished in the new publicity. By the final weekend of the primary an electoral contest between two men of genuine workaday political tolerance had become in the reporting almost a religious clash; and not only in out-of-state reporting, but also in local reporting, where its effect on voter reaction was immediate.

The vast investment of the Columbia Broadcasting System in a scholarly pub-

lic opinion analysis of Wisconsin came out Sunday morning on the public air as a stirring account of tense Protestant-Catholic cleavage. NBC, not to be outdone, matched CBS in what had come to be accepted as realistic analysis. The *Milwaukee Journal,* the dominant newspaper of the state and as fine a newspaper as any in the country, adorned a superb Sunday story by its perceptive political correspondent, Ken Fry, with a map breaking every county in the state into its precise Catholic-Protestant percentages. On the Sunday before election, when almost three hours of television drenched Wisconsin with the political story, the TV screen seemed to be reporting not a contest for the sublime office of the Presidency but a sporting event in which the Protestant 9th Congressional was pitted against the Catholic 8th Congressional.

This correspondent leaves doorbell-ringing and the scientific analysis of loyalties to other, more qualified men. I only know that in my own taxi-driver poll a month before the election the common responses were "I'm gonna vote for Humphrey, he's for the workingman," or "I like Kennedy, I like the way he talks." But on the day of voting I could get the unabashed reply, "I'm voting for Kennedy—I guess it's because I'm a Catholic" or "The Catholics aren't democratic—Hubert ought to talk about it." The climate of opinion we had all helped make had created a new kind of reality.

A wise and veteran politician once said to me, "American politics is a puzzle—a jigsaw puzzle of nationalities.

God should paralyze the hand of the man who tries to break up the jigsaw." For this next decade we must face openly, in the press and our hearts, the cleavage between white and Negro Americans; this is enough for any political system to digest in a decade. To examine publicly and self-consciously all the other elements in the jigsaw could be too much. It may make great, colorful, and truthful copy; but truthful reporting and wisdom are not always synonymous.

SATURDAY REVIEW April 23, 1960

PERSPECTIVE 1960 #4

The Harlem Fox

Now that Congress has committed to law its massive new act of Negro enfranchisement, I offer for consideration Mr. J. Raymond Jones, "The fox of Harlem."

Tall and oak-limbed, dark-brown and handsome, his silver-gray hair and pencil-thin moustache establishing an air of aristocratic dignity, J. Raymond Jones scarcely seems like a revolutionary.

Yet that is what he is in American politics. It is he, as much as any other individual, who has reduced to anarchy the great machine of Tammany, over whose wreckage Mr. Carmine De Sapio now nervously presides. And his revolt in the huddles of Harlem is important not only for New York but also for Chicago, Los Angeles, and the most distant parishes and counties of the farthest South where Negroes vote or are about to vote. For Mr. Jones is a Negro political leader finally beyond the white man's control; and how he uses the power of the Negro in American politics may determine our culture for years to come. We shall be facing this power in the next decade wherever Negroes learn their strength.

In the last decade, 900,000 white people have fled from New York City—net. In the same period the net inflow of dark Americans (Negroes and Puerto Ricans) has mounted to 300,000. Today, of New York's 8,000,000 people, an estimated 1,000,000 to 1,100,000 are Negroes, and another 700,000 to 750,000 are Puerto Ricans—between them, almost a fifth of the population of a city where, a generation ago, they may have totaled 5 per cent.

It has taken almost thirty years for this depth-change to show in the structure of municipal politics—and J. Raymond Jones has lived through the entire change.

Time was when the clotted blocks of Harlem were plantation districts of Tammany, to be bought, sold, and distributed like baronies to the white favorites of the Chief of the Hall. The Tammany clubs of Harlem segregated their overwhelming Negro membership in cellars below or attics above their clubrooms. Time was when a white overlord could openly say in a Negro's hearing to the Tammany overlord downtown, "Alright, if you want us to run one, I'll run the blackest, ugliest one in my district and I know just who he is." Time was when the white political proprietor of a Harlem Negro district would run a puppet black face for the judicial bench, yet drive Negro politicians from his office in wrath when they sought the job of Judge's Clerk—a rich political plum—for their own race. Such plums were reserved for white men. Negro political leaders were paid off with the right to run police-protected crap games or backroom speakeasies.

Each Negro victory in New York in the past thirty years has been won by the law of tooth and fang. First, the fight to let Negro ward heelers become captains in their own right; then the fight to let Negroes be elected district leaders and sit in Tammany conclaves in person; then the right to choose which of their fellow men they would nominate for office; then the right to control their own patronage. In each of these struggles, for thirty-five years, J. Raymond Jones has played a vital role, learning the techniques of politics as he went, earning from his own people the title of "The Fox." In his personality and emotions, J. Raymond Jones, a proud man, still bears the scars of each humiliation and expression of contempt.

J. RAYMOND JONES now sits in victory in Harlem. For it was he, beyond the flamboyant, race-baiting Adam Clayton Powell, who organized the 1958 voting which broke totally all white control in Harlem. It is he who has organized the superlative Negro political machine which has now finally welded the five Negro districts of Harlem into the largest single deliverable voting bloc in the largest state of the union in the elections of 1960.

Yet J. Raymond Jones, fox and revolutionary, artist in political technology and the intricacies of election petitions and patronage manipulation, is more than a racial silhouette of one dimension. He is the only Tammany leader in the private rooms of whose clubhouse (the George Washington Carver Club) rest a copy of Toynbee, a collection of books on Africa, a study of American sociology. At home in his apartment on the cliffs where New York's Negro elite live above the valley where their brethren swelter in the slums, his library runs from the complete Balzac and complete Shakespeare to the memoirs of Harry Truman embedded in a vast collection of books on economics and science. Tough and hard, a former coal stoker in the Caribbean, a former ice peddler in New York, a former Red Cap in Penn Station, Ray Jones, now sixty, is also a man of distinguished mind and great learning. He can play it low, tough, and cunning; or play it way up high where men speak of America's ultimate purposes. With equal eloquence he can talk in the vernacular of pressure or the vernacular of the egghead. Yet all he wants at the moment, he says, is "fair shares"—fair share of education and schooling, of patronage and public jobs in the Tammany share-out.

What makes Mr. Jones so interesting is that he is not alone in his captaincy of the revolution that has swept Harlem in the past two years. He is joined on the one hand by his political partner, front-

man, and banner carrier—Congressman Adam Clayton Powell, a man of
passion and flamboyant race bitterness
who may possibly be the most dangerous political figure in New York, either
black or white. He is joined on the
other hand by the meek and plastic Hu-
lan Jack, Borough President of Manhattan, one of the more inept men ever cast
by Tammany as an ethnic emblem to
catch votes. Jack, humiliated and out-
cast by Tammany finally as a fool, has
joined the new Harlem bloc for survival.

These are three Negro types that
Americans will meet in our new politics
for a generation—both in the big cities
of the North and in the Deep South
where Congress this year promises to establish Negro voting. Mr. Powell is a
racist extremist, explosive and danger-

ous. Mr. Jack has been a puppet and
hence useless either to his people or to
his masters. Between them is J. Raymond Jones, a master political technician, picking his way through a tangle
of pressures within his domain and
without. He can remain master of his
coalition, and keep it just this side of
violence, only so long as he gets from
white politicians and delivers to his voters their full fair share. Which of these
three types the American Negro will
choose to follow, and which way they
will go, is as much the white man's responsibility as the black man's. But the
responsibility for both groups in choosing leadership on the urban frontier of
race tension is inescapable.

SATURDAY REVIEW May 14, 1960

PERSPECTIVE 1960 #5
The Degeneration of Command

We shall probably never know the name of the officer who ordered Francis Powers to fly his plane over the Soviet Union. Nor is his identity important. What is important is to locate the exact organization box he inhabits on the great chain-of-command chart responsible for war and peace and then erase it. It is certain that neither President Eisenhower nor Christian Herter,* and probably not even Allen Dulles,** made the precise decision to send this man at this time over this route. Yet someone did give the order. And however low or high this someone ranks, he represents what the worried school of defense scientists calls "The Degeneration of Command," a phrase that labels one of the more doom-laden dilemmas of our time.

The dilemma is simply put: we live in an age of increasingly complex defense systems, so intricate, so automated, so swift-moving, that their technologies require instant decisions at levels and in time-sequences ever farther removed from political responsibility.

*Secretary of State
**Director of the Central Intelligence Agency

We operate today in the closing months of a defense era that relies on the piloted bomber; this era has already seen the time of decision between alert and retaliation in air war reduced to some four and a half to six hours. Although this is a frighteningly short period to decide whether to end civilization or not, it still permits Strategic Air Command at Omaha to seek political guidance from the White House before speeding our bombers beyond the present geographical limits of the fail-safe system. We must presume, and indeed Mr. Khrushchev's statements indicate, that a similar Russian system still offers Russia an equivalent few hours for political decision to judge and control firing decision.

But this age of the piloted bomber, of the B-52 and B-47, is already ending, making way for the age of the intercontinental ballistic missile. The Russians, it is reported, already have two operational ballistic bases. And our first ICBM bases, each with its cluster of nine silver petals of Atlas missiles coded for specific Russian cities, are being installed.

These new bases, the Russians' and

ours, change the nature of war by one more step. Missiles arrive in thirty-five to forty-five minutes; they cannot be called back. They must be countered instantly. Thus, they chop the time of decision after first warning from the present four and a half to six hours to a fifteen- to thirty-minute time span—and make even fainter the faint prayer that the red telephone at SAC headquarters can connect with the President in time to let *him* decide whether the world must be blown up or not. One prays that the observers in the Russian detection system have similar luck in reaching their center of political decision, too.

ALL THE wizardry and ingenuity of American electronics are now being channeled into that marvel of science which is our air warning net in order to preserve this minimal time between warning and decision. Yet however much the art develops, however sensitive and sophisticated the warning systems become, there remains always a human being who must read the information the radar brings and judge it. There remains always an ineradicable element of chance when an individual must decide whether an unidentified signal is caused by heat inversion turbulence in the air, by meteorites, by sea gulls (as has indeed happened), or whether the signal is caused by a hostile missile hurtling on with desolation which requires instant retaliation before the power to retaliate is wiped out twenty minutes later.

Our own systems of defense and detection are marvelously effective; yet so worried is one group of our greatest defense scientists about their own work that they have this spring organized, on their own initiative, apart from government, a summer conference at the Massachusetts Institute of Technology to examine what they call the "technical instability of peace," the accidental, self-triggering potential of the new war technologies.

It must be assumed that the Russian warning and retaliation system is at least as much and probably more "technically unstable" than our own. The Soviet war doctrine of "preemptive war"—the code that calls for first strike when they believe American intention clear to attack—reflects a more trigger-happy mentality than ours. And the Russians live in the same world with our Strategic Air Command. It is estimated that our 1,500–2,000 strategic bombers make 100,000 individual missions a year, all of them for training, but many fully armed with nuclear bombs. In five years, half a million such individual missions will have been flown. Even the tiniest percentage of accident allowed for human fallibility, for a pilot gone berserk, for instructions misread, is too great to contemplate. For accident must trigger the Russian defense-retaliation system.

It is this that makes the thought of American planes flying over the Soviet Union so frightful. Espionage, unhappily, must go on indefinitely if this nation is to maintain effective defense. But the tools of espionage require examination. When such a tool as the Lockheed U-2 is used—and how many? One? Two? Ten?—it teases the trigger mechanisms of Russian retaliation.

WE LIVE still in those months of history when technology permits time for an Eisenhower or a Khrushchev to be informed that the hostile signal is probably a photo-reconnaissance plane and need only be shot down. Yet such a plane could be a bomb-carrier. Several at once could be strays of the Strategic Air Command. And at some indefinable month in the next year and a half, as we slip into the maturity of the missile age, technology will reduce the warning time to its approaching twenty-to-thirty-minute span for decision. It is then that some anonymous Russian brigadier, unable to reach Khrushchev in time, may respond to an anonymous American brigadier's decision with an act of intercontinental violence simply because they have accidentally triggered each other off.

This is what is meant by Degeneration of Command; this is the problem posed by Francis Powers's flight. If this country must face death it should be by decision of the man the people choose— the President of the United States or his Secretary of State. Neither of these two men can decide the time and course of each individual flight over Soviet air. But since each such flight puts the trigger-mechanism in anonymous hands, each such flight curtails and mocks their constitutional responsibility for our destiny. It is that that makes it technically imperative that such a flight over enemy soil never take place again. If this country and Russia are to be devastated, we should have, at least, the miserable consolation that it happened by design and not by accident.

SATURDAY REVIEW May 28, 1960

PERSPECTIVE 1960 #6
The Republican Predicament

The fireworks of national elections all too often obscure far more than they clarify.

Thus it is quite probable that this year's contest for the Presidency may conceal from today's voters what tomorrow's chroniclers will see as one of the most dramatic events in American political history: a testing of the Republican party, for survival or death.

This testing will take place far below the level of popular attention, for at the level of national excitement where the personality of President is chosen the Republicans can still mobilize their last great resource—their dominance in the vast arena of mass communications, of TV, of radio, of press and magazines, where images are marketed for national consumption. It is quite possible that this dominance may help manufacture a Republican victory at the Presidential level in November, 1960—but what worries many of the most sober and concerned of Republicans is whether they, or any other party, can long survive as a party such unfulfilled triumphs as those of 1952 and 1956.

———

IT IS PERSPECTIVE that gives best the dimensions of what worries the ablest Republican thinkers. Never in American history has a national party been so long and so persistently denied the right to shape national policy. For thirty years—since 1930—Republicans have managed to control Congress only twice. Never has any President so continuously been denied the opportunity to write his own legislation in Congress and across the land as Dwight D. Eisenhower, thrice deprived by Americans of a Congress of his own partisan faith.

As one shortens the perspective, the Republican predicament grows worse. In the off-year Congressional elections of the last decade, where parties are tested apart from the Presidency, the Republican base has shrunk with a remorseless, almost irreversible trend, from 49 per cent in 1950 to 47 per cent in 1954 to 43 per cent in 1958 to what some Republican analysts gloomily estimate as a 40 per cent base today. From 1950 to 1958, as the nation grew, Democrats added 5,500,000 voters to bring their base to 25,500,000; Republican votes were fixed in 1958 at 19,000,000 as they were in 1950.

Bringing the perspective to a still narrower focus, to the roots of politics in state and community, the reading is even gloomier. Not since the zenith of the New Deal in 1936 have regional Republican fortunes been lower at statehouse levels where they control only fourteen of the forty-eight governorships and seven out of forty-eight state legislatures elected in 1958.

OVER AND over again, from coast to coast, below the effective reach of the mass media which they dominate, Republicans have seen a terrifying pattern of erosion repeat itself. On the Atlantic Coast, the 13th Massachusetts Congressional District, south of Boston, Republican since time out of mind, once full of shoe factories and old-line Yankees, now full of electronics and suburbanites, showed 60 per cent Republican in 1952, 58 per cent Republican in 1954, 55 per cent Republican in 1956—and then, flip, a Democrat elected in 1958 and Republicans reduced to a 45 per cent minority. Across the continent, on the Pacific, the same pattern: the First Congressional of California, fir-forested and tawny of slope, sprawling down the coast from Oregon to San Francisco Bay—no Democratic candidate at all in 1952, 59 per cent Republican in 1954, 53 per cent Republican in 1956 and then, flip, a Democrat elected in 1958 and Republicans reduced to a 45 per cent minority. Nor are these isolated examples. Similar patterns of unbroken erosion repeat in Iowa, Kansas, North Dakota, South

Dakota, Illinois. Indeed, of the scrawny present Republican House delegation of 153 members, no less than thirty-nine hold their present seats by the scant margin of 53 per cent or less.

IT IS NOT the cold figures of the last decade's elections that alone paint the picture; it is the quality of conversation of responsible Republican leaders in Washington, conversation which runs the range from melancholy to demoralization.

Time was when Republicans, even in defeat, spoke with a ring of absolute conviction, a blind sense of inner indefinable moral purpose. Time was when almost any Republican echoed that ringing sound of authority attributed to Senator Hoar of Massachusetts, who in 1890 declared: "The men who do the work of piety and charity in our churches, the men who administer our school system, the men who own and till their own farms, . . . the soldiers, . . . the men who went to war and stayed all through, the men who paid the debt and kept the currency sound . . . and saved the nation's honor . . . commonly and as a rule, by the natural law of their being, find their place in the Republican party; while the old slave-owner and slave-driver, the saloon keeper, the ballot box stuffer, the Ku Klux Klan, the criminal class of the great cities, the men who cannot read and write, commonly and as a rule, by the natural law of their being find their congenial place in the Democratic party. . . ."

———————

SUCH SOUNDS of natural righteousness and deep confidence have not been heard from Republicans in Washington for years. Instead, the Republican sound today is one of confusion and uncertainty and, in the past few months, of a strange new note—bitterness against Dwight D. Eisenhower. In another six months, Eisenhower will be out of the heat of battle. With his coming, many Republicans once hoped, would come a restoration of purpose and program from which the party could build again as the Democrats built from Franklin D. Roosevelt's partisan leadership. Instead, on Eisenhower's departure, he leaves a party weaker than when he found it, with a dwindling base of voter loyalty, deprived of troops, workers, visions, dependent entirely on the mechanics of mass communication.

This hushed bitterness of authentic Republicans can be found everywhere— on Capitol Hill, in Republican National Headquarters, and even, where it is most guarded, in the entourage of Vice President Nixon. For it is Nixon who faces a possible future as President with the inescapable legacy of a bitterly hostile Democratic Senate and a probably hostile House. It is Nixon who must win not only for himself but in such a manner as to save his party also; it is Nixon now who must do what Eisenhower was supposed to do eight years ago. And, even for a man of the Vice President's formidable talents, the problem is a desperate one, as we shall see on examination in a later dispatch.

SATURDAY REVIEW June 11, 1960

PERSPECTIVE 1960 #7
The Republican Predicament: II

Nowhere is the Republican predicament (see *SR,* June 11) more acutely brought to focus than in the offices from which Richard M. Nixon conducts his campaign for the Presidency of the United States.

For if the deep strategic purpose of any candidate must be to arrive at the White House with a clear image of leadership, a popular mandate, and the Congressional base to propel the American people forward, then the tactics of Nixon's campaign clash starkly with his deepest strategic needs. The clash can be simply put: Nixon's chief tactical advantage in the campaign of 1960 is the personal popularity and laying-on-of-hands of Dwight D. Eisenhower. Yet his chief strategic burden is the political legacy of the Eisenhower Administration and the unresolved party problems that Eisenhower leaves behind. How to rid himself of this political legacy without, at the same time, stripping himself of Eisenhower's friendship and reserves of personal popularity is, without doubt, the gravest problem Nixon faces.

———

UP TO now, and all through the spring, the Nixon campaign has been dominated by the anticipated Rockefeller blitz. Rockefeller, serious or not about his candidacy, has long since publicly divorced himself from the Eisenhower Administration to appeal to the liberal center; thus Nixon has been forced, tactically, to find shelter in the President's approval and the friendship of the Republican regulars. The Vice President has thus been frozen into that rigid partisan posture and must stay frozen until the last roll call of the convention frees him to step out on his own. It is only then, and quite late in the season too, that Nixon can address himself openly to his fundamental strategic problem— how to win not only for himself but his party, how to plan effective new programs for the nation yet face a Senate that will be irrevocably Democratic and deeply hostile, how to offer the nation perspectives and banners different from Eisenhower's, yet retain the old general's vigorous patronage in the campaign.

This is only partly a matter of campaign timing, at which Mr. Nixon is a master. It is even more an exertion in political philosophy. And it is this exertion which, if Mr. Nixon is nominated, will give the Republican campaign its historic flavor. For, if Mr. Nixon is to revive his party and be elected in a way that will let him govern effectively, he must distinguish for Americans once more between the Republican and Democratic parties.

The vast and real differences between Democrats and Republicans have always been seen vaguely by political analysts and understood only intuitively by American voters. The Democrats as a party, by and large, are held together by a faith that government is there to be used as an instrument of action, that power is to be enjoyed, that leadership is an invitation to experiment and adventure. It is this unspoken faith that is the most effective recruiting agent for the brilliant young men who, all over the country, have given the Democrats their preponderant and growing strength.

Republicans, as a party, have mistrusted government as a thing in itself; deep in their philosophy lies buried the noble concept of the individual's responsibility for community action apart from government. Yet even in this philosophy, government must play a role to make possible the exercise of this individual responsibility in schools, on farms, in communities, in business, in new and effective form. And it is here that Eisenhower has most weakened his party. He has blurred the Republican vision; whether for want of executive skill or intellectual energy, he has given no banners to his party around which recruits may gather.

No NEW institutions or departures in any area of American life will reflect, at his leaving, the problems that have swollen in Eisenhower's Administration. Republican orators will have no TVAs, no social security, no farm legislation, no labor legislation, no Marshall Plans to talk about. In Eisenhower's eight years the fantastic and wonderful world of science has come to pose for the American Government a management problem of crisis dimensions—yet 80 per cent of America's lavish expenditure on science is still fed through the bureaucracies of the Pentagon and the AEC with no attempt to marry science and government in any way the future demands. A feeble attempt has been made to dismantle the Democratic structure of farm subsidies—which has cost the Republicans their traditional farm loyalties yet has in no way solved the problem of the fields. In foreign policy the world has changed as Europe has achieved equality, Africa has become free, and China has become a giant—but the "new look" of the Eisenhower Administration has erected no new institutions or policies to meet these changes; instead, it has rigidly administered the once-brilliant, now-obsolete old Democratic policy of containment. Even in fiscal management, which has so absorbed Eisenhower's personal emotions, no creative way has been found to defend the value of the steadily eroding dollar. No glow of supreme purpose draws young people after Republican leadership as Rooseveltian and Stevensonian leadership drew young vigor into party work.

ONE CANNOT talk, even briefly, with the tiny band of young lieutenants who manage Nixon's closely held campaign without sensing in them an awareness of this problem; they already search for ideas and answers in those corners of the great university campuses which the Democrats have not already foreclosed on them. Nor can one ignore their vitality and energy, reflecting so vividly the personality of their chief, contrasting so sharply with the tired, caretaker quality of the Eisenhower entourage. For Nixon is a man with a personal zest for government as a process and for politics as an adventure. In almost every area of national concern, one feels the itch of inner-circle Nixon men to be at work on foreign policy, farm policy, science, and defense on their own. Such energy could promise for the beginning of a Nixon administration a new outburst of a "hundred days"—if only it were free to act now and recruit the Congressional base now.

It is possible that the Eisenhower personality magic, plus the mass-media amplification of the "peace and prosperity" chant, can make Richard M. Nixon President. But it cannot make him President in any way that will let him govern effectively. This he must do himself, balancing tactics and strategy as he goes. And, since Nixon seeks not only to preside but to govern, the way he meets this problem is central not only to 1960 but to the politics of the entire decade to come.

SATURDAY REVIEW June 18, 1960

PERSPECTIVE 1960 #8
The Eisenhower Valedictory

It is sad that the last of President Eisenhower's voyages about the world has ended where the first began—in Asia, and in failure. Yet out of each failure comes something learned. And if the fiasco of the President's intended visit to Japan causes Americans to re-examine the role of our President in international affairs something nonetheless will have been gained.

Somehow, in the past decade, and particularly in the past few years, a notorious confusion has grown up which can if unchecked warp the effective practice of our diplomacy and diminish the importance of our leadership. This confusion rests on the myth that somehow the President, and the majesty of his office, grow with the size of the cheering mobs that line the streets of dusty foreign capitals as his procession sweeps by bearing the American message. Corollaries of this myth are that he is our ablest bargaining agent and that his presence abroad automatically expresses American goodwill.

Persuaded by such myths, our President in the past eight months has traveled faster and farther than any leader in our history—to Paris in October, to India-the Middle East-Greece-Italy-France in December, to South America in the spring, to Paris again in May, to the Philippines-Formosa-Korea this month. Nor has he been alone in such travels. Statesmen have been rocketing and crisscrossing about the globe this year like satellites in eccentric orbit: DeGaulle to England-Africa-America; Macmillan to France-Germany-America; Khrushchev to America-France-Asia-France; Chou En-lai to India, Kishi to America, Adenauer to France and America, and lesser chiefs of state everywhere like American students in tourist season. In this circus, the American President has been one of the star performers and it is not inappropriate to ask whether the majesty of his office and the purpose of America in the world have been amplified or diminished by his exertions.

A brief historical perspective is not out of order as one reflects on the roots and origins of this enveloping confusion. And such a perspective at once silhouettes the British and the Russians as chief authors of the myths of conference summitry and personal diplomacy.

For the British, summitry is an art

brought to its peak by Winston Churchill. In their memory ring the names of such conferences as those of Newfoundland Bay, Arcadia, Quebec, Casablanca, Teheran. At such meetings, the British, a relatively minor power, were elevated by their valor, war experience, and the consummate skill of Winston Churchill to equality with the two power giants of the twentieth century. British survival dates from such summit meetings. And a blur obscures the later failures of Yalta and Potsdam.

The Russians nurse from another tradition—one dating as far back as the days of Lenin and Trotsky and the first Bolshevik diplomacy of Brest-Litovsk. Ignored during the Stalin era, the earlier Communist doctrine of the founding fathers is again honored—the doctrine that sees each international convocation not as a forum of negotiation but a propaganda platform from which Communism appeals to masses of the oppressed over the heads of their leaders.

AMERICANS, HOWEVER, must look at such matters differently and through the lens of our own experience. From Wilson's unhappy journey to the Versailles Conference down to Eisenhower's humiliation in Paris and Japan, summitry and personal diplomacy have proven a miserable manner of conducting American diplomacy. In the postwar era almost all American triumphs of substance, from such minor triumphs as the ending of the Berlin Blockade and the evacuation of Austria, to such major triumphs as the Marshall Plan were all achieved by quiet, patient, covert negotiation before being confirmed in public. Where memory recalls a successful wartime summit—such as Casablanca and Teheran—it recalls only an administrative conference on tactics for managing a war in which purpose and policy were already agreed before meeting; such conferences as Yalta and Potsdam at which our Presidents discussed issues, were failures.

It is not that our Presidents are lesser men than other chiefs of state, or that our diplomacy is clumsier than that of other peoples. It is simply that summitry and Presidential diplomacy do not fit our Constitutional needs.

Dwight D. Eisenhower, a man of enormous personal courage, of radiant good will, of vast experience in international affairs, has so often proven himself wiser than his professional counsellors in diplomacy that one cannot question his international competence. Were the Eisenhower family the British Royal Family and, like them, only an emblem of honor to be carted around the world opening bridges and ennobling trade fairs, his exertions in travel this year would be justified.

But the President of the United States is more than an emblem. He is at once High Priest of our secular democracy and the Magistrate of its power. So vast is the nature of his power and so complicated its mechanics that he cannot, constitutionally, be brought to a table of negotiation and pinned down in detail. Though his power is greater than that of other chiefs of state he cannot exercise it with the certain, quick precision of parliamentary premiers or dictatorial chiefs. Nor can he be offended personally without suffering offense for all Americans. If the President chooses to bargain with foreign powers he can most wisely bargain through deputies. Deputies can be repudiated, countermanded, second-guessed. The President himself cannot. About the President there must always be an air of remoteness and distance to make majestic American power. When the President submits this majesty to overexposure around the world, to challenge by street mobs, or to scorn by other men at a table, he diminishes it. Though the President of the United States may, as a person and a leader, seek to be loved and make friends—as all Americans at home and abroad wistfully seek to be loved and make friends—this is not his proper duty. His proper duty in foreign affairs is the deployment and disposition of American power in the outer world. This requires a cold, exquisitely nice, unflustered exercise of intelligence at headquarters, not at the front. It is a job performed best from Washington, not in competition with other wandering road salesmen of state.

In one of his recent polls, Mr. Gallup asked the nation which candidate for President is best equipped to sit face-to-face across the table from Khrushchev. Mr. Nixon won by a substantial margin. Too many Americans now accept this thinking as the frame of our diplomacy. If the candidates accept this thinking then they, too, have swallowed the great myths. For the question is not who is the best gladiator to put in the world arena, but how and on what terms the President should choose to exercise his authority in foreign affairs. This is the valedictory of the Eisenhower voyages of the past year and what he has contributed to public experience by his trials.

SATURDAY REVIEW July 2, 1960

PERSPECTIVE 1960 #9
Census and Politics—1960

It is rare that a Presidential campaign falls in a year that furnishes so clear and startling a description of change as the year 1960.

For 1960 is not only a quadrennial Presidential year, but the year of the Federal Census. And as the first, raw, still-unevaluated data begins to cascade from the Census Bureau it is already apparent that it offers Americans an opportunity for self-recognition as important and historic as that offered by the great Census of 1890.

The Census of 1890 was our official farewell to the American frontier. That year, the men of the Census announced that the great plains and prairies were so covered by settlement that no one could any longer draw the frontier line which had been the horizon of American life for two and a half centuries.

The Census of 1960 is equally important. It marks the passage of the crest of the great city, the first turning of Americans decisively away from a community institution which has dominated our culture and politics for half a century.

In gross terms, of course, the census records the continuing miracle of American growth—the swelling of our country by 28,000,000 people in a dec-

290

ade, or by almost as many new Americans as America held people at the outbreak of the Civil War a century ago.

But it is not the growth that is important in this decade. It is the change in the pattern of growth. For the great cities which, decade by decade, as if by some unchangeable law of history, have grown without a hesitation through every census, have stopped growing.

Instead, from coast to coast, they dwindle. This year, according to the first census figures, the downturn becomes official. In all but one of the fifteen largest metropolitan areas in the United States (those with approximately 1,500,000 population or more), the core city, the central municipality, has lost population. From New York through Washington, Cleveland, Buffalo, Baltimore, Chicago, Detroit, clear across to San Francisco, all our major cities but one have lost citizens, in a sweep so broad as to define not an individual local crisis but a universal phenomenon. The sole exception to this sweep has been Los Angeles, which gained some twenty-four per cent in population. But then Los Angeles never presented itself as a city in the classic sense. The chief loser (fifteen per cent) has been Boston, city of my birth. Memory carries this writer back to the days when he was a boy in Boston's public schools in the Twenties and our teachers taught us to expect, as certainty, that Boston (then 750,000) would some day reach 1,000,000. Boston reached 800,000 in 1950 and has now fallen to 677,000, or less than when I was born.

Two-thirds of all the massive growth of American numbers has, it appears, come in this decade in the suburban girdle of our cities, great and small. This change in the American pattern of living has, of course, become already perhaps the most overworked subject of humor, politics, sociology and analysis in what passes for American intellectual discussion. Yet the change is so vast, so all-embracing, so profound, that it is fair to say that the political exploration of the subject has not yet even begun.

This new pattern of American life for example, no longer needs the railway facilities of the past; and only 800,000 men work on the nation's railways today, where 1,326,000 found jobs on the rails eleven years earlier. Suburbanites drive to work; and Jimmy Hoffa's teamsters carry the freight out to their supermarkets. As the logistics of the suburbs require, increasingly, rubber-wheeled transport, Hoffa's power in American affairs grows to rival that of railway barons of the 1870s and 1880s. The new nation now uses gas and oil in the suburbs (the consumption of natural gas in the country has doubled in the past decade). But in West Virginia, only 200,000 miners work in mines that employed 400,000 ten years ago; 350,000

people in West Virginia are fed by means of Federal government food parcels and the state is seen as a problem state, not as an area under strain in a period of national growth and change.

From the crude figures of the 1960 Census, a crude logic draws some of the perspectives that will frame this campaign of 1960. To build the vast girdle of suburbia about each of our withering cities has required a national exertion greater than that of clearing the wilderness; housing has thus become our largest single industry. We built approximately 1,400,000 new dwelling units last year and, it now appears, we will match that mark this year. This is the largest chunk of new capital investment in American life and the exertion affects our entire credit structure. Since the war the corporations of America have drawn only $90,000,000,000 from the credit system of America to finance their huge expansion of production facilities, and another $36,000,000,000 for mortgages on factories, office buildings and commercial structures. But Americans have used $116,000,000,000 to finance their new homes.

Suburbia, then, is mortgaged to the hilt, a drain not only on our present resources, but a massive claim against future resources. Nor is it only a general public claim. Suburbia is a claim against the future of all the individuals who live in it. Americans, today, are marrying more youthfully than any other civilized Western people—and these young marriages must be equipped and financed out of credit, not savings. Where, before World War II, only one dollar out of every fourteen in take-home pay was pledged against in-stallment payments, today, it is esti-mated, one dollar out of every nine in take-home pay is obligated for the ap-pliances, the tools, the cars that make possible comfortable or decent living in suburbia.

The growth of the nation has thus come in suburbia, and suburbia rests upon credit. But this credit, however magnificent its use has been, has not just happened. It has its roots in the past and in government policy—first the New Deal Housing Laws, then the New Deal credit laws, later the Veteran laws. Just as the Homestead Laws of the 1860s, by throwing the lands of the West open to free energies, finally erased the frontier thirty years later in 1890, so has the social legislation of the early 1930s changed the America that appears in the Census of 1960. In each case, the wise and far-seeing policies of one generation succeeded—and suc-ceeded so spectacularly as to pose an en-tirely new problem of politics for the generation that follows.

What is called for thus, by the Cen-sus of 1960, is a re-examination of the nation in the new idiom of the Sixties— a re-examination of ways to preserve the vital essence of the city before it decays in chaos; a re-study of the suburbs and ways to give them roads, schools, hos-pitals which neither private credit nor community budgets can supply; a re-appraisal of all national transportation in terms of the three-cornered rail-truck-air war; a fundamental reshaping of our institutions of government, state, municipal and regional.

Such a re-examination has, to be

sure, already started, and the national debate over the use of national resources had begun even before the first prelimi-nary census figures were available. Up to now, however, the debate on our na-tional product and the use of our re-sources has been given a spurious vitality chiefly by locking it to the de-bate on foreign affairs and our contest with Communism. The mythical fig-ures of Gross National Product and the equally mythical estimates of growth rates here and abroad have been volley-ing back and forth as if it were chiefly Russia's challenge that would determine the shape of our future, and the chan-nelling of our energies. The Census comes to remind us that it is not Russia which should be central to the debate on the use of our energies, but our own needs. No nation can change so pro-foundly as ours seems to be changing without requiring new institutions and new thought, in its own spirit and for its own good.

It took some ten years after the clos-ing of the frontier before the new rela-tions in American life became clear enough to require Federal action. It was only the discovery of individual com-munities that they could not grapple on a state level with the railways, with the food packers, with the trusts, that fi-nally brought the problems of that era to Washington—and resulted in the historic re-examination that ran from the first Roosevelt through the early Wilson years. One hopes that it will not take so long in our time; and the year 1960 is a good year to begin the task.

SATURDAY REVIEW July 9, 1960

PERSPECTIVE 1960 #10
The Changing of the Guard

LOS ANGELES

It was a subdued convention.

The eye and ear caught the usual surface sights and sounds of carnival: there were bands, banners, street floats, demonstrations, the flags of every state, girls, limousines, police sirens, and two competing delegations of Puerto Ricans who enlivened the lobby of the headquarters hotel with steel-band music and dancing. Oratory drenched the air of caucus and convention, and for three days the last loud pilgrims of Adlai Stevenson* ringed the convention hall in an endless chain, chanting to the evening skies with a noise and enthusiasm unmatched since the days of Willkie.** But for the delegates themselves, and for those who take their politics seriously, it was a flat gathering. The most important emotions, except for those of the Stevensonians, lay beneath the surface—intense, but voiceless to express themselves.

The Biltmore Hotel, convention headquarters, was thronged—as all

headquarters are thronged—with the curious, always seeking to poke their faces into the TV camera, and, among them, the staffs of the candidates, the convention personnel, the press. But the delegates themselves were scattered over thirty-five miles of Los Angeles's palm-starred boulevards, few of them willing to trust their driving skills on the city's mad freeways, and most of them reluctant to spend the five or ten dollars for a taxi ride from one center of their sprawling dispersion to another. (From Pennsylvania headquarters in Pasadena to New York headquarters in Hollywood was a fifteen-dollar taxi ride, which discouraged casual visiting between these two traditionally friendly delegations.) It was a balmy week, the weather as perfect as it must have been before man's smog fouled Los Angeles, so delegates caucused in their individual hotels by states, or lounged near swimming pools and sent their wives and children off to Disneyland while they followed proceedings largely by TV and the hourly extras.

A national convention, always a universe in itself, is usually bound together in a compact huddle of downtown hotels in some compact, clotted city so

*Unsuccessful Democratic Presidential candidate in 1952 and 1956

**Unsuccessful Republican Presidential candidate in 1944

293

that geographical nearness throws delegates together until they can simmer into a common boil. But this convention was a diffuse one with only two focal points, the Biltmore Hotel and the Sports Arena; it was difficult to create the emotions to stampede such a convention; had it been otherwise, Adlai Stevenson might have had a chance. The universe of this convention was atomized and dispersed—as was the greater universe of reality outside and beyond it.

Those delegates who might have flown to Los Angeles in 1956, and the press corps which did fly en masse to the Republican Convention in California four years ago, could only have flown on the now obsolete prop-pulled planes, which then took nine to twelve hours to span the continent. The delegates who flew from the East Coast for this convention made the flight in the new jets—five hours from coast to coast, the continent spanned in half the time. So much had America shrunk since 1956, as the world had shrunk.

This shrinkage of the world, this changing world, this world of challenge and Communism, was indeed the central theme all orators seized upon. They not only seized upon the theme; they repeated it, hammered it, flattened it until the entire convention seemed a continuous drone of great worries dimmed by overlapping clichés. Whenever one tuned the inner ear to attention to separate words from the drone, the same phrases came shimmering through the blur: ". . . the ramparts of freedom . . . this world, half free and half slave . . . this, the most powerful nation on

earth, reduced to . . . leadership . . . uncommitted nations . . . the revolution of technology . . . the revolution of rising expectations . . . the people who look to us for an example . . . twenty-five minutes away from the pushbutton on Khrushchev's desk. . . ." All the great concerns were reduced to a common patter, and, with the exception of John Kennedy's brilliant closing address of acceptance, the speeches bored the delegates and made them fidget. The delegates already knew the burden of the times: on Monday, the day the convention opened, Khrushchev rattled his rockets in support of Cuba, Castro spat on us again, the Congo broke into chaos.

The world was, indeed, changing. This every delegate knew; these were remarkably sober, earnest delegates, with fewer drunks among them than in living memory. They brooded, and many of them actually read in their hotels. From Beverly Hills to Pasadena, the booksellers had a run on stock. Three of the most important bookstores in Los Angeles (Hunter's, Pickwick, Brown's) sold completely out of Kennedy's "Strategy of Peace," two sold completely out of Adlai Stevenson's "Putting First Things First," and Kennedy's "Profiles in Courage" was also all but cleaned out. (Pickwick, Hollywood's great bookstore, sold out of "American Freedom and Catholic Power," too.) Thus it was not only the outside universe that was changing, but the universe of the convention, too.

A convention is usually made up of older, if not wiser, men than the voters who send them there. In most states, party leadership chooses delegates who are long-time, trusted party servants; or men of eminence in culture, diplomacy, and the professions who can adorn the delegation; or, in many cases, those who contribute the big money to the local party and now wish the honorable symbol of a delegate's badge. Most of those who come to a convention have earned, over long years of achievement at some level, the right to come. Delegates from the primary states are usually younger than the machine-picked delegations, but all of them, in one way or another, are older men, their ages averaging over fifty.

IT WAS THESE older men who felt most poignantly—and with expressive melancholy—their familiar universe changing about them. One could see drifting through the lobbies such former powers as James Farley, or Tommy Corcoran, or Scott Lucas, or Claude Pepper—but they were powerless relics. Even currently active politicians of an ineffectual age—Carmine DiSapio and Mike Prendergast, leaders of New York's huge but impotent delegation—stalked about together, almost hand in hand, as if dazed and lost and afraid to be alone. The strenuous applause for Eleanor Roosevelt, the applause for Sam Rayburn, the tumultuous applause for Adlai Stevenson was not only for these people as individuals but also as symbols of a familiar past, a safer, victorious past. Even Averell Harriman, a man who has earned much credit from the Republic and wasted most of it in the local barbarian wars of New York poli-

tics, received a round of sincere, heart-warming clapping and cheering. It was as if only his triumphs in Moscow, Washington, London, and Paris were remembered from a larger, more glorious past.

It was when they faced the future (to which every orator summoned them, saying we must boldly and fearlessly face the future) that they were perplexed. Time had passed them by. Perplexity was of the essence of this 1960 convention: perplexity at the great unclarified issues of the world which the headlines told about, and perplexity as they contemplated the only candidate their party had cast up who might face this future, John F. Kennedy.

IN THIS PERPLEXITY the convention was right. They could opt for the familiar past, or for the unknown future with Kennedy. Conventions in America are a stage where, quite often, the naked political act takes place in public; delegates like to imagine that each convention makes history as did those of 1932 and 1952, and, thus, that they too help shape history. But the shape of this convention had long since been determined before it gathered. It had been determined in Wisconsin and West Virginia, where Kennedy had stumped through the snows and spring grasses to show his magic with the simple voters. Now, in Los Angeles, he continued to stump, addressing every state caucus open to him down to noon on balloting day—and he used the same phrases, the same anecdotes, the same themes he had used to tow-haired youngsters in the school gyms of Wisconsin and to grimy miners in the hollows of West Virginia. He need not have stumped in the areas of critical convention strength—the urban delegations of the powerful Northeast—because he had long since compelled the handful of men who control the big state delegations to acquiescence and support. He had compelled them by showing his vote-pulling muscle in alien primaries, in farm state and urban state, in New England and the Pacific, in Catholic state and Protestant state. Yet he stumped now nonetheless.

Seeing him now in action, every group at the convention was perplexed by him.

John F. Kennedy impresses one as a high-spirited stallion—tense, handsome, graceful in actions of power, with hidden, dazzling reserves of intelligence, strength, and resiliency. Yet these are not qualities that necessarily create likableness; the perfection of performance created an awe—and a touch of fear. One can be inches close to Kennedy, yet always the last inch shelters a concealed reserve, a hidden barrier. Adlai Stevenson drowses when he is bored, for he does not suffer fools gladly. Yet when Stevenson gives himself, with all his wit and all his warmth, men leave with a sense of intimacy. With John Kennedy it is different. It is easier to approach Kennedy than any other major figure in politics; and his candor when he speaks is startling, the operation of his mind fascinating. But no man ever enters Kennedy's presence without total alertness, as if he were being tested by Kennedy's alertness.

To politicians, Kennedy is a strange phenomenon. He can discuss the four Pennsylvania districts that bothered Governor David Lawrence this spring, the composition of various wards in Boston, the problems of Governor Rossellini's ticket in Washington. But then, after having mastered politicians with his knowledge of the mechanics of their trade, he will befuddle them by an intellectual generalization out of a culture they have never perceived. He can also discuss American historiography with scholars, the qualities that make a good book, the character of the great Marlborough (quoting as he goes and speculating on Churchill's motives in writing the work)—and then baffle the intellectuals drawn to him by the grubbiest details of campaign housework and intrigue. The youth of the Democratic nominee, contrasting with the range of his practical and intellectual experience, creates perplexity—and thus the convention of older men accepted him, turning their generation over to another generation and an unknown master whom they could not understand, yet a master nonetheless.

PERHAPS THE highest point of the convention, and certainly (with the exception of Kennedy's closing address) the most eloquently moving moment was the speech of Senator Eugene McCarthy pleading that the convention consider the name of Adlai Stevenson. Its eloquence, its nobility, its sense of people were superb. It was flawed only by the logic that held it together, for he pleaded with the delegates to ignore their instructions and vote for Stevenson. Yet Kennedy had invoked these instructions from the common people to their delegates in New Hampshire and Wisconsin, in West Virginia and Maryland, in Indiana and Oregon. He had piped up control over scores of such delegates with his own voice, by his own exertions in village square and basketball court. Then, having won in the far reaches of America, he had skilfully summoned the big-city bosses of the East to surrender to the strength he had shown. They had no choice. The primaries—those most primitive and homely of political instruments—were the club he had used to beat into submission the big-city bosses, who once thought him only a boy. Like most defeated chieftains, they proved after defeat his trusted allies, the necessary men to carry the convention. As when Caesar conquered the Gauls, and the Gallic cavalry brought to his banners after defeat the outriders and moppers-up necessary to harass Pompey in the following civil war, so Kennedy used the submissive chieftains of the big city to mop up Stevenson.

I think there will remain with me always a scene that followed immediately after Kennedy was nominated. Wyoming's vote had given Kennedy the official majority in the balloting and so, swiftly, the politicians darted from their seats on the convention floor, up the stands, and across the few hundred feet to the prefabricated cottage adjacent to the Arena, which had been converted into Kennedy's floor headquarters and command post.

John Bailey of Connecticut, bald and happy, boss of his state, was the first to arrive; he alone among the big-city bosses had been a Kennedy loyalist from the moment the campaign had been conceived. There arrived next the short, stocky Governor of Ohio, Mike DiSalle, the first reluctant chief conscripted by Kennedy in the winter. There arrived next Dick Daley, mayor of Chicago, boss of Illinois Democrats, short and stocky, too, dragooned to service only weeks before the convention opened. Then came the equally short and stocky Pennsylvanians, Governor David Lawrence of Pennsylvania and Congressman William Green, boss of Philadelphia. One by one, long and short, they arrived, for the word had spread that Kennedy would stop here for a moment of privacy before going to the rostrum of the convention itself. It was certainly the greatest convocation of Democratic political power in one room that this correspondent has ever seen. All wanted to be visibly and demonstratively present as the candidate arrived from his North Rossmore hideaway en route to the convention rostrum, to show that now, after their earlier surly neutrality, they were his people.

Several of them gathered in the balmy evening about the pool of the prefabricated cottage, drinking. They drank Coca-Colas and beer, for strong drink is frowned on by John Kennedy at his headquarters (Kennedy is a soft-drink man himself). They waited, chatting with each other, and then one of them—either Bailey or DiSalle, I forget which—said, "There he comes now."

A hush fell on them. Far off in the distance they could see a winking row of tiny red lights serpentining across a Los Angeles boulevard. All of them recognized it, for they were bosses, mayors, governors, masters of police themselves. It was a police cavalcade, bearing possibly a future President of the United States, approaching from the hideaway where Kennedy had spent the evening.

Kennedy loped into the cottage, with the light, dancing step that is his manner, and for a moment they surrounded him. Green of Philadelphia hugged him—perhaps ignorant of the fact that Kennedy is a man who hates to be touched, gripped, hugged, taken by the lapels, or accosted in any of the gestures which are so common among Republican and Democratic politicians alike. Kennedy seeks reserve always, a little distance between him and the public. Then Kennedy gently left the hug and was alone in a corner of the room with his brother Robert and brother-in-law Sargent Shriver. The others surged forward on impulse to join him. They then halted. A distance of perhaps thirty feet separated them from him, but it was impassable. They stood apart, these older men of established and decades-long power, and watched him. He turned after a few moments, saw them watching him, and whispered to his brother-in-law, who approached to invite them across the space. First, Averell Harriman. Then, Dick Daley. Then Mike DiSalle. Then, one by one, in an order determined by his instinct and judgment, he let them all congratulate him. Yet no one could pass the little open distance uninvited because there

was this separation about him and the knowledge that they were there not as his patrons but as his clients. They could come by invitation only.

After a few moments of conversation it was time to go to the convention hall, which, an hour before, had witnessed the delegates choosing Jack Kennedy.

Outside the cottage, the instantaneous throng had gathered, the mob which always coagulates about power. The mob was thick over the few hundred feet from the cottage to the convention and it was, conceivably, dangerous as all mobs are. All of them, then, mayors, governors, bosses alike, clustered together and formed a flanking escort about Kennedy, led by the white-helmeted police of Los Angeles, to protect Kennedy as they offered him to the convention. There were the short—DiSalle (Ohio), Daley (Chicago), Green (Philadelphia), Wagner (New York)—and the tall—Harriman (New York), Williams (Michigan), John McCormick (Boston), and many others; but all of them alike put their heads down to plunge through the crowd and protect him, bowing to a man of another age and a new era. No one of them, perhaps, could remember six months or a year back to the day when they had other candidates, other dreams. Kennedy was now *their* candidate; he had compelled their loyalty, as he had compelled the loyalty of this entire convention which had no other choice.

SATURDAY REVIEW August 6, 1960

PERPSECTIVE 1960 #11
Republicans Revisited

CHICAGO

An accident of politics caused the Republican convention to follow the Democratic convention in the calendar of the Presidential season; and from this accident, here in Chicago, the Republicans suffered. They suffered because what was at issue at the Republican convention was ideas, not personalities; and because the 2,000-odd newsgatherers—of radio, TV, press, and agency—who must mirror a convention to itself and the nation brought with them from the excitement of Los Angeles a fatigue of nerve, perception, and energy too heavy to meet the subtleties of the Chicago proceedings.

Outwardly, of course, the carnival trappings of the two conventions were almost the same, mocking with their vulgarity the gravity of what must happen at a Presidential convention. The surface differences were trivial: The Republican bands were larger, brassier, and more numerous than the Democratic music-makers. The dresses of the girls in Los Angeles, fluttering in the summer wind, seemed, in memory, prettier; but the Republican convention was adorned with several beauties in breath-taking tights with more immediate impact. Chicago was breezier and cooler than Los Angeles on its good days, ˜hotter and muggier on its bad days. But the caucuses, receptions, statements, and press conferences of both conventions were the same—and by providing the same kind of news they obscured the strange differences between the two parties that govern America.

One can always draw a reasonably satisfying wiring diagram of the Democratic Party, from center of power to center of power, from the big-city bosses of the East to the citizen groups of the West to the Bourbon oligarchy of the South. No such wiring diagram is possible for the Republican Party; its structure and physiology are entirely different from those of the Democrats. And it is this difference in physiology and structure that makes it so difficult, even now, to assess the obscure clash of wills and ideas that has just closed here in Chicago.

It is best, perhaps, to see the Chicago convention as one more chapter in the centuries-old civil war that has split the Republican Party from birth.

For almost half a century—from the days of Abraham Lincoln and Thurlow Weed to those of Theodore Roosevelt and William Howard Taft—this civil war went on openly and visibly between reformers and stalwarts, between idea men and organization men, in convention and in party caucus. But from 1912 on, with the public breach of the Roosevelt and Taft wings of the party, a permanent distortion has come about. One half of the drive and tradition of the party is always starkly visible in a conservative, nationalistic, cement-bound organization that controls its machinery of operation, while the other half of the party's drive and tradition persists amorphously, completely outside the machinery, in a system of ideas, ideamakers, and reformers of liberal tradition who make themselves felt only at quadrennial intervals.

Over and over again in the past twenty years, since Wendell Willkie's triumph in 1940, the regulars who make up the party's bony structure have assembled in convention ready to nominate a president in the tradition of William Howard Taft, and have then been overwhelmed by a mysterious swoop from the outside. This, of course, has only confirmed the regulars' conspiratorial theory of American history once so ably expressed by Joe McCarthy of Wisconsin. And this is what baffled and confused the regulars in the convention just ended, when they saw a man they believed their own turn against them. For never has the external swoop of the liberals on the convention seemed so nakedly conspiratorial as in the Compact of Sixty-second Street when, on Saturday morning, it was announced that Richard Nixon and Nelson Rockefeller had met on the fourteenth floor of a triplex apartment overlooking Central Park in Babylon-by-the-Hudson and there settled the course of the convention 800 miles from the convention proceedings themselves.

IT IS WORTH pausing to examine the Rockefeller operation for a moment. The Rockefeller operation rested on the belief that the ideas that Nelson Rockefeller so eloquently voiced in the spring months of 1960 could, of themselves, create a situation where he might be chosen President. Its strength lay in the personality of Nelson Rockefeller himself and in the enormous and imaginative work of his brain trust, led by the brooding and brilliant Emmet Hughes. Its weakness lay in its apparent ignorance of the grubby details of politics, its inability to cultivate delegates, organize delegates, or deliver, in mechanical terms, the enormous political potential that existed in Rockefeller down to the weekend that preceded the convention opening. The sole and superlative pragmatist in the Rockefeller camp—Lieutenant Governor Malcolm Wilson of New York—had been immobilized for months by personal reasons. Rockefeller's other pragmatists were, by far, more amateurish than the men who mounted the Stevenson drive in Los Angeles a few days earlier.

Since the Rockefeller candidacy thus lay solely in the strength of its ideas, it could be wiped out by anyone who expropriated those ideas and abolished the distance that Mr. Rockefeller and Mr. Hughes were trying to keep between themselves and the party regulars. This, of course, is what happened when Mr. Nixon met with Mr. Rockefeller and accepted his ideas. There was, thereafter, no longer any possibility of an open dispute between the two, nor a possibility of type-casting the one and the other in the leading roles of the traditional Republican feud, as the Rockefeller camp had hoped. Had Mr. Nixon really remained the conservative he was in 1952, or had Mr. Rockefeller's managers been shrewder in practical politics, the convention might have burst into open war. When it was all over, one of Mr. Nixon's young and able Californians—who resemble so much in age and style Mr. Kennedy's young men from Massachusetts—murmured, "What a beautiful political property that Rockefeller is—if only he'd had somebody to manage him."

The dismay of the Rockefeller inner circle when its members realized on the Saturday before convention that their candidacy had evaporated was equaled only by the dismay of the regular Republicans when they examined the full text of the compact and the full range of liberal thinking that Messrs. Nixon and Rockefeller had sealed in New York on Friday night. And the dismay broke most sharply in the platform committee.

The Republican platform committee had been chosen haphazardly, which is to say traditionally, by the machinery of the party which belonged to the fossilized regulars. Its 103 members had been in full session for a week before the convention opened, hearing witnesses, discussing and polishing the platform which had been drafted long in advance, fondly imagining that their proceedings were of real weight and real influence. (Why they should so have imagined is probably a matter of self-delusion—the critical subcommittee on national defense had heard only four witnesses, two strangelings and two fortress-America advocates, before going into executive session.) When these grass-roots conservatives discovered that one midnight session in New York was to reshape the platform beyond all their powers of protest, they felt not only personally affronted in pride and exposed as buffoons but also betrayed by Mr. Nixon, whom they had seen for so long as their own flesh and blood.

The problem that faced Mr. Nixon on his arrival at the opening Monday of the convention was, therefore, simply to prevent the party from tearing itself apart in open civil war. And though his success in this effort gave the convention its murky and often dreary appearance, it concealed a private political performance of absolute mastery.

The outer Mr. Nixon, followed everywhere by the mobile jungle of television wires, cables, cameras, and microphones, was the boyish, affable Mr. Nixon whom the public saw. This was the Richard Nixon who managed to shake hands and have his picture taken with some 2,200 of the 2,400 delegates and alternates to the convention. This was the Mr. Nixon who unnerved both his staff and the Secret Service by plowing through the always dangerous mobs of well-wishers to shake hands, say hello, and be friendly. This was the Mr. Nixon who, entering the convention hall on Thursday to make his speech of acceptance, could explain to the little cluster of microphones how he had prepared himself for this climactic speech not only by studying the great acceptance speeches of the past but also by spending a full week reading books "on history, philosophy, and literature."

Then there was the other Mr. Nixon, the operational Mr. Nixon, whom the public could never see. Each move he made, in haste and under strain, was right—in timing, in degree of pressure, in the intricate meshing of convention tactic and electoral strategy. There was never any doubt, from the weekend on, that Mr. Nixon had the nomination; the only doubt rested on whether he would have it on terms that offered him a chance to win the election that followed, and, if elected, an even chance against Mr. Khrushchev in the years thereafter.

Mr. Nixon faced, first, the problem of quelling the rebellion in the platform committee. This was a tactical-strategic problem of separating and subduing the two halves of the revolting coalition— the Southern hostiles and the Midwestern conservatives. Here, Mr. Nixon chose as his battleground the issue of civil rights, and in a thirty-six-hour period from Monday evening to Wednesday morning he succeeded in breaking

the back of the opposition by dividing it. This was backroom work, hard work, and it required, as one of his lieutenants said, "the collecting of every political IOU we held over the past eight years." Once that was done, Mr. Nixon had established the strategic base for his election campaign, a campaign which his lieutenants hinge on his ability to carry the great industrial states of the Northeast where the Negro vote is so critical.

A lesser man might have been content to rest there. But Mr. Nixon, in full knowledge of the bruising the older Republicans had taken, went on. He went on not only to enforce his previous choice of Vice President, internationalist Henry Cabot Lodge, but also to pivot his acceptance speech on what is certainly the most unpopular issue in general American politics—the continuance and re-invigoration of American aid to the outside world as the major instrument of American foreign policy. When he had finished, Mr. Nixon had separated himself by several light-years from the old regular and isolationist thinking of the Republican Party, yet he held their machinery under stricter control than any man since Robert A. Taft.

In retrospect, the chief drama of John F. Kennedy's nomination lay in Kennedy's spring ordeal as he fought in the primaries across the nation and subdued the bosses of the big cities. The drama of the Nixon nomination lay in a brief period of three or four days and was worked out on the second and third floors of the Blackstone Hotel in Chicago. The Kennedy drama ended in an act of surpassing political clarity. But the Nixon drama ended in a series of gambles as bold and hazardous as any Presidential candidate has ever undertaken.

By Thursday evening, when the Republican convention of 1960 was adjourned *sine die,* it had accepted all of Mr. Nixon's gambles. The Republican campaign was to hinge on foreign policy—thus committing its fortune, to a large extent, to the turbulent world of international events and mortgaging its chances to the calculations and miscalculations of Soviet policy in the next three months. It had chosen to yield the South to the Democrats and gambled that it must sweep the entire industrial Northeast as well as Richard Nixon's native West. It had gambled, with Nixon, that only the posture and promise of a liberal philosophy could let it win in such a manner as to govern the nation in cooperation with a certainly Democratic Senate.

If, in any of these gambles, Mr. Nixon should prove wrong, it is certain he will have ended his own political career—and possibly, also, the nature of the Republican Party as it has existed in American politics since 1912.

SATURDAY REVIEW August 13, 1960

PERSPECTIVE 1960 #12
With Nixon in Georgia

The drive from Atlanta's airport, over the throughway had been carefully slow, the shape of the city gradually growing on the ridge, handsome new buildings appearing on its crest, chunky towers rising in profile from their midst, the gold dome of the State House glittering—and no one in the Vice President's hopeful cavalcade knowing quite what to expect here in the heart of the Deep South.

But the moment the procession climbed the incline to turn on to Peachtree Street, the gossip of politics and whispering of hope instantly became substance. The Atlantans were there not in the twos and threes of ordinary, orderly political demonstrations, but in five-deep, six-deep ranks that first blotted the sidewalks and then poured into the streets. From the windows above, a storm of confetti, paper streamers, torn scraps, red, blue, and gold spangles rained down, gathering to a blizzard as thick as Wall Street ever offered returning heroes. People waved their banners, shouted, screamed, and crowded thicker and thicker until the procession slowed to an ooze. At Atlanta's Famed Five Points, where Peachtree turns left on to Edgewood to descend to Hurt Park, the cavalcade halted completely as the crowd surged out to mob the open convertible of Dick Nixon and his wife.

By the time the white-helmeted police had cleared the way again, the mob had swarmed thick after the car, breaking the cavalcade. They trotted after the Vice President, in the center a herd of young girls in white skirts and red-white-and-blue hats, jiggling and hip-wriggling, and after them a pell-mell horde of old and young chasing him all the way to the park. At Hurt Park, there were two or three acres of them, yodeling and yipping rebel-yells, crowding over the limestone parapet above, sitting on the ledges of the pool, spilling over the streets, waiting to be taken, yearning to listen. It was, Dick Nixon was later to remark, the most impressive demonstration he had seen in fourteen years of campaigning. It was, said Ralph McGill, publisher of the *Atlanta Constitution* and sage of the modern South, "the biggest thing in Atlanta since the premiere of 'Gone With the Wind.'" For what we were seeing was mood become fact; we were seeing discontent with the sudden impact of reality.

———

THERE WAS organization to it, of course. Organization had gone to work at mid-morning on Monday preparing this Friday demonstration. The lady volunteers had undertaken to call every name in the 600-page Atlanta telephone directory and had all but succeeded. The College-Youth-for-Nixon had covered every supermarket and shopping center with announcements two days beforehand. The teen-agers had circulated through all downtown office buildings in the morning, reminding people of the excitement to come and distributing bags of confetti. Two airplanes buzzed overhead carrying sky-streamers that read "It's Nixon Day in Atlanta." Yet no four-day frenzy of preparation could, by itself, have brought together 150,000 people out of a population of 1,000,000, one in seven of the entire population—or created this mood.

For the mood, as one circulated through the crowd, while friendly, warm, and happy, was not the adoration or hero-worship one gets in a Kennedy crowd at peak intensity. It was a mood of revolt—and the friendly beneficiary of this mood was Richard Nixon.

You could touch and taste the sense of revolt at any level. The man who introduced Nixon to the crowd was James V. Carmichael. Once James V. Carmichael had aspired to a political career in Georgia and run for Governor; he had won the primary by a clear 3,000 popular votes; yet the rigged machinery of Georgia's Democratic primaries, which reduces the great city of Atlanta to equality with the lowest hillbilly county by the unit-rule system, had de-

prived him of a nomination rightfully his. Carmichael, a Democrat, now announced he was going to work and stump for Richard Nixon. The crowd roared approval.

And as one circulated through the crowd, one picked up the refrain: no one here in Atlanta or this crowd seemed to hate Kennedy as a man. But they did hate the state machine, the redneck gang descended from the Talmadge family which denies suffrage or voice to the new and growing cities of Georgia. Wherever you could sample it, the crowd rang the changes on the theme. A local newspaperman: "We're gonna scare hell out of Talmadge and his lousy machine with this." A lawyer, Democrat, who had helped organize the demonstration: "We've pleaded and tried to get our own Democratic Party system to do something about this electoral system and this unit-rule of theirs; but they won't do it." A smart, middle-class lady: "They've got to stop taking the South for granted; Southern whites are the biggest minority in the country, we need a two-party system." Another local newspaperman: "They say they want a two-party system—but here in Atlanta it only means they want to lick Talmadge and the State House crowd."

THIS IS THE mood of the city. And this mood has to be superimposed on the mood of the dominant Southern rural vote to see what disturbs Democratic strategists. Normally the overwhelming Democratic rural vote can swamp the revolting city vote in the South. But this season the rural vote is being divided by the deep and dangerous split over religion. How widespread this native hate of Catholics in the Deep South may be is still impossible to measure. It is still possible that fundamentalist preaching against Catholics can provoke a test between bigotry and tolerance, as it did in West Virginia where Kennedy won more because of than in spite of the religious issue.

But it is the mood of the cities, joined to the religious civil war in the hill and farm country, that is perplexing in this election—and, probably, is of more permanent importance. For the cities of the South have grown and swollen in the past decade with a new industry and a naturally conservative middle class. Their instinct for citizen-participation in politics, a local reflection of a new national development, is all but choked by the ancient machines that have dominated Southern politics for so long. It is impossible for Atlanta, grown by an enormous 40 per cent in the past decade to a metropolitan area of 1,000,000, to sit still and be held artificially subordinate to hill counties of seventy-five or a hundred thousand, as the Democratic Party here insists it should. If Atlanta seeks full expression and can find it only in the Republican columns—then the inclination of this city is to seek it there.

It was hoped by some Democrats that only Eisenhower's personal glamour led to the urban revolt that carried six Southern states in 1956. Now, Nixon on his Southern tours has demonstrated that this is not so. In perspective, Eisenhower has been a bridge over which hundreds of thousands of Southern Democrats have traveled into the Republican camp; they speak of it now without apology, with an air of fashionable defiance. If Nixon can hold them for the next two months he will have created the base for a real two-party system in the South, and for a realignment of American politics.

At the end of Nixon's day of triumph, I spoke to the mayor of Atlanta, William B. Hartsfield, one of the most distinguished and progressive officials of the nation, and a Democrat. I asked him whether Kennedy would get the same kind of demonstration if he came to Atlanta. The mayor avowed that Atlanta was a very hospitable city and Kennedy would get a warm welcome. "But," he added, "I won't be around when he comes." I asked why. "Well," he said, "Kennedy will be taken over by the State House crowd. I won't be allowed even to get near him. I'll be kept way off there on the fringes with the crowd."

And this, in a sense, is not only Atlanta's problem and Mr. Hartsfield's problem—but Mr. Kennedy's problem, too.

SATURDAY REVIEW September 17, 1960

PERSPECTIVE 1960 #13
Ranging the Target

WITH THE KENNEDY
CAMPAIGN

There are always two audiences to the ordeal of a man seeking the Presidency as he journeys over this vast land.

There is, first, the national audience, reached through the two score or more newsmen, broadcasters, analysts who doggedly trail in his wake to feed the great opinion-making press and networks with their distillation of his speeches, film clips of his action, sound-snatches of his voice. Not for days or weeks can the exhausted candidate learn what posture or image he has established in the mood or emotions of this national audience, which votes him, ultimately, to power.

Then there is the personal audience that gathers in the flesh, in shirt sleeves and house dresses, to listen to the candidate as he pauses in his travels. This is so small, statistically, as to be almost beneath measurement—yet its importance is almost as great as that of the national audience. For it is the personal audience that gives the candidate the response of warmth or frost, of applause or indifference. And since the candidate, whoever he is, sits at the center of

a web of affairs so complex as to be dehumanized, the human response of the personal audience shapes him and his campaign almost as profoundly as all the statistical and strategic planning of his staff. The laughter of the personal audience, its scowl, its silence, its cheering are the only clues in the mystic communication between the leader and the led that tell, truly, whether he has reached those he seeks to lead.

Becoming President is an utterly personal business, the candidate must feel the beat of the people he hopes to lead; their heart is his target; and by their immediate response, whether they be a thousand at a whistle stop or ten thousand in an auditorium, he knows whether he has ranged the target or failed.

SLOWLY, OVER the first week of his campaign, with the heart-squeezing beauties of this beautiful land in harvest season flicking by, John F. Kennedy has been ranging his target—and, in ranging it, giving shape to his campaign.

Each minute of his time since the close of Congress has been counted like

307

a bead; no leisure now lets anyone explore his inner thinking. Nor is there any reflection of this inner thinking in the carefully prepared speeches and programs, mimeographed and handed to the press with meticulous efficiency in advance-speeches and programs for the most part never uttered or spoken, to the exasperation of press and staff writers alike. One can only observe the groping process of Kennedy's thinking by listening to him before his personal audiences and noting the change that the days and the response make in his "all-purpose speech," the daily litany repeated three, five, sometimes ten times a day before ever-fresh audiences on the trail.

There are homely changes, like his first mention of the baby. Out of whatever sense of delicacy, Kennedy was silent about his wife's pregnancy for the first few days of his campaign. Then, in the warm sun, at noon, before the colorful new courthouse of the little town of Eugene, Oregon, he was suddenly impelled to offer a courteous excuse for his wife's absence because "she was otherwise committed." A friendly ripple of laughter followed. The next morning in northern California, he had changed it to "my wife has other responsibilities," and a warmer laugh followed. By afternoon, his excuse for his wife's absence had become a forthright "my wife is going to have a baby." By Friday, in the San Joaquin Valley, it had become, as he excused her absence, "my wife is going to have a boy in November." It had become a certified gag, and that evening in Los Angeles, it became a press conference question which ended a passage of tense and delicate questioning on religion. "How do you know it's going to be a boy?" asked the questioner. "My wife told me," said Kennedy. The audience laughed again, and the conference had departed from the somber area of religion.

The response of the personal audience shapes something far more important, however, than a certified exit line. It establishes in the candidate's mind what Americans want to hear; and so, slowly, the much-despised "all-purpose speech" reflects, as it changes, his own reading of the people's mood and their stirrings.

The Kennedy all-purpose speech at the beginning of his campaign was a collection of loosely jointed themes and anecdotes, some fresh, some left over from the primaries, a jumble of issues with no cohesion ("the importance of the Presidency" . . . "the world cannot exist half-slave, half-free" . . . "only the President can lead" . . . "farming is our number one domestic problem" . . . "automation can be a blessing or a curse" . . . "we must move" . . . "I ask your help").

Gradually, as applause told him where he hit, as questions from the audience voiced their concerns, the speech took shape and unity. One could sense gradually, as the candidate sensed, that the strength of the Kennedy campaign lay with his party's posture on domestic affairs, and that its vulnerability lay in the vast area of foreign affairs. (His aides report that 90 per cent of all questions are "issue" questions—foreign affairs overwhelmingly first, medical aid to the aged next, aid to education third.)

Through the first week of campaigning, applause and indifference shaped the speech to a pattern. A call to sacrifice and a warning of the perils ahead now usually comes first (always to sharp applause); then Kennedy draws the profile of the two great parties as he sees them, basing himself on Democratic bedrock strength ("We believe this is a great country—but it can be greater; this is a great state—but it can be greater. Republicans believe things are as good as they can be"). From this base he goes then to the transition: that an America moving forward at home, creating an impact of domestic dynamics as it did under Wilson, Roosevelt, and Truman, sets up a dynamic which causes the rest of the world to look to us for leadership; and then comes the transit to war and peace, to survival in a world of enormous destructive capacity—the greatest question of all (loud applause)—and termination with America must move again; "I ask your help."

The all-purpose speech, sometimes given in three minutes, sometimes in ten, is now a drone in the ears of reporters who have heard it for weeks. But given with growing passion, it reflects in the candidate a growing sense of his own authority, a sense of sureness, and most of all his own picture of the nature of his campaign. Extemporizing in Los Angeles, at the end of the California swing, Kennedy could suddenly peel off such a passage as this: "Mr. Nixon and I, and the Republican and Democratic parties, are not suddenly frozen in ice or collected in amber since the two conventions. We are like two rivers that flow back through history, and you can judge the force, the power, and the direction of the rivers by studying where they rose and where they ran throughout their long course." This is not only eloquence; this is a change in a man's perception of his role; this is the inner dynamic of campaigning.

HERE, IN THE moving combat headquarters of the Kennedy campaign, with the candidate, the early mood is one of determination, optimism, confidence. The basic problems that must be met and which, at this writing, are still unsolved are, first, the approach to the bitterly divisive religious question and, next, a substantive position on foreign affairs. But the response of the personal audiences on the tour has been so warm, so good, that these grim problems are seen as manageable—difficult but not impossible.

Not all in the Kennedy camp agree. The deputies to the roving headquarters from staff headquarters in Washington grumble that Kennedy, in addressing himself to the personal audience, is missing with the national audience. His voice and purpose, they say, as carried by the networks in the big industrial centers of the East, sound rushed, hasty, often shrill. They insist that the national image given is one of an impatient man—and the mood of the country is not so much impatience as perplexity.

In his first ten days of campaigning (from Washington to Maine to Alaska to Michigan to Idaho to Washington to Oregon to California) Kennedy has covered some 16,000 miles and seen, perhaps, a quarter of a million people. At this furious pace, he will have been exposed to about 2,000,000 out of the 180,000,000 Americans by election day. Only then will we know whether his reading of the mood of the 2,000,000 reflects the true concern of the 180,000,000.

SATURDAY REVIEW October 1, 1960

PERSERCTIVE 1960 #14
Campaign and Reality

Perhaps never before, at this late stage of a national campaign, have all prophets, analysts, polltakers, and principals been so completely in agreement— their agreement being that no American election of recent times has been so completely baffling, mysterious, and unpredictable.

That this should be so is a combination of two rare factors. The first is the compulsory irrelevance of both candidates as they address themselves to the key issue of the campaign; the second is the conjunction of this irrelevance with the extraordinary shift in power and legitimacy that will be established in America by January of 1961.

THE PRESIDENCY IS an office rarely won in open contest as it is to be won this year. It is an office whose descent, despite all the carnival trappings of campaigning, is hallowed by a legitimacy broken only three times in this century.

The nature of this legitimacy can be simply described: The office of the President is so close to that of high priest of our secular society that voters set for it standards different from those of all other contests. The President is elected to conduct affairs of history; thus the voters habitually seek their Presidents from among the men who have become familiar as figures on the national scene in Washington's temples of history. Ordinary men will not do. Legitimacy thus transfers power, irrespective of party labels, almost automatically from one man to another on the Washington scene unless some accident or total upheaval happens to intervene.

Thus only the Republican split of 1912 brought Wilson to power; legitimacy preserved him there, even though his was the minority party, for eight years. The postwar upheaval of 1920 brought in a twelve-year period of Republican legitimacy. The collapse of our economy brought in Roosevelt in 1932, and the legitimacy he established has persisted for nearly thirty years, through Truman and Eisenhower, both men his appointees, both endowed publicly with competence in matters of history.

ONLY ACCIDENT, the deepest shaking of events, or a near cataclysm interrupts this succession of legitimacy; and such a

311

cataclysm is in the making now, the first since 1932.

But the nature of this cataclysm is entirely different from that of 1932. Then it lay in an internal breakdown which was visible on every bread line and felt in every mortgaged farmstead, and which could be debated openly among Americans on the basis of commonly visible evidence, in a magnificent demonstration of wise, free, informed popular choice.

Today the shaping cataclysm lies in America's foreign affairs. Wherever one wanders this fall in the wake of the candidates, whenever one sifts through crowds listening with the same strange earnestness in Oregon or Virginia, Michigan or Iowa, New York or California, he finds the dominant concern the same: war or peace. "War, war, go away," the crowds seem to murmur, or, in Emmet Hughes's jingle, "Force be evil, Force be good, Force stay out of my neighborhood."

And it is this that makes the present epochal election so baffling and so unpredictable. For the crisis is apparent to all. Yet it is a crisis of slow erosion, with the evidence confusingly spread around the globe from the Congo to Laos, from Berlin to Cuba. And the tragedy, the inescapable tragedy, is that neither candidate can bring clarity of speech or utterance to the crisis because reality forbids it. No man who hopes to be elected President can responsibly discuss in public or propose in open speech either his plans or his solutions for our tangled affairs; by so doing he would reveal to restive adversary nations and

sensitive client states those matters which, as President, he must handle by stealth, secrecy, and surprise.

It is obvious, for example, that our thinking about the United Nations must soon be revised. It is increasingly packed with half-finished nations, fully equal voting members in a rotten-borough General Assembly where Gabon (417,000 inhabitants), Cyprus (549,000), and Iceland (169,000) vote on a par with nations several hundred times their size. Someone must blow the whistle soon. What is good in the U.N.—and what is good is vital to our security and world peace—can be preserved only by general charter revision. Yet no reasonable public discussion of this is presently possible without seeming to offer public comfort to Mr. Khrushchev.

Both candidates know, and their entourages will privately discuss, the need of revising our thinking on China. But neither can discuss a realistic China policy because open discussion would reveal our private planning to the Red Chinese with whom we must later negotiate.

It is obvious, further, that Mr. Khrushchev's present major difficulty with his Chinese ally gives us a maximum opportunity for negotiation with him. He is a man in a bind. This opportunity may be gone by next spring when the new President is ready to do business. But no new approach or hint of approach can be openly discussed, for any such approach requires secrecy and stealth to the uttermost degree.

One can run down the full list of

America's problems overseas, the areas that sputter with threat of war—Africa, Cuba, Berlin—yet few or none can be discussed in an open election. Thus irrelevance becomes compulsory. Thus Mr. Nixon is reduced to saying that the crisis does not exist; and Mr. Kennedy insists that the crisis will naturally solve itself once America moves forward on the home front again. And the nation listens to both, aware that the danger is real, but baffled as to what either candidate proposes on this, the overriding issue.

DESPITE THE quickening and strengthening of the Kennedy campaign in the past few weeks to a point where the magicians of poll-taking put him abreast of the Vice President, the advantages still lie with Nixon. In any blurred choice between the legitimate and the aspirant, the American people tend to choose the more legitimate, the more familiar figure. Thus Mr. Kennedy must either wait for events in the outer world to turn the American sense of peril in his favor in the next few weeks; or he must himself bring a clarity into matters at whatever risk, domestic or foreign, to make the crisis turn, in the popular mind, in his favor. Until he succeeds or fails in doing this, this epochal contest offers no clue as to its outcome to seer, prophet, mystic, or poll-taker.

SATURDAY REVIEW October 15, 1960

Chapter 9

Politics USA III: Local Style

There are basically two kinds of national political reporters: those who pretty much stay in Washington, D.C., covering the happenings on the Potomac; and those who range the nation, uncovering and defining national trends from an accumulation of local events. White, of course, was very much of the latter school, traveling widely, rarely spending more than a week or two consecutively in the nation's capital, always keeping tabs on the local pols, good guys and bad guys.

His initiation into this fraternity came serendipitously from a three-month round-the-country automobile trip he took in 1946. His immediate goal: to learn how the Americans of the Eleventh Bomb Squadron he'd known in China were fitting into postwar America. Their stories finally proved too diffuse to make an article, but one stop on the trip, McMinn County, Tennessee, proved to be the genesis of his ultimate career. It was his first exposure to dirty American politics, and resulted in the dramatic "The Battle of Athens, Tennessee," published by *Harper's*. Later he would note ruefully that he (the tyro) had failed to recognize that what he saw in Athens and elsewhere on this trip marked in fact the beginning of a new political era—the entry into politics of a host of returning veterans, "the undiscerned story of the elections of 1946."

By 1955, when he did a two-parter on Texas politics for *The Reporter,* he had clearly learned his "lesson." With great originality he used his insights into political life in the Lone Star State to warn of national trends that might well be in the making. Some of today's readers may be stunned to see how deeply McCarthyism had penetrated the American scene.

The other two "local" articles that comprise this chapter are quite different in nature, but both have, by extension, significant national context. One analyzes the complexities of California politics in 1956; the state was just emerging as a "new power source in our national life," and White chronicles four dynamic politicians, any of whom might one day be president. The other deals with a much more intimate situation for the author, the 1965 election for mayor of New York City, his home; as he argues vividly, the winner "must face questions larger than New York—questions that touch all Americans, in every big city, as the same coiling frustrations strangle the vital centers of American civilization."

THE BATTLE OF ATHENS, TENNESSEE

The Sweetwater River, a pleasant mountain stream that falls into the basin of the Tennessee, cuts through McMinn County beneath a canopy of high tension wires. The people of McMinn County, like the taut, coppery wires, hum with subdued peaceful activity until they are disturbed; and then, like the wires, they snap in a shower of sparks and violence. It took several killings, ten years of extortion and thuggery, a world war and an official invasion by legal gunmen to bring on the violence of August 1, 1946, and the bloody siege of the Athens jail. But when it was over, democracy was firmly established and authority once again rested with the citizenry.

The people of McMinn County are God-fearing men and women. When the Robert E. Lee highway climbs out of the Shenandoah Valley, which can take its religion or leave it, into east Tennessee on the road to McMinn the highway is sprinkled with signboards telling the godless wayfarers that "Jesus is coming soon" or warning them "Prepare to Meet God." McMinn itself is relatively free of such shrieking witnesses to faith; McMinn's religion is Methodist and Baptist, quiet, bone-deep, and so-

ber. On Saturday afternoon when farmers throng the town, preachers are allowed to call sinners to repentance in the shade of the courthouse at the county seat. But most of McMinn meets God in the serenity of Sunday morning at the red brick or white board house of worship in peace and devotion. The church-goers have made liquor illegal, and Sunday movies are unlawful, too.

Next to religion, politics is the most important thing. But until 1946, religion absorbed so much of the spirit of right-thinking people that politics fell automatically to the bad. First, it was the Republicans. They had McMinn County for years and years. The Republicans would let a Democrat get elected now and then, but the sheriff was theirs and they held tight to the county trustee who disbursed funds and issued poll-tax certificates. Then, from 1936, when Paul Cantrell won the election and established an eastern outpost of the Crump machine, it was ten years of Democrats.

PAUL CANTRELL, state senator from the McMinn area and boss of the county, was a medium-sized, bespectacled man

317

of sallow complexion, a big head, and little neck. Cantrell loved two things; money and power. He had a nervous, fidgety way about him; he rarely looked directly at a man when he talked to him; towards the end, an armed deputy accompanied Cantrell as guard when he strolled through Athens, the county seat. Pat Mansfield, his sheriff, was a tall, handsome man from Georgia. Pat was kind to his family and gave money to his church. He might have been popular but many people resented the sour troop of plug-uglies he had recruited to be his deputy sheriffs. Pat did Cantrell's bidding.

The Cantrell forces were hard, well-connected people. Cantrell was allied with Burch Biggs in neighboring Polk County; the pair were tied tight to the Crump machine, and Crump ran all of Tennessee. They were so close to the Crump machine that George Woods, who represented McMinn in the state legislature, was speaker of the house in the legislature of the State of Tennessee.

THE MACHINE bossed the county with a rough hand. The sheriff had sixteen regular deputies and about twenty or thirty other men he would deputize in "emergencies." Three of the deputies had served penitentiary terms. One of them had been convicted of taking a little girl out and violating the age of consent. It wasn't rape, but then it wasn't good, either; and God-fearing people like those who farmed and worked in McMinn didn't like it. When the deputies arrested a man they often slugged him until he was sensible. No-

body talked back much in public because it wasn't safe. The deputies threatened to kill people they didn't like. They were brutal men, ready to beat, blackjack, or bully anyone. One GI who was home on leave during the war was shot and killed by a deputy at a public entertainment house near Athens; a sailor home on leave was killed at the other end of the county.

The gambling joints and bootleggers were all tied to the machine. They paid off the proper people and operated punch-boards and slot machines, sold liquor, did as they pleased. As a matter of fact, if someone was in the pen the best way to get him out was to work through the small-time racketeers to get the machine to go easy.

The take from the bootleggers and gamblers wasn't the only source of revenue for the machine. The county was directed by fee-grabbers. A tourist comes riding down the highway; maybe he has a bottle of beer. The deputies arrest him and take him to court. In the court is a little man, called "the informer," who says he is a lawyer. He advises the tourist to plead guilty, pay his fine, and go his way. Sixteen dollars and a nickel. No one will ever know how many people paid their sixteen dollars and a nickel, over and over again, to support the sheriff and his deputies. The sheriff was paid five thousand dollars a year and expenses, but he got seventy-five cents a day for every man in jail that had to be fed. When a drunk was arrested, he was put back on the street next day with a clear head and an empty stomach, but the charge to the county was two days' food at seventy-five cents each. In ten years, county expenses for the sheriff's office had run to over three hundred thousand dollars. McMinn has an audit committee working on the books now.

There was nothing that could be done about it, because you couldn't vote the machine out of office. The machine had taken the county from the Republicans by a famous vote-grab in 1936; some people still tell how the last ballot box from a normally Republican precinct was fixed to show just enough lead to carry the county.

From then on, no matter how people voted, the machine counted the votes. In the key districts when the polls closed the deputies took the ballot boxes to jail, or another safe place, and counted them without any opposition watchers present. Then they would announce the results and always the Cantrell men won. There was nothing that could be done about that either. Appeal to the courts was useless; the Republicans tried that but no suit-at-law was ever won by the opposition.

THINGS HAD been that way for a long time when the war came, taking thirty-five hundred boys from McMinn homes and flinging them across the face of the earth. Folks kept writing to their sons about affairs in McMinn County; sometimes the boys would visit on furlough and then write to their friends in camps all around the world. There were four years to think about McMinn County, and Ralph Duggan, who was a lieutenant in the Navy, says he thought a lot more about McMinn County than he

did about the Japs. Many were thinking as Ralph did—that if democracy was good enough to put on the Germans and Japs, it was good enough for McMinn County, too. It got to be a saying in Athens: "Wait till the GI boys come home."

By spring of 1946, the GI boys were trickling back to McMinn from France and Germany and Italy and the Pacific. The people of McMinn say there is nothing but what some good doesn't come of it, and what happened afterwards in McMinn came from the war. The boys learned a lot about fighting and more about patriotism in the Army; when they came home they were ready to do something about democracy in Tennessee.

IN FEBRUARY they set to planning. They met secretly because the Cantrell forces had the guns, the blackjacks, and the law; and the deputies could make life hell for anyone they could catch. Once in the summer campaign, they seized one boy, locked him up, took his poll-tax receipt from him, and then, threatening his life, made him sign a statement that no such incident had ever taken place. There were five GI's and one civilian in on the first secret meetings. They decided that in the summer election for sheriff and county officials the GI's would put up a complete slate of their own. Mansfield, Cantrell's sheriff, was going out of office and Cantrell was running for sheriff himself.

The veterans sounded out general feeling and in May they called a mass meeting. To get into the GI meeting you had to show your discharge papers, or your membership card in the American Legion or VFW. The veterans picked a non-partisan slate: three Democrats, two Republicans. Knox Henry, a tall handsome boy who had been hurt in North Africa and ran a filling station, was the man for sheriff. He was Republican, but the county trustee was to be Frank Carmichael, a farmer and a Democrat. Carmichael had been a major in the war and was badly wounded at Saint Lô. The other candidates were GI boys, too, except Charlie Pickel who had been in the first World War and had returned with his wounds to be a carpenter. Jim Buttram, a sturdy, solid chunk of combat infantryman, was to be campaign manager. Jim's family had a grocery store in Athens and Jim was new to politics.

With the slate chosen, the campaign picked up speed. Ralph Duggan, who had come back from the Navy to his law practice, was legal adviser and they pored over the Tennessee Code to see what the laws allowed them. The business men who feared the Cantrell forces contributed money secretly. They were afraid to give openly because the machine could raise the taxes, or arrest them, or generally make life hard. But eight thousand dollars came into the campaign fund and soon loudspeaker trucks were rolling over the hill roads, the *Daily Post-Athenian* was carrying campaign ads, and the local radio station was putting out fifteen minutes of talk a day. Up and down the pockets and roads went GI's calling meetings in evenings at schoolhouses or homes, begging, urging, pleading with everyone

to get out and vote. It wasn't hard to pin scandal on the Cantrell forces; McMinn County had lived with the scandal for almost ten years. Nothing had been done about it for two reasons: first, the only alternative was the old Republicans; and second, it did no good to vote because the Cantrells always counted themselves to victory anyway. So over and over, like the beating of a drum in the darkness, the GI campaign chanted its theme: "Your vote will be counted as cast, your vote will be counted as cast."

"Everybody knew we were trying to do the right thing," said Jim Buttram. "We had twelve public meetings and we knew they were damned good. About three weeks before elections we knew we had won the votes and the hearts of the people of McMinn County. But the hardest thing to do was to build an organization to help us see we got a fair count on election day."

The GI's asked the governor for help; but the governor was elected with Crump backing and was silent. They asked the Attorney General in Washington for help; he did nothing. They made contact with the FBI office in Knoxville; the FBI agent said he couldn't do anything unless Washington told him to, and Washington wasn't telling. The GI's were on their own.

II

Election day dawned sweet and clear over McMinn County. McMinn numbers twelve voting precincts but the decisive vote is cast in two townships,

Etowah and Athens. Etowah is some ten miles in the hills from the main highway, but Athens, the county seat, is dead center. Athens sprawls fragrant and green about the old white courthouse; the Robert E. Lee hotel sits on one side, Woolworth's and a movie house on another, stores and offices on the other two sides. One block up from the courthouse lies the red brick county jail. Maple trees and green lawn surround the courthouse; old people sun themselves on the benches, children romp on the grass, blue-denimed farmers stroll casually about buying supplies for home and land.

Election day saw Athens an armed camp. As the voters came to the polls, they found the Cantrell machine in ominous demonstration of force. Almost two hundred armed deputies strutted about, pistols and blackjacks dangling from their belts, badges gleaming. The deputies were strangers. Mansfield claims he asked the governor for National Guardsmen to help him, and the governor authorized him to get deputies where he could. The machine had turned up a sodden gang of plug-uglies, most of them from foreign counties some from as far as Georgia. Fred Puett, the Chamber of Commerce secretary, said that they looked as though they were drugged; their eyes seemed as cold and arrogant and hard as those of a band of Nazis.

By the Tennessee Code of Law, each polling place must be staffed with watchers from both parties, and the GI's had chosen boys of the best families, with the best war records, to stand as their representatives at each place. As

the polls opened in Etowah, one of the GI watchers asked to see the ballot box opened and demonstrated empty as required by law. "Hell, no," said one of the deputies; an argument sputtered, a highway patrolman was summoned and Evans, the GI poll watcher, was hauled off to jail.

At 9:30 trouble flickered in Athens; the machine charged Walter Ellis, a GI watcher, with an unspecified federal offense, took him from his appointed place at the polls and put him in jail, too. At three in the afternoon Tom Gillespie, a colored man, appeared at the eleventh precinct complete with poll-tax receipt. "You can't vote here," said the machine watchers.

"He can too," contradicted the GI spokesman.

"Get him," yelled one of the deputies and someone slugged Gillespie. Gillespie broke for the door and ran down the street. As he ran, a deputy at the door drew his pistol and shot him in the back. Gillespie was taken to the hospital. Fifteen minutes later, Bob Hairell, another GI watcher at the twelfth precinct, was in trouble. The machine wanted to vote a nineteen-year-old girl; Hairell objected. One of the deputies settled the argument by pulling his blackjack and laying Hairell's head open. Hairell was off to the hospital. The *Daily Post-Athenian* sent a reporter to get the story on Hairell. He, too, was slugged and told not to ask questions.

AT FOUR, THE polls closed. In the eleventh precinct, the two GI watchers, Charles Scott, Jr. and Ed Vestal, were thrust to one side as the machine prepared to count the vote. Through the plate glass door of the polling place, the people could see the two boys penned in their corner of the large room. By this time, Jim Buttram, the campaign manager, had decided that the vote of the eleventh precinct wasn't worth trading off against the lives of two of his men. Twelve armed deputies had cleared the sidewalk in front of the eleventh precinct polling place, but hundreds of people stood on the opposite side. They watched Jim and Mr. Scott, father of Charles Scott, cross the street to speak to Mansfield, the sheriff.

Mansfield was sitting in a red 1946 Dodge. There were six men in the car. Buttram offered to give him the precinct in return for the release of the watchers.

"Are you trying to tell me how to run this election?" asked Mansfield. "You go over and get them yourself if you want them."

"You wouldn't want me to get shot, would you?" said Jim. A deputy sitting beside Mansfield lifted his thirty-eight from his lap and said: "Buttram, I ought to shoot you right now, you're the son-of-a-bitch who started the whole thing."

Mansfield knocked Moses' gun down and told him to shut up, he was doing the talking.

Mr. Scott leaned over and said: "If you won't let my boy out of there and anything happens to him, you'll have to pay for it."

Pat grabbed his gun, snarled "Let's settle this right now," and started to open the door of the car. Buttram

slammed the door on him, and he and Scott hastily made their way back to the cover of the crowd.

A few minutes later Neal Ensminger, the editor of the local paper, strode over to the precinct door to see if he could get a tabulated count. As he asked one of the deputies a question, the two GI's in the polling place broke for safety. With his shoulder down, young Scott burst the door and pounded out, followed in a moment by Vestal. Bleeding, they ran across the street to the crowd as the deputies trained their guns on the boys. By this time women were screaming, children were crying, and the veterans—still unarmed—stood cursing and shouting from the opposing pavement. The deputies held their fire as the two boys slipped among the people.

It was five now, and following their practice the Cantrell forces removed the ballot boxes of the eleventh and twelfth precincts to the security of the jail for counting.

III

The GI's had promised to get the vote counted as cast, and they gathered at their campaign headquarters around the corner to confer. As they stood in the street, two Mansfield deputies approached to break up the group. Otto Kennedy was watching from his tire store as the deputies walked up the street. With Otto was his brother Oley Kennedy, just out of the Navy, and his brother J. P. "Bull" Kennedy, just out of the Army.

"Pat Mansfield said he was going to give us a fair and square election," said

Kennedy, "and then we saw those sons-of-bitches from Georgia, walking around with their guns and badges, telling us to kiss their neck. They'd put our boys in jail, they were running all over us. I stepped up to the door. I saw them coming. I just couldn't take it. I said to my brother: 'Bull, let's get them.'"

As the deputies stepped into the crowd, the GI's closed about them. They hit hard and high and low. The guns were taken and distributed among the GI's. Three more deputies, then two more walked into the crowd. All were disarmed and the guns handed out. The deputies were loaded on cars, taken to the woods, stripped of their clothes, and left to walk their way out.

The GI's were still indecisive and the Kennedys became cautious. They had struck the first blow; they were vulnerable. Otto decided to go home, telling the veterans that if they decided to do anything the Kennedys were ready to come back; otherwise they were staying away. Dusk was settling and the vets talked. A city policeman walked by to say that Mansfield was coming with tommy-guns and tear gas. Then something happened.

FROM DUSK to dawn, the story of the siege of Athens dissolves into anonymity. The people had voted the GI ticket, trusting the GI guarantee of a fair count. Five districts which had been fairly tabulated by evening had already given the GI's almost a three-to-one lead. But the ballot boxes of the eleventh and twelfth precincts were being counted in the jail. Tomorrow the Cantrell forces would have victory and no one would be safe. On the one hand, the Common Law says that every citizen has the right to prevent a crime or felony from taking place; on the other hand, to take the jail by storm against the lawfully deputized thugs seemed perilously close to insurrection. A very fine point of law is involved and Crump still runs Tennessee. Therefore, no man knows or tells who played precisely what role in Athens on the night of Thursday, August 1, 1946.

Down the highway from Athens is one of the armories of the National Guard. By eight o'clock rifles and machine guns were held by dozens of the veterans. It was a quiet movement. There was no raving or shouting. They collected at their headquarters and gravely, under cover of darkness, walked the two blocks to the jail where the sheriffs had taken the ballot boxes. Behind the jail is a barbed wire enclosure. Facing it, across the street, is a low hill covered with vines and several houses and buildings. The deputies had made a mistake that the battle-wise GI's recognized immediately: they had concentrated forty or fifty of their number in jail and left no reserves in town. The GI's deployed in the darkness in a semicircle above the jail, on the hill behind the cover of vines, on rooftops. A veteran strode into the street and yelled at the silent jail a demand for the ballot boxes and the release of the GI prisoners.

A voice answered, "Are you the law?"

The GI yelled back, "There isn't any law in McMinn County."

A lone shot went off from within the jail. The man that answered from the hill answered with a tommy-gun.

There were several hundred veterans in the semicircle and hundreds of boys and civilians. Some had rifles, a few had tommy-guns, others had bird guns and hunting pieces. The fusillade rose and fell above the night, echoing into the suburbs and hills. Bullets spattered the Chamber of Commerce and the newspaper office a block away. A block down the road, a man standing on the corner of the courthouse square was nicked in the arm.

The local radio station had sent a reporter with a microphone to cover the action; up and down the county farmers tuned in to the running account. Some of them put their clothes on, got their guns, came to join in the shoot. Boys too young to cock a rifle came down to see the fun and remained to learn how to shoot in the night.

THE DEPUTIES were safe behind the thick brick wall of the jail, and the bullets of the GI's could do no more than cut out chunks of the wall. As the sporadic shooting dragged on hour after hour, the veterans realized with a sick feeling that night was wearing away and, with daylight, state patrolmen—perhaps even the National Guard—might be called in to reinforce the garrison of deputies. Defeat would mean that McMinn County would never be safe again for any man who had taken part in the night's firing. It was go through with it, or get out of town.

At midnight a detachment went over to the county farm where a case of dynamite was located. During a lull, the veterans yelled that unless the ballot boxes and prisoners were released in twenty minutes they would blast the jail. An hour went by and the jail made no answer. Somebody fitted a cap to a stick of dynamite and tossed it into the street. A second stick followed. On the third throw, two sticks were tied together and thrown across to the sidewalk of the jail. The fourth throw of two sticks landed on the porch of the jail and tore it wide apart. Somebody had learned about demolition in the war; for the last try they decided to prepare a homemade satchel charge of the rest of the case and place it under the jail wall. But before the charge could be placed, the jail was yelling surrender. It was 3:30 in the morning.

"We're dying in here," came a call. "Don't use any more dynamite, we're giving up."

No one was dying. Four of the deputies were pretty badly hurt and required hospitalization; ten of the GI's were wounded in the day's action; but the war was over.

The vets ordered the deputies to march into the courtyard with their hands up, leaving their guns behind. As they marched out, the crowd gathered round, yelling, cursing, and booing. Someone in the crowd reached out with a razor and slashed at one of the deputies, laying his throat open. Duggan tried to stop the man; the man explained that the deputy had arrested him before, taken him to jail and kicked in four of his ribs. Duggan tried to reason with him, but he made another razor pass. Then Duggan slugged him into obedience and led the deputy off to the hospital. Behind them a file of deputies, guarded by GI's, paraded through the street to the courthouse and back so that the people might see and taunt their unthroned impotence.

By this time dawn was lighting the county and the radio station, broadcasting the victory, was bringing farmers in from all the hills to see what was happening. The state capital had been alerted and the State Commissioner of Public Safety, Lynn Bomar, called up to locate a GI to negotiate. Ralph Duggan answered the phone and spoke to George Woods at the state capital. Woods, who was Election Commissioner of the county, promised—if given a safe conduct—to return to Athens on Monday and certify the election of the entire GI slate. Duggan announced the victory to the crowd at six in the morning and then went home.

VIOLENCE FLICKERED on for several more hours. The GI's had had their fill, but the civilians and boys were carrying on. They smashed in windows of the deputies' automobiles, turned them over, burned cars indiscriminately. It was the GI's now who had to restrain the civilians and protect their prisoners. By ten o'clock, however, the fury had spent itself and the GI's were carefully escorting their prisoners out of town. At three, a giant mass meeting was held in the courthouse, men jamming the as-

sembly hall, overflowing onto the steps and the lawn. The Reverend Bernie Hampton read the twenty-third psalm and asked the body of citizens what their will was. Someone suggested the appointment of a three-man committee to administer the county till things settled down. The three-man committee was elected immediately and from Friday to Monday it conducted the county's affairs on a volunteer basis.

It summoned the county court—the local legislative body—to a meeting on Monday morning. The county court declared vacant the offices held by machine contestants in the elections and declared the GI slate duly elected. Six of the twelve precincts' votes were thrown out entirely, for no fair count had been given there. When the GI's broke into jail they found that some of the tally sheets marked by the machine had been scored fifteen to one for the Cantrell forces. Where the GI's witnessed the count, the margin was three to one GI. Thus it was decided that only in those precincts where both parties had watched should the count be accepted. By Monday afternoon, Knox Henry was sheriff of McMinn County and the law was safe.

IV

McMinn is quiet and peaceful again. The courthouse has been painted for the first time in years, and the big clock has been fixed so that it strikes the hours loud, clear, and free over the entire town. The jail has been repaired but it is curiously empty. Within a month Henry was running McMinn County with eight youthful GI deputies. Saturday night no longer filled the cells with fifty or sixty men waiting to be fined; by the end of the month, Saturday night found only three men in jail. The four city policemen had been fired and replaced by veterans. Pat Mansfield was back in Georgia, working as a fireman on a railway. Paul Cantrell was in Nashville and didn't want to come back.

The gambling joints have been closed down, the bootlegging ring has been smashed, fee-grabbing ended. There are no more slot machines or punchboards. Henry has pledged the new regime that the sheriff will live on his lawful salary.

The GI party, too, has been disbanded, but a Good Government League has succeeded it. The Good Government League has branches in fifteen different communities of the county and is the public whip. The county court still has a majority of old Cantrell men, but they don't come up for election till next summer. Meanwhile the Good Government League suggests various actions to it, and the court pays heed.

The first thing the county court was persuaded to do was to establish an audit committee. The Good Government League wants to see what resources are available for the two most pressing local problems: schools and roads. Schools are pretty bad in McMinn. Pay for teachers is so poor that all the best teachers are leaving. In some places in McMinn, teachers get eighty-five dollars a month

for the eight months they work; that averages less than fifteen dollars a week, year-round, as take-home pay. Even a waitress at the hotel makes more than that. Highest pay is at the high school and that comes to only thirty dollars a week for a teacher with a master's degree. The Good Government League wants to divert money from the sheriff's heavy budget to the education budget. When the schools and school buses are fixed, they want to do something about the roads. Maybe after that the League will move on to such long-range plans as a permanent county-manager system and a new structure of government.

The GI's like McMinn and they think they can keep it healthy. There will always be bootlegging unless the church people let the county make liquor legal. But now the government will be master of the bootleggers instead of the bootleggers masters of the government. The GI's say they aren't interested in "issues"; they aren't interested in unions or poll-tax laws or running the country. This was a McMinn matter, strictly a battle to give McMinn fair and square elections and force Boss Crump back to Shelby County.

It is true, of course, that Crump still runs the rest of Tennessee and that Crump helped send back to Washington a man named Kenneth McKellar. And until November 1946, McKellar was president of the Senate of the United States of America, called the greatest deliberative body in the world.

HARPER'S January, 1947

TEXAS: LAND OF WEALTH AND FEAR

I. Blowing the Bass Tuba the Day It Rained Gold

All day the wind blows. It blows in easterly from the Gulf, or swings arid-hot, blowing from the west, or shifts, hollering down from the Great Plains to the north, dropping the temperature twenty degrees in an hour.

The wind carries dust. Dust in your throat, dust in a haze over the gray-rimmed horizon, dust twirled in fountains that sift and dance across the road. Even now in spring when the plains should be green, they remain gray—the hills yellow-gray, the rocks red-gray, the mesquite black-gray.

For five years now, since the drought began, this wind, scouring the soil from the face of Texas, has been uprooting and hurrying plainsmen toward the cities. But for twenty years before the drought, the plainsmen had been coming—by bus, by train, by old farm truck—sucked irresistibly in toward the cities by the new industry and new wealth of oil as more lately they have been pushed relentlessly out by the parched waste of the plain.

The villages that once drowsed in the sun about the placid center squares of courthouse and schoolhouse, Woolworth's and the J. C. Penney store, have become towns. The towns have become cities whose cubes and towers thrust abrupt and unannounced from the plains. Between, in any direction across the map, men thin out year by year. The empty fields are speckled by the silent pumps, whose rocking beams glide up and down, up and down, ceaselessly sucking oil from the depths and feeding the air with the faint, aromatic fumes of escaping gas.

Twenty-five years ago, three out of every five Texans lived on farms or in villages. Today Texas has eight million people, and only one out of four still live on farms or in villages—the rest are city people. The population of Texas has jumped two million since 1940, yet more than half its counties have lost citizens.

Most of the new city people are plainsmen or cotton farmers or ranchers from the Southwest. But many are distant arrivals from New York or California, Tennessee or Illinois. All have come here for the same reason: to seek their fortune. Many have found it. But whatever their luck has been, all are strangers, rootless in place or time, in the nervous new civilization of the Texas cities.

————

WITHIN THESE new cities, bursting with energy and throbbing with the skills of modern industry, the ancient manners and morals of the American frontier still have superficial currency. From the old Southwest, the citizens have remembered (or conform to) the pattern of casual good manners, of easy courtesy in reply, the friendly "hello" in the street, the kindliness and helpfulness to wayfarers.

And yet, alone in the air-conditioned stillness behind the Venetian blinds, alone with their new wealth, these people know that the bonds that tied them to the frontier, that tied the frontiersmen to one another, are gone. Within, there broods uneasy doubt as to their own role and that of their fellow citizens. A sense of menace, of unease runs through their conversation as if the great wheel of fortune might turn and suddenly deprive them of the wealth they have so lately won. And the menace may be anywhere—in a neighbor's home, around the corner, on the other side of town at union headquarters, certainly in Washington and New York. In the heat of modern American problems, the prairie emotions tend to curdle— neighborliness becomes an excuse for the prowlings of slandering busybodies, and the sheriff's posse is corrupted into a lynching party for careers and reputations.

The Climate of Distrust

This emotional climate would be no more than a matter of morbid or humorous interest to other Americans as they watch a growing community fumble its way to maturity were it not for another set of facts:

▶ That millions of Texans are convinced that their primary enemies are other Americans and that the American experience in this age and generation has been a total failure, their own prosperity notwithstanding.

▶ That within Texas the machinery of government, from the person of the Governor down through the structure of both major parties, has been captured by a nameless Third Party; obsessed with hate, fear, and suspicion—one of whose central tenets is that "If America is ever destroyed it will be from within."

▶ That a handful of prodigiously wealthy men, whose new riches give them a clumsy and immeasurable power, seek to spread this climate and their control throughout the rest of the United States.

Ardent and devout states' righters at home, bellowing and snorting that the "sovereign" privileges of Texas must not be disturbed, these men see no contradiction in a Texas political imperialism that intervenes with its money in the domestic politics of thirty other "sovereign" states from Connecticut to Washington, from Wisconsin to New Mexico.

There is an element of cruel exaggeration in approaching the colorful diversity and complexity of Texan life through such men and the industry that made them rich—oil. There is much more in Texas than oil. Texas is not only first in oil (over $3 billion annual production); it is also first in sulphur, first in cotton, first in rice, first in roses, first in chemicals. The industrial crescent along the gulf coast, where natural gas is delivered at tidewater, is the freshest frontier in American industry and one of free enterprise's proudest achievements.

But the exaggeration is thrust on any inquirer into Texas politics because the men who have made their money out of oil are so immeasurably wealthier than any others, because on the American scene their special privileges have become an anachronism, because with their riches they have tried to push the state of mind that is Texas across the nation. Furthermore, oil has captured the imagination of Texans in this generation the way cattle did a century ago, and all Texans, whether poor or rich, whether in oil or in no way remotely connected with it, are caught up in the excitement, turbulence, and emotions of an industry that feels its privileges menaced.

Spindletop to the Panhandle

The oil industry of the United States was half a century old, John D. Rockefeller had long since made his fortune, and Standard Oil was already a giant trust when a brilliant Montenegrin engineer named Captain Anthony F. Lucas, defying the most expert geological advice of his day, drove a 1,160-foot hole down through a sand hummock near the Gulf coast and, on the clear morning of January 10, 1901, saw rise a black, stinking fountain that spilled 25,000 to 100,000 barrels of oil each day over the surrounding countryside. Spindletop, which was the name of this discovery, was eventually to prove out at a hundred million barrels, or one-tenth as much as all the oil produced in America in the previous half century of the industry's existence.

With the eruption at Spindletop, the entire structure of the American oil industry was ripped apart. The resources that gushed from the fields of the Southwest were too vast even for the mighty power of the Standard trust to cap. Though Standard and its offshoots and rivals (Humble, Magnolia, Gulf, Sun) were to follow the oil down from the old fields of the Northeast to the Southwest, their control of pipelines, markets, refineries, and research never gave them more than a collective suzerainty over the new empire.

The real vigor and animal excitement of the industry was in the hands of a new breed of men, the "independents," the boomers, prospectors, wildcatters, producers, and would-be producers. Out across Texas, Oklahoma, and Louisiana raced the treasure seekers, drilling in swamps, in deserts, on ranches and farms. By chicanery and rascality, vision and daring and courage, they created the industry of the oilfields. They leased and drilled and stole and cheated and fell from icy drilling platforms in blizzards to die finding the new gold. Riggers and roughnecks, leasemen and scholars, horse traders and gamblers, engineers and adventurers chased one another and chased oil for half a century in an industry that is still today the easiest to enter, the easiest to get rich in, and the easiest to go broke in.

OIL SEEMED to lie everywhere in Texas, as it seems to lie everywhere on the great slope down from the Rockies to the Gulf. By the mid-1920's Texans had found oil from the Panhandle in the north to the border in the south, from the fringe of the Gulf to New Mexico in the West.

Those were the days when "depletion" was born. "Depletion" is a sensitive word, and when talking to an oilman you must approach the topic as cautiously as you would approach a discussion of his womenfolk's virtue.

Depletion is the root of Texas oil fortunes, a loophole in the income-tax laws of this country that gives oil millionaires magic exemption from tax burdens that all other citizens must bear.

Depletion, when written into the tax laws of America in the early 1920's, justifiably expressed the anarchy of the early oil business. In those days, once a pool was discovered, as many men as possible bought the right to drill in it. Like half a dozen children with their straws in one soda, each sucked oil as fast as possible to get the most while the getting was good. In their frantic and uncontrolled haste they wrecked the early fields, letting the wonderfully valuable natural gas fizz off into the air to be flared as a waste product while salt water crept in from underneath to ruin a well before a fraction of its predictable life had run.

In those days, when a well's life might end in four, ten, or eight months, farmers, ranchers, producers, everyone with oil rights argued that income from oil was not just ordinary earnings. It was, they said, the depletion of a natural resource, the wastage of accumulated natural capital which when gone was all gone, like savings spent. So the Federal tax laws gave oilmen a depletion allowance, which made 27.5 per cent of all income from oil free and clear of any income tax, like money drawn from a bank. Later we shall see how depletion permits men to have incomes of millions of dollars without paying any tax at all.

The next climactic event in oil, an event that shook the industry almost as completely as Spindletop, took place a hundred and fifty miles to the north in the peanut and sweet-potato patches of Rusk County, near Turnertown. There in October, 1930, a broken-down old wildcatter named "Dad" Joiner had sunk his last few pennies in a ramshackle drilling rig which, at 3,600 feet, suddenly hit oil.

What "Dad" Joiner hit was the largest single oil pool ever to be discovered in these United States before or since— the great East Texas pool, which, with some five billion barrels, overmatched in lush, easy wealth the wildest dreams of fantasy.

The East Texas pool drenched the shrinking markets of America in depression, and they promptly collapsed. Prices dropped from forty to twenty to ten and in some places to five cents a barrel. Drowning in oil, crippled with abundance, Texas called out its National Guard and proclaimed martial law in the fields. Near riots broke out, men ran "hot oil" against regulation, shot and killed each other, while for two years the state sought to establish order with new laws.

F.D.R., Noninterventionist

Finally, one Sunday in April, 1933, in the Chinese Room of the Mayflower Hotel at Washington, all the representatives of the nation's oil industry gathered to memorialize Franklin D. Roosevelt, President for a month, asking him to appoint a czar to take over the entire oil industry and control it for its own preservation. Mr. Roosevelt, whose name is now a cuss word among oilmen who preach of states' rights and freedom from any control, refused— and insisted that Texas and other producing states work out their own controls. This Texas did, in some of the wisest conservation laws ever passed.

These laws ordained "proration," which simply established the right of the State of Texas, through its Railway Commission, to conserve the natural resources of the state. The commission now establishes the "allowable" amount of oil each individual may take daily from any well he drills, penalizes operators for wasteful practices, and makes the utilization of natural gas compulsory. In short, proration guarantees that oil and gas will be withdrawn from the ground only under conditions that guarantee maximum longevity and maximum yield for the field. The deple-

tion percentage is still 27.5, which arbitrarily averages a well's life at less than four years; but oil wells may last ten years, twenty, thirty, or more under the new regulations.

With order established, the industry was mature. That is, it could be financed. Previously no bank would lend money against a field that might be depleted in months. Now, with reserves scientifically judged, and allocated, oil underground was bank collateral. Banks could finance a hit, and one lucky hit meant that the underground collateral would finance ten or twenty more tries. It meant that fortunes could be pyramided quickly, which they were.

MEANWHILE, TOO, the price of oil was rising (a barrel of oil is now worth $2.56), scientific methods of discovery were bringing in ever more numerous fields, war boomed production, and income taxes for the wealthy climbed to the confiscatory levels that national defense made and still makes necessary.

These new taxes superimposed on their new wealth made Texas oilmen explore another area of special grace accorded them under the industry's peculiar tax laws, a benefit equal to or greater than depletion in importance. In the oil industry all new drilling expenses may be charged off against income as current expense. Let us suppose that an individual has an income of $5 million from oil. Depletion's 27.5 per cent gives him a cool $1,375,000 free and clear of any tax at all. This he may pocket. The remaining $3,625,000 is subject to tax. But why let it accumulate to be taxed away by the Federal government at eighty-five per cent? Why not, as the phrase runs, "go out and drill it up"?

To "drill it up" means you spend the $3,625,000 in vastly expanded drilling and exploration for more oil. If you lose, the money spent would have been taxed away anyhow. If you win and hit, you have discovered reserves of hundreds of thousands of barrels that are a capital asset, as good as money in the bank. If you sell such a discovery, it is taxed as a capital gain. No other industry can make such capital investments and write them off out of pocket.

There is a defense to be made of depletion, of course. For oil removed from the ground *is* "depleted" and gone, a natural asset reduced. Some allowance, even the Federal tax collectors argue, is necessary. The question is, how much? Shall depletion be permitted at 27.5 per cent only until the original investment in exploration and drilling is recovered and then be sharply reduced to, say, ten or twelve per cent? Or shall it be flatly reduced across the board to match the estimated life of the field?

Oilmen make another defense: that depletion and other benefits are needed to keep risk money flowing, to keep men gambling to find the new oil we require. For all the recent stabilization of the oil industry, it still involves a vast element of risk. It is a game of chance in which chips—wells—cost from $30,000 to $1,000,000 each. Of every seven holes drilled, six on the average are "dusters." Tens of thousands of men

have gone broke punching dry holes. Scores of thousands, from New York to California, have pooled their savings behind a wildcatter or driller for just one try at the rewards depletion promises and have lost everything. For every man who has made his millions, hundreds have vanished penniless. Even old "Dad" Joiner died broke, bargained out of his discovery by the sharpest operator of all, H. L. Hunt.

'The Day It Rained Gold'

All this is controversy. The facts are that with oil coming in all over the map of Texas with tens of thousands seeking it, with pools of it to be found one out of seven times, it was mathematically predictable that a certain number of men, protected by depletion and capital gains, would become fantastically wealthy, and that depletion and capital gains in their present form would become their main articles of faith.

The thing to remember about most of the very richest is that twenty-five years ago they were flat. They were poor only yesterday, won their wealth during the hated New Deal's "twenty years of treason and shame," and now are the richest men in the world. They feel and insist that they won their wealth by their own exertions, which of course they did, in a rough fight in which courage as well as luck was vital. But as one Texas elder statesman puts it, "They were standing there blowing the bass tuba the day it rained gold."

Now, for reasons some of which are in

their pocketbooks and some of which they could not rationally explain, they feel themselves acutely menaced. Over and over again, Northern Congressmen make mumbled noises about doing something to subject oilmen to the same tax burdens as less privileged citizens. Over and over again the Federal government proposes to regulate the natural-gas industry more strictly. Washington is, has been, and can be dangerous. And this has made most oilmen states' righters—which means, said a Midwestern businessman recently arrived in Texas, "They want the Federal budget balanced, but they don't want it to be balanced with their money."

Finally, the Texas tycoons of oil have missed the great maturing experience of American businessmen, which is the management of labor, of human beings en masse. The oilmen are "producers"—and in no other field of human endeavor can so much wealth be gotten with the employment of so few human beings. Theirs is a business of buying and trading in leases, hiring rigs and sinking holes with twenty-odd men, selling crude to big companies by telephone. Once a well is in, it works almost untended feeding oil or gas from the ground to the pipelines. The American businessman or manufacturer, no matter how ferocious and bitter he may be about unions, has had as a matter of efficiency to learn to deal with human beings in mine, mill, factory, and department store as employees and as unions. This experience the Texas oilmen have skipped.

It is of course unfair to speak thus of a whole group of people. Texas oilmen are no more cut of one pattern than are the steelmen of the Ruhr. Among them one can find men of remarkable erudition and culture, such as Everett Lee De Golyer, greatest of living oil geologists and patron of the arts. One can find men like J. R. Parten, alternating between public service and the oil industry, whose loyalty to the America of this generation outweighs parochial loyalty to the industry that gave him wealth. One can find Texas millionaires who import snow from the Rockies for their parties, and others who buy masterpieces of French painting.

The Export of Fear

But the community of oilmen as a whole is a community gripped by fear that Washington may erase its privileges. Along with them in this fear, the oilmen have swept farmers, landowners, merchants, lawyers, all who have stakes or hope to place a bet on the roulette wheel of oil. They have persuaded their fellow citizens, as one public relations campaign phrased it, that "If you're a Texan, you're in the oil business." Together they have muddied the image of their fears, so that the fear of Washington is blurred with fear of Communism, fear of war, fear of other Americans.

Not only that. Being vigorous, aggressive men who have won their fortunes by doing and acting, they feel the best defense is a good offense. Thus they have entered politics as they have entered oil, staking a bet on a Representative here or a Senator there. Most are little operators with thousand- and five-thousand-dollar chips, whose belief it is that the Congress of the United States may be manipulated or cozened as is a backward state legislature. Occasionally a number pool their cash to take out advertisements in political campaigns as far afield as Denver and San Francisco.

Among these political dabblers, however, are four whose wealth is so prodigious that their fumblings with national politics cannot be ignored. Country boys all, strangers in the big city, their efforts, sometimes naïve, sometimes shrewd, to remold America to their image are worth more than a casual glance.

HUGH ROY CULLEN of Houston, at the age of seventy-two, is the dean of the group. A man whose education stopped at the third grade, Cullen was brought up on a farm in Denton County. His elevation to the eminence of local sage and sachem can be dated almost precisely from the day when his drillers, in 1934, brought in the Tom O'Connor Hill, whose half billion barrels of reserves Mr. Cullen now shares with the great Humble Oil Company.

A large, raw-boned, handsome old man, whose face glows with the ruddiness usually associated with the steady drinker, Cullen is an authentic primitive. Even in Houston, Cullen is a character, a figure both of affection and of friendly jest, of whom it is irreverently said that he has reversed the old Texas

gag from "If you're so smart, why ain't you rich?" to "If he's so rich, why ain't he smart?"

The affection for Cullen in Houston is easy to understand, for his status as a benefactor is unmatched in local annals. He has spent money lavishly on hospitals, churches, orphanages, old people's homes, and schools. His most favored charity is the University of Houston, to which he has given oil properties he considers to be worth $160 million and which even other oilmen appraise at around $80 million. These gestures, gratifying as they are to the inner man, have also produced a steady stream of local headlines, intoxicating to ego and pride. They have further produced in the community of Houston a desire to pamper the testy, often tearful old man in his foibles just as far as can be done.

Thus the University of Houston boasts in its student officer corps a unit called the Cullen Rifles for which Cullen provides the uniforms. In the days when he was the largest contributor ($20,000 a year) to the Houston Symphony, the orchestra would play "Old Black Joe" to soothe its benefactor at otherwise austere concerts. Even when, at the university commencement exercises, Mr. Cullen became angry at the invocation of the preacher and pushed him bodily away from the microphone, no one protested very much. Cullen had found the preacher's invocation "doleful" and besides, "he was just a little fellow anyway." But when finally one night on the radio Mr. Cullen called Dean Acheson a "homosexual" even the local stations had to cut him off.

Cullen became interested in politics

during the late New Deal (which he loathes with incandescent fury), and war years, while Jesse Jones, grand master of the local political scene was in Washington feuding with the Messrs. Wallace and Roosevelt. Since the return of Jesse Jones to Houston after the war, Mr. Cullen has gone into a slight eclipse as a local oracle—an eclipse probably hastened by his famous published protest that "Jones has been away from here for the last twenty-five to thirty years and has come back to Houston and decided, with the influence of a bunch of New York Jews, to run our city."

'Ike . . . Attend to This . . .'

In national politics, however, Mr. Cullen's interest has been unflagging, and he takes a constant, meticulous interest in affairs of state. He showers President Eisenhower, Senators, and Congressmen with telegrams and letters whenever the mood seizes him.

"You know," he explained in January of this year, "I groomed Ike for the Presidency. He's a swell fellow. But he's got some damned people around him who are inexperienced." In March he elaborated: "In my opinion, Eisenhower, the Republican Party, and the country itself would be a lot better off if the President listened more attentively to Joe Martin and Joe McCarthy than he does to Dewey, Lodge, and Stassen."

Harold Stassen, Director of the Foreign Operations Administration, has particularly aroused Cullen's ire, not only for his politics but as an ingrate. "You take this Stassen," Cullen said recently. "He's a likable cuss. I furnished

him some money to run for the nomination so he could then give the votes to Ike. He almost didn't. I said, 'Harold, you won't do. Mentally you're a conservative, but at heart you're a socialist."

Most lately, since the President has opposed the Bricker amendment, an increasing exasperation has been creeping into Cullen's telegrams. One recent communication to the White House ended, "Ike, I hope you will not wait but attend to this important matter immediately."

If it is quite clear down in Houston that Cullen is giving the President one more chance to be good in these last few months, it is equally clear in which direction his allegiance has shifted. Cullen, when he sponsors a man, does it up well and usually starts by arranging a triumphal introductory tour through Texas for his choice. Senator Taft was so honored by Mr. Cullen in his heyday, as were Generals MacArthur and Eisenhower. Cullen's favor has most recently settled on Senator Joe McCarthy, whom he styled "the greatest man in America," a few weeks ago when he personally sponsored the Senator's visit to deliver the commemorative address on San Jacinto Day.

Coming from another man, such mouthings might appear to be an advanced case of senile dementia. In Mr. Cullen's case, they are not. They are immodest and perhaps untruthfully boastful, but they are buttressed with a purse and with action that make him, even in his fumbling, untutored crudity, one of the nation's most ambitious investors in political futures.

RESENTING AS he does the slightest trace of Northern money or influence in sovereign Texas, in 1952 Cullen persuaded his conscience to put money down in no less than twenty-three other states beyond his native soil. His contributions went to campaigns in Wisconsin (McCarthy), Indiana (Jenner), Idaho, Maine, Connecticut, New Mexico, Washington, Nevada, Utah, Missouri, Montana, California (where he financed five candidacies, including that of Representative Ernest Bramblett, since convicted of kickbacks and extortion), Virginia, Illinois, Maryland, New York, Ohio, New Hampshire, North Dakota, and New Jersey. His sons-in-law went into Wyoming, Michigan and Arizona. His political gambles were even better than wildcat drilling. In some thirty-four campaigns where Cullen money was staked, twenty-two of his choices were winners, and only a dozen were losers.

In 1952 Cullen recorded direct contributions of $53,000 and his sons-in-law $19,750 more. Since it is axiomatic in American politics that recorded contributions are like the tip of the iceberg, revealing only the smallest fraction of what is spent in elections, it may be assumed that Cullen has tried to influence many others. His contributions to Harold Stassen have been noted. He has been credited with a share in the defeat of former Senators Scott Lucas of Illinois, Frank Graham of North Carolina, and Claude Pepper of Florida. In Houston, one informed estimate of his total political expenditures during 1951 and 1952 comes to $750,000.

Mr. Cullen is essentially a simple man fortified with the perhaps naïve belief that with enough money he can engineer passage of the Bricker amendment, make Presidents, and control Congressmen. It is doubtful whether he has any theology or ideology about how he would change and remake the United States. The only thing that seems certain is that he wants it changed.

Just Two Country Boys

The next two in the grand quadrumvirate of Texas oilmen are Sid Richardson of Fort Worth and Clint Murchison of Dallas. Richardson and Murchison are different, in essence, from Cullen in that while Cullen is intoxicated with politics Richardson and Murchison can take it or leave it alone. Close friends ever since their boyhood in the little cotton town of Athens, Texas, both still assume the air of homespun country boys. "Sid and Clint," said one Dallasite, "are both nice guys. They have only the simplest, most innocent desire in the world—to make money. All they want is more."

In this pursuit of "more," Sid has outstripped his chum Clint by several leagues, as he has outstripped, probably, every other living individual in the United States. There is an almost monastic purity in Richardson's single-minded devotion to the pursuit of wealth. A country trader who graduated from trading in bits and pieces of land, he entered the oil industry almost inevitably as a "leaseman," a specialist in the brokerage and huckstering of oil leases.

Today Dallas is full of men who claim to remember when Sid Richardson wore patches on his pants or had to borrow bus fare to get from Fort Worth to Dallas. The turning point of his career seems to have been reached in the cold December of 1933, when, wildcatting out in Winkler County in West Texas, his fortunes reached so low a point that local grocers refused him credit to buy food for his drillers and Sid had to go all the way to Fort Worth and truck borrowed groceries to his men for Christmas.

Sid hit modestly on that one, but the big money did not flow until he hit the Keystone sands in 1937. From then on Sid rolled. By the time he first met Dwight D. Eisenhower (who had just been made a brigadier general) on a train from Texas to Washington, Sid's income was over $2 million a year or, in terms of oil, eight thousand barrels of "allowable" a day. The find that projected him into the stratosphere of wealth did not come until 1943, when on a tract of leaseholdings he had purchased for $332,000 the famous Ellenberger lime was discovered. The reserves there were estimated at 250 million barrels. And, as if fortune were not yet tired, when Sid moved his operations on to Louisiana in the postwar years he made another monster strike at Cox Bay (estimated at 250 million barrels) which makes him far and away the richest American, with the possible exception of his Dallas neighbor H. L. Hunt, who may be his only rival in the billion-dollar bracket.

Nothing seems to have interfered with Richardson in his quest for trea-sure. He is unmarried and has no children. He lives alone in an apartment in the Fort Worth Club, with a collection of Remington and Russell paintings. Philanthropy holds little, if any, interest for him. Once during a trip across the country after the Keystone discovery had already made Richardson rich, a traveling companion asked him, "Sid, why don't you give Dallas a children's hospital? Dallas hasn't got a children's hospital." Said Sid, "Now if I do that, why, everyone in the world will come around asking me for money and I just don't want to be bothered." Sid's friends accept this attitude, for the man has no pretense. "Why, Sid has no more civic responsibility than a coyote," one of them said, "but he's a nice guy."

No particular connection can be made between Richardson and any of the grosser forms of political manipulation. Texas Democrats of both the Shivercrat and the Loyalist persuasions consider Richardson still a Democrat: his friendship with Sam Rayburn is warm and enduring: along with a small minority of the Texas rich he has shown no enthusiasm for Joe McCarthy. Politics, for him, seems to be simply the pleasures of association with the great and the respect the stark and massive dimensions of his wealth can earn from them in return. His association with Elliott Roosevelt in a Texas radio station was good for several meals at the White House before Sid took over the property when Elliott went off to war. His early meeting with Eisenhower has flowered into a fine friendship. When Sid flew off to Paris, to visit Eisenhower at SHAPE, the trip had none of the flavor of a self-appointed political mission, but was rather a call on the general by an old friend who advised him to run for the Presidency as a Democrat. Sid has since been a guest at the White House (perhaps a return invitation for the vacation he gave the Eisenhowers in 1949 on his private island off the Gulf coast), and his loyalty to Eisenhower remains undiminished. Content with his friends, an occasional drink, and an evening of canasta or poker, Sid Richardson behaves like a thoroughly happy man.

Clint

Clint Murchison is by all odds a far more complex human being than his crony Sid. A stocky, rumpled man with an open and seemingly friendly expression, Murchison is described by some Dallas businessmen as a genius. "Like all geniuses and near geniuses," one of them has said, "Clint is a successful neurotic. Except where some geniuses paint paintings and make music, Clint makes deals."

The base and core of the Murchison wealth is oil. Murchison's interest in oil began in the early 1920's, when, lured into it by his boyhood friend Sid Richardson, he began to play around with leasing, drilling, and wildcatting. Like H. L. Hunt, Murchison achieved his present stature in the East Texas oil pool, where he seems to have been a front-rank performer in running and dealing in "hot oil" in the days when proration was being established under National Guard bayonets. Murchison

went on to found the Delhi Oil Company, to pioneer some of the first big natural gas developments in north Texas, and was far, far above the field when the classical forms of oil accumulation began to pall on him and he lifted his eyes beyond the confines of the state.

UNTIL HIS recent sortie into Wall Street's Battle of the New York Central, Murchison's business ambitions seemed to be satisfied with biting off a series of small-sized $2- to $20-million properties. The cadence and diversity of these acquisitions is reflected only in part by the headlines in the business section of the local paper: DALLAS MAN OPENS BROWNSVILLE BANK, MURCHISON BUYS VAULT FIRM, MURCHISON BUYS CONTROL OF CARGO LINE, DALLASITE, PARTICIPATES IN VENEZUELA PURCHASE, HEDDEN BAIT FIRM BOUGHT BY DALLASITE, MURCHISON BUYS MAGAZINE, LOCAL OILMAN WINS PLACE IN CANADIAN LINE, TEXAS OWNED CALIFORNIA HOTEL TO OPEN FOR BUSINESS, TWO TEXANS BUY BIG NEW YORK CENTRAL BLOCK.

The records of Murchison's eleemosynary activities provide a rather odd counterpoint to this drumfire of headlines. The Murchison enterprises in philanthropy best known to the public are the erection of seven prefabricated huts to house students at North Texas State College; two "opportunity awards" to be given annually for five years to students at Texas Agricultural and Mechanical College; a gift of 197 stuffed birds (coastal Texas specimens) to

Southern Methodist University; and, finally, prizes totaling fifty dollars in a contest for left-handed fiddlers. The latter were carefully stipulated as twenty-five dollars for first prize, fifteen for second, and ten for third—win, place and show.

The headlines have omitted mention of enterprises Murchison has dabbled in and then withdrawn from, or which he has dabbled in and controlled without publicity. They have not mentioned his abortive effort to buy a chain of a hundred Texas newspapers during the Second World War, his control of Henry Holt & Co., New York publishers. They have also ignored what is common knowledge in Dallas: that "Old Clint" is an "equity man," his finances entangled in a bookkeeper's mare's nest of bank credit and stock deals. Sometimes believed by Northerners to be the wealthiest of all Texans, Murchison is considered in Dallas the most vulnerable of the really "big rich." To keep his status Clint must keep going—in business as well as in politics.

In extenuation of the fact that Murchison, like Cullen and Hunt, has been publicly associated with Senator McCarthy for the past four years, his friends plead the simplest of excuses: that it's necessary for business. They say that if he put money in the New Mexico gubernatorial race it was because he had utilities there; that when he tried to get pipeline transmission rights to bring Canadian natural gas down to the United States, he made a strenuous effort to contact the Duke of Windsor, believing that the Duke had valuable Canadian contacts. If Murchison supports McCarthy, they say, it's simply because he's looking for winners in Washington.

All in all, Clint told a reporter recently, he has put something less than $40,000 into McCarthy, including expenses for the private airplane Murchison has several times provided to fly the Senator into and around Texas. Murchison's first contact with McCarthy occurred in 1950, when a relayed request from the Senator found Clint ready to put up $10,000 in the famous campaign that licked Senator Millard H. Tydings of Maryland with faked photos of Tydings and Earl Browder in a chummy attitude. In 1952, Clint put up money to help McCarthy defeat William Benton in Connecticut, and for McCarthy's broadcast attack on Stevenson from Chicago.

Murchison's friends insist that he does all this without any particular passion or malice. And, despite Murchison's hospitality to McCarthy during the San Jacinto Day visit, they say the relationship is cooling. As evidence, they point out that Murchison took the Senator sternly to task last October for not defending Air Force Lieutenant Milo J. Radulovitch when the latter was accused of disloyalty because of his family's leftist tendencies. They stress that Murchison is no fanatic, no monomaniac, no ideologue; the same year that Clint put up $10,000 to help McCarthy lick Benton, he donated $1,000 to the Democratic National Congressional Committee. If Senator McCarthy starts to slip, they predict that Murchison will discard him. He will turn out to have been a political dry hole.

SEVERAL ATTRIBUTES BESIDE the immeasurable extent of their wealth bracket these three country boys who have made good. All three have earned a certain reservoir of affection from their fellow citizens, whether through their generosity, as in Cullen's case, or their homespun charm, as in the case of Murchison and Richardson. Their political ventures have in common an old-fashioned directness, typified by the belief that influence can be achieved simply by money and key contacts.

The fourth man in the quadrumvirate, Haroldson L. Hunt of Dallas, is set apart from the others, first by the quality of foreboding and distaste that his name arouses even in the very rich, and second by the fact that he has learned that nowadays massive wealth, to defend itself, its prerogatives, and its principles, must have at its disposal massive means of communication.

THE REPORTER May 25, 1954

II. Texas Democracy— Domestic and Export Models

Haroldson L. Hunt of Dallas, a tall, white-haired, green-eyed man of sixty-five, differs radically from such other Texas political operators as Clint Murchison and Hugh Roy Cullen. While Murchison and Cullen apparently persist in the old-fashioned idea that money talks loudest in politics, Hunt has discovered that there is something more important to politicians, namely the pre-packaging of public opinion to deliver votes en masse when and as necessary.

It is not that Hunt is contemptuous of the simpler uses of money in politics. Like his colleagues, he operates far beyond the boundaries of Texas, not only in his avowed financial support of such national endeavors as the MacArthur-for-President movement but in individual state campaigns such as those in Maryland ($3,000 for Glenn Beall in 1952), Montana ($3,000 for Zales Ecton), and West Virginia ($2,950 for Chapman Revercomb). And these, of course, like most such public listings, probably represent only a portion of his out-of-state political commitments— Texans believe he was also deeply involved in both the 1950 campaign of

Richard Nixon against Helen Gahagan Douglas in California and that of Frank A. Barrett against Joseph C. O'Mahoney in Wyoming in 1952.

Such direct operations are, however, vastly overshadowed by the political power Hunt has packed into the family of radio and TV shows associated with Facts Forum, the nonprofit foundation he supports. Seen at first hand, the headquarters of Facts Forum, on the seventh floor of Dallas's Mercantile Securities Building, close enough to Hunt's own offices in another building to receive personal attention, is not at all imposing. The door is marked only FACTS FORUM DISPELS APATHY. Behind are no floor receptionists, anterooms, or appurtenances of power such as adorn Madison Avenue enterprises of one-tenth the influence. Instead one finds a cheery, disorganized series of rooms with books, pamphlets, and magazines stacked helter-skelter on tables, shelves, and cabinets.

The air of bustling optimism is well justified. For Hunt's fascination with the mechanics and engineering of public opinion seems to grow each month as he completes the transition from his fantastically profitable past to the self-given role of elder statesman.

OVER THIS past, as over Hunt's future, rests a cloud of speculation and uncertainty. The first record of his name in Dallas was a casual social note in the Dallas *Morning News* for January 16, 1938, announcing that "Quite the nicest family imaginable has come to Mount Vernon of Dallas to stay . . ." and going on to report that Mr. H. L. Hunt, with wife, four sons, and two daughters had just arrived from Tyler, Texas, to purchase an oversized replica of Mount Vernon in Dallas's most fashionable suburb.

To this day, Dallasites know little more for certain about the tight-lipped, mysterious Hunt than what he has vouchsafed in occasional interviews: that he was born in Vandalia, Illinois, stayed in school long enough to acquire a fifth-grade education, was a wandering ranchhand and lumberjack before settling down on a farm in Arkansas in 1911, entered the oil business around 1920, and in 1931 won his first big stake in the East Texas pool.

About these bare facts, however, there swirls gossip so persistent as to be impossible to ignore. Sometime between the acquisition of his farm in 1911 and his entry into the oil business, H. L. Hunt acquired a reputation as a professional gambler known up and down the Mississippi. His first major oil leases were acquired, according to legend, in a poker game.

The late 1920's found him a minor and inconspicuous oil operator in Arkansas and Texas, with no great finds to his credit until the East Texas pool came in in 1930. No one to this day knows precisely how Hunt got "Dad" Joiner's original field away from him, but men who operated in East Texas in those days consider it one of the sharpest bits of business in an industry known for slick dealing.

"Dad" Joiner went on to die broke, commemorated only in the name of the town of Joinerville, Texas, and H. L. Hunt went on to acquire one of the greatest fortunes in modern times. During the New and Fair Deal days, Hunt stretched his empire through Texas, Louisiana, Alabama, Oklahoma, and Wyoming. Today, with an estimated 300 million barrels of oil reserves, he is bracketed with Sid Richardson as a candidate for billionaire rank.

The growth of his fortune to such dimensions seemed unable to still his persistent gambling instinct. From Tyler he bet on horses around the country and frequently dashed off to Florida to follow the races for months at a time when any winnings must have been made grotesquely unimportant by his oil wealth. Indeed, Hunt's unquenchable delight in the ways of chance persists. It was only last year at a dinner party in Dallas that he pulled out several lists of football games around the country which he had been doping out and offered to bet against anyone at the table on three out of five contests. The odds, someone noted, were stacked 3–2 in favor of the house—the house being one of the half-dozen richest men in the world.

Helping the House Odds

To American politics Hunt seems to have brought the same desire to underwrite his simpler gambles in individual campaigns by newer techniques for improving the house odds. In Facts Forum he has found a way of doing so. The namesake radio program, "Facts Forum," begun in 1951 (see *The Reporter*, February 16, 1954), can now be heard on 246 stations from Portland, Maine, to Portland, Oregon. The Facts Forum organization sponsors "Answers for Americans," carried free on 139 ABC radio and 13 TV stations across the nation. To these have been added a TV version of "Facts Forum," carried by 67 stations, a companion show, "State of the Nation" (free time on 131 MBS stations), and, this spring, the nationwide "Reporters' Roundup" acquired from MBS (free time on 216 stations).

Facts Forum seems to reflect only a part of Mr. Hunt's ambitions in his progress to eminence as a manipulator of opinion. Last year Hunt won an FCC license to operate a commercial TV station in Corpus Christi. Twice this year he has visited New York, held press conferences, and scanned the nation's word capital in search of opportunities. He has tried to acquire control of *Collier's* and *Coronet* and been rebuffed in both cases. He was spurned by NBC this April in his attempt to wring free time from the network for another Facts Forum nation-wide show. Currently, gossip in the word business holds that the undaunted Mr. Hunt is readying a

national news magazine for fall publication.

Meanwhile through Facts Forum Hunt commands a national grassroots organization whose influence almost every Washington Senator has felt in the push behind the Bricker amendment, and whose power any small-town Texas editor can explain by pointing to the flood of Facts Forum-inspired letters supporting Senator McCarthy.

There is a final thing that should be said about Hunt and Facts Forum. They did not create the climate of opinion that they now foster. The ideas they push are the common currency of the men who shape Texas thinking and run Texas politics. Hunt may not have developed these ideas into a system of politics, but he has brought his remarkable gifts for business organization to exporting them across the country as he exports oil and gas. He does it cheaply, too—with $3 million worth of free air time wrung out of the big radio networks. Hunt may be serious when he estimates his annual outlay on Facts Forum at only $20,000.

America has been so long bombarded with concepts, prejudices, and symbols that have been loaded and aimed from emplacements in New York, Washington, and Hollywood that it has difficulty recognizing Dallas, Texas, as a contender in this field. This is unfortunate, because the voices of Facts Forum are recurrent native American voices, tracing their descent from the Know-Nothings, of yesterday. These ideas have persisted in the fluid, ever-changing life of America almost as te-

naciously as the ideals of American freedom and tolerance. But they have
always hitherto been minority voices.
What happens when they gain the upper hand in a community is nowhere
better demonstrated than in Texas itself, whose governor, Allan Shivers, is a
member of the advisory board of Facts
Forum and governs the state by the code
that he shares with it.

Politics by 'Proper People'

On the surface, Texas politics has a
breezy, wide-open appearance. Texans
like to boast that their state has no machine and politics is a free-for-all. What
they mean by this disclaimer is simply
that nobody has ever defined the kind of
machine that runs their state. It is true
they have no machine in the recognizable Eastern form of patronage, spoils,
and bloc-delivered votes.

Texas politics rests, instead, on a series of autonomous self-winding groups
in each community, consisting of the local aristocracy of enterprise and commercial achievement. These close-knit
social groups are the respectable
people—merchants, lawyers, bankers,
publishers, contractors, businessmen,
oilmen, and their wives—who run their
cities as if the cities were clubs in which
they constituted the nominating committees and the electorate-at-large the
herd. Some of these little oligarchies (as
in San Antonio) may at times be as corrupt and crude as Frank Hague's old ca-
marilla in Jersey City; others (as in

Dallas) may be distinguished by the
most extraordinary civic responsibility
and honesty. But their common characteristic is a ruthlessness that arrogates to
them sole control of local political life.

The men who direct community affairs are not the Big Rich but the Little
Rich. The Big Rich are far more interested in national politics with its ever-
present threat to their tax privileges.
The Little Rich, swept by their emotions of fear and insecurity, see in every
school-board contest, in every independent candidate who repudiates their
leadership, the hand of Moscow or of
the CIO bent on destroying Texas institutions.

The No. 1 Shivercrat

Upon this loose federation of local
"businessmen's machines" rests the
power of the present dominant figure of
Texas politics, Governor Allan Shivers,
a tall, dark man of extraordinary ability
and vindictiveness. A lawyer, born
poor, Shivers entered politics at twenty-
seven from the highly industrialized
Port Arthur area, voted pro-labor consistently during his early years in the
Texas Senate, and then went on to sponsor the "millionaires' amendment" to
limit Federal income taxes to a maximum of twenty-five per cent.

Succeeding to the governorship by
death of the incumbent in 1949, Shivers, by the end of his present term (and
he is seeking another), will have governed Texas longer than any other man
in its history. An intimate of the Big

Rich (Shivers is friendly with both Cullen and Hunt) whose contacts with the oil companies are excellent (Humble Oil occasionally puts its executive plane the "Flying Jennie" at his disposal for flights about the state), Shivers nevertheless represents a force basically independent of both the Big Rich and the big oil companies. Made substantially wealthy by his wife's orchard and cattle properties on the Mexican border (among the more consistent employers of wetback labor in the area), Shivers's instinct of government is the generalized instinct of all the men and community groups who form his political base.

Like Thomas E. Dewey, with whom he has been compared, Shivers is an excellent technician at every level of politics. He is slick enough to import high-powered professional talent to help him with radio and TV appearances, has been in control long enough to have filled all of the 116 appointive boards and commissions of Texas with nominees from every stratum of his statewide support, and is adept enough to have swung Texas to the Republicans in 1952 on the tidelands issue and now to prepare for a breach with the Republicans over both the Benson farm program and President Eisenhower's opposition to the Bricker amendment. Unlike Dewey, Shivers does not pretend to a philosophy of growth and development or to an understanding of the great outer world and its problems. While Dewey has flatly opposed outlawing the Communist Party, Shivers, tackling the problem with a sheriff's

posse, has advocated the death penalty for Communists.

New Law West of the Pecos

Perhaps no facet of Shivers's government in Texas is more illuminating than that fear of Texas labor which was climaxed this March in the anti-subversion bills before the Texas legislature.

Organized Texas labor has long constituted both the most conservative and most cowed body of unions in the country. AFL and CIO together count no more than 400,000 members out of 2,651,000 nonagricultural workers on the state's payrolls. As manufacturing has soared nine times in value in fifteen years, industrial labor has grown from 163,978 in 1939 to 464,105 in 1953. And as labor has grown, laws have been fashioned to hobble it.

Starting in 1941, the Texas legislature has piled law on law until by now every form of union security—closed shop, union shop, maintenance of membership—is outlawed. Unions are subject to all commercial anti-trust legislation: picketing is unlawful if there are more than two pickets every fifty feet: union officials and organizers must be registered with the state and carry identity cards; all unions must file complete financial reports with the state (thus exposing their strength and resources); no felon can be a union official—and Texas laws permit the branding as a "felon" of any union man who gets into a brawl on a picket line. It should be noted, too, that such laws have far more than state-wide impact; no less than a half dozen other states in the region have followed Texas's lead, remodeling their laws either precisely or approximately on its labor code.

TO CAP THESE laws, Texas this spring passed a new set of Loyalty and Subversion Acts. These make "Communism" (never precisely defined) a felony punishable by from two to twenty years in jail. They establish penalties for "subversives" (undefined) that permit stripping these unfortunates of any privileges of citizenship and enjoining their exercise of any business or profession licensed by the state. Under the new laws, upon the affidavit of one "credible" witness and the application of a District Attorney, a local judge may order the search of any establishment and the seizure of "books, records, pamphlets, cards, recordings, receipts, lists, memos, pictures or any written instrument." If the establishment to be raided is a private home, the affidavit must come from two "credible" witnesses.

One episode during the hearings on these bills is as revealing of the atmosphere in which they were passed as any disquisition. Surprised and upset by the large crowd at a hearing, Representative Bill Daniel (brother of U.S. Senator Price Daniel) rose suddenly and demanded, "Is there a Communist in the room?" He glared about him, then snapped: "You've all got your coats on, how do I know you're not carrying guns?" (Representative Daniel had his

coat on himself.) He was finally pacified only when the chairman ordered a paper passed around the room to newsmen and spectators, ordering all to write their names and addresses for security purposes.

IN THEIR PRESENT form these bills represent a negative triumph for labor and other groups that opposed them. One of the bills originally specified the death penalty for Communism, and the bill's sponsor, Representative Robert Patten, refused any whittling down of the death sentence; he wouldn't even accept life imprisonment as a substitute, he said, because he didn't want those Communists hanging around the penitentiary to corrupt Texas prisoners. Likewise defeated was the original proposal for a State Loyalty Review Board, an administrative tribunal that might, without judicial process, have declared any man disloyal and thus have deprived him of all rights of citizenship down to his hunting, fishing, and driving licenses.

Code of the New Southwest

Such acts and such legislative leadership would be easier to press into the more familiar patterns of American state politics if they *did* spring from the calculations of a smooth-running party machine. They spring, however, from no blueprint but only from what has been called the "anarchy of the radical Right"—the distemper of spirit that

Texans share with a still unmeasured percentage of American citizens.

This distemper is nation-wide and its symptoms are familiar: the belief that labor unions and foreigners are dangerous; that the New Deal was not a debatable episode in American history but a conspiracy of aliens; that our Allies are bloodsucking America into bankruptcy; that the American government is honeycombed with spies; that the United Nations is a compact with the devil, written and conceived by Alger Hiss, on orders from Moscow; that UNESCO, its changeling child, is an institution preaching free love, racial miscegenation, and death to American traditions; that Joe McCarthy is the senior patriot of the nation; and that both older American parties are legitimate objects of deep suspicion.

This set of convictions is the code of what has become an unrecognized third party in American politics. The leadership of this third party has, to be sure, long been familiar nationally in the roster of solons that starts with McCarthy, Jenner, McCarran, and Velde in Washington and ends with such purely regional luminaries as Jack Tenney in Southern California. Its birth has been heralded by such seers as Colonel Robert R. McCormick of Chicago, whose *Tribune* is presently hailing its boss's latest efforts to make out of such men a "For America" political pressure group to contend with the older parties. Its antecedents run back through Rankin and Bilbo to the Klan and even remoter origins.

What makes this third party gener-ally difficult to recognize is the fact that it is so far not an organization but a state of mind. This state of mind flourishes, either quietly or exuberantly, in almost every part of the United States— with special vigor in Southern California (another newly developed area of numberless uprooted), in the *Tribune's* "Chicagoland," and certain strata of Detroit, New York, and Boston life. But it is only in Texas that this state of mind has crystallized so completely that the third party has reached the status of a governing force.

Texas elects to the national Congress such distinguished men as Sam Rayburn and Wright Patman, but they come from rural districts rather than from big cities. They are a small minority of Texas's Congressional delegation. The great majority of Texas Congressmen, like the government of their state, speak not for the Democratic Party whose label they bear but for what Governor Shivers has called the "Texas Democratic Party." When Governor Shivers nominates Senator McCarthy, as he did last year, an honorary citizen of Texas, he merely dots the "i's" and crosses the "t" in proving the affiliation of the "Texas Democratic Party" with a nation-wide group, namely the third party.

Slice of Paradise

One travels through the beautiful suburbs of Texas cities, the clean new houses where children play on the green lawns, the innocent voices laughing in the evening, the dogs frisking. One reads in the newspapers of meetings of Parent-Teachers Associations, of Dads' Clubs, of Citizens Councils, of Flower Clubs. To a traveler returned from years in Europe, this seems a slice of paradise where no evil could lurk.

The traveler learns differently.

San Antonio is considered the most tolerant and easygoing of Texas cities. Yet this was where the Minute Women put the Catholic Archbishop under surveillance because he had been heard saying he was going to vote for Adlai Stevenson. In Houston, largest of Texas cities, the central council of the American Legion has set up a local patrol committee "to watch for any subversive groups or organizations which might come to Houston to hold meetings under the auspices of churches, school or other organizations." Houston is where Legionnaires brawled with Quakers in an attempt to break up a Friends Service Committee meeting because it looked "subversive." Houston is the city where a slate of school-board candidates running solely on an anti-UNESCO plank filled two of four contested seats. Houston is the city where the university decided not to give broadcast lectures on American history this year for fear that the subject matter would be called "controversial."

Dallas is Texas's self-proclaimed capital of culture. Yet some of the ladies there have learned how to use the telephone to hound neighbors for supposed subversion or to call the FBI when they dislike someone, as happened to a widow in a Dallas suburb who told me her story.

It was seven in the evening when the bell rang in the little white frame house where she lives alone. A clean-shaven young man showed her his credentials and told her he was from the FBI. He had received reports, he said, that she was in correspondence with people abroad. She explained that she had read a recent travel book on Yugoslavia and had written to one of the women mentioned in it and had been answered. All this, she said, had happened since Tito became our ally. Here in this box were all the letters. Would the FBI man like to read them? No, he didn't want to read them, but had she ever written about China? No, she hadn't, she said. And the FBI man said not to worry and went on his way.

Emeny and the Enemy

Such gossip can reach up to imperil even the most distinguished and conservative. Only this spring Dallas witnessed one of the most curious attempted character assassinations ever to occur even in Texas. In 1951 a Cleveland industrialist transplanted to Texas named Neil Mallon organized a Dallas Council of World Affairs. Despite the fact that its roster of speakers included, among others, former Senator Henry Cabot Lodge, it aroused suspicion.

One of Dallas's moderately wealthy citizens set himself up to investigate the Council, and it was not long before he hit pay dirt. The executive director of the Council, an attractive young man named Glen Costin, was traced to a meeting at a hotel in Cleveland last January that had been sponsored by the Foreign Policy Association, Inc., of New York. Here, it was ascertained, had come Brooks Emeny, president emeritus of the Foreign Policy Association. Now Brooks Emeny had once been on the board of directors of the Institute of Pacific Relations. And so had Alger Hiss, Q.E.D. From Alger Hiss to Brooks Emeny to the Foreign Policy Association to a Cleveland meeting of the Foreign Policy Association to the Dallas Council on World Affairs to its executive secretary to Neil Mallon, a clear Red trail was drawn. Furthermore, whispered the gossips (with no proof), Mallon was selling industrial equipment to Russia (which he was not).

Now all this may sound too preposterous to believe. Yet for one full month while this correspondent was in Texas, the Dallas Council on World Affairs fought for its life. And only because on its board sit honorary members from the city's largest banks and most respected businesses could it get a fair hearing from the citizenry and be cleared, after declaring its formal disaffiliation and disassociation from and any lack of any connection with the Foreign Policy Association—of which Secretary of State John Foster Dulles is a member.

The Perils of Growth

If this climate has developed in Texas to such a uniquely morbid degree, the reasons are not too hard to discern. The dominant factor is, of course, the peril that Texans share with all Americans in a country locked permanently in a struggle with the forces of Communism around the world. And in Texas nerves have cracked generally worse than elsewhere in the United States because to the emotions of that struggle have been added all the other strains which that state is experiencing. For it is an enormous strain on human minds and long-cherished traditions to change as swiftly as Texas has changed.

Texas is a state where only a generation ago cotton was king—and of sixteen million acres once in cotton, only six million are still sown to the fiber. Odessa, a Far West village of 500 persons in 1930, today counts 45,000. Houston, a city of 250,000 in 1930, today counts 750,000, boasting that in each year but one since the end of the war it has led the nation's cities in construction and capital investment. Dallas thirty years ago was a drowsy cotton-trading and wholesaling center. Today it is the Southwest's financial capital, with two of the nation's top twenty-five banks, boasting the establishment of more new insurance companies last year than any other city in the country. Each month, the recorded influx to Dallas comes to 1,700 job seekers, without counting their families and those who arrive without being recorded.

At the mercy of the more modern forms of communication, these new Texans find, with one or two magnificent exceptions, all the papers and radio and television stations drumming at them with incitement to be afraid and to conform. Not quite sure of themselves, they fall silent or get in step.

Conformity in Texas finds ready-made clothes, the flashiest of which is the incredibly exaggerated form of local patriotism called "Texanism." "Texanism" is different from the pride of a Bostonian in Boston, or a Californian in California. It is a form of nationalism that began more or less as a joke, as simple braggadocio about the biggest state with the prettiest girls and the fightingest men in the Union, and has ended by making Texans literally believe that there is a difference politically between their state and other states and that that Union is always a potential menace to Texas rights and privileges. Though it is untrue, as one Northern mother claimed, that Texas children are taught more Texas history than American history, it *is* true that Texas, its legends, its history, and its heroes, is taught to its children with far greater intensity than a Boston child is taught of the Battle of Bunker Hill or an Illinois child of the settling of the prairies on which he lives.

IN ADULT LIFE this provincial nationalism can be capitalized on by either such state politicians as the one who boasted, "I am a Southerner before I am an American, and a Texan before I am a Southerner" or by industries such as the assembly plant at Dallas that advertises its cars as "Made in Texas by Texans." For Texans, Texanism is a synthetic faith that lets them oppose all the controls and exactions of the Federal government in Washington as an invasion of sacred and immemorial rights, while at the same time providing with its frontier and vigilante memories, a complete answer to the newer problems of minorities, labor, and the complexities of city living. Very frequently, it should be noted, Texanism is strongest and most vocal among those who have arrived in Texas from out of state, while those who prefer to be Americans first and Texans second are as frequently descended from the oldest and most distinguished families in Texas history.

These elements—the common national struggle, the unsettling effect of rapid change, the myths of Texanism are in themselves almost enough to explain why Texas politics has taken on such a peculiar cast. But when all these elements are manipulated by clever men and by the kind of money the Little Rich—the prosperous car dealers, the contractors, the bottling concessionaires, the little oilmen, the real-estate men—can make available to state candidates of their choice, these emotions can be made to stand up and march.

Practical Politic$

Practical Texas politics, the mechanics of electioneering, starts with the truths that, first, more money is needed, vote for vote, to win a hard-fought campaign there than in any other state of the Union and second, that the almost complete communications blackout in press, radio, and television deprives a shoestring candidate for state-wide office of any chance of making his voice heard above the blatant blare of phony emotions.

Two hundred and fifty thousand dollars is the minimum estimate for any easy state-wide campaign, a million for a hard-fought one. The shoestring candidate must travel to make himself heard until his voice is hoarse, and traveling in the vast distances of Texas with two sound trucks is expensive. Direct mail is more expensive—$96,000 for a single mailing to each registered voter in the state.

An adept like Allan Shivers, well heeled himself and even more lavishly supported by little businessmen across the state, can scientifically survey, cross-check, and resurvey public opinion moods. Salesmen and district men of large state-wide firms will go from gas station to gas station along their routes of call spreading gossip. ("This man Yarborough [Shivers's opponent in 1952 and again this year] is a nice guy," one rumormongering campaign ran. "He speaks nice, too, but I don't hold with his idea of mixing Nigger kids with white kids in school.")

IN THE GAME of Texas politics, the trick is always to tag the other fellow as "Red," "left-wing," or the "tool of the CIO and powah-hungry pohlitical bawsses of the Nawth." This is a technique that can be readily applied to anybody by such masters of political public relations as John van Cronkhite Associates of Austin and Watson Associates of Dallas. Watson Associates was slick

enough even to brand Homer Rainey, the distinguished former president of the University of Texas, an atheist in his campaign for governor in 1946. Trapped by a planted question during his campaign, Rainey said that he would have to consider the circumstances before firing out of hand any hypothetical atheist who might be discovered on the campus. His answer, rebroadcast around the state, was converted to a charge of atheism against Rainey himself and the man was crushed.

The classic assembly of all these elements was best executed in the Texas campaign of 1952, a political orgy on which the neat statistics of votes throw little light. Actually, the Democrats, with 970,000-odd votes, pushed the Republicans, who got 1,102,000, hard. It was not money alone that wrenched Texas out of the Democratic column for the second time in eight years, lifting the Republican score from its 1948 total of 282,000 to four times that, even though the Eisenhower-Shivers campaign used an estimated $6 million and the Stevenson forces raised only $180,000. The critical factor in the Texas campaign was pressure, the power of community leadership to make a vote for Stevenson not only unpatriotic but un-Texan and downright dangerous.

Eisenhower was Texas-born to begin with, and the billboards screamed VOTE TEXAN—VOTE IKE. One night a group of residents of one of Dallas's better suburbs hired a sound truck that circled around the home of one Stevensonian blaring, "H. R. Aldredge, are you a

Texan? H. R. Aldredge, are you going to vote for Ike? H. R. Aldredge, how are you going to vote?" Across the state the campaign took on the hue of a carnival and religious revival. "I spent $15,000," said one lady ranch owner (with oil royalties) to this correspondent, "but it was such fun. We had two cowboy bands and girls dressed up as cowgirls and we went up and down the county for Eisenhower with those bands." Where cowboy bands and cowgirls did not work, there was social pressure—at the country club, in the office, in business, through the banks. Of a hundred loyal and fairly well-known Democrats who were requested by the Democratic National Committee to sign their names to a Stevenson appeal, only fifteen dared do so. Licked before he started, even so powerful a man as Senator Tom Connolly did not dare offer his name in the Senate primary race.

Burning Oil on Troubled Waters

The tidelands oil issue, of course, dominated the Texas campaign of 1952, and no better illustration could be offered of the dovetailing of special interest with burning emotion. The economics of the tidelands issue was relatively simple. If offshore oil was to be developed under Federal jurisdiction, the Federal government could require payment by producers of a royalty of $7.5 per cent as it does on oil discovered on other public lands. If offshore oil was to be developed under Texas jurisdiction, producers would be required to pay only 12.5 per

cent, as on most Texas state lands. For the oilmen it was preferable that tidelands be controlled by state rather than by Federal government, but this was not a very exciting issue to debate before voters.

It was obviously better to dress the issue in Texas patriotism and emotion. That was easy, because royalties from Texas state lands go to support of the public schools, and the children of Texas could be described as the true victims of Federal control. This could be done, and was done by Watson Associates, in a campaign newspaper (financed by Clint Murchison) which showed a beaked and civil Stevenson sneering at a classroom of Texas children, saying "Tideland funds for *those kids?* Aw, let them pick cotton." Or it could be done by imported Hollywood film and TV technicians who ran off documentaries on the tidelands to be shown over and over again in the last few weeks of campaigning until, as one baffled parent put it, "My kids came running in from the TV set like Paul Revere, tears streaming from their eyes, saying 'Pa, they're trying to take our tidelands away!' "

The Tide after Tidelands

As the passions of the 1952 campaign have ebbed, many of the mingled elements have untangled themselves, and Texas politics now presents a relatively simple pattern.

There is, first, a small and respectable Eisenhower branch of the Republican Party, strong chiefly in Houston and

among expatriate Northerners generally.

There is, next, a much larger "loyalist" or Stevensonian Democratic body in
the state.

And, finally, there is the third party,
which controls the machinery of both
Republican and Democratic Parties in
Texas (the Republican and Democratic
state chairmen were law partners in the
same Dallas office until last month,
when the Democratic chairman resigned to run for Congress) and whose
vigor stems not so much from cold
planned organization as on the crystal-
lization of a mood into a system of politics.

Texans who recognize the power of
this third party like to outline it against
the past of Texas's turbulent political
history. Enormous gusts of emotion
have swept through Texas politics again
and again to reach a peak and then fade
out. Texas was split down the middle
feuding over Joe Bailey fifty years ago;
it was split again, in bitterness and
emotion, over Pa and Ma Ferguson and
the Klan in the mid-1920's. Texas democracy survived each of these emotional toots and in between went on to
elect great governors, create the best
school system of the South, tackle the
Negro problem with greater tolerance
than any other Southern state, and write
some of the soundest laws on natural-
resource conservation in the Union.

TEXAS HAS BEEN off on another of its
emotional toots in the past three years,
an emotional toot not quite so sharply
defined as that over the Ku Klux Klan,

not so easily recognized as was the symbolism of the white nightgown and
hooded face, yet fundamentally part of
the same tradition. Just how deep this
emotional toot goes, how accurately the
shrieking, frightened, vocal community leadership represents the millions
and millions of politically silent Texans,
no one can tell. Perhaps the oddest contrast to the attitudes of the dominant
community aristocracies is revealed in
several private surveys recently conducted by pollsters in Texas. These
show that cross section for cross section,
weighing the big and little, loud and
silent, Texas attitudes are only slightly
more extreme on questions of Communism and domestic politics, and are
lightly *more* liberal in matters of racial
tolerance and respect for civil liberties
than those of the nation as a whole.

Currently, Texans who make a study
of such things seem to feel that sometime between the campaign of 1952 and
the passage of the Subversion Acts in
Austin this spring, the influence of the
third party may have leveled off and
may even be abating. Any number of recent events are offered as omens. Senator
McCarthy's quarrel with the Army
seems to have reduced the Wisconsin
Senator momentarily to something a lot
less than infallibility in the press, for
the Army is one of the few Federal institutions that Texans recognize as both
patriotic and American. Moreover, it
should be noted the Army, with its numerous posts and installations, is one of
Texas's largest cash crops; and even Governor Shivers found it convenient to
have an appointment elsewhere when
Senator McCarthy spoke on San Jacinto

Day in Houston. The determined fight of the labor unions against the establishment of a star-chamber Loyalty Review Board resulted in victory at Austin. The collapse of cattle prices and distress on the farm have sweetened the memory of the Federal government, whose onetime lavishness with farm aid now strikes many Texans as quite American again. In this rural discontent with the Benson farm program, the chief sufferer, politically, seems to be Allan Shivers, who is blamed in the countryside for throwing Texas to the Republicans and is hurt in the cities among the former country dwellers who still get letters from the folks on the farm.

There is growing resistance to the third party among both Democrats and Republicans. Among Republicans, leadership is coming from the Houston *Post,* owned and controlled by Secretary of Health and Welfare Oveta Culp Hobby, which in the past two years has not only provided the most courageous and tolerant reporting in all Texas but has also gained circulation in the process, overtaking and pulling abreast of the stodgy Houston *Chronicle.* Yet, if the Houston *Post* reflects Eisenhower policy, it does not reflect the realities of Republican Congressional politics. During roll-call votes, Republican political strategists today count on at least sixteen out of twenty-two nominally Democratic Texas Congressmen. They can have these votes without asking and without patronage; to challenge these men and to challenge Shivers throughout the state with candidates of their own the Republicans consider unthink-able. Even the Houston *Post* will support Shivers in this year's campaign.

Democratic Rumblings

The true contest with Shivers lies, therefore, in the Democratic Party. The Democratic National Committee has now authorized the first organization to oppose the present dominant state machine. This organization, just established this spring is called the Texas Advisory Council to the Democratic National Committee. Its purpose is twofold: to tap Texas money for Democratic candidates across the nation and to provide a catch basin and leadership for the 970,000 Texas voters who in 1952 remained faithful to the national party. Fragile and as yet unsure of itself, this Council starts with the tremendous resource of the 1952 "loyalist" voters and the leadership of some of the oldest Texas family names.

Its weaknesses are twofold: It lacks any echo in the press and communications of the state, and it now lacks the funds to overcome this press blackout. Although its leaders will contest the state elections of 1954 (with slim chance of winning), its real sights are fixed on 1956 and control of the Texas delegation to the National Convention.

At the moment, Governor Shivers, his machine and its supporting community groups, and the oil money set the political tone of Texas, which, far more importantly than any formal organization, control its elections and its government.

If these elements are politically vulnerable—as this correspondent believes they are—they are vulnerable because the changes that have brought them to strength are producing dynamic counterforces of their own. The wealth that Texas has poured into great universities and cultural institutions inevitably produces professors who teach and students who think. The most effective protest against Senator McCarthy's address on Texas Independence Day came from students of the University of Texas.

JUST AS IMPORTANT, the great Texas industrial boom has created a growing and powerful, if politically untutored, body of industrial workers. The vigor of the anti-labor crusade and the harsh restrictions upon unionism have begun to force organized labor into Texas politics on a Northern scale in self-defense. For the first time, in the Texas Advisory Council, a body of practical politicians in Texas has begun to organize not apart from or in hostility to labor, but with labor unions and federations as an integral part of the organization.

Beyond these are other factors. There is, to take one, the growing importance of the Negro and Mexican vote. Negroes and Mexicans together account for one-quarter of Texan population. In practice, say the hard-boiled politicians, many of these votes can be controlled or cowed in any municipal or local election—but in state-wide contests, and certainly in national elections, these minority votes can no longer be bought.

As Texas Goes—

These are the perspectives of the contest. To maintain its control, the present Texas leadership must go on from extreme to extreme in an effort to keep the thinking of a modern industrial community bent to the code of the vigilantes. Its efforts are of more than local interest. In American politics certain states periodically acquire an influence, sectional or national, far beyond their geographical limits. Virginia and Massachusetts in the early days of the Republic, Ohio and Pennsylvania in the post-Civil War era enjoyed such power. No one in modern times has been able to ignore the impact of New York, Illinois, Wisconsin, and California on the nation in both leadership and legislation. In the roster of the great and dynamic states Texas has now won a place. The struggle for control of its bursting energy and industrial power cannot leave American life unchanged; whichever way it goes, the rest of the nation will be tugged to follow—or to resist.

THE REPORTER June 8, 1954

THE GENTLEMAN FROM CALIFORNIA

Nixon, Knowland, Knight, Warren—any of them could become President. That's why the political struggle in our fastest-growing state has assumed national importance.

The time is August, 1956. The place is the Cow Palace, San Francisco. Out of the seething, milling thousands on the floor of the Republican National Convention a man rises, leans into a microphone as radio and TV suck his words out to the nation: "California casts seventy votes for . . ."

For whom?

For Eisenhower, to be sure, if he is a candidate. But if not Eisenhower, for whom?

Upon the unpredictable answer may hang not only the Presidency of the United States but also control of the prime new source of political power in America—the state of California.

Rarely has one party in any one state faced so perplexing a question as does the Republican party of California this year. Out of its bosom it has nourished to massive national importance four men, each with a major claim on the Presidency of the United States. And though one (Chief Justice Earl Warren) has declared himself categorically out of consideration, two (Senator William F. Knowland and Governor Goodwin J. Knight) are already avowed candidates for the Presidential nomination, while the ambitions of the fourth (Vice-356

President Richard M. Nixon) are masked only by a well-behaved silence. These ambitions cannot all be served at the same time. Only one can win. Skillfully handled, this depth of talent could let California decide who will lead the Republican party for the next four years. Played wrong, it can blast the Republican party apart and turn California, the nation's new political titan, over to the Democrats whom the Republicans have so consistently outwitted for 20 years.

This new power source in our national life is, indeed, almost as important a prize as the Presidency. No longer is California what it was only four years ago: a faraway scouting ground for Eastern leaders seeking collateral strength beyond the Rockies. This year, symbolically, the Republican leaders will convene in San Francisco. Politically, the age of California independence has begun.

With its 13,250,000 citizens, California is already the second largest state in the nation. By 1965 at the latest, statisticians tell us, California with 18,000,000 will have outpaced New York by at least a million. By then it will be sending to Washington 43 or 44 congressmen, or one tenth the whole House of Representatives; its politics will touch all of us. And one way or another, these politics will be settled this year by what the California Republicans do to one another.

The story of the California Republicans is, indeed, one of the most intriguing in the nation. Up to now, they have brilliantly solved the root problem of Republicans everywhere in the country—how to win elections despite a permanent minority status in a state where Democrats outnumber them by more than three quarters of a million. Yet they have done so without bosses, without organization, without disciplinary machinery.

It was a defeated Democratic chieftain who described them most aptly to me. "What they've got," he said, "isn't a party. It's a star system, it's a studio lot. They don't run candidates—they produce them like movie heroes, every one cast in just the right part. But sometimes," he said, suddenly brightening, "you get swell fights on a studio lot."

IT IS WORTH a fleeting glance at the personalities of these stars before one examines the substance of the struggle which Democrats so gleefully anticipate and Republicans so desperately hope to forfend.

Goodwin J. Knight, fifty-nine, governor of California, is the newest of them. Type-cast as a politician of the older, earthier American school, he is one of the most instantaneously charming men in American public life today.

A robust, broad-shouldered, barrel-chested man, whose rugged face is plowed by a hundred friendly wrinkles, he has found in the carnival of politics delight, joy, intellectual sustenance. It has fascinated him all his life. He remembers playing hooky from high school as a boy and slipping a hard-earned dollar to a janitor just to hide in the wings off stage and listen to William Jennings Bryan orate to a ladies audience from which men and boys were barred. He was in politics at high school, in politics at Stanford, wrote his graduate thesis on the American Presidency at Cornell (where he remembers listening to a young New York politician named Franklin D. Roosevelt talk to the boys about party loyalty). A successful businessman, a successful lawyer, a successful judge—all these careers were prelude; his real life was people and politics. "I remember when Goody was making it," reminisced one Republican old-timer to me, "if there was a driving rain, if your speaker broke on you at the last minute, even if you had to drive out to Riverside at ten at night to make a speech—you could always call on Goody at the last minute, and he'd be there." Goodwin Knight now sits in the beautiful air-conditioned governor's office in Sacramento, having got there the hard way.

Richard Nixon, the dark, handsome, boyish Vice-President of the United States is a politician of completely different stripe, one of the most modern political technicians in the United States. Originally type-cast as a clean-cut young hero, he now fills the role of junior-executive statesman. No escalator of local county activity, state legislative seat, judge's bench or service in Sacramento carried Nixon up to fame. "Dick," said one of his friends, "is the first lateral entry into California politics. Why, the first time Dick ever visited the legislature at Sacramento was when he came back from knocking off Alger Hiss in Washington." Nixon's true base is a mastery of modern communications, of radio, television and public relations. He is part of an age and community entirely fresh, where detergents compete with soap, plastics with glass and baby formulas with mother's milk.

Tense, moody, introspective, Nixon is the antithesis of Knight. They set up in each other the cat-dog bristling effect so common between extroverts and introverts. Both are magnificent speakers, with but one difference. Where Knight leaves an audience friendly and relaxed, Nixon leaves them fused and charged with emotion.

Senior Senator William F. Knowland represents an older California than either of the other two—the older conservative California whose politics, before the tide of Democratic migration, was run like a feudal barony. Dressed in a flowing toga, he could play the part of a Roman senator with no coaching at all. He comes of the Knowlands of Oakland, a name as imposing in California politics as that of the Roosevelts in New York, the Lodges and the Kennedys in Massachusetts, the Tafts in Ohio. Yet one must not think that Knowland holds his Senate seat by inheritance alone. From boyhood (he was finance

chairman of Alameda County's Coolidge-Dawes Republican club at the age of sixteen) until today, when he is the principal national executor of Robert Taft's political estate, he has labored as hard at politics as Goodwin Knight, mounting every rung from Assemblyman through state Senate to national committeeman before receiving his Senate seat by appointment from his family friend, Earl Warren. (He has held it by election twice since—in 1946 and 1952.)

In contrast to his two nimble rivals, Knowland seems solemn and forbidding ("When Bill tries to unbend," quipped a friend, "he creaks"). Yet he is, nevertheless, an exceedingly pleasant and cordial man to meet. His enormous outer self-possession may make visitors squirm and fidget in embarrassment, but on the platform, his huge frame with its precisely featured head gives the impression of a man of solid, obstinate honesty.

The fourth and greatest of the Californians is, to be sure, Earl Warren. In California politics, Earl Warren combined the role of benign father and trusted family counselor. Even today, after he has abandoned all active participation in California politics and declared himself irrevocably out of the Presidency which the other Californians so desperately seek, Warren towers above them *in absentia.* Yet, to explain Earl Warren and the impact he left on the California mind, one must go back to California politics as he found them on arrival.

————

EARL WARREN came to power in 1943 as governor of a state with the oddest political structure in the Union and a staggering problem of social dynamics.

The political structure Warren inherited was the legacy of a waspish Bull Moose Republican hero named Hiram Johnson. In 1911, Hiram Johnson, a wrathful man, had led the Californians in a revolt against the corruption of both their major parties and their bosses. His revolt, coded in law, wiped out patronage as it is known everywhere else in the Union, endowed California's cities with nonpartisan governments, forbade conventions to nominate candidates, threw primaries open to everyone, and finally wiped out every crevice and cranny by which conventional party bosses build and control machines.

The problem that Warren discovered was simply people—newcomers. From 1930 until 1953, when Earl Warren said farewell to California, its population almost tripled. They came in hordes. First the Okies, Arkies, Texans, fleeing the Dust Bowl on restless, sorrowing impulse. Then the drift tide of the war—workers, soldiers, Negroes (there are now 600,000 Negroes in California). Then the army of workers and professionals sucked in by the industrial draft of the Korean boom—to work at the esoteric electronic mysteries of great bombers, guided missiles and radar in which California industry specializes.

As they poured in, California politics changed like the crust of its earth buckling in an earthquake. Until 1930, the Democrats of California had been little more than a cult, sending to Washington one congressman out of the state's 11, sending to Sacramento 13 legislators out of 120. But the newcomers were overwhelmingly Democratic. By the time Earl Warren came to power, the Republicans were swamped by a Democratic majority that outnumbered them by a million registrations—and which still outnumbers them by 850,000.

The Republicans of California had good reason to be scared as the deluge began. For the rootless migrants of the thirties arrived in a misery of spirit even more acute than was general in the troubled America of the depression. Friendless and hungry in a strange land where the grapes of wrath hung bitter, they were prey to some of the most frolicsome schemes advanced even in an American age that took Huey Long and Father Coughlin seriously. "Technocracy," "Ham 'n Eggs," "$30 Every Thursday," "End Poverty in California," the Townsend Plan, all swept the state in gusts that made the emotions of rich and poor tremble like a lute in the winds.

To meet their problem, the Republicans thus began to develop a technique which, in California, has since been carried to a more artful level than anywhere else in the Union. This is the technique of formal or informal political public relations, whereby great firms of specialists undertake to merchandise ideas and candidates by every modern device of communications. Such masters of the craft as Whitaker & Baxter of San Francisco, Murray Chotiner of Los Angeles (a lawyer by profession), Harry Lerner & Associates, Consultants, Inc., and D. V. Nicholson & Associates, regard politics as a science which, to paraphrase Clemenceau, is too important to be left to politicians.

In a state of so many strangers, where there is no party organization in the older American sense, where there are few precinct workers and these change residence as rapidly as do the voters they must contact, in such a state people's ideas are particularly susceptible to slogans, movies, billboards, radio and TV.

Though this technique is expensive (Whitaker and Baxter alone have administered more than $10,000,000 in public-relations funds in campaigns over the past 20 years), the public-relations engineers can provide a candidate with complete political valet service—scripts, speeches, issues, strategy, market surveys, campaign clubs. These masters of the open forum of public opinion are as potent political factors in the West as the old-fashioned political boss is in the closed forum of conventional politics in the East. Richard Nixon probably owes as much of his swift rise to fame to Murray Chotiner, and Goodwin Knight as much of *his* to Whitaker & Baxter, as Adlai Stevenson owes to Jake Arvey, and Averell Harriman to Carmine DeSapio.

This evolving technique fitted beautifully into the legacy of Hiram Johnson and, particularly, into something he had invented called cross-filing—an electoral law which left California's newly arrived uninformed voters completely confused by primary ballots devoid of any party designations (*see box page 368*). Technique and cross-filing were not, however, enough to guarantee Republican control of the state as the Democratic tide swelled, and, in 1938, for the only time in 60 years, the Californians elected a Democratic governor— the dour and sputtering Culbert Olson. Olson lasted until 1942, at which time Earl Warren replaced him and demonstrated that wisdom and strategy, as well as technique, were necessary to solve the great dilemma of Republican minority status. Warren's strategy was simple: to give the state a Republican government liberal enough to swing to his support hundreds of thousands of moderate Democrats and independents.

EARL WARREN had already won statewide respect as a brilliant prosecutor and effective attorney general when he first became governor. But he was still, essentially, a minor figure, waiting to be measured when he began his lifework. Slowly and surely, however, he grew in stature with the growing problems of his state. In a decade when its doubling population might have wrecked orderly government, he gave the state one of the most superb state administrations in America.

But beyond that he had the indefinable human "call" to ordinary people that makes great politicians. Tall, husky and handsome, father of six glowingly beautiful children, he was a family man who shared fathers' problems with all family men.

When Virginia Warren, driving back

to school at the University of California, was hurt in an accident and Warren immediately announced an intensified highway safety patrol, everyone knew it was a father speaking, not politics. When Warren slugged it out with the Assembly for his medical insurance program (he was licked by the doctors' lobby), thousands of family men on salary felt he was striking for them. A civil libertarian by instinct, he battled against the teachers' oath at the University of California until he won. He balanced California's budgets, fought the local liquor lobby, stood with calm impartiality between labor and business.

Somewhere along the way, in 1948 and 1952, Presidential ambition caught him—so feverishly that in the political hunting season the taste was sharp enough in his mouth to bite. Yet by 1953, with the failure of his try at Chicago, this passion seems to have burned itself out. In the grand office of Chief Justice of the United States, his powerful talents have found a job stately enough for his measure.

Californians still love Warren. But his old California friends all bring back from Washington the same tale—that he will not run, under any circumstances, for political office again. Indeed, to one such visitor, he genially said that if Adlai Stevenson were interested in hearing so, word could be passed to him, too.

Yet, even in California, where his turndown of the nomination is accepted as fact, men hope against hope that a direct personal appeal by Eisenhower can persuade him to run. Only the War-

ren candidacy could guarantee the California party against the fight that threatens to tear it apart. For California has changed much since Earl Warren left it only two years ago, and its new leaders are not agreed on his heritage.

WHEN HE WENT to Washington, Earl Warren left behind him two great legacies. He left, first, the lesson that good government is smart politics. He left, also, a Republican strategy which had reduced California's Democratic party to anarchy—but with which, nonetheless, many Republicans disagreed. In a rough sense, these disagreements reflect both California's geography and the changes of the past 20 years. For California, locked against the vast rolling Pacific by its rugged mountains and bare, tawny hills is really two states.

There is San Francisco in the north, flung over its tumbling peaks, sparkling in the night above the reflecting pool of the Bay with a thousand necklaces of golden light. It is a place of beauty, queen over a metropolitan area of 3,000,000 people. It is a city of tough unions; girdled with universities that touch and stimulate its thinking as do universities about New York, Chicago or Boston; a city of tolerance, traditions, culture and a homeborn aristocracy.

Los Angeles in the south is different. It is a sprawling expression of the automobile age flung over a 4,071-square-mile saucer between mountain and ocean, with no core, no center. It is a working-class giant of timid unions, a

Pittsburgh-with-palms (as someone has called it), smarting continuously under the acrid industrial pollution of its smog, the biggest industrial center between Chicago and Tokyo. It is overwhelmed with strangers who huddle together in Negro districts, Jewish districts, Mexican districts, pure-white districts, full of suspicions and fears. It has no aristocracy. One powerful family, the Chandlers, towers above all the rest; and the Chandlers' crown property, the Los Angeles Times, is the most potent single instrument in shaping the opinions of Los Angeles' 5,000,000 citizens, who cast 48 per cent of the state's vote.

Until the end of the war, Republican leadership in this strange state lay in the north. Until then, the north supplied most of the funds of the party, the leaders, the strategy—and Earl Warren. The strategy, as we have seen, was to accept Democrats as friends and fellow Americans, temporarily misled by their party affiliations, and seduce them from their party labels by middle-of-the-road humanitarian candidates.

But Republicans of the "Southland," which is what Los Angelenos like to call their region, had been nourishing an alternate strategy. This strategy held that the Democratic party conceals secret and malevolent enemies of the nation; that to win Republican elections, Democrats must be scared away from their own party, not lured away by the caressing hand of friendship.

As the postwar years brought Los Angeles its tremendous industrial growth, the balance in the state's politics began to shift. And, in 1946, in the person of Richard Nixon, the Southland found its true political leader, a skilled tactician whose philosophy holds, as conscious policy, that the minority party can win only by supercharging enough zealots to ignite thousands of apathetic neutrals.

The early rocketing career of Richard Nixon is germane to the present hassle in California politics only as it shows the development of a political stance. His first opponent, Democratic Congressman Jerry Voorhis of the Los Angeles suburbs had, in 1946, after 10 years in Washington, a seemingly unbreakable grip on his district. Voorhis, a hardworking liberal, an effective member of the Dies Un-American Activities Committee, who had fought Communist penetration of the CIO-PAC, suddenly found himself pinned against the wall by a handsome young Navy veteran named Richard Nixon. Nineteen forty-six was the year of the veterans' eruption into American political life; Nixon, as his campaign leaflets billed him, was a "clean, forthright young American who fought in defense of his country in the stinking mud and jungles of the Solomons" while Voorhis, said the leaflets, had "stayed safely behind the front in Washington." Voorhis had accomplished nothing in 10 years in Washington, said Nixon; moreover, said the Nixon leaflets, striking a note then still fresh in politics, the campaign against Voorhis was a campaign against "the PAC, its Communist principles and its gigantic slush fund." The telephone campaign, ascribed to Nixon's supporters, was blunter. "I just want you to know," the anonymous phone callers would say, "that Jerry Voorhis is a Communist." Then the phone would click dead.

Nixon won that election, with 65,000 votes to Voorhis's 49,000, as one of many veterans across the country upsetting established political strength. His next big step was in 1950, when he challenged Helen Gahagan Douglas for the senate and handcuffed her to fellow-traveling New York Congressman Vito Marcantonio in speech and pamphlet. ("Is Helen Douglas a Democrat?" was one of his most effective brochures.) Though Warren refused to endorse Nixon in his campaign, Nixon won by 670,000 votes.

With the election of 1950, Nixon emerged as the senior figure cf southern California and chief of a group of southern California congressmen and Los Angeles Republicans of his own philosophy, chafing to seize leadership of the party from the northern Californians.

Richard Nixon has, by now, become one of the most emotional symbols in American politics, for his exceptional and unbeatable abilities provoke at once the most ferocious loyalties and fiercest hatreds. But it was not until the great campaign of 1952 that these emotions began to rowel the Republican family of California.

NINETEEN FIFTY-TWO was the year of Earl Warren's last try for the Presidency. With the looming Taft-Eisenhower deadlock shadowing all

preconvention politics, Warren's strategy was to outwait the deadlock, disrupt it, use his 70 California delegates to snatch the nomination for himself or secure the nomination of the man he wanted. As co-chairmen of the delegation pledged to him, he had selected both California senators, Knowland and Nixon.

Now, neither Knowland nor Nixon was a man unstirred by ambition himself—and in the merciless preconvention dueling between Taft and Eisenhower leaders, these lesser California ambitions offered Eastern politicians opportunity for the most subtle and primitive deals. Robert Taft, not once but several times, offered Knowland the Vice-Presidency on his slate if Knowland would canvass the California delegation to throw its second-ballot strength to him. Knowland refused, saying he could not honorably make such a deal so long as he was California's co-chairman, pledged to support Warren's own try for the nomination.

The Eisenhower forces had more luck. Even before the California delegates detrained from their special 18-car Pullman in Chicago, Eisenhower's backers felt they could boast as many as 50 certain California votes, once Earl Warren should release his pledges.

It is hard to say on what precise day the deal was knit. But the precise moment when the California party began to come apart was nine thirty on the evening of July 4, 1952. All the previous day, the happy California delegates on their special train had been journeying from Sacramento, the governor's daughters dancing lightheartedly in the lounge car, the piano pounding, the gayer spirits shooting off firecrackers and cap pistols to celebrate the Glorious Fourth.

At Denver, at nine thirty, the train paused to receive a newcomer doubling back from Chicago to report on the bubbling gossip mills of the gathering convention. It was Richard Nixon. Within minutes of his arrival, the train sputtered with rumors. From the cars where rode the southern California leaders who were Nixon's battle guard, a new convention strategy rose. Eisenhower could not be stopped, California must not waste its votes, it must go for Eisenhower; in return, Nixon's name would be suggested to Eisenhower as possible Vice-President.

Angrily, some Warren supporters insisted Nixon be told the train held no berth for him. Calmer heads prevailed, however, and a berth was found. To the press, Nixon characterized talk of himself for Vice-President as ridiculous. But 15 minutes before the train pulled into Chicago he slipped off at a suburban station; his picture was missing from the group photo showing California's delegation arriving united to support its governor for President.

The campaign-train intrigue of 1952 had affected only Warren and Knowland. Almost immediately, however, Nixon was to add another to his list of ill-wishers, a man far more dynamic than the other two. This was Goodwin J. Knight, then lieutenant governor of California.

It was a tiny episode, to be sure, that sparked the great feud. All the dignitar-

ies of California had been summoned to Los Angeles Airport to greet Nixon on his triumphal return as Vice-Presidential nominee. Among them, glowing, was Goodwin J. Knight— who had helped sponsor Nixon's earlier career as boy congressman. But now, according to Knight's aides, the lieutenant governor suddenly found himself being physically pushed out of the welcoming party and forced to stand on the side lines, like a yokel, while photographers snapped the important political pictures of Nixon with local personages.

This rankling incident might have been forgotten in the heat of the day; but the breach widened to final rupture two years later. By then, in 1954, Goodwin Knight, as governor, had carefully agreed with Senator Knowland and Nixon's chief of staff, Murray Chotiner, on the distribution of party honors within the state—a deal, Knight's partisans insist, later confirmed by Knight personally with Nixon. The deal hinged on the naming of Howard Ahmanson, a respected Los Angeles businessman and builder, as vice-chairman of the state party acceptable to all three chieftains—Knight, Knowland and Nixon. But Knight was about to take off from California, first for a governors conference in New York, next for a honeymoon with his sparkling second wife. In Knight's absence, Nixon's field staff decided to unstitch the deal and substitute for the neutral Ahmanson a 100-per-cent Nixon supporter.

Again, the telephone technique was used. This time, the phones buzzed with the story that Ahmanson was being investigated by the Senate for collusion and corruption in the "windfall" contracts then making the headlines. The charge, as it later developed, was completely baseless. But the broken deal and the use of the telephone techniques within the party itself infuriated Knight and aroused Knowland. Knight interrupted his honeymoon to bring his yacht to wharfside and organize a countertelephone campaign across the state. Knowland flew back from Washington to take floor leadership personally in the state committee fight. On the floor, the Knight-Knowland forces crushed the Nixon guard and Ahmanson was named by acclamation. On the practicing politicians of the party, it left the conviction that no deal with Nixon sticks unless it can be policed.

While the strain between Knowland and Nixon has since been well smothered by dignified silence, the feud between Nixon and Knight has grown in heat and intensity. Neither will discuss it publicly. But their aides and associates are unrestrained. The Nixon campaign line is that Knight is a clown ("one of California's best-known comics," is what Nixon called Knight one evening at an august private gathering in Washington). The Knight response is even more cutting—that Nixon is a dangerous man, relentlessly pursuing his personal ambition at whatever cost.

WHEN SEEN from the far side of the Rockies, in terms of the national office they both seek, the Knight-Nixon struggle seems no more than the screeching collision of two vivid personalities. Yet it is more than that. Under the surface it is a struggle for control of California. And the battle over the posture and strategy of California's Republican party can either confirm them in power over the Union's most powerful state—or finally lose the state to the Democrats, who are counterorganizing.

For if the Nixon zealots speak for the Southland Republican strategy of scare-and-fear, Goodwin J. Knight has taken to himself the Warren position of the broad middle road.

Many California Republicans find it odd indeed to discover Goodwin J. Knight in this position. All through the long years when Knight, as lieutenant governor, had played second fiddle to Warren, his office had been the rendezvous of Warren's enemies, his open ambition the peg on which they hung their hopes of a new brand of Republicanism. They had waited his coming as the day of the new broom.

Today, in Los Angeles where he was raised, Goodwin J. Knight is considered a traitor by Old Guard Republicans. For not only has Knight, seated in power, pursued a Warren policy—he has done so with flair, bravado, vigor, retaining all Warren's excellent department chiefs, making excellent new nonpartisan appointments, adopted as his own Warren's personal staff and secretariat.

One of the rare Republican leaders who can talk labor's language, Knight has won the exuberant support of California's Federation of Labor against the Democrats. Always a personally tolerant man (he resigned in his youth from the Los Angeles Bar Association because it would not admit Negroes), he has

now, as governor, made it a misde-
meanor for local school boards to refuse
to hire qualified Negroes on account of
race. His budget is balanced, he has
driven through final legislation crippling the power of California's local liquor lobbies, has upped sharply funds
for highway safety and mental-health
research.

Many Californians regard Knight's
record in office as an expression of basic
opportunism. As lieutenant governor,
he pleased many ultraconservatives by
fighting to establish the teachers' oath
at the University of California. As governor, he has angered many of them by
proclaiming himself in violent opposition to Joseph McCarthy and all the
techniques the Wisconsin senator introduced to American life. Again, in October of 1954, while running to retain
the governor's seat, he was caught in the
cross fires of California's violent emotions about the UN. Summoned by one
group to proclaim a UN Day and by another group to proclaim a U.S. Day, he
refused to proclaim either. (He tells a
story particularly apropos in this connection of the priest who came to give
last rites to a dying sinner. "John," said
the priest, "you're dying now; are you
prepared to denounce the Devil?" "You
say I'm dying, Father," replied John.
"Faith, I'm in no position to antagonize
anybody.") Yet, when reelected, Knight
proclaimed UN Day without a quiver;
and, in conversation, shows not only affection for it but a good grasp of world
affairs.

This charge of opportunism, whether
valid or false, can be laid against any

man who takes politics as his profession—and for Goodwin Knight, politics is a demanding, intricate, skilled
occupation. His private library is that of
a man preoccupied with its principles
and mechanics at every level. It ranges
from endless biographies of Theodore
Roosevelt and Lincoln (his heroes), to
such high-brow classics as Ortega y
Gasset's The Revolt of the Masses, from
Harold Laski's Liberty in the Modern
State, to Russell Kirk's The Conservative Mind. In his bedroom is a dog-
eared copy of Machiavelli's The Prince.
He reads Norman Vincent Peale. But
his favorite reading, he says, is Thoreau's Walden.

Shrewd enough to protect himself
from the epithet of egghead by a won-
drous platform collection of jokes and
anecdotes, he is, nevertheless, a scholar
of American politics in its deepest
sense. Whether he has switched as an
opportunist, or acted out of conviction,
Knight's record as governor must be accepted as his own calculated summation
of the mood of America today and what
Americans want. On this record, he
held his governorship by 551,151 votes
in 1954, when other Republican candidates across the nation were being
knocked off like ninepins. With this
election, as governor of the largest Republican state in the Union, he moved
into the front rank of contenders for national office—if Dwight Eisenhower
should throw the Republican convention wide open.

It leaves him in the front rank, however, only if he can control the 70 delegates of his home state over the intense

enmity of the Nixon forces. And the outcome of this struggle depends, in turn, on the tactics and ambitions of the fourth gentleman from California— senior senator William F. Knowland.

KNOWLAND FITS oddly into the three-way strain that rives the California party. For he, like the other two, also has a career which seems to reverse itself. Except that unlike the other two, he began as a middle-roader and ended as the acknowledged leader of the extreme Republican right.

It is difficult now to remember the first mark made by Knowland in the American Senate in 1945. In those days, he was a friend of Britain, protected the OPA when most Republicans sought immediate postwar liquidation, held forth with lofty nd enlightened speeches on modern labor-management relations. This posture continued, moreover, down to January of 1949 when, as the darling of the liberal Republicans, he unsuccessfully contested the Taft forces for Republican floor leadership and was backed by such future Eisenhower Republicans as Senators Flanders, Ledge, Saltonstall, Aiken and Ives.

Nineteen forty-nine was, however, the hinge year of Knowland's political career, the year when he acquired his nickname, "Senator from Formosa." It was then he was seized by the searing conviction that America's destiny must be staked, in this age of hurtling destruction, on the fate of Chiang Kai-shek alone. On tour through the Orient

that fall, Senator Knowland and his wife arrived in November of 1949 in Chungking, that romantic and fog-shrouded city above the Yangtze gorges, just as the Communist columns of Mao Tse-tung closed about its cliffs and hills. There he visited Chiang Kai-shek, who is never more heroic than in defeat, in the macabre atmosphere of a doomed city about to fall to a merciless enemy. He left with Mrs. Knowland on a night flight, as panic bubbled, the day before the Communist armies entered to hoist the Red flag and claim the destinies of his friends.

When Knowland emerged a few days later on the China coast, he was a changed man. Bristling with anger, he demanded that Douglas MacArthur be named High Commissioner for Asia and that America immediately impose an air-sea blockade of the entire China coast.

He returned to Washington to find new friends waiting for him in that wing of the Republican party which has always used tragedy in the Orient to accumulate quick political capital. By the logic of politics, he soon found himself divorced from his middle-road friends and working with the most extreme right, up to and including Senator McCarthy (he later defended McCarthy against the Senate's vote of censure).

On domestic roll calls no other senator has a higher record of support of the Eisenhower administration—94 per cent. But on foreign policy, Knowland has been the administration's itching hair shirt. It is said that Dwight D. Eisenhower, a man slow to anger at personalities, cordially dislikes Knowland both as a person and policy maker.

This White House animosity Knowland recognizes, and it galls him. Knowland is not a man to squander words or bleed in public. But his pride has been deeply wounded. His deep concern with aggressive defense of Formosa—even at the risk of war on the Chinese mainland—is considered by most administration policy makers the surest way to atomic holocaust. But Knowland feels that his deep convictions have been twisted by slicker men to make him appear like a narrow warmonger. The wedge between himself and the White House, he feels, has been driven there by artful intriguers closer to the President. "He wanted to play ball with them," says one of his closest friends. "He beat his knuckles bleeding trying to get into the White House, but that damned palace guard closed the door on him and wouldn't let him in. If there'd been any way to get in, he would have joined the family."

Whatever the roots of his feud with the White House, as an avowed candidate for the Presidency Knowland has now emerged as the eminently respectable leader of all those forces that once marched behind Robert Taft. He plans to enter primaries in Oregon, South Dakota, Nebraska and Minnesota as a fundamentalist Republican; he will claim old Taft loyalties elsewhere too.

But this out-of-state strength is available only if he proves he still holds strong in his home state, California. Which leaves him, as it does Nixon and Knight, contemplating the alternatives of a difficult reconciliation within the private councils of the party—or an all-out battle in the primary of June 5th.

THESE WEEKS in California politics squirm with a complexity and intrigue that defies reasonable analysis.

Between the fifth of March and the fifth of April, any man who wants to claim California's 70 delegates in the primary of June 5th must officially file a slate of 70 names pledged to him. But no one, at this writing, can guess when or what President Eisenhower's decision will be.

How Cross-Filing Works

California's cross-filing primary law is unique in American politics. Originated in 1909, by protesting political reformers, it sought to wipe out the power of party bosses by permitting any candidate for office to file in any party's nominating primary. Further, until 1954 it was not necessary for him to inform voters of his own party affiliation by labeling himself on the ballot. A candidate was required to win the contest in his true party's primary; but if he did that, and led in the other party's primary also, he won *both* nominations. Thus, all four of the state's major Republican Presidential possibilities for 1956—Earl Warren, William F. Knowland, Goodwin J. Knight and Richard M. Nixon—have at one time or another been selected in *Democratic* primaries as *Democratic* candidates. In some years, 80 per cent of all candidates elected to state office in California have been elected on both tickets. In one year, when two Doyles were on the ballot, a Communist, Bernadette Doyle, filed in the Democratic primary and ran up 450,000 votes from Democrats innocent of her party affiliation.

Continued

In a state where the daily press of the great metropolitan centers is overwhelmingly Republican, where Democratic names and platforms consequently lack resonance, where most voters are strange to California issues (60 per cent of Californians are out-of-state born compared to 16 per cent of New Yorkers and 12 per cent of Pennsylvanians) the great struggle of the Democrats has been to make their identities known to fellow Democrats.

During the New Deal days, Democratic fundamentalists in one large city prowled the streets by night scrawling across campaign posters of opponents the word "Republican" as if it were a dirty word. And Republican zealots chased after them, rubbing it out, as if it were, indeed, a dirty word.

It was not until 1952 that Californians voted a modest amendment to their system of cross-filing, approving a referendum which still permits cross-filing but requires candidates filing in primaries to label themselves on the ballot with their authentic party designation. The 1954 election, the first since the reform, thus became the first in modern California history in which all candidates chosen in Democratic primaries were really Democrats, and the Democrats could offer their first all-Democratic state-wide ticket.   —T.H.W.

This makes Knight's position the happiest. Knight is for Eisenhower. But as governor of California he already has announced that he will file his own name as favorite son. If the President decides to run again, Knight, at the convention, will simply deliver to Eisenhower on the cheering first ballot. But if Ike withdraws, Knight will irrevocably control the 70 delegates pledged to him. With this core strength, he can mobilize political friendships already developed in Pennsylvania, Missouri, Wisconsin and New England. Though the Presidency is admittedly a long-shot try for Knight, his chances are excellent, as a Californian and a liberal, for nomination for the Vice-Presidency.

Knowland's position is more difficult. Knight has already offered Knowland a substantial share of the delegates on his favorite-son slate of 70. Despite their contrary philosophies, both men operate by the same code of political honor, and Knight would like to see their rival ambitions settled not by open fight in California but by who can raise more out-of-state strength. Knowland, of course, would like nothing better than to run an individual clear-cut, unaffiliated slate. But to do this would tear wide open the party his family has done so much to make great. Caught thus in apparent indecision, he has not, at this writing, clearly announced what his tactic in his home-state primary will be.

The toughest decision of all is Nixon's. For Nixon's career and future depend, above all, on Eisenhower. With impeccable good taste the Vice-President has, up to now, waited the President's decision and kept his local leaders on leash. Some of his Los Angeles lieutenants profess to be unworried. The decision, they insist, will be made back East, by the big powers and then, said one, "these seventy California delegates won't count any more than seventy Chinamen." Others say that, with the assured backing of the Los Angeles Times, with complete control of the Los Angeles County organization, with unlimited funds, any slate they enter in a three-way race, no matter how late, will win. A Knight-Knowland combine, they acknowledge, will be tougher to face. But, they point out, Nixon is a magnificent campaigner and always shows best as an underdog battling against odds.

At present, the analyses of all California's most eminent political sages tangle back and forth like rabbit trails in the snow. All three candidates are under the heaviest pressure to compromise and present a "harmony" slate. No one knows whether this pressure can quench their ambitions or change the tactics these individual ambitions may demand. No one can predict with certainty whether the fight will erupt in the June primary or on the convention floor itself. Only one prediction is sure: if Eisenhower's decision throws open the Presidency, California will produce the noisiest political brawl since McKinley licked Free Silver.

COLLIER'S February 3, 1956

THE BIG CITY FACES ITS DECISIVE MOMENT

In New York next week, voters will pick a mayor who must cope with the crises that grip all big American cities. Here Theodore H. White examines the candidates and the problems the winner will face.

Now is when the Big-City looks at itself again. As the glowing skyscrapers rise like golden honeycombs in the quickening dusk, the voice of the politician from the sound truck warns, above the incessant screech of traffic, that all is crumbling underneath.

Each morning, as its citizens awake, yawn, stretch, bolt breakfast and send the children off to school, New York City takes the self-renewing web of daily miracles for granted: the 1,000 custodians heating the 860 school buildings for the 51,500 teachers who are on their way and the 1,073,000 students who will follow; the 1,200 garbage trucks, grinding gears to pick up the 9,000 tons of garbage; the subway workers assembling 670 trains to swallow and disgorge 9,500 bodies every minute of the two rush hours; the computers of the power centers, winking red, green and amber as they respond to need, calling on the generators to build the electric pulse from 2.5 million kilowatts at 7 a.m. to four million two hours later.

Only an expert might detect from day to day, under the roar of this primordial routine, a new rhythm sounding the first faint shrill of crisis. For, in the great cities of the nation, crises come rarely by emergency. They sneak up so slowly that they are, perhaps, insoluble by the time the citizens or even the mayor can recognize them.

The daily report on major crime, for example, if Mayor Robert F. Wagner calls for it, will show that two murders have happened within the past 24 hours. No different from yesterday. But that average number is twice what it was when Wagner assumed office 12 years ago, to govern a city whose population has remained practically the same. Since 1954 he has added 7,000 policemen to an original force of 19,840. Today, New York City has more cops per capita than any major city in the country—but lives in growing fear.

Or, again—the daily water report. It, too, changes only slightly daily. But four years ago at this season the reservoirs held 68% of capacity, a year ago 43%—and today 37.5%. The city has spent $400 million to increase storage capacity—already up 52% in 10 years. Yet today the city is in a desperate water crisis. What if a quick December freeze crystallizes the water in the hills above the reservoirs and *actually* no more water flows in the mains in February? What then?

What then? Bob Wagner would not be human if he did not relish the prospect that, by next year, it will be someone else's problem.

SO, TOO WILL be the biennial charade of New Year's Eve, when Mike Quill of the Transport Workers Unions threatens to strike the subways. Every two years Mike Quill keeps the mayor up around the clock, at some midtown hotel, insisting on *personal* negotiation until he sweats out a pay raise large enough to show the men in his union he is still old "Iron Mike." The last time Iron Mike Quill did that, on New Year's Eve of 1963, Susan Wagner, whom Bob Wagner loved so deeply, lay dying of cancer at home. Wagner had promised to be with his wife on their last New Year's Eve together. But in the end the mayor's pledge to keep the city running was overriding and he sweated out the evening with Quill. The subways ran. This New Year's Eve it will be someone else's responsibility . . . along with all the problems of the school system, the troubles in Harlem, the rats in the tenements, the dwindling water supply, the endless rounds of dinners, parades, ceremonies, greetings, favors.

For Robert Wagner has had it. He is leaving. Let the three men who seek to replace him argue their lungs out. He knows that at stake is far more than control of City Hall. The mayor-to-be must face questions larger than New York—

questions that touch all Americans, in every big city, as the same coiling frustrations strangle the vital centers of American civilization: Can any great American city still be governed efficiently under the old American constitutions of state and country? Can either party come up with answers that do not make the cities helpless and beggared wards of a distant central government? Can any man, or group, call into being new human resources, to make our great cities clean and peaceful places in which to live?

Bob Wagner tried. Any examination of New York's mayoralty race begins with the root fact that the effort of this decent man was absolutely honest, thoughtfully intelligent, and completely dedicated; but that, despite this, the crisis the city faces as he leaves is the largest in its history.

The struggle Bob Wagner led as mayor was, at the end, graven in every line of his face and feature, as if a bone-weariness had invaded his spirit. It was as if in the last few years the executive will to dominate, to make the city respond to command, had been drained from him. "His face," a cynic once said, "would make a bloodhound's look happy." Yet when, in June, he announced withdrawal from the race, the city woke with shock. Love him or despise him, who else could do the job? Or, simply, who else could hold the country's largest city together?

Since then, three candidates have emerged, all equally ardent in Wagner's denunciation, all equally sure they know the answer to the nation's No. 1 problem—the turmoil of city life; but all unique, with the particular exaggeration of color that only New York politics gives its candidates.

There is, first, Mr. William F. Buckley Jr.—39 years old, journalist, wit and philosopher, emblem of the newly created Conservative party of New York. His fundamental thesis is that the cities should quit trying to do what is impossible; that the quality of urban American life will be improved only after the city promises *less* rather than *more* to its citizens and clients.

There is, next, Mr. Abraham Beame, 59, Democratic candidate—trained over 19 years in the New York City bureaucracy (he is, presently, comptroller of the city). Beame has broken with the Wagner administration but accepts its goals. He insists all will be cured if only the next administration can muster the zip of decision Wagner seemed to lack.

And, lastly, there is U.S. Congressman John V. Lindsay, 43, Republican-Liberal candidate, an indignant man. Returning after seven years in Washington, he is convinced that his city's needs have been too long ignored not only by federal and state governments but by its own people—who have withheld from it the brains and spirit without which it cannot thrive.

William Buckley offers the clearest political philosophy—and a program of forthright negatives. Abraham Beame offers the longest record of municipal experience—and a program of efficient continuity. John Lindsay offers an appetite for command and a dazzle of proposed new solutions.

Since Lindsay, untested by any administrative experience, is the largest gamble offered to the electorate, it is best to start with him.

John V. Lindsay, six feet three inches tall, sandy-haired and blue-eyed, endowed with the energy and endurance of an athlete, the zest, earnestness and civic impulses of an Eagle Scout, is a member of the smallest minority in the polyglot megalopolis of New York City: the Anglo-American remnant of native-born New Yorkers who have refused to give the city up. His would be a totally hopeless candidacy were it not for the fact that he is also Congressman Lindsay, Republican, and that his record is one of the curiosities of recent American politics.

As representative of New York's 17th District, Mr. Lindsay is a walking political paradox. For the chief political characteristic of his Manhattan district is that so few of its luminaries give a damn about New York while Mr. Lindsay desperately does. The 17th, to be specific, is that tiny part of the great city which the rest of the world thinks of when it says New York: skyscrapers and nightclubs, discothèques and garment center, beardies and bankers. Those who live and work in the 17th prescribe daily the kinds of dresses women will wear around the country, dictate what kinds of movies Hollywood will make, publish the national magazines, choose the best-sellers, select the prime-time evening shows on television, manipulate the value of the pound sterling, the prices of stock, the flow of petroleum around the world. Their chief product is ideas: their chief talent is problem-solving. For decades, however, they have abandoned the city's problems to the people who see the huge metropolis as home while they have been content to use the city chiefly as their executive or artistic forum. They have now, finally, like the home-dwellers, come to realize that New York may soon be not only unlivable as a dwelling place but unworkable as their forum—and, with some astonishment, have come to realize that their young congressman has preceded them in this recognition.

The question now is whether the rest of New York can be brought to take Lindsay seriously, too. Elected first as a maverick in 1958 and reelected despite the Kennedy sweep of 1960, Lindsay began more as a political ornament than a political leader. It was during the Kennedy administration that Lindsay began to take on dimension. It was a time of ideas in American politics; and Lindsay, whose district was a forcing-bed of ideas, found himself more at home in the New Frontier than most of his colleagues on the Democratic side of the House aisle. From his first pro-Kennedy vote in the battle to break conservative control of the House Rules Committee, step by step down through the critical struggles over the civil rights bill and Medicare, Lindsay was part of the dramatic turning of thought which has made the tragedy of the cities the central subject on the current agenda of American politics. To this record must be added that something which politicians call "clout" and intellectuals style as "charisma."

Roughly translated, both clout and charisma add up to the same thing—

voter response. And the voter response to the Lindsay record has gone like this: an 8,000-vote majority in 1958, up (27,000) in 1960, up (53,000) in 1962 and, then, climax in 1964: three-to-one victory, by a margin of 91,000, in a year of Democratic landslide. Sweeping every election district of his circumscription, from the fringe tenements of Puerto Ricans to Greenwich Village's bohemia, as well as the executive citadels of Park Avenue, Lindsay became the nation's leading Republican vote-getter of 1964.

The fact that, at 43, Lindsay is already considered one of the liveliest potential Republican presidential nominees of the future is, of course, thoroughly recognized by him—which is what has made his subsequent behavior all the more startling and daring.

In this nation, quite the most painful way of short-circuiting one's political future is to become a mayor. Mayors, by and large, are among the most unhappy specimens in politics. U.S. senators, governors, Presidents are, in the American pantheon, men of dignity, substance and nobility: they speak of large matters, demand sacrifice, call out the National Guard and wave the flag. But mayors collect the garbage, sweep the streets and never have a cop on the block when you need one. Americans expect to give to their country—even their lives. But from their city they expect to take—which explains the basic plight of New York and all great American cities.

———

IF, HOWEVER, a man is silly enough to want the miserable job of mayor, he has to be doubly silly to run as a Republican in any of the major cities where Republicans are so hopelessly outnumbered by Democrats; and silliest of all to try in New York, a city where Pavlovian Democrats outnumber registered Republicans by three and a half to one and think "Republican" is a dirty word. Generally, every four years some hapless Republican politician in New York City is conscripted by the party elders, by appeal to duty or promise of future appointment, and sent forth to political annihilation. To run for mayor of New York as a straight Republican is, thus, absurd. Yet for any Republican to reach deliberately across party lines and court the restless ones inside the Democratic party is counted as treason. Any Republican who plans a larger future within his national party knows it. It is hopeless one way—and a desperate risk the other.

Why John Lindsay chose to take the risk is as difficult for him to explain as for any man. Perhaps the best answer is heard at small meetings whenever Lindsay grows angry, which has been more frequent as the campaign has drawn to its end. There is a question, open or unspoken, that exasperates him: Why should anyone who, by playing it safe, might become a presidential candidate do such a silly thing as want to be mayor of New York? His answer: "I like being a congressman. It's a good job, an exciting one. But you can't sit there in clinical detachment in Washington, passing housing bills, schools bills,

Medicare bills, antipoverty bills for the cities, and then wash your hands of the job at home. We've given the cities the tools to fight—now someone has to use them."

A simpler explanation is given by his wife Mary. It was off-again, on-again, the idea growing for months, like yeast in his mind. It was off-again as late as the Sunday evening before the Wednesday of his decision—and then he explained to her simply that he couldn't look at himself in the mirror, shaving in the morning, if he *didn't* run.

It must not be construed from all this that Lindsay is naive. To run for mayor, given his handicaps, required the deftness of a Machiavelli, the nerve of a second-story burglar—and luck.

First, it was necessary for him to win the full support, financial and organizational, of the Republican party in New York State—yet disassociate himself publicly and completely in the eyes of the Democratic city from his national party, to run as a nonpartisan. With the help of Governor Rockefeller and Senator Javits, this first step was awkwardly accomplished. The next step was to snatch the endorsement of New York's minority Liberal party—deftly accomplished with the help of its master, Alex Rose. Then, it was hoped, ignition would take place as Lindsay, champion of the new, urged the city to face forward. By the end of June, however, Lindsay's luck had run out. His first campaign posters ("He is fresh and everyone else is tired") had taken a direct bead on a precise target—weary Robert Wagner.

But when, in June, Wagner withdrew, this target vanished. Instead of facing a symbol of weariness, Lindsay now faced an incomparably more formidable opponent—the faceless, ancient and entrenched Democratic party of New York City.

TO SEE JUST how formidable an opponent this is, one must travel across the bridges arching from John Lindsay's Manhattan to the Bronx, Queens and Brooklyn, where dwells another New York. There, entwined in the hearts and habits of six million people, lie the taproots of the oldest continuing political institution in the world—the Democratic party of New York City. This party, founded by the "Society of St. Tammany" two weeks after the Constitution was put into effect in 1789, is as old as our republic itself—and, in New York, until recently, has commanded almost as much loyalty. Today, however, it boils with a restlessness of its own, which led to the choice of Lindsay's chief opponent, "Honest Abe" Beame.

To understand the sources of this restlessness, it is best to seek out Beame's base. Driving across the old Manhattan Bridge, over the filthy East River and past the doomed Navy Yard, down the garish and decaying main channel of Flatbush Avenue, you come to the monument to Civil War heroes that marks Prospect Park. You are now in Brooklyn, largest of New York's boroughs (2.7 million citizens), the most important Democratic county in the nation.

You peel off to the left, at the park, to enter Eastern Parkway—a broad and handsome boulevard lined with trees, the mainstem of a constellation of little neighborhoods, all of which, in this instance, happen to be Jewish. Sedate, neat, clean, Eastern Parkway resembles Grand Avenue in Des Moines far more than it does the turmoil of the Lowest East Side of its origins—or the towers of Manhattan of its dreams. And there, at 739 Eastern Parkway, a chocolate-colored, fine-lined, three-story brownstone displays a sign which says, simply, "Democratic Club 18th A.D."

This is the Madison Club—Abe Beame's club or, more accurately, the club of which Abe Beame is a member. The club is the family inheritance of Assemblyman Stanley Steingut, who received it from his father, Assemblyman-Boss Irwin Steingut. In some parts of New York such clubs have been in family possession for almost 70 years. There is a club on Manhattan's West Side (the Eugene E. McManus Club) that has been the property of the McManus family—son, father, and grandfather—since the turn of the century. These are what their enemies call "the machine," and what its members call "the organization." Of New York's 100-odd Democratic clubs, perhaps 60 still belong to "the machine," clinging to their original ethnic kinships—Irish clubs, Negro clubs, Italian clubs, Jewish clubs. Years ago, many were run by racketeers; a few are still frequented by ordinary crooks; but most are run by people like Messrs. Steingut and Beame—neighborhood people for whom the club is a central institution and for whom, as at the Madison Club, the big event of the year is nothing more sinister than the annual bridge game. All together these clubs have a collective loyalty which transcends race, religion, class or previous condition of servitude. In 1957, when Episcopalian John Cashmore, the machine's man, ran against Jewish Harris Klein, the insurgent, in a primary contest for the borough presidency, Abe Beame was an election-district captain of the Madison Club and he was responsible for just one block in his neighborhood. Fifty-one-year-old Abe Beame, a tidy, indefatigable doorbell-ringer, delivered his solidly Jewish block for the organization's Cashmore over the insurgent Klein by 242 to 6 on election day. Multiply such captains and such neighborhoods citywide and, in a national election, they explain why Lyndon Johnson could carry New York City alone by 1,387,245 over Barry Goldwater.

But clubs like the Madison Club are in trouble now, as is the entire old Democratic machine, for they have largely outlived their usefulness. Their strength came simply from "taking care of people." Over the past century they enfranchised, in order of their arrival in the city, the Irish Catholics first, the Germans next, the Italians and Jews thereafter, the Negroes and Puerto Ricans only yesterday. They got the immigrant's boy out of jail, whispered in the judge's ear, fixed a job here, got a peddler a license there—and sold their votes and power in a squalid and sordid traffic of crime and dishonor. They commissioned the bridges (and collected the graft) which makes Manhattan an engineer's wonder; they commissioned (and thereby got rich) the underground and underwater highway links which taught the entire world the technology of tunneling; they built the hospitals which pioneered world research on tuberculosis. But government of New York was theirs—a private and clandestine enterprise from which all outsiders were excluded.

TODAY, THIS kind of government no longer suits the grandsons and granddaughters of the immigrants the machine Americanized. The young lawyers, executives, schoolteachers they have bred insist on open-style American government; and, year by year since 1948, such young "reformers" have claimed clubhouse after clubhouse from the old machine until finally, in 1961, they claimed the loyalty of Bob Wagner himself—by defeating, on his behalf, the bosses who had originally nominated him and sought to unseat him.

The revolt of the reform clubs against the machine clubs can be characterized as a war of ideas against the heritage of the past. For, the condition of New York and every other city is such that municipal life cries out for new ideas—and the old machines, everywhere, are as devoid of ideas as an egg is of hair. The weakness of the reformers of New York, as elsewhere, is that they cannot agree either on their ideas or on personalities. Thus, in the Democratic primary this September, the reform Democrats split—putting up three men against the one man, Beame, whom the old clubs put up. Taken together, the reformers outvoted the old clubs 54 to 46; but Beame outdistanced their top runner, Paul Screvane, Wagner's choice to succeed himself, by a handy 59,000 votes—and, for the first time in 12 years, the old machine could look forward to having City Hall solidly in its grasp again.

The machine, of course, can be and has been defeated in New York City's history. Over and over again, when the stink at City Hall nauseated even the tenements of the immigrants, the good citizens of mid-Manhattan would saddle up a white charger for a lance-bearer, and the lance-bearer would thunder down on the crooks. Seth Low did it in 1902. Fiorello LaGuardia did it again in 1934. But the lance-bearers have always had, in the past, a magnificent target: corruption. This year, Lindsay has been deprived of the traditional target. For the outgoing administration of Robert Wagner was scrupulously honest; and, in Abe Beame, this time, the machine has been sensible enough to offer a man of unimpeachable personal integrity.

Of Abe Beame, as a candidate, several things must be said: there is the man, first; five-foot, two inches tall, graying of hair and sad of eye, he is not so much unassertive in a group as completely inconspicuous. He is an accountant by profession but a kindly accountant, the friendly bookkeeper type, the little fellow against whom the fat lady in the crowded bus always poses

herself because she expects him to give up his seat to her; and, of course, gentle Abe Beame would do so. The mind is good—but focused on figures, and the chief passion in his conversation reflects the abuse his accountant's mind has suffered from years of serving in a city's administration (as Mr. Wagner's comptroller) which has outspent its means and is now living off the cuff. Having broken with Wagner on the issue of deficit financing, he campaigns with sturdy, dogged persistence on budgetary rectitude. But it is difficult to imagine Abe Beame exercising command of the city during a race riot.

Beyond that, most importantly in New York, Beame is Jewish. Jews, although approximately a quarter of the city's population (an estimated 1,836,000), are its most enthusiastic voters—they cast an estimated 33% of the city's vote. Since Lindsay's intellectual appeal to Jewish voters in his own district has always been as great as Adlai Stevenson's was for Jews everywhere, his great hope had been to carry the majority of New York's Jews; the Beame candidacy thus strikes directly at the base of Lindsay's expected strength. How New York Jews will split on Election Day is a mystery.

There is, next, the fact that, with commendable candor, Beame refuses to repudiate the "organization" from which he comes. He is part of them; he grew to manhood in the Steingut clubhouse, his friends are there; he is loyal to them. This loyalty seems to him in no conflict with a mayor's duty. As mayor, he will try to run the city neatly, efficiently and balance its budget. But politics, in his book, should be left to "the organization." Why should the men who have labored so hard in the clubhouse, he asks, not have their fair share of jobs and nominations at City Hall?

It is just this candor which explains the ferment in the Democratic party as it examines Abe Beame. For the mayor trails a shawl of influence over all city government—he appoints commissioners of police and hospitals, welfare and prisons, housing and antipoverty. He hands out judgeships and magistracies. But how will Beame share them out? In his background, for example, stands owlish and tyrannical Boss Charlie Buckley of the Bronx; the young Democratic reformers had—by this year—all but finished off old Boss Buckley, sending to Washington over his opposition two fine new Democratic congressmen, Jonathan Bingham and James Scheuer. If City Hall, under Beame, returns control of the Bronx to Charlie Buckley—as he will—does this mean the end of Bingham and Scheuer? Will years of work in purifying the party be undone? On the other hand, in voting for Lindsay might they be helping a Republican on his way to the White House? Does New York need a change that badly?

For important-name Democrats, such questions are irrelevancies. Beame is the party candidate; they must support him. The most important of these is, of course, U.S. Senator Robert F. Kennedy who, with exquisite niceness, has so far stayed clean of the dirty undercleavages and deals of the city's politics. But when Kennedy travels the city to stump for the Beame team, the wild applause and enthusiasm he draws at rallies makes vivid, by contrast, the pallid support of the men he accompanies. John Lindsay's problem is how much of that pallid support he can cause to crumble between now and Election Day.

THE ESSENCE OF Lindsay's plight as he attacks this Democratic base is that he is running not so much against the personality of Abe Beame as against the spirit of the city; and the city is so overpowering that against its background all individuals are pygmies. New York is a roar and a rushing in the ears over which no single voice since Fiorello LaGuardia has ever come clear. For 20 years New Yorkers have watched their local contests with indifference born of hopelessness; and this continuing boredom has been for Lindsay from the very beginning Lindsay's underlying problem. For his endeavor has been not only to make himself, personally, known in the outer boroughs, but to inject *belief,* a sense of credibility that he, or anyone else for that matter, can change things in New York. And in his trying he has mounted, win or lose, two efforts that have lifted his campaign to national significance.

The first of these has been Lindsay's organization. Since May he has called into being, out of nothing, a system of volunteers that far outnumbers the troops of the established Democratic clubhouses. Under the direction of a brusque, vigorous, virtually inexhaustible young lawyer, Robert Price, 33, no less than 114 Lindsay clubhouses have been created in street-level, flag-decked storefronts across the city which, on any given evening, direct a volunteer army of between 8,000 and 10,000 doorbell-ringers and missionary canvassers.

What Lindsay has going for him is a national phenomenon: the deep and urgent yearning for participation in government is changing American politics all across the country—from university campuses, where left-wing students riot, to counterpart right-wing uprisings, such as the Goldwater volunteer effort in Los Angeles in the primaries of 1964. Lindsay's people are young, full of energy, fresh to politics, overwhelmingly (in New York) Democratic, but seeking any opportunity to *act,* to *do* something about their community. The Lindsay election strategy has been to offer such volunteers action, *now.*

The second effort of the Lindsay campaign has been equally remarkable: a mobilization of brains unprecedented in the city's history.

Under the direction of the candidate's brother, George Lindsay, on leave from his law firm, eight original volunteer task forces of thinkers have grown to 25 task forces—on air pollution, on crime, on water supply, on municipal finance, on civil rights, on transport, on police methods. Scholars of medieval art have tramped the waterfront, mile by mile, exploring ideas for parks and grottoes. Research analysts of investment banks have given their evening time to analyze

the general economy of New York; management consultants have examined the operation of City Hall as if, at last, they thought it as important as the management of a minor brass-and-copper firm. Nowhere on the Democratic side in New York City does any comparative ferment go on except in the senatorial offices of Robert F. Kennedy, where the old Kennedy intellectual tradition continues and similar scholarly thinking has begun. As yet, however, it has not influenced in the slightest the thinking of the old machine.

ORIGINALLY IT was hoped by the Lindsay planners that the work of the volunteers in the neighborhood clubhouses and the expert task forces would mesh, and an ignition of enthusiasm would take place. For the most part, this magic has been slow in developing, and Lindsay strategists are at a loss to say why. Tactically, of course, Lindsay's plan was crippled by the three-and-a-half-week newspaper strike, which blinded the city just as the task forces were preparing to roll out their pageant of ideas. More fundamentally, what has happened is that the Lindsay exploration has revealed a family of problems so complicated that the candidate has found difficulty fusing them into a single credible call.

The range of task-force work has been so vast that it is as if an enormously tangled organism were bared for inspection. It has not been easy for Lindsay to capsulize, for example, the elaborate study of crime in street and park, and the technical proposals for police mobility and communication; nor has it been easy to summarize the school study's warm, understanding suggestion for freeing teachers in the classroom from bureaucratic entanglement. The dilemma, however, is not only one of public relations but of reality. And two task forces spell this out best.

There is, on the one extreme, the committee which began simply as a committee on municipal architecture. Its guiding spirit is Architect Philip Johnson. Under his leadership the committee has expanded not only its personnel but its vision, until it has become, of all things, a committee on municipal beauty. As Johnson talks, he makes one behold the city as it might be. New York is a water city, the greatest harbor in the world—only no one sees it. Can the soot-grimed, green-rotted waterfront be restored to beauty? Can the waters be used to bind rather than divide the city? Can the barricades of automobile junking yards, the rusty derelict coaling stations, the decaying pier sheds be torn down to reveal the beauty of the islands again? Can the ravage of Staten Island be stopped in time to preserve for tomorrow this last wooded enclave of the city? Sketching future vistas, Johnson makes one see how an *architecte du roi* could create of New York's natural beauty something more splendid even than Paris.

But beauty costs money—which leads one to another equally impressive task force at Lindsay headquarters, the task force on municipal finance.

The finance task force is headed by Eugene Becker, a banker-volunteer. Mr. Becker has put together, in a thick-indexed, massive black volume, one of the most paralyzing documents a sober citizen can examine. The result of his committee's research reveals, in effect, that the city is living on the threshold of an emergency. There is no money at the moment either for long-range programs or for beauty—no money even for the common everyday running expenses of the city. New York might, conceivably, even have to face payless paydays for city employees next spring, no matter who is mayor.

Between this short-range emergency and the long-range vistas of the city-beautiful, as it might be, lies the fundamental challenge: What resources has the city got to cope with both current emergency and future need? And it is only in standing back from the detail of the campaign, only in viewing it from a national level, that one can see what is really happening.

Under the Kennedy-Johnson administrations the national government finally completed the revolution of the New Deal-Fair Deal years, ushering the nation to the threshold of a new revolution. The jungled frontier of this revolution is every congested city. The federal government, insists Lindsay, must help feed this revolutionary front. But beyond that, a greater resource must be exploited; citizen energies must be massively involved to make communities better places to live in.

Lindsay's campaign thus has given the impression of groping—a wild flailing about to give a new shape to the chaos of the ongoing American revolution. It has confused the hopeless New Yorker by its very diversity: by its potpourri of ideas and goodwill, its visions of beauty and architecture, its insights into the bedlam of classrooms and bureaucracy, its stiff management analyses of departmental confusions, its unquestioning and orthodox acceptance of current doctrines of civil rights. And it is precisely at this point that Lindsay is vulnerable to that brilliant and savage counterrevolutionary, William F. Buckley, Jr., third candidate for mayor, who bears the banner of the newly formed Conservative party.

MR. BUCKLEY (no relation to the Democratic boss) is, like Mr. Lindsay, New York-born and Yale-educated. He is the most sparkling philosophical mischief-maker ever to stoop to a mayoralty race. His candidacy for mayor is nonsense in any practical sense—yet he is anything but frivolous. His purpose is not to govern the city but to reshape the Republican party in city, state and nation by destroying John Lindsay.

The thrust of Buckley's campaign is clearer than that of either Lindsay or Beame. The two major candidates contend with each other to say who can do more for the people of New York as their mayor. Buckley calls this kind of contest "a taffy-pull." He believes that government should do *less* not *more* for its people—not only city government, but federal and state governments, too. Knowing himself to be absolved from the dreadful prospect of actually governing the city, Buckley revels in candor: he can muse aloud that New York would be better off if it had less, rather than more, people—if it shrank from eight million to six and a half million; he can openly discuss the decomposition of Negro family life and its financial burden on the city—he expects no votes in Harlem anyway; despite his devout personal Catholicism, he can accept a program of birth control for non-Catholics; he can insist that people should pay for what they get from the city, whether it be parking space or water.

The Buckley candidacy threatens Lindsay on three levels at once.

First comes the dramatic level. The easy forum of politics is television. On TV Buckley is a star. His haughty face, its puckering and hesitation as he lets loose a shaft of wit, would have made him Oscar Wilde's favorite candidate for anything. In television debate Lindsay is normally flanked by Beame, who wants to talk about budget figures. But when Lindsay can free himself from Beame's figures to loose any of the visions of his task forces, there, on his other flank, is Buckley, puncturing the dream or hope with a witch's shaft of rhetoric.

Next comes the hard-nosed level of the Buckley campaign. Buckley is out to split the Republican vote. For him, Lindsay is a traitor to the Republican party—and must be punished. But if Buckley can accumulate 300,000 right-wing votes, he will not only have punished Lindsay—he will have made future endorsement by his new Conservative party a major weight in New York politics. With 300,000 votes, Buckley will be able not only to cripple Lindsay but control as many as 20 Republican nominations for State Assembly, City Council and U.S. Congress in the New York metropolitan area. This is no mean target for any egghead, and with 300,000 votes, the seismic effect of Buckley's impact on Republican politics could be nationwide.

Yet it is the third level of the Buckley campaign which is the most serious: It is a series of questions posed to the nation and the Republican party. What, in effect, asks Mr. Buckley, is the purpose of city government? What are its true constitutional functions? Is it really to care for the worn and the tired, the huddled and hopeless, the refugees who, today, come from the Black South or Spanish Puerto Rico, as 90 years ago they came from Europe to pass through Castle Garden and Ellis Island? Has the city—has, indeed, all American government—promised too much? Should government, therefore, cut and run from its promises?

AND THUS, ONE returns to Robert F. Wagner—12 years mayor of the greatest city in the world, against whom all three candidates run in absentia. He tried to meet the promises. But what happened? Was the failure his, personally? Or is the problem too big, simply, to be solved?

The answers lie in the sterile digits of the city's budget. But one must tap the digits to make them come alive as the

teacher of physics, in the old experiment, taps iron filings on a piece of paper, then thrusts a magnet under the paper and thereafter, in a twinkling, the iron filings line up about the hidden lines of magnetic force. If one taps to find the hidden lines of force in the bizarre figures of New York's near-bankruptcy, one can tap them into sudden clarity.

What emerges, starkly, is the shock and cost of the racial confrontation between black and white in the big city. For in America it has been left to the big cities of North and West to pay for centuries of wickedness and degradation imposed by other men in other places at other times on black-skinned Americans. And New York, most lavish of cities, has gone broke paying for other men's sins against the human conscience. The rising anger of Negro-Americans in New York, their insistent demands speak in figures, thus: welfare—up from $183 million in 1954 to $502 million in 1965; the cost of hospitals—up from $181 million to $493 million; cost of police—up from $104 million to $296 million; cost of schools—up from $319 million to $814 million—and all for a city of stable population in a time of prosperity. Year by year, to meet the growing social crisis, Wagner had to tax; and the more he taxed, the more the city's restlessness grew, the faster became the departure of its white, middle-class citizens to the neighboring suburbs. Year by year—by four, five, or six percent—the city's expenditures grew as the budget crept up from his original

$1,639,000,000 in 1954. And then, last year, the budget became totally unhinged, rocketing up by *half a billion* dollars to a staggering $3.87 billion.

Faced finally with risking fiscal insolvency or riot-in-the-street, Wagner chose to risk insolvency. He would borrow, off the cuff, another $250 million beyond what taxes would furnish simply for daily running expense—which is the same as a family pawning its furniture to buy groceries. "The strongest force," he wrote officially as a foreword to his half-a-billion-dollar extra demand for the city's needs, "in the upward surge of our expenditure requirements is the plight of that major sector of our population which, until now, has lacked equal access to, and opportunity for, significant participation in the benefits of urban life and living. . . . The costs of their maintenance (especially that of the children and of the aged) is a factor which defies limitation or control. Under the law, we have no alternative but to maintain the needy. . . ."

To accept the digital story as told by the budget is, however, to read only half the story of New York's crisis. The figures tell only of the challenge the city tried to meet. The other half is the story of the challenge it could not afford to face—the challenge of its confrontation with technology, the disruption of the city by life in the changing 20th Century.

New York, like every other American city, is at once fevered and overwhelmed by the wizardry of American productive and technological exuberance. A national prosperity, for example, has flooded New York with automobiles. Shortly after World War II the daily count of automobiles entering the downtown Manhattan cordon was 320,000; today, their daily number is over 600,000 in the same inelastic street space. But who will pay to clear a public way for these private automobiles? A national boom has peaked in New York, creating more than 64 million square feet of new office space (more than Philadelphia, Los Angeles, Chicago and San Francisco combined). But this achievement defeats itself because no one knows how to get people efficiently to their offices and back, how to protect them from violence at night, or protect their lungs from soot-fall and sulfur dioxide by day. The air, the water, the streets, the entire environment of New York is congested and polluted by a metropolitan community of 15 to 20 million people who use the core city at will—yet less than eight million stay to pay its burden.

The American system of government does not permit any city to solve its regional problems under its own leadership. New York cannot require Scarsdale to pay for the use of New York as a forum, any more than Los Angeles can require Beverly Hills to pay for the use of Los Angeles as a forum or contribute to the help of riot-torn Watts. Nor can the city export the present net cost (and the higher future cost) of the civil rights revolution to the greater nation—so, it bears alone the largest charge of the racial confrontation.

Cities, traditionally, are where the

stresses of civilization come; and revolutions break when old forms of government can no longer bend to meet the stresses. Historians may well probe New York's crisis and next week's election to find whether American constitutional revision began here, giving American cities authority and financial resources to meet burdens and functions they can no longer support alone. They will examine it to see whether men could devise a way to decentralize bureaucracy and let the sprawling city's constituent communities develop with personalities of their own.

But this kind of speculation is very remote right now for those who crowd the sidewalks of New York. There, for years, New Yorkers have been irritated by visiting cousins who chant: "It's a great place to visit, but I wouldn't live here for a million bucks." New Yorkers yearn for a man who can make their town a great place to live in again; for if someone does not, it will become a tragic place to visit. This is what they are groping for in the election of next week. Only after they vote will anyone know whether they are willing to give any mayor their vitality, heart and goodwill—the last, untapped resource for hope.

LIFE October 29, 1965

Chapter 10

The Action Intellectuals

In all his reporting White sought to illuminate the powers behind the powers. Who were the men and women who brought ideas to political leaders, and, more importantly, who then put such ideas into action? In an earlier time, the "action" people were most often themselves politicians—ward heelers, city or state bosses, party faithfuls—or big campaign givers; and while intellectuals have to a greater or lesser extent always had a role in our government, rarely were they in positions of governmental authority.

By the mid-1960s, however, this balance had changed drastically. Beginning with Franklin D. Roosevelt in 1933, more and more intellectuals were recruited to government to actually *run* things, not merely advise. Their number reached a peak in the Kennedy and Johnson administrations, a phenomenon that intrigued White, and prompted him to chronicle it in a three-part series for *Life* in 1967. "For intellectuals," he wrote, "now is a Golden Age and America is the place. Never have ideas been sought more hungrily or tested against reality more quickly. From White House to city hall, scholars stalk the corridors of American power."

Nothing he wrote filled him with more pride than this series, "The Action Intellectuals," which is presented here in its entirety.

THE ACTION-INTELLECTUALS
Part 1

From the Editors' Precede: "A brotherhood of scholars," writes Theodore White, "has become the most provocative and propelling influence on all American government and politics." He is describing the action-intellectuals, the large and growing body of men who choose to leave their quiet and secure niches on the university campus and involve themselves instead in the perplexing problems that face the nation. They sit today in the highest councils; their ideas are molded into policy; the judgements they make are crucial. Who are they? Where did they come from? And in what direction are they taking America? In the first article of this three-part series, White explores the workings of the action-intellectual community, the bases from which it draws its power and the men who belong to it. Next, the involvement of American intellectuals in matters of state from the earliest days of the republic will be examined. In a final installment, White explains the dilemma the action-intellectuals themselves face in dealing with the future of the nation.

This is the story of a new power-system in American life—and the new priesthood, unique to this country and this time, of American action-intellectuals.

In the past decade this brotherhood of scholars has become the most provocative and propelling influence on all American government and politics. Their ideas are the drivewheels of the Great Society: shaping our defenses, guiding our foreign policy, redesigning our cities, reorganizing our schools, deciding what our dollar is worth.

Change has called this new power-system into being—raw, dislocating change rushing over us in such torrents that the problems left in its wake overpower our understanding. As the world outruns its comprehension of itself, inherited knowledge and tradition no longer grip onto reality. "Folk-wisdom," said the late Robert Oppenheimer, "can cry out in pain. But it can't provide solutions."

Yet governments must have solutions. They cannot let change simply happen; their duty is to place a discipline on events. Thus, with almost primitive faith, American government has turned to the priesthood of action-intellectuals—the men who believe they understand what change is doing, and who suggest that they can chart the future. For such intellectuals now is a Golden Age, and America is the place. Never have ideas been sought more hungrily or tested against reality more quickly. From White House to city hall, scholars stalk the corridors of American power:

▶Last year one half the Cabinet of the U.S. was drawn, not from politicians, but from the brotherhood of learning: Secretaries Gardner, Katzenbach, Weaver, Wirtz, McNamara, Rusk—all were, at one time or another, college professors or teachers. One catches best the temper of the time as HEW Secretary John Gardner begins a sentence with a slip of the tongue: "When the faculty gets together—I mean, when the *Cabinet* gets together . . ."

▶For decades, the largest office in the West Wing of the White House, facing out on the Executive Office Building, has usually been the lair of the President's most important assistant. During the last seven years, however, it has been chiefly occupied by Theodore Sorensen, Bill Moyers, Joseph Califano—the successive chiefs of the task forces that ceaselessly scout the campuses and foundations of the nation in search of brains and ideas; and, from basement to third floor of the White House, professors and scholars have sifted what the scouts have brought back. The Presidency, in fact, has become almost a transmission belt, packaging and processing scholars' ideas to be sold to Congress as program.

▶No political reporter travels the campaign trail today without realizing that backroom bosses are steadily being pushed out by backroom professors who define the issues, draw up position papers, draft the speeches the candidates will voice. "We are a new establishment without initiation rites," says one of them. "You never know when you're in, but you certainly know when you're out."

▶By now, beachheads of scholarship are being set up even in the city halls. In his first year in office, Mayor John Lindsay of New York City appointed no fewer than 17 college deans, professors and lecturers to his staff. "If you got together all the books they'd written," says an old city hall hand, "they'd fill every shelf in this room."

No one can describe to any intellectual's satisfaction what the word "intellectual" means—let alone define the elite new category of action-intellectuals who generate such waves of impact on the American government. Yet, broadly speaking, intellectuals are men for whom ideas provide more than the thought patterns that weave connections among facts—as ideas do for most thoughtful men. For the true intellectual, ideas have an electric vitality of their own which is sensed only by other artists-of-the-mind; ideas engaged his passion more than reality or humanity itself.

In the classic—or pure—intellectual, this distinctive passion commonly voices itself in tones of outrage or despair as he looks down from the ivory tower on man-in-action and scolds the hypocrisy or compromise which action forces on dreams. But the new action-intellectuals have transformed the ivory tower. For them, it is a forward observation post on the urgent front of the future—and they feel it is their duty to call down the heavy artillery of government, now, on the targets they alone can see moving in the distance. Courted by politicians and press, suspected alike by men-of-affairs and ivory-tower colleagues, the action-intellectuals worry about the contradictory tugs of pure contemplation and contaminating involvement. Yet they cannot draw back.

Says Richard N. Goodwin, one of the youngest and most creative of the new breed, former adviser to Presidents Kennedy and Johnson, now at Wesleyan University: "The ultimate commitment to ideas is to act on them; action can involve a commitment to an idea that the most brilliant thinking never approaches. It's easy to be pure when you're detached. But Goethe said to act is to sin, and so you have to be willing to sin a little. It's only when the necessity for compromise or accommodation begins to drown the ultimate conviction that led you to act in the first place that you have to withdraw—and that's a matter of individual conscience and judgment."

IF THE action-intellectuals recognize that peril is hidden in their new roles, so, too, does government. For the flood of new learning flows in no patterns tested by the past; it flows in separate streams, bubbling wildly from separate sources of restless curiosity.

By now, to be sure, the authority of those scholars who explore the stream of science and technology has been fully established in Washington. More recently, with greater difficulty, the government has learned to absorb the wisdom of economists whose way of thinking in symbolic aggregates colors all Washington decision from defense to urban housing. Today, with utmost difficulty, government is groping to find guidance from a third category of scholars—social scientists, the men nominated by history to explain how communities shall master the changes provoked by the physical scientists and economists. And it is just here that controversy blisters. Do social scientists yet know enough to guide us to the very different world we must live in tomorrow? Do they offer wisdom as well as knowledge?

Says Professor Edward C. Banfield of Harvard: "The premium of scholarship for a professor is all too often originality—not correctness. A politician or businessman must pay a price for being wrong; the academic never does. The college professor has no knowledge of what people want now, or what they are going to want; he deals in generalities, and there is no way of applying a general theory to a unique event. I think it's a national tragedy that people in decision-making roles turn over to intellectuals or computers the right to make their decisions. And it's bad for scholarship, too. No one should tell a professor what to think about. A good professor is a bastard perverse enough to think about what *he* thinks is important, not what government thinks is important."

To all of which the action-intellectuals might reply: in the Kingdom of the Blind, the one-eyed man is King. Man must find his way across the buckling landscape of the changing world either by instinct and tradition—or by knowledge and ideas.

No tactical manual or operational guide describes how the action-intellectuals operate. Chance, impulse, ambition, discontent and public spirit all lead such men by a dozen different paths to the seats of power. Yet all paths start from the dynamics of modern knowledge. Learning today accumulates at such an accelerating rate that no one can keep up with all of it. Monographs and books, papers, and surveys, statistics and theories pour off the press in avalanche-flow until the desks of professors frequently resemble the snow forts that children make—white dens over whose barricades of tumbling, still unread documents, the eyes of the professor are barely visible.

Truly revolutionary ideas, as always, are rare in this flow, because authentic, historic geniuses—like Newton, Darwin, Einstein and Keynes—are rare in any age. Yet within the disciplines carved out by the giant thinkers toil thousands of brilliant minds, primary producers of really good ideas.

Between such idea-producers and government stretches a gulf, and across this gulf the action-intellectuals throw a bridge. Government, pressed by change, calls for information, explanation, analysis. The action-scholar first perceives how the ideas of the primary producers can be given the dimension of time and program that may guide action. Stirred by government's call, he responds.

From White House, from state houses, from city halls, from Washington departments and agencies, scouts continuously reach across the gulf to the action-oriented scholar. At times, as last summer, the White House will send its scout-packs to tour the country and hold audience in the great idea-centers. From one such tour last summer, White House staffers Joseph Califano, Harry McPherson and Douglass Cater returned to package a black loose-leaf volume of 19 separate families of ideas—which were promptly assigned to 10 announced task forces (and a number of as-yet-unannounced task forces) already processing these ideas into the raw stuff of legislation.

Some action-intellectuals cross the bridge as messengers or consultants, returning to their studies between campaigns. Others take leave from scholarship for a year or two to accept government posts with the sure knowledge that they can always return to a university or pick up a foundation grant afterward. Still others cross to the government side and then never return to teaching; the experience of action transforms them into executives.

FRANCIS KEPPEL, former dean of the Harvard Graduate School of Education, for example, was among a group of economists and political scientists who seven years ago joined a mission to Nigeria to advise on what should be done about education in that emerging African state. Out of their thinking came a theory that has shaped Keppel's professional perspective since: that education is not simply a moral matter of providing equal opportunity; it is a national investment—as much so as roads, bridges, dams, defense. Education nourishes strength. As a national investment it cannot be left entirely to local budget-makers: it requires a national policy of research and development, to modernize it, stimulate it, make it better.

Returning in 1960 to join a task force of scholars in the Kennedy campaign, Keppel was able to thread this theory into the rhetoric of the election. In 1961, the new President stated the theory to be his policy. Then, nothing happened—for ideas require political motors. Scholars, in their jargon, call the junction between ideas and power "the interface." But the unfortunate scholar appointed by Kennedy as his first chief of education could not penetrate the interface or master the art of gaining a busy leader's attention; and so, frustrated, he resigned after 18 months. When Kennedy was informed of the resignation, he asked, "Who is he? I never heard of him." To which his assistant, McGeorge Bundy, replied, "That, Mr. President, is just the trouble."

If, then, someone is disposed to translate an idea into action, he must be willing to soil himself in politics. Thus Keppel, crossing the bridge in 1962, decided to resign from Harvard to accept the post as chief of the Office of Education for a three-year adventure in the mechanics of government.

His first task was to mobilize within Kennedy's inner court the necessary political and administrative support to revitalize the original idea and make it move—for the President's new education program lay fragmented and trapped in the lobbies and corridors of the 87th Congress. With the help of Ted Sorensen, J.F.K.'s intellectual chief-of-staff, Keppel nailed this down. Then Keppel began his own crash course: learning which committees of Congress to court; how to convince the statisticians of the Bureau of the Budget that the theory of investment was valid; how to neutralize the educationists' massive lobby, the National Education Association. Another professor-in-government, Wilbur J. Cohen, father of Medicare, wise with decades of Washington lore, contributed the analysis and theory which, at once, helped to solve the church-state conflict and channeled the new funds where they were most needed.

By 1965, five years after his journey to Nigeria, Francis Keppel, now an accomplished administrator and operator, could watch as President Johnson signed the $1.3 billion Elementary-Secondary Education Act of 1965. He could, if he wished, boast that he and Cohen, two professors, had led the federal government across the watershed that made Washington, for the first time, responsible for modernizing education all across the nation.

Drawn by conviction, other scholars have followed the same route on state and city levels. Dr. William Ronan, a burly, soft-spoken professor of government, was first called 10 years ago to consult on revision of New York's constitution. He caught the attention of Nelson Rockefeller and became his chief-of-brains-staff, then last year was appointed chairman of a new Metropolitan Transportation Authority—New York's massive $2 billion project to untangle the mass-transit and commuting problems of the lower Hudson metro-politan jungle.

AUGUST HECKSCHER, the sensitive and urbane director of the Twentieth Century Fund, was first called to government as consultant on the arts to Eisenhower and Kennedy. But Heckscher's book on the civilized use of leisure (*The Public Happiness*) indicated where his true interest lay. Thus, when called by Mayor Lindsay, he resigned his foundation post and, as New York City's bicycle-pedaling Parks Commissioner, has set out to put his theories to the test of practice.

Over the past 10 years, theories incubated by such action-intellectuals have: reshaped the basing and strike patterns that deploy SAC's bombers around the globe; led to the great nuclear test ban treaty of 1963; cut our taxes, reshaped our economy, lifted national income by 50% in the past seven years, made us rich. In the *next* 10 years, their theories will change America even more: changing how we travel, how we live, how our medicine is given us, how we make war, how we seek peace, the air we breathe, the water we drink.

Yet the community that produces these ideas—its geography, its power centers, its interstrands—remains largely unknown.

Of the 300,000 or so American college professors, only a handful—probably no more than a few thousand—claim membership in the action-community. But they have subtly transformed our old tree-shaded campuses

from transmitters of knowledge to brokerage houses of ideas. And no one has even attempted to guess how many action-intellectuals cluster in other institutions, for they wear no uniforms, carry no badges, and glide back and forth between centers of deceptive names and origins. Some make their base in foundations. Others are housed in new-fashioned "think-factories," commissioned by the government to think for it. All, however, are bound together by the dominant philosophy that no idea is neutral, no fancy so pure that somehow it is irrelevant to life.

THE FORD FOUNDATION, for example, wears the mantle of an old-fashioned, "do-good" charity, chartered "to advance human welfare." It has been described by cynics simply as "a large body of money completely surrounded by outstretched hands." Actually, it is the world's largest investor in new ideas—big ideas, little ideas, oddball ideas, foolish ideas, seminal ideas; and its president, McGeorge Bundy, is, in function, director of the "Federal Reserve Bank" of most new American intellectual enterprises. Each year from his wood-paneled office on Madison Avenue he must suggest to the trustees how to gamble and give away $200 million on ideas that somehow, for better or worse, will influence the thinking of the men who make American policy. Since 1950 he and his predecessors have spent nearly $3 billion on such ideas.

Ten years ago, for example, the Ford Foundation sensed that the easing of tension between Russia and the West was creating a moment for the "uncorking" of pressure—and began to finance an exchange of scholars between the world of Communism and the West. It proceeded next, in 1960, to initiate unprecedented meetings and conferences between Soviet and American leaders in science, education, industry; proceeded next, in 1963, to draw Western European leaders into the discussions on war, peace and disarmament. If the détente between East and West is today a fundamental of world politics, the Ford Foundation can boast that its $6 million investment in an idea first explored the opportunity to unlock doors for a tentative handshake across the threshold of friendship.

Or again: way back in 1952, before demographers alarmed the world with the phrase "population explosion," the Ford Foundation made a tiny grant ($60,000) in this problem area. Year by year the Foundation increased its investment in birth control until, by 1959, it had begun to assemble scholars in conferences on reproductive biology, on the motivations and communication of family planning. By 1960 it was financing adventures in birth control—from the laboratory work that developed the intrauterine coil to staffing the birth-control programs of India, North Africa, Egypt and Pakistan. Fifteen years and $90 million after Ford's initial effort, the Foundation can boast that the subject of birth control has almost ceased to be controversial and that its financial support has possibly been the largest energizing factor in the wave of public acceptance.

McGeorge Bundy's present dreams

go even further. Three programs now top his agenda: a family of plans, all designed to break the commercial networks' domination of American broadcasting by creation of a competitive, imaginative public television system; a massive expansion of the Foundation's support of Chinese studies—with the long-range hope of breaking through to an understanding of Red China; and an overriding research effect on the confrontation between black and white Americans which Bundy calls "the most urgent domestic concern of this country."

From the Ford Foundation, a hundred threads lead out to support or subsidize spin-off and dependent foundations: to a score of research centers studying Russia, Africa, the Middle East, the Atlantic Community; to the Brookings Institution, which drafted a law that governs presidential transition and, even before the Ford Foundation began to help it, structured the Marshall Plan and first conceived the idea that the U.S. must have a central Bureau of the Budget; to an agricultural research center in the Philippines, where scientists have discovered startling new ways to multiply rice production in Asia; to a scholarly research foundation in Princeton, which is exposing the extreme cost and squalor of political campaign financing.

If the past record is any guide, any of the 2,500 projects and ideas the Ford Foundation is now financing may someday result in new laws passed by legislators who will never know it was the Foundation which first moved the ideas on the way to their in-basket. "Our job is *not* to do what government does," says onetime professor Joseph McDaniel, secretary of the Foundation. "Our job is to help those who experiment and think *ahead* of the government."

ONE MUST cross the entire continent, to the cliffs of Santa Monica by the broad Pacific, to observe another archetype of new intellectual center. The RAND Corporation, first and greatest of the "think-factories," was created by the federal government in 1946 to gather thinkers who would ponder the nature of modern war.

Housed in a totally undistinguished complex of concrete-and-glass buildings, RAND is as ugly as any of the flat, new electronic plants of New England. One enters by appointment only; security guards check identity at every gate and issue visitors' permits. In its red-tabbed safe are to be found every secret of American security: our intelligence on China and Russia, the number of our bombs, the deployment of our missiles, the design and technology of the thermonuclears. Out of such information RAND's economists, physicists, engineers, social scientists have woven theories that have already changed American history.

BY NOW, OF course, RAND's triumphs are legend within government: its perception in 1953 of how the ICBM could be fashioned long before official Washington believed it feasible; its spectacular analysis of intercontinental bombing strategy, which saved the Strategic Air Command some $10 billion while at the same time increasing its power; its cost-effectiveness studies of strategy, which led to McNamara's reorganization of the Pentagon; its analysis of the resources and policies of Russia and Red China; its predictions of China's nuclear capacity.

RAND insists that the *way* its scholars think is just as important as *what* they think about or what their thinking has produced. "We have bred," says its new president, Henry Rowen, a tall transplanted Bostonian, "a new generation of people with a new kind of problem-solving skill. So few people can structure a problem: What's the hypothesis? What are the data? What are the alternatives? By what criteria should government assess alternatives? How much should we decide now—how much later?"

It is as difficult to measure RAND's ultimate influence as the Ford Foundation's. From RAND have developed a series of spinoff "think-factories," such as the Hudson Institute and the System Development Corporation, authorized—like RAND—to think for government as public-service, nonprofit corporations. RAND's graduates have left to spread their way of thinking at Harvard, M.I.T., Chicago—even to France. For a while, in the early '60s, they prowled the corridors of the Pentagon with such authority that one observer likened them to the Jesuits at the courts of Madrid and Vienna three centuries ago. When RAND talks, government need not obey, but it listens.

IT HAS BEEN relatively easy for American leaders to adjust to the input of ideas from its new "think-factories" and from the public-service foundations. It has, however, been far more difficult for American leaders to adjust to the changing nature of the parent source of the new elite—those great universities where first bubbles up the learning which the activists impose on policy. The adjustment is all the harder because the American universities of yesterday are still so familiar to the American memory, so washed in nostalgia that examining them today is as if one woke to find Frank Meriwell of Yale commanding an airborne division in Vietnam.

The University of Michigan at Ann Arbor, for example, is picture-book pretty. Its lithe girls and lean boys, its campus elms, its sprawl of bookstores and hamburger joints offer the tranquil portrait that most middle-aged Americans like to think of when they think of the Old School. The fact that NASA has placed $17 million in continuing contracts at the university is, of course, acceptable—that is science. The fact that the final validation of the Salk vaccine which conquered polio was announced from Michigan's Rackham Building is also acceptable—that, too, is science. The fact that GIs in South Vietnam use techniques developed by Michigan's post-World War II studies of battlefield surveillance is also acceptable—that is public service.

But beyond all this, the Ann Arbor campus pulses with such vitality that the very nature of its original mission seems, to some old graduates, to have changed. At the north edge of the central campus squats the Frieze Building, home of Michigan's School of Social Work. It is also the base of Professor Wilbur Cohen, now Under Secretary of HEW, and of Dean Fedele Fauri. The thinking of their school has overhauled, revised and rewritten this nation's social security laws; has fathered both Medicare and Medicaid; is changing our national standards of relief and welfare; is currently devising and shaping the comprehensive new legislation for an all-embracing National Youth Act.

Nearby stands the white brick building of Michigan's Economics Department. Its erstwhile chairman, Professor Gardner Ackley, like Professor Cohen, is on leave in Washington, overseer of the national economy as Chairman of the Council of Economic Advisers. On the fringe of the campus stands the cubist monolith of the Institute of Social Research, presided over by Dr. Rensis Likert, master of opinion-survey techniques. Every year the greatest corporations in the country send their economists to the university's November seminar on consumer-buying plans; the production schedules of General Motors and Ford respond to the institute's survey findings. Of Likert's institute's $4.5 million budget, only 10% comes from the parent state of Michigan; more than half comes from federal agencies, the rest from giant businesses and foundations that feel they simply must know what he learns before they can act wisely.

Some 25 to 30 new centers and institutes have been created at Ann Arbor since World War II, adventuring into such fields as computer techniques, mental health, water resources, nuclear engineering, the ecology of man. Each sets up a new impact wave. Dean William Haber of Michigan speaks from strength when he says, "The leadership of this country today lies on the campuses. It is the businessmen who are alienated from the revolutionary change of our life, rather than the college community."

All this is, without doubt, a kind of glory. Yet the Michigan legislature, which provides funds for this state university, is disturbed by the strength that builds from such intellectual energy. When courtly, aristocratic President Harlan Hatcher, soon to retire, pulls up before the state house in Lansing in his chauffered limousine and pleads for money for his university—its old buildings are too cramped to hold the burst of students its fame has drawn—does he plead as functionary or as master? Does the dominance of this one overpowering center of excellence at Ann Arbor contradict Michigan's egalitarian tradition? Should the Ann Arbor campus be reduced in size, as some legislators feel, and the state's nine other universities and colleges be developed to equality in excellence? In short, is their university getting too big for its breeches?

Such uneasy mutterings and mumblings of politicians are heard in states all across the nation—but louder and with most resentment in Washington. Who do the professors think they are? And, since the Boston power-center of

Harvard and M.I.T. stands to the entire nation as Ann Arbor stands to Michigan, it is well to examine what that remarkable energy cluster does, and to consider its dimensions. It is more than an archetype; it was the seedbed of the new elite, and it rises above all other intellectual centers as tall as Washington does above the state capitals.

THE CHARLES RIVER oozes down from Watertown, Mass. to divide Boston from Cambridge and, as it broadens, enters what is probably the greatest single gathering place of academic minds in the world. It passes the gypsy-colored turrets of Harvard's Houses on the one side, the neo-Georgian campus of Harvard Business School on the other; then opens into a basin as it skirts the blockhouse-modern outline of Boston University's new buildings, then streams toward the Atlantic, past the gray-limestone Roman temples of the Massachusetts Institute of Technology.

This complex of scholars has for generations been part of American history. Harvard is the oldest university in our country and its robust tradition of patriotism and involvement goes all the way back to the Revolutionary War, which its graduates triggered. Harvard's tradition of involvement has always been, however, a matter of individual response—whether by scholars, students or graduates—to outside calls for participation in public affairs. Today, though participation at Harvard is still individual, it has a new twist: a matter of aggressive initiative, a response to discovery in the halls of learning that forces scholars to act outside in the halls of power.

No catalogue of billboard names can give the full dimension of the current participation of Harvard's scholars in national affairs. But today, for example, back again teaching on campus are three former U.S. ambassadors: John Kenneth Galbraith (India), Edwin O. Reischauer (Japan) and Milton Katz (the Marshall Plan). Back on campus are Professors Archibald Cox (former Solicitor-General), Abram Chayes (former legal adviser to the State Department), Adam Yarmolinsky (former Special Counsel to the Department of Defense), Daniel P. Moynihan (former Assistant Secretary of Labor), Richard E. Neustadt (adviser to Truman, Kennedy and Johnson), Don K. Price Jr. (former Chairman of the Research and Development Board, Department of Defense). Away on leave in Washington or recently resigned are Harvard professors presiding over our income tax strategy, our policy in Latin America, our experiments in urban living.

Backing up such platoons of front-line operators are the support elements of great scholar-illuminators, equally influential on national policy. For example, Professor John K. Fairbank, America's most distinguished China-watcher, a former OSS man, never set foot in the new State Department building until this winter, when he gave his headlined public testimony before the Senate's Foreign Relations Committee. Yet this reflects his influence less than his private correspondence or the unan-

nounced comings-and-goings to Cambridge of U.S. senators who seek his wisdom on Asia's revolution. Professor Merle Fainsod has lifted American study of Soviet society and politics to entirely new levels of sophistication. Professor Simon Kuznets, by developing periodic measurements of U.S. economic activity, has delivered to Washington the analytical tools that are making Keynesian theory work.

Beyond these are the names, yet again, of the professors who, as consultants, make their influence felt on a per-diem or per-assignment basis in the military, in industry and in medicine as well as in government. A quick glance at Harvard's files one morning turned up a random and incomplete list of 50 names, but their range of penetration covered everything from national strategy (Professor Thomas Schelling, who urged on the government the hot line between Moscow and the White House) to steel-pricing (Professor Otto Eckstein, whose research braced John F. Kennedy for his crackdown on Big Steel). And beyond these were the Harvard laboratory men whose quiet, unpublicized work, generally benign, has been able nonetheless to deliver to the world such masterpieces of fright as napalm (Professor Louis Fieser) and LSD (first explored by the Harvard Medical School in 1952, then prostituted by Lecturer Timothy Leary, who was fired by Harvard before becoming high priest of psychedelics).

Now broaden the focus to include Harvard's chief partner in public adventures, M.I.T., and examine the substance of their joint contributions to American policy.

Most major universities casually credit themselves with acts of Congress or of their state which their professors have written into law. The University of Chicago proudly asserts that in the halls of its Law School, its scientists and law professors drafted the first version of the McMahon Act which placed control of atomic energy in the hands of civilians rather than the military. Berkeley can boast of atomic legislation and of enforcing federal land laws. But Harvard and M.I.T. together are responsible for an almost unbelievable range of statutes.

As EARLY AS 1954, for example, a group of Harvard and M.I.T. professors began to get together privately on Friday afternoons. Their knowledge told them the world was at the rim of nuclear destruction, and they felt it was their duty to peer beyond the rim and think about arms control. By 1956 the original group had grown to a formal seminar in which defense scientists, political scientists and historians joined as a working group. By 1960 they were hammering their ideas into the speeches of John F. Kennedy's presidential campaign. By 1961 four of the members of their seminar (Jerome Wiesner, Mc-George Bundy, Arthur Schlesinger Jr., Carl Kaysen) held White House posts. By 1963 they had seen their ideas written into international law as the test ban treaty. In response to pleas from presidents, senators, congressmen, the

Harvard-M.I.T. professors have by now written a dozen major laws, from investment-tax credits to labor legislation, from civil rights to education and model cities and metropolitan development.

The outburst of public activity, as we have seen, disturbs other scholars, even at Harvard and M.I.T., who interpret it as a subtle betrayal of the real purpose of scholarship, the pursuit of truth for its own sake.

In Washington and at other political centers, however, it disturbs other men for different reasons—not so much for the power that Harvard and M.I.T. wield in national thinking (or the right and wrong of their contributions) as for the way this great center links together with the other centers at Ford, in California, in the Ivy League belt, in Washington itself. "If I had my way," burst out one of the highest executives of the Johnson Administration, "there wouldn't be another federal dollar going to those schools or laboratories in Boston and California. They're draining the rest of the country of its brains."

Those who see a brain cartel inexorably taking over the nation's thinking can trace, like all amateurs of cartel theory, neat and precise interlockings and directorates: Harvard Dean Mc-George Bundy leaves Cambridge to go to the White House as presidential security assistant, then emerges as president of the Ford Foundation to be central banker for all American ideas. Carl Kaysen teaches at Harvard, is simultaneously a consultant at RAND, then leaves for the White House as a

Kennedy assistant, then emerges to become head of the Institute for Advanced Study in Princeton. Dean Rusk, professor of government at Mills College in California, enters government during World War II, leaves it 12 years later to become head of the Rockefeller Foundation in New York, then returns to become Secretary of State. Kermit Gordon leaves Williams, becomes a member of the Council of Economic Advisers, then Director of the Bureau of the Budget, then emerges to become head of the Brookings Institution. Charles Hitch goes from Oxford to RAND to Yale and to RAND again, achieves distinction as a RAND economist, becomes comptroller of the Department of Defense at the Pentagon, then emerges at Berkeley as a vice president of the University of California.

John F. Kennedy sets up a task force in the election of 1960 to screen names for candidates to run his Department of State. Of the first 82 names on the list handed him, 63 are members of the Council on Foreign Relations in New York. Johnson succeeds Kennedy and creates a new Department of Housing and Urban Development. Its No. 1 man, Secretary Robert Weaver, is an ex-professor at Columbia; its No. 2 man, Under Secretary Robert C. Wood, is a professor on leave from M.I.T.; its No. 3 man, Assistant Secretary Charles M. Haar, is a professor on leave from Harvard.

Those who like to draw lines between boxes with names in them ask: Is this truly a community of scholars? Or a new kind of political machine?

NOTHING ANNOYS the senior action-intellectuals more than this kind of cartel diagram. They see themselves as a community, with recognizable community centers across the nation. But a community is different from a cartel. A cartel sets out to exclude; a community reaches out to include. And their community, they insist, is the most open in the U.S. Credentials for entry are, simply, brains—plus the ability, the cunning, or know-how to get their ideas listened to in high places. No one gets rich. Scholars start as consultants to government at $50 a day (plus $12 per diem) and reach a peak of $100 a day (plus $16 per diem) as top advisers to the White House or the Atomic Energy Commission. Any good professor can earn more as a consultant elsewhere.

"My fee to industry is $250 a day at home, or $300 a day plus full expenses if I have to travel," says Robert Machol, professor of systems at Northwestern University in Chicago. "The post office pays me $75 a day when I advise them—and I lose money on expenses—but it's the government of the United States. There's nothing like it."

No ethnic barriers, no financial-means test, no geographical origin prevents a scholar from entering the intellectual community and, with luck, making his way via Harvard or RAND or M.I.T. or Michigan to the very top. No professional seats are inherited the way that executive leadership of business, estates and sometimes labor unions is. No dynastic names open the ladder to the top, as do the names Kennedy, Taft, Stevenson, Rockefeller or Roosevelt in politics.

Instead of dynasties, there are traditions; instead of conspirators who guide a cartel, there are only father-figures, great teachers who pass on to younger men not only old learning but the zest for application. A Robert Oppenheimer or Ernst Lawrence of California, a Julian Levi of Chicago, a Rensis Likert at Michigan, a Felix Frankfurter of Harvard—teachers like these breed and recruit their talent from the rawest of student material, then select the best, place them, and guide them over the years on the zigzag escalation back and forth between campus, foundation and government to leadership. How such father-teachers have affected American government over the past 20 years could be demonstrated by taking any one of a dozen of them. Professor Edward Sagendorph Mason will do as well as any.

PROFESSOR MASON of Harvard is still, at 68, a large, burly man, his balding head a Daniel Webster dome, his high cheekbones and Roman nose giving him a senatorial visage, his virile Midwestern voice strong enough to fill any lecture hall. Appointed a junior economics instructor at Harvard way back in 1923, when Harvard was a bastion of the most conservative economic views, Mason found his thinking changed by the Depression and then went to Washington as a consultant. The New Deal was first reaching out for scholars then, and the Labor Depart-

ment asked him to do a study of the inflexibility of industrial pricing. By the time World War II broke out, he had learned something of Washington ways; and when his colleague, Professor William Langer of Harvard, became chief of research and analysis at OSS, he was ready to serve as that office's chief economist.

To be chief economist of the OSS was a new level of academic experience, for Mason's economic analyses were to guide the heavy bombers of the 8th Air Force in target selection, locating the guts of German industry so that the planes could pick those guts apart and destroy them. To assist him, Mason chose 10 or 12 young men for what, at a university, would be called a graduate-student seminar; half a dozen were sent to London where they became "the Jockey Committee" of the combined Allied Air Forces. These young scholars were to learn early the terror that can coil in ideas—that ideas can not only create but kill. "Those last few months," recalls one of them, "when we were choosing the last cities in Germany, we knew we were just killing them, murdering civilians, and we had to go on." They were to learn responsibility, too. They read the secret cables and knew that one three-star general was telling Eisenhower that the D-day invasion would fail and *he* could not take responsibility. Yet the bright young men had to assume theirs.

Professor Walt W. Rostow, now chief White House security assistant to President Johnson, was one of Mason's young assistants and became secretary of the Jockey Committee. He remembers: "We were all kids. Guys our age were being sent to die over Germany. I couldn't qualify for the Air Force because of my eyesight. It was important to me that if my friends died over target, they should die well—on a worthwhile mission." Professor Carl Kaysen, onetime deputy security assistant to John F. Kennedy, was another of Mason's young men and he remembers: "It was a dedicated, passionate group. We were kids, captains and majors, telling the whole world what to do. We knew more about what was going on in German industry than the whole apparatus of regulars. We worked harder. We lived it around the clock, four or five of us in one big house in London, talking shop all through the day and night. I was 22 or 23, seeing high politics and government from the inside."

None of the young men ever forgot the experience—or the excitement of what ideas, linked to government, could do. Of Mason's young OSS recruits, at least six went on to become professors: Charles Kindleberger and Walt Rostow at M.I.T., Carl Kaysen at Harvard, Moses Abramovitz at Stanford, Kermit Gordon at Williams, Tibor Scitovsky at Berkeley. All passed on to their students, in turn, the lore of government as they had acquired it from Mason when they too were young.

Mason was to train not one generation of young men but several. With the war over, Mason went back to Harvard to study the economics of the postwar world, in particular, the economic problems of emerging nations. At Har-

vard's new postwar Center for International Affairs he created an advisory committee for underdeveloped nations—and recruited another generation of young men to reorganize the finances of Pakistan and Iran, to examine the educational system of Nigeria, to survey and help (as they are doing today) the economies and problems of Ghana, Colombia, Liberia, Greece, Malaysia.

Not since 1946 has Mason spent a year without a government assignment, obligation or consultancy. But he still teaches Economics 287 in Room 217 of Harvard's neo-classic Littauer Center. His career is summed up in no specific piece of legislation. It has crested, rather, in the attitudes of a generation of young men now grown to command positions in American policy and power. His famous graduates include not only his OSS boys. Postwar protégés include Kingman Brewster, now president of Yale; Anthony Solomon, now Assistant Secretary of State for Economic Affairs; Donald F. Turner, antitrust chief at the Department of Justice; David Bell, former chief of AID, who now heads the Ford Foundation's vast international division; Lincoln Gordon, Assistant Secretary of State, about to become president of Johns Hopkins University.

What Mason has taught, over and above pure economics, is not only what governments *do* in public affairs, but what they *should* do, and how. Nor does he find his career strange, any more than would James Bryant Conant, Edward Teller, William Langer, Charles Hitch. This, they all feel, is the duty of a scholar—to take part in public affairs. But if their present influence is now so great, it is chiefly because of their time and generation—for it has been the jolt and sweep of change as much as their instruction which has created the community of action-intellectuals.

Always when there comes a periodic deep shift in mood, a great undefined need to alter the structure and shape of American life, the American system has sought and found idea-men to guide it. Thus the present obtrusive eminence of American intellectuals in practical politics presages, like the flocking of geese in the fall, a movement of political climate. They have been the heralds of change since the beginning of American history.

LIFE June 9, 1967

ACTION-INTELLECTUALS

Part II: Scholarly Impact on the Nation's Past

From the moment they dropped anchor in the shelter of the bay, they knew it was to be different. There was the winter forest of New England in its darkness, hiding God-knew-what savages, beasts and dangers; and beyond, more wilderness ridged by mountains, folded with more wilderness running to unknown oceans; a geography written on by no one, a history unmade—an entire land to be filled with people in a pattern that ideas could shape.

What ideas they did not yet know, except that those of the old country would not do. So in the captain's cabin of the *Mayflower* the Pilgrims signed their Compact: to let themselves be governed by whatever new ideas should seem wisest to them once ashore.

It was a century and a half before they had educated the men and fashioned the ideas which created the phenomenon of the United States. The skies were high, the king in London was far away, and the colonial thinkers had to work out for themselves the problems of man, government, frontier and environment by rubbing education against reality. In colonial Williamsburg, a young law student named Thomas Jefferson would linger at the doors of Virginia's House of Burgesses to hear the debates of men interested in raw politics, not court politics. Harvard graduates led the Boston Tea Party in 1773. A year later, the boys of the Boston Latin School mustered out America's first student-protest delegation to call on the British general because the Redcoats had cindered the snow slopes of Beacon Hill and ruined their sledding.

Protest was in their blood; their grandfathers had left England after a century of war when the word "Protestant" meant exactly what it said. For them, ideas involved action. Yet ideas and learning had always to be tested against the experience of free men in a new land. Thus, in a collective burst of genius, their thinkers came to fashion a new invention: the Constitution of the United States.

This Federal Constitution was something totally new on earth—a theorist's dream which, for the first time, freed men from imposed authority and made power the instrument of man's will, not the King's. Its stubbornest problem was the demand of Order for a strong central government, contradicted by Freedom's demand for liberty of the individual. The constitution-makers neatly settled the question by dividing power between a federal government and state governments in a balance sufficient for their own generation, yet leaving the precarious balance for other generations to debate in the future.

The best scientific thought of the day colored the making of the American system; and science at the time was based on Newtonian mechanics, a clockwork view of a universe checked and balanced by invisible wheels and pulleys. The core idea, the mainspring, of the early American theorists was that free men, acting each in his own best interests, would by some magic law of politics always find the right solution. When tried, the idea seemed to work like clockwork, too.

HISTORIAN Arthur M. Schlesinger Jr. points out that revolutions are always made by intellectuals, who sooner or later are always replaced by practical men. Intellectuals see new problems first, they are gifted with the words to write manifestos and speeches, can inflame the passions of ordinary men with visions of what may be or what ought to be. And then the pragmatists take over as revolutions dispense with their theorists. In America it took a full generation, until the election of rough-hewn Andrew Jackson in 1828, for the practical men to take over—men who simply wound and re-wound the clockwork mechanism the Founding Fathers had devised.

The vitality of the system is best demonstrated by what followed Andrew Jackson. For 70 years, with the brief moral interruption of the Civil War, men seeking their private interests worked within the frame of the founders' dream. Trappers penetrated the wilderness, gunslingers followed them to make a frontier, pioneers cleared the land, immigrant hordes poured in after them knowing that what one worked for or got or grabbed might, in this country, be held. In the process, they created at once the world's most effective get-things-done civilization and system of politics of unmatched squalor and vulgarity.

By the middle '80s of the last century, greed and grabbing, spoils and corruption soiled Washington, where florid and baroque men of action used the national government simply as an instrument of their appetites. The greatest American historian of his day, Henry Adams, a sensitive dandy, grandson and great-grandson of Presidents, mourned: "No period so thoroughly ordinary had been known in American politics since Christopher Columbus first disturbed the balance of American Society. . . ."

It was the mid-point of this era, a century ago, that Justin Morrill, a Vermont storekeeper-merchant-financier, unknowingly triggered what was to become the present blast of academic penetration into government. The wartime Congress of the '60s was swept by what we would call a giveaway mood—free land for homesteaders to fill the empty map, free land for the railroads to build tracks to get them there. Thus in 1862 Congressman Morrill achieved another giveaway—free land to endow state colleges whose leading purpose would be "to teach . . . agriculture and the mechanic arts. . . ." America was then the land of the farmer—and whatever could be done to help him would help business and railways, too. Morrill's "land-grant colleges" were to be "service institutions," offering higher education to ordinary people for the first time. They were a complete break with the European tradition of the university as an institution for training a young élite, to govern empires, to serve God, or to be clerks, for those who did. After prolonged debate Congress acted on his idea and approved.

Morrill, a spare-framed Yankee with trim side whiskers, was a "sound dollar" man whose thorough-going conservatism was unblemished except for a delightful and aberrant interest in the beauties of Washington architecture. By 1890, Morrill could see the first flowering of his dreams. Railways crisscrossed the continent, farmers filled the land, and the census of that year reported that, at last, no man could draw any frontier line between settled America and the wilderness. And Morrill's land-grant colleges were truly beginning to serve the farmers, teaching them in each state the best seeds for each climate and soil, increasing yield per acre and poundage on the rumps of beeves. But some of the colleges had developed an astonishing vitality and would go even further in exploring what "service" meant. In particular, the University of Wisconsin.

———

IT SEEMED TO the academics gathered at Madison, Wisconsin, that the farmer had other problems besides insects, hail, frost and the sterility of his prize boar. For example: railways whose rates gouged him, banks and money-lenders that cheated him. The University of Wisconsin had begun to study such other problems, too, as part of the human ecology of the farmer's life—or, as later wordsmiths would say, his "sociosphere."

In 1892 the university set up its first department of economics and began to assemble a most remarkable energy-cluster of early social scientists whose professorial studies—of the social problems the strong and organized might cause the weak and unorganized—were causing fever in the blood of the state's politics. And when, in 1900, this fever produced a political tribune, Governor Robert La Follette, it was natural that he should turn to his old school, the University of Wisconsin, for guidance on writing its professors' ideas into law. "Professors on University Hill in Madison," one historian was to observe, "were only a mile away from the politicians on Capitol Hill."

What happened in Wisconsin between 1900 and 1906 was viewed by the established Eastern order as revolution, socialism, or just plain tomfoolery. The university's scholars researched, then helped draft for La Follette, laws that limited the railways' ability to discriminate on rates, that made industry bear the same property-burden in taxes as individuals; they went further and intruded into politics with laws that set up direct-election primaries and established a state civil service system. And when, in 1906, La Follette moved to Washington as senator, he carried with him a system of "progressive" ideas that was to change national politics.

Within a decade, the word "progressive" was the label on a ferment that ran from coast to coast—but the yeast in that ferment came from the campus at Madison, Wisconsin, and could be traced directly back to such professors as Commons, Ely, Ross, Meyer. From that original ferment were to come, much later, Social Security, TVA, Unemployment Insurance and regulation of the stock market.

The large consequences of the new ideas bubbling among American scholars were not immediately visible, however, in the early 1900s; for no historical development proceeds in a straight line from given point of origin to final climax. Periodically the stream of academic penetration in American politics was to broaden, then choke to a trickle—but never entirely to dry up in modern times. Mostly, it fluctuated in force with the nature and style of the man who sat in the White House.

Thus, it was entirely natural for a patrician Theodore Roosevelt—author, historian and adventurer—to invite scholars to his White House. His elegant taste could summon Cellist Pablo Casals to play there, enjoy the table-talk of Sculptor Augustus Saint-Gaudens, make a companion of historian Henry Adams. And as Progressive demands rose in politics, it was natural for him

to invite Professor John R. Commons (Wisconsin) to discuss labor laws, Professor Richard T. Ely (Wisconsin) to discuss tax law, Professor William Z. Ripley (Harvard) to discuss railway legislation, and Nicholas Murray Butler (Columbia) as a generalist, much as Kennedy later used Arthur Schlesinger Jr.

The influence of scholars on government was, however, not always predictable by the background of the Chief Executive. Woodrow Wilson, himself a professor of government and university president, displayed to other scholars the attitude of a country-school superintendent toward apprentice-teachers. His administration reflected this parochialism. When, for example, the U.S. entered the First World War, the American Chemical Society sent a deputation to visit Newton D. Baker, Secretary of War, and offered the full mobilization of their resources to prepare for the violence that might come. Baker thanked them, asked them to return the next day after he had contemplated, received them again and dismissed them. He had, he said, made an inquiry; he did not need them; the War Department, he had learned, already had *a* chemist.

But Woodrow Wilson's First World War was, in American history, a climactic trauma—the hour of loss of innocence. It required America to make contact with and thrust itself upon an outside world in which the nation had previously been only an observer. War required the first modern mobilization of men—in vast numbers and aggregates under a logical, central direction. And for this, it required academic participation—but within precisely defined limits. Businessmen (under Bernard Baruch) organized the war economy—but book-bearing economists and professors were also needed to sift and pattern the figures. Above all, war brought America face to face with strange people speaking strange languages. Thus came about the first specialized task-force, then called The Inquiry, to prepare our positions for the ultimate peace gathering at Versailles.

THE PROFESSORS and academicians who largely staffed this committee could trace boundaries in Central Europe back to the Byzantine Empire, and they could indicate the documents in Greek or Latin that supported or contradicted what Woodrow Wilson and Colonel House thought might be proper borders in the Danube Valley. Such professors were, however, only specialists, technicians—not policy-makers; American statesmen paid as little heed to them as did the British delegation to the wisdom of John Maynard Keynes of Cambridge.

Nevertheless, the national innocence lost in the First World War could never be recovered. A succession of three presidents—Harding, Coolidge, Hoover—tried to bring America home to live on the simple straight-way of Sinclair Lewis' Main Street. But Main Street was doomed, as were the ideas it had sprung from, outworn by time. Though Main Street businessmen still swore by the

theories of Adam Smith and John Stuart Mill, that simple faith was already obsolete.

Smith and Mill had shattered Pharaonic economics with their belief that the invisible hand of private interest would always guide free-enterprisers in their own selfish interests, to produce what society needed most. By the early '30s, this idea had run its day and failed—America hungered, industry had collapsed, farmers burned crops and pitch-forked sheriffs, 13 million unemployed shuffled in the desolate streets, and the greatest of all depressions in history had begun.

Thus entered Franklin D. Roosevelt and the first brain-trust.

TODAY IT IS accepted as entirely normal that scholars should contribute ideas during political campaigns. But the use of scholars in coarse, active campaigning was fresh when, in January of 1932, Franklin D. Roosevelt set out to run for president. His obvious issue had to be the Depression. Yet, what would he say? His confidant, Samuel Rosenman, replied they could best learn what to say by talking with the scholars of the universities, where economists, lawyers and thinkers abounded. Enthusiastically, Professor Raymond C. Moley became captain of a Columbia University task force to provide ideas.

"We were," says Professor Adolf Berle, reminiscing, "freaks—like phrenologists. A politician who talked to a professor in those days kept it a deep, dark secret. And you couldn't get the best professors into politics—politics were dirty and squalid, they thought." Others took a dimmer view of professors. "Economists," remarked Charley Michelson, the Democrats' chief speech-writer of the 1932 campaign, "economists are like the buttons on the sleeve of a man's jacket. They're useless, but they look good. You have to have them."

Roosevelt, of course, would have won his election had he been advised by Aimee Semple McPherson or Karl Marx rather than the professorial brain-trust. It was what these men contributed to the nature of American government *after* the election, however, that marked a watershed; and it is important to measure the development of their ideas: how far and in what stages they stretched through the years of American life to their present triumph; and why, perhaps, these ideas will, like Adam Smith's, now stretch no longer to meet the problems of our times.

The early academic brain-trusters were merely a corporal's guard during the campaign—Moley, Berle, Tugwell. But they could recruit—they were webbed into the intellectual underground of the nation at all the great campuses where ideas, untapped, had been accumulating. Universities were places where scholarly discipline required men to study the changes of times past, and to contemplate new changes; suddenly professorial names like Thurman Arnold, James Landis, George F. Warren began to appear in headlines.

These were all senior idea men. But

beneath them was a janizariat of younger men, mostly lawyers, all fresh from the classrooms, with no practical experience to cramp them, in whom burned theories taken fresh from professors' lips or books. One catches the flavor of the period best from a young Harvard Law School lawyer, James Rowe, since grown to be one of the authentically great men of American politics, adviser to Presidents from Roosevelt to Johnson.

"Tommy Corcoran sent me up to Harvard Law School in 1935," Rowe recalls, "to bring back 20 graduates. Times were hard then; even the brightest young men couldn't find jobs. We came in as lawyers, on working jobs; then we brought in the economists; then we coalesced and spread out. We were a community.

"At parties we brought our girls or our wives and we'd sit debating until 2 o'clock in the morning—no dancing, 10 guys all sitting on the floor arguing. The question then was whether people were going to eat or not. Back in Montana, where I came from, in Rosebud County, 90% of our people were on relief. We had leaders and gods, men like Ickes and Corcoran, Cohen and Jim Landis, Bill Douglas, Thurman Arnold, Jerome Frank. And we had an enemy— the businessman was the enemy."

The idea that knit this community, professors and law clerks alike, was a simple one. It was that the invisible hand which Adam Smith had seen directing all economic affairs was now dead. People starved because the theory required them to starve. So the hand of government, from Washington, must replace the invisible hand. The young lawyers had clients who, though anonymous, were real: the hungry and unemployed; workingmen trying to organize unions; farmers dispossessed of land; little investors cheated of savings by Wall Street bucket-shop operators. And for such client groups they were the intermediaries between ideas that could save them and politicians who could enact ideas into law. Crudely and blunderingly, they went to work.

Two emotions infused these young thinkers. The first was an optimism about achieving direct social change through the instruments of central government. The second was a disquiet, in some a disgust, with the underlying premises and foundations of American society as it was.

It was the experience of World War II that separated these two emotions, subtly dividing the activist American intellectual from the alienated and the ivory-tower intellectual, a cleavage that persists to this day. By the time the war broke out, the Harvard Law School graduates held almost every general-counsel post in the government's cabinet-level departments; and the young men had matured. They had, in the early '30s, seriously debated whether to nationalize all America's banks and business. But the war-effort made them partners with American industry, bringing them into contact with men like Harriman and Hoffman, Lovett and McCloy, Forrestal and Patterson—the best in American business.

"There was this growth of under-standing in the war," recalls Kermit Gordon, the new head of the Brookings Institution, "between academics and business. They came to terms with the foundations of our industrial society. They found we didn't need to shatter the premises of our society to make progress." The distrust had disappeared; the belief in direct government action remained; and in such wartime agencies as OSS (Office of Strategic Services), OWI (Office of War Information), OPA (Office of Price Administration) scores of younger scholars were beginning to learn the trill of government action, all sharing a new, unworded philosophy; that men of ideas and theories were almost a Fifth Estate of government. Recognizing the Lords Temporal of political power, they were to be the Lords Spiritual of theory.

World War II amplified the influence of academics further, with a new and genuinely revolutionary development—the organization of American science for war by scholar-leaders. For, in the late '30s and early '40s, scholars began to foresee, long before the military, what modern war would require. And it was the Harvard-M.I.T. center of scholars that led the invasion of the war effort by American learning.

HARVARD PRESIDENT James Bryant Conant and M.I.T. Vice President Vannever Bush had both recognized early that the war was coming; both had had junior experience with the bungling organization of American science in World War I; and both now had access to the court of Harvard-man Franklin D. Roosevelt. Their idea, which Roosevelt accepted so enthusiastically, was that scientists and scholars could best serve government if they skipped all military or other bureaucracies and were organized independently in what came to be known as the Office of Scientific Research and Development. The hardware inventions and developments that came from this office are history: atom bombs and radar, antibiotics and sonar, explosives and napalm. Yet their greatest invention was, perhaps, political: a new way of using brains. For the OSRD decided not to centralize or mobilize brain-power within government, but to build on existing strength outside government—and to do so by the novel method of subcontracting thought. M.I.T. was to develop radar; California Tech was to study rockets; the University of Chicago was to explore sustained nuclear reaction; the University of California was responsible for developing the bomb; and the large industrial corporations—Du Pont, General Electric, Union Carbide—were to machine, as hardware subcontractors, what the scientists dreamed of.

What they produced dazzled Congress, the world, even the military. Professors were in. "We ran around after the war," says a Pentagon general, "collecting professors like butterflies. Everyone wanted the flashiest collection of butterflies for his branch." Congress had been so impressed that, in an outburst of enthusiasm, it wanted professors to solve everything—from cancer to the common cold—by creating one enormous, centralized government department to oversee all scientific effort.

Conant and Bush scotched this effort and, departing, left behind what, to the administrative eye, seemed like the most wasteful, confusing and overlapping system of government aid to learning ever devised. When asked one day many years later about its apparent confusion, Conant replied, "We planned it that way so that the NSF, the AEC, the NIH, the Army, the Air Force would all have independent funds for science—so that no one government agency could turn off all the spigots at once."

The breakthrough had been made; government was now to intertwine itself through American learning—through its universities, laboratories, social research centers and science—in a complexity never approached by any other country, in a lavishness which now runs at some $15 billion a year. By corollary, any university where a group of professors seized on an idea remotely describable as of national concern knew where it could be financed. The defense scientists had the first finger in the pie—but social scientists, students of foreign affairs, mathematicians, linguists could follow their lead. Government money, then foundation money, enriched the imagination and enlarged the ambition of scholars to totally new dimensions. The ability to sell explorations or ideas to government became a fundamental disturbance in academic life as many professors swiftly learned that a good promoter advanced as quickly as, or more quickly than, a good scholar.

"All you have to do is call yourself an 'Interdisciplinary Center' or, better yet, an 'Institute,' to qualify for a national defense grant. And all you need for a center is one warm body, a good idea, a couple of assistants—and you're in business," said one rueful professor recently. Thus, those who knew best the ways of Washington and the routes to the money-spigots of the various government agencies entered into a bizarre new world where they were, at once, supplicants for largesse, yet guides to government thinking.

No hard-and-fast generalization can cover the 15 years between the end of the war and the advent of John F. Kennedy, but the orthodoxies of the era can be roughly summarized:

▶The governing conviction of the action-intellectual held, unquestionably, that Washington was where the action was, that the central government alone was staffed with the quality personnel needed to launch great new programs. Washington also conferred a matchless campus prestige on those it summoned to its use ("There's nothing that impresses a seminar—or the faculty—more than to be called from the room because the White House is on the phone," said a Princeton professor not long ago). State and city politics bored the scholars. Washington was The Scene. If a man had influence in a Washington agency, his ideas might someday run as writ across the country.

▶Professors fundamentally were still advisers rather than policy-makers. The great Robert Oppenheimer was never once invited to meet Franklin D. Roosevelt or talk with him all the while his mind directed the shaping of the first A-bomb; Oppenheimer met Harry Truman, in a group conference led by Secretary Henry L. Stimson, only once before the bomb dropped.

▶Overwhelmingly, the activists were Democrats. The older men had learned the ways of government under Roosevelt, the Democrat, during the war. They passed their lessons on to younger men. An occasional Kingman Brewster (now president of Yale) could and did serve government (in the Marshall Plan) and remained a Yankee Republican; as did James Bryant Conant, president of Harvard. A scholar like Malcolm Moos might serve Eisenhower in the White House (Eisenhower's brain-trust was once described as "Mac Moos in a room with mirrors around him"), but such men were rare. Home, for the intellectuals, was the Democratic Party—the party of Roosevelt, of Truman, of Acheson, above all the party of Adlai Stevenson.

▶All through this period, moreover, knowledge was exploding as research quickened—not only in defense science and nuclear energy, or in astrophysics and space. There were the grating new problems of men in changing communities—new inner and outer frontiers which only scholars, now so generously funded, explored and from which they brought back first reports to influence policy.

Scholars began to illuminate the condition of the Negro. A solitary child psychologist, Kenneth B. Clark, by his research on the psychological crippling of child minds by segregation was probably as important an influence on the Supreme Court's historic desegregation decision of 1954 as all the NAACP's mobilization of legal talent. Overseas, the familiar globe blistered with the names of new, independent nations about whom tradition gave us no knowledge or understanding—but at home, old universities had already incubated an array of interdisciplinary centers to study the developing nations of Asia, Africa and Latin America.

Where else could government go for guidance in an increasingly complicated world except to the scholars who graphed the complications?

IT IS COMMON and quite easy to draw a sharp distinction in technique and style between the Kennedy and Johnson administrations—and the contrast cuts.

But what binds them together historically is more important—for the continuum of their administrations was to close the Rooseveltian phase of American history, to see the triumph of one set of ideas and to force the groping search for another set still undefined.

Revolution had swept around the outer world since World War II; but the world of Americans-at-home had changed almost as dramatically. Mass education had altered the climate of the nation. During Franklin Roosevelt's second term, in 1938, only 1,350,000 college students strolled the campuses. And they were then outnumbered by

the union proletariat of two industries alone—the railways (958,000) and the coal miners (538,000). A generation later there were six million college students in the country; and this campus proletariat had reversed the numerical proportion to a staggering 8 to 1 over the diminished handful of 782,000 laborers who still worked automated mines and railways.

Intellectuals had worked their way into the fabric of government itself. From the New Deal on, the increasing receptivity to ideas of the Executive Departments had magnified the intellectuals' influence. But by 1960, education had begun to change Congress itself and create a receptivity there, too.

"We used to look at Congress as a bunch of C-plus students," says one professor-in-government. By 1960 the Senate boasted no less than five ex-professors—Douglas, McGee, Mansfield, McCarthy, Fulbright. (It has since added three more, Miller, Tower and McGovern; by 1966 the House, in addition to 226 law degrees, held 19 members with advanced academic degrees.) Both Executive and Congress were on the right frequencies to pick up new messages.

It remained for Kennedy, entering this changing scene, to make brains fully operational by wiring his Washington senatorial office directly to his natural political base in Massachusetts. As early as 1958, he dispatched his chief-of-staff, Ted Sorensen, to an evening meeting at the Commander Hotel off Harvard Square in Cambridge to set up an Academic Advisory Committee.

A year later, formed up in ranks by Professors Arthur Schlesinger and John Kenneth Galbraith, the campus corps could deliver to Kennedy not only speech material, position papers, guidance, but also personalities such as Wiesner and Bundy, Cox and Keppel, Chayes and Rostow, Kaysen and Hilsman, Tobin and Nitze, who would go on with him to Washington, not just as advisers to policy-makers but as policy-makers themselves, *their* hands on the levers of power.

What Kennedy began with his volunteer study group in 1959, Johnson lifted to a new level with his task forces. The Johnson task forces of 1964 and 1965 were government groups in which scholars were paid for their time and bracketed with budget officers and bureaucrats, so that ideas might come off the line ready for shaping into law. "Johnson has a talent for power," observes Bill Moyers, once his closest personal aide. "Power these days is brains, and he goes for it." Only a man with such a taste for power could have his White House check out, late last fall, his intellectual score as against Kennedy's and come up with this incomplete yet flattering Executive nose-count: five Rhodes scholars at top level, 77 intellectuals badged with a Phi Beta Kappa key (five in the Cabinet, one in the White House, one in the legislative branch, 13 ambassadors, 23 in sub-Cabinet positions, 29 appointed in independent or regulatory agencies, five as bureau chiefs), plus 33 major appointments fresh from professorships and 40 more with other specific scholarly background.

A reporter, visiting Washington again and again in the Kennedy-Johnson era gradually found his old political sources of information being rivaled, then outmatched, by his academic sources of information. On reflection this, too, seemed natural; for the windows the academicians offered a reporter to look through were the same windows through which the Chief Executive himself peered. A new syllogism could be made, embracing all politics from Platonic root to American experience:

Men always have the choice between chaos and order, and generally prefer order. But order requires power, and all power is exercised, in final analysis, by individual men. Every President is subject to the traditional danger of the prince-in-his-court—that he will be suffocated by the flattery of his servants, his information choked by what his bureaucrats report. The leader thus desperately needs an independent check. A free press once provided this check. But knowledge now increases at such speed, with such complexity, that the press is inadequate to the responsibility. Only in the universities or the foundations are men paid to study, year after year, all those issues which a Chief Executive must grasp. Thus, without scholars, an American Chief Executive can no longer operate, or supervise, his bureaucracies.

IN ANY ONE of the last three administrations one can reach into the record to see the Chief Executive turn to scholars for help in judging his bureaucracies, then see the scholars slowly changing roles from specialist or medieval wise man to operator, and then policy-maker. One can trace it best, however, in the life of an individual like, say Professor Jerome Wiesner of M.I.T., whose service to the nation spans all the administrations from F.D.R.'s through Eisenhower's to Kennedy's and Johnson's.

Wiesner, now provost at M.I.T., is by profession a student of electronics and by repute a genius in the field of communications theory. Like so many young engineers and physicists of the time, the suction of the Manhattan Project in World War II drew him to Los Alamos, where he worked on what he now vaguely describes as "the electronic guts of the bomb." He went on to supervise the electronic monitoring of the first postwar Bikini bomb tests, then masterminded the Lincoln Laboratory's security-shrouded communications breakthrough which linked computorial science and electronic relays in the DEW (Distant Early Warning) network and is now the backbone of the American field communications in Vietnam. Occasionally in the period of the late '40s, back at Cambridge, he would meet on Sunday mornings with a group of Harvard and M.I.T. professors at the Irving Street home of Professor Arthur Schlesinger to discuss problems of peace and war. Yet, officially, Wiesner was only a consultant and specialist.

During the '50s, however, came the spectacular series of scientific break-throughs—computorial control of military systems, the thermonuclear warhead, the development of rockets—which revolutionized intercontinental

war. Yet the scientists, like Wiesner, who created these wonders still operated as directed by the bureaucracies in patterns framed by the political information of other men. In 1957, for the fist time, Wiesner graduated to a higher level, as scientific member of the Gaither Committee, whose presidential commission from Eisenhower empowered it to examine all national defense. National defense at this level means total and rigorous examination of the motivations, the facts, the planning of all the bureaucracies serving the President in defense.

The President, for example, had declared officially to all the world that the U.S. would never strike first with nuclear bombs; but at SAC headquarters Wiesner was told by generals that, of course, Americans had to strike first, and any president who didn't was out of his mind. The President had been informed, and believed, that he had 400 massive bombers on 15-minute alert; Wiesner found that only 20 to 40 of the big bombers could get off the ground in any hour.

"I was shocked," he recalls, "by how ill-informed the President, the Department of Defense, even the Secretary of the Air Force were about our country." Even more was he shocked by looking, for the first time as a supreme policy-adviser, at the outer fringe of the terror he had helped create. America was certainly able to destroy all Russia; but if the Russians were capable of even 50% of the American effort (which they were), they could so punish America as to end its civilization. At the most optimistic estimate, 30 million Americans would die in the counterstroke, 150 million in the most pessimistic estimate—and those who survived would "live in a radioactive desert."

The only personality in government who seemed to share Wiesner's overwhelming concern was the President, who had to think for all the people. Eisenhower, profoundly tormented by the possible accident of nuclear warfare, was a man of peace. He sought arms control. But he was surrounded by a court where his military bureaucracy, as it had to, sought maximum strength; and his diplomatic bureaucracy was frozen by the concept of "massive retaliation."

Wiesner vividly recalls visiting Eisenhower at the White House in the fall of 1957 and hearing him talk about the need for arms control. "If we have a war," said the President, "there won't be enough bulldozers to scrape the bodies off the streets. But I can't get them to understand it. They won't help me. I need help."

There was very little help that Wiesner could give Eisenhower beyond his electronic competence and advice. But already the original Harvard-M.I.T. defense study group had acquired a throbbing vitality of its own (see Part I). By 1960, they were wired into Kennedy's campaign, and Wiesner's passion for peace could be voiced in the Democratic platform of 1960 as a promise to set up an arms control agency. By 1961, as chief scientific adviser to Kennedy, Wiesner, no longer a consultant, could impose such an agency on the old bureaucracies, and negotiate, then push through the test ban treaty he had long dreamed of.

If one is to try to trace, however, through both the Kennedy and Johnson administrations, the uncertain line along which the scholars brought to a close the vital work of the New Deal and provided the take-off line for the new, uncharted era of the present, one would have to seek it in the work of the Keynesian economists, and not only in their impact on national affairs but on national thinking.

In the 25 years since Roosevelt's New Deal had man-handled control of the economy away from New York's complex of bankers and brought it back to the capital, economists had learned much. Economists are scholars who like to think in terms of "aggregates." Through statistics, they grope for reality; elaborate symbolic formulae parade through their dreams costumed as truth and promising abundance.

IN THE GENERATION since Roosevelt, they had devised elegant new tools of statistical measurement, precise gauges of national produce and income, survey techniques for probing consumer impulse and demand. They had tamed and made useful the high theories of John Maynard Keynes. They were compulsively eager to test such theories on the American economy and thus, when John F. Kennedy gave them their chance, the door was open to that spectacular quantum jump of activity which introduced the new Era of Abundance.

All three original members of the Kennedy Council of Economic Advisers, the high command of the New Frontier's adventure in economics, were children of the Depression, moved by compassion—Walter Heller of the University of Minnesota, James Tobin of Yale, Kermit Gordon of Williams. All three were rather gentle men, but James Tobin, handsome and silver-haired at 50, expresses their feeling best. His mother had been a Depression social worker in Illinois and, he says, "My childhood house was full of talk of unemployment and relief, and people suffering. I went into economics because I thought it would save the world. People like me thought that the application of intelligence to government was the only way of doing good."

All three men were fortunate in being connected with a President who sought to do good and knew enough history to realize that politics, to do good, have to serve ideas rather than ideas serve politics. When, in January 1961, President-elect Kennedy telephoned Tobin at Yale from Palm Beach to invite him to be a member of his Council of Economic Advisers, Tobin demurred. "I'm an ivory-tower economist," he said. To which, according to Tobin's recollection, the President-elect replied, "That's fine. That's the best kind. I'm going to be an ivory-tower President." To which Tobin, in turn, replied, "That's fine—that's the best kind, too," and accepted.

The ideas these Kennedy economists fed into the bloodstream of government were to change all the perspectives of American business activity. Lifting the gross national product by 50%, in the longest continuing boom in our history, these ideas were to gorge the American system with an abundance it has not yet learned how to absorb. This triumph was to lead to what one of their number calls "the intellectual imperialism of the economists"—a desire on the part of many scholars to apply the aggregate techniques and arithmetical methods of the economists to the entire range of national problems. And it also has led to the belief, on the part of too many of them, that figures and statistics can illuminate the wordless aspirations and perplexities of American life.

LIFE June 16, 1967

ACTION-INTELLECTUALS

The expert's role is not to dictate answers to problems but to suggest approaches and alternatives.

Part III: Chartmakers for Our Demanding Future

Not since the barbarian princes of medieval Europe surrounded themselves with astrologers and theologians has any sovereign office so completely given its trust to or taken its guidance from official wise men as does the American Presidency today.

And not since that visionary, Christopher Columbus, spread his maps before Ferdinand and Isabella of Spain to explain his theory that the earth was round has any court had so much reason to be grateful to its wise men—or so much reason for caution.

Columbus was to lead the Spaniards to a new world he had not dreamed of, just as American scholars today are leading us, by their theories, to a new world whose dimensions their imagination cannot yet circumscribe. And as appetite for the gold Columbus found ultimately destroyed the Spaniards, so the new abundance which scholars are pouring into old American forms imperils the life it is supposed to enrich.

For in America today the new abundance—of knowledge, of technologies, of material things—has strengthened old appetites but shaken old values. It has filled leisure hours not with contemplation, but with temptations. It has congested places of repose with crowds who disturb each other's tranquillity. It has freed citizens for motion so frantic that neither our streets, our roads, nor our landing fields can manage the traffic of vehicles loaded on them. It has incubated a consumption so extravagant that the physical metabolism of our communities cannot carry away or absorb the wastes.

Most of all, however, the new abundance has changed the drives of the nation's politics. Americans have left behind the historic era of scarcity, where the cleaving thrusts of politics rose from how to share among all people what there was to share. Today the Politics of Distribution is being replaced by the Politics of Innovation—abundance invites us to the Age of Experiment.

The new wealth teases the imagination of both state and individual; and as many of our oldest standards of judgment crumble, into the void has come the new elite of American scholars— the action-intellectuals, who not only define for government what problems change has brought, but are expected to offer solutions.

419

This, says Professor Samuel Beer of Harvard, is the distinctive character of the new politics—that its goals are less and less set by old pressures and pressure groups; more and more by the invitation of pure learning and research knowledge. Information, as it accumulates, provokes intervention in politics all by itself.

"If a man knows more than anyone else in the country about retarded children," says Beer, "and there's money to do something about it, how can he be silent?"

Equally, if government calls for knowledge, how can scholars hold aloof? At a long evening's talk-session of professors in Los Angeles, a professor of the UCLA Law School voiced his credo: he was a devout Democrat, just back from a hitch in Washington at the advanced liberal headquarters of the War on Poverty. Asked whether he would serve conservative Governor Ronald Reagan in California if called on, he replied, "If Reagan asked me— why, of course I'd have to say yes. That's what a professor is for." None of the others demurred.

Old-fashioned pressure groups, inspired by ideas born 30 years ago, may press their local congressman, say, for legislative approval of a new $5 million housing project. Yet an astronomer, sweeping the night skies by himself, may lay down in the offices of NASA a set of charts and photographs that will trigger an expenditure of $50 million by administrative decision alone.

As we move further into this new era, who is to decide what opportunities are to be explored? Who is to judge a complicated idea as being good or dangerous, as feasible or simply fanciful? How will national resources be assigned to the widening range of experiments?

Adolf Berle has said that all political priorities must flow from an over-all system of philosophic values: only when a political system has decided what is good and what is beautiful can it take the intermediate steps and set the priorities for reaching its goals. So it is that, as one examines the scope and excitement of what the action-intellectuals ponder these days, one moves through stages of enthusiastic anticipation, to perplexity, to alarm—depending on how clear are the goals framed by their ideas and the values that guide them.

ESSA, FOR EXAMPLE, has clear goals. ESSA—Environmental Science Services Administration—is the governmental flesh on an idea that over the years grew among scholars to provoke political action in 1966: the perception that all the environment of man seemed interlinked. The outer space that envelopes us, the ocean depths and the air we breathe, the shores we bathe on, the earthquakes that rock us, the sunspots that blot out radio communications slowly assembled themselves in scientists' vision as one interlocking, quivering web of nature. Government, through the Department of Commerce, responded. By administrative decision, its Weather Bureau, its Coast and Geodetic Survey, its National Bureau of Standards, all its environmental activities were focused in one new institution, ESSA, with a clear goal: to harness all weather, ocean, space, river, solid-earth sciences and services in a team that might make the great globe and America's share of it a better place to live.

Few men but other scientists can understand ESSA's scientific programs and esoterica. Yet the importance of the agency's service is already accepted by all Americans. Says Dr. Robert M. White, ESSA's director, "Man *must* live in harmony with nature. But modern living presses on the environment beyond its capacity to tolerate—industry, population, pollution disturb it. And at the same time, as our civilization grows more complex and sophisticated, it becomes more sensitive—so that old-fashioned phenomena like earthquakes, floods and hurricanes become more devastating. If we don't learn to live in harmony with the environment, we're in trouble."

In 10 years' time ESSA's leadership hopes to launch not only new adventures in monitoring man's environment but the first tentative adventures in positively managing it. An international weather watch may permit accurate weather forecasts two weeks in advance and a central natural-disaster warning system would alert citizens to every disturbance, from hurricane and flood to radio blackouts and tsunamis. ESSA hopes to learn enough to lay before political leaders possible methods of clearing fogbound airports, augmenting rainfall in parched areas, even modifying brutal storms.

ESSA's goals are so clear, indeed, that its scientific ambitions have already become the commonest editorial clichés, and today it is politically more fashionable to denounce air pollution than the man-eating shark or Communist imperialism. The only question is, how much of our resources, what priorities we will let ESSA's scholars claim for their experiments.

What is true of ESSA is true of all government's great scientific agencies—AEC, NASA, NIH and others. Their goals, too, are clear. Likewise, the only question the scholars serving these agencies pose is how much of the total of our new abundance government will give them, how slow or fast we will permit them to conduct those experiments which lead us to the moon, or the inner energy of the atom, or the solution to cancer.

A stupendous gulf, however, separates scholars concentrating on such goals from equally dedicated scholars in other still-unfocused disciplines who may deliver us to political problems more frightening than did the physicists who gave us nuclear bombs. Within 20 or 30 years, for example, the biologists may be able to convert matter to life. They may conceivably learn enough of nature's code of heredity to give boys to couples who want boys and girls to couples who want girls. They may permit us to breed the kind of successor generations we want, or to eliminate "ordinary" offspring along with potential idiots, criminals, degenerates.

What kind of people do we want to have? What kind of people should be eliminated? The American value system does not yet press government to guide or slow or speed the curiosity and experiments of the biologists; so they probe decades away from the threshold of political decision.

Where the impact of learning presses most brutally on current political decision is in the middle ground. For between ESSA, NASA and AEC on the one hand (where values are clear and controls established) and the biologists on the other hand (in whose field it is too early to speak of values and controls) lies the area explored by the social scientists. The social scientists study man's relation to man; they offer a bewildering output of fact and research on how swiftly these relationships are changing—in our communities, cities, moralities. But do their facts add up to wisdom? Does their description of the problems automatically lead to solutions? Can they, for example, give a grizzled mayor or harassed city council useful guidance without clear values which they all accept?

IT IS THE wild and rumbling rhetoric of the alienated intellectuals of what is called "The New Left" which, paradoxically, illuminates best the dilemma of the action-intellectuals. There is very little new about the ideas of the New Left except for the sour and hopeless quality of their talk. To the New Left, the enemy in America is some faceless "they" who control events. "They" are persecuting Negroes. "They" are building not a Great Society but an idiot so-

ciety. "They" have ruined our cities. "They" are crushing individuals, depriving them of identity, denying them the opportunity of achievement. If only the anonymous and malevolent "they" can be purged, implies the New Left, America will find its way to a new, freer, humanitarian society.

The action-intellectuals, as we have seen in Part II of this series, left this philosophy behind 30 years ago. They have become participants, and government is their instrument of expression; change must be governed or civilization will destroy itself in an anarchy of technology. Yet, the action-intellectuals have no certain answers for tomorrow. Thus, even in the most specialized laboratories, the scholars grope for a "coherent doctrine" embracing both sociology and technology. And it is just here, in this search for "coherent doctrine," that one comes to the quandary of today's social scientists—for the best of them stands at the dawn of a self-doubt unknown to earlier generations of scholars who preceded them to Washington.

Their activist predecessors had not only the enormous advantage of a stored-up capital of ideas, but within their disciplines they had the certainty that comes of a "coherent doctrine." The physical scientists could see themselves as nature's agents, revealing nature's laws, which could not be challenged; Einstein had given a theory about the nature of the physical world, and they were its oracles, as little to be doubted as were the theologians of the Middle Ages, the only men then licensed to explain God. The academic economists of the past 10 years could operate under the roof theories of John Maynard Keynes with the tools of analysis and statistical measurement developed in the previous 30 years.

THE SOCIAL scientists, however, when they look at America today, know they are not the mouthpieces of nature proclaiming oracular truth. No master has given them the magical human equivalent of Einstein's $E = mc^2$. They must wander *across* disciplines—in economics and psychology, in health and psychiatry, in images and heritages, in arithmetic and beauty—dealing with human beings whose genetics and aspirations defy the techniques of all the sciences that preceded them.

Crutched by the measurement techniques of the economists, many social scientists fumble to define—in figures—emotions, yearnings, resentments, groups, classes and movements. Surveys and studies—some spurious, some genuine—explode to epidemic proportions. Pollsters and researchers tramp from door to door, office to office, flood the mail with questionnaires to be encoded on computers in the hope that truth will result. (One estimate is that over $500 million a year is spent on such surveys.)

To the best of the social scientists, however, many such surveys are now seen as dangerous, or as wasteful as they are useful. For to measure something does not mean to understand it. Figures alone, said a French social scientist,

would indicate that tearing down the Louvre and expanding in its place Les Halles, the central market of Paris, would be the most efficient economic use of space in the French capital. But what would Paris be without the Louvre? Again and again, scholars recognize that figures and measurements have deceived earlier scholars who led government to blight what it sought most to save or create:

▶ *Item*—Thirty years ago the best New Deal intellectuals urged an aggregate, economists' strategy to save the farmers of the nation. There were 6,812,000 farm families at the time, pressed to the wall by dead theories which held that the laws of the market must prevail, however cruelly, over their agony; only new theories could lead government to alter these laws. The farm family could be seen as an integer in the global market, a production-consumption unit, a symbolic junction of figures on acreage, prices and yields. Or it could be seen as a family—a man with dirt under his fingernails, enjoying the dew and the clear sky in the morning, hoping over the short-range for a good crop this season and, over the long-range, to pass on 160 acres to his son. Intellectual strategy might have focused either on saving the family in the village, as a community, or on the figures which defined its problem on charts. The easier—although in those days the bolder—solution was to focus on figures: stabilize the price of the crop and then raise it; save the price and save all—which was, indeed, the intellectual solution the government adopted.

For a generation since, undeviatingly, men in Washington who have thought about farms have thought of them in terms of price-supports. Not the family, but the bushel has been the unit of measurement—prices pegged for all farmers alike, at rising rates, no matter how few or many their acres. And as prices rose (they are now three times what they were in the Depression), science and efficiency led the big farmer to gobble the small. Result: of the original 6.8 million farm families who were to be saved, 3.2 million remain today.

▶ *Item*—Urban renewal was a lovely idea, which sprang from scholars 18 years ago. Today, a score of cities show the triumphs of urban renewal in new vistas and glistening buildings that open to the sun. But for each center this program created, it wiped out three or four living communities, and with them the old neighborhoods that gave the city its vitality, diversity and flavor. Urban renewal has succeeded superbly in its theoretical, or numerical, purpose—reducing density of population per square foot in the core city. But along the way no one remembered that, for every family driven out of what is called a "blighted neighborhood," balancing housing had to be built, communities created. By 1964, urban renewal in our big cities had given new shelter to only 28,000 families, but driven from their homes 176,000 families, pushed out to seek dismal rooms in strange neighborhoods or to crowd into new slums.

Figures and facts are the building blocks of intellectuals' theories—yet what reading is to be made of contradictory facts? The overwhelming weight of most research, several years ago, indicated that the condition of the Negro in Los Angeles—measured by figures on housing, wages, income, delinquency, family life—was better than in any other big city of the land. A minority report was brought in by the scholars of the UCLA Institute of Industrial Relations, probing such measureless resentments as public indignities, lack of transportation or hospitals. Neither the State of California nor the City of Los Angeles heeded the minority report—and, in 1965, Watts exploded.

Further, when scholars begin to extrapolate from one environment to another they make errors as gross as ordinary men. Brilliant scholarship in economics and history guided the thinkers of the Marshall Plan to force Europe toward unity in the spectacularly successful Common Market. So, from Harvard's Center for International Affairs scholars pushed this concept of European unity into American diplomacy of defense and it took the shape of NATO's polyglot Multilateral Force (MLF)—an absurdity that satisfied no European ally's instinct for control of its own defense and thus paralyzed Atlantic diplomacy for three years until discarded and buried in 1966.

CLICHÉS ALWAYS show where the action boils. Thus if today the condition of our cities has generated the most overworked set of clichés in American public talk, it is not because the scholars, with their overwhelming deluge of statistics, are guilty of intellectual "over-kill." It is because they are truly baffled by the amoeboid growth of a new kind of American life where the old sociological tools can detect no recognizable pulse or beat. They are baffled by the creeping, centerless sprawl of a Los Angeles or Nassau County as much as by the nameless development in the South Chicago-Gary area of the greatest, yet unrecognized, Negro metropolis in all history. They are baffled because what they are really trying to probe is the nature of a new civilization.

Today, as cities are jostled by the impact of technology and swollen by new arrivals, we face a future in which, by the year 2000, 80% of all American growth will happen in metropolitan clusters, where more than 280 million Americans will be crowded. Will they crush each other's dreams, will they suffocate each other's identity? Yet, in precisely those university centers where the best scholars gather to answer such questions, one finds the most concern among action-intellectuals about the validity of their own thinking.

The two centers of greatest prestige in this country are the urban-study centers of M.I.T.-Harvard and the University of Chicago. Rivals for years in the same field, the same wordless confusion now binds them. "We used to think," says Professor Richard Wade of Chicago's Center, "that give us enough money and we'd solve the problems of education, tear down slums, clean up cities, begin real job-training. Now we have the money, and we find our assumptions weren't right. Our academic theories and framework were unreal. No university has the answer to the problems that perplex you and me."

A thousand miles away one can listen in Cambridge and hear Professor Daniel P. Moynihan of the M.I.T.-Harvard Center echo the same thought: "We have to find out what's happening. We know that uncontrolled introduction of technology is spoiling city life. We have to find out how it works in order to manage it. We know, for example, there is an Urban Lower Class—but how do you absorb it, eliminate it, control it? We have to know more. And Washington . . . Washington will call on you endlessly for ideas—they're demanding ideas faster than they come. But you don't get good ideas every day; three good ideas in a lifetime is enough for any man."

Nowhere is the quandary of the urbanists better reflected than in the new departments of Washington government—Housing and Urban Development, Health-Education-Welfare, Transportation. These are the most exciting departments of the Johnson Administration, headquarters in the search for ideas that may turn the key to the future. The new departments and their academic elite know that whatever hopes are summed up in the Great Society are theirs to make real. Their mandate is all-encompassing, their funds generous, the challenge immediate. All they need are answers. Yet, all they can offer are experiments.

Professor Robert Wood of M.I.T., for example, is Under Secretary of Housing and Urban Development. He is a sandy-haired, wiry man of 43, who graduated from combat soldier in a World War II infantry division to a Harvard scholarship, and thence over the years, as a student of urban affairs, to the M.I.T. faculty. A talk with him reveals all that is best, hopeful and unsettling in the Politics of Innovation.

As chairman of two scholarly task forces on the cities, set up by President Johnson in 1964 and 1965, he helped conceive the legislation written into the laws of 1966 as the Model Cities Act— legislation which gives federal money to a few American cities to devise and coordinate the services that would make living communities out of slum jungles. When the Administration asked him to leave M.I.T. and become an official, he could not refuse. "If I believed what I wrote," he said, "I had to put my money where my mouth was."

Now Wood is passionately concerned with making operate the programs he helped stimulate—both the Model Cities legislation and the more far-reaching Metropolitan Areas legislation. Worried about persuading this year's Congress for the money necessary to continue the department's experimental programs, Wood equally worries, he admits, "when everyone starts yelling for more money. I'm not sure we know how to *use* more money.

"What we're trying to do is to prove that the American city can be made livable again. But if you focus only on schools, only on Head Start, only on race problems, it just doesn't work. Somehow we're trying to start a self-generating, self-renewing process of community action. But every city is different—Seattle is different from New York, Boston from Los Angeles. They can't work these programs by themselves—but we can't run them from Washington either. What cities are for is to provide people with choices—so people can live, play, shop, go where they want. We don't want to prescribe a Utopian City for America. We want to give it choices in urban life."

What is happening among the action-intellectuals is a vast pinwheeling motion, as if a ghost-like army were maneuvering in the dark, unfolding to take up new positions for new action. The problem of the city is only the pivot of this redeployment; a larger historical strategy is developing. For the first time in 60 years, since the scholars of Wisconsin took their ideas to Washington (see Part 2), the action-intellectuals are beginning to doubt whether the central government in Washington is the appropriate instrument for the needs of the new generation of problems.

THE NEED of American communities today is for a diversity of solutions, a diversity of expressions that will be paralyzed if controlled from Washington, or unwittingly cruel if imposed by fiat. A totally new orchestration of services, a new chain of responsibility is required. And if Washington is no longer the place to press for action, where should the action-intellectuals go?

Thus, at the forward fringe, the best thinkers among the scholar-elite meet the New Left thinkers back to back. Neither can find a real "they" to press to do their will. But whereas the New Left believes that once the sinister, conspiratorial "they" in Washington or New York is eliminated all will be well, the action-intellectuals know the real "they" is *us*—and the kind of government *we* may create. Thus, the action-intellectuals bring us to re-examine the nature of American government itself.

William Scranton would not consider himself an intellectual. He was a politician, a working governor of the state of Pennsylvania. Yet he was able to frame the problems. In the late summer of 1965 a group of friends were visiting him for the weekend at his home at Marworth. He was leaving Pennsylvania in excellent shape and was already looking forward to the end of his term in the statehouse. Sitting on his terrace, overlooking the green slopes of the Appalachians, he talked about the job of being a governor.

He always felt sorry, he said, for the governor of New Jersey—whichever man it happened to be. New Jersey simply couldn't be governed logically; you couldn't even run an efficient political campaign there—there wasn't a single television station in the state by which you could reach all the people at any one time and explain matters to

them. New Jersey really ought to be split up: Hudson and Bergen counties ought to be peeled off and attached to some new state-to-be-fashioned that would include New York City and adjacent Connecticut—perhaps to be called the "State of the Lower Hudson"; it was the only efficient way of handling some of the biggest problems of the metropolitan area—transportation, commuting, pollution, crime.

And the whole area around Trenton, naturally, could best be governed if it were attached to the Philadelphia area. And the border between Massachusetts and Connecticut—what point was there in that arbitrary line? Southern New England was, in effect, already one community.

Even the borders of his own state might usefully be redrawn. The problems of Pennsylvania-beyond-the-Alleghenies were Ohio Valley problems, and the counties of southeastern Ohio and northern West Virginia have far more in common with Pittsburgh than they do with Columbus or Charleston.

Geography is one of Scranton's hobbies, so it was not difficult to urge him on. And, in half-serious, half-comic mood, he rearranged the map of the U.S. as far as the Great Lakes—at which point his professional knowledge of governments and geography ran out.

Scranton's thoughts were not entirely new. As long ago as 1787, at America's first Constitutional Convention, old Ben Franklin suggested the delegates forming their new union abolish and revise their state borders. The echo of the idea can be heard today in conversations with governors, mayors, lawmakers all across the land. For they talk, most of them, like men trapped—trapped by fossil forms and ancient theories hardened into law, trapped by boundaries drawn in Elizabethan, Puritan or Restoration London, by courtiers who granted blocks of land in a distant wilderness to favorites who had never seen America. Or they were trapped by surveyors' lines drawn straight as a ruler across the Louisiana Purchase and the Mexican conquests more than a century ago.

Within these old state borders, drawn for a rural, muscle-powered people, have grown the vibrant, humming new centers of American civilization—and within these centers have developed a people full of dreams, ambitions, desires entirely different from the simple life of the 18th Century. But the services they need and seek cannot be delivered within the old constitutional rules by any leader, no matter how hard he tries.

NEW YORK State and New York City have, as governor and mayor, two outstanding and equally dedicated men, both Republicans, both staffed with scholars who define with meticulous accuracy and common agreement the problems before them. Yet constitutionally they must be enemies—they snarl at each other, make peace, grow bitter again, make compromise. For John Lindsay, constitutionally, is cast as beggar; his city is the financial capital of the world, yet he cannot tap its resources for its needs without permission from Nelson Rockefeller in Albany, or mercy from Washington.

To dare to question the validity of the Constitution of the United States is heresy in American politics—though the Founding Fathers themselves anticipated the need for changes ("The Congress, whenever two thirds of both Houses shall deem it necessary, shall propose Amendments to this Constitution, or, on the application of the Legislatures of two thirds of the several States, shall call a Convention. . . ."). Even state constitutions have, until recently, been sacred—with only 10 of 49 states revising their constitutions in the half-century up to 1960. However, a restlessness of growing force has begun to sweep the nation. In the past three years, Michigan, Tennessee, Connecticut, New Jersey have all revised their constitutions and 13 more states have set up official constitutional study commissions. In New York, Maryland, Rhode Island, Pennsylvania, constitutional groups are gearing for or are already at work.

No such fundamental ferment has swept the nation since the Civil War—and at its source is the yeast of science and scholarship. Few scholars go as far, say, as Professor Wentworth Eldredge of Dartmouth who calls the Federal Constitution "a mudbank left by the receding tides of history," a relic of the "era of the ox-drawn sledge." Nevertheless the research, the probings, the information that scholars bring back about man's relationship to man, and his relationship to nature, and the changes in both nature and man shake some of the most sacred assumptions of that Constitution.

It is not only the boundaries and functions of states and cities that they question. Legal scholars question the universal validity of the hallowed jury system. Can an institution developed by Henry II of Anjou and applied in 12th Century England as a simple system of establishing facts to which an itinerant king might apply his rule of law—have bearing today on traffic courts, on pollution problems, on scientific discoveries where no jury of laymen can satisfactorily weigh facts for the law to govern?

Other scholars question the traditional process of American elections. Can government carry its appeal to the people in any rational sense when the great forum of appeal is, today, television—and television is open only to those with the largest purse, and its impact dependent on carnival artistry and staged happenings?

STILL OTHER scholars question the entire current structure of the U.S. government. Are the federal bureaucracies of the 18th Century appropriate, some ask, for the tasks of tomorrow? Is central authority too limited to plan effectively the use of scarce resources like water and leisure land? Is the U.S. government so large and so extortionate in taxes that it must yield to some new kind of federalism which would give local authorities their proper share of revenues?

The oldest bureaucracies in America are, for example, the Department of State and the Department of War— both founded when the diplomacy of the Renaissance had just matured and rules of civilized warfare were being shaped. In the past 50 years, new and more complicated forms of war have developed—and the pandemic violence of partisan war, incubated by agitation and subversion, is just as revolutionary as nuclear war. Since none of the older bureaucracies can cope with the new immorality and new terror of partisan war, the CIA has been drawn into the empty shadow-ground where a new development—perhaps a "Department of Political Warfare"—should exist. But as the CIA flounders, doing of necessity those unpleasant things someone has to do, it shocks the traditional morality of the nation.

Scholars examine the world about us, too, and illuminate fresh problems overseas. Is it wise that, in a shrinking world, the economy of the United States should be manacled to gold? Is it not best, the scholars say to government, that a new scheme of universal currency, divorced from gold, be devised to unify the monies of all the world? And what, they ask of government, are you to do about the newly defined problems of population control abroad as well as at home?

One returns from a long wandering around the country with no detailed blueprint of the future of American civilization. The intellectuals offer no pattern as clear as St. Augustine's City of God, or Plato's Republic. They offer no certainties except that, in the future, change will come swifter rather than slower. And it is in the questions they ask and in the information they deliver that they raise, finally, the question of their own role.

The ribs, the stones, the vaults that shape the states and communities of the world all began as dreams. For the duties and rights assigned by constitutions to ordinary men have all descended from the imaginations of unknown visionaries in a forgotten past, hardened by age into law.

Yet states and constitutions can be changed and destroyed, too, by dreamers.

It is not that any serious scholars question the values of the American Constitution—the Bill of Rights which guarantees freedom; the underlying commitment to rule of law, to peaceful transfer of executive power; the balancing checks on all forms of power. It is only that the information, the research, the questions of the intellectuals are slowly challenging the validity of the old mechanics of government, casting doubt ever more gravely on whether the old Constitution, unless overhauled, can adequately grapple with the new obstacles to the pursuit of happiness.

Just here, perhaps, the new scholar-elite offers its greatest service—and suffers its greatest temptations. The scholars have arrived at the junction of history where their role in politics demands definition. For it is as teachers, as cartographers only, that they must be seen. Their studies and surveys, however imperfect, are the only road maps of the future showing the hazy contours

of a new landscape. It is vital work—so long as the map makers do not confuse themselves with tour directors. How Americans shall move across the panorama they describe and what structures shall be erected there is work for other men.

THUCYDIDES, 2,400 years ago, first put his finger on the danger these scholars pose in politics. It was, he said, frequently a misfortune to have very brilliant men in charge of affairs: they expect too much of ordinary men.

Politics is an art that requires faith from the people in their leaders; without such faith, governments crumble, wars are lost, riots burst, no vast social experiments can be undertaken; and scholars who seek to impose logic on a people too fast, before they have provided the education and understanding to which leaders can make appeal, understand little of the art of government.

American intellectuals began their journey to power as teachers—explaining and illuminating the revolutionary changes of our time. Today the new age invites them, as experimentalists, to a new step forward. Yet, we are to be the raw stuff of their experiments; and men are not particles to be wrapped up from micro-model to macro-model by an Einsteinian theory, not random units whose drives can be summed up by the aggregate equations of economists. In the new age, more than ever, the humility of the old-fashioned teacher becomes them best. There will be much pain and wrenching as we cross their maps to the promises beyond; and only leaders whom the people themselves choose and trust can judge the costs and rouse the faith to make the journey—a long road of common experience, common learning, common understanding, before we reach common consent.

LIFE June 23, 1967

Chapter 11

One Shot: The Middle East

White was born and reared a Jew. He learned Hebrew so well (see Introduction, page 00) that years later he could still translate fluently. He arrived at Harvard a fervent Zionist (a fervor that did not survive his freshman year, however). And throughout his life he cared deeply about the nation of Israel, went there on occasion, was fascinated by Middle East politics. Yet, for unknown reasons, he published only one magazine article about the area—in 1967, when he, accompanied by Time Inc.'s Richard Clurman, covered the Arab-Israeli Six-Day War for *Life.**

*A decade earlier he had been at work for *Collier's* on the 1956 Arab-Israeli War, but the piece died aborning when the magazine suddenly went under. See also Chapter 1 footnote, page 3.

Recalls Clurman: "He and I made our way in a rental car up to the head of an Israeli tank column advancing to fifteen miles outside Damascus. Along the route, stopping frequently, Teddy shouted questions in his Talmudic Hebrew to joyous civilians who answered this overflowing journalist with flowers and embraces as he struggled to get it all down in his tattered notebook. Years afterward he glowed whenever he told about those days."

Completed in less than a week, "The Armor Churns Up the Syrian Hills" is a typical White Fang account (see Introduction, page xvi), with a brilliant first paragraph that in a few words movingly sets the historical backdrop.

THE ARMOR CHURNS UP THE SYRIAN HILLS

Down the slopes of Tiberias, Herod's city, came rumbling Israeli Sherman tanks en route to battle. Beneath them lay the placid waters of the Sea of Galilee—and on the Syrian bluffs, above the waters where Peter fished, was the low haze of artillery smoke and the high, black, waving plumes of air strikes. A helicopter in the sky above the memorial to Mary Magdalene drew one's gaze. Ferrying wounded from the battlefront across the lake, it flew low over the green grove of the Mount of Beatitudes. There Christ had preached the Sermon on the Mount, and at its foot he caused the Miracle of Loaves and Fishes. The eye followed the slowly moving helicopter across the barren hills, strewn with black basalt boulders and purple thistles, until it disappeared between the Horns of Hattin where, one July day 900 years ago, Saladin met the Crusaders in their heavy Frankish armor, routed them and put them to the sword. This perspective was too large to grasp.

Only within sounds of shellfire, across in Syria, did the perspective become real again—tanks and trucks lurching up the slopes on a freshly bull-dozed trail; the dead beside the road under their tarpaulin covers, with helmet-capped stakes to mark their place; a platoon of Israeli mortar-men examining a Russian-built Syrian truck, tinkering with it, then dancing with glee as one of their number made it roar alive; a deserted Arab village, its honey-colored walls silent except for the echo of gunfire; the call, down the line of jammed armor and trucks: "Clear the road, clear the road! Wounded coming back!"—and then the ambulance delicately, slowly seeking out the gentlest ruts in the rocks.

We came down from the front in late afternoon to wash and rest in Kibbutz Dan, northernmost of Israeli settlements. Kibbutz Dan has lived in strain for years—its silo mortared several years ago, its electric generator also hit from the Syrian slopes. Kibbutz Dan raises chickens, cows, apples, honey-bees and has a fishpond for breeding carp. Mobilization had taken 50 able-bodied men and women from Kibbutz Dan's 500 souls two weeks earlier. Thus, when the Syrians hit them on Tuesday morning, June 6, at 7:30, only 24 middle-aged men were left to hold the trench line, with teen-agers to run the ammunition. Baruch Fischer, a stocky, 50ish, middle-aged apple specialist, was in command of the two 8-mm mortars close by the chicken coops in the rear. When the Syrian company attacked, the four automatic rifles in the forward trench line pinned the enemy in the meadow under the grove; then the trench command post called for mortar fire and Baruch's two mortars, firing 150 rounds in 20 minutes, chopped the enemy up.

Some might see it as a miracle, for the answering Syrian shellfire dropped within the chicken coops only 15 yards from the mortar pits. A direct hit might have ended Kibbutz Dan's resistance. Baruch Fischer did not see it as a miracle. "There was no place for us to go," he said. "We stayed here or we died." Later, he added that, of course, even if the Syrians had overrun the settlement, the Israeli army would have been there an hour later to recapture it. But by then, he said, they would have found everyone dead, so they had to fight.

This is the feeling in Israel. No one here doubts that America would, ultimately, have arranged to end the blockade of the Gulf of Aqaba. But, said a Foreign Office official in Jerusalem, by the time they opened up the Gulf, they would have opened entry to a country that was dead.

THIS IS A country still suspended between a nightmare and a dream, relishing a moment of ecstasy. And it would be unreasonable to try to write reasonably about what has happened to people here.

Legends have been born that fathers will tell children to tell their children after them. Prophecy has come true. A flag of Zion floats over Jerusalem for the first time since the Romans leveled the holy city 1,900 years ago.

To be a Jew in Jerusalem is to watch the dawn come up through the dark sky and silver the ridge and fortress walls of the Old City in the East—and know that now no threat lurks behind the hills. No muezzin calls from the minarets of the walled city. They will again; the Israelis have promised so. But, for the moment, the beat and pulse of the entire ancient capital lies in Israeli hands. Where legionary and crusader, pasha and commissioner, once made law, Israeli soldiers patrol. Amiably alert, on guard at every crossroad and holy place, in desert battle dress, their Uzi—submachine guns—slung over their shoulders, they pace the streets, check passes and say "*Shalom*"—Peace.

BUT THIS IS a peace that is still unreal. The Israelis themselves wonder how to absorb their victory, what can be done with it. Their armor stands an hour's push away from a naked Damascus, two hours from Amman, four hours from Cairo. They are confused by the prospects. It is difficult to look forward—and impossible to look back. Had the cast of history gone the other way, they would be victims, not victors.

To separate the facts of the past fortnight from the growing legends is difficult, especially in this cradle of legends. It is best to start with the largest emotional reality and the mood of the nation that grows from it.

ON THE SLOPES of Mount Zion, by David's tomb, is a memorial to the nameless millions of Jews murdered in Europe by Hitler. In the underground grotto, by the light of flickering memorial candles, one can read, smeared in black ash on the wall, in the Bible's Hebrew, "The voice of your brother's blood screams to me from the ground."

Israelis are Jews who have declared they will not ever again be victims— and their army is an expression of this will. In this nation ordinary politics are even more addled than elsewhere—too many tongues, customs, experiences, superstitions, brought from the lands of exile, divide it. Gossip and ideology splinter it. But the army expresses the fundamental politics of survival. As such, it unifies a people who will not die.

Girls of 18, called by draft for their 20 months of service, are ushered forth by families as if to wedding or to nunnery. It is a folksy army. Boys and girls meet and marry in the army, and the army provides rabbi, service, wedding dance and banquet. Yet it is supremely efficient, too. The mobilization process, the most sensitive in the world, can call up 10% of all Israel's 2,300,000 Jews in just 48 hours—every reservist at his station, behind gun, at the tank, at the wheel—all ready to fight, or die.

The army which defends Israel takes this emotion for granted. It must also take for granted the strategy forced on it by geography. The psalm says to lift up one's eyes to the hills whence cometh strength. To the Israeli army, however, the hills have been hills of peril. On the eastern front, two enemies—Syria and Jordan, emplaced on ancient ridges, commanding every yard of Israel's narrow coastal plains. To the south, the Sinai desert; and then, behind Suez, the strength of Egypt, armored by the Russians. Beyond this close-in ring lie Iraq, Saudi Arabia and other Arab nations— in all, some 80 million hostile Arabs. This was a situation to be borne with constant attention even while the Arab states continued quarrelsome and divided among themselves. But if they united for war, and if Israel could be caught before mobilization—before its regular army of 50,000 men might reach its mobilized strength of 300,000—the Arabs might inflict on Israel instant death. Thus, for 10 years, the continued strain on Israeli nerves, the burden on Israeli intelligence and political judgment.

A year ago, when this correspondent last visited Israel, war in modern fashion had already broken out—irregular war of familiar style. From the Syrian heights above the Galilee an occasional mortar shell fell on an Israeli village— an artillery round, no bombardment but sporadic fire. There were also the saboteurs, mining roads within Israel; the night ambush—one settler killed here, another there; a water line cut, a telephone line ripped out. Casualties few. Yet politically unsettling. The Syrian raiders sought, without success, lodgment in the villages of the Arab minority within Israel, for if Israel's 10% of peaceful Arabs might be converted by terror to an internal guerrilla force, no orderly state could function. Among themselves Syrian Arabs charged Jordanian Arabs with cowardice—Amman, they insisted, must be made another Hanoi, a base for irregular warfare *à la* Vietcong.

A year ago this correspondent found all northern Israel smarting from the pinpricks of the guerrillas. The Israel army command, however, held back. The most important enemy, it insisted, was Egypt, with her Russian armor. Let Israel's government negotiate in any international forum for peaceful settlement of border flare-ups—but if Egyptian armor moved across Suez to take up positions in the Sinai desert, Israel must mobilize.

Thus, the climate last summer. What caused it to change so swiftly, one cannot yet fully understand. Perhaps rivalry among the Arab states for leadership in the holy war against the Israelis; perhaps a misunderstanding by Nasser of a promise of Russian backing; perhaps a general feeling that America was too tied down in Southeast Asia to support Israel effectively.

IN MID-MAY, as Israelis tell it, began the nightmare days. On the 15th Nasser's armor began to roll north across the desert, digging in on Israel's southern frontier—seven divisions, 900 tanks. On May 22 the U.N. Emergency Force was finally withdrawn; the day following came the blockade of Elath, Israel's only southern port, as Nasser closed the Gulf of Aqaba. On May 30 Jordan's King Hussein flew to Cairo and, returning to Amman, announced that his state, too, was joined with Egypt in the holy war. From Iraq a new division was marching to bolster Hussein's Arab legions on the western hills.

All this to the obbligato of Radio Cairo and Damascus, both promising, in Arabic and Hebrew, death and extermination to Israel. An Israeli doctor tells of a middle-aged woman asking him for suicide pills to take if necessary—she had lived through Hitler's concentration camp, and she could not live through another. A father tells of his 10-year-old son coming home from school saying that if the government would not fight, he would not want to be an Israeli any more—he would go to America and become an American. In the Israeli press, fury. Men tell of other grown men crying in exasperation as the cabinet debated whether to wait for American support, or to act on its own.

By the first week of June, with their army almost fully mobilized, the Israelis were coiled like a spring in full compression. And now there were almost daily Egyptian over-flights of Israel's handful of five main airbases. The southern borders began to sputter as sporadic Egyptian mortar fire set wheat fields ablaze on Friday, June 2; on Sunday, June 4, two Egyptian commando battalions arrived in Jordan. Command of Jordan's army had passed, at last, to Nasser.

Thus, finally, on Sunday afternoon

the Israeli cabinet faced decision: to wait for diplomatic help, delay which might mean death; or let the army decide time, dimension and method of response to Egyptian attack. Eighteen men met that afternoon and voted yes.

What happened on Monday, June 5, 1967 was more in the nature of paroxysm than war—or rather, as if an awkward and ignorant hand had been toying with the fuse of a strange explosive of unknown power, and thus been blown to bits.

THE SHATTERED remnants of the Egyptian army are now flung across the sands of the Sinai desert for 200 miles, from Israel's southern border all the way to the Suez Canal. Under the blue and merciless skies of the desert, strewn across its sifting dunes, a museum of war's infinite agony is spread out. There, along the road one drives, held timelessly and silently in place, are 14 Russian tanks—six to one side of the road, eight to the other side, as if on perfect tactical deployment, yet all black and silent. In the sun an Egyptian soldier lies as if asleep, his poncho covering his head, shading him from the sun. Three others are nearby, grotesquely rigid, legs spread, toes pointing stiffly up in an antique Pharaonic frieze. Israeli scoop shovels cover the bodies with sand, for the only things that move now in the desert are Israeli. Along each road there are dead Egyptian tanks and more tanks, trucks and more trucks, tracks in the sand showing the agony of hopeless flight. By the airfields are strewn the burned-out MiGs.

So are fragile helicopters, their rotor blades squashed as though someone had stamped on spiders.

Thus one comes to Mitla Pass—four miles of destruction in the desert mountains, main route of the Egyptian flight, swathed on either side for hundreds of feet with tipped-up trucks and burned-out tanks. The wriggling tracks show how they tried to thread the bottled pass, were stuck in sand and then caught. Circlets of black show where fuel spilled and blazed. A single pass of the observer's plane cannot encompass it; one asks for a second pass, and a third. High up in a cleft there is a single truck which could not possibly have mounted over sand and roadless rock so high into the mountain. Terror must have urged it up—to no avail; the black of burning fuel surrounds it.

Then back from the desert via Sharm el Sheikh, a spit of land where desert sand covers coral reef, pointing out into the beautiful green-blue waters of the Gulf of Aqaba. Here is where the blockade was closed. The reef stretches out into translucent waters with the tempting iridescence of coral anywhere.

A beautiful place to bathe, observes one of the Israeli soldiers stationed there. Too beautiful a place, one notes, to have triggered such a war.

THE CENTRAL front also has its tormented showpiece—Jerusalem.

All Monday morning, at the outbreak of war, the Israeli government, through local agencies of the United Nations, had sent messages to Hussein of Jordan asking him to hold fire. If he would keep his peace, so too would they. Israeli sources are convinced the messages were received; but they believe that by Monday Egyptians so completely controlled the Jordan army that Hussein could not reply. Yet Israelis were surprised nonetheless when Arab artillery opened fire that day from Jordan's ridges on both Tel Aviv and Jerusalem. Surprised, as one Israeli says, but not dismayed.

For if the war with Egypt was long prepared, action against Jordan was opportunity itself. To fight for the holy city of Jerusalem was the chance to fulfill prophecy.

Now one can trace the course of prophecy through the blasted hundred yards beyond the Mandelbaum Gate. Around the circuit of the old wall, with its pretty gardened foreslope, there are fallen poles, upended buses, burned sedans and cairns of stone, already wreathed in roses, to mark where soldiers fell. On to the Gate of Lions, where dangles a single, huge, timbered door—the other torn off as Colonel Mordecai Gur's lead tank butted through.

In 1948, during Israel's war of liberation, Mordecai Gur had fought as a company commander under Brigade Commander Yitzhak Rabin to hold Jerusalem. They had lost, and Ben-Gurion had predicted that for Israelis the loss would be "a lamentation for generations." Thus it was fitting last week for Gur, now Brigade Commander himself, to report to Uzi Narkiss, Sector Commander, to pass on to Rabin, now Chief of Staff, that all Jerusalem

was in his hands. All three—Gur, Narkiss and Rabin—were men born in Jerusalem, who never hoped to see the Wailing Wall again. And now they might.

FOR THE PAST few hours, as I write this, looking out over the walls of Old Jerusalem, there have been continual explosions and puffs of smoke from beneath the crenelated wall of the Old City built by Suleiman the Magnificent. Israelis have been clearing land mines. Tomorrow, on the Jewish festival of Shavuot, celebrating the harvest of the first fruits, Israelis will be allowed to enter the Old City and pray once again at the Wailing Wall, the last remaining outcropping of the temple destroyed by Titus of Rome in 70 A.D. As high as a man can reach by lip or touch, its stones have been polished smooth by centuries of kiss and stroke. Above men's reach grow the tufts of shrub which have found roots in the crevices of the gray and mellow stone. A few days ago, when correspondents were first admitted, the Israeli army had already placed at its foot a wooden ark of the scrolls of the Bible. Lest anyone mistake what it was, the crude Hebrew lettering of an army sign said, "Beyt Knesseth"—This is a temple.

The Old City, at this writing, is being kept as a temple of all faiths. Signs on every holy place proclaim: "Holy Place. Unauthorized Entry Is Forbidden." Other signs, in Arabic and Hebrew, warn that the penalty for looting is life imprisonment. And nowhere is security tighter than in the garden of the Mosque of Omar, no place more difficult of access than this exquisite octagon of green and blue and yellow tile mosaics. Mortar shell fragments and spent bullets litter its paths. A few days ago there were pools of blood, and some stains are still wet. But the mosque itself is totally unscathed, immaculately beautiful. The Israeli flag waves everywhere else. Above the Mosque of Omar, however, still stands the golden crescent; no Israeli flag profanes it. The Israelis are treating this victory gingerly.

THIS SENSE OF caution is now the prevailing mood in Israel. Yet it should not be mistaken. Under it is glowing pride and a sense of muscle. Ten years ago Israel celebrated another such victory—and then, like a cormorant used by fishermen, was forced by larger powers to choke up the fish once caught. This time Israel will not disgorge without a fight.

What Israel should retain and should give up is now being debated from parliament to *kibbutz,* from Dizengoff Circle in Tel Aviv, where miniskirted girls are welcoming back their boyfriends, to airstrips in the desert, where reservists argue endlessly. Israel has no blueprints. Task forces of the Foreign Office are hastily preparing contingency plans for any overture of peace from any Arab state, or any new event.

Several main lines of thought emerge and blur. There is the thinking of the Foreign Office—that not territory but peace is what Israel wants; thus, above

all, let Arabs and Israelis sit down face to face and work out peace. The military thinking is that peace rests on defense and defense on borders that can be held. The military yearns for a state widened at its waist to the banks of the Jordan, the Syrian heights above the Galilee occupied, the Sinai desert held in force down to the canal. More sophisticated thinking sees the matter as a delicate balance between how much land Israel needs for defense, and how many of the one million Arab civilians just conquered can be retained without upsetting the nation's social structure.

On certain points all thinking coincides: that the Gulf of Aqaba must be forever open to all nations, that the ridges above the Galilee must never again be in hostile hands, that King David's Jerusalem must be forever held as one—not because of its commanding heights, but because emotion simply cannot yield it back.

A final scene comes back from a visit to Bethlehem a few days after its capture. In the dark chamber where, supposedly, Rachel lies buried, Israelis of every diverse strain had gathered—from the bearded "tremblers" in their long black caftans to the husky paratroopers from Tel Aviv and the *kibbutzim.* In the gloom one of the orthodox "tremblers," swaying back and forth, broke into the ancient Hebrew chant for the dead: "He who maketh peace in His heavens, He will make peace for us and for all Israel—and say ye amen." Even the irreligious paratroopers bellowed "Amen!"

It was in this cruel and lovely land,

2,000 years ago, that peace and mercy were first preached by a Jew of Nazareth as universal doctrine. Every artifact and ruin, every ancient terrace hardened to stone, every fallen pillar and tumbled fortress, from Acre in the north to the marshes of Sinai in the south, bespeaks the alternation between man's mercy and man's animal fear. It is Israel's turn now, for the first time in two millenia, to seek a balance. Said an Israeli official this week: "We have plunged back into history."

LIFE June 23, 1967

Chapter 12

Politics USA IV: The Later Years

From 1960 on, White was primarily occupied with writing books. But he still liked occasional magazine assignments, particularly when they dealt with national politics. This chapter completes our look at such stories.

His articles on the deaths of Robert Kennedy and Lyndon Johnson make clear his very different feelings about the two men. Two opinion pieces—on direct presidential elections and on granting the vote to eighteen-year-olds (both bad ideas, he contended)—show the once-liberal author moving toward conservatism.

Spiro Agnew, he argued in 1973 on the occasion of the vice-president's public disgrace, cheated us all, but particularly he cheated his own conservative cause; White had been looking forward to a 1976 campaign that would have been a "real outspoken debate between an intelligent conservative force [Agnew] and an intelligent liberal resistance."

White's last "Making of the President" book covered the 1972 race, but he continued to chronicle the presidential elections.* In 1980 he traced for *Life* the vast differences that had occurred during his quarter century of observing this nation's process of picking a Chief Executive. Four years later, in "New Powers, New Politics," he further analyzed the huge new influence of blacks and women in American politics; the former, he found, was a whole lot easier to comprehend than the latter.

* Including the book *America in Search of Itself* in 1982, a retrospective of presidential elections 1956–80.

THE WEARING LAST WEEKS AND A PRECIOUS LAST DAY

All that week he had been tired. The deep tan, burned in by weeks of campaigning in the sun in the open car, lay over the exhaustion: the hair bleached blond, the fine fibers on the forearms almost flaxen. But he did not show the weariness except when you talked to him alone.

The Tuesday of the Oregon voting had been the worst day in weeks. He used the day to barnstorm through California's southland, from Los Angeles to Lakewood to Santa Barbara to Ventura to Oxnard to Los Angeles; and the crowds, as usual, were wild. They fed him the adrenalin to carry on; but in the plane, in conversation, the exhaustion was always there, under the determination.

He had few illusions. His last Oregon poll had shown him 30–29 over McCarthy, but the undecided vote was huge. And, usually, he knew, the undecideds came down on the other side. He rambled on about Oregon, returning constantly to its beauties and the spectacle of its fir-covered slopes and green valleys. But it had been a cold state to him; Oregon, a great white suburb, had no problems, he knew he frightened

Oregon by what he spoke of and his visions.

It was going badly back east too. Pennsylvania's delegation had been raided by Humphrey the night before. He had felt he had a pledge from Mayors Tate of Philadelphia and Barr of Pittsburgh to wait before committing to another—to wait and give him the chance to show his strength with the voters at the polls, in the primaries. Governor Hearnes of Missouri had been for him. But Hearnes was switching too. He thought Mayor Alioto of San Francisco had been with him—but Alioto also was now learning to Humphrey.

He talked: about the huge crowds in California and crowds as a serious index of response; about Vietnam—the negotiations should have begun much earlier, but he trusted Harriman to make the case. If we *did* have a case in Vietnam, this was the way to show it to the world—by talk, not by bombs. He felt we had already gained much in Paris by exposing the intransigeance of the enemy; but he was not hopeless of solutions—perhaps cantonment in South Vietnam, some new frame to give both

445

sides in the fighting the security they needed.

Yet, always the conversation came back to the exercise in power which is a campaign for the Presidency. Oregon was lost, he already feared. So he *had* to make it big in California. Then, showing his strength in the most populous state in the Union, he might turn back east to deal with the local power-brokers. We haven't begun to fight that battle yet, he said. New York was uppermost in his mind. Unless he could show real muscle in California, his own faction-ridden state would be the arena of the most bruising clash this season.

People criticized him, he knew, for this extravagant spending of energy in the primaries. But, he kept saying, "Is there any other way of convincing them? Can you think of any other way?" If California went well, then he would rethink it, and might get those four or five days of rest before plunging into combat in New York. But now he was worn to the bone.

Then, that evening, winging north to Portland on a plane crowded with newsmen and cameras, with no crevice for privacy, the returns from Oregon had come in. Ethel gently held his hand, her fingers entwined through his or curled about his muscular wrist. He would not show his hurt; he smiled, talked to friends, strolled the aisle, encouraging the downcast, making clear he was going on with it.

THE LAST WEEK began badly, but he carried it off with courage, skill and an-

imal energy. When, on Sunday, California began to turn up—when he could sense, as a politician does, the return of enthusiasm in the surge of the crowds—he would not slacken his pace.

For he was an old-fashioned man of politics. And politics were people, a concept descended to him from his grandfather, who had known that truth three generations ago. He understood as well as any man the new technology of media and organization. His California campaign, pulled together finally, was running smoothly. The themes, pouring out of radio and television, were coming clear: an end to war in Vietnam; a new orientation for the federal government—which had come to him, after he could view the Executive from the outside, seeing government as cold, overcentralized, needing to be brought back to the people in their communities; and—a third theme—law-and-order, an end to violence.

Yet, the old politics meant this message had to be brought directly to people—by talking to them; had to reach their hearts and yearnings in person. Thus the last crescendo of barnstorming.

When he moved through a black district, or a Mexican-American district, the campaign reached a terrifying frenzy. It frightened one to drive in the open car with him—the screaming, the ecstasy, the hands grabbing, pulling, tearing, snatching him apart. To them he was The Liberator. In the other districts, always he pleaded—trying to explain America to Americans and show them the direction in which it must move. His staff insisted that he cool it; they, too, were frightened by the emotions he raised.

But he could not completely cool it. Briefed and briefed again on how to meet McCarthy in TV debate, he did so visibly with superb control. But though the voice and words were calm, his hands were moving, reaching, pleading.

Even when his polls in the final weekend turned upward, he kept at it until one or two every morning, then rose after five or six hours sleep, again to reach out, be with people. Until, finally, on Monday night, having barnstormed through San Francisco, Long Beach, the southland and reached San Diego, he collapsed. He could not finish the last speech; the enormous vitality had reached its end. He must rest.

ELECTION DAY he slept late at the beach home of Evans and John Frankenheimer. Six of the children had been flown out to be with him, giving him the solace of a family day. Shortly after noon, he went out on the beach to frolic with them. It was no time for a solitary friend there to talk politics. So they kicked the rubbery, dark green kelp on the sand, and talked of the pollution of this beautiful coast and the disappearance of the great old kelp beds; they compared the Pacific to the Atlantic, and he preferred Cape Cod.

The sun would not break through, a chill mist hung heavy; but he stripped his flowered sunshirt and plunged in nonetheless. A huge roller came in and

the bobbing heads of two children went under. Bobby dived; for a moment one could not see him in the surf, until he came up with David, whom he had pulled from an undertow. A large red bruise now marked his forehead. He had bumped either sand or the boy, but the boy was safe.

Now they came back up the beach to the pool, and children tumbled over him. Max, the 3-year-old, wanted to walk the beach and bury coins in the sand. So they did. Then back to the pool, where Bobby tossed little ones through water, one to the other, as their glee rang out. Ethel, as tired as he, her hands placid in her lap, watched as he growled, teased them, let them roughhouse him.

Only once did he talk politics. He porpoised up, swam to the pool's edge and, with the inevitable curiosity of one politician about another, discussed his opponents' style and tactics—bitter about one of them, fond of the other. Yet, as always during these last few days, his conversation came back to New York, his home state, and how difficult it would be unless California turned out good, today.

It was not until after 3 in the afternoon that he received a private first flash. CBS had done some early sampling of voters as they left the polls and now guessed it might wind up as high as 49/41 Kennedy over McCarthy, with 10 for the Lynch-Humphrey slate. He sat there in the mist, in blue pullover and flowered beach trunks, and did not react to the news. Ethel asked whether it was good enough. He made no response. He wanted to know about South Dakota—were any early returns in yet? If South Dakota, rural, and California, the nation's most urban state, both went for Kennedy on the same day—*then* there was a real chance, not only in New York but with the key brokers.

By now Richard Goodwin and Fred Dutton had joined him; they were pleased. Slowly the warmth and taste of victory came over him—and hope, too. He yawned, stretched his arms, suddenly drowsy, and said he thought he would take a nap. He left relaxed and confident.

IT WAS THE last time one would see him alone again. That evening in his huge suite, the rooms thronged with old friends, campaign workers, newsmen, there was no escape to share the joy privately with Ethel; friends and newsmen hunted them down from room to room as they tried to be alone for a moment, together. But the script of election night dictated otherwise. The votes were slow, but what was coming in was good and strong, a solid win, and the TV nets demanded their time. So he must wander from studio to studio to talk, answering again and again the old questions.

At midnight, ritual demanded that he go down to the screaming throng in the Embassy Room where, before the cameras of the nation and his supporters, he would accept victory. Then, after that, there would be a real party—Pierre and Nicole Salinger had invited

the old friends to a celebration at their discothèque, The Factory. So they watched him go down the corridor, moving in a boiling mob through the entanglement of television cables—to the people, who were waiting downstairs.

The people. To him they were not numbers, nor digits, nor blank faces to be manipulated only by the new techniques. They were the very essence of politics. Impatiently, furiously, he had fought for them, and the passions he stirred were a response to the emotions inside himself, the deep feeling that the very purpose of government is to do things for people. For this, they called him "ruthless," an epithet that seared his spirit.

Once, overwhelmed by a Midwestern mob, he quipped: "All this for a *ruthless* man? Just think what they would do for a kind one." Although he joked about the word, it cramped his thoughts and public behavior.

Robert F. Kennedy wore his heart open at all times, and though strangers hated him with a venom almost irrational, it was what this impetuous heart dictated that they feared. All those who knew him best knew its kindness and courage, gallantry and tenderness. Its outer shell was the armor and lance he bore in public; and the style others hated was that of a man who jousted for the things he loved and never wavered in his faith.

There was no party at the end. His friends rushed to the hospital or to the hotel where the forlorn children slept. One could not explain this faith to the brave youngster, still awake, fighting back his tears at the horror he had seen on television. One could only hold the child, order hot chocolate for him, try to comfort him, fighting back one's own tears while recognizing the father's image in the good strong face of the child. And hope that he would keep the faith, as all his family had, in his country and people, hard now as it might be.

LIFE June 14, 1968

DIRECT ELECTIONS: AN INVITATION TO NATIONAL CHAOS

Last September, in a triumph of noble purpose over common sense, the House passed and has sent to the Senate a proposal to abolish the Federal System.

It is not called that, of course. Put forth as an amendment to the Constitution, the new scheme offers a supposedly better way of electing Presidents. Advanced with the delusive rhetoric of *vox populi, vox Dei,* it not only wipes out the obsolete Electoral College but abolishes the sovereign states as voting units. In the name of The People, it proposes that a giant plebiscite pour all 70,000,000 American votes into a single pool whose winner—whether by 5,000 or 5,000,000—is hailed as National Chief.

American elections are a naked transaction in power—a cruel, brawling year-long adventure swept by profound passion and prejudice. Quite naturally, therefore, Constitution and tradition have tried to limit the sweep of passions, packaging the raw votes within each state, weighting each state's electoral vote proportionately to population, letting each make its own rules and police its own polls.

The new theory holds that an instantaneous direct cascade of votes offers cit-

izens a more responsible choice of leadership—and it is only when one tests high-minded theory against reality that it becomes nightmare.

Since the essence of the proposal is a change in the way votes are counted, the first test must be a hard look at vote-counting as it actually operates. Over most of the United States votes are cast and counted honestly. No one anymore can steal an election that is not close to begin with, and in the past generation vote fraud has diminished dramatically.

Still, anyone who trusts the precise count in Gary, Ind.; Cook County, Ill.; Duval County, Texas; Suffolk County, Mass.; or in half a dozen border and Southern states is out of touch with political reality. Under the present electoral system, however, crooks in such areas are limited to toying with the electoral vote of one state only; and then only when margins are exceptionally tight. Even then, when the dial riggers, ballot stuffers, late counters and recounters are stimulated to play election-night poker with the results, their art is balanced by crooks of the other party playing the same game.

John F. Kennedy won in 1960 by the tissue-thin margin of 118,550—less than 1/5 of one percent of the national total—in an election stained with outright fraud in at least three states. No one challenged his victory, however, because the big national decision had been made by electoral votes of honest-count states, sealed off from contamination by fraud elsewhere—and because scandal could as well be charged to Republicans as to Democrats. But if, henceforth, all the raw votes from Hawaii to Maine are funneled into one vast pool, and popular results are as close as 1960 and 1968, the pressure to cheat or call recounts must penetrate everywhere—for any vote stolen anywhere in the Union pressures politicians thousands of miles away to balance or protest it. Twice in the past decade, the new proposal would have brought America to chaos.

▶ To enforce honest vote-counting in all the nation's 170,000 precincts, national policing becomes necessary. So, too, do uniform federal laws on voter qualifications. New laws, for example, will have to forbid any state from increasing its share of the total by enfranchising youngsters of 18 (as Kentucky and Georgia do now) while most others limit voting to those over 21. Residence requirements, too, must be made uniform in all states. The centralization required breaches all American tradition.

▶ Reality forces candidates today to plan campaigns on many levels, choosing groups and regions to which they must appeal, importantly educating themselves on local issues in states they seek to carry.

But if states are abolished as voting units, TV becomes absolutely dominant. Campaign strategy changes from delicately assembling a winning coalition of states and becomes a media effort to capture the largest share of the national "vote market." Instead of courting regional party leaders by compromise, candidates will rely on media masters. Issues will be shaped in national TV studios, and the heaviest swat will go to the candidate who raises the most money to buy the best time and most "creative" TV talent.

▶ The most ominous domestic reality today is race confrontation. Black votes count today because blacks vote chiefly in big-city states where they make the margin of difference. No candidate seeking New York's 43 electoral votes, Pennsylvania's 29, Illinois' 26 can avoid courting the black vote that may swing those states. If states are abolished as voting units, the chief political leverage of Negroes is also abolished. Whenever a race issue has been settled by plebiscite—from California's Proposition 14 (on Open Housing) in 1964 to New York's Police Review Board in 1966—the plebiscite vote has put the blacks down. Yet a paradox of the new rhetoric is that Southern conservatives, who have most to gain by the new proposal, oppose it, while Northern liberals, who have most to lose, support it because it is hallowed in the name of The People.

WHAT IS WRONG in the old system is not state-by-state voting. What is wrong is the anachronistic Electoral College and the mischief anonymous "electors" can perpetrate in the wake of a close election. Even more dangerous is the provision that lets the House, if no candidate has an electoral majority, choose the President by the undemocratic unit rule—one state, one vote. These dangers can be eliminated simply by an amendment which abolishes the Electoral College but retains the electoral vote by each state and which, next, provides that in an election where there is no electoral majority, senators and congressmen, individually voting in joint session and hearing the voices of the people in their districts, will elect a President.

What is right about the old system is the sense of identity it gives Americans. As they march to the polls, Bay Staters should feel Massachusetts is speaking, Hoosiers should feel Indiana is speaking; blacks and other minorities should feel their votes count; so, too, should Southerners from Tidewater to the Gulf. The Federal System has worked superbly for almost two centuries. It can and should be speedily improved. But to reduce Americans to faceless digits on an enormous tote board, in a plebiscite swept by demagoguery, manipulated by TV, at the mercy of crooked counters—this is an absurdity for which goodwill and noble theory are no justification.

LIFE January 30, 1970

THE 'THEOLOGY' OF THE YOUTH VOTE

I have been studying the Supreme Court's majority rulings on voting rights: henceforward, in all Federal elections, full franchise is granted to illiterates and eighteen-year-olds. The rulings are lucid, convincing and legal as can be. But somehow they do not make sense.

It is not the practical mess they make of our election procedures that bothers me most—although that is serious. Over two centuries Americans have come to vote as citizens of both state and nation at the same time, same place, same polls. Now, in at least 47 of the fifty states, we will vote with split citizenship. One file of our polling places will hold illiterates and eighteen-year-olds, voting on the most complicated offices of national destiny. Another file of those who can read, write and are older, will be entitled also to vote on local governors, mayors, sheriffs.

Nor am I overwhelmingly upset by the tone-deaf political quality of these decisions. This November, fifteen states entertained propositions to lower the voting age. Only one, Alaska, voted to lower the age to eighteen, Montana and

Massachusetts dropped it to nineteen, Maine and Nebraska to twenty. The ten others threw such propositions out. It would have been wisest, politically, for the Supreme Court to leave so fundamental a decision to all the people of the Union, by the same amendment process used earlier to outlaw discrimination by race, sex or poll tax. But the Court did not do so.

What bothers me most, however, what nags at reason like a tooth just beginning to ache, is less immediate. It is the quality of political thinking that moved the Voting Rights Act through Congress to the Supreme Court. It is a quality of thinking I begin to call "theological liberalism" or "moral absolutism."

Moral absolutism is an entrancing logical construction of thought where, if one starts with a certified moral premise, then one occupies Moral Base A. Logic then leads to Moral Base B, Moral Base C and thus to Zed—each step logical in progression, but absurd in final result.

The Voting Rights Act of 1970 is a pure specimen of such thinking. It takes off from a certified immorality—

the brutal historical fact that black people in the South have been abused beyond the tolerance of conscience. Many blacks are illiterate because they have been deprived of any opportunity for education. This injustice must be rectified—Moral Base A. But to proceed from this base to the Supreme Court's conclusion that reading and writing are no longer necessary to qualify a man to vote for Federal office anywhere in the nation is unreasonable. I cannot be convinced that wiping out literacy as a qualification for voting on the President is the best way of righting injustice done to blacks in the South or Indians in the Southwest.

The provision that eighteen-year-olds must vote will probably debase the voting pool less; but it is another classic example of the dynamics of theological liberalism. Historically, it was Georgia that first permitted eighteen-year-olds to vote—in 1943. To Georgians it seemed that a man who must fight and die for his country should have a say in its leadership. True then, and still true. This truth could well have been stated flatly by an act of Congress, giving men who volunteer or are drafted the right to vote—whether at eighteen, seventeen or sixteen. But from this Moral Base A the new act proceeds, zip, to Zed. All eighteen-year-olds, in uniform or out, are enfranchised for Federal elections.

This thinking, and the Supreme Court reasoning, is unsettling—age now becomes a touchstone of discrimination, a prejudice of "class," in a muddle where civil rights and political

rights are confused. Nature has it that people mature at different ages—there are fools of thirty who will be fools at sixty; and youngsters of sixteen or seventeen as wise as any voters of middle years. Some arbitrary political choice must be made of the age of suffrage, and any political choice is an act of discrimination.

Thus, wisely, most state laws arbitrarily fix 21 as the age when men and women can dispose or manage their own affairs—and also as the age when they may share in the management of national affairs. But the thinking of the Supreme Court now affirms that discrimination by age is also morally wrong. It leads to some tantalizing questions: Are rules for mandatory retirements at 60, 65, 70 also discriminatory and illegal? Is denial of the vote to seventeen- and sixteen-year-old citizens also wrong?

Congress, which passed the Voting Rights Act of 1970, established Moral Base A in the Civil Rights Acts of 1964 and 1965. In moving this year's act, it hoped to receive the applause of the moralists while anticipating (as did the President) that the Supreme Court would restrain goodwill by common sense. This did not happen.

"Credo Quia Absurdum Est" ("I *believe* because it is absurd") chanted the devout in the Middle Ages. At this point I find myself unable further to believe "because it is absurd." It is not the substance of the decisions that threaten us—the inclusion of eighteen-year-olds and illiterates will not immediately alter the tilt between the two parties or

basically warp judgment on the issues. It is the theological quality in the thinking of the Court that upsets me more. Such thinking begets heretics.

NEW YORK TIMES January 6, 1971

A CONSERVATIVE BETRAYS HIS CAUSE

Of all the absurdities of American politics, none is more absurd than the choosing of a Vice President.

From Truman to Agnew—through Barkley, Nixon, Johnson and Humphrey—all have been imposed on politics in the turmoil of conventions, either by Executive fiat, or the hasty compromise of exhausted factional leaders. And, though the country has been governed by such accidental men for fourteen of the past 28 years, each has been treated as a ceremonial figure of little consequence and no meaning.

Spiro T. Agnew was different. He was a man who finally gave the fossil office meaning—not as a figure of government, but as spokesman for one of the grand neglected causes of American history, the cause of American conservatives. And, thus, of all the crimes charged against him by the Justice Department, none can match in national importance his betrayal of that cause, for which he spoke so eloquently.

One must look back on history, beyond the mandate of 1972, to measure the hurt he has now inflicted on American politics. For generations, the conservative cause in America has been an impulse lacking either a respected voice or coherent philosophy. American history gives conservatives neither an honorable tradition nor great heroes. Where British Tories can look back on such men as Disraeli and Churchill who added glory to the empire and pride to Englishmen, American conservatives have had to reach all the way back, past Calhoun to Hamilton to find a hero. The dull and tongueless men who paraded through American politics from Garfield through Harding and Hoover left us no more impressive descendants than Robert Taft, of starchy courage, and Barry Goldwater, of outraged integrity.

Image of a Watershed

The election of 1972 was thus—or so it appeared then—a watershed. For the first time since 1928, a conservative leadership appealed to the American people on clear issues—and won overwhelmingly. The conservatives, under Nixon, had read the mood of America better than the Democrats. They had read the times as signaling a halt in experimentation, a moment for curbs on power that affected the lives of common people.

The revelations of this spring and summer have profiled political tragedy. They have described a Nixon Administration, despite its creative historic achievement, as a conservative Administration worm-eaten by men who could not tell right from wrong.

The Americans had voted, in 1972, for a curb on power—in Vietnam, in their cities, in their schools. They had voted for "law-and-order," a civilized purpose. Then, all through the summer of 1973, they learned that what they had voted for was most abused by those who had promised it most solemnly. The first Attorney General of the Administration, it turned out, would be charged with violating the law he was sworn to uphold. The clean-cut young men who directed the mechanics of the Republican campaign were exposed as bungling knaves, as stupid as they were criminal. "My wounds save with the cold can not more ache," wrote Wilfred Owen of the men who held the line against adversity in Flanders in 1917; so might American conservatives have spoken until the unmasking of Spiro T. Agnew. But now, indeed, their wounds ache more.

Out of the Darkland

Spiro T. Agnew was chosen on Thursday morning, Aug. 8, 1968, at the Hilton Plaza hotel in Miami Beach, only a few blocks north of the Doral Hotel on the ocean, where, four years later, the Democrats were to repeat absurdity in choosing Tom Eagleton. Agnew's name had been tossed up to the weary Republican candidate, Richard Nixon, after four long and inconclusive round-the-clock sessions of Nixon's counselors and party leaders. Southerners had vetoed all liberal candidates for the Vice Presidency—Lindsay, Percy, Hatfield. Northerners had vetoed all conservatives—Reagan, Tower, Bush, Baker. Nixon's personal choice had been Robert Finch, but Finch refused the honor. Nixon was left with a choice between two men whom his closest advisers called "the political eunuchs," both of whom had survived the elimination contest: John Volpe and Spiro Agnew. And Nixon chose Agnew.

Agnew, however, turned out to be anything but a political eunuch. He had a gift of rhetoric, an authentic cadence to his speech which no other American conservative even approached. He had courage. He seemed, above all, intelligent and perceptive. He had come up in Maryland, out of suburbia, that darkland of American politics. Agnew understood and spoke for the emotions of homeowners, strivers, Middle Americans. His assault on the press, the most self-important power system in American life, was the most vivid public examination of its functioning by a political figure in recent years. Without doubt, after the mandate of 1972, Spiro Agnew was the leading candidate for the Presidency in 1976—a conservative with style.

And then he turned out to be a

cheap, common crook—a man who accepted cash for a fix even as he sat in the Executive Office Building; an income-tax chiseler who put campaign contributions into his own pocket; a small-minded man who could not, in his own conscience, recognize cheating for what it is.

In doing so, he betrayed the conservative cause. A novelist may bring sympathy to this son of an immigrant family, hardened by the struggle to make a living, polluted by the radioactivity of money all around him, finally achieving the poise, the presence, the personality of a major man of state.

But a historian can bring no sympathy to Spiro Agnew.

There has come on us a turning point in the flood of American ideas; the mandate of 1972 accepted and welcomed it. The Liberal Idea, which had overborne American thinking in the previous fifteen years, would have been stronger, tougher, more fruitful had it been forced to examine the reality of the country once more in 1976; it is strong enough to have warranted decent opposition. Had Spiro Agnew—the publicly perceived Agnew of a few months ago—run in 1976, the country would have been the better for it. The political system would have been refreshed by real outspoken debate between an intelligent conservative force and an intelligent liberal resistance.

Losing a Choice

Spiro Agnew, as the ablest spokesman of the conservative cause, has now and for some time to come deprived the country of this choice. No one else in our time who again uses the honorable words that Agnew so slickly mastered can speak them without arousing instant suspicion. No one who challenges the institutions he made his enemies—the press, the television networks, the great foundations, the universities—will be able to examine reasonably their power and their manner of using it. Far more than the scoundrels of Watergate, he has warped the structure of our politics. Almost as disastrously as Hoover's Depression hushed conservative voices for one generation, Agnew's felony may hush them for another. The conservatives deserved better than this.

NEWSWEEK October 22, 1973

THE MAKING OF THE PRESIDENT AIN'T WHAT IT USED TO BE

The thicket of primaries, the demands of TV, the complex new rules about money and delegates make accountants, lawyers and computers essential to the game of getting to the high seat of power. The author, after 24 years of President watching, provides a penetrating review of politics.

The map remains the same, of course; and so does the wise old Constitution that counts up our votes in communities, by states. But all else has changed. And I find myself 24 years down the road tracking the old story across strange turf, in a game with rules that neither I nor anyone else completely understands.

The old bosses are long gone and with them the old parties. In their place has grown a new breed of young professionals whose working skills in the new politics would make the old boys look like stumblebums. The transcontinental playing field still stretches from Maine to California—but in every back room, besides the old electoral map of the states, there now hangs the Map of the Major Media Markets. This new map decides how and where candidates travel, carves new political regions around the sprawl of great interstate television centers, pinpoints demographic audience targets.

Specialists now conduct campaigns. The men who understand the Media Map are the media masters. In the back rooms they are joined by other specialists—in public-opinion polling, in direct mail, in street and telephone canvassing, in ethnic analysis. Anyone who has the direct ear of the candidate is now called a "strategist"; the old-fashioned hatchet man out on the road is now styled a "surrogate." And the road itself has changed. Secret Service men protect the candidate's body and armed police patrol rallies from rooftops, scouting for assassins; their protection wraps a declared candidate in a cocoon that all but separates him from the people; and the friendly club of political reporters, which would once develop over a campaign year from a handful to a busload, now starts with a horde that chokes reporting and ends with a mob that overwhelms its story.

Political parties no longer control the delegates who choose the presidential candidates: the people do so in the primaries, swayed and brainwashed by the new professionals. Campaigns are more expensive than ever, but governors, senators, congressmen find that money is easier to come by, too. Such candidates run their own campaigns, hire their own professionals, win their seats independent of party support or discipline—and are quite willing to flout presidential leadership, which weakens both President and party. Most of all,

459

the primaries, which were devised to let ordinary people clarify their choices, have grown into a set of 35 ambuscades in 35 states, a six months' elimination contest that may well bore, confuse or disgust the voters before this year's long race is run.

A bloodless revolution has torn down the old power structures

In 1960 two notable candidates, Kennedy and Humphrey, fought two bitter primaries in Wisconsin and West Virginia that decided the Democratic nomination. In 1964 two Republicans, Goldwater and Rockefeller, clashed in three major primaries. In 1968 the Democratic field widened to three candidates and six critical primaries. By 1972 there were five Democrats battling in 12 states. By 1976 two Republicans and eight Democrats fought in 15 states, all of which were crucial.

This year, however, 13 men—10 Republicans, three Democrats—are facing off in 35 states, as well as Puerto Rico and the District of Columbia, in a free-for-all that is supposed to produce a reasoned and popular choice for President of the United States.

Is this a worse or better way of choosing Presidents than the old way? Do people have a larger or only a more confusing choice? How did we get Here from Back There? Above all, where is Here in the flow of American history?

THE BEST WAY of getting at the answers is to recognize that no master plan designed the curious and frantic way we now choose candidates for the presidency. Instead, a bloodless American revolution has, over the past 25 years, torn down the old power structures of American politics, substituting an unplanned, unfinished new structure. Finally, it is only by tracing the underlying revolution step by step, presidential year by presidential year, that one can understand how the present bizarre system came into being.

The time to start would be after World War II, with America the victorious and proud world power. In those days voters still came in "packages," a Republican and a Democratic package for most big cities and states, within which were smaller packages of ethnic groups, union groups, county groups and regional groups, most of them organized or tied together by traditional leaders.

The press of those days (controlled by Republicans) called the Democratic party's masters "bosses," their Republican counterparts "leaders." Republicans had "organizations," Democrats had "machines." New York had its Tammany, Chicago its Cook County machine, the southern states their courthouse gangs, California its Publishers Mafia. Together such bosses or leaders chose a majority of the delegates to the national conventions, where they made their deals and chose nominees from among their betters—some of whom, more often than not, made great American Presidents—Franklin Roosevelt, Harry Truman, Dwight Eisenhower.

Such bosses or leaders could safely ignore, and did for years, an idea that had first ruffled American politics at the turn of the century—the idea of a direct primary, which proposed that the people, not the bosses, should choose the two parties' candidates. Once the bosses had learned, however, that it was as easy to deliver the voter packages at the polls on primary day as on election day, they could relax. From 1901, when Florida put on the first primary, and for half a century thereafter, primaries were as useless as the rows of buttons on the sleeves of the well-tailored statesman—decorative but purposeless.

Until 1952.

In 1952 came the first flicker of change, and it was the Republicans who tickled it. Eastern Republican "leaders," in their traditional feud with midwestern Republican "leaders," decided to launch Dwight D. Eisenhower, "Mr. Hero," against Robert A. Taft, "Mr. Republican." The New Hampshire primary was their launching pad. Ike's primary showing convinced the party bosses at the Republican convention that he could win an election. His own record convinced Americans he could govern them.

I happened on the presidential scene four years later, in the New Hampshire primary of 1956, having recently come home, after 15 years, from the murderous cruelties of Asian politics and the cold rigidities of Europe. I did not know then, watching Estes Kefauver in New Hampshire, that he was trailblazing both a theme and a process in American national politics.

Kefauver was a disarming man—tall, burly, fond of women, even fonder of good whiskey, formidably learned, masquerading as a coonskin backwoodsman. Somewhere in his Tennessee youth he had run up against Boss Crump of Memphis: it had made him a reformer. As he sloshed through the snow and muck of "mud season" in New Hampshire, he denounced Adlai Stevenson as the creature of the wicked Cook County machine ("We can't turn our party over to Stevenson and the Chicago gangsters"). He won in New Hampshire six to one. A week later, he beat Stevenson in Minnesota—three to two. Whereupon, Stevenson, a doughty warrior, decided he must fight—and went on to baby kiss, handshake and plead in Florida, in Oregon, in California, beating Kefauver in these late contests and proving to the bosses that he was the Democrats' best vote getter. But together, Stevenson and Kefauver had made the primary contest the coast-to-coast marathon it still is starting in New Hampshire and ending in California.

*I*n 1964 two historic forces met to dominate our political future

All American presidential campaigns are both farewells and beginnings and it would be good to say that that most romantic of modern campaigns, the triumph of John F. Kennedy, was more beginning than end. Its gallantry, however, lay in Kennedy's elegant fight against the past and his triumph over that past, while the beginning of the great revolution in American politics had to wait until his administration, once installed, opened the gates. To understand what that revolution was to do to American politics it is best to skip directly to the campaign of 1964, and watch the revolution in America grunt its way forward by several giant steps.

IN 1964 TWO historic forces met and married to dominate America's political future—television, whose producers were beginning to explore its full reach and impact, and the black people of America, whose leaders insisted that national politics be opened to all races.

My memories of television's explosive entry bring back most vividly the Republican campaign of 1964. At the Cow Palace in San Francisco, Nelson Rockefeller prodded and taunted and mocked the raging Sunbelt Republicans, denounced Barry Goldwater, laughed at their fury while the audience howled in fist-shaking frenzy. ("You lousy lover, you lousy lover," I remember one woman screeching through Rockefeller's allotted five minutes on the platform.)

It was true spectacle, apparent savagery, drama that TV directors could show live, then cut and edit for showing again and again. Just such scenes of real savagery in Chicago, four years later in 1968, ruined the Democratic candidate, Hubert Humphrey. Television, thus, would dominate all national conventions forever after. "If I had had a pint of brains," Barry Goldwater told me later, "I should have known in San Francisco that I had lost the election right there."

But television was not through with Goldwater. There was, first, the new stage on which he, as all other candidates ever since, had to perform: the network half-hour evening news shows that had begun only the year before, in September 1963. Goldwater was a man of such stark candor that he could usually be relied on to produce a prickly and quotable truth that would arouse millions and enrage more. TV murdered him. All national campaigns after the coming of the evening news shows have been aimed directly at the nightly news—major speeches and statements must be made before three o'clock in the afternoon (East Coast time) to reach their target, the national TV viewers, by nightfall.

The choice of a media manager is critical to the candidacy

Television's evening news entered American consciousness so effectively that it was an institution within a month after its beginnings, and the accepted prime forum of politics six months later. No so, however, with the other great television intrusion into politics that year—the adversary commercial.

The adversary commercial arrived like a clap of thunder, the brainchild of William Bernbach, chief of Doyle Dane Bernbach, Inc., one of New York's more creative advertising agencies. Bernbach demanded from Lyndon Johnson, and surprisingly won, complete control over the party's advertising. Bernbach did not want to be bothered by political second-guessers. ("Politics," he said once, "is about survival.") Bernbach is a mild-mannered man, almost sweet, usually smiling. But his commercials were of absolute savagery, with a slash that television had never known before. Best remembered is his Daisy Girl spot—the beautiful child plucking petals, counting in a high trill, is drowned out by the deep male voice of a missile countdown. The mushroom blast blots out the end of the commercial, with the unspoken message that Goldwater is for bombs, Johnson against them. A second spot followed 10 days later—a deliciously beautiful little girl is licking an ice-cream cone, while in voice-over comes a tender, motherly voice explaining how bad nuclear fallout is for children. Then, in lullaby tones, comes the message, "There's a man who wants to be President of the United States who . . . wants to go on testing more bombs. His name is Barry Goldwater. . . ." Such commercials all but branded Goldwater as a babykiller. Outrage limited both to only one show-

ing on national TV, but other commercials followed. The one Republicans hated most, coast to coast, was a clip of a pair of hands tearing up a Social Security card, *your* Social Security card, while in the background a voice repeated one of Goldwater's horseback opinions on the uselessness of Social Security. The commercial made Goldwater the enemy of the old people—and old people vote.

Goldwater had been created as a national candidate by the tactical skills of his early campaign chairman, F. Clifton White, the last grand master of old-school, back-room politics. White knew how to tie up the packages; but he was dismissed the day after Goldwater's triumph. Television and its new professionals thereupon undid his packages. Lyndon Johnson would have defeated Goldwater anyway—but television destroyed him.

From 1964 on, the choice of the media manager of a presidential campaign has been critical to the candidacy. From William Bernbach of Madison Avenue in 1964 to Gerald Rafshoon of Atlanta in 1976, the choice has ranked with that of campaign manager, chief fund raiser and chief brain truster as a first imperative of candidacy. The media manager must be artist, whore and businessman all at once. He must be able to shoot film and catch the voice that gives his candidate nobility, force, regular-fellowship or statesmanship in either 30-second, 90-second, five-minute or half-hour exposures. He must know how to edit the film, where to buy the time slots and precisely what local or network audience he hopes to reach—earnest citizen, common slob, rock 'n' roll fan or union man.

THE CAMPAIGN of 1964 would have been memorable enough if only for its illustration of television's power. But history that year was to put on another demonstration that far outdid television's impact on American politics. For that, one must move from the Cow Palace of San Francisco to the convention hall in Atlantic City, where the Democrats met the same year.

Many reporters came to the Atlantic City convention from the "Mississippi Summer" of that year, where northern students, white and black, were trying to register blacks to vote—and failing. The convention itself was ringed with such students chanting that the Democratic National Committee must unseat the all-white regular Democratic Mississippi delegates. Television caught that. But it could not catch the shudder in a hot muggy hearing room where a black woman, Fannie Lou Hamer, told the Credentials Committee what had happened in Mississippi when she tried to register to vote.

". . . It wasn't too long before three white men came to my cell. . . . I was carried out of the cell into another cell where they had two Negro prisoners. The state highway patrolman ordered the first Negro to take the blackjack. . . . I laid on my face. The first Negro began to beat, and I was beat until he was exhausted. . . . The second Negro began to beat and I began to

work my feet. . . . I began to scream, and one white man got up and began to beat me on my head and tell me to 'hush.' One white man—my dress had worked up high—he walked over and pulled my dress down and he pulled my dress back, back up. . . . All of this on account we want to register, to become first-class citizens, and if the Freedom Democratic Party is not seated now, I question America. . . ."

Three days later, the blacks of the Mississippi Freedom Democratic Party had invaded the convention hall and occupied the seats of the all-white Mississippi Democratic Party. The blacks were clearly illegal. The whites were clearly immoral. Party leaders that evening offered a compromise, quickly accepted. The blacks of the Mississippi Freedom Democratic Party would get two votes at this convention, and beginning with the next convention in 1968, no delegation would be seated from any state where the party process deprived citizens of the right to vote because of race or color.

It was considered an interim compromise—but it was to change the entire character of American politics from then on. Somehow, someday this ban on *exclusion* would become an insistence on *inclusion*.

We should pause over the Compromise of 1964, for, at the time, its effect was incalculable. Until then the great American parties had been a crazy quilt, a patchwork of like-minded people, each state choosing its delegates by its own rules, sometimes boss controlled, sometimes slated entirely by one man, sometimes bought out by one big corporation, sometimes the marionette show of one great labor union. The national conventions accepted the delegations sent, and sometimes in rowdy, sometimes in frolicsome circumstances, the back-room boys worked out their deals.

Now, however, for the first time, a national party had binding national rules. States must obey—or be excluded. If the rules insisted on the inclusion of blacks, why not Hispanics? Why not women? Why not youth? Why not, finally, seat every group that the national party reform committees decided had a claim on the power, jobs and spoils that went with the presidency? Step by step, convention by convention, television would present the spectacle outside and on the floor, while in the committee rooms the rules were rewritten—as if to provide a new script for the show four years hence.

Memory is pocked with the scenes and emotions—and the residue left behind in rules.

*D*emocratic leaders winced at the impact of woman power

It is Chicago, 1968. Enter American youth, protesting. It is Vietnam-time. Blood and tear gas foul the streets. Just as the youngsters seem about to overwhelm the headquarters hotel at the corner of Michigan and Balbo Drive,

Mayor Daley's cops with tear gas and nightsticks sweep the streets of the insurgents. But in the committee rooms, the insurgents win their cause. Shamed, confused in the din of the floor, the regular delegates accept a Minority Report on Rules that they do not understand. It demands that all Democratic voters get "full, meaningful and timely opportunity to participate in the selection of delegates" to the next convention and sets up a commission to rewrite party rules.

It is Miami in 1972—the year the women break through. They encamp at the Betsy Ross Hotel, caucus, organize, nominate a woman for vice-president, demand and get a woman as Democratic National Chairperson, make Democratic politicians wince at the impact of woman power. Five weeks later, as the Republicans also meet in Miami, the crazies try to entice television away from Nixon's convention by baring their bosoms in Flamingo Park and jouncing their lovely breasts for the camera eye. But the real breakthrough had already been made by sterner women.

*T*he curtain rises this month on the first act in New Hampshire

It is New York, 1976. Jimmy Carter saunters down the aisle of Madison Square Garden. He is choreographed to pause, turn, greet Richard Daley. But he ignores Daley, mounts the platform—and holds the whole party in his hand. The convention roars. He has come there by the primary route, by the new politics. These delegates on the floor are entirely new people, the Daleys are old and fading. Another reform commission will follow this convention, but already a new breed dominates the party—people who know how to win primaries, manage caucuses, use computers, gear organization to media. They move in clusters, like roving guerrilla bands, and get out the vote wherever they go. "Political junkies" they call themselves—people who in their 20s were protesting the Vietnam war, hardened in the campaigns of Clean Gene and Bobby in '68, in Cesar Chavez's boycotts, in McGovern's Army of '72, in a dozen individual state battles. They and the media men are the new professionals. Like the old professionals, they know all about politics—except how to govern.

In both parties—in the Republican party less, to be sure, than in the Democratic party—these are the men and women, now in their 30s or early 40s, who dominate the field commands of 1980.

THE CAMPAIGN OF 1980 has now been under way for over a year—the candidates crisscrossing the country in their transcontinental mating dances with the voters, straw poll following straw poll, caucuses tuning up for rehearsals. But the curtain rises on the first act this month. February, when New Hampshire, as always, votes first; then a week later, Massachusetts and Vermont. Then follow all the others until Sweepstakes Day, June 3, when eight states (including California, Ohio, New Jersey) vote, to round out a total of 37 primaries, electing more than three fourths of all the delegates to the two national conventions, both now swollen to almost twice their size of 20 years ago.

Three major regulatory changes will separate these 1980 campaigns from those of years gone by. And it is important always to bear in mind that each set of laws or regulations was fostered by good intentions and then undermined by the Law of Unintended Consequences. A fourth change is the most important so we will come to it last.

THE FIRST MAJOR change abolished the old unit rule. Down through the 1960s, each state could decide either by custom, law or its delegation's decision to vote at the convention in one solid bloc. This unit rule gave bosses, kingmakers, dominant publishers as well as little states their clout, as blocs of power shifted on the floor like chess pieces played by one hand. Starting in 1968, however, the Democrats have insisted that each delegation represent all the people in its state, that all delegates vote as individuals. The Republicans, too, have now outlawed the unit rule—except for the state of California, where a winner-take-all state law governs its party primary and has withstood all petitions and attempts to abolish it. With the exception, thus, of the Republican delegation from California, all the other delegates of both parties are up for grabs in an unprecedented free-for-all. What this free-for-all means is that every candidate has to fight for his share of delegates in every state, in every single congressional district—with no cop-outs, loopholes or graceful courtesies to favorite sons. It means, for example, that Senator Kennedy cannot yield any Southern state to favorite son Jimmy Carter. Jimmy Carter is odds-on favorite to carry Alabama's primary—but if Kennedy gets 20 percent of Alabama's vote, he will probably get 20 percent of Alabama's delegates, which could prove critical in convention balloting. Similarly, Carter will fight for New York. If he gets 30 percent of New York's popular vote in the congressional districts, he can probably claim 30 percent of its massive 282-man convention delegation. And if Governor Brown gets 10 percent of the popular vote here, 20 percent there, up to 50 percent in his native California—then Brown may have up to 25 percent of the convention delegates and become, if not the candidate, the convention's power-broker-in-chief.

The abolition of the unit rule makes the Democratic contest a spirited one; but it can make the Republican convention a chaos. With 10 candidates, among whom no less than four major personalities mean to hang in, this convention could turn out to be the most intricately brokered one since Republican "leaders" chose Warren G. Harding on the 10th ballot in 1920.

Abolition of the unit rule makes the long primary route an ordeal, with no mercy for the weak or faint of heart, but it probably is a good thing. Even though it puts a premium on a candidate's glands and endurance rather than his thought, still it has opened the process. And even though the sequencing and management of the primaries desperately need some national law to bring order out of chaos, the direct primaries probably accomplish what their dreamers set out to do—involve more Americans directly in choosing the national leader.

THE SAME CANNOT be said of the second set of changes, the so-called outreach rules. With these, the Law of Unintended Consequences has translated a genuinely noble concept into a hodgepodge of racism, sexism and special interests.

To understand the outreach rules, one probably ought to fix first on a little-noticed decision of the Supreme Court, *Cousins* v. *Wigoda,* handed down in 1975, with political consequences almost of the same order as *Brown* v. *Board of Education.* Back in 1972 the McGovern people had thrown Dick Daley's white ethnic Chicago delegates out of the Democratic convention, a political decision neatly characterized by the Chicago *Daily News'* political wise man Mike Royko: "Anybody who would reform Chicago's Democratic party by dropping the white ethnic would probably begin a diet by shooting himself in the stomach." Three years later the controversy ran all the way up to the Supreme Court, which finally ruled that since a national party was a free association of people, Daley's delegates had been properly excluded, Illinois law to the contrary notwithstanding. A political convention of a national party can therefore now decide, if it wants to, just who is a qualified delegate and who may be excluded, whether or not sent there by the common voters.

Today the Democratic Party sets racial standards for delegates

In making the rules of the two parties paramount over the laws of the states, the Supreme Court hastened a yeasting that had been working in American politics for generations—the slow, undeniable, growing demand of minority groups to share in the power and spoils of high office. And the paradoxes that now govern selection of Democratic delegates by skin color and descent are so enormously complicated that they defy simplification. But what was heard on the floor of the Atlantic City convention of 1964 as a scream for racial justice has climaxed, 16 years later, in a cruel bureaucratic division that sets one American heritage against another. In Atlantic City the old faith of America as stamped on its coins, *e pluribus unum,* was still valid: it has become now, in presidential selection, *ex uno plures.* After three reform commissions, the Democrats' official manual honorably urges all state parties to reach for "ethnics, youth, persons over 65 years of

age, workers . . . the physically handicapped." But it also orders that the states' Democratic parties shall practice "Affirmative Action," shall weight their search in favor of "women, blacks, Hispanics and Native Americans." If the voters, who usually vote by congressional district, do not choose the proper names preordained by the affirmative action rules, the entire delegation may be hauled up by the Compliance Review Commission. And if the Credentials Committee of the convention decides the Compliance Review Commission has rightly challenged the choice of the state's voters, they can throw them out of the Democratic convention as was done with Dick Daley's freely chosen delegates in 1972.

We can take, for example, the case of New York State with its 39 congressional districts and 282 Democratic delegates. Covering New York politics today makes a reporter almost long for the old days when a Tammany source would tip him off: "This time we'll choose an Irishman from Brooklyn for the mayor's slot and fill the other two spots with a Jew from the Bronx and an Italian from Queens." The coarseness of such reality offended the civic sense that New York, like the nation, should be governed by the best qualified, the ablest persons.

Today the Democratic party *mandates* such racial qualifications. On March 25 each of New York's 39 districts will vote for a Democratic candidate for President. A month later, Democrats will gather in caucus in each district and choose names, real people, as delegates to fit the proportion of votes their candidates got in their district.

If this seems complicated, it is. But it gets more so. If the voters in the caucus choose all white males, or all black females, or all Jewish Talmudic students, or all WASP schoolteachers—what then? Then, says the intricate law, the State Democratic Committee will choose 64 at-large delegates designed to balance the choice of race, sex and ethnic origins so as to reflect the social composition of the state as a whole, as well as its preference for the Democratic candidate.

No one quite understands how all this will work out this spring, and New York's politicians, a quarrelsome lot, are ready to sue at the flip of the polling-booth curtain. Under pressure, the State Democratic Committee has allotted a fixed quota of delegates to blacks (19 percent), another to Hispanics (7.2 percent) and is considering a quota for Asian-Americans. New York's Democratic delegation will go to the national convention in 1980 split by race, color, sex and ethnic origin. No Jim Farley will swing them as a bloc, either to support or oppose a candidacy or extort privileges for the Empire State.

THE THIRD SET of technical changes, without ever intending to do so, separates the President from control of Congress and divorces party control from national purpose. This set of changes brings us to the inescapable, if dirty, subject of money and the inescapable, though historic, connection at all times, everywhere, between money and politics.

*M*oney buys access to the men who make the laws

There is nothing that politicians, old and new, left and right, utopian and pragmatic, hate more than the new laws that govern the use of money in American politics. All agree that much in these new laws is necessary—but that, as a whole, they are indigestible.

One has to start, again, with the past to understand these new laws. ("Money," said Jesse Unruh, once a young Stevensonian idealist, now the hard-bitten treasurer of the state of California, "is the mother's milk of politics.") In times gone by it was quite accurate to say that the Southern Pacific Railroad owned the California Assembly, the Pennsylvania Railroad owned the State House in Harrisburg, the big oil companies owned Texas politics, and the Rockefeller family owned the New York Republican party. Money in politics buys attention or access to the men who make the laws or, quite frequently, it buys laws and officials themselves. But riding the crest of the liberalism of the '60s, new federal laws began to come off the legislative assembly line.

The first laws, those passed in 1971, insisted that candidates report where and how they get their money. These early laws revealed that one generous Chicago insurance man, W. Clement Stone, had been so moved as to give Mr. Nixon's 1972 campaign no less than $2,051,643.45; further research revealed that in 1968 he had contributed $2,813,699. For these huge sums, Mr. Stone received in personal favors apparently nothing. He simply *liked* to give his money to a President he could talk to.

Similarly, Stewart Mott, a dashing young man and heir to a goodly chunk of the General Motors fortune, gave $400,000 to George McGovern's campaign and, in aggregate, more than that to other liberal candidates of 1972, for a total of $822,592. Like Republican Stone, Democrat Mott apparently sought nothing for himself. But there were others who wanted something, such as fugitive-from-justice Robert L. Vesco, who put a secret $200,000 in cash into the Nixon campaign; groups like the milk dealers, Northrop aviation, Gulf Oil; sinister characters determined to buy influence at the White House or an indulgence from the IRS. The 1971 laws led to the unraveling of the flow of campaign money to Mr. Nixon; which led to the unraveling of the Watergate scandal; which led, in a burst of indignation, to the election laws of 1974. Which then led to further revisions in 1976. Which will lead, undoubtedly, to further and further revisions until, perhaps, no one will understand the rules of campaign financing.

What the new laws attempt to do is to limit the ability of rich men to buy attention or indulgence. No individual can now give more than $1,000 to any one presidential candidate. For Clement Stone and Stewart Mott this is like trussing up a brood cow in milking season. It is so for scores of other six-figure givers. A few candidates, as well as some givers, welcome the change. Said one of George McGovern's closest advisers of the campaign of 1972, "If the law had been in effect then, we wouldn't have had to go out to Max Palevsky's house for a lecture every time we passed through Los Angeles." Palevsky, a computer genius, contributed or loaned $373,875 to McGovern before his nomination in 1972.

Far more important than the curbing of individual money was the curtailing of group money power. For years there have been those who put up big money for causes they held dear: Texas oilmen for their interests; the steelmen of the Midwest for theirs; the farmers and schoolteachers; the Jews of New York and Beverly Hills for civil rights and Israel. With the new laws such groups can no longer harvest a million dollars at one evening's dinner, as they did in Los Angeles for Richard Nixon in 1972; or a million dollars at one small breakfast, as did a handful of liberals for Stevenson two days after his nomination in 1956.

But not even the giving of the present $1,000 maximum is simple; it must fit the overall law of "matching funds." This year a presidential candidate is allowed to spend a legal limit for the primaries of almost $16 million, half of which will be matched by government money if the candidate meets certain rules. The maximum you can give a candidate is $1,000, but no more than $100 of that can be in cash; and no more than $250 will be matched by the government. And, whether in cash or by check, the donor of $100 or $1,000 must fill out a form stating his name, home address, business address and occupation. This frightens many people who do not want to be officially recorded on a "givers" or "suckers" list— or, worse, be caught on the wrong side, officially, if their candidate loses and a vengeful victor checks up. Candidates must file reports monthly, keep books open for inspection and meet so many intricate rules of how much money was collected where, in what denominations, from how many individuals in how many states, that the head twirls. John Connally of Texas has already decided to give up government matching funds in order to run his campaign as he wants.

professional accountants anticipated, it was more quickly staffed than were the advance-schedule unit or the field-organization unit. Behind their plywood partition, young men and women opened mail, extracted cash, photostated checks, sent out requests for further information on contributions, compiled lists and arranged for an on-line computing center to process their data batches. The Kennedy team in 1980 means to be in full compliance with all laws—and so do the staffs of all other candidates. No candidate wants to leave a loose thread for unraveling such as led to the Nixon disaster of 1972–73.

But the new laws have created such complications that, at times, it may be useless for a campaign to accept an honest 10 dollar bill if it is unaccompanied by name and address—the bookkeeping costs too much.

*H*ow to make the crucial decisions on where the money goes

*N*ew laws encourage the formation of powerful action groups

Perhaps the best way of getting at what recent changes in laws have done to politics in 1980 is to pay a visit to the headquarters of presidential candidate Edward Kennedy. The first fully operational unit of his campaign, within a week of its announcement, was its accounting staff. With two lawyers, unnumbered volunteers and 15 to 20

In 1960, several weeks before the convention, John Kennedy remarked that he thought it would cost $750,000 for all his campaign expenses from primary through convention. Now, 20 years later, it may cost his brother almost that much in bookkeeping expenses alone.

THE NEW MONEY laws change entire campaign strategies. Do you shoot your legal wad in the early primaries to gain attention—and then run broke, as did Henry Jackson in 1976, in the middle primaries? Or do you save your money for national television on Sweepstakes Tuesday in June? And even then you must watch the state-by-state rules, some of which are absurd. For example: one regulation details the allowable expenditures of a candidate state by state; in each state it comes to a ceiling of 16 cents times the number of the voting-age population, adjusted for inflation. Thus, in next month's New Hampshire primary, each candidate may legally spend only $264,600 as his total. But how does a candidate divide his New Hampshire costs from his Massachusetts costs, when every dollar spent on Boston television reaches over the border to the critical voting belt of New Hampshire independents on that state's southern rim? John Connally originally planned to reach New Hampshire Republicans by heavy spending on Boston television. George Bush has tried shoe leather, sweat, hard work and hand-shaking—but also had spent $190,000 by the first of this year to spread the message by radio and television across New England. The greater portion of his media budget he will save for primaries later down the road. Then there's the critical Texas Republican primary. Any airplane trip within Texas must be considered an in-state expense, and a campaign jaunt from El Paso to San Antonio to Dallas to Houston must be recorded against the Texas state limit set at $1,899,193. But if candidate Ronald Reagan, say, flies from California to Dallas, Texas, that is an interstate, not an in-state, trip; and if he campaigns that night in Tulsa, Oklahoma, and flies back to Houston, Texas, these also are interstate trips that do not count against his legal Texas limit. Or perhaps they do. No one knows whether he might be declared a lawbreaker or not for a decision that, 20 years ago, was a candidate's to make as he saw fit.

What the new laws of financing have done, finally and disastrously, is to weaken the leadership of a presidential candidate over his party—and strengthen the influence over Congress of special groups whose interests may conflict directly with the President's vision of the future.

The new laws, for example, encourage the formation of Political Action Committees: not only labor groups, cause groups and environmental groups, but also corporations, trade associations, kooks, freaks and special-interest gatherings are all invited to form PACs and put money into politics. Though you can give only $1,000 to the presidential candidate of your choice, you can give $5,000 to any Political Action Committee of your choice—or to a number of them. These in turn can then hand out your money to candidates at every level as they wish. In the old days I discovered that a crusty old Texas oil-man named Hugh Roy Cullen, an ardent supporter of Joe McCarthy, had put his money into congressional races in no less than 23 states, as well as Texas—and I found this shocking. But today the law *requires* a PAC to qualify as a receptacle of honey money by investing not in one candidate but in at least five. There were 650 PACs in 1975; there are 1,910 now. They range from the giant aerospace firms to such special-interest groups as pro- or anti-abortion, pro- or anti-smog, pro- or anti-rifle. Thus, while presidential candidates must go the primary route, seeking money by bits and pieces, by media appeal, by direct mail and by qualifying for federal matching funds, the congressional candidates may go another way, dependent more and more on PAC money.

This separation between a President and his party bothers thoughtful people. "The terrible thing," said Vice-President Walter Mondale one recent afternoon, relaxing in his rounds as chief surrogate for Jimmy Carter, "is that a President has *got* to do unpopular things, knowing the party is not responsive, that you have to face the uncontrolled fury of the people in the primaries." Mondale reflected on how Truman could count on the bosses to deliver the old packages in the primaries and the Congress. "But," he said, "there's been this whole sea change of issues," and went on to tick off the changes in his 16 years in Washington—inflation, the growing Soviet threat, the need for managing and housekeeping the reforms of the '60s and '70s, the need for huge immediate expenditures on energy investments, which will pay off only many years later. Every one of the things that *had* to be done, thought Mondale, was unpopular. And there was no way of controlling the party in the primaries ahead: "The

revolution in the party's nominating process has weakened the presidency more than people perceive."

POLITICAL HISTORIANS, looking back on the sweep of American history, like to identify what they call Critical Elections—elections that set new directions, elections that made people see hidden problems as clearly obvious, elections that suggested solutions. Lincoln's election in 1860, Wilson's in 1912, Roosevelt's in 1932, Kennedy's in 1960 are now all seen as signals of turnings. And so the election of 1980 may well become a Critical Election—if only one of the candidates can in the next few months make his choice of direction clear.

It is easy to explain how television grabbed, then dominated the political process. Easy to explain how the passions of the '60s forced Americans to stand apart and look at one another, dividing delegations by race, sex, origin. Easy to explain how the "open" process has made the conventions a mob scene where, instead of the 1,300 or 1,500 manageable delegates of 20 years ago, the parties now assemble 2,000 to 3,000 in unmanageable hordes. Easy to trace how the new laws, the new technicians, the new specialists of elections have divorced candidates from party, Presidents from control.

But all these are technical changes.

The fourth and last change is the most important of all.

What has changed most is America's place in history, our sense of American power and its reach . . . either overseas in Tehran or at home in the ruins of the South Bronx.

*I*n the past the victor was always the man with the clear message

In the last week of his 1956 campaign for reelection, President Eisenhower, in one of the great blunders of his career, chopped off his wartime allies—England and France—in their attempt to keep control of the Suez Canal and thus retain access to the oil of the Middle East. We Americans did not then need Middle Eastern oil, so his dramatic act, wrapped in the moral rhetoric that always drapes the last week of a presidential campaign, seemed fitting. One could not foresee, in 1956, any shortage of the gasoline we would need for the new suburbs and supermarkets that were growing up around Eisenhower's interstate highway program. Besides—if it came to trouble—we could, by the flick of a finger, settle any Middle Eastern disorder. Indeed, two years later, in July of 1958, Eisenhower deployed 70 warships of our Sixth Fleet. On a hot summer afternoon 2,000 Marines landed in turbulent Lebanon, with no opposition, to support a friendly government against an imminent communist coup. During a gradual buildup to 15,000 men, one U.S. soldier was killed by a sniper's bullet. But within

months the troops were pulled out. Such, then, was our power. Carter should have it so good.

This power is no more, and this, more than any other change, affects the way the election of 1980 will run. Dwight Eisenhower in 1952 and 1956, John F. Kennedy in 1960, Lyndon Johnson in 1964 all spoke for a nation whose power was, fundamentally, unlimited. The unspoken question in those campaigns was whom should the people choose to use it. The victor was always the man with the clear message, the man who could drive the spike of his direction through the blurred issues to a national purpose.

*T*he great strength of the U.S. election system is its power to educate

As I write, two great issues weigh on American politics. The first is the humiliation in the Middle East; this, we can hope, will pass as other thunderheads have passed. But the second is far more terrifying—the intertwined phenomena of inflation and energy shortage, the sickening realization by Americans that money and savings are worth less and less every year, that all the virtues taught in childhood are eroding. Every conversation at every level is invaded by price talk: What did you pay this week for oranges or meat?

For a pair of shoes or a car? Inflation, like the threat of war, makes all private planning a gamble and renders public planning powerless to protect any individual from the future.

These issues—inflation, energy and foreign policy—are, of course, locked one to the other. Our foreign policy built a world of hope after victory in World War II. Now the needs of this world affect everything from the vital food prices at the supermarket to the casual pennies at the newsstand. The most backward people have learned they need not starve—thus they bid up the price of our food. A billion people in Asia and Africa are learning to read and write; they need textbooks and newspapers. So we must share with them the resources of paper pulp we once monopolized and pay a quarter for the newspaper that used to cost a dime. These are problems our own goodwill invited and we must accept.

But many of our problems reflect an ugly outside world where a growing contempt for and hostility to America are a new reality. An open trade war is being waged against America by the oil-producing countries. An undeclared trade war has been conducted against America for the past two decades by a defeated enemy, Japan, that America helped restore to prosperity. These realities must be recognized—and dealt with.

The great and residing strength of the American election system is its power to educate, and problems crowd the agenda in 1980. It is not only inflation and the Ayatullah and oil policy that seek definition. The decay of our inner cities, the crumbling of our borders by silent penetration of illegal immigrants, as well as the promise of molecular biology, the vision of control of rain, wind and weather that seems almost in our grasp—all these, too, need to be defined. Then a message must sound that offers an approach to them. No amount of media management or scientific polling can give an answer to what really bothers us. That is for the candidate himself to say. The conventional 20-point platform, five-point solution, bold new answers that usually make up the dreary oatmeal breakfast of a campaign are all but irrelevant. The answers to all the problems the candidate senses will seem different to the President after six weeks in office—and his campaign promises will, as always, be left to wither. What is characteristic of a great campaign is not that the candidate has precision answers to precision questions, but that he makes clear the direction in which he hopes to find the answers.

At this early stage, what the campaign of 1980 lacks is what Critical Elections are remembered for: a clear call in a clear *direction* by someone who knows where he wants to take the American people. American elections are history's greatest dice game with fate. It is an occasion when ordinary people are given not only the illusion but also the right to control the governance and events of their lives. These elections are the opportunity to send, or return, a leader with the authority to govern at home and act abroad. If any of the candidates, from favorite Jimmy Carter to dark horse George Bush, can give a clear choice of direction and get the voters to agree—this election may, after all, be called Critical. With luck, its victor has a chance to be a great President.

LIFE February, 1980

NEW POWERS, NEW POLITICS

Blacks and women, says the author, are altering the political landscape.

I am flying from Chicago to New York, as I have so often. The runway lights of O'Hare fall away beneath. Then: up and over the lake and, once airborne, I usually drowse. But not tonight, for something is disturbing me—a paradox is unrolling below. Detroit is the same light blur to the north, Cleveland the same ground glow to the south; then over Pennsylvania's dark hills and finally the sea approach to La Guardia, with the carpet of New York's lights sparkling in greater splendor than ever before. The spectacle proclaims a robust civilization, alive and thriving, the same as ever, only bigger, better, more beautiful.

Except that it is not the same as ever.

I fly between these two cities regularly. But what my eyes tell me from the sky, my ear to the ground contradicts. Winds are blowing down below that have not stirred American politics in just this way in a half-century. Down there, one system of politics is giving way to another still unnamed, unshaped. In Chicago, they tell me it is simply the breakup of the old Daley machine as the locals fight for control of its parts, patronage and pieces. But a

visit to the City Council says "no" to that easy answer. Pictorially, the Council offers a study in black and white.

There on the platform is the black Mayor, Harold Washington, handsome, gray-haired, majestic in appearance, a man of mottled record. Below the platform, before the hemicycle of aldermen, struts Edward R. Vrdolyak, debonair and pinch-waisted, the best-tailored machine politician in America, almost taunting as he saunters between his honor the Mayor and the machine's white majority. Almost all 50 aldermen used to dance like marionettes to Mayor Daley's beat, the blacks full and willing participants in the chorus line of the machine. This new Mayor controls only 21, mostly black, a sprinkling of white allies among them. But Vrdolyak's 29 are the majority, ethnics all in this paradigm of ethnic cities—Slavs, Irish, Italians, Germans. Together they paralyze the city. This is more than a struggle for spoils or control of the machine. This is stark; black against white; and that is new. Chicago was not like this before.

In New York, it is different, too. On the clutter of my desk as I return, my

eye falls on the headlines of The Amsterdam News, the most important
black newspaper in America. "Black
Mayor in Philly," shouts the headline,
"When Is N.Y.C.'s Turn?" That headline would not have run in New York 10
years ago; it, too, is new. Boston, Birmingham, Los Angeles, Atlanta, Hartford, Flint—on and on come new
names as the black surge rolls up to the
city halls.

I can sense winds shaping new forces:
the women, for example, whose impact
on politics in this decade will be at least
as great as the impact of the blacks, perhaps greater. Together, the unlikely
combination of blacks and women insists on sharpening the definition of
"equality," the fundamental faith of our
nation. But so much else is new, too.
The homosexuals have moved, as a
force, into politics. New tides of immigration and ethnic pride are changing
the cities; environmentalists and ar-
dents of nuclear freeze add voices of
doom. To which is added the turmoil in
the old, orthodox "special interest"
groups such as labor, farmers and banking. Altogether they bewilder politics
in 1984, almost midway through a decade seeking definition. What rolls loose
now in American politics are forces of
emotion and resentment completely
outside the conventional old political
system.

Historians, whose wisdom is usually
enhanced by hindsight, may be able
later to sum up all these new stirrings
and their effects in an epigraphic Zeitgeist. We who follow elections as they
happen also recognize that it is the

spirit of the times that usually prevails
over formal politics, that undermines
old policies or sets forth new directions.
But we shall have only a few months,
from now to the end of the year, to find
a phrase for styling this decade of dis-
continuity. We cannot yet measure the
winds and counterwinds that may make
the formal counting of numbers in the
election of 1984 all but irrelevant. But
whatever is coming in this decade has
already begun. The election will only
test the strength of these new forces
against the old; the winner, whoever he
is, must read policy and direction out of
the scrambled numbers of the election.

Within the swirl, candidates control
mechanics in a way unknown when I began reporting politics 30 years ago: a
sophistication of demographic analyses,
technologies of direct mail, tricks of
money raising, instruments and specialists of television and radio. Candidates
can no longer, as Franklin D. Roosevelt
did, harness the forces they seek to
guide by dealing with half a dozen
bosses and several labor leaders, or win
over Texas and California at a convention by an overnight deal with power
brokers. Nor can they, as John F. Kennedy did, by his instinctive mastery of
television, make a few simple themes
come clear.

America, punished from abroad by
pressures of trade, torn at home by a variety of resentments, is too complicated
now—and thus the winds and forces are
more important than all the new mechanics of organization, or the staffing
and rustling in candidate camps as they
push to power. This election depends far

more on how the earnest candidates read the mood of the country and how the victor translates his victory than how the Iowa caucuses, the New Hampshire primary or the 12 primaries and caucuses in the sweepstakes of March 13 are won or lost.

OF THE TWO major "movements" disturbing the atmospherics of 1984, the blacks and the women, it is easiest to start with the former because the black movement lends itself better to measurement.

One must start from back of the beginning, for in politics nothing sprouts overnight, without its back-root in time. There is, of course, the classic earlier history—slavery; Civil War; Reconstruction; the increase of blacks in the cities; black family dissolution. But the current chapter of politics cannot help but start with the march from Selma, Ala., in 1965, which forced the Voting Rights Act of that year from conscience to law. And it is now as if the Voting Rights Act had been a delayed, slow-burning fuse that is reaching explosion point only this year. Blacks eligible to vote, once the most underrepresented in appearing at the polls, have, since 1978, begun to register and vote all across this country.

For sweep, breadth and passion, nothing like today's surge of black registration has been experienced recently in American politics. In Illinois, in one 18-month period, 200,000 new black voters registered and helped to give Harold Washington his 1983 mayoral

victory; black and Hispanic registrations in Texas gave Mark White his governorship in 1982, and blacks gave Mario Cuomo his in New York in the same year.

The sweep of this registration drive is so immense that figures can give only a gross outline of its potential; they cannot give the inspiring fervor. The figures read that of us 235 million Americans, 25 to 30 million are of African descent. More than 17 million are eligible to vote; in 1966, 4.4 million voted; by 1980, 8 million. From 1980 to 1982, however, 573,000 more registered to vote. Since 1982, 600,000 more have enlisted. And, if black leadership meets its targets this year, two million more will have been registered by November. These are not casual voters being registered; these are "cause" votes being recruited with the same emotional dynamics as civil-rights activists were in the 1960's. Ninety percent of black voters vote Democratic; thus their registration presses on Republican hopes like lead. In seven states, they can, in 1984, with their new registrations, overturn President Reagan's slim 1980 majorities and give those states to the Democrats.

The potential of the black vote has been growing since at least 1948, when, in three key states (Ohio, Illinois, California), it gave Harry S. Truman his margin of electoral votes. But always, previously, black politicians have been invited, or forced their way, into the old political system to share a piece of the action: black councilmen in black wards, black Congressmen in black districts, black mayors in increasingly black cities, black appointments at top city, state and Federal levels.

What makes the black vote different this time is the nature of the movement's leadership, its repudiation of all the old rules of bloc leverage that black politicians once accepted. And the quality of the new movement is best embodied in the flaring personality of Jesse Jackson, who has seized the spokesman's role (over much internal opposition among black leaders). He proposes to change the American political system and the structure of the Democratic Party.

The Rev. Jesse Jackson is much less, yet far more, than a realistic candidate for the Presidency of the United States. He comes out of the black history in America, where for generations two leadership groups have contended—the minister-evangelist and the pragmatic politician. He unites the two streams. Only once before have these two different styles been displayed in one man—by Adam Clayton Powell Jr. of New York, who was, at once, a divine, a politician and, alas, a reprobate. Mostly, in the postwar world, blacks have given their hearts and hymns to evangelicals like Martin Luther King Jr. and their votes to such skilled professionals as Willie Brown, majority leader of the California Assembly, or Charles Rangel and his 20 fellow black Congressmen in Washington, who can deliver the share of jobs and welfare that the black poor need.

Jesse Jackson is different. He is, of course, like all politicians—white and black, male and female, Protestant, Catholic and Jewish—interested in the share-out. "We have the key to the White House door," he told the black caucus at the 1980 Democratic convention; "we should hold that key until we have at least three Cabinet members. . . ." In 1983, his rhetoric escalated. "We want it all," he called out in momentary exuberance on the night of Harold Washington's primary victory in Chicago. But he is also the first to demand a specific black voice on national policy, whether it be in Medicaid, Social Security, defense or our dealings with the peoples of the third world. His coup in Syria, winning the release of an American captive, has given his campaign a dramatic value and vigor that lifts him out of the "pack" of candidates. It makes him a major, even if ultimately momentary, figure in national politics.

In effect, Jackson is demanding that the Democrats propose to the nation a coalition government, not just of interests and regions, but of race and of ethnics—the famous "rainbow coalition," which, if accepted, could remold the contours of classic politics.

This is new. Jackson can more decisively affect who will be President of the United States than any black before him. He can, by mobilizing hard delegate votes behind his demands, compel the Democrats to become the party of black interests in the United States; or, by withholding his votes or running independently, give the election to the Republicans.

————

NOT ONLY ARE the power and aspiration of the black movement new, so is the edge to it. It is not the edge of hopeless rage that slashed the cities of the United States with riot in the 1960's. It is a cool rage, an intelligent slicing at white male dominance of politics and society.

As, for example, in New York. No more polyglot city survives in America than New York. For 30 years, ever since Robert F. Wagner Jr., a series of liberal mayors has tried to make this a city of peace and tolerance. In healing the wounded, nourishing the sick, housing the homeless, caring for the fatherless, they have made this city the shelter of all the world's minorities. Whites are now, in total, only one minority among many. Yet the momentum of the black movement seeks to remove Koch from his mayoralty. Thus, from Michigan, comes black Representative John Conyers Jr., with a posse of aides and associates, to investigate Koch and the New York City police on charges of brutality. Most cops are rough; they have to be. So, too, are New York's. But New York's "finest," though pilloried by black leadership, are probably as sensitive to race relations as any police force in the country.

Koch has momentarily eluded the wrath of the movement by appointing a thoroughly competent black to be chief of his Police Department. Yet that will probably not appease black leadership; and, if they can unseat him, then, of the six largest cities in the United States, the roster will read: New York—black mayor? Chicago—black mayor. Los Angeles—black mayor. Philadelphia—black mayor. Houston—woman mayor. Detroit—black mayor. Practically a clean sweep. Nor did this happen by accident. It is laudable that blacks are encouraged to vote; and so they must, as should whites. But the freedom call of black registration, "black must vote for black," can easily backfire. Some white politicians in the cities will sooner or later give the countercall of "white must vote for white."

The blacks are only the most conspicuous of the movements fashioning the *Zeitgeist* in which the election of 1984 unrolls. What black leadership shares with most of the other movements, astride or aborning, is a common purpose—to transform the traditional credo of American politics, "equality," into the credo of "group equality." While economic inequities prod almost all the new groups in motion, what blacks want most is public acceptance of equality, not only on the basis of individual merit, but of group results and group shares—in short, "quotas" or "goals and timetables."

At some point, of course, the black movement, as all the others, must compromise with reality: All men are not born equal, though the Declaration of Independence so states. Within every group, talent is shared unequally by its members; the old notion was that opportunity should be open equally to all individual talents, from which followed the thought that barriers of race and sex to such opportunity must be torn down. But, for the moment, the black movement has introduced a new thought:

that America is not a nation of equality of individual opportunities, but a coalition of races, each required to be equal in group results or entitlements. Down the road, if America so divides, lies the "Lebanonization" of the American political system.

If the new demand for "equality" comes sharpest from the blacks, it comes fuzziest from the women—whose movement into politics is at least equal in pressure, and perhaps more so than the movement of the blacks.

IT IS DIFFICULT to think of women as a distinct political force in American politics.

Women?

It was once assumed that whatever a man's fate, his mother, his wife, his daughter shared in it. Thus, those of us who write of American politics once held that no more than three great issues dominated all Presidential elections, singly or in combination. They were the issues of white and black, bread and butter, war and peace. But, in the climate of 1984, the women, or those who claim to speak for them, have added what may be another: women against men, gender against gender.

Any politician who ignores the ancient resentments and new ambitions behind the thrust of the women is blind to what probably is the most formidable new force in American politics—and the most difficult to define. One can ignore the self-appointed representatives who purport to speak for all, or a majority, of our women. But women, even

more than the blacks, press on all of us the need to redefine the meaning of equality.

What is equal? How far can one press equality in politics when nature itself has differentiated between the sexes, forcing on women burdens, hazards, and commitments essentially different from those of men?

THE SPEED OF the women's movement in the last 10 years is only vaguely measurable in votes. The number of women legislators in state assemblies has doubled in the last 10 years. They hold one-quarter of the seats in New Hampshire's Legislature; and across the country, in Oregon, their seats in the Legislature have almost doubled: from 11 out of 90 some 10 years ago to 20 out of 90 today. Women now hold 24 seats in Congress, as against 15 in 1971; they held the mayoralties in 76 cities (population over 30,000) last year as against only seven in 1971. They have surfaced occasionally as governors in the last 10 years. But these are only formal figures of surge. They do not give depth. At the grass roots, women have multiplied in power and in voice beyond measurement: town councilors, community commissioners, selectmen, first selectmen. Enter any suburban town or small village and one is as apt to find a woman in the chair as a man.

It is not really at the upper political levels, where such organizations as the National Women's Political Caucus or the National Organization for Women or the venerable League of Women Voters purport to speak for women, that one bumps against the underlying dynamics. Behind them trail associations of women lawyers, women doctors, university women, women analysts, who themselves represent only an elite among the wave upon wave of ordinary women who have in the last 20 years entered the labor force. The American labor force now counts 48.8 million women to 63.3 million men. In six million working American families, the woman earns more than the man.

When politicians mourn the decline of excellence in American education, they mourn unconsciously for the dedicated schoolteachers of their youth who have gone into advertising, marketing or retailing rather than to the classrooms they once knew. Everywhere women challenge old rules, sensible and stupid alike; New York City's Fire Department has, thus, substantially redesigned weight-handling competence tests so that women, who must lift the heavy and thin alike and carry them down a ladder from a burning building, may qualify for firefighter training.

Across the country another kind of tomorrow is taking shape. The speed of women's entry to higher education is comparable only to the speed of black registrations to vote. In the late 1950's, twice as many men went to college as did women. In 1972, just 12 years ago, colleges still counted only 74 women for each 100 men. By 1981, women outnumbered men in colleges by 108 to 100; and the proportions have probably increased since then. This penetration of American leadership by the majority

sex, women, moves through corporate boards, through establishment law offices, through administrative appointments, through university faculties, through all systems where brains, not brawn, count. And their movement for equality hammers on politics.

One must pause to consider the realities in the surge.

Reality One: Women not only have been separated from men by biology, but also have been abused by prejudice and tradition. They are underpaid in equivalent job responsibilities; they are refused as individuals equal access to credit. Age-long denial of their dignity has grated on feminine sensibilities that once could vent only in private bitterness within the family, personal depression or the intrigue of palace politics. It does not matter that the United States traditionally has been the most sensitive of nations to this inequality and was the first to move to correct the abuse of women. In the long struggle to correct inequalities in treatment of the sexes, the United States has led. But the old white male dominance of public politics has now, decisively, been challenged; millions of American women are convinced that the white males persist in oppressing them or are reluctant to "liberate" them.

Reality Two: The resentment of so many vocal women leaders is directed at the discriminatory laws and regulations that are necessary to protect them against the hazards visited on them by nature. Women are vulnerable when they are pregnant—to fumes in factories, to heavy weight lifting, to certain physical duties. Regulations *must* discriminate to protect them. A cardinal and universal discriminatory law is that against rape, which all civilized societies adopt to protect their women. So, too, are the laws defining age of consent—adolescent young women *should* be protected against would-be seducers. War, too, requires discrimination. Women can be extraordinarily valuable in war, as the British proved in World War II. But, as the Israelis found to their sorrow in 1948, women cannot be used in hand-to-hand combat on the battlefield.

But all biological realities are swept into confusion by the feminist push to propose once more and ratify the equal rights amendment. Equal rights imply equal responsibilities. And such responsibilities as in combat, firefighting or even football cannot be distributed equally by sex. Yet the symbolism of the equal rights amendment sways the virtuous, sincere or hypocritical, to voice assent.

Which brings us, finally, in vote counting, to:

Reality Three, known as the "gender gap."

The "gender gap" is a relatively new term introduced by the influence of television exit polls in 1980, when women apparently voted for Reagan by only 47 percent to 45 percent, while men supported him by a thumping 56 percent to 36 percent. Having been heralded as the "gender gap," the gender gap thus becomes a reality of media politics and, like all new realities, must be endowed with roots, causes, reasons.

The generally accepted explanation has been that, though husbands and wives generally do vote alike, the issue that separates them is war against peace.

Although every war in this century has been launched by a Democratic President, women are now "perceived" by the national public-opinion polls as marginally favoring Democrats, whom they see as ostensibly wanting peace, against Republicans, who allegedly may bring war. This differential vote of the gender gap may amount to three million or four million of the estimated 50 million votes to be cast by women in 1984. If women can be persuaded that men "enjoy war," while women cry "peace," this differential vote can be critical. Added to the black vote, this gender gap may be impossible for the Republicans to surmount.

From Elizabeth the Great, to Margaret Thatcher, from Golda Meir to Indira Gandhi, women leaders have made war as unpredictably as men. But that is not the perception current in American politics in 1984. The perception is that women will vote marginally for the person who talks peace most eloquently. From this perception rises the feeling that the dismay of women (and men) at the prospect of war requires at least the consideration, if not the nomination, of a woman as Vice President.

It is impossible, thus, to give a name to the *Zeitgeist* of the 1980 decade, which includes women and blacks in the same package. It is impossible not only because political leadership is perplexed over what to do about these two main forces running loose outside the traditional political arena, but because so much else is running loose at the same time.

SOME OTHER stirrings must be at least noted, if not defined, to give the sense of the current fog in American politics as the candidates lurch into the primary, or definitional, stage of the Presidential season.

▶ Consider, first, an absolute novelty in national politics: the issue of variations in sexual life styles. It is certain that no candidate wishes to press on homosexuals the biblical curse of Moses. In the civilized tolerance of educated American life, homosexual men and women are accepted by many now as, at worst, merely psychologically handicapped. Majority mores still find their ways repugnant, yet in the large cities where homosexuals cluster, their votes are critical. Closeted for so long, they insist that they be accepted now as they are; and that approval be voiced publicly by one or the other of the great parties. The Democrats must meet this year in San Francisco, the Mecca of homosexual congregation. The Democrats must face them, perhaps permit them onto the floor as homosexuals have so long sought—or repudiate them. And, if the Democrats invite them on the floor, then the Republicans will take the alternate stand. In a close election, the vote of homosexual men and women might swing the results in California and New York.

▶ Consider, next, ethnics. Ethnics are no longer simply "ethnics." Time was when "ethnics" meant Americans of eastern or southern European descent— the Italians, the Jews, the Slavs chief among them, with the Roman Catholic Irish included for good measure. These were people of cultures different from the old northern European Protestant stock. But all, except the Irish, are being galvanized to self-identification by the regulations of the 1970's, which define other special categories of Americans entitled to special privileges by race alone (Afro-Americans, Hispanics, Asians, American Indians). The old ethnic balances in politics sway like a mobile in the wind. The old "white majority" becomes increasingly a fissiparous coalition of many minorities. Italian-Americans, working-class Catholics, are moving so fast up the American social scale that they find any remaining barriers of prejudice in corporations and colleges more offensive than ever. Slavic-Americans, among the most discriminated-against groups of whites, are moving to express their interests. Jewish-Americans, who once swung so much weight in American foreign policy, find themselves for the first time countered by the growing Arab-American citizenry. And, subtly, the spectacular increase of the Asian-American population weaves its way into politics as an entirely new element. More conservative in life style than most others, they are as sensitive to prejudice as any.

▶ Economic "special interests" that once seemed as steady as the flow of milk from a cow are now splitting. The protection of farmers through price supports now runs to $28 billion in Government subsidy a year—more than the farms earn. City Congressmen protest; their clamor adds confusion to the old farmer-worker alliance. Great industries and their workers divide. American industry is being attacked, sometimes dismantled, sector by sector, by foreign competitors. Those who can withstand the winds of foreign trade (like I.B.M., Boeing, Caterpillar Tractor) cling to the old doctrine of a free and open world of trade. Those who see themselves put out of jobs (like steel, garment, textile, automobile workers) demand protection. It has been 50 years since trade and tariffs were an issue in American life; but they have become so again; and the candidates who need a general theory of national trade policy are, themselves, confused.

Add up only these new stirrings and the election of 1984 would seem to be a turbulence confined to the Democratic Party. Since 1932, half a century ago, new ideas and departures have largely centered in that party. The ethnics, the Southerners, the blacks, the labor movement have been their clients. And it is tricky business for the Democratic candidates, in the swirl, to make new friends without losing old ones, to make commitments that will bind the nation to a clear course if one of them is elected.

But such deep stirrings require more than political tactics, or the collection of political credit cards, to resolve. A new culture is struggling to be born, or to capture the Democratic Party. And it must face the formidable resistance of

the old traditional culture of the nation, which has so much to recommend it, and which the Republicans will set out to defend.

THE REPUBLICANS have their problems, too, for the old culture is as difficult to define as the new.

The base of the Republican vote remains, of course, the old stock of the country, the Protestant vote. Yet the call of the old culture reaches through all other ethnic groups—it is what makes so many young men (Democrats and Republicans alike) volunteer for the Marines; and makes so many young women still hope to start families, rather than to seek work as computer programmers, social engineers or to serve hamburgers at fast-food restaurants.

The Republicans in 1980 tried to sum up their call with "getting government off the backs of the people," then simplified it in their five-point slogan: "Family. Neighborhood. Work. Peace. Freedom." It turned out, however, not to be as simple as that: government means control; no party can shrug off that responsibility; and that responsibility has brought the Republicans to the limits that reality forces on leadership.

It is difficult to praise Ronald Reagan among most East Coast intellectuals; and he has, indeed, wandered in trying to apply old thinking to new reality. But to underestimate Reagan's real accomplishments is a mark of intellectual snobbery. He has, with unexpected mastery, undeniably slowed inflation; he has incubated a recovery which, though slow, is working. Four million more Americans are in jobs than a year ago. In the upper classes and segments of the middle classes, a euphoria of consumption reigns. Equally undeniable is a nightmare budget deficit acquiring the metaphysical dimensions of a thundercloud—the deficit cuts a cleavage within the Republican Party itself, one that will burst later rather than sooner and, almost certainly, not until after the election.

But the Republican leadership is subject to the same winds as the Democrats; and control of events at home means, increasingly, adjusting to an unstable world abroad. The Republicans necessarily inherit President Reagan's record, and will face a foreign policy election, and in foreign policy the old culture no longer serves to guide. To re-examine foreign policy means to question old shibboleths, from the Middle East to NATO, which American ethics have enshrined as sacred since World War II; and no domestic problem of any consequence can be separated from foreign policy.

Item, for example: Immigration. America has lost control both of its borders and qualifications for citizenship. The Statue of Liberty still declaims, "Give me your tired, your poor/Your huddled masses yearning to breath free." But very large groups of the American people no longer believe in such poetry. The Republicans support the mild revision of the immigration laws as set forth in the Simpson-Mazzoli

bill, which is designed to limit the Hispanic inrush on American jobs. It is opposed stubbornly by the Hispanic-American caucus in Congress (11 members). And, since the blacks will vote, overwhelmingly, against any Republican, the Republicans must hold on to some slice of the second largest minority vote, the Hispanics. To support the bill means that Republicans may not only alienate critical Hispanic votes in Texas, California and New York. It means further that they may alienate Mexico, Central America and all the Latin countries south of the border where foreign policy is at stake. No clear sound comes from the White House because the White House believes in the old culture of the open country; and the realities require otherwise.

Item again: Trade and industry. We are under attack as an industrial nation. Always, historically, the Democrats have been the party of free trade, the Republicans of protectionism. By some magic of transformation, the Democrats seem to be moving to protectionism while the Republicans are hung on the free trade dogmas of Adam Smith. There is no longer any foreign policy on this matter. What the bipartisan teams of Hoffman-Harriman/Vandenberg-Marshall achieved in reorganizing world trade in 1947–49 neither protects peace nor our jobs one generation later. So the Republicans are stuck with the conventional trade folklore of the 1940's that no longer serves us in a world that has changed.

Then, finally, the superitem: missiles, nuclear bombs and peace. A Russian rearmament program, beginning in 1963, reached high gear in 1977, frightening the Carter-Mondale Administration to an American countereffort in the holocaust game. There is nothing Mr. Reagan has been able to do about this except sit tall in the cowboy saddle and hope that more missiles on more launching pads will alter the minds of the men who control Russia. But, because Soviet bureaucracy is locked, he must face the serious underlying debate among both the thoughtfuls and the crazies of American politics. Can diplomacy reach the Russians? We are the only power that can maneuver and shift ground; the Russians, frozen by a fear as large as ours, cannot shift. So we stalk and wander around their stonelike position in negotiation, hoping that one approach or another, one meeting with Andropov or his successor, will trigger a reasonable reaction from the adversaries. Intricate problems of strategy, accuracy and throw-weights are involved; but the apocalyptic quality of the menace can fill the streets with protesters; such people are more likely to vote than most. Those of both the old and new cultures do not welcome senseless death.

EMOTIONS LIKE these make the weather of American politics in 1984. They hang overhead like clouds waiting for a Benjamin Franklin to string a kite aloft and bring down the tensions of the skies to a key that forks electricity,

which may some future day be given purpose.

That is the business of politics in its highest sense—to translate moods into majorities, majorities into power, power into new laws and direction. It will not be the candidates' "horse race" of 1984, however exciting it is, that changes history. The horse race is the story of the largest participant sport in the country. But the distinctions between "pack" and "front-runner," challenger and champion, that enliven our daily dispatches will soon be forgotten. It is what the winner does with his election and, more importantly, how he reads the storm winds and silent undertows that will make history.

Thirty Presidential elections have come and gone since Abraham Lincoln came to power in 1860. Some of these are recognized as "great" elections, some as simply datemarks in a drift. It is not, however, "landslides" or "squeakers" that make "great" elections, not the total or margin of the votes, though the final count does confer legitimacy. Lincoln and Kennedy were both elected by what we call squeakers; both were actually minority winners. They could, however, read the forces that brought them to power and, so reading them, move the country to action. Harding and Hoover both won their elections by landslides—and left behind nothing but dust. Franklin Roosevelt, on the other hand, with his great landslides, could read his victory clearly enough to reshape the political contour of the country, then lead it to war and victory. Johnson and Nixon misread their landslide mandates—and, in both cases, tragedy followed.

So, then, we come to the election of 1984—not the Orwellian but the American 1984. It is a testing time, with much old folklore to be discarded and many new frustrations, real and imaginary, screaming for attention. It will be, as always, a reaffirmation of popular controls over a powerful and effective government and a testing time of limits. It is a testing time of how far the Americans are willing to go, and at what cost in life, to maintain peace in a sputtering globe. It is a testing time for industry, those who own it and those who work in it, and of how much they must yield to keep it competitive in cost, benefits and technology. It is, perhaps, most of all, given the black and feminist drives, a testing time of the meaning of the word "equality."

Equality is the only theology of this country which was founded on faith. The Constitution may be amended; laws can be changed. But no one can change such articles of faith as, "We hold these truths to be self-evident; that all men are created equal." Or the Gettysburg address, which held that "our fathers brought forth on this continent a new nation, conceived in liberty and dedicated to the proposition that all men are created equal." These tenets cannot be amended by law or vote—but they require reinterpretation. Does equality mean, as it originally meant, "equality before the law"? Or, as the 19th century read it, "equality of opportunity"; or, as the new readers of "equality" interpret it, "equality of results," requiring quotas, goals and timetables, and judgments of men and women, not by individual excellence but by group?

Serious matters are involved in the election of 1984. Only the candidates' race will be over on Nov. 6. After that comes history—the meaning the winner reads into his victory, however narrow, however large. But the voting citizens will be, thereafter, primarily an audience as the new President tries to find direction in what they said. If he goes only with the winds, he must tack and sheer; and may, like a good sailor, survive his four years. If he chooses rather to navigate by the stars, sensitive always to the winds he must greet or avoid, he may transform this after all into a Great Election.

And then we may be able to give a name to this uncertain decade, and let the historians later identify its *Zeitgeist*.

THE NEW YORK TIMES MAGAZINE February 5, 1984

LBJ: HE "TRIED SO HARD TO DO GOOD—AND LEFT BEHIND SO MUCH BREAKAGE" *

Though Lyndon Johnson achieved notable social gains as President, he will be remembered most for his role in our Vietnam debacle.

He was, in retrospect, larger than life—as perplexing and awesome as a force of nature. Six feet 3 inches tall, cowboy-lean in his youth, jowling as he aged, pointed of nose, restless even when sitting, Lyndon Baines Johnson, 36th President of the United States, left no neutrals in the wake he cut across American politics. And it would be a mistake to bleach from his memory the gusto, the vivid language, the high aspirations with which he colored his Presidency.

He could be the imperious, ugly, callous boss of his staff. He could be the conniving, wheedling, bargaining architect of some of the most famous deals in the United States Senate. He could be the high visionary who finally enfranchised the blacks of America and nursed the suffering of the aged. He used language more earthy than any President since Lincoln. Of one of his senatorial allies, he chirped, "Why he wouldn't know how to pour _____ from a boot!" Of one of his successors, he quipped, "Jerry Ford couldn't walk and chew gum at the same time." He stigmatized his Vice President, Hubert Humphrey, in a sentence, "He cries too much."

On the campaign trail, we reporters who followed him as he stumped for a second term noticed that he switched hats when his plane crossed the Alleghenies: west of the Alleghenies he waved his Texas Stetson; in the East he wore a fedora. But he was always and at all times President of the United States. And historians will find no 20th-century President more puzzling than this same Lyndon Johnson who tried so hard to do good, and left behind so much breakage.

No President, except Franklin Roosevelt, will have left deeper marks on American history in this century. But no one will be able to assess Johnson's Presidency without understanding how very much the politics of that Presidency were shaped by the Congress of the United States. For he was, as he said himself, "a man of the Hill." And his world, even after he became President, revolved around the Congress on the Hill, which he alternately revered and despised.

He had come to Congress first at the

* This article was written by White and accepted by *TV Guide* eight years earlier, but was published posthumously.

juvenile age of 23 as assistant to a Texas congressman, and had fallen in love with Roosevelt's New Deal. By the age of 28 he was a congressman himself. By 1948, in one of the most scandalous primaries in Texas history, he had squeezed out an 87-vote margin, ensuring his election as United States senator and earning him the nickname "Landslide Lyndon." By 1955 he was not only senator but majority leader, one of the great majority leaders of Senate history.

His problem was that he thought that the Congress of the United States was, in itself, the world of reality. If he could pass a law, then that law thus became reality. If he could stitch together a majority on the Hill, then that became a majority of the people. If he could cozen the Congress and conceal reality from it, he felt he could conceal reality from the people, from the press, from history.

HIS PREOCCUPATION with Congress sometimes worked and history was changed by much of the masterful legislation of his Great Society program. Millions of aging Americans today enjoy Medicare because Lyndon Johnson willed it so. Millions of black Americans vote today because Lyndon Johnson pushed through Congress the Voting Rights Act of 1965. Millions of young Americans go to college today because of Lyndon Johnson's provisions for Federal aid to education. Old immigration quotas were abolished, environmental bills were passed, new Government departments were created.

He loved his role as ringmaster of

Congress. He could make it dance, jump and twirl. But he was more than ringmaster of the circus. He behaved as if he owned it—until the tragic spring of 1968 when Congress, caught between the pressure of the President and the pressure of the people, broke from his grip, and an era of American history came to an end.

It was the revolt against the war in Vietnam, chiefly, that broke the grip of his Presidency over events, and broke his heart, too.

Lyndon Johnson had cheated in the election of 1964. He had told the American people that he was not going to send their sons to die in Asian wars. And then, after the election, with a Congressional resolution in his pocket authorizing him to act, he *did* make war.

A CASE SHOULD and must be made for his war. He acted in high purpose and good cause, with no malice and no imperial design. He did not enjoy the killings, and the chant of the demonstrators, "Hey, hey! LBJ, how many kids did you kill today?" hurt him. But he bungled the war, mismanaged the war, did not understand the reality of Asian politics. He thought that by punishing the enemy, he could win—but in Asia, wars are won not by punishment but by extermination; and Johnson had no stomach for extermination. So he lied about the war. He told Americans we were winning when we were not. He lied about the costs, burying them in the budget, and sowed the seeds for the inflation that surged when the climate of the world changed.

It was then called "the credibility gap," but the credibility gap simply meant that the American people no longer trusted their Government. For all the good Lyndon Johnson did, this was his major legacy to the American people—a distrust of their Government, and the recognition of the first major defeat in war in all American history.

In an appearance before Congress in 1965, he said, "A President's hardest task is not to do what is right, but to know what is right." Lyndon Johnson tried, indeed, to do what was right. But his knowledge of the world was limited to Congress; outside that world he did not know what was right. The verdict of history will probably read: a big, lusty, hungry man, trying to do good—but a bad President.

TV GUIDE January 31, 1987

Chapter 13

The Ugly Ways of Racism

As White notes in his autobiography, three great changes in American life confronted him when he returned from Europe in 1953: prosperity, which was manifest everywhere he looked; the rising pervasiveness of television (when he left the United States in 1948 he had never been in a private home with a television set, now all his friends had them); and, most unsettlingly, the racial problems that were beginning to emerge as blacks moved into the mainstream.

His first article on this new world of race relations was for *Collier's* in 1956 and dealt, appropriately enough, with the expected role of the Negro voter in that year's presidential election. He would often return to that subject as part of broader themes (e.g., see "New Power, New Politics" on page 477). Then, in the mid 1960s, he wrote three powerful articles for *Life*—a perceptive two-parter on the racial wars in U.S. cities, and (a year later) a forthright analysis of a subject most white Americans didn't talk about publicly: white backlash against Negro demands (the term "blacks" had not yet entered our lexicon).

THE NEGRO VOTER—CAN HE ELECT A PRESIDENT?

Editors' Precede: *Negroes now hold the political balance of power in America's five biggest cities. These cities in turn dominate states that cast 156 electoral votes, three fifths the number needed to elect a President. The drama of this month's national conventions will revolve in large part around the efforts of both major parties to convince American Negroes that politically they do not stand trapped, as one of their leaders has said, "between the known Devil and the suspected Witch." Whichever party succeeds best may well swing the crucial vote—and the 1956 election next November . . .*

Chicago, evening on the South Side, in the black belt, and the 2d Ward Republicans are meeting in the made-over store that holds their club-room. Outside, through the open door on 35th Street, the sound of loiterers, chatterers, high-pitched laughter. Inside, 50 or so people on the shabby folding chairs, watching television, waiting.

The meeting opens with a hymn ("Pass Me Not, O Gentle Saviour"), and the Reverend King S. Rains rises to talk. He's just been down to Memphis on a "mother-trip," the way he has gone to see his mother down South every year for 30 years.

"Been to a meeting down there of ministers," proclaims the Reverend Rains; "heard more talk about voting in two hours than I've heard in Chicago in two years. Down there, they're pledging themselves to get 70,000 more votes than ever before and they said to me, 'What you doing in Chicago?' I said we're raising money to send to the bus strike in Alabama. You know what they said to me? They said to me, 'You Northern Negroes don't know what you're doing. You're like a man running to put out a fire with a bucket of water in one hand, bucket of gasoline in the other. That's what you're doing, raising money for the strikers in Alabama with one hand, voting Democratic with the other.'"

Long pause.

"And they're right," says the Reverend, his voice rising and breaking. "What are we doing up here? These knock-kneed ministers, eating chicken, getting fat, telling people to vote Democrat—and people listen to them! They know they're lying when they tell the people to vote Democrat." (Audience groans, murmurs, "That's right.") "Do you know we've got the balance of power in our votes? What are we going to do with it? The president of the NAACP, he told you the other day, he said we're between the Devil and the Witch. He couldn't come right out and say it because of his job. But I tell you what he meant—he meant you've got to vote Republican. I say so."

The meeting goes on and I wander out. It is a long way from Chicago to the deep South—Eastland and Talmadge, Emmett Till and Autherine Lucy, bus boycotts in Montgomery and Tallahassee, all far away. But the winds blow hot off the embers of hate and carry strong to the North. How strong, one asks? Are they strong enough for the 2d Ward Republicans to stir a revolt of Negroes against Democrats in Chicago because Democrats in the South savage their kinfolk?

It is only three blocks east on 35th Street from the 2d Ward Republicans to the 2d Ward Democratic Club, but the Democratic answer to these questions comes squirming alive as one strolls: children on the street still playing long after bedtime, men sitting on the stoop, men eddying about the taverns. People oozing from the five-room flats where three families share each flat (inside, the penciled signs, three to a door—"For Barrett, Ring Once," "For Patterson, Ring Twice," "For Henry, Ring Three Times"). Trash between the houses, paper litter, the sick stink of the stock-

yards staining the air with every shift of summer wind. Here the cold figures of census boil vividly in human congestion: Great Park Census Tract, 65,000 human beings per square mile, Douglas Tract, 48,000 (in white neighborhoods only 17,000 per square mile). Fifteen to 25 per cent unemployed here; one quarter of families in some tracts without fathers; of 17,000 Negro births in Chicago, an estimated 4,000 illegitimate.

Statistics cascade through the mind here, each with a face and a sorrow; of all the women in Chicago's county jail, 69 per cent are Negro; of all the men, 62 per cent; of all the forlorn on relief, 72 per cent Negro; of all the clients of public housing in Chicago, seeking shelter of the government, 70 per cent Negro. And in Detroit, Philadelphia, New York, kindred figures grimly repeat themselves.

Of all the strollers on 35th Street this summer evening, 65 per cent are Southern born, brought North by hope and fancy to the jungle of the city, with less than five years of primitive village education—less, as sociologists point out, than functional literacy for city life.

Wandering and trapped, compelled and pressed by the white world around them, flailing out in anger and desperation, frightening and perplexing their white neighbors (who flee to the clean new suburbs where Negroes cannot follow), they have become a group, a voting bloc, a community conscious of its wants and strength. These are people whom Northern politicians all too frequently like to consider as a regional, distant, Southern problem—a problem to be deplored and denounced as a faraway offense against American morality.

BUT THEY ARE HERE, now, in Chicago, groping to make up their mind about what kind of President of the United States suits them best, weighing their power, weighing their need, here in Chicago, against the hate that prickles them as they read of Mississippi, Alabama, Georgia, their states of birth. Republicans rouse their conscience. But 2d Ward Democratic headquarters is here to help, now, in Chicago, where they live.

Up one flight is the office of Congressman William Dawson. I had been to see him that afternoon—a sturdy, powerful man of seventy, of golden voice and flowing eloquence.

Dawson is a Democrat neither by birth nor upbringing, but by conviction, which is stronger. "I was born in Dougherty County, Georgia," he says, "just one step this side of Hell. I stood guard with my father all one night to stop a lynching when I was fifteen. I hated the word Democrat when I came North. I saw them bring Negroes up from the South in World War I and stuff them in here, into 4½ miles of black belt, until it was the most populated spot on the face of the globe. I saw them ripping basements out of stores, pushing people to live in rat-infested filth until the black belt was the damnedest pesthole ever conceived by the mind of man."

What made him a Democrat? Roosevelt, it seemed; Roosevelt cared. Roosevelt brought assistance, relief ("Negroes would have died like flies if he hadn't kept his hand on the money until it got to them").

In the party which Dawson joined, he found leverage, dignity, power. Power, finally, as the strongest Negro boss in the country; power to dump a mayor of Chicago (Martin Kennelly) because of the way that mayor's cops were treating his people; power to appoint, promote, reward—and help.

Dawson's headquarters is open 365 days a year to service the people of the South Side's squalling streets. Service for mothers who need public aid for dependent children, old folks who need pensions, families seeking public housing, bright young men wanting appointment; defense of the rights built into Negro thinking by a generation of welfare agencies ("My people got rights. They're entitled to consideration. Some of the biggest Simon Legrees there are work in these relief agencies," says Dawson). Service, here in Chicago, not crusades against the dragons of the South has made Dawson's base solid. From this base his control has spread to a five-ward empire; and the largest deliverable bloc of votes in Illinois has made him the most powerful Negro in American politics, chairman of the House Government Operations Committee, vice-chairman of the Democratic National Committee. But still he remains ward chairman of his 2d Ward, answering his phone, providing service.

Yet there is a rumbling on the South

Side now. Younger people and labor people call him a "white-man's Negro" or, worse, "bandanna-head." What's he done about civil rights?, they ask.

Dawson bridles at the implication. Mississippi is a long way off. Speeches on Chicago street corners won't help. Hysteria has brought a whole lot of new leaders all trying to prey on his people's emotions. Only experience, knowledge, above all, politics can help. And if you're in politics, you try for all you can get for your people ("all that ain't tied down"); but above all you remain loyal to party and country. At times indignant, then gentle, then solemn, then crafty, his words cascade out, and by any standards this is a big man. He sticks by his philosophy: "I'm a congressman first. I happen to be a Negro, and the question of race comes second."

How well will this philosophy stand up in the race of '56?, one asks. How many 2d Ward Negroes will stay with the 2d Ward Democratic Club in exchange for the services Dawson provides: the sewing classes for mothers, the children's drawing classes, the protection from police? How many will abandon the Democratic ticket in Chicago because only by striking at Democrats everywhere can they strike at the party that gives power to Senator Allen J. Ellender of Louisiana, Senator James O. Eastland of Mississippi, Georgia's Herman Talmadge and the other men they hate in the South?

Few of the Democratic delegates who assemble in Chicago this month will have the time to wander the pavings of 35th Street less than a mile away from the stockyards convention hall. But their actions and decisions will be magnetized, nonetheless, by such rumblings as stir the 2d Ward. For these are questions that reach far beyond Chicago's 2d Ward, or the parishes and hill counties of the South. The relations of white man and black man in our country have become in this year, 1956, for the first time since the Civil War, one of the central imponderables in the great struggle for our Presidency.

In the past 10 years, all American politics have buckled under one of the great movements of history—the mass migration of millions of American Negroes from the lands of humiliation in the South to the democracy of the big cities of the North. Here, bewildering and perplexing the crowded cities, they have found finally the power to alter the shape of American life.

The new political power of the Northern Negro rests upon two things: his irresistible growth in numbers, and a fresh, superbly gifted leadership.

Up until 1910, only one lifetime ago, the Negro was strictly a Southern resident and Southern problem; 90 per cent of all American Negroes then lived in the South. Today, two wars and an industrial boom later, 35 per cent of the nation's almost 18,000,000 Negroes live in the North and West. Each year, in their paths, follow scores of thousands more.

Between 1940 and 1950, the Negro population of our great cities jumped by a phenomenal 66 per cent, while in some (Chicago, New York, Philadelphia) the white population actually declined. Since then, according to Collier's current survey, the movement, rather than slowing, has speeded. By the beginning of this year, Chicago's 1950 count of 492,000 Negroes had grown to an estimated 670,000 (an unbelievable 32 per cent jump in half a decade; University of Chicago statisticians predict a Chicago one-third Negro in texture by 1980); Detroit's Negro population had jumped 100,000 or 33 per cent (to 400,000) in this half decade; Los Angeles' by 48 percent (to 254,000); Cleveland's, Boston's proportionately. A score of smaller cities—San Francisco, Gary, Buffalo, St. Louis, New Haven, Baltimore, Toledo—have seen similar or sharper rises.

What suddenly draws all political attention to the Negroes in 1956, however, is their phenomenal concentration in the queen cities of five of the biggest voting states of the country: New York, California, Pennsylvania, Illinois and Michigan. These states cast 156 electoral votes, or just 110 short of a Presidential majority. And in the great cities of these states, the Negro population percentage runs from a high of 21 per cent in Philadelphia (Mayor Richardson Dilworth unofficially sets it higher, at 25 per cent) through 19 per cent in Detroit, 17 per cent in Chicago, 11 per cent (excluding Puerto Ricans, who represent another 6 per cent) in New York, 11 per cent in Los Angeles.

For almost 20 years, this vote has been the most solid property in the political estate of the Democratic party.

YEARS AGO, TO be sure, the Negroes, still wedded to the memory of Abraham Lincoln, were just as solidly Republican and regarded the Democrats among themselves as freaks. ("I remember," says Roy Wilkins, executive secretary of the National Association for the Advancement of Colored People, "when I was young in Kansas City, the kids threw rocks at Negroes on our street who dared vote Democratic.") But Franklin D. Roosevelt changed all that; his New Deal was aimed directly at Americans in distress, and distress has been house companion of the Negroes since their history began. With Roosevelt, government came to mean Social Security, relief ("Let Jesus lead me and welfare feed me," was a depression chant of the Negroes), unemployment compensation, housing, strong unions open to Negro membership. In overwhelming, earthquake proportions, the Negro vote became Democratic in 1936 and 1940.

As war and boom sucked Negroes north to the big industries and the Democratic tutelage of the great unions they joined, as Harry Truman, one of their favorites, broadened the Roosevelt tradition, their vote became ever more solid. By 1948, when Truman squeezed out his hair's-breadth win over Dewey, carrying Illinois by 33,612 votes, California by 17,865 votes, Ohio by 7,107 votes, no practicing politician could ignore the fact that the Negro vote in these states was one of the vital margins by which the Presidency of the United States had been won.

Varying from state to state, the Negro vote now usually runs Democratic by margins of three to one, four to one, and, in some cases, nine to one. In many states, this vote is absolutely indispensable to Democratic strategists. The ardent civil rights position of Governor G. Mennen Williams of Michigan and Governor Averell Harriman of New York springs from deepest conviction, to be sure. But a Democrat without such convictions would have a tough time being elected in those two states. In the 1954 gubernatorial election Harriman carried the whole Empire State by only 11,125 votes, while just one of New York City's five Negro districts (the 12th A.D. in Harlem) gave him a majority of 20,221! Governor Williams' state-wide margin of victory in 1952 was 8,600 for all Michigan; but the solid-Negro 2d, 5th and 7th Wards of Detroit (by majorities of 91 per cent, 92 per cent, 91 per cent) gave him a margin of 28,123 votes alone.

POTENTIAL POWER as great as this is too stupendous a fact to be concealed—least of all from those who shape and lead it.

And what has happened is that American Negro leaders have become aware of their strength; and they are determined to use it this year.

Any white American in whose mind the image of Negro leadership is still yesterday's fuzzy picture of Booker T. Washington is today completely out of touch with reality. A whole constellation of action groups has matured among Negroes of the North in the past 10 years of progress; they operate on every front of what Negro leaders like to call "the power structure of America." The NAACP is the senior, legal arm, prying open opportunity after opportunity through the courts; the Urban League fights on the industrial front, wrenching open closed jobs in field after field; the Negro church has come alive, vibrant, passionate, inflaming politics with religion; prosperity has brought the Negro community businessmen of wealth and prominence; the labor unions have trained and educated men of depth and drive; a Negro press of constant and effective indignation amplifies and magnifies them all among their own people.

At the summit of these groups stand leaders too brilliant and diverse to be capped by any single figure: Thurgood Marshall of the NAACP, victor of the historic Supreme Court decision on school integration, tall, sardonic, gay, almost mischievous; Roy Wilkins, executive secretary of the NAACP, polished phrase maker, eloquent, calculating; Alex Fuller, the solid, burly, easygoing vice-president of the Wayne County CIO; bitter, brooding, delicately handsome Edwin Berry of the Chicago Urban League; the grave, solemn, grizzled veteran Julius Thomas of the National Urban League; Congressman the Reverend Adam Clayton Powell, Jr., flamboyant, graceful; or City Councilor the Reverend Marshall Shepard of Philadelphia, dedicated, robust, untiring; and others, too many to note.

Long gone are the days when the support of many Negro clerics was considered a standard article of political merchandise. (Landon campaigners of '36 rushed $20,000 in cash to Harlem on election weekend to try to buy the support of Father Divine.) Dead, too, are the days when Negro politicians could be described as racketeers, bootleggers and crooks who could be bought for a five-dollar bill. Today's Negro leaders are men of fire and passion, almost unique in this bland age of moderate contentment. Rarely have I met with a more impressive pool of talent and ability.

These men know their strength and they recognize their moment. For, in the past two years, there has been a flare-up of Negro emotions in America unprecedented since the days of Reconstruction. This flare-up dates precisely from the Supreme Court's decision to desegregate the public schools of America; which, in turn, provoked the last-ditch reaction of the white South—the murders in Mississippi, the white Citizens' Councils—which, finally, has shaken Negroes North and South to the resistance and reaction that now daily make headlines all across the country.

In Chicago, a Negro social worker organizes a handful of Negro housewives in a voter-registration campaign. Her pamphlets say: "Don't Get Mad—Get Smart, Register!"; and in two years her volunteer committee has jabbed Negro registration in the South Side up from 200,000 to 275,000. In Detroit, a Negro doctor decides to invite a few friends for dinner to raise money for the Montgomery strike; the dinner grows in a few weeks to a community affair and $32,000 is raised in an evening. Says Senator Jim Watson, New York's only Negro state senator, "Why, I'll be walk-

ing down Amsterdam Avenue and a stranger will grab my arm and say, 'What'cha gonna do about that Miss Lucy girl, man?'" Pastor Martin Luther King, hero of the Montgomery bus strike comes to speak in Brooklyn and thousands crowd the church to overflow the sidewalks outside. The temper shakes family loyalties. In Detroit, the aged and ailing father of Congressman Charles Diggs, Jr., tells me, "We've got to get rid of Eastland and I don't care how—even if it costs my son his seat."

The temper goes deep. Traditional political loyalties teeter-totter in slums, at bars, in poolrooms, on street corners. In one day's doorbell ringing on the South Side, I interviewed 21 people (too fragmentary a cut from which to draw final political conclusions, but one learns that the Negroes are disturbed). Five weren't going to vote or wouldn't say ("Neither party is worth a damn," said one auto worker on the street corner), nine thought they'd stay Democratic, seven thought the Republicans would do more for civil rights ("I read everything I can get my hands on," said one. "I'm a Democrat, but I'll go for Ike nationally. We got to do something about this Eastland; and that Talmadge, he's worse.").

Julius Thomas of the Urban League sums it up: "The events that have followed desegregation have affected the Negro community more than anything else in my lifetime. The communications have been so vast on TV, radio, the press that it's right there at the top of consciousness. You'll hear it all the way down to the poolroom and the barbershop, men saying, 'Those S.O.B.s, do they think forever they're gonna push black people around because they think we got no brains?'"

However deep this indignation is, it should be recognized that, for the moment, it is governed by responsible leadership. As Thurgood Marshall says, "We sit on the lid." Beyond this is other, almost sinister leadership. The whole structure of organized Negro leadership today flinches at violence; but on the fringes of the Negro community are other violently intemperate men, as racist as the white Citizens' Councils, who can rouse full savagery against any hapless white minority engulfed in Negro slums.

Conscious thus of their voting power, of the indignation underlying it, Negro leadership has this year worked out a precise program to be wrung from both major parties.

UNDERLYING THIS program, first of all, is a principle again most aptly put by Julius Thomas: "It is not any longer a question," he says, "of how a white man feels a colored man should be treated. It's now a decision of law that he should be equal. The question is how we interpret the laws of the country— it's what the South *must* do to conform to the law of the land. The Negro now has a completely different status. The law is on his side now. Whoever discriminates against him is a criminal, is breaking the law."

Coupled with this principle is the tactic of legislative enforcement. In practice, this year, Negro leadership fastened on the civil rights bill, HR 627, a bipartisan measure, as the acid test of every politician's good will. To press it, the NAACP's Washington director, the astute Clarence Mitchell, fashioned the first full-blown lobby for Negroes, a group of 40 or 50 congressmen known as the civil rights bloc (California's James Roosevelt and Chet Holifield, Pennsylvania's Hugh Scott, New York's Edna Kelly, Massachusetts' John Heselton among others) whose members caucus regularly and carefully mesh their action with the NAACP legislative program. On the floor this bloc might influence 200 to 250 votes. By the time this article appears in print, HR 627 will have passed or failed and the congressmen who supported or opposed it will be marked in the NAACP's books for future support or retaliation. Neither party will be able to wriggle out of blame among Negroes if this bill fails. Said Roy Wilkins to the NAACP convention a few weeks ago: "The Republicans will say that they proposed the legislation but the Democrats would not pass it. The Democrats will say that they had little chance to pass it because the Republicans delayed so long in submitting it. Both parties hope we will be fooled by this double talk . . . they have been busy scratching each other's back while we have been left out in the cold."

HR 627, the bill in which so much Negro emotion was invested, was an omnibus bill of many good intentions. But its operational mainspring was the power it gave the federal government by injunction and intervention to defend the Negroes' right to vote in the Southern states—and prosecute white men who stop them. Any substitute civil rights measure denying this objective is, in Negro thinking, only a palliative, however enlightened. For, from this tactical objective of Southern voting rights, as from some commanding salient on a battlefield, hangs the Negro strategy of the future.

This strategy is as simple as it is profound. It is to alter totally the patterns of Southern custom and life. "It does no good," the leaders of the NAACP say almost to a man, "to send a rescue party south or mourn a colored man murdered in Mississippi. But if the federal government guarantees the Negro the right to vote down South, everything changes. No outsider can do anything about a Negro-hating sheriff in Tallahatchie County, but if Negroes vote they can change the sheriff. Arguing about segregation up North does little good—but if Negroes sit on school boards down South, they can act for themselves."

Negroes speak of this objective from their own parochial point of view. But on the broad scene, the attainment of this objective will change our national politics at a stroke. For the Old South, with its familiar voices in Congress—so often distinguished, so often antique—will be dead. The new men it sends to Congress, to be elected in large part by colored votes, must speak in different accents entirely. Then, truly, the roots of Congress change and politics lurch into new, uncharted seas.

And this, fundamentally, is what Negro leadership is demanding of both national conventions this month.

IT IS THE Negro politician of the Democratic party who will quiver most intensely under strain in the next few weeks. For, after 20 years of loyalty, Negroes have won high place and power in the Northern Democracy. All three Negro congressmen—Powell (New York City), Dawson (Chicago), Diggs (Detroit)—are big-city Northerners, and Democrats. All of Michigan's nine Negro legislators are Democrats; so are all five Negro Aldermen of Chicago, both Negro City Councilors of Philadelphia, the two Negro Assemblymen of California. They have served their party well and, in turn, their party has served the needs of Negroes.

Yet the very achievements of Negroes in the past 20 years have cut away the base of unthinking devotion to the Democrats. The growth of a Negro middle class, in their good homes, their clean suburbs has opened an audience for "Republicanism." Eisenhower has proved a remarkably humane and tolerant President, deft, wise and firm—if not bold—in every area of civil rights. Years of education have developed an entirely new class of young Negro intellectuals, college graduates, who know that Roosevelt is dead, but that Senator Eastland, a Democrat, still thrives, and why vote Democratic any longer? Overwhelmingly, Negroes still occupy the bottom rungs of the economic ladder; but the lash of economic need has been cushioned, and conscience has been pricked by the reports from the South. These are the people waiting to see how the conventions come out, and their vote will be cast as conscience calls regardless of party.

Most Negro politicians still confidently expect an overwhelming Democratic vote in all Northern local and state contests. What they fear is ticket-splitting at the top of the ballot, if the Republicans go all out to win. Willoughby Abner, Education and Political Action Director in Chicago of Walter Reuther's solidly Democratic United Auto Workers, said: "For the Negro, straight-ticket voting is too expensive a luxury this year."

This is the year, many Negroes feel, to pick and choose on the ballot, rewarding friends and punishing enemies, regardless of party label. Los Angeles Negroes in 1954 showed best how ticket-splitting can work. In that year, in 30 solidly Negro precincts of Los Angeles, Democratic candidates rolled up their normal three-to-one margins in all contests except one—for the governorship. For the governor's office, the Republicans had provided that cheerfully positive man, Goodwin J. Knight, one of the nation's most eloquent and ardent exponents of civil rights. And "Goody" split the vote, running his Democratic opponent a neck-and-neck seven-to-eight race in the final count. Any such Negro split-voting in this fall's campaign in New York, Philadelphia, Chicago or Detroit would doom the Democrats' hopes of carrying these states for the national ticket.

At the moment, Republican chances of gain seem best in New York, worst in Detroit, indifferent in Philadelphia, Chicago and Los Angeles.

Republican prospects in New York look good because of a variety of factors. There is, first, the high percentage of middle-class and intellectual Negroes among New Yorkers. Next there is the clever leadership of Republican County Chairman Tom Curran, Tammany's archenemy, whose simple but cutting slogan against Democratic U.S. Senator Herbert Lehman, if he runs again, will be "A Vote for Lehman is a Vote for Eastland." (Curran's chief gripe at the moment seems to be against his own Republican National Committee, which, he thinks, is indifferent to Negro emotions and unwilling to provide resources to get the good message across.) There is, further, the prospect that that energetic and effective liberal Jack Javits, New York State's Republican Attorney General, may carry the Republican senatorial standard at the head of the state ticket, and Javits's pulling power is prodigious. Lastly, there is the turmoil in the mind of Congressman Adam Clayton Powell, Jr., now a Democrat, but willing to go over to the Republicans at the first "emphatic demonstration" that they will push civil rights faster than will his own party.

In Detroit, nothing short of contrived stupidity can lose the Negro vote to the Democrats. The Democratic party of Michigan is one of the most effective political organizations in the nation, and is faced by a singularly inept

Republican opposition. If there is a split here, it will be a split away from the residual Republican Negro vote. Even Charles Roxborough, the oldest Negro Republican leader in Michigan, an Eisenhower man, says he guesses he'll have to vote for Governor Williams in Michigan, because "these local Republicans don't want intelligent Negroes."

Philadelphia Negroes will have a contest of loyalties—a Negro Republican is running for Congress in the preponderantly Negro 4th Congressional District against a white Democrat. But Joseph Clark, former mayor and a demigod in Negro thinking, heads the Democratic ticket for Pennsylvania U.S. senator. In Philadelphia, as in Los Angeles and Chicago, there will be a breakaway from the Democrats—but how seriously in all these cities depends entirely on the "ifs" and the behavior of the two great national parties, in convention assembled before us this month.

IT IS THESE "IFS" and the calculations politicians make of them that will rowel the Democratic party convention on Chicago's South Side. For six months, sensing the distemper of the Northern Negroes, Democratic leaders have been trying privately to weave the party to compromise. Their efforts have been moderately successful and many Southerners seemed resigned to accept the inevitable. Said one Mississippi politician to me: "In 1948, we went to the convention wanting to get kicked out. This time we want to stay. We'll accept almost any resolution so long as it's worded in nice language and so long as we know it doesn't apply to Mississippi." Yet whether or not a preconvention compromise on the resolution heads off open-floor warfare at the convention, the Negro's vote and Negro's attitude will cramp each speech and maneuver. Some Northern Democrats believe it is more important to keep their home base secure by a dramatic appeal to the city Negroes than to win the Presidency; while still others believe that the Presidency cannot be won without the Negro (said one to me: "We can afford to lose Mississippi and South Carolina and still win; but if we lose the Negroes in the North, we're through.").

The dilemma the Democrats face is stark and of the essence of drama—a truly hot civil rights resolution, with teeth in it, calculated to rivet Negro loyalties to the party can easily drive the white South entirely out of the party. But a mild, nobly moderate resolution can expose them to a flamboyant counterappeal at the Republican convention a week later—or to a White House gesture timed and phrased to rouse maximum Negro support.

Paradoxically, no matter what the Democrats do, the big "if" of the campaign is not up to them but to the Republicans. For if the Republicans choose to make the Negroes Target A from convention through campaign, nothing can protect the Democrats' vulnerable moral flank from a Republican breakthrough. ("I don't know how we can go about persuading these people that Eastland ain't a Democrat," said one Tammany chieftain to me.)

AT THE MOMENT, however, there is little apparent evidence that the Republicans do consider the Negro Target A—for this is basically a White House decision and Eisenhower has been ill. Eisenhower's behavior, his administration of desegregation in the armed services and the District of Columbia have won him unqualified praise from all Negro groups; but what they have sought and still seek of him is some one bold, unqualified, dramatic gesture jostling the South on the road the laws and the high court have defined. For whatever reasons, medical or political, the President has not, as this is written, made such a decision.

In the absence of a bold stroke from the White House, the Republican play lies in the hands of its state and regional party organizations and its national committees. And although the sagacious Republican National Chairman, Leonard Hall, is planning to rifle-shoot for the election of at least two Negro Republican congressmen running against white Democrats in Philadelphia and Cleveland with all the resources he can throw in, he has been unable to energize the state organizations on a nation-wide basis to mobilize the Negro potential. ("Some Republicans," the candid chairman once said, "have their feet stuck in concrete.") Basically and sociologically, Republican state organizations are unlikely to go out for the predominantly working-class Negro unless flogged into it by the White House.

WHETHER OR NOT the conventions and campaigns of 1956 deliver to Negro leadership their cherished goals this year, they will mark another milestone toward the inevitable. For with the power and leadership the Northern Negro has accumulated, the surge of the Negro to full equality everywhere can hardly be turned back.

Basically, for the Negro, what is at issue in this campaign is not principle, but timing—which party's candidate will go faster, which will move sooner. Nor are the Negroes themselves insistent on explosive immediacy. "We walk a tightrope," said Roy Wilkins. "We want to move, but there must be no explosion, no bloodshed. If there's bloodshed, our people down South get hurt worst of all. There mustn't be bloodshed. If there's bloodshed, it's disaster, for it wipes out all the middle ground of white good will down South, the very people we need as friends if we're to succeed."

It would be missing part of the enormous drama of American life, if the Negro surge of 1956 were seen only in terms of one campaign. To see its historic meaning one must draw back and see the Negro migrant to the Northern city against the political development of all the migrant groups who have gone before. For the Northern cities of America, with all their squalor and violence, have been radiant centers of freedom and democracy for all the world. Each immigrant group that has found dignity and freedom there has been educated to use its power to give the same values to its folk at home. Thus did the Germans of the 1848 migration work for the freedom of Germany; so did the Irish of Boston, New York and Chicago help to create a free Ireland; so did the Jews of the East Coast help to create a free Israel; indeed, in Pittsburgh in 1917 the Czechs of Pennsylvania actually outlined the structure of the first free Czechoslovakia. Each group has used its vote and power to sway American support for American ideals everywhere in the world. And now the Northern Negro is using his vote and power to do in America what other minority groups have done for their brethren overseas.

COLLIER'S August 17, 1956

RACIAL COLLISION IN THE BIG CITIES

The Negro-white problem is greatest in the North where the Negro is taking over the cities—and being strangled by them.

Part I: Rushing to a Showdown That No Law Can Chart

Richard Daley, three times mayor of Chicago, is aging now. Under the shiny black vest, his girth has thickened; but the China-blue eyes in the wide, pale face still stab as he leans forward to talk to a visitor about the Negroes of Chicago.

Civil rights? Daley rumbles. Civil rights in Chicago? Negroes can vote, can't they? They can register, can't they? They can go anywhere they want, can't they? He talks of the jobs they hold, their numbers among his cops (14%), the phenomenal improvement in their education. This is Chicago, he says proudly—not Birmingham.

All that Mayor Daley says is true. Everything promised by the civil rights bill now before the Congress has long been granted to Negroes in his city. Negroes can, indeed, freely enter any hotel or restaurant in Chicago (downtown, that is, *not* in the suburbs). Negroes can indeed vote (seven South Side Negro wards alone provided 118,000 of the 139,000-vote margin by which Daley won re-election).

No distant federal government need intervene, as suggested by the civil rights bill, to protect Chicago's Negroes. They have their own aldermen in the city council, and it stands clearly on the record of history that Daley was the first big-city political boss to grant full equality and loyalty to the Negro captains of his Cook County machine. Out of loyalty to them—as well as to President Kennedy, whom Daley reveres—the mayor has just compelled a bitterly resentful city council to pass a bill which, if enforced, opens housing to Negroes anywhere in Chicago.

Yet, in the South Side Negro wards of Chicago, Richard Daley's name is today hissed and booed: his Negro aldermen are nicknamed "the Silent Six" by other Negroes, and scorned as part of the white man's machine. No Negro leader in Chicago can define what it is they want—except that they want action. "Dick Daley," says one leader, "is a man surrounded by tame Negroes. The mayor of this city doesn't need silent Negroes—he needs an action committee."

Daley is not the man to unburden himself to a stranger. But the fact is that he has cashed every claim he held on the loyalty and obedience of the machine in order to pass this housing bill for Negroes; it has cost him votes all through white Chicago, which resents the bill. How will he defend the action in the white wards next year—the Polish wards, the Irish wards, the Italian wards, the Jewish wards? In the gravelly, rough voice that seems to style all mayors of Chicago, Daley says he'll ask the white voters how many of *their* folks came over on the Mayflower. All men are equal, aren't they? And there follows, then, a recitation of the noble prose of the Declaration of Independence.

But the crisis that Daley will not discuss goes far beyond the arithmetic of voting in 1964, either in Cook County or any other big city of the U.S. For Richard Daley and the men who really lead the Chicago Negro community are out of contact: they simply do not understand each other. Whites and Negroes in his city, as in every city of the North, have passed far beyond the simple legal remedies provided by the current civil rights bill. Whether they want to or not, they must explore a future no law can chart.

DETROIT'S MAYOR IS 26 years younger than Chicago's Daley. Handsome and articulate, Jerome Cavanagh, at 35, glows with the engaging freshness of the young new politician. His perspectives for the nation's fifth-largest city are large and visionary. But he wilts as he estimates that 65% of his time is spent on Detroit's Negro problem. "You come home," he says, "after one of these days and you're desolate. You've spent

the entire day putting out fires—but what about the other important things?"

In Los Angeles, a woman voices the perplexity in a woman's way. Rosalind Wyman of the Los Angeles City Council: "What can you do? You sit there watching what happens in the South and you rack your brains. My God, what can you do right here in your own backyard?"

These are fragments from this reporter's notebooks after six weeks of travel through the nation's cities in a season of trouble. For, as black Americans and white Americans began, in 1963, to move toward an ultimate showdown, there were actually two stories to report. One was the battle for simple decency, fought from Birmingham picket lines to Capitol Hill, and now moving to formal climax in the civil rights legislation before Congress. But beyond this headline story looms the larger, more important, yet frighteningly obscure story of race ferment and change in the great cities, where the American Negro increasingly lives and seeks his future. There, all that the new civil rights bill promises has already been won—from the Negro's right to vote, to his right to eat hamburgers sitting beside white men.

In the big city the story of the Negro is one of unshaped perplexity—the perplexity of the Negro with the city, and of the city with him. The city's promises to him are as large as freedom itself, but delivery on those promises is another matter. In the North, the happy, traditional refusal of the American temperament to admit that any problem is insoluble is confronted by the equally traditional but unhappy refusal to look facts squarely in the face.

White and Negro urban leaders both know that a bad situation has to be changed—all the while refusing to examine what the situation really is.

The very questions that explore this larger story have an ugly ring to them: Why, really, are white people abandoning their big cities? Will Negroes take over—and if so, when? If the centers of the cities become black and the suburban rings around them become white, what kind of metropolitan civilization will we have? Do Negroes want this? Can the cities alone support the burden of Negro need? What do northern Negroes demand and what responsibilities are they prepared to assume? Will the election of 1964 turn on the race problem and, if so, will this obscure or illuminate the nature of this crisis in American civilization?

Every story, great or small, is a story of individuals and individual decisions; and this story can begin, as this reporter began it, on a Saturday afternoon driving through Los Angeles, Calif. I was following a blue, rust-streaked sedan that was weaving with the stop-and-start uncertainty of a stranger looking for something, when I suddenly realized that the driver was looking in the wrong place.

The driver was a Negro; and he was four blocks east of Alameda Street. The children in the back seat pressed their noses against the window, peering at the palm trees of the Promised Land. But

the Texas license plate said the family was migrant, too newly arrived from the South to know that in Los Angeles the Negro boundary is fixed at Alameda Street. In the South, discrimination is as sharp as a knife-edge and every Negro knows where the cut comes. But in the big city it is subtler and it would probably take some time for Mr. Texas Sedan to get the message and rattle back across Alameda to the black ghetto if he wanted shelter for his family.

About a thousand Negroes like Mr. Texas Sedan come to Los Angeles every month from the South, mostly by auto. But I had also seen them come into Chicago, at midnight, up from Mississippi on the brown-and-orange special of the Illinois Central, and come into New York and Philadelphia on buses from the Carolinas and Virginia. And whether they come by car, bus or train, they all look as innocent, as hopeful, as puzzled as Mr. Texas Sedan and his wife beside him and the children in the back seat: singularly undramatic.

Yet they are the stuff of high drama—for they are history moving to a crest, feeling its way into an uncertain future, producing by accumulation these simple facts of change: Washington, D.C. is, today, almost 60% Negro in population. Within 14 to 16 years, *if present population trends are arithmetically projected into the future,* Negroes will be in the majority in Detroit, Cleveland, Baltimore, Chicago and St. Louis; and, in the decade following, in Philadelphia. Such arithmetical projections have, in the past, both underestimated and overestimated Negro growth figures in the big cities. But if, by the decade 1980–1990, which is almost tomorrow in the eyes of history, these unchanged trends *do* give America a civilization in which seven of her ten largest cities (all except New York, Los Angeles and Houston) have Negro majorities, then that civilization will be transformed.

One must look back to grasp the full dimension of the change in the nation's urban life and the direction in which it points—for this change surges from a national adventure that may, some day, be seen as romantically as the migration of the covered wagons. Until 1940, 75% of U.S. Negroes lived in the South, the great majority of them func-

tionally illiterate, primitive, excluded from society and so cruelly policed as to have no respect for law but fear. But World War II made the North into a great industrial furnace—and the draft of the furnace sucked Negro labor by the scores of thousands up the Mississippi valley, up the east coast to the forges, foundries and factories of the war effort. The postwar boom and the Korean war kept the furnaces blazing and the migration northward continued. In some years in the 1950's as many as 200,000 southern Negroes moved North or West to the big cities in search of jobs and freedom.

Where they pooled, Negro death rates fell and birth rates rose. In the 20

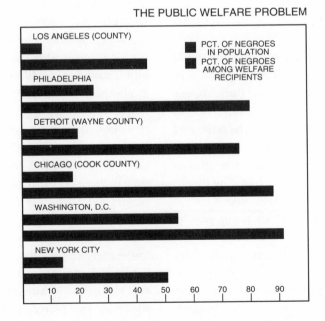

THE PUBLIC WELFARE PROBLEM

Chart of welfare costs (for general relief and aid to dependent children) shows the disproportionate amount paid to non-whites. In Los Angeles County, for example, Negroes make up 7.6% of population, get 43% of relief funds.

years 1940–1960, the Negro populations of New York and Philadelphia
doubled (to 1,100,000 and 529,000
respectively); the Negro populations
of Chicago and Detroit tripled (to
812,000 and 480,000 respectively),
and that of Los Angeles multiplied by
five (from 63,000 to 335,000). Though
migration from the South has now
slowed, the urban Negro crude birth
rate—approximately 40% larger than
that of whites—continues to swell their
numbers. In Chicago, for example,
where Negroes have risen from 278,000
in 1940 to approximately 900,000 today, their natural-growth rate is nine
times faster than it was before the war.
The fertility rate of Chicago Negroes increased in the 1950–60 decade three
times as fast as that of Negroes generally. We are, in short, witnessing in our
cities one of the great population explosions of all time.

Something has to give. And what
gives is the neighborhood pattern in
big-city living as Negroes, bursting out
of inhumanly crowded slums, fleeing
the smell and the rats and the noise and
cackle, like flood waters under pressure,
squirt and spill over adjacent neighborhoods. Street by street, block by block,
neighborhood by neighborhood, solid
black precincts crunch their way year by
year through the hearts of our cities.

In 1956, on a similar survey, I remember that the white people in Chicago still hoped to hold "them" (the
blacks) to a few small beachheads north
of the Chicago River which would then,
as an internal Mason-Dixon Line, divide
the city into a white north and a black

south. This fall I found the Negro
beachheads north of the Chicago River
had developed into a breakthrough.

Ninety-sixth Street was to be the line
protecting the "perfumed stockade" of
East Manhattan, the most fashionable
all-white enclave on the island. But Negroes have begun to appear on the East
Side as far south as the 80s. In Boston,
"they" were supposed to stop at Franklin Park; "they" have by now completely
outflanked the park in Dorchester and
have closed in on Blue Hill Avenue. In
Los Angeles, in Philadelphia, in Cleveland, too—everywhere the For Sale and
For Rent signs on lawns and apartment
houses mark the moving edge of Negro
frontiers. And everywhere the problem
is seen shortsightedly in terms of lo-
calities, of individual blockbusters or
block-moppers—not as an elemental
force bursting dikes.

"Where are the whites going to stop
running when they know they can't
hide?" asks Loren Miller, the great Negro housing champion of Los Angeles.

The answer is, of course, as clear as
the maps that chart Negro expansion:
"they," the whites, are going to the suburbs. There, a white population explosion in the suburban ring matches the
Negro population explosion in the central city.

In Chicago, in Philadelphia, in Boston—everywhere except New York
City—the same pattern repeats itself;
the suburban "white noose" tightens
about an inner city that is becoming
more and more rapidly Negro while,
within the strangulating city, a turmoil
begins that feeds on fear and hate.

To understand what is happening inside the major urban centers, one must look freshly at the city—for city-Americans behave in silent patterns which are familiar to all of us, yet totally at variance with what is publicly taught us about the metropolitan melting pot.

The melting pot melts different minorities at different rates. Also, from Boston to Los Angeles, most urban Americans live in neighborhoods of their own "kind," with people of their own origins and traditions. One usually leaves the "old neighborhood" to move up. Thereafter, most racial and ethnic groups in America sort themselves out by income and class. In the new neighborhoods they "mix" with "strangers" only as education grows, and then by seeking out people of kindred interest: businessmen with businessmen, professionals with professionals, union leaders with union leaders, politicians with politicians. The lower the educational level, the more people tend to cluster with their "own kind," seeking social life with those who live nearby.

WHAT MAKES a neighborhood different from a ghetto is simply that a man can always choose to leave his neighborhood—but in a ghetto he is locked in.

When Negro leaders call their neighborhoods ghettos, they mean that they are locked in; and thus the black ghettos become, for sensitive and aspiring Negroes, prisons. Most Negro leaders are convinced that if Negroes were free to move anywhere they want, they—like most other ethnic groups—would prefer to live with their own and sort themselves out into the quiet and the noisy, the diligent and the shiftless. But Negroes are given no elbow room.

Most Negro communities expand only by crude pressure of numbers—the resistance outside usually determining the rate and direction of growth. Across the country Negroes usually gobble up Jewish neighborhoods first, then Italian neighborhoods. In the folklore of the big city, Negroes meet their toughest resistance in Polish or Irish neighborhoods, so that police watch the frontiers of a Polish-Negro or Irish-Negro neighborhood as a potential flash-line.

In the big cities, thus, two primordial emotions confront each other: one is that of the Negro who wants out, who wants room and dreaming space; the other is that of the white workingman who has the deep emotional need and hunger to live comfortably with others like himself. For many a white workingman, his two-family house represents the dream-end of life. He plans to live on the lower floor, rent the upper floor and add the rent to Social Security or pension, finishing his life in modest contentment near his friends, watching his grandchildren grow up. For him, the Negro neighbor ravages the dream.

When the Negroes' tormenting need for housing rubs against the tormenting need of other American groups to live with their own kind, trouble comes; and very few men in the big city, as we shall see later, have had the candor to examine this problem in public and explore practical solutions that may meet both needs.

Any solution, or any approach to a solution, must begin with commonly agreed facts. Yet the facts attack any reporter who examines the Negro community with this paradox: the progress of Negroes in the North breathes hope into the meanest of men; at the same time the internal decomposition of Negro society frightens the most hopeful of men. In the big city things are better than ever for the Negro—and they are also worse.

The big city is a street called "John R" in Detroit—a dirty, trash-littered cord of filth running through the center of the Negro ghetto. John R. is the cen-

ter of one of the two worst crime districts in all Detroit (the other is Twelfth Street, also an all-Negro neighborhood). But just three miles away is a district called Conant Gardens. There elm trees arch over the street, the white churches nestle on green lawns, teenagers shyly court each other on porches; the smell of fall makes the air fragrant. This is the kind of suburb Longfellow might have envisioned as an American future. Conant Gardens is a working-class, lower-middle-income district distinguished for two reasons: it is the most crime-free precinct in the most crime-free district in the entire city of Detroit; and it is also 100% Negro. What makes the Negroes of Conant

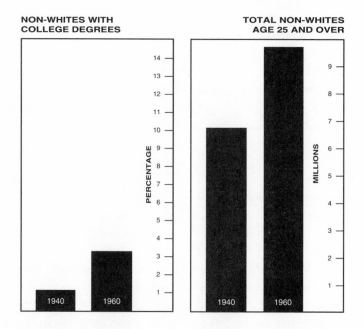

Number of college-educated non-whites (above) has risen to a still inadequate 3.5% of the adult non-white population (among whites it is 8%). Nevertheless the number of college graduates is rising rapidly at faster rate than non-white population (right).

Gardens such superb citizens, and the Negroes of John R. such a menace to society? No one can answer more adequately, as we shall see later, than to say that these outer differences measure the distance between self-respect and despair.

In the big cities of the North, Negroes have found success and disaster at the same time. Success is the political power to claim in one recent year over 30 judgeships in New York City. Success is as tangible as Baldwin Hills in Los Angeles, with its slickly modern homes and their ground ivy, their fiber palms, their dichondra lawns. Success is Pasadena, with its small colony of Negro scholars, engineers, scientists. Success is education—in 1947 U.S. colleges and professional schools counted 124,000 Negroes; in 1961 they enrolled 233,000. Success is Negroes directing embassies, leading orchestras, commanding Army units. In the decade of the '50s alone, the number of Negro engineers jumped fivefold. Since 1940 Negroes have claimed government jobs more and more insistently—and won them, particularly in the big cities. In that period Negroes employed in government jumped from some 4.5% to almost 13% (in Philadelphia, to about 50%). Success has found the Negro in the big city and delivered to him not only a solid, educated middle-class but given him a leadership group of dazzling achievement in the arts, in writing, in politics, in sports and in their own community affairs.

But disaster also has found him in the city. The Negro who migrated to the North came chiefly to work at the heavy jobs—the steel mills, the packing houses, the assembly lines. For the past 10 years these jobs have been evaporating as automation has condemned scores of thousands of middle-aged Negroes to discard, and scores of thousands of their youngsters to a future that holds nothing.

In Detroit proper, for example, the largest employer of labor is Chrysler—and until late this summer, before the new-model boom, in the automated metals division of Chrysler, layoffs under union seniority rules affected every man hired after February 1948. Automatically and without prejudice the great mass of Negroes who migrated to Detroit in the '50s was eliminated. In Chicago, erstwhile "Hog Butcher for the World," the packing houses once employed 20,000 workers, heavily Negro. Today Chicago no longer butchers hogs for the world, for the packers have moved out to new and more efficient plants and their South Side workers will never be employed again. In Chicago the Urban League estimates that 18% of all employable Negroes are unemployed.

Generally, across the country, unemployment averages 5.6%, but among Negroes the figure is double that—11%. Next year, 1964, is not only an election year—it is 18 years from the baby boom of 1946, and the number of untrained and unskilled Negro adolescents will almost double. As late as 1948, in the adolescent years between 14 and 19, unemployment was worse among white youngsters than it was among Negro youngsters; but this summer, in our new technological society, 24% of all Negro youngsters were unable to find work, while this was true of only 9% of all white adolescents.

THESE STATISTICS begin to live and breathe on the pavements of the ghetto: the wino on the street, lurching from side to side; the mid-morning drunk with his bottle in a brown paper sack, the three, four, five hopeless ones leaning against the corner post or sitting on the curb at high noon watching the world go by. And these, unfortunately, are the ones whom the white neighbors of the Negroes in the city see and re-

member. Ignoring Conant Gardens or Baldwin Hills or St. Albans, N.Y., and all the known evidence of Negro achievement, the emotions of white people fix on the spectacle of decomposition and its effects.

Here, alas, the reporter must contend with an issue that, when raised, so embitters Negro leaders as almost to hush friendly dialogue. But the inescapable truth is that, just as the challenge of the city has led many Negroes through education to breathtaking achievement, just so has the challenge of its industrial civilization caused many others to collapse in squalor. And one must report squalor if one is to begin identifying problems.

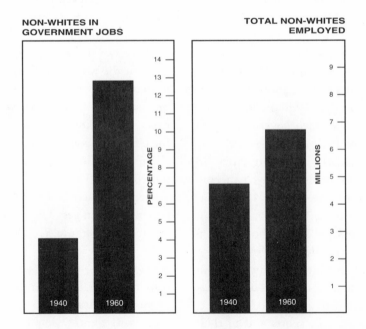

Key role of municipal and federal governments in broadening Negro opportunity shows in this comparison: non-whites in government jobs almost tripled in 20-year period (above). Non-white employment rose only 44% (right).

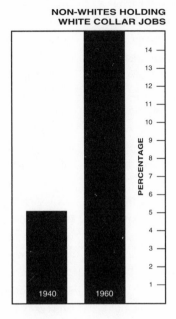

**NON-WHITES HOLDING
WHITE COLLAR JOBS**

Non-whites holding white-collar jobs have risen 150% in 20 years, while total of employed non-whites has expanded 44%—a sign that a Negro middle class is emerging.

Crime, of course, is the most immediate charge against the Negro community. In the past five years Negro crime rates in the cities have risen four times as fast as the white crime rate—which is rising too. Some hitherto unpublished figures for the rise in Negro crime in urban areas over the five years 1958–62 read: murder, up by 25%; robbery, up by 32%; larceny, up by 43%; forcible rape, up by 13% (narcotics, *down* 28%). More than half of such Negro crimes are perpetrated against fellow Negroes, much of their wrath at the world being spent on each other.

What is more disturbing to those who plan the future of the big city are the pathetic and frightening figures on out-of-wedlock births. In general,

across the country, Negroes bear 10 times as many babies out of wedlock as do white families. Nationally, one fifth of all Negro children are illegitimate. But in the big city this figure soars—so that in central Harlem more than a third (37.5%) of all children are born out of wedlock and in Chicago the figures come to 27.3%.

Where one can analyze the problem—and pitifully small work of analysis has been done—it is not at all a calculated pattern of brood mothers scheming to bring up babies on relief. It is rather a pattern of the drifting, unemployable Negro male who abandons his mate as soon as she becomes pregnant, because he cannot support her; of the lonesome southern-born girl in the big city, too ignorant to consider what a night's warmth will cost in the future. Still, however innocent or pathetic are the reasons for such out-of-wedlock births, they pose a real, pragmatic problem as their number increases steeply. The city must become father and provider for such children; and if one generation of illegitimate children proceeds to breed another and larger generation, the perspectives are endlessly gloomy. In Chicago, for example, it is estimated that the city spends $7,000 to raise each such child to the age of 17, and last year Cook County was supporting 51,000 such illegitimate Negro children. In New York City, last year alone, the number of illegitimate Negro children *increased* by 10,000.

There begins to swirl, thus, in the ghettos of big northern cities, a pattern of twin cyclones—an upper cyclone carrying some families up in aspiration and ambition, another cyclone carrying others down to decomposition. In the big city the Negro community begins to take on a weird hourglass configuration: an educated middle-class at the top and a "subculture" of despair at the bottom: Negroes beginning to "make it" (only 5.7% of Negroes earned more than $5,000 in 1948; by 1961 this figure had grown to 28.4%) at the top; and at the bottom Negroes in hopeless misery. The Negro community, in short, lacks "structure."

The needs of these two groups of Negroes are as different as the needs of whites who go separate ways of life. But both groups are teased by the dreams and visions offered by the white man's culture, thrust on him by the white man's television every night—and both groups are tormented at their own levels by the frustrations that come when they try to touch what those dreams offer.

"You sit there," says Alex Fuller, a vice president of the A.F.L.-C.I.O. in Detroit, "and you listen at night to these people selling suburban real estate: 'Come see Goldenwood Manor,' says the announcer, 'where the water of your swimming pool turns gold in the moonlight at night.' You sit there with your kids, listening to this manure, and as they grow older, you wonder."

"She says," reports a Chicago relief worker of her client, "'I'm 16. I'm pretty. Why can't I have nylons like the other girls? I need a new compact, I need a dress.' She sees it on TV, and she wants it and she's going to do *anything* to get it."

"For the middle-class Negro in Chicago," says Professor Ray Mack of Northwestern University, "there's no way out. The movable generation can't move. There's no Beverly Hills or Scarsdale or Highland Park waiting to take him. The middle-class American Negro—it's his kid that gets beaten up by the lower-class Negro. It's he who pays the price of the ghetto. He's followed the rules, he's gone to school, he's got a good steady job. But he can't leave. He's won in the sweepstakes—but when he goes to the window, he finds they won't pay off on his ticket."

IT IS THIS conjunction of educated Negro leadership and Negro working-class misery that gives the Negro problem of

COMPARISON OF FAMILY INCOME

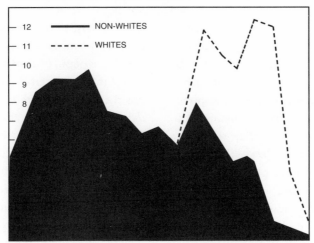

Graph shows sharp difference between family income of non-whites (shaded area) and whites (dotted line). Differing pattern of white and non-white family income is emphasized by scale which shows income in $500 steps up to $5,000, in bigger jumps for higher income categories.

the North its punch, its confusion and its menace. For, just as much as ordinary people needs jobs, a certain number of men in every group need to lead. It is a hunger in them, as song is a hunger in the musician and creativity is a hunger in the heart of the artist. And the Negro middle-class, for all its achievement, has been—and remains—as excluded from general leadership as the Negro workingman is generally excluded from the skilled unions. Most Americans with a leadership urge express it in private business and industry, where the nation's executive talent so brilliantly flourishes. But this world of private enterprise is largely closed to leadership Negroes by prejudice, and only rarely have Negroes tried to penetrate it, as other groups have done, with ventures of their own.

Thus Negro leadership talents turn inward. And as their educational levels, horizons and abilities rise, they find they can lead only one way—against the common enemy they perceive in all white people.

THE MOST BITTER—and perhaps the most eloquent—of these talented Negro leaders have arrived thus at what can be called the conspiratorial theory of American life: that there is a conspiracy, somewhere, to lock Negroes in ghettos and exclude them from the general white life of the metropolitan center. When asked to pinpoint the "conspiracy," they can occasionally finger a racist like Mayor Orville Hubbard of Dearborn (Detroit) Mich., ex-Marine, ex-unionman, who believes in "complete segregation one million percent on all levels." (His police wagons carry two signs—one of them his euphemistic racist slogan, "Help Keep Dearborn Clean"; the other, just below it, "Be Nice to People"). But generally when one seeks for evidence of this conspiracy in the North, the charges dissolve into the anonymous "they." For the white "they," just as the black "they," have conspired at nothing, planned nothing. "They," both white and black, have been—and continue to be—incredibly irresponsive to each other's real needs and fears.

Dr. John A. Morsell of the N.A.A.C.P., who is one of the most thoughtful Negro leaders of this country, likes to explain the race demonstrations of the past year by analogy with nuclear physics. "It was only a question of time," he says, "when it was going to happen. At a certain point when you enrich a mass of uranium enough, it becomes fissionable. When you add enough educated people to any contained group, when you add enough leaders—then you get a fissionable mass and it goes off by itself. The year just happened to be 1963."

The growing mass of Negroes in the northern urban centers is already fissionable. By 1970, estimates the Urban League, 18 million Negroes (more than the entire population of Canada) will be living in the big cities of the U.S. Unless their demands are met—and unless *they* meet the demands of their white neighbors—we face a continuing moral and constitutional deadlock new in the history of our country. It is, therefore, vitally important to scrutinize, as we shall next week, the demands that the Negro leaders are leveling against white society, and their dilemma in leading their own people; to measure how greatly the presidential election of 1964 can complicate, by partisan politics and political requirements, the tentative search for solutions; to consider how greatly that election turns on the present civil rights bill before Congress; and, finally, to report the general consensus of men of goodwill as they reflect on where and how American life has wounded the Negro most deeply—and what responsibility Negro as well as white leaders must bear in healing those wounds.

LIFE November 22, 1963

The angry U.S. Negro's rallying cries are confusing his just and urgent cause.

Part II: Power Structure, Integration, Militancy, Freedom Now!

In the American South the Negro has a relatively simple goal: to wring from hostile white men an end to legally imposed indignity. But in the big cities of the North, where Negro Americans increasingly seek their future, no such simple objective rises from the dialogue between white and Negro leaders. The nature of America's future civilization depends on clearing up the bitter tangle of misunderstanding between whites and Negroes; yet the noise of the present dialogue deafeningly confuses the real issues they pretend to discuss.

The historian of the future will, of course, see the ferment and change caused by city Negroes more clearly than we do today. His report will start, as ours must, with an account of the centuries-old injustice of the white man to the black, of the crippling of emotion which every Negro suffers every day as he tries to live in a white world that prefers to ignore his existence.

With the advantage of hindsight, the historian of tomorrow will coolly strip the noise from the action to measure how well or ill Negroes fared in this episode. But those Americans who try in this decade—*now*—to meet Negro demands live with a dilemma of understanding. The problem is compounded by the reluctance of well-intentioned whites to bring up harsh but inescapable facts. No one can describe this dilemma better than to offer for consideration four of the key words or phrases of the bitter dialogue—each reflecting one facet of the many-faceted confusion.

MILITANCY IS A word that today reflects a special posture or a type of person. A Negro leader must be known—first and above all—among his own people as a "militant." Not to be "militant" exposes a Negro to the charge that he is an "Uncle Tom." Once known as an "Uncle Tom," his career is over.

"Militancy" thus makes the public confrontation between the races chiefly a dialogue of black demand on white guilt. On occasion the "militant" Negro can be a man of incandescent, self-denying heroism—a Martin Luther King. But the "militant" Negro can also be one who substitutes pure flamboyance for leadership. Congressman Adam (We-Got-the-White-Man-on-the-Run) Clayton Powell is, for example, the single Negro most strategically placed (as chairman of the House Committee on Education and Labor) to operate on two of the greatest problems of his people: jobs and schooling. Not a hint of creative thinking or leadership in these supremely vital fields has come from Powell. Yet, as New York's leading "militant" Negro, he is politically invulnerable in Harlem. Powell called for "a Birmingham explosion in New York City" this fall.

"The word 'militancy' detonates such a charge," says one Negro leader, "that you simply can't afford *not* to be a 'militant.' Of course, this has a crippling effect on strategy. You ask in a closed meeting, should we go all the way, even to insurrection? And everybody says, no, we haven't got the force. If that's so, shouldn't we try to make progress with the help of the best elements of white society? But if you *say* that, it sounds as if you won't do anything unless you're sure of white support. You're not 'militant'—so where are you?"

It thus takes far more courage for a Negro leader in the North to compromise in the open with white leaders on a given program than for him to hold firm as a "militant." A charade then ensues whereby "militant" Negro leaders gather at various city halls; sympathetic white leaders listen to their demands and respond with promises that sound as if they were written by the Negro abolitionist Frederick Douglass. And then, as the promises slowly vanish in a

blur, the banners wave and the audience chants: "Freedom *now!*"

FREEDOM NOW! is a mood phrase that links the militant leader to the passions of his followers. It is almost as difficult to quarrel with this phrase as to denounce The Star-Spangled Banner or Caroline Kennedy; it is as impossible to reply to it as to the question, "Have you stopped beating your wife?"

But "Freedom *now!*"—no matter how wonderfully it lends itself to the emotional mood of orator and crowd, no matter how bravely the placards wave the phrase above good people softly singing *We Shall Overcome*—is a phrase with explosive potential. For the problem of bad housing and education, unemployment and lack of opportunity cannot be solved anywhere near fast enough to satisfy the cravings generated by orators who chant: "We want it *now!* We want it *all!* We want it *here!* Freedom *now!*"

By wiping out reasonable public discussion of steps and procedures, the phrase "Freedom *now!*" blinds rather than clarifies. It could conceivably deliver leadership of the Negro community to demagogues who, if they insist that "now" is 1964, will force the major parties to polarize on this demand to the peril of both Negro and white.

Only when one attempts to pin down what "freedom" really is does one begin, for the first time, to grapple seriously with the Negro dilemma. For, the definition of "freedom" becomes "real integration," and the word "integration" itself remains to be defined.

INTEGRATION IS A word of substance that covers goals and ends, but no one has ever defined it except as the opposite of "segregation." Segregation originated in the South as a system of laws which imprisoned a man by the color of his skin at birth. From hospital waiting room, through school and work, to the grave, segregation shut Negroes out of community life. This system, long recognized as morally wicked, is now— thankfully—illegal. In the northern city it has been outlawed almost as long as the whipping post and thumb rack— though replaced by a system of white hypocrisies and subtleties which erects before Negroes an invisible web of prejudice that excludes them from the promise explicit in the laws.

"Segregation," being a legal term, can be outlawed by courts, supported— if necessary—by armies. But courts cannot define its opposite, "integration," nor can armies enforce what courts cannot define. Thus confusion— since "integration" has as many meanings as it has champions.

"Integration" can mean, for example, jobs. But in jobs it can be a demand as solid as opening locked unions to fair opportunity for Negroes—or as silly as the unblinking complaint, on opening night, by pickets that Cleopatra, an African heroine, should have been played by a Negro rather than by a white woman—Elizabeth Taylor. "Integration" can also be applied to the symbol-ism of American life—it can support the insistence of Negroes that TV, movies and stage begin to show the Negro in true achievement rather than as permanent servingman; or it can invite the absurd proposal of some Los Angeles Negroes that they organize a protest march of 10,000 if no Negro girls are included among the beauty queen finalists for the Tournament of Roses parade on Jan. 1, 1964.

Chiefly, however, "integration" enters the public dialogue in two areas of real demand: schooling and housing. Yet "integration" as applied to schools in the North defines an emotion, not a program.

No one has yet constructively and pragmatically defined what "integration" in the schools requires. Clearly, by the historic decision of Judge Irving Kaufman in New Rochelle, N.Y., separation of children by color, when *purposefully* practiced by school boards in the North under hypocritical cover phrases, is as illegal as the South's openly acknowledged practice. But, equally clearly, parents are not inevitably bigots if they prefer to have their toddlers attend schools in their own neighborhoods. In between these two clarities, however, is the large expanse of gray battleground where "integration" triggers off automatic demands on the school system.

Enough survey work has been done to show that Negro parents, like white parents, are more interested in the quality of education than in the chromatic proportions of the classroom. Yet in every city so much emotion is spent weighing the numbers, the percentages, the admixture of black with white, that Negro leaders have convinced far too many of their own people that Negroes sitting together in one classroom retard each other's education. In cities like Washington, D.C., where 80% of children in public schools are Negro, or areas like Manhattan, where 69% are Negro and Puerto Rican, "integration" could be achieved only by the most mechanical and arbitrary importation of white children from distant areas.

So in the name of "integration" some Negro leaders, notably in Los Angeles and New York, are demanding that white children be transported into Negro slums to achieve the proper chromatography. In New York the most advanced proponent of this impractical proposal is Dr. Edward Lewis of the Urban League. Talking to this good and genial man, one has difficulty believing he takes his own demand seriously. One has the feeling that he would like to get off the hook but that he is hung there by the word "integration" and the need for "militancy." Few Negro leaders in New York dare denounce the idea publicly for fear they will be blasted by others of their race for being against "integration." Meanwhile white parents can be tormented by a magnificently emotional appeal: "Integration means your kids will be forced on buses and shipped to Harlem schools with all those illegitimate and backward kids."

The kind of confusion set up by the word "integration" as applied to education is best reflected in a conversation with a bitter young Negro student leader in Chicago who began by listing as his No. 1 demand of American society: "separate but superior education for Negroes—if we could get it." Then, after increasingly emotional talk for an hour, he took up the matter of cross-busing white children into Negro districts and said, "The white kids got to pay for what their parents did to us. Even at the age of 6, they got to pay—because they're going to pay one way or the other. Besides, it'll be good for them."

"Integration" as applied to housing leads to hypocrisy. Outside of New York there is no substantial evidence that any neighborhood of mixed colors, if left unprotected against the pressure, has ever been successfully and permanently stabilized against the torrent of in-migrating Negroes. If there is any consensus in the heated race confrontation, it is this: in the crowded central cities, given the bursting need of Negroes for housing, Negroes can be introduced to white neighborhoods in orderly fashion only by quotas or, as the University of Chicago nicely puts it, "managed integration."

THIS SOMBER judgment was shared by at least 50 of the 60 white and Negro leaders to whom this writer has spoken in the past few months. But almost no one will speak this judgment aloud. Alone among public agencies, the New Jersey Advisory Committee to the U.S. Commission on Civil Rights has this fall courageously spoken up for "benign quotas" to lead Negroes out of their ghettos in orderly manner. In Chicago, Saul Alinsky, one of the Negroes' great white champions and a man who favors quotas, has said, "An integrated neighborhood—that's a neighborhood between the day the first Negro family moves in and the last white family moves out."

But elsewhere public statement and private view contradict each other. One of the most respected of American Negro leaders recently testified officially to this view: "I think any quota is odious, and I don't know how you maintain a quota." But the same man told me privately this fall that he feels quotas have "pragmatic value." White officials in New York City who deny publicly that any quota system exists in the public housing system will tell you, privately, how they work to maintain a balance.

Yet for all its haziness the word "integration" does, somehow, represent a genuine goal—the day when whites and Negroes will enjoy equal opportunity in the nation's life, will "communicate" with each other, will ignore the color of their skin and become friends. This greatly desired end will not, naturally, come about by itself; thus both strategy and tactics are necessary—and both of them are knit into the operational phrase of the present Negro unrest: "power structure."

POWER STRUCTURE is the commonest phrase on the lips of every Negro thinker and political analyst. Where the phrase originated is known only to scholars, but today it emphasizes the gap between two different visions of reality.

The word "power," to white politicians, means votes, police, armies, a government's power to compel. But as Negro leaders use the phrase, it means the entire structure of American life. Whoever has any privilege (either public or private) to give or withhold is part of the "power structure."

To Negroes "power structure" means not only government but the men who control the banks, industry and insurance companies; the men who control newspapers, magazines and television; it means the schools and their administrators; it means the churches and their hierarchies; it means the labor unions and their leaders.

Of these elements of the "power structure," Negroes have leverage only in one: government. This leverage they have won by translating the growth of Negro population in the big cities of the North into solid blocs of votes that swing six to eight of our greatest states one way or the other. Exploiting this strength, Negro leaders insist that government use *its* leverage on all the other elements of the "power structure," private and public. They propose that government press itself into *every* area of decision, that it penetrate and dominate everywhere that discrimination in any form is practiced.

ALL NEGRO leaders, whether of the intransigent radical fringe or the most docile and mendicant timidity, demand that the "power structure" be opened to include them at every level, right up to the policy-making summit. This, they insist, is the most important single transaction of this generation of Americans—the single overriding priority for all the nation's effort.

One should pause over the phrase "power structure" because it leads directly to the hard, true needs of the Negro community: the often-repeated trinity of demands—jobs, housing, education. And none of these problems, Negroes say, can be cured except by pressure on the "power structure." In New York City, for example, it is estimated that the construction unions control over 100,000 jobs. At the present rate of admitting apprentices in, say, the Steamfitters Union, if Negro applications are accepted beginning right now, it will be eight more years before the first Negro fills an opening as apprentice in that union. This, Negroes point out, is patently unfair and completely unrealistic; they argue that the union must be forced open to them, now, preferentially or not.

NEGROES IN big cities across the country also want to pressure the "power structure" to force open the schools, public or private, to their students—or to force into their schools the best teachers available. As for housing, federal financing for more than 30 years supported the "power structure" of real estate developers who insisted that new suburban dwellings be covenanted against Negro occupancy; why,

then, should not federal power now be used, asks Loren Miller, the Negroes' outstanding housing expert, to break open those suburban rings that trap Negroes in their urban ghettos?

The Negro community has needs as urgent as hunger, as hard as rock—yet the rhetoric of today's dialogue hides the reality. There is, for example, the clear national need that human beings eliminated by automation from industry, black *and* white, should not be dumped on the slums of our cities like animal refuse awaiting garbage removal. This urgent need can be expressed in several ways.

It can be expressed in the words of Louis Martin, a Negro journalist, who says, "After the civil rights bill goes through, what next? We have to take care of the guy out of work. He's mad. He won't lend himself to morality. This guy being tossed out by automation— you have a quarter of a million of him in the big cities. If you let him linger in poverty too long, you're developing another kind of culture in the city, a culture you can't reach with nonviolent preaching. I say you've got to take a billion dollars a year, if necessary, and toss it into the pool and say that any Negro—*or any white man*—who makes less then half the national average income ought to be able to find government work. I say that this basically illiterate guy has got to have another choice besides crime or relief."

Martin is now deputy chairman of the Democratic National Committee and is, therefore, relatively free of the pressures of interior Negro politics. Inside Negro politics, however, few men can speak of the problem as one shared by both races. Instead they speak in the dogma of the civil rights movement, of "reparations." As voiced by the National Urban League in its demand for a national "Marshall Plan for Negroes," the concept of equal opportunity must be expanded to include the "concept of indemnification"; and there is the warning that, if such sin-gold is not paid by white Americans to black Americans, the "power structure" is inviting "social chaos."

THE INFLAMMATORY language of the indemnification proposal illustrates a troublesome political paradox. The Urban League, led nationally by the brilliant Whitney Young and in Chicago by the distinguished Edwin C. Berry, is perhaps the wisest and most responsible of Negro civil rights groups; it knows best the internal problems of the Negro community in the city; it is most willing to accept Negro responsibility for what must be done—and is consequently suspect among extremists within the Negro community as "a front for the white men." The Urban League must, thus, advance its share of extreme public demands—and, once these demands are voiced, all other groups, in order to be "militant," must back them too.

This militancy of language—supported by moral indignation yet coupled with total confusion about what practical steps must first be taken—has brought into the crusading Negro movement a fringe of extremist followers, white and black, moved by many other inspirations, both domestic and alien.

Some of the wildest civil rights militants are descended from America's native radical tradition, which goes all the way back to the Boston Tea Party, to Thoreau and the Abolitionists, and descends through Populists and Wobblies to the radicals of the '30s. These are people learning, with zest and wonder, how delicate is the meshing of big city civilization. Their sit-ins and demonstrations have kept police forces across the nation strained for months. They have dumped garbage on City Hall in New York City, picketed a Chicago newspaper whose editorials they disliked, closed up construction sites in Philadelphia. Some of the leaders and participants in the civil rights movement insist that direct action, whether it works or not, is the only form of therapy which can reach Negro despair. Others find a simple joy in what can be done by mischief: "What if," mused a Chicago direct-actionist, "we all went into Marshall Field's, by the hundreds, and ordered parcels shipped C.O.D. all over town? I'll bet we could wreck them if they didn't negotiate with us."

The most remarkable thing about this past summer's protest demonstrations has been the ability of responsible Negro leadership under the most desperate cross-pressures to keep such extremists under control.

The central and most responsible vehicle for direct action in the country is the Congress of Racial Equality—

CORE. CORE is led by some of the highest-minded, most dedicated men of the Negro movement—and it believes, with magnificent simplicity, that it alone can decide for its members which laws they shall obey, which disobey. Disciplined and well indoctrinated in the techniques and philosophy of civil disobedience, CORE represents a thoroughly American, though thoroughly disturbing, tradition of protest by direct action.

There are other direct-action groups—sometimes organized, sometimes not—who are far less reputable. For example, in Detroit this summer a local, unaffiliated university group called UHURU (an African word for "freedom") on its own initiative sat in at City Hall to demand, among other things, that the mayor immediately arrest the prosecuting attorney of Wayne county and appoint a Negro chief of police.

Still more sinister groups are also interested in direct action. One is the Communists, who again are trying to mount an important penetration into American politics. One staff member with definite Communist ties was uncovered in Martin Luther King's southern office this summer and was fired; but a continuing outside Communist effort—so far frustrated—to penetrate King's leadership circle is known to exist. National officials of CORE have already warded off Communist infiltration in chapters in Pittsburgh and in San Francisco; but Communist efforts to penetrate the Los Angeles group remain of concern to them.

A MORE SERIOUS penetration by unidentified elements is believed to have been made in S.N.C.C.—the Student Non-Violent Coordinating Committee. On two occasions—once in Jackson, Miss., once in Birmingham—agents of this group tried to convert a peaceful march into a violent *Putsch* on government offices; both times they were headed off by responsible Negro leadership acting in time.

One of the most chilling documents this writer has seen recently was the draft "battle plan" discussed by S.N.C.C. (and rejected by Negro leaders) for use this fall in Alabama. It advocated a march on Montgomery in "nonviolent battle groups," with their own insignia and flags. These "battle groups," trained in street-battle tactics, were to cut Montgomery off from all communication with the outside world—presumably to provoke "nonviolent" combat between Alabama and the U.S.

It cannot be overstressed that such lunatics and aliens are, at the moment, no more than irritants in a vast and inspiring thrust of Negroes toward dignity. But the confusion of the dialogue over civil rights magnifies what these irritants can do. Consider the riots in North Philadelphia on the weekend of Oct. 28. They were triggered off, after a Negro was shot by a policeman in self-defense, by one car roving the Negro districts with a loudspeaker and calling for "an eye for an eye" retaliation. The loudspeaker-equipped car was proved, on later investigation, to have been manned by a member of a Communist splinter group. But several hundred angry Negroes took to the street in response to the call.

As THEY TRY to sort out historic, long-range problems from short-range tactics, the Negro leaders face their largest dilemma in the elections of 1964. A quick analysis of the last presidential election explains both their dilemma and their power.

Of Kennedy's 303 electoral votes (Nixon received 219), 57 came from states of the Old South. But no less than 100 more of Kennedy's electoral votes came from states where his majority was less than 51%, shading down to margins so thin as to be an electoral twitch—indecision transfixed during a momentary count.

Under the discipline of conscience, Constitution and history, President Kennedy, in the role of 1964 candidate, must now grimly contemplate sacrificing as many of those 57 southern electoral votes as are necessary to move this country forward in race relations. He cannot, however, afford to give up also the 26 electoral votes of Illinois (his 1960 margin—9,000 out of 4,757,000 votes cast), the 21 of Michigan (1960 margin—67,000 out of 3,318,000), the 12 of Missouri (1960 margin— 10,000 out of 1,934,000) and be re-elected President. Yet whether he gains or loses votes in such big city states (his prospects, it should be said, are much brighter in New York, Pennsylvania and California) depends almost as much on

the Negro leaders as on his own behavior and performance.

For everywhere in the big city states the edge of friction cuts where Negro and white workingmen jostle each other—in jobs, in schools, above all in white working-class, home-owning neighborhoods. As a union man, the white worker has generally voted Democratic. But in local election after local election this fall season of 1963, wherever the Negro issue can be sensed in working-class votes—from Boston through Cambridge, Md. through Philadelphia—the white workingman has voted increasingly anti-Negro in defense of his neighborhood base.

As Negro leaders continue to press the white liberal leaders of the North (Republican and Democratic alike) for the demands that rise from the inner torment of the Negro community, they also press white liberal leadership further and further away from the white working class—and the working class itself toward the temptation offered by anti-Negro demagoguery. By pressing hard enough the Negroes can as thoroughly wreck or alter the nature of the present two-party system as did the Democratic radicals of the 1890s. (The battle cry of those radicals is oddly evocative of the Negro uprising of 1963: "If we can't all sit at the table together," said 'Ma' Jones of the Populists, "let's kick the legs off the goddam table and all sit on the floor.")

Much of the urgency with which Administration leaders and many Republicans endow the civil rights bill now before Congress comes from this perspective on the elections of 1964. If the bill is defeated, or filibustered to death, or compromised to nothing, it will inevitably strengthen and feed the passions of the most extreme Negro militants, boil over into the presidential politics of next year, and thus divert the nation's attention from the far more complicated next step, which is the effort to solve the over-all problem of the Negro in the big city.

IS THERE ANY area of this problem in which men of goodwill, both white and black, do agree privately if not publicly? Perhaps the most encouraging discovery this writer made in journeying across the country is this: that among themselves the more farsighted of Negro leaders have come to recognize that if they press responsibility for community behavior on the white, they must accept a black community responsibility too.

But they can only speak openly of their own responsibility, they insist, if the white man first moves to pick up his. The white power structure, they say, must first show by massive public and private effort its willingness to cope with the human fallout of automation, must demonstrate by massive public and private effort an intent to raise the quality of education and opportunity for Negro children. Then—*and only then*—they say, can Negroes face what they euphemistically refer to as their "housekeeping problem." In the discussions of "housekeeping," one of the words used

by Negro extremists offers a helpful point of departure. It is the ugly word "castration."

When Negro intellectuals use the word "castration," they mean the lack of pride of so many Negro men which has come down from the days of slavery. Marauding white men and African black chieftains conspired, centuries ago, to tear apart Negro family life by buying and selling human bodies. For two hundred years thereafter in the New World, white men defiled the bodies of Negro women and violated the spirit of Negro men powerless to protect the women and children they loved. A great many American Negroes bear on their faces the signature of the white man's lust and ancestry; and so, the theory goes, the responsibilities of parenthood and family have become less important to Negro males than to white males.

To this historic "castration," say the Negro intellectuals, has been added the newer "castration" of industrial city life. Most of the brawn-and-back jobs for which Negroes originally came north are fast disappearing; in an automated world the robust, masculine heave of shoulder and muscle earns less. Negro women can become school teachers, collect tolls on highways, become clerks or secretaries. But for Negro males the doors are closing. In the U.S. three Negro women attend college for every two Negro men; among white people the proportion is just the reverse. In the big city, the father of the Negro family becomes less and less able to support his family—or to care for it.

And fatherless babies grow up in a world with no family standards of decency, a burden and menace to all about them, white and black.

Many of the problems that beset the big city Negro are problems that plague other Americans too; and the purpose of the nation's politics is indeed to frame laws in which all people have equal opportunity to solve their problems. But the particular problem of Negro family life can only be solved by Negroes themselves.

In South Los Angeles last year, the Reverend Douglas Ferrell became the first Negro to win a seat in the state assembly from his district. His all-Negro neighborhood is a delight to the eye and, on Christmas week, white people drive through its streets to see the competition over Christmas decorations among blocks. Ferrell is no intellectual, but he has a shrewd answer as to why his neighborhood is so attractive while other all-Negro areas just a few miles away are both an eyesore and a stench.

"The root of the problem," says Ferrell, "is despair. A man says to himself, 'I've been down so long till down don't bother me.' Something happens to him. Defeat sets in like a disease. It's like a cancer; it eats away his will power. He gives up. He wants to be with other people like himself, no matter what level he lives on. He's got no design for living, no pride, no courage, no ambition.

"What happens to make a neighborhood like ours? I'll tell you—somebody has got to 'want to want.' It begins with one individual usually. One man and his wife begin improving their house. And if two of them on one street start, it catches on."

ACROSS THE continent, in a setting as different from South Los Angeles as a trash barrel is from a palm tree, stands a grime-coated, red-brick building on Harlem's 135th Street. Within this building an experiment is being conducted by three Negro intellectuals—Kenneth Clark, Cyril Tyson, Kenneth Marshall—men as different from the Reverend Douglas Ferrell as the settings they inhabit. But their reading of their people is the same. The Harlem experiment, called HARYOU (Harlem Youth Opportunities Unlimited), is supported by New York City and the President's Committee on Juvenile Delinquency, and it is the most successful exploration of Negro youth problems done in this country up to now.

Though HARYOU has no final answer yet, it has learned this: little can be done *for* Negro youth from the outside; but almost anything can be done *with* Negro youth. Given hope, leadership and opportunity, they can confront and tackle—as they are already doing—the dope pushers, the hustlers, the winos, the despair within their community with the same fervor they have shown in mobilizing their resources against the white enemy downtown. One of the oddest discoveries made by the HARYOU leaders in talking to their Negro youngsters is that some of the most popular teachers in the much-denounced schools of Harlem are the toughest teachers—those who insist that the children toe the line and measure up to the work. Such teachers apparently care.

"What these kids need," says Cyril Tyson, the talented director of the project, "is to begin to look at themselves in different ways, not the way they've been taught to look at themselves. They need what all Harlem needs—structure and discipline. Money alone isn't the answer—it's what you do with it. We're trying to use the internal resources of Harlem to create a new kind of community, something with self-sustaining inner energy."

HARYOU is some 2,800 miles from Los Angeles. Yet, if there were a consensus that stretched over white and Negro leaders from New York to California— covering almost every city in between, including cops in uniform, clerics in collar, sociologues with surveys, politicians in office—it would be this: before the big city and the Negro community finally adjust to each other, despair must be pushed back to give room for dreaming. Only then can Negro family work be reconstructed and responsibility within the family established. And if there is any one point where the cycle of despair must be broken, it lies in the juvenile-adolescent years, where hope and education must be made to take root.

But the white man of any city is, alas, badly equipped to bring the healing quality of hope into the Negro ghetto of the big city. History has pressed white man's cruelty so vividly on Negro minds that the friendliest of Negroes find difficulty in trusting white people. The white man in the slum is the enemy; he is the cop; the relief administrator; the boss; "the man." The white man must open the gates of opportunity, keep them open, beckon the Negro in—but only Negroes can lead their communities through those gates to hope and respect.

One calls thus, finally, on the mayor of America's largest city, New York's Robert Wagner. Now in his third term, Mayor Wagner has changed from the pudgy, benign man elected in 1953 to the rather gaunt and perpetually exhausted official he is today. No one has ever accused Wagner of blinding eloquence, but warmth of heart, patience and growing courage have slowly established him as one of New York's greater mayors.

After an hour's talk of Negro problems, of jobs, of housing, of commitment, of all that the city is trying to do, the mayor ends by talking about children: "That kid in Harlem who lacks skill, that kid who lacks the will to go on. He just isn't going to rush into a youth worker's office and say, 'I want to be trained.' You've got to go out and talk him into coming in. And that can't be done by government. Government has to have help. It's got to be done by leaders in the local community. Those kids in Harlem—they're discouraged, they're living off the bottom of the well; somebody's got to give them the spirit to climb up into the sunshine."

It is morning and the mayor is still in bathrobe and slippers, wearily facing the trip downtown to City Hall. At

City Hall statistics and budgets will confront him; at City Hall, he knows, it is estimated that the Negro community requires two and a half times as much expenditure from the city for each Negro child as does the white community for a white child—and children eat up more than half of the city's entire $3 billion annual budget.

The sun in Gracie Mansion is warm and bright; the mayor knows how limited is the power of the city to deal with matters of spirit and hope. Yet he must do his part. He bends his head and doggedly faces the unpopular decision: "We're just going to have to spend more, a lot more. That's the job of the elected official—to go out and explain why we need the dough."

All over the country, in every big city, councilmen and mayors, congressmen, governors and greater officials know that they must now go out and explain why they will need "more dough." And they must explain the problem knowing that all the money in the world will not be enough. For, as Mayor Wagner put it, the job the nation faces on the urban frontier is not a job for government alone, nor for whites alone—or blacks alone.

IT IS A JOB, first, of thinking, of examining where American life must change as well as where it must be guarded. It is a job of sorting out the short-range problem of guaranteeing opportunity for the Negro and separating it from the long-range problem of reaching commonly accepted standards of behavior and morality in the big city. It is a job as practical as apprentice-training, as delicate as the rules of love and marriage.

No other free system of politics has ever before coped with problems of spirit and of reality so complex. History offers no other precedent to guide Americans—except their own. In America the children and grandchildren of immigrant hordes, acceptable nowhere else in the world, joined to transform existing tradition and create one of the wonders of Western civilization—the self-governing American city. The agony of the tongueless immigrant arriving in the strange land has never been adequately chronicled—nor the agony of the city that received him. But we know that the adventure succeeded. The immigrant, finally recognizing what he must learn, learned to strive; and the city, responding to his effort, finally accepted him for the rites of citizenship. The Negro's problem with the city and the city's problem with the Negro are, today, far more complicated. But the first step to solution must be found, surely, in the tradition of the American city itself.

LIFE November 29, 1963

BACKLASH: IT HAS A WRENCHING GRIP ON LOCAL ISSUES

On election day, what will be the impact of the hidden anti-Negro feeling?

Southridge Development rises in rose-red brick, six stories high, 10 acres broad, on the approaches to New York's LaGuardia Airport. Fringed with ground ivy and green shrubbery, hollowed with sunny interior play space for the children, Southridge in the Borough of Queens is a community of 1,320 families who have found the Good Life in the Big City. For some of its young couples, Southridge is only a way station to the even better life of the green suburbs; but for most it offers what they always dreamed of having—a short subway ride to the job downtown, a good school, a quiet and pleasant place to live and see their children grow.

It is impossible for the casual passerby to conceive of Southridge as a political storm center. Yet it is. And, as Election Day closes on the nation, politicians not only in New York but in every great city of the eastern seaboard will be watching Southridge to see whether the continuing headlines of municipal confusion, of bus strikes, of turbulence in the schools themselves, of parental revolt, riots and patrol wagons in the once-tranquil community

have their repercussion in the voting on November 3rd.

The storm had been brewing all through spring and summer until, finally, it burst on school-opening day, September 14th. The pickets arrived early that morning in front of Public School 149, flanked on both sides by the great development; and by half past eight, under gray skies, they trudged in continuous circles before the neat, four-story schoolhouse.

"LOCKED OUT OF OUR NEIGHBORHOOD SCHOOL," read one sign.

"THIS IS NOT A GAME OF CHESS—DO NOT USE MY CHILD AS A PAWN," read another.

"NO FORCED TRANSFERS," "KEEP OUR CHILDREN IN OUR NEIGHBORHOOD SCHOOL," "INTEGRATION YES—PAIRING NO," protested others.

The kerchiefed mothers filed in silence in front of the school which, until this day, had been *their* school. Now, however, *their* school had been "paired." By dictate of the city's school board, their five-, six- and seven-year-olds this year would be compelled to go to first and second grades in the Negro district

534

six blocks farther away, while the Negro eight-, nine-, 10- and 11-year-olds of P.S. 92 would be compelled to cross into their district to attend third, fourth, fifth and sixth grades.

But approximately a mile away, where P.S. 127 (previously 94% Negro) and P.S. 148 (previously 87% white) have also been paired, the distance between schools ran to 14 much longer blocks and parents were correspondingly more bitter despite the prospect that buses would transport children living at the district's perimeter.

Business-suited white fathers were picketing outside P.S. 127, deep in the Negro district. "I've got a little girl," growled one. "She's either gonna have to take the bus or walk 18 blocks, and if she walks she's got to cross Astoria Boulevard and that's *six* lanes of truck traffic. Integration is okay with me. I'm for it. But if they think sending my kid to their school is gonna improve *their* education—not me. I'm gonna register my kid into private school. How much? Twenty-five a month, and we'll just have to cut down somewhere."

Outside P.S. 149 there had been other pickets: "What do you come to any neighborhood for?" asked one. "You buy a house because it's close to the school, the church, the shopping center you like. And when they say you can't send your kid to the school across the street—that's why I'm picketing." "I got three kids—7, 3, and 1½," said another. "We moved in here because the kid could go to school on the same block. Now he can't go there anymore. So all right, so my wife can walk the

kids and push the carriage eight blocks to the other school—but what does she do when it's a winter day and the snow's falling? How does she get the kid to school?"

And then the picket's sign—slowly, ominously passing: PARENTS—REMEMBER SEPTEMBER 14TH ON NOVEMBER 3RD.

Few politicians in New York that evening were unaware of the signs; and for those who ignored it, the drumbeat of the front pages since September 14th has come as a daily reminder: "REJECT PLEA AS 8,000 PICKET"; "SEIZE SIT-IN PARENTS, ARREST 65 IN QUEENS SCHOOL"; "WEIGH NEW PLAN FOR ASSIGNED INTEGRATION."

The angry mood of Southridge today chills the blood of every municipal official in the city; but for none is the chill more ominous than Ed Sadowsky.

ED SADOWSKY IS a man of sparkling intelligence and genuine goodwill. At 35, he is a city councilman of New York and, until this year, he was one of the most promising young political figures in the big city. But Ed, who lives in Southridge Development, is the original man-in-the-middle. He believes in civil rights and the need of America's races to understand each other. This earns him little credit with civil rights extremists, who say Ed "finked out on them" last year; he would not let his children boycott the schools when the Negroes did so to demand greater integration. This year, his white neighbors denounced Ed because he did not support the white boycott of schools to protest the pairing plan. ("Eddie," said one tragic voice on a recent telephone call at night, "I couldn't believe a nice Jewish boy like you would let them do this to us.")

For Ed, compulsory school pairing is a personal as well as a political problem. He and his wife, Jean, have three children—7, 5 and 2 years old. Jean must now take the 5-year-old seven blocks to P.S. 92; at the same time she has to get the 7-year-old to P.S. 149. Same problem picking them up after school. The Sadowskys personally are willing to go through with the pairing—seven blocks, they think, is a small price in inconvenience to pay for a great goal. But they are realistic, too. "I don't know how I'd feel," Ed says, "if it were 14 blocks." For he is unwilling to call his white neighbors bigots. Southridge is an integrated development where Negro, mixed and white couples have dwelt peacefully together for several years; their school already held 12% Negro children even before the pairing. "They aren't afraid of Negroes as such," says Ed, ruminating about his neighbors. "They're afraid of the unknown."

And so, too, is Ed—for his political future now hangs in the balance. This year's election does not immediately bother him; he personally does not run again until 1965 and Johnson, he is sure, will sweep the councilmanic district by a huge majority in November. But he was recently voted off the board of directors of his Southridge cooperative because of the school-pairing plan;

and when it comes to his own candidacy next year, he is sure he will lose votes heavily in his home blocks; how many other irate parents elsewhere will vote against him, he cannot tell. So, the pattern of events in his life is being watched closely by other political leaders in the nation's largest city; for Ed Sadowsky is a symbol, and his fate will be typical of scores of local political leaders across the country who must eventually face the polls to test the strength and depth of the "white backlash."

Just what is the "backlash"? What are its elements? Is it simply localized reaction to the three classic and rising Negro demands—for better jobs, better housing, better education? Or is it a national upwelling of indignation, about to spill over into the presidential choice of November? Is it a fashionable cliché of the 1964 political season? Or is it something more lasting, a development in American history that cries for answers—and finds none?

ONE MUST BEGIN, of course, with the word itself. "Backlash" as a word entered politics just as "Cold War" (Walter Lippmann) and "egghead" (Steward Alsop) did, through the midwifery of a Washington column—in this case, the New York *Herald Tribune* column of Rowland Evans and Robert Novak—as shorthand for white resentment against the pace and tone of Negro demands everywhere. Evans and Novak, however, had taken the word fresh from the mintage of a one-time journalist, Eliot

Janeway, an old friend of Lyndon B. Johnson, who has evolved over the years into a consulting economist. Janeway, an aficionado of Washington politics since the high noon of Franklin D. Roosevelt's New Deal, had been quite precise when he coined the word. Reflecting one day last year on the breakup of the classic liberal coalition which powered that New Deal, Janeway was frightened by the growing competition between white and Negro workingmen as automation squeezed out the jobs of both. Janeway felt that, in any significant downturn of the economy, this competition might well break up the political partnership of labor unions and Negro groups on which so much of the Democrats' power has traditionally rested. The white workers, he felt, would lash back at the Negroes the next time crisis pinched—and thus the word "backlash."

By the summer of 1963, when the word was coined, America was well along in the Negro revolution that had begun with the first use of police dogs in Birmingham on Sunday, April 7th. At the time, white resentment of Negro demands was still thought of as a narrow southern prejudice. During the Democratic primaries in the spring of 1964, however, as Governor George Wallace of Alabama carried his message of bigotry to the big industrial centers of the North, it was clear that white workingmen could, indeed, be stirred deeply enough—in Milwaukee, in Gary, in Baltimore—to give Wallace 34% of the vote in Wisconsin, 30% in Indiana, 43% in Maryland. After that,

with the summer rioting of Negroes in the big cities, backlash became the most perplexing emotional issue of this year's political campaign—a nightmare for some politicians, a tantalizing enticement for others, a confusion for all.

For backlash is a northern big-city phenomenon—as invisible, yet as real, as air pollution. In the South, where racial attitudes have been frozen by three centuries of slavery and indignity, the politician deals with recognizable prejudice. But in the North, where the surging growth of the Negro population is changing every big city's life, attitudes are still elastic. Men of earnest goodwill and men of spastic bigotry, alike, grope in moral confusion—trying to decide what they think of the Negro's revolution as it touches them.

Nor is this a sudden, overnight conflict in the American conscience. Politicians, as a matter of their trade, recognized this discord between ideals and realities long before the sudden fashion of the term "backlash"; they could see with what difficulty their cities were seeking to adjust to the Negro population explosion. And, like men of any trade, they have measured and registered within their fraternity each pressure point on the scale of protest, and the opportunity or peril of satisfying it.

THE FIRST AND most basic Negro demand, politicians recognize, is for job opportunity—in private industry as in government. This, by now, they believe they can handle. Backed by such progressive trade unions as the United Automobile Workers in Detroit, the Garment Workers' in New York, the Packinghouse Workers in Chicago, they crunch away, bit by bit, at the resistance of the narrower craft unions and pry open, through government intervention if need be, at least token Negro admissions all across the country.

Politicians recognize white resistance, but they are convinced it is resistance short of backlash. The ugly pockets of prejudice that remain among workingmen can usually be explained, they say, by specialized fears or specialized traditions. Steelworkers, for example—from Gary, Ind., through Pittsburgh, Pa., to Sparrows Point, Md.—sensitive to seniority rights and the ravages of automation, are, as a group, particularly resistant to Negroes, whom they fear as job competitors. Barbers and hairdressers show another face of fear. They are upset these days by the barber shop provisions of the 1964 Civil Rights Act, convinced—erroneously—that every corner beauty salon and two-chair haircutting shop may now face the need to employ a specialist in coiffing Negro hair. Taxi drivers also are frequently anti-Negro. Prey at night to dope addicts and hoodlums, so many of whom in large urban areas are Negroes, they indiscriminately fear all Negroes; and the cab drivers spread their fears, in telling and retelling their stories, to all who travel the big cities or arrive from peaceful towns.

Yet, such sputterings of fear upset few politicians; they know that, by appealing to a rough code of fair play, they can defend Negroes on the job front. Reality demands that Negroes get a chance to work; the American ideal demands fealty; and the voters will go along. This year, for example, propaganda against the civil rights bill was specially pointed in virulence to reach working men and women. But in a series of closely watched primary elections, congressmen who voted for the bill, with its Equal Employment Opportunity provision, have almost everywhere defeated enemies of that bill who attempted to purge them by backlash.

POLITICIANS KNOW they get hurt in response to the second great Negro demand: access to good housing. Here the pressure for change clashes with the sense of kinship and neighborhood that so many ethnic groups cherish—as well as with the individual property owner's fear that his life-investment in his home will shrink, overnight, in value. Again and again in the past three years, champions of open-housing have tasted defeat as they brought their measures and convictions to the test of voting. A number of big cities have managed to get antidiscrimination open-housing measures approved by their city councils—notably Chicago, where Mayor Richard Daley exerts a one-man discipline, and Philadelphia, where Negro voters pack a massive punch. But at a broader, state-wide level, the defense of neighborhood living and property values, when carried to legislative verdict, has resulted in defeat, everywhere, for open-housing advocates. In the past two years, Ohio, Michigan, Iowa, Indiana, Illinois, Washington, Wisconsin and Rhode Island, among others, have either killed fair-housing bills in legislative committee or voted them down on the floor. And when carried further, to the people themselves, the few referendums permitted the voters have all resulted in defeat for open-housing—in a cultured university town like Berkeley Calif., as well as in Seattle and Tacoma.

Referendums, it should be noted, are the horror of all politicians, for a referendum offers only a crude "yes" or "no" to what, usually, are the most complicated and intricate problems of government. With the utmost difficulty, Democratic politicians in Illinois managed this summer to choke off a petition for a housing referendum signed by 545,616 citizens. But in California, next month, voters will judge a referendum to repeal the Rumford Fair Housing Act on the same day they choose their President—and politicians regard this as the only major threat to a Johnson victory in that state.

One can judge at once how potent, yet how sharply focused, are the politics of housing by examining a single state, Michigan, over the past three years. In 1962, the 14-year Democratic dominance of that state was put to an end by George Romney, admittedly the best candidate the Michigan Republicans have put up in years. But Democratic politicians, in analyzing the many factors contributing to the defeat of Democratic Governor John B. Swainson, fasten with particular emphasis on the voting pattern of the suburbs. Here,

Swainson was particularly vulnerable as champion of Housing Rule 9, which forbade real estate dealers to discriminate by race in selling houses. Voters in the all-white suburbs—fearful of Negro penetration—punished him heavily. A 1960 Swainson margin of 5,402 in Dearborn became a 1962 loss of 16; suburban Macomb County cut his 1960 margin of 38,243 to 12,605; and thus across the board in an election in which Romney squeaked through by a plurality of only 80,573 votes of nearly 2,800,000 cast.

No metropolis has offered a more precise picture of contrary voting impulses than did Detroit in this year's September primaries. Democratic voters in the 16th Congressional District, which includes Dearborn, were summoned to choose between John Lesinski (the only northern Democratic congressman to vote against the civil rights bill) and John Dingell (who supported it). Backed vigorously by the United Automobile Workers, Dingell won handily—but at the same time, in citywide balloting, Detroiters chose to lead their slate for the city Common Council by voting for Thomas L. Poindexter, who drafted an ordinance permitting Detroiters to refuse to rent or sell housing to Negroes if they so choose.

IF RESPONSE TO Negro demands for job opportunity brings approval to politicians and response to Negro demands for housing brings peril, then the third Negro demand—for "integrated" education—causes politicians to flee to the hills. No politician in his right mind will get himself involved in the problem of big-city school integration if he can avoid it. Schooling is an emotional issue. The passion it arouses sears the most sensitive nerve ends of parental love and affection. Politicians, unanimously, try to toss the problem to school boards—and piously look the other way as the school boards wrestle with the pressure groups. But from Max Rafferty in California, through Ben Willis in Chicago, to Louise Day Hicks in Boston, the most firmly entrenched school officials of the country are those who are adamant in favor of neighborhood schools.

What happens when a school board crumbles before the pressure of demonstrations or the passion of the streets is shown most vividly by the plight of New York City's Board of Education. Here, in the most tolerant of all American cities, a distinguished group of citizens was set up three years ago as an entirely new school board. Under their earnest care, an imaginative open-enrollment plan has been expanded, until now 15,000 Negro children a day are carried from schools where *de facto* Negro concentration prevails to white schools, whenever individual Negro parents so request. This voluntary plan was accepted with remarkably good grace and no trouble. But when Negro demonstrations this year panicked the school board, it accepted the crude "pairing" solution of the "Princeton plan" in order to placate civil rights groups, and attempted to impose this invention of a bucolic New Jersey uni-

versity town on the complex life of the world's largest city. The result has been dismal. The most tolerant of northern big cities is now host to a Parents and Taxpayers Association (PAT) that claims, with its affiliates, a quarter million to a half million members and showed, last month, enough muscle to pull a quarter of a million pupils out of school. Thus, New York City's Board of Education has become the whipping boy of both Negroes and whites.

POLITICIANS EVERYWHERE have for a long time recognized the backlash potential in the Negro pressure for jobs, housing and education and have measured them as local troubles to be handled by local leaders. This year, however, the long train of Negro street demonstrations, climaxing in the summer riots that boiled up in the anarchy of Negro ghetto life, have stirred white resentment to an extent that cannot be localized; fear and indignation have generalized into a morbid, brooding concern of millions of Americans for law and order itself.

It is this last development that intrudes on the political planning and strategies of the current presidential campaign. Exactly how agitated are the American people in reaction to the violence of this summer? Do they feel that Negro rioting poses a threat to the stability of American life as we have known it? Do they now put such concern above their sense of economic well-being or fear of war?

For possible answers to such questions, most national political strategists turn to public opinion polls, and politicians in the United States read such polls the way farmers and fishermen read weather reports—not as guarantees of tomorrow's weather, but as the best forecast of probabilities at a given moment. Polls today, in this open season of politics, gush from every source in the nation—private, political, local, national, academic, industrial. And, after some initial confusions and contradictions, the polls have gradually acquired the sound of a harmonious chorus:

▶In Milwaukee, a brewery firm tells its beer salesmen to sound out the talk in the saloons of south Milwaukee, where Polish-Americans gave Governor Wallace so heavy a vote in the spring. The poll is brought privately to the White House and its burden is that Lyndon Johnson need not worry: Sure, they voted for Wallace in the spring, just to show the blankety-blanks. But they're going to vote Johnson in November because they think "Goldwater is a nut."

▶In Connecticut, a public utility doing a market survey of its customers tacks on a "shirt-tail" of political questions—and reports that Johnson is a runaway in a white-collar city like Hartford although backlash is eating away the blue-collar vote in working towns like Bridgeport, Waterbury, New Haven.

▶In Baltimore's 2nd and 6th wards, where Wallace scored so heavily in the Maryland primary, the steelworkers seem to be coming back to Johnson. A local candidate's poll reports that three out of four of those who say they voted for Wallace in the spring will vote for Johnson in November.

▶A plant-gate poll of white steelworkers by the Chicago *Sun-Times* in July showed Johnson only 53/47% over Goldwater; but an early September poll showed Johnson's margin over Goldwater had widened to 63/37%.

These are fragments of local polling. Nationally, the major pollsters work with a finer mesh and greater subtlety. Newest of the major pollsters is Oliver Quayle, whose reports, paid for by the Democratic National Committee, go directly and officially to the White House. Quayle makes a major distinction between *potential* backlash and *real* backlash. Potential backlash he defines as the index of fear among white people in the big cities: real backlash is the measure of avowed Democratic switchers to Goldwater, switching *because* of fear of Negroes. In New York, for example, late this summer after the riots, Quayle found a measure of fear—slight or great—among no less than 69% of Democratic voters. But when wrung down to actual voting patterns, only 6% of these same voters indicated they would switch from Johnson to Goldwater. Parenthetically, it should be observed that the "frontlash," a phrase invented by Quayle and now one of Lyndon Johnson's favorite words, the defection of Republicans to Johnson, vastly outweighed this Democratic defection. No less than 39% of New York Republicans who voted for Nixon in 1960 plan to vote for Johnson in '64.

Still other regional and national polls pour into the White House—and though they vary from state to state, they point, all of them, in the same direction. Said one White House analyst, "We find backlash everywhere—but it runs from a low of one-tenth the frontlash in some places to a high of only one-third in other places."

Reading such polls, the Johnson strategists have come to a basic conclusion: that backlash will not affect their candidate's prospects this year; that "backlash" is an unease whose impact will be felt not as much now as over the long range. Their advice to the President is that he should cling simply to his three great harmony themes: Peace, Prosperity and Justice-for-All. Where Democrats find local problems of backlash more complicated, they are being urged to favor the obvious answers: in working-class districts, the bread-and-butter issue ("You never had it so good"); and in white-collar districts, the peace issue ("Do you want Goldwater's finger on the atomic trigger?").

If the Democrats' euphoric response of the moment is to ignore backlash, the Republicans, underdogs at the moment, can permit themselves no such easy answer. For them, backlash is torment. "It's like the Catholic issue against Kennedy last time," said one veteran planner at Republican headquarters. "We know it works for us. But if we work it too hard, it can explode like dynamite against us." Said another: "It's there. We know it. You know it. But can you tell me any practical way of getting a handle on the issue?"

The working Republican solution is, of course, at once as obvious and deli-cate as the performance of a man walking the high wire. Goldwater must talk "law and order," without talking anti-Negro. Goldwater, a man of personal goodwill, has no desire to be elected as a race-baiter. His basic appeal in the South rests on his passionate belief in States Rights and an embittered suspicion of the federal government as a whole. But his appeal in the northern industrial states is limited by just this assault on the federal government which has, over the years, protected the labor unions, financed the new suburbs with federally guaranteed mortgages and provided Social Security.

IF THERE IS to be any hope at all of a Goldwater victory, it must come by adding to his basic expectation of triumph in the South and the Mountain States, a breakthrough in the great industrial belt that holds 80 million people in the Boston-Baltimore-St. Louis-St. Paul rectangle. And the breakthrough must come by emotion and by fear. Goldwater's most solid appeal in this geographical area seems to be the wrath with which he scourges gang-rape and switchblade hoodlums. But it would take only a trifling twist of eloquence or of phrase, a single film clip of Negro rioters on TV accompanied by an appeal for law and order, to make this theme anti-Negro. With great decency, Goldwater has shrunk from this open racist appeal, while his lieutenants rely on events to work for him.

But events have not worked for Goldwater since July and early August, when the national voicing of his law-and-order theme at the San Francisco convention was followed, as if to prove his point, by the riots in Harlem, Brooklyn, Rochester and New Jersey. For the riots, rather than spreading, have stopped; and local resentment of Negroes, rather than being fused into a national hate, has frayed and returned to local levels—where it remains firm, morbid and possibly growing. (A September poll in Indiana, for example, shows a jump in intense, local anti-Negro prejudice from 8% in the spring to 22% now, following the summer riots.)

The White House has acted discreetly but irresistibly both on civil rights leaders and their sources of financing among northern whites. The word is out to "cool it." At Atlantic City, federal surveillance extended as far away as Philadelphia to pinpoint chartered busses that might be carrying known troublemakers to the Democratic convention. National Democratic money for Negro registration has been carefully delayed, and even more carefully watched to make sure that it is responsibly used for registration of voters and not for hell-raising. Above all, responsible civil rights leadership has itself got word through to the streets. Thus, in this fall season, the riots have, indeed, been cooled—and with them the national backlash that might have spread epidemically through the northern cities.

And that is how Barry Goldwater has come to face his historic dilemma: whether to grasp desperately for victory,

by pushing to exploit the backlash, which seemed so potent in the sultry days of rioting; or simply to keep hammering away broadly at the need for law and order, and hope voters will translate their local fears into presidential ballots. To choose the former course is to push the Republican party into a racist mold; to persist with the latter, since there have been no new Negro uprisings, holds no promise that devastating defeat can be avoided. With Goldwater's apparent persistence in the second course, the omens seem to point to a Lyndon B. Johnson sweep to the greatest victory since Roosevelt's in 1936—while backlash spends itself in local elections, where fear so largely influences voters' choice.

Yet, however large or small the Johnson victory in November, backlash will remain. For backlash is not just the slang of this election year, backlash is the confused reaction of a majority of Americans to a nation changing almost too rapidly to describe. They are unsettled by the remorseless progress of a technology that makes muscle power obsolete; by the hordes assembling in the great metropoles, who press on each other's privacy and custom; by a gaudy profligacy frothing on an incredible prosperity—all the more galling to the underprivileged as they see it flickering on their television screens, as if they lived in a prison with glass walls. And, in the very heart of these metropoles, explosive congregations of Negroes, fresh from the humiliations of the past, will not abide further delay in sharing the good things they see about them.

SWEPT ALONG by such changes, jostled by the dreams and needs of tomorrow, the natural communities of American life grasp for some necessary sense of stability and order. For America lives by a system of silent understandings among communities of men which have never been defined. In their unions, their churches, their ancestral gatherings, Americans find a warmth and togetherness which is written nowhere in the Constitution or the charters of local law. But each community has a life of its own, which politicians salute when they inspect cattle at the state fair, when they march in St. Patrick's Day parades, appear on the reviewing stand on Columbus Day or Pulaski Day, refrain from campaigning in Jewish neighborhoods on Yom Kippur. No arbitrary homogenization of America can replace the strength that comes from these many roots, nor any amount of high-rise public housing eradicate delinquency as effectively as a close-knit, harmonious neighborhood. And as urban planners rip down such neighborhoods, both Negro and white, or the dogmas of school boards tear families apart, they create fears that beloved ways of life may be threatened in ways undefined, in a future over which individuals may have no control.

All across the country this fear of the unknown prevails among whites, and thus the classic question on people's lips, "What do they want—what will they ask for next?" and the more precise, yet perplexing question on the lips of politicians, "What will they settle for?"

The emotional response of the white majority, proceeding from the insistent Negro demands, has rarely, if ever, been adequately discussed.

The tragedy is that no one has the answers; the shame is that no one, in all the long turbulence over civil rights, has yet assembled the nation's leaders, either political or academic, to examine where the Negro community is now, where we hope to bring it in the next 20 years—and by what steps. Not even the Negro community's own leaders have yet agreed on an overall program which, with distant yet sure goals, could be presented to the white community and would include a program for educating whites out of their fears and Negroes to the pattern of their future.

TO TAKE ONE major example of confusion: Most white citizens of America grow indignant when they hear of Negro demands for "reparations"—a demand first voiced last year, though fuzzily, by the Urban League, which set its sum at approximately $20 billion for a domestic "Marshall Plan" to be directed by community leaders. Yet, upon investigation, one learns that the U.S. Department of Health, Education and Welfare already spends approximately $2.5 billion annually out of its $6.5 billion total budget in payments directly to Negroes for welfare, health and education. To this expenditure must be added at the very minimum another $2.5 billion already being spent annually by welfare and community agencies in individual cities and states. Thus, the relief and welfare tab for Negroes, across the country, now runs to at least $5 billion a year, or $50 billion in a decade—simply to keep affairs at their present level of simmering discontent.

The $20 billion figure suggested by Negro leaders is therefore certainly not extravagant; actually it is probably a gross underestimate of what will be needed over a generation of effort to improve matters. But even $50 billion will be useless if dogma, rather than fresh thinking, directs the distribution. And, at present, no such fresh thinking can be found, either at HEW in Washington, or in New York City, or in any other large city. The triad of Negro demands—for jobs, for housing, for education—have become by now almost clichés. No group of civic leaders agrees on just how housing can be opened to Negroes without creating or expanding ghettoes, or what is meant by "quality education." No public authority has ever addressed an inquiry into the conditions of Negro family life, all but destroyed in the big city and generating the violence that terrifies big-city whites. No one has pursued an inquiry into the unique conditions of Negro political leadership in a white society, or into the possibility that some effective form of self-governing authority might be set up in the Negro community—an authority Negroes could trust more than they do the white. The racial "numbers game," both of classroom chromatography and trade union tokenism, remains profitless for lack of long-range thinking—as do the preachings on Sunday and the demonstrations in the streets.

And so, in the vast confusion, backlash whips back and forth. It is conceivable that a Johnson victory as huge as Democratic euphoria assumes it will be may give the President more political elbow room in both houses of Congress than any Chief Executive of modern times. And then, perhaps the restless energy of the President may address itself to this greatest problem at a level where his enormous art as a political leader can bring forth the long-range programs and goals that America must have, whatever the cost.

It is also conceivable that the election of 1964 could alter the entire nature of America's two-party system—forcing the great Republican party, born in racial strife, to choose whether it abandons its tradition and becomes the white man's party or refreshes its tradition by designing a program of social harmony.

Only one political certainty can be stated now which will outlast next month's election: If, at this time when the nation is so rich and strong, both parties ignore the need for constructive answers to the question "What Do They Want?" then disaster lies ahead—and backlash—the politics of chaos—will carry over, its snap growing in violence from 1964 to 1968 and all the elections beyond, until the question *is* answered.

LIFE October 16, 1964

Chapter 14

One Shot: Freedom of the Press

That freedom of expression is the *sine qua non* of a free nation was unarguable for both White the reporter and White the historian. The Joseph McCarthy–led blacklisting craze that shamed the country after World War II affected him personally. Largely because of his conclusions about the Communists in China in *Thunder Out of China,* he found himself being called a "pinko" (in fact, he was always staunchly anti-Communist), which in 1948 meant, as he wrote later, that "no large or distinguished magazine or newspaper would hire [me]." Thus, when he looked for a job in Europe (see Chapter 5), he could find one only with a "marginal news-feature service." And, as a free-lance in the early 1950s, he discovered that, with the notable exceptions of *The New York Times Magazine* and *The Reporter,* U.S. magazines would publish only his nonpolitical writings—on such subjects as "the best restaurants in Paris and the falling Irish birthrate . . . which I loathed." Then, in 1952, White's younger brother Robert, a scientist, wired him that he, Robert, was about to lose his U.S. Air Force security clearance because he was the brother of a well-known subversive (never mind that the subversive—Theodore—had been cleared repeatedly in those days by "every security agency of the U.S. Army"). The matter was eventually cleared up, but its impact was compounded a year later by an event at the USIA library in Berlin: McCarthy henchmen Roy Cohn and David Schine found copies of *Thunder Out of China* there and promptly had them purged and burned. "I was on the public list for discard," he wrote later. It was an accumulation of experiences that rankled him all his life and made him especially sensitive to anything that threatened a free press.

Though First Amendment principles were often part of White's political analyses, only once did he devote an entire article to the subject of journalistic rights and responsibilities. At issue was the jailing of a *New York Times* reporter for refusing to disclose his sources for a series of stories on the strange deaths of thirteen people in a New Jersey hospital. The implications deeply disturbed White, as the following article makes clear.

WHY THE JAILING OF FARBER "TERRIFIES ME"

The reporter's right to protect his sources protects the rights of the public, too.

M. A. Farber of the *New York Times* has now been freed from Bergen County's Hackensack jail. For a total of nearly six weeks he sat in a cell block adjacent to a man who had allegedly murdered his own mother and facing an accused German sodomist awaiting deportation. Farber was there simply for practising the reporter's calling—charged with both civil and criminal contempt of court for protecting the honor and tradition of that calling.

The fact that M. A. Farber is now free pleases me. But the issue raised by his imprisonment will not go away. In fact, his imprisonment terrifies me more and more. For if the Supreme Court does not, in the next few months, rule on this issue, I may follow him to jail. So may any honorable man of our craft. And if our craft is to be made subject to a new jurisprudence that can compel all of us to become official public informers, not only will the press suffer for it—so, too, will the public good.

The Law of Unintended Consequences has a dynamic of its own—and the willful refusal of the courts to understand how the American political system and the reporter's craft interlock may some day mark the Farber case as the beginning of a paradigm of Unintended Consequences.

To MAKE CLEAR what I see at issue here, I would like first to summarize the summerlong story.

In the mid-1960's, 13 people died in a hospital in Oradell, N.J., under strange and unexplained circumstances. The local county investigation found nothing actionable in these deaths and the matter was dropped. Ten years later, acting on a tip, the *New York Times* assigned reporter Farber to investigate the series of incidents again. His stories provoked a new prosecutor to reopen the case and, as a result, a Dr. Mario E. Jascalevich was charged with killing five (later reduced to three) patients by injecting them with curare. After a 34-week trial, Dr. Jascalevich was found innocent, but before his acquittal, on June 30 of this year, William J. Arnold, the local judge hearing the case, issued a subpoena to reporter Farber (and another to the *New York Times*) ordering him to deliver to the court all the "documents" on which he had based his stories, including "statements, pictures, memoranda, recordings and notes of interviews of witnesses."

The subpoena was a sweeping, indiscriminate, vacuum-cleaner order. But I think it was the use of the word "documents" that first upset me—that and the blithe and callous legalese which held that it would not "cause undue hardship to said Myron Farber to be compelled to attend and present" the unspecified documents desired by the court. To believe that it causes no hardship to a reporter to violate his confidences is a monument of ignorance of the reporter's critical role in American public life.

A good reporter is a cross between a beggar and a detective, a wheedler and a prosecutor. This is how he collects facts. But the essence of his trade is to know how to sift out of rumor, gossip and hearsay the essential facts and then to arrange those facts so that a story comes out as close to the truth as he can make it.

Most of us take notes as we go. Or, if note-taking cramps the person we are talking with, we jot down notes as soon as we can get away and catch breath. We take notes on stenographer's pads, folded copy paper, margins of dinner menus. Sometimes we take notes with ostentatious flourish, either to bully people or to flatter them. Sometimes, after feigning uninterest, we take notes surreptitiously—on a paper napkin under the table, even on toilet paper in the washroom.

But these notes can scarcely be called "documents." A large part of what goes into our notes is nonsense—or worse, misinformation, People use us to plant lies, float allegations, bring others into suspicion or contempt. The most vivid of our notes are often records of indiscretion, indignation, hysteria or malice—in no legal sense "evidence." And I should hate to see men condemned, exonerated or betrayed by the jumble of notes I have piled up in 40 years of reporting.

Recently I have had the experience of trying to weave some of my old reporter's notes into a book. I found in those notes so many falsehoods, so many wild conversations, so many confidences of people who trusted me, that I am appalled by how much harm could be squeezed out of them by a smart lawyer, a smart politician, a smart propagandist.

I have some wartime notes of a conversation in 1942 with Gen. Douglas MacArthur. In them he excoriated George Marshall and Franklin Roosevelt with such bitterness that, had his remarks been uttered by a second lieutenant, the lieutenant would forthwith have been court-martialed. MacArthur relied on a personal trust in me to let himself spout without being quoted. It was at a low point in his career; nor did he really mean what he said, because there is no reflection of his charges in his own memoirs years later.

I have notes, tantamount to an invitation to blackmail, of a conversation in 1960 with a friend of Lyndon Johnson who offered to get me pictures of Jack and Bobby Kennedy in drag at a gay party in Las Vegas if I would promise to publish them. The notes are explicit, but the story was a lie and to print it would have been unconscionable because I believed then and believe now that Lyndon Johnson had nothing to do with the spreading of so false a rumor.

My notes contain, however, other, far more important materials and recollections which demonstrate, I hope, a reporter's higher function—to bring to public attention matters of common concern which should be thrust on the agenda of government for official action. I once wrote a story about a famine in the Chinese province of Honan in which millions of people died. The story was printed in *Time* magazine and its publication saved countless lives. But not until now, writing this piece, have I told anyone that I came across the matter because friends in the United States Embassy in Chungking wanted someone to explore the story in the field. The embassy had received letters from American missionaries in the famine-struck area telling of a desolation and corruption concealed by censorship from the whole world. One of the young diplomats at the embassy called me in, simply put a batch of letters on the table between us, let me read—and said nothing. It was essential to conceal his name, for he was the key "leak." The "leak" was his way of appealing to American conscience beyond the bureaucratic channels of the State Department. Had I exposed him, he would probably have been purged at the time—in 1943—or later by John Foster Dulles or Joe McCarthy when they were blinding the State Department by cleansing it of alleged "Reds."

———

THE WORD "LEAK" has a derogatory connotation. But some day, perhaps, some school of journalism will give a special course in "leaks" to young officials and aspiring journalists alike, awarding the process called "leaking" the dignity and importance it deserves.

We all live in a world increasingly thicketed with bureaucracies. They spread like giant fungoids; no one, not even Congress or the President, understands completely what goes on within these fungal monsters; and among them the medical and hospital bureaucracies come closest to baffling understanding. Without an inside leak, penetration of these thickets is almost impossible. Doctors, nurses, hospital administrators all too frequently cover up for each other. But in their charge lie the weakest and most helpless of our citizens— the ill, the old, the poor, the sad of spirit. Someone must patrol the custodians who are supposed to care for them.

In the Oradell hospital case, only a leak could have alerted such a patrol. That leak turned out to be a woman who in 1975 called the *New York Times*'s attention to the fact that helpless people had died, no one knew how, at Riverdell Hospital. The *Times* assigned the story to Farber, who pursued the story with devotion and diligence for four months, springing other leaks as he went. The *Times* then called the situation to public attention by printing a story on its front page, naming no names but placing the matter on the agenda for official investigation.

We reporters have to get our information where we can—usually by eyeball observation or legwork; sometimes from libraries and scholars; more often by coaxing politicians, officials and cops to talk; and sometimes by trading information with people in power, offering them our legwork in return for their confidences and superior investigative resources. We are responsible for what we write; they are responsible for official actions at law. We bring matters to attention; they must decide whether to act. And absolutely essential to the entire process is the reporter's code of honor: Once you pledge that you will protect an informant, the pledge is as binding as the Hippocratic oath on doctors, or the pledge of privacy given to witnesses by grand juries. Even among gangsters, "squealing" is considered a disgrace.

MUCH MORE, however, than a reporter's honor or disgrace is at stake here. The Farber case is touched with history, which the courts do not seem to understand. For if Farber had been compelled by imprisonment to name his sources, to hand over his notes, all of which are only hearsay evidence, then the unintended consequence of his punishment could have reshaped—and may still reshape—American political history.

For longer than anyone can remember, it has been accepted in American politics that a reporter's protection of his sources could not be violated. No law said so; no ruling said so; it was simply taken for granted. All politicians, from Presidents down, have accepted such shelter. One cannot, for example, write American history from

the turn of this century on without writing of what the great "muckrakers" accomplished. There would have been no urban thrust behind the Progressive movement had not Lincoln Steffens reported in his "The Shame of the Cities" on big-city corruption—and protected his sources. People might have eaten filth and offal for another generation had not Upton Sinclair relied on thinly disguised reporter's privilege in "The Jungle." Without Ida Tarbell's reporting of the strangulating oil trusts, they might have persisted in full vigor for another generation; and she could not have pursued her investigations had she not been able in clear conscience to protect her sources from reprisal.

The protection of sources by reporters has been so long accepted that it is almost superfluous to repeat the reasons for it here—except that the bureaucratic clotting of our lives today makes this privilege even more essential. More and more, individuals must live in corporate groups, public or private, in a "lock-up" of hierarchies where the whistle-blower, the protester or the just plain conscience-smitten is increasingly subject to dismissal or vengeance— whether in the United States Navy or the Teamsters Union, at I.B.M. in Armonk, N.Y., or in a hospital for the infirm and aged.

Often there is no possible way safely to call attention to wrongdoing unless the protester is assured of his anonymity. There would have been no exposure of the My Lai massacre had it not been for the ability of a brave reporter to persuade a handful of men in the United States Army to tell the truth. The civil-rights movement of the 1960's would have been stalled for years had there been no reporters to tell its story and defy local courts which sought to intimidate them. The revelations of Watergate might never have come about had not two reporters discovered a source, or several sources, whom they protected under the name of "Deep Throat." Had the jurisprudence that threw Farber into prison prevailed in 1974, the attorneys of Messrs. Mitchell, Haldeman and Ehrlichman could have demanded that Mr. Woodward and Mr. Bernstein give up their notes and so reveal the identity/identities of "Deep Throat"—or go to jail.

In short, the conduct of American public affairs has for a century or more rested on the right of the American press and its reporters to tell their stories within traditional privileges and with traditional restraints. Now the courts, in a new departure, seem bent on erasing a protection built into the very functioning of the American system. And, since the Constitution is being invoked, we should go on to the Constitutional issues debated in the Farber case, which is presented as a clash between the First and the Sixth Amendments.

NEITHER THE First nor the Sixth Amendment actually declares what the debaters have attempted to persuade us they say. The First Amendment says most briefly, "Congress shall make no law . . . abridging the freedom of speech, or of the press. . . ." Around that curt phrase volumes of law have

grown up; under its shelter television, publishing, cinema, pornography, polemic and poetry have all flourished; within its protection the American public has become better informed than any other. All reporters and editors have considered that this phrase guarantees the protection of sources, because such protection is essential to the newsgathering procedures of a free press.

The Sixth Amendment has been similarly enlarged from its sparse phrases. It has been expanded in common talk to a Constitutional guarantee of "fair trial." Yet the phrase "fair trial" nowhere occurs in the Sixth Amendment. What is promised is simply "speedy and public trial"; the right of the accused to be confronted by the witnesses against him; and that the accused shall have "compulsory process for obtaining witnesses in his favor." So far in the Farber case, the judges of the bench—from Hackensack, N.J., to the Supreme Court in Washington—seem bent on enlarging this last phrase to an entirely new dimension, compelling newsmen not simply to bear witness themselves but to finger other names which may help a shrewd criminal lawyer discover further witnesses to clear his client. Thus any reporter, by this stretch of interpretation, can become an agent of the court in any criminal process of law.

LIKE ALL GREAT ISSUES, the Farber case is wrapped in a tangled husk of immediate circumstances that make it immensely difficult for a man of conscience to judge.

First is the circumstance that Dr. Jascalevich was being tried for murder. New Jersey has no death penalty, but he could have been imprisoned for life; natural sympathy leads everyone to lean toward the man on trial rather than the abstract concept of press privilege. Every decent person rejoices that the innocent has now been cleared and goes free.

There is, next, the circumstance that M. A. Farber has a contract with a publisher to write a book about the Oradell affair—and may, indeed, make money from the book. I, as a reporter who makes his living writing books, do not find this at all dishonorable. But neither Farber nor the *New York Times* concealed the fact that Farber was writing a book. It was a matter of court record as early as May, six weeks before Farber was violently excoriated in open court by a Federal judge, Frederick Lacey, for sacrificing his responsibility on "an altar of greed"; and the actual manuscript was turned over to the court after much fuss before Farber was carted off to jail for a second time in October.

And underneath all comes the final circumstance: the insistence of the court on making Farber an agent of the law in defense of the accused—an insistence proven unnecessary, finally, by the jury's verdict.

THE PRESS HAS been accused of much in the past 10 years, and much of the accusation smarts because it is true. Some of us have tried to penetrate grand juries, which we should not have done. Some of us have tried to provoke inci-

dents to make good film or good copy, which we should not have done. Some of us have become swollen with our power and have earned fully the opprobrium implied in the term "arrogance of the press."

But none of us claim that reporters are above the law. Most of the press would agree that no law protects or should protect a reporter from being called to bear witness in open court. A reporter, like any other citizen who has witnessed an act of violence, a riot or a crime of any kind, must testify to what he saw. Any reporter who steals or burglarizes a document should stand trial for the crime. Nor should any privilege protect a reporter from the laws for libel or the penalties for defamation, if proved. But Farber has broken no law, nor has he refused as a citizen to give testimony. When called to the witness stand by a defense subpoena, he responded for five days to every question—except those demanding that he divulge confidential sources or produce confidential notes.

The full power of the court and its compulsions have always been available to the defense to seek out its own witnesses and force them to testify publicly—and in this case such power was used successfully. But the New Jersey court insisted that Farber fully expose his journalist's sources or go to jail for his refusal. Whereupon the Supreme Court refused to accept for judgment this case where the First and Sixth Amendments apparently clash—and, by its silence, not only remanded Farber to jail but expanded the arbitrary power of lower judiciaries everywhere in the Union in an unprecedented manner. So it becomes central to the Farber story to examine to whom this new grant of power is being made—and its consequences. It becomes central to face the fact that the phrase "tyranny of the judiciary" is as unpleasant a truth as "arrogance of the press"—and possibly more dangerous.

Every observer of American politics recognizes that, since the early 1950's, the power of the courts has increased enormously. But every veteran reporter knows that not all judges are spiritual descendants of Holmes, Brandeis and Warren. All too many judges, wrapped in the black robes of court, are graduate politicians, neither scholars nor Solons; and, as one descends the hierarchy from the Federal to state to local levels, one finds more and more of them are hacks. Appointments to the bench, in New Jersey as elsewhere, are born of politics; they are influenced by ethnic and racial groups, by labor and business interests, by political clubhouse connections, snobberies of bar associations and law schools—occasionally even by the Mafia. To extend to all these men, through the precedent of the Farber case, the same right to squeeze information, confidences and hearsay out of reporters converts the Sixth Amendment into an instrument of judicial extortion.

Judges, like reporters, executives and politicians, suffer from an institutional appetite for more power; they are as sensitive, too, to the judgment of their peers; and thus, by the conjunction of these pressures, they can reduce high justice to tragedy. The great decision, *Brown v. Board of Education,* which wiped out all legal grounds for racial segregation in American schools in 1954, was a stark and beautiful act of American high justice. But in the 20 years since, it has been completely wrenched about. Stretching that decision year by year, a scattering of judicial tyrants across the country have destroyed communities, eviscerated cities and succeeded in dividing children and communities by race and color more effectively than ever before. The men of the Bergen County courts and their consenting but silent fellows of the bench may be of perfect faith in believing that the implications of the Sixth Amendment override those of the First. But they may someday find themselves as appalled by the consequences of the Farber decision as the authors of the Dred Scott decision were by the consequences of theirs.

ALL AMERICAN life is veined by a web of interlocking privileges, privileges exempting some groups from taxation, privileges protecting other groups from discrimination, privileges excusing yet other groups from regulation. Among the most important of all are the exemptions traditionally granted certain people ever since the Revolution from the majesty, pursuit and cruelty of what passes for justice. No wife, it is held, can be forced to testify against her husband; no cleric against one who confesses to him; no doctor or psychiatrist against his patient. None of these privileges are written into the Constitution any more than a reporter's privilege to protect his informants from reprisal is. But they are part of the American way of life.

Over the past decade the courts have been closing in on the press—ruling in the 1972 Branzburg decision that a reporter must testify to hearsay within the privacy of a grand jury; ruling in the recent Stanford Daily decision that a newspaper is always open to unannounced search and seizure of its records and files, whether it is a party to an action at law or merely a possible source of information. But now, under the precedent of the Farber case if the Supreme Court allows it to stand, no one is safe. Certainly not the small-town newspaper for whom a $5,000-a-day fine could mean disaster unless it yields up all its confidences at the behest of the local judge; probably not the psychiatrist, the priest or the doctor, all those who have enjoyed for so long the unquestioned privilege of confidence and have had that privilege upheld by the courts; and possibly not even the lawyer. Under the Farber ruling, even a Mafioso lawyer or a corrupt official has the right to compel a newspaper or reporter to trace the trail of his reporting from name to name before a black-robed man called "judge" who will then de-

cide whom to expose and whom to protect.

In due time, the Supreme Court must decide whether to hear the appeal of the *New York Times* from the punishment imposed on it by local magistrates in New Jersey for refusing to open its files to government. I await the decision with trepidation, not because I fear for the *New York Times*—which does as well financially as it does editorially, thank you—but because I am afraid for myself. If the Farber decision stands, I should at once go back to my files and start burning up my old notes. The denial of reporter's privileges could reach into my home whenever any politician styled "judge" decided to invade my home. And I am equally—indeed, more—afraid for the many innocent people who could be hurt if I were forced to make public all the nonsense and privacies I have learned from or about them. The First Amendment, in final analysis, was not devised to protect any reporter or publisher from the law or to give us special entitlements. The First Amendment is listed as the First to protect the people—because only an informed citizenry makes our kind of republic possible.

THE NEW YORK TIMES MAGAZINE
November 26, 1978

Chapter 15

Southeast Asia

In 1940, early in White's China years, he was asked to spend "three or four months" in Southeast Asia gathering background material for *Time*'s morgue in New York. On the surface it was the realization of a young reporter's dream: a new world to explore, no specific deadlines, unlimited expense account. But it was, in all, a depressing experience. He concluded that the French colonialists in Hanoi in fact "hated the people they ruled"; the Japanese, in the process of bloodlessly coercing the French administrators into submission, were "bullies" and even more contemptible; and the Vietnamese people, whom he found extremely unattractive, were not about to die for any country but their own. It was certainly no place, he concluded, for American military involvement.

While none of this newly acquired knowledge led to any bylined story at the time, it proved to be extremely valuable when during his 1950s European stint he reported on French policy in Indochina. And when the French forces had to surrender to the Vietminh at Dien Bien Phu in 1954, White was able to write a most perceptive explanation of what had gone wrong. It is the first of two articles in this chapter.

The second, for *Life,* was written on the eve of major South Vietnamese elections in 1967. Though he had in 1961 privately urged President Kennedy to get out of Southeast Asia, White had come to accept JFK's policies there; now, however, he found himself in a quandry—as were most Americans. Was it time to rethink our commitment?

INDOCHINA—THE LONG TRAIL OF ERROR

On February 19, 1954, General Henri-Eugène Navarre summoned together a group of newspapermen in Saigon and there, as Commander in Chief of the French Expeditionary Forces in Indo-China, permitted himself one of the most fatuously optimistic situation reports ever made by a military leader on the eve of disaster.

The efforts of the Communist enemy, Navarre said, had reached their maximum; the next few months of dry weather would give the French every opportunity to exploit their advantage; the following year would probably bring about the decisive defeat of the enemy.

In precisely the same week, only two days earlier, the Chairman of the U.S. Joint Chiefs of Staff, Admiral Arthur Radford, and the Under Secretary of State, General Walter Bedell Smith, had appeared in Washington before the House Foreign Relations Committee and declared with equal certainty, according to Representative Walter Judd, that Communist prospects of "any decisive immediate success are slight, while their prospects of ultimate victory are nonexistent."

Three weeks later, the four best divisions of the Communist army of General Vo Nguyen Giap opened their assault on Dienbienphu and turned the pressure on the Hanoi delta. Less than three months later, Dienbienphu fell, after an agony of hopeless heroism, and the Hanoi delta seemed open to catastrophe.

Although Hanoi can still be considered, in technical military terms, a beachhead defensible for months, there is nothing in the Indo-China war that gives the western world the slightest reason for comfort today. The chief reason for the increasing peril in Indo-China is the kind of thinking that led to General Navarre's classic blunder at Dienbienphu and to the casual optimism in Washington.

For almost fifteen years the Asian Communists have been developing certain types and styles of war, tailored not only to their terrain but to the politics of their villages. And western soldiers and statesmen, all the while paying lip service to the overriding importance of political direction of modern war, have continued to deal with it in the most parochial military terms.

The Face of the Battlefield

Wars unroll over hard and stubborn physical features of the earth's face. Indo-China is a 1,550-mile curve along the southern bulge of Asia's flank, opening north and south into two river basins.

The southern basin of Indo-China, where French penetration began over a century ago, is the watershed of the Mekong River, shared by two native peoples, the Cambodians in the interior and the Annamites on the coast. Here in the south is the heart of French colonial wealth—the rubber plantations, the trade, the huge rice surplus that makes Indo-China so tempting a prize for Communism.

To the north a mountain range paralleling the sea divides the interior people of Laos from the coastal Annamites on the east. Still further north this coastal strip broadens into the two provinces of Vinh and Thanhhoa, and then into the great basin of Tonkin adjacent to China. Tonkin is a forty-five-thousand-square-mile mountain region cupping a small deltaic plain through which the Red River flows to the sea. From the air these mountains look neither very high nor very forbidding. On the ground these low ridges are sharply folded, cut with limestone cliffs that demand a sharp uphill climb or steep descent in any direction one chooses to move. It is here in the northern basin of Tonkin that the war is being fought; and it is here that both terrain and human resources seem most perfectly arranged to aid the guerrilla tactics that the Com-

munists of Asia have been refining for fifteen years.

To this correspondent nothing has been more evocative of years gone by than the photographs of battle scenes from the Tonkin delta front. Almost any of these scenes could have been North China in the years 1939 to 1945, when the Chinese Communists were learning, as they fought the Japanese, how to pit superior politics and organization against superior weight of enemy metal. It was there in the laboratory of North China in those years that the present commander of the Vietminh forces, Vo Nguyen Giap, learned his trade.

The Mountain Refuge

Guerrilla war, in China and later in Indo-China, started in the hills, away from the roads that could bear trucks and artillery. Hill people are poor people; they are used to gunmen in their midst, for bandits usually dwell in the hills and are protected there because they raid only in the lowlands. Amid the misery of Asia the line between banditry and honor is blurred, and many a man crosses it both ways in his life. The Communists climbing into the hills seem no different from other men in flight or hiding.

Guerrilla strategy starts with this concept of the mountain base, called in Communist jargon "the liberated area." The first move is logically and invariably the cutting of the roads by means of deep ditches, one after the other, at every entry to and exit from the mountain lair. If the enemy fills one ditch, there is another two hundred yards beyond, then another, and another. The enemy can make a raid, send a patrol of seventy men, once, twice, three times. The guerrillas vanish. The fourth time, when the patrol has been reduced to twenty men, the guerrillas ambush it. Months may pass. The enemy commander tires of exhausting his troops on patrol. He *knows* the cities, towns, and railways are important. These he holds firmly, and temporarily he is content.

POLITICS AND guerrilla tactics fit together like the spear in its shaft. Within the mountain redoubt, the Communist leaders call meetings—meetings for youth, meetings for women, meetings for students, meetings for tillers. In the primitive uplands, the Communist leaders have much to teach: They can teach simple weaving and sandal making, they can teach elementary hygiene, they can teach reading and writing. They give names and ascribe causes to all nameless aches and grievances of the peasants—it is the landlord, or the Japanese, or the white man, or imperialism that makes them hungry. When the enemy, provoked, makes a raid into the redoubt, peasants and guerrillas warn each other. They protect each other, fight together, until peasant and fighter become indistinguishable. Together they learn how to make hand grenades, how to make mines of hollowed rock and black powder, how to ambush and fall back. Ambitious young intellectuals sneak out of cities and schools to find careers in the hill governments;

sturdy young peasants graduate out of the paddies to join them in leadership.

It may take years, as it did up in northern China, before the guerrillas acquire their first radios, their first mortars, their first artillery, before they begin to coagulate out of the guerrilla reservoir the little units of "regulars" in company formations of three to five hundred. Always the strategy is the same—never to sit still; ignore the railways, the cities; when the enemy pursues, flee; accept battle only on one's own terms; nothing need be held seriously—no point, no ridge, no gap is important, so long as politics welds the people firmly to the army. Gradually the "liberated areas" spread into the lowlands. The shadowy areas of condominium between enemy garrison by day and guerrilla garrison by night are reduced to the zones of fire about a blockhouse or fort on the outskirts of the big town, at the bridge, on the railway.

In China, by 1945, the Communists had spread their "liberated regions" like a film, invisible but all-powerful, down within rifle range of every major Japanese garrison, railway line, and city wall. Flying over the North China plains on bombing missions against Japanese bridges in the closing months of the war, we Americans would look down from the air and see a countryside that recalled medieval Europe. Huge ditches, built by the Japanese for protection, flanked the railways for hundreds of miles. Each Japanese strongpoint was a turret, frequently with a dry moat, always with a necklace of barbed-wired gun pits ringing it round, facing out on an invisible enemy who could not be seen but was always there.

Guerrilla war comes to its climax when artillery and shells to feed it are at hand. By then the enemy commander has become so exasperated in years of struggle with ghosts that he yearns to catch the elusive guerrillas just once, to have them stand and fight in a dug-in pitched battle where his metal can pound them. He exposes himself, takes risks, and then one day, out of the unknown, the guerrilla army appears equipped with all its collected artillery and delivers the climactic blow. For the Communists of China the moment arrived at Changchun in Manchuria in the fall of 1948, when the enemy had long since ceased to be the Japanese and had become Chiang Kai-shek, who had seeded off his garrisons in isolated pockets across the land. For the Vietminh Communists and the French, the moment arrived in 1954, at Dienbienphu, when the guerrillas ceased to be guerrillas and became an army.

The Long Road to Dienbienphu

It is extraordinarily difficult to recall, after eight years of struggle with Communism, how the war in Indo-China began. Yet it is essential to remember that the problem facing the French has never been that of putting down an "uprising" or "rebels," but of suppressing an independent government.

When, in the summer of 1945, the French returned to the deltas of the Mekong and the Red Rivers, they returned not as conquerors, but as secondary occupiers to relieve the British and Chinese armies in their task of disarming and repatriating the defeated Japanese. Not only that, but the French found that in the long absence of their own occupation and the turbulent closing months of the war in Asia, the Annamites had established governments of their own in both the great river basins, policing villages, vocally protesting their independence and ready to defend it.

In the Mekong basin of the south, the return of the French was greatly aided by the British troops of General Douglas D. Gracey, a pukka sahib of the old Indian Army, apparently unaware of the purpose and politics of the new Labour Government in distant London. General Gracey would tolerate no nonsense from natives; he cleared them from the government buildings in the heart of Saigon, leaving them in the suburbs for the incoming French to mop up—a task that a French general estimated would take "about a month."

In Hanoi, the return of the French was much more difficult. Tonkin and Hanoi were in the Chinese zone of occupation. In the Governor General's palace sat a frail and goateed little Communist named Ho Chi Minh, leader of a revolutionary league called the Vietminh. On September 2, 1945, Ho Chi Minh proclaimed to the cheering people of Hanoi a new Declaration of Independence which began with a paraphrase of the great passage: "We hold these truths to be self-evident, that all men are created equal . . ." While the first delegates of the returning French were confined to quarters like prisoners, two U.S. Air Forces planes buzzed the crowd to add glory to the ceremony, and the "Democratic Republic of Vietnam" was proclaimed.

The conspicuous American approval of the proceeding was quite natural. Ho Chi Minh and his military right arm, Giap, had for months been working under the guidance of the O.S.S. during the Japanese occupation to aid American intelligence and aviation units. In the mountains of north Tonkin the first guerrilla bases had been organized with arms from America, and thus the roots of an organization never since dissolved were thrust down.

IT TOOK SIX months before the French could persuade the Chinese Nationalists to leave Tonkin and another eight months of futile negotiation in Indo-China and Paris before they could muster enough troops in the Orient to blast Haiphong, the delta's port, seize Hanoi, and drive Ho and his fragile Vietminh government back into the hills whence they had come. From that day—December 19, 1946—to this, the war has gone on.

Four French commanding generals have come to Asia, chanted of victory, held and lost garrisons, lunged fruitlessly at a vanishing enemy, and departed leaving behind an enemy stronger than when they came.

By the end of 1950 the French had suffered their first major reverse when the entire string of border garrisons on the frontier of Red China was snuffed out, permitting the Vietminh and Red China unimpeded communication with one another. By 1951 the late General de Lattre de Tassigny, after seeing his major outposts fall, had established a surface stability with the famous *ceinture* (belt) of forts and blockhouses that defend the triangular wedge of the Hanoi-Haiphong delta, a *ceinture* that might have been drawn from the blueprints of the Japanese in North China in 1945. French courage never failed; only the political direction to give it meaning was lacking.

By 1953, Paris had sent General Henri-Eugène Navarre to Asia; he proposed to bring the elusive enemy to battle once and for all. He dispatched ten thousand of his finest troops by air to the mountain pocket of Dienbienphu, far beyond his own ability to supply or relieve. Chiang Kai-shek had similarly begun his disastrous campaigns in the Chinese civil war by isolating his spearheads in garrisons far beyond his communications. And, just as Chiang Kai-shek had, only much sooner, Navarre learned that at a certain moment Communist guerrillas coalesce and become formidable armies.

Now, in the aftermath of Dienbienphu, we are learning from French sources the full strength of the army that has been gathered in the hills. The Vietminh now count eight regular divisions of three regiments each—the 304th, 306th, 308th, 312th, 316th, 318th, 320th, and 325th. The firepower of these units in automatic weapons is stated to be greater than that of equivalent French divisions. Their artillery consists mainly of 75-mm. recoilless rifles, but their 120-mm. Soviet-made heavy mortar is heavier, it should be noted, than the standard French 81-mm. mortar. Like the Russians, the Vietminh mass their heavier artillery firepower in separate divisions, and at Dienbienphu the Viets unleashed their new 351st Artillery Division. This division, trained in China, is largely equipped with American 105s captured in Korea.

At Dienbienphu, Communist General Giap stacked four infantry divisions (including the crack 308th and 312th) with their organic artillery, added the bulk of his artillery division plus his new 37-mm. anti-aircraft unit, some newly furnished twelve-barreled "Katyusha" rocket launchers of Russian origin, then sat in the encircling hills and let the French have it. Whether or not the French were ignorant of this power, as some say, or whether they knew of the power but believed the Viets could neither supply nor handle it, is immaterial. French intelligence reckoned on forty enemy 105s plus forty to seventy enemy 75s or heavy mortars. What the gallant General de Castries faced instead was over three hundred enemy "*bouches du feu*"; little wonder that the French artillery colonel at Dienbienphu blew his brains out.

In INDO-CHINA today, the Vietminh can probably summon a total of 320,000 "regulars" for cohesive operation; this figure leaves out their coolie supply corps and a political organization that can graduate veteran peasant fighters in a few weeks into the ranks of "regulars." Against this, the commonly accepted figure of Allied strength is 520,000-odd. Backing this force is an overwhelming superiority in armament: Unchallenged in armor, sea power, planes, and trucks, the French troops can draw on depots in the delta crammed with U.S. supplies. This superiority in supply and numbers is, however, sharply reduced when its composition is more closely studied. The troop figure includes quartermasters, M.P.s, and signal transportation, and medical corpsmen to a total of perhaps half its effectives. And most of the effective combat troops are in the blockhouse or garrison points. It includes, moreover, only about 180,000 men of the French Expeditionary Force (about 75,000 Frenchmen, 20,000 Foreign Legionnaires, the rest Africans) while the "loyal" Vietnamese who fill out the French ranks make up almost 300,000. These "loyal" troops are mixed levies, some very good, some very bad, and the further the military situation deteriorates, the less loyal they will be. To hold them, to raise more, to instill in them the vigor, skill, and will to fight against their Communist-led compatriots is the very heart and soul of the problem today, as it has been ever since the war broke out.

A Flag to Fight For

The Indo-China war cannot be divorced from politics. Whatever the real or professed purposes of the French government when it reentered Indo-China, the natives of that country could interpret them only against a century of colonial rule. Colonial rule, even at its best, requires the constant threat of force to maintain itself, and for a century in Indo-China the French had been suppressing revolt, uprising, and conspiracy—in 1884–1888, 1893–1895, 1908, 1914, 1916, 1930—as all colonial uprisings must be suppressed, by quenching them in blood. The French were more extravagant than the British in reprisals, in extortion, in denial of personal and civil liberties, and they reaped a double harvest. On the surface there was an appearance of greater tranquillity, but beneath lay a political chasm between them and the people, bridged by no such groups as India's Congress Party.

The French ruled over a people whose emotions spanned the range from deep apathy to profound hatred. If the Annamites lived quietly, they did so because their lives were no more miserable than those of other Orientals and because the French brought medicine and hygiene, learning and science, roads and jobs, tools and cloth.

The lasting legacy of the Japanese triumph in the Orient was that Orientals could now hope to possess all these secrets of the white man, and his power, without paying the white man's fee of servitude. When the French returned in 1945 and 1946, they found the country speckled with nationalist groups of every hue, all of them convinced that they need never again submit to the colonial rule that had evaporated in the few months between Japan's collapse and France's return.

The French proclaimed on their return that theoretically they were willing to give the Indo-Chinese what they most wanted—independence and unity of their country. But in 1945 France suffered from the same constitutional maladies it suffers from today. The French Government was a grouping of parties, no two of which meant the same thing by the same word. The French Government in March, 1946, promised Ho Chi Minh the unity of the three Annamite states, Cochin China, Annam, and Tonkin, and that it would station no more than 15,000 troops in his country, to be reduced twenty per cent each year until by 1952 no more French troops would remain, with the possible exception of those guarding bases. Yet there were "details" to be worked out, and the country still had not been "pacified." So, even as French and Vietminh conferred in Paris in the summer of 1946 on the "details," French and Vietminh patrols clashed and killed each other in deciding just who would "pacify" what.

While Ho Chi Minh negotiated at Fontainebleau from July through August about the unity of the various Indo-China states, the French proconsul in Asia, Admiral Thierry d'Argenlieu, stage-managed a separatist puppet movement he had set up as the "Republic of Cochin China" the very week Ho Chi Minh left for France. Independence to the Vietminh meant a share in the control of their own exports and imports. When the French set up a virtual blockade of Haiphong, shooting broke out in November, 1946, and the French Navy moved in to shell the city over open sights, killing thousands of the inhabitants.

France itself, emerging from the humiliation of German occupation, was rededicating itself to all those liberties of conscience and mind that still flourish so brilliantly in that land. But what went on in the distant colony was almost unknown in Paris. No French newspaper had a correspondent in Indo-China in the critical months of November and December, 1946; only twice between 1945 and 1950 did the French Assembly even debate the subject of Indo-China. Political direction from Paris flickered and contradicted itself as the diverse parties in the French Government ignored or disagreed on what should be done. Administration in Indo-China was in the hands of semi-autonomous civil servants, some good, some bad, split among themselves by career jealousies, their policy guided by old colonists who "knew how to handle the natives." When after the uprising of Annamites at Hanoi in December, 1946, with full-scale war almost inevitable, Ho Chi Minh cabled a final plea for compromise to French Premier Léon Blum, the local French censor held up the cable until it was too late.

The Vietminh forces driven out of Hanoi in 1946 were not then the organized force they are now. They had displayed not only treachery and bad faith but also their inability to control the wild bands of fanatics, hating white men, who rallied to their banners. When the Vietminh forces were driven out, they left behind a diverse array of other nationalist groups whom they had alienated—partly because of their ruthless assassination of rivals, partly by their outright espousal of war to gain what others thought might be won by further negotiation.

Bao Dai

The French now had a war on their hands, but the prospects would have been far from hopeless if they had chosen to emulate the British in staging an orderly withdrawal from Asia. What the French wanted, however, was something utterly schizophrenic—to withdraw yet to stay, to offer the fiction of independence yet to maintain the substance of control. Later, French opinion came to desire nothing more than a robust national leadership to shelter the rear guard so that France could stage a graceful and gradual exist. But by then the Communists had liquidated or absorbed almost all other nationalist elements. And the French were stuck with the "Emperor" Bao Dai, the man they had chosen to lead the "Associated State of Vietnam" against the Vietminh-controlled "Democratic Republic of Vietnam" in the hills. To avoid confusion, the western world speaks of the Communist state simply as "Vietminh" and Bao Dai's state simply as "Vietnam."

IT WAS NOT until 1949 that the "Emperor" Bao Dai was proclaimed Chief of State by the French. A vigorous young man of forty endowed with a supple intelligence, Bao Dai is more an object of pity than of distaste. Educated by the French as a native princeling, he was brought up to be pliant and infirm of will, ready to serve any master. Having sworn loyalty to the French Republic, he next pledged loyalty to the Vichy state, then cheered the Japanese when they removed the French, next pledged loyalty to the Government of Ho Chi Minh in 1945 (assuming for the occasion the title of Citizen Van Thuy), and finally, after a brief exile, offered his loyalty to the French again in 1949. Though he is depicted as another King Farouk, his vices are much exaggerated. He does enjoy the French Riviera, but his romantic escapades there have been minor ones. In Indo-China, his mistresses are neither numerous nor grotesquely housed; they dwell in modest villas, as he does himself, in a society that has fresh recollections of princes with hundreds of concubines. It is not these pleasures of the flesh that make him incapable of leadership as much as his seeming total lack of vigor and purpose. For in order to rally the thousands of young, hopeful, educated people in the land to build the structure of government, some vision must be offered them. Few dedicated officials will risk death at their posts to serve a ruler who during the disastrous defeats of 1950 was disporting himself on the Riviera, and who in today's moment of peril is to be found again in the fashionable resorts of France.

For the complete failure of Bao Dai to give leadership to his people against the Communists both Bao Dai and the French must share the blame. Bao Dai's fault lies simply in that where statesmanship has been called for he has never exhibited more than a petulant desire to be left alone by the French, by Ho Chi Minh, and even by his own advisers.

FRANCE'S FAULT lies in that it has never given Bao Dai what was promised him. The basic documents of French relation with the "independent" Associated State of Vietnam that Bao Dai rules are still the accords of March 8, 1949. These leave in French hands control of Indo-China's finances, justice, foreign trade, and foreign affairs; the Government of Bao Dai must still accept French advisers at every technical and administrative level; French citizens and enterprises are still given special safeguards. In the years since Bao Dai's return in 1949 the French have again and again promised to "perfect" Vietnamese independence. The details are, to this day, always to be worked out later. Within this framework, neither Bao Dai nor the French have been able to foster native institutions in which young leaders may develop; corruption and maladministration in the countryside, cities wide open with legal opium dens, brothels, and unpunished racketeering have disillusioned all those who once considered Bao Dai a possible alternative to Ho Chi Minh's Communism. He has been destroyed as a symbol of independence against an enemy who flaunts a banner of independence that the unfortunate Annamites cannot easily recognize as spurious.

There are millions of Vietnamese and thousands of potentially able junior leaders who either hate or fear Communism, yet find no hope in Bao Dai or his Government. They are the *attentistes,* the waiting ones. They have waited too long. At this writing, the Government they are asked to support has left them leaderless, with not only the Premier, the Vice-Premier, the Foreign Minister, and the Economics Minister, but the Emperor, the Empress, and their two sons visiting or negotiating in Europe.

Enter America

It is at this point, on the edge of military disaster, that the United States is considering entering the Indo-China war. It has, to be sure, long been involved both politically and logistically in this war. But what has been under debate the past few weeks is whether the United States should inject its armed might—and blood—into a situation where the French Assembly has not ventured to ask its people to send draftees.

The most remarkable thing about this debate in Washington is the fragmented, unco-ordinated quality of discussion as each individual bureau or agency discusses the mechanics of the particular phase of the problem that concerns it. One hears what Admiral Radford thinks, what the Ground Forces think, what Mr. Dulles thinks, what CIA thinks, what Senator Knowland thinks. Rarely, if ever, does one hear mentioned the views of the Presi-

dent—he who, from his supreme position and unique experience, should alone see the matter whole and shape the policy of the government he heads.

The primary burden of policymaking is divided between the State Department and the Pentagon. Yet, here again, both great guardian Departments are split by the most diverse opinions, which apparently are as yet unreconciled.

At the State Department one is confronted with the most melancholy choice of judgments: either that the State Department, in its upper echelon, was abysmally misinformed about the situation in Indo-China, or that it deliberately misinformed Congress and public when in February it told them all was well. It is not only more charitable but correct to assume the former. Yet if one assumes that the senior echelon of State was misinformed, in the teeth of the masses of reporting on the deterioration of the situation in Indo-China during the past two years, both within State and from the CIA, one can only be further depressed at the extent to which domestic political passions have wrecked our government's mechanisms of information.

"When I first came to State," said one man formerly intimately associated with policymaking, "if a man thought and studied and knew his facts he would have had a hearing. The State Department would listen to an intellectual approach from any qualified person who thought what he had to say was right for the United States. After that it might be rejected for technical reasons—because Congress wouldn't stand for it, because it couldn't clear SWNC [the State, War, and Navy Committee], because our Allies wouldn't go along, because the public wasn't ready. Now, you bring the same equipment to the same problems and if what you come up with is politically unpalatable, you will not only be misunderstood but you'll have your patriotism questioned.

"Any suggestion you may make of yielding any territory to the Communists is equated with moral approval of Communist aggression; any suggestion you may make about negotiating with China runs into Senator Knowland's veto on acknowledging that China exists. In Indo-China we have had a policy based on fiction, not facts. It was based on the fiction that Indo-China was independent when it was not independent. It was based on the fiction that the men we recognized as native leaders in Indo-China were real leaders when they were not leaders."

YET THIS atmosphere, arising from the fear of many gifted men that they will receive the reward of Absalom's tidings, can only be a partial explanation of State's misjudgment. A greater part seems to come from its failure to review all the experience America acquired in Indo-China under the previous Administration, so that its New Look, rather than being New, is simply a quick gloss on Democratic strategies and miscalculations—some of which had been in process of reevaluation before the Republicans took over.

A flashback on American policy in Indo-China shows how difficult it was to avoid the trap in which we have been caught. During the war, the United States came to the conclusion that empires in Asia were finished. As early as January, 1944, President Roosevelt had told Lord Halifax that in his opinion Indo-China should not be returned to the French but should be administrated under an international trusteeship. "France has had the country—thirty million inhabitants—for nearly one hundred years and the people are worse off than they were at the beginning," he said.

This conviction stemmed naturally from our ancient hatred of colonialism. It continued in vigor down through the first year of the Marshall Plan, whose funds were carefully forbidden to be used in colonial wars. The anticolonial policy of America reached its successful climax in the pressure that forced the Dutch out of Indonesia, thus saving Holland from bankruptcy and Indonesia, so far, from Communism.

This policy died in 1949, not because of the considered abandonment of an American tradition but because in that year the Communists in China triumphed, rolling to the border of Indo-China. At that moment, any self-proclaimed anti-Communist became an ally of America, without question as to his effectiveness or ability. Thus, in 1949, to balance the massive Communist victory in China, the United States set its solemn seal of recognition on Bao Dai.

However much justification there

was for this recognition—and a good case can be made that the experiment was worth trying—it had clearly failed by 1951. Bao Dai had proved his incompetence, and the French, by their refusal to give more than lip service to independence, had provided the Annamites no reason to oppose Communism. We had, moreover and most tragically, found that the most promising political gambits of American ingenuity within Indo-China were opposed by the French. The ECA in Indo-China found, for example, that American-financed health stations in villages at the very fighting front had enormous political impact; villagers would cross the lines at night from the Communist hills to have their eyes smeared with the magic aureomycin that cures trachoma in five days. But these and other avenues of political approach to the development of native leadership could not be explored because the French, or rather General de Lattre de Tassigny, did not approve.

Believing then that it was essential to support the French in Indo-China in order to get them to ratify EDC in Europe, not realizing that France's weakness in Asia made it too weak to join EDC in Europe, the Democratic Administration nevertheless realized that the war was moving slowly toward disaster. Thus, in the fall of 1951, secret military staff talks were initiated with the British, French, Australians, and New Zealanders to devise joint plans for the military defense of Southeast Asia. These plans, after initial foundering for lack of diplomatic groundwork, were straightened out at the Lisbon Conference in 1952, and then permitted to lapse. They lapsed because Mr. Truman announced he would not run again and thus his Administration became for the next nine months a caretaker régime without the power or desire to initiate policy.

It is this concept of a Southeast Asia Military Defense Pact, born in 1951 and allowed to lapse in the spring of 1952, that in the spring of 1954, in desperate haste, the Administration is trying to revive by bilateral talks with all interested parties. What is sought is simply a statement from a number of partners of intent to defend themselves. This could be approved by the Congress in a joint resolution, avoiding the delay of treatymaking. It is to this end that all Mr. Dulles's energies are bent at the moment, as a necessary prelude to any intervention.

It is realized now at last that Bao Dai is useless. (In the words of one high State Department official, "We've known it for weeks—even months.") But the necessary planning for the emergency reorganization of politics in French-held areas of Indo-China is difficult to discern.

Along with the illusion of Bao Dai, the illusion of Indo-China as the key to all Southeast Asia also has begun to fade. The old concept of Indo-China's strategic position was usually sustained by huge charts showing how the Japanese had jumped off from Indo-China to take the Philippines, Malaya, and Indonesia. It is, however, now remembered that the Japanese thrusts were all made by sea under covering air power, not by overland ground assault. Their advances even in Burma and Thailand could only be sustained by their unchallenged control of sea and air. But today sea and air power remain all through Southeast Asia incontestably in western hands. It is still politically too early to stress this point, but sober thinking now recognizes it.

The Soldiers' View

Part of the confusion of thinking in Washington is due to the conflict in views between America's senior military men. When there is no strong civilian guidance, as there is not today, military opinions become extremely important in making policy.

The two chief points of view are first that American air-sea intervention, or the threat of it, will be enough to stabilize the fluid situation, and second that air-sea intervention, as in Korea, will inevitably prove insufficient and must be followed up by ground troops.

The air-sea position is commonly associated with the views of Admiral Radford. This school believes that air-sea bombardment from land-and carrier-based planes can choke off the supplies of the Communist army. It believes that American ground forces will be unnecessary, hoping that the present French forces and their native supporters can retain cohesion on the ground and fight back. The politics that have brought the contending forces to their present gloomy imbalance are only casually con-

sidered. This view seems at the moment to be dominant. The State Department appears convinced that Congressional leaders who will not tolerate ground intervention have been brought around to accept air-sea intervention. Thus, with its eyes on the domestic political scene and the reluctance of Congress to go all out, before elections, the U.S. government seems backing into action with a military program that can be advertised as both cheap and approved by high military authority.

THE GROUND-FORCE soldiers who oppose this view believe that the present position of the French in Indo-China is such that air-sea intervention must inevitably result in ground intervention as well. If ground intervention must come, their belief is that the best place for it is not in guerrilla-rotted Tonkin but across the narrow waistline of Indo-China, the 150-mile belt between Vinh and Hué, where with a few divisions a line can be pinned on the South China Sea and the Mekong. Yet the ground-force generals do not want to intervene, for the politics of the New Look have cut the Army down to the point where it is questionable whether even those few divisions are available. Further, in global strategy it is folly to disperse reserves around the periphery of the globe, fighting Communism on its distant flanks rather than stabbing for its heartland. The ground commanders, too, are far more sensitive to the politics of the villages in which they must fight than any other group of people in Washington, and are uneasy about intervention without a political approach that can bring about true Vietnamese support.

Geneva and the Delta

At the moment of this writing, Washington is suspended between news from the front and from Geneva. The interim decision of the State Department is to give the French their way at Geneva, accepting any settlement that is satisfactory to the tottering Laniel Government. In the threatened Red River delta, there is at the moment no lack either of arms, ammunition, fuel, armor, or planes. The French have an estimated 70,000 to 80,000 combat troops in the delta area, plus many more Vietnamese in the battalions of Bao Dai to defend a perimeter of 250 to 300 miles. There are also some ten crack French Union battalions and five good Vietnamese battalions as mobile reserves. French intelligence believes that the four enemy divisions that captured

Dienbienphu will be in place by June 15, ready to fight, as will be two more columns of enemy troops advancing from north and south, totaling twenty more battalions. Within the delta as many as seventy thousand armed Communist riflemen may be concealed among the seven million inhabitants. In purely military terms the delta can be held. But this is not a purely military war. If the seven million rise on the enemy's call, or if the loyal Annamite battalions are infected by the rot of disaffection, nothing can hold. And the political formula to hold the loyalties of the Annamites has not yet been found.

If settlement or partition is agreed on at Geneva, there will be long months ahead to consider the next political steps, to salvage what remains of Indo-China. If it is not, a decision must be made in the next few weeks whether to hold at the delta, hold at the waistline, or fall back for strategic regrouping on a line excluding Indo-China.

THE REPORTER June 22, 1954

BELL OF DECISION RINGS OUT IN VIETNAM

It is night, and the monsoon pours down, pelting and slashing the city, drumming on the iron roofs of the Tan Son Nhut base where Americans sleep, thrashing the mat shacks of the refugees. The lightning stabs, the thunder cracks and in between crumples an occasional softer thud. In the corridor of the hotel, the 3-year-old child of the English diplomat next door runs out barefoot, sobbing in fear. I try to soothe her with a few words of English; her dark-haired Vietnamese amah pads out to rock and comfort the child, cradling blond curls against black pajamas.

All across Vietnam one knows women are clutching children just like this, trying to still fear, just as grown men are clutching earth and mud for safety, too. Day belongs to us, but night is the killing time we share with Charlie, our patrols stalking the countryside for raiders, their raiders probing to ambush us or rush a village for the murder mission of the night. Whatever moves then is target, and from American bases one knows artillery is racketing and slamming, bursting at random in free-fire zones.

Thus, slowly, one hears the monsoon in diminuendo, and only the softer thud remains. The ear lingers on this softer thudding—is it thunder fading? Or our artillery? Or their mortars?

As one cossets sleep, and even the softest thuds vanish, the echo lingers. Logic asks, "What are we doing here? What are we doing here?" As the mind restlessly tries to sort out facts and sights in answer, memory recalls the vision of the city outside, now dark.

It is election time, and raddled, flaky walls on every street flaunt the banners of candidates. White posters, peeling in the monsoon rain, show unsmiling faces of unknown leaders above the slates of the water buffalo, the palm tree, the rice sower, the white star, the white dove. Soon the bell-ringer will be clanging off the allotted time at the rallies where they hope to voice their message. Out of these mysterious faces must come, we hope, leadership to purge this melancholy city, gangrenous with the swollen human wastes of war; to cleanse the mounds of garbage, decay, trash in the street; to bring order to a community where pimps, prostitutes and corruptionists earn more than government ministers.

The images of the countryside beyond recur. Jeeps and trucks are rushing cartons of green voter-registration forms to every hamlet; tons of paper ballots will follow. Will the experiment work? Can this election heal this broken land, refresh the empty fields abandoned by farmers where rice should be planted, where beasts now graze untended? In 1963 this land exported 300,000 tons of rice; this year it will import one million tons. Now through the richest paddy land of Asia rumble American trucks bearing rice bagged in Houston, Texas. One remembers the moonscape panorama from the air—mud-ball forts and stockades by every village gate, the pockmarks of artillery on hills around. One remembers the sight along the coast of what is left of the old French railway that once ran from Hanoi to Saigon, its bridge spans snapped in "V"s, its rails ripped out by peasants to melt for iron.

WITH THE memory of the old French railway, the spool of recollection begins to unwind the first thread of an answer. For it is with the French and their legacy of evil that the story of America's presence here begins. The climax of the story and America's gamble will come within the next few days, when these tormented people must choose leaders to govern their nation. But the roots of the story go back to the French and the ruins of the nation they destroyed.

I remember coming down this coastal railroad 27 years ago to rest on the veranda of this same hotel in Saigon. It was the first colonial enterprise I had

ever seen—and the worst I was ever to see. It was not the classic avarice, extortion and expropriation of colonial life that offended so much. Nor the fact that the French budgeted their opium monopoly at a larger sum than the budget for hospitals, schools and libraries combined. It was the sight of people—the causal quality of cruelty, the simple slapping by white men, smack across the face, of grown Vietnamese rickshamen and servants as if they were naughty children. The sullen quality of native faces repudiated the beauty of the city: the splendid French boulevards ran like causeways above a basin of hate.

For the last 20 years this basin of hate has been openly boiling. Today the hate of the round-eyed white man is the greatest propelling fuel of the enemy's resistance. When little Vietnamese children smile at American soldiers and shriek "Hello, hello," it is a triumph of major proportions. Yet the Americans are too few to occupy even a portion of Vietnam's 12,500 hamlets and prove to the people that white men come of varying traditions. Too many Vietnamese know Americans only as bomb-droppers and burners.

We deal with what the French left behind a dozen years ago—not only this ancient hate of white men but the crippled shape of society. In their schools the French trained schoolteachers, mandarin-type clerks, parish priests, a handful of doctors and lawyers. But no men who could govern a country. Major businesses the French controlled themselves. The more grubby enterprises were turned over to

Chinese traders. No business leadership, no political parties were allowed to develop. When today Americans talk, as they do endlessly, of the "thinness of the crust" or "the leadership problem," they mean simply that the Vietnamese on our side lack anything like the trained leadership in numbers, talent or experience needed to make a nation work. This was the way the French wanted it.

To the French, Vietnam was a crazy quilt of villages of Viet-Cham-Khmer-Thai culture with a historical overlay of Buddhist priests, another overlay of Confucian mandarins, upon which they imposed a final overlay of native clerks and French bureaucracy. The only links between the villages and the government in Saigon were tax collectors and police; there was no opportunity for the men of Vietnam to graduate to dignity except as servants of French purpose.

VIETNAMESE RECOGNIZE their own wounded incapacity. I asked a member of the present cabinet why his government did not seize the French-owned rubber plantations which pay taxes to the Vietcong. He answered, "Because we don't have the people to run them. We seized the French rice plantations and now they run at a deficit. We don't know how to run rubber plantations and we need the money from rubber exports. As soon as we have the people who can run them, we will seize them."

The Vietnamese have no one who can run the antique waterworks of Saigon, or its electricity system or its com-

merce. We are hothousing the training of Vietnamese: university students have multiplied from 13,000 to 32,000 in six years; primary-grade students have jumped from 1,200,000 to 1,750,000 in the same period. But Vietnam cannot even print its own primary schoolbooks. Of the 12 million textbooks pumped into Vietnam schools in the past few years, 90% had to be printed abroad. It will be decades before this year's college graduates reach maturity and responsibility.

When the French collapsed in 1954, Americans entered this sick ward of social pathology in total ignorance. This ignorance has conditioned all our blunders since.

We are learning, but very late. Not until 1957 did the first State Department officer begin studying Vietnamese. Even in 1962 State's Foreign Service Institute was training only five young diplomats in the language—four officers and one wife. Not until 1966 did State put Vietnamese language training on a crash basis; hundreds are now learning the language in Washington. But in all Vietnam today the embassy commands only 13 language-trained officers (10 months of instruction). The American press corps here is more disadvantaged: not a single American newspaperman speaks or reads the language at all. Neither embassy nor Army can offer a basic handbook of fact or history about this country, though one has been in preparation for 10 months. We still lack a manpower survey to give us a clue to Vietnamese resources in skills and education. "We have," said one young U.S. officer, "no institutional memory. Every man who comes out starts learning from scratch all over again." Thus we fly blind, blundering through rumor and gossip, groping for statistics because simple facts elude us.

But, somehow, over the recent years millions of Vietnamese have grown entirely dependent on us—their leaders to be imprisoned or massacred if we leave. Strange shapes and groups float through their murky politics—sects such as the Cao Dai (a powerful religious group that worships Confucius, Buddha, Jesus Christ, Victor Hugo, Thomas Jefferson and Winston Churchill), the Hoa Hao (with other strange beliefs), Buddhists, Catholics, militarists, petulant intellectuals—all anti-Communist, yet distrusting or despising each other. But we know little about them or how their antagonistic energies can be channeled to provide effective resistance.

Through this fog of blurred information, there has finally seeped an action imperative that we have mouthed so long as a glib phrase: that we control political problems in Oriental sociology: that to win, it is not sufficient to win on the battlefield: that to win we must challenge a charismatic adversary for the minds of Asian peasants who are half mesmerized, half terrorized by a condition of political warfare as devoid of classical morality as of classical tactics and as deadly as it is invisible.

One must try to grasp the nature of the enemy to understand anything, for his great strength lies in the grasp his imagination holds over Vietnamese

peasants—just as the elusive prize we seek in the coming elections is a government that can match this invisible control of popular emotions.

One way to sense the invisible quality of the struggle is, say, to look for what we identify as COSVN. COSVN—Central Office for South Vietnam—is the enemy's mobile capital, seat of the National Liberation Front.

A helicopter lifts one from Saigon to Cu Chi, where the American 25th Division defends the approaches to the capital; another helicopter lifts one north toward Tay Ninh province, and in a few minutes the round green breast of Nui Ba Den, a 3,000-foot mountain cone, rises sheer from the water-logged plain. "We know there's V.C. radio somewhere in that mountain," says the major. "He'll pass the word to them we're flying north." North of Nui Ba Den begins triple-canopy jungle—a coating of thick underbrush, a second tier of hardwoods poking through the brush, a third tier of jungle growth soaring high above.

Last spring in Operation Junction City two of our divisions penetrated, then occupied, COSVN's lair here. They chopped up the enemy's Ninth Division, forcing it and COSVN headquarters to flee across the border to Cambodia. We found abandoned hospitals and staff schools, underground arms factories, tons of documents, a base installation that may have held from 5,000 to 12,000 troops. Then, since it was useless to waste two American divisions in garrisoning several hundred square miles of empty jungle, we withdrew.

NOW THE JUNGLE has closed over the victory. We know that COSVN is moving in again. But from the air absolutely nothing is visible. There are the air strips we cleared ready to be used again. There are our tank tracks already full of water. There is the swath of B-52s left in the jungle one day when we had intelligence of a politburo meeting—a belt of bomb craters, now filled with turquoise blue pools of water. But nothing moves. Back and forth we crisscross the air seeking COSVN's new lair, but we see nothing. Only infantry on foot can poke it out.

Yet infantrymen are equally frustrated in their search. Several hundred miles north one watches a major general of the Marine Corps at his evening staff briefing. Seven enemy battalions are scattered through his sector, all directed by radio from some regimental headquarters in the border mountains. We have a fix on one of them, a pink uncertain blob on the operations map. We know that the best part of an ARVN division is attempting to strain out this one battalion of perhaps 500 men. But if they kill 30 we will be lucky. "They are like grease," said a French officer to me years ago of their war against the Viets. "You squeeze them in your hand and they ooze through the fingers." As our troops move, bamboo sticks will clatter in villages, gongs will sound, a native telegraph system will warn the hunted battalion. It will dissolve to

companies, companies to platoons, platoons to squads, to be sheltered in huts, caves, underground tunnels. When our troops reach the fix the enemy will be gone. And even those villagers on our side will be too terrorized to point out their hiding places. It is an environment we fight—not an army; and it is this environment we must liquidate before we will be able to silence the guns.

THE ENVIRONMENT we battle is people—caught or transfixed by a sinister, yet masterly, achievement: the romance-terror web of the Vietcong. One must respect the imagination that created this invisible government. Born of hate of French dominion, it has created a moral imperative: that whoever takes the hand of the white man in friendship is traitor to his own people. To this it has added a supreme triumph of organization: the ability to find, train and elevate from the drowsy villages a native leadership which, over 20 years, has given scores of thousands of once uneducated peasants access to careers, dignity and status. All of this is capped by a final discipline of terror which, in the areas of its reach, denies any other leadership the opportunity to offer people a rival choice. Over the past seven years, this unrelenting terror has exterminated 12,000 civilians—more than have been killed in the bombings of Hanoi.

During the past two years, our forces have ground down the military arm of this invisible government until today no major formation of enemy dares face us in the field by day in any corner of the country. But the environment of romance and terror persists; it shelters the hidden dispersion of their troops everywhere; by night in thousands of hamlets it punishes any who openly or quietly reject their message. The Vietcong, in ultimate analysis, is the first native institution created and shaped by Vietnamese themselves in this century. We cannot match their knowledge of their country; only a rival native institution can do this.

It is with this that American policy reaches the limits of its power. Progress, in American terms, has been spectacular—enemy killed, bases built, roads cleared, tonnages delivered. American generals debate whether any more troops would be useful; Westmoreland says yes, and makes a convincing case; other generals say they literally have run out of stand-up targets. Yet we all agree that never has any army performed better in the field than the American forces in Vietnam. All that valor and technique can offer is being delivered. Our troops can move anywhere, occupy just about any place. We can do almost anything we want in this country—except govern.

American policy thus faces two choices: either to adopt a policy of extermination, the classic way of ending guerrilla wars; or to invite into being a native counterforce to isolate the enemy from the people. And, since extermination has been decisively rejected, the American effort today is pinned to the great adventure of fostering a political alternative to the Vietcong: a new government to offer peasants in their villages the sense of a secure tomorrow, free of terror and corruption. All that America can do to bring food, shelter and hope, schools and medicine, cement and roads to the myriad hamlets is being accomplished. The machinery of progress is being installed; yet it still lacks the spark of ignition to set it in motion.

The spark must come from Vietnamese themselves. And it is thus one must see the elections of next week—a first awkward step of a people struggling to find national leaders who will offer an alternative between slavery to white men and Communism.

Nothing could be more preposterous than to apply American standards to this election. An election involving millions of illiterate peasants who vote by symbols, a handful of intellectuals who know politics from reading Plato's *Republic* in French, and a tough-nut army officer corps must produce strange sights. Sound trucks blare in Saigon, slogans stream out. Programs occupy full pages in newspapers promising heaven and hereafter immediately: peace, social security, old-age pensions, land reform, medicare, urban renewal, education and science for all—visions which the economy of this racked land cannot achieve for generations. A comic-opera quality coats the touring carnival of candidates—all candidates must travel together in the same government-provided plane, addressing the same rallies rounded up for them by military officials awkwardly trying to reproduce a facsimile of American practice.

Yet to dismiss the procedure as nonsense is to misread history. The most important and encouraging facts are simple: vitality and courage. The contending candidates for the senate have exposed themselves to Vietcong assassination. Intellectuals who months ago regarded the enterprise as farce are scrabbling, dealing, fighting for their candidacies as if life depended on it. The air is full of anticipatory charges of coercion, crookedness and corruption; but what is offered in these elections is recognized by all as real: a chance to run their own country.

Both the venom and the rhetoric of the campaign are creating a consensus, an expression of national will. All candidates use some variation of the phrase "social justice" to describe their program and no speech, by any candidate, is complete without a denunciation of corruption. Corruption in this country is total—it runs from the cop who collects 100 piasters to let a taxi enter the Saigon airport, to the field police who take a slice of peasant produce on the way to city market, to the district chief who takes a slice of American cement and food intended for peasants, to the topmost ministers themselves. I spent a day touring with Premier, now vice presidential candidate, Nguyen Cao Ky, whose fragile regime has presided over such corruption. He could not act, he explained, until now—but the elections would provide a legal basis for government, and with legitimacy would come action. "Corruption starts at the top," he said, "not the bottom. Now we have no legal basis for getting rid of corrupt officials: they all claim political support. But if we win support direct from the people, we can act against any of them"—and he made a chopping motion with his hand.

Equally encouraging is the attitude of the American Embassy. Every pressure, every warning the Embassy can exert to keep these elections honest and minimally decent is being exerted. The temptation for Americans to intervene is enormous and the invitation comes most warmly from the thin layer of Vietnamese intellectuals themselves. We are the power here. Why, they ask, do we not use it to elect a civilian president? The campaign manager of one of the leading civilian candidates, a man of great dignity and education wanted a message carried to Ellsworth Bunker, our ambassador, and said to me: "Tell Bunker secretly I will do whatever he wants. I will switch to any candidate the Embassy wants me to support." To which the only reply that could be made was: categorically, publicly and privately the American Embassy supports no one—a puppet state is to us useless. Our Embassy wants any government any president, who can wean romantics from the V.C., free the peasants from terror, give them a sense of confidence in leadership—and give us a legitimacy to defend. For better or worse, all our might is pawn to what comes of these elections.

THE RANGE OF choice this election offers is limited. There is the military ticket—and then come all the others. Generals Nguyen Van Thieu and Nguyen Cao Ky are the uneasy partners who head the military ticket—and both only four years ago were junior colonels, chart flippers and table setters for their seniors. Of the pair, Thieu, at 44, is far more impressive. A rather large head surmounts his diminutive body; the forehead is broad, the eyes usually sad, pouched with weariness. When he speaks, in excellent English, it is slowly, gravely, thoughtfully, with strangely convincing sincerity. Ky is totally different—flamboyant, dapper, lavender-scarved, bepistoled, yellow-gloved. Although Ky makes sense in private conversation, a public audience or press conference is to him what catnip is to a cat—his snappy wisecracks, outrageous rejoinders, public contempt of the civilian opposition remind one all too much of dragon lady Madame Nhu of the ill-fated Diem regime.

Both generals are untutored in history or government except for what the last two years of responsibility have taught them. Thieu, now a converted Catholic, comes of a Confucian mandarin family, finished junior high school, then entered a French military academy. Ky, whose father was a primary school teacher, flunked out of high school, then was trained by the French as a military pilot. Their regime today rests on a skeleton of perhaps 500 or 600 young officers, like themselves equally untutored in politics, and an inner group of military cronies who hold the key ministries. This inner group ranges from the distinguished Nguyen Duc Thang, a university student of mathematics and the head of revolutionary development, to Nguyen Ngoc Loan, head of the secret police. Both

Thang and Loan are cadet classmates of Ky (as is the incompetent minister of information, Hguyen Bac Tri). But whereas the robust, outgoing Thang is the most admired and idealistic man in Vietnamese politics, the slovenly, unkempt Loan is the most despised man in Saigon. Whether personally corrupt or not, he heads what is considered the most corrupt organization in government and is the person most loathed by civilians. The relative fortunes of Thang and Loan, if the Thieu-Ky ticket wins the election, will be one of the clearest indexes to the future.

It would be unfair to dismiss the military ticket as unfit because of their uniforms. Years of war against Communism have taught them an inescapable lesson: unless they get the people actively with them, then they are doomed. Said Thieu sadly, one afternoon after a campaign trip, "To pacify this country by military we need two million troops to occupy the villages. What must happen is they should have confidence in government. They must trust us. After elections we must act so quickly against corruption that people will know we govern *for* them." One cannot help but be attracted by Thieu. He reminds one of the best and most devoted officers of Chiang Kai-shek's Kuomintang. There is little question of his good intent—only of what he can deliver if elected.

Of the 10 civilian candidates, Mr. Tran Van Huong is commonly considered the chief contender, and so one calls on him. One finds a gentle old man of 63, round tummy protruding, iron-gray hair close-cropped, his bare toes wriggling in his sandals. His supporters have found him a little walkup apartment on a trash-littered street. Wet wash hangs from the lines in the courtyard, refuse is piled there. His poverty advertises itself. Once a primary school inspector, his gallant opposition to the hated French is a matter of record. Briefly, under the Diem regime, Huong was called to be mayor of Saigon, then resigned in a demonstration of stubborn integrity, later was reduced to earning a living as clerk-typist for the Dentists' Association. His supporters—mostly schoolteachers and university people— seem slowly to be building strength. After a long conversation with him about his program and platform one gets to the final question—if elected, how would he go about purging corruption and helping the peasants? He replies saying he is afraid—not of Vietcong assassins or of the military opposition, but simply of the job itself. Could any man, he asks, be adequate to clean up the stink of corruption, the gangrene of Saigon? One notices that the old man is softly weeping—as only a decent old man can weep.

Thus one asks; if I were a Vietnamese would I vote for this soft and lovable old man to govern so cruel a country? Or for tough and battle-hardened military men?

ONLY AFTER the elections will Americans be able to judge whether we are approaching the end of the beginning. Not only is the presidential slate being elected, but also a senatorial slate to balance the executive. And the overall quality of senatorial candidates is far more promising than the executive candidates. An experiment in leadership is taking place, and on this experiment rests all America's commitment. For whatever comes of these elections, the next phase in this agony requires that the Vietnamese themselves assume responsibility. Our arms and presence have slowly ground the enemy down from mortal military threat to morbid political epidemic. To deal with this political epidemic, only Vietnamese can act.

Any visitor to Saigon can find solid portents to read the future either with gloom or hope. If another coup replaces a civilian government, or if no action is taken by the new government against the structure of corruption, or if no link is made by the new government with the emotions of the peasants, we can do little more. American arms, valor, money, goodwill have carried our adventure as far as it will go. If the victors in this election make a farce of their victory, it will be time to rethink our commitment.

Yet one must underline the fact that the dominant sentiment here among most pragmatic and hardheaded Americans is one of cautious hope: hope that the election itself has indeed involved enough Vietnamese to think about their own future: hope that the coarse and awkward procedures of electioneering will meet those minimum standards of decency and honesty to give a crude expression of national will; hope that whatever leaders are elected have learned enough from peril to get through to the people.

Several snatches of conversation linger after a month's visit to this country. An American officer said to me, "The only immorality is to kid ourselves. If there's no light at the end of the tunnel, it's up to *us* to say so. But if there is light at the other end of the tunnel, we have to stay." A State Department officer said, "It's not more troops, or more money, or more supplies we need—it's more time. It takes nine months to make a baby; it takes longer to make a nation."

What follows in the next three or four months, therefore, becomes first-act curtain. A respectable new government may be able to open direct talks with Hanoi. Or Hanoi may accept our offer and negotiate. Both possibilities at the moment seem unlikely and thus the best that can be hoped for is that the new government will provide the first relatively solid political base from which to conduct the struggle, whether it be three, four or five years more. Only if this new government demonstrates that capacity will the American people next year in *their* election face the hardest question of all—whether they want to stay the course for what may become the longest war in American history.

LIFE September 1, 1967

Chapter 16

One Shot: Japan

Watching at close hand the Japanese pillage of China and East Asia during World War II left White with a lifelong mistrust of that nation. And, with one exception,* until very late in life he chose not to write about Japan. Privately, however, he fretted about Japan's economic "miracle," which seemed to him to come increasingly—and unfairly—at the expense of the United States. Finally, in 1985, he decided to speak out. His highly opinionated article, which follows, argues with gusto that Japan's manipulative business practices are nothing less than a weapon of war.

*In 1970 he recalled for *The Atlantic* the 1945 Japanese surrender to MacArthur in Tokyo Bay, which he had witnessed. Excellently written, it is, however, purely a reminiscence after twenty-five years; its essence is included, indeed expanded upon, herein.

THE DANGER FROM JAPAN

Today, 40 years after the end of World War II, the Japanese are on the move again in one of history's most brilliant commercial offensives, as they go about dismantling American industry. Whether they are still only smart, or have finally learned to be wiser than we, will be tested in the next ten years. Only then will we know who finally won the war.

No sense of irony stained the spectacle of victory about the U.S.S. Missouri, no sense of shadows to rise years later.

We were all too bedazzled by the splendor of the day—for here was American power at its zenith. We had won the war, totally, and the men who had won it, soon to become legend, were all there on the veranda deck in pressed suntans or navy whites. A band had been swinging through "Anchors Aweigh" as we gathered that morning, but as the climax approached a hush fell; silence stretched like a blanket over our murmurings.

None of us of course knew what America would make of the victory, or the Japanese of their defeat. But the power was all ours and stretched, visibly, as far as the eye could see. The Third Fleet had come in from offshore and now crowded Tokyo Bay—flattops and battleships, cruisers and destroyers, guns trained on the land we had laid waste. There was no question but that we had won this war.

It was Sunday, Sept. 2, 1945, there on the other side of the dateline, and the skies, after a Saturday drizzle, stretched gray. But this was no guarded and hid-den schoolhouse, with only a handful present to watch, as at the surrender of German forces only four months earlier at Rheims. Douglas MacArthur's sense of drama insisted that all the world be there to witness, and we were several hundreds thick on the foredeck.

The Missouri had been swept clean. The Stars and Stripes above the main-mast was the same that had fluttered over the Capitol on the day Japan attacked Pearl Harbor; it had just been flown out from Washington. The flag of Commodore Perry, who had pried Japan open to the West 90 years before, was draped on the rear turret, with the 31 stars of the then half-grown union faded but clear. And on each of the three 16-inch guns clung our sailors in white, holding on by a handgrip, or with their legs curled tight about the barrels.

Just in front of the turret was the sur-render table, draped in a navy-blue cov-erlet, bare but for the documents. There the Japanese would sign. A few minutes before the appointed hour we heard the piping that announced the launch car-rying the Japanese was alongside. We watched them come aboard: Mamoru Shigemitsu, the Japanese Foreign Minister, in morning coat and striped trousers; Gen. Yoshijiro Umezu, Chief of Staff of the army, in his starched brown uniform. Shigemitsu limped, for he had been crippled years before by Japanese terrorists who had tried to kill him, considering him a man of peace. But that brought him no sympathy from us now as he grasped the rail to pull himself up, then limped to the table of surrender.

I bristled at the sight of them. I had seen the Japanese blast and flame Chungqing, the city I had lived in years before, then bring their planes down to machine-gun people in the streets. Japanese had shot at me, I had fired at them, and so the luxury of this moment was one I enjoyed. Others, too, hated the Japanese—perhaps all except Douglas MacArthur, who saw them as he saw all Orientals, as errant little brown brothers who must be rebuked, but then brought into Western civilization. Yet that day he was taskmaster and conqueror.

A few minutes after 9, General MacArthur himself appeared, and the Japanese came forward. No one helped Shigemitsu, but some Americans more generous than I brought him a chair to sit on as he signed the surrender. Next came Umezu, the brown pock marks on his cheeks swelling and falling as he clenched his jaws. He wanted no chair; he stood stiffly, unfolded like a jackknife, then bent and signed the paper. Neither said anything. Then MacArthur spoke, for peace and conciliation—rather well, I think now as I read his text 40 years later. Then all the others signed. I notice, as I follow the notes I made on my copy of the text, that when the Dutch representative signed, the sun broke through the clouded morning, and the scene began to glisten.

At this point happened the episode that stands out sharpest among the memories of that day—the flyover. As MacArthur intoned "These proceedings are closed," we heard a drone and looked up. It is difficult to recall now, after years of floundering and blunder, how very good we were in those days, with what precision we ordered things. Four hundred B-29s had taken off from Guam and Saipan hours before to arrive over the Missouri at this precise minute of climax. They stretched across the rim of the horizon, and their heavy droning almost instantly harmonized with a softer buzzing as 1,500 fleet aircraft from our flattops joined them. The B-29s had burned out Japan's cities, dropped the two big bombs; the fleet aircraft had sunk the Japanese Navy. Now the killing arms of our power, the air forces, slid down from their height in the sky to circle low over the armada of American ships. Then, still very low, they disappeared across the sky, over two cities they had left in ruins, first Yokohama, then Tokyo, as if brandishing our power over the people who had dared, without warrant and with planned deceit, to attack and bloody us at Pearl Harbor.

We had won out over them. We lost more than 100,000 men to prove we could not be lacerated without warning, without seeking revenge.

Except that America's revenge on Japan was of such an extraordinary character as to befuddle all scholars who claim that history has a logic of its own. What we are faced with now is the idea that events contradict history's logic. Perhaps we did not win the war, perhaps the Japanese, unknown even to themselves, are the winners.

IT HAD TAKEN us years to get to Tokyo Bay. But that story had begun with an idea, as all wars do.

As a very young reporter, I had gone to Asia, and there became acquainted with the crowning Japanese idea: "The Greater East Asia Co-Prosperity Sphere." The slogan was scrawled across the walls of all the regions I visited, from Manchukuo to North China, down finally to Hanoi in 1940, when the Japanese took over Vietnam. And they meant to go further: to Thailand (with its tin), Malaya (rubber), Indonesia (oil and timber). The Japanese idea was simple: that Japan was the leader of East Asia, and so it should harness Asia, with its resources, its genius of mind, its hundreds of millions of people, and all would grow prosperous—Japan most of all.

But the Chinese, both Nationalist and Communist, had resisted. And, as the Japanese did their best to beat the Chinese into submission, America said: No. Franklin Roosevelt imposed his embargo on Japanese trade—no scrap metal, no oil, nothing that would help Japan pursue its purpose of conquest. The noose had thus tightened about Japan in 1941, whereupon they attacked us and hoped, having hurt us, that we would negotiate on their terms. Tactically, the attack on Pearl Harbor was one of the most brilliantly executed strokes of the war. But politically, it was most unwise, for America fought back.

Today, 40 years after the end of World War II, the Japanese are on the move again in one of history's most brilliant commercial offensives, as they go about dismantling American industry. Whether they are still only smart, or have finally learned to be wiser than we, will be tested in the next 10 years. Only then will we know who finally won the war 50 years before.

So we must go back to Japan at that weekend of surrender and see what we made of it.

The eye recalls almost nothing sharp of those first three days. Both Tokyo and Yokohama were wasteland. Here and there was a speckle of corrugated iron shacks where the bombed-out victims of our raids lived. Spikes of smokestacks rose above rubble. In the streets trudged the Japanese—forlorn and shabby. Along the country roads trickled the first of their demobilized soldiers, their belongings slung over their shoulders. All of Japan was open to us, except for the Emperor's palace in Tokyo, behind its moat and earthen walls. The 11th Airborne Division had arrived to protect him from all intruders—Americans and Japanese alike.

A few days before we entered Japan, an intelligence officer had briefed a few of us correspondents on how delicate that mission would be; Japan was still fully armed, with 57 divisions in the home islands. Some units were violent. There had already been one assault on the Emperor's palace in the days since he had radioed his submission to us; it had been beaten off. The Emperor was our key. "In essence," concluded the officer, "we've achieved a coup d'état. Our coup has been to take the Emperor. We've given him the widest latitude in telling his people how to take defeat. But, when they learn he takes orders from us, that we're using him to restore order, there's no telling how the mechanism will react."

So, when we flew in on Friday, Aug. 31, before the surrender, the soldiers in my plane were taking apart, fingering, reassembling their guns as soldiers always do before assault, ready to shoot if this surrender was a trap.

But it was no trap; the Japanese *had* surrendered; the Emperor had defused the Japanese war machine, still capable of one last explosive bloodletting. The airfield perimeter had been guarded immediately by the 11th Airborne. The Japanese had not only obeyed our orders to remove all propellers from their planes at Atsugi Airfield, our point of descent, but the planes themselves had been bulldozed into a junkheap at the far corner.

That first weekend of reconnaissance and tingling fear we roamed the streets of Yokohama with strut and swagger. We took over the new Grand Hotel on the Bund—just up the street from the offices of the House of Mitsui. So I strolled down to visit it.

The House of Mitsui was one of the grand *zaibatsu,* those great Japanese merchant trading houses that we meant to abolish but did not. I walked in with Jim Stewart of the Office of War Information, who spoke fluent Japanese, and we were ushered into an executive's suite.

His face I have forgotten; in my notes his name reads simply "Fujiro," and he spoke fine English. When he understood that we had come not to arrest him but to talk, he relaxed. I wanted to pick up the threads of the story of defeat and surrender.

Fujiro told it well: It had been four months since the last ocean-going vessel of Japan's far-flung merchant marine had made it safely back to Yokohama, Japan's largest port. It had been more than a year since Kawasaki, the nation's oil port, had received a tanker from the East Indies. Yokohama was prostrate, he said. He guessed that 200,000 people had been killed in our bombings and 700,000 had fled.

But the Americans were not hated, he assured us. The people hated their army. "Why no planes, no guns to defend us?" He spat out names like Tojo, Oshima, Shiratori. The people expected them to be executed. People hated the United States bombers, but the first Americans to land were well-behaved. Jim Stewart remarked that, unlike the Japanese, American soldiers did not rape. Fujiro acknowledged this.

Then to his plea. Hunger. Food. Let Japan work to support herself. Japan could still make ships—"let us make ships to earn our way." Some textile mills remained; the Japanese could still make cloth to earn a living. But Japan needed food most of all—one-third of all its food in the closing days of the war had come out of China. Japan could sell us tea and silk, but it needed food.

What were the plans now of the House of Mitsui? we asked. He replied: "Frankly, gentlemen, until your military tells us what to do, we have no plans." Before we left, he poured us a toast: "To your safe arrival!" We drank, the House of Mitsui bowed as if we were not only liberators but allies.

These days, the House of Mitsui is thriving again, its trading net spread from steel mills in China to refineries in Iran to operations in America—the whole world has become its "Greater Co-Prosperity Sphere."

FOOD, THEN, that weekend and that month was of the essence.

There is a strange and wonderful thing about Americans, of which I am proud. In war we bomb, we kill, occasionally our solders are savage, too—although when an American officer goes berserk, we try him in our own military courts, as we did Lieut. William Calley for the massacre at Mylai. But Americans abhor starvation, and they are very good at organizing to help all starving people—defeated Germans, defeated Japanese, Ethiopians subject to Marxism.

So, in the first few days of occupation, our rage evaporated in the task immediately at hand: to feed the Japanese people we had conquered.

What MacArthur was up against

were the essentials that geography forces on anyone who governs Japan. Japan is a nation of four rocky islands—with a combined area that is smaller than California. Seventy-two percent of the land is mountain and rock, useless for anything but tourism and scenery. Only 16 percent is tillable. When, a century ago, the Japanese were a nation of 30 million people, they could barely feed themselves and infanticide was a common practice. Their internal history has thus been scorched with savage civil wars. Then, when Japan was opened, the coiled aggressions so long turned against each other turned against their neighbors—China first, then the Russians, then Korea.

But the Japanese add to their poverty of physical resources two extravagantly useful conditions. They have, first, a sharply indented coastline, with natural ports inviting deep water to their shore. England has the same advantage, which once gave that nation, and now gives Japan, access to all the world's resources of ore, oil, foods, timber; by cheap shipping, Japanese can draw raw materials from anywhere and can send competitive manufacturers anywhere, too.

To this gift of geography is added a gift of genetics, a striking quality of mind. We often think of the Japanese as less than innovative but, technically, they are superb adapters and producers. We learned that in the war against them: their torpedoes were better and faster than ours . . . until we learned to make ours better. Their initial combat plane—the Zero—was a superlative machine; it could turn, dart, wheel away and mock American flying machines. No matter that Americans had invented the airplane and the flattop; when the war started, Japan had in several arms superior, if derivative, technology. What licked them was American bravery, the mobilization of then-superior American science and industry, and their own blundering politics that led them to challenge us.

Whether Americans made an equal blunder in entering Asia in 1945 is something historians will debate for decades to come. But if we *did* blunder in that fall season of 1945, the blunder stemmed from mercy and generosity. Both mercy and generosity proposed a peace the like of which had never been granted before to any conquered nation—except, perhaps, the Germany defeated only months before.

Our first challenge in those early weeks was, of course, the simple mechanics of occupation. But then we faced the problem of how to govern the now-abject nation—above all, how to feed it. Japan's hospitals were full of the diseases of malnutrition. MacArthur ordered at once that our occupying forces distribute their rations to Japanese civilians from Army kitchens. He then ordered that all the 3½ million tons of food stockpiled for our own armies for the projected landings of October and November be rushed in. Yet still there was not enough. He himself described it best in a cable to the War Department in the spring of 1946—a spring of imminent starvation. We must either feed the Japanese or starve them, he wrote, and then we must face the conse-

quences. "Starvation breeds mass unrest, disorder, violence. Give me bread or give me bullets," he finished in the grandiloquent MacArthurian flourish.

The next paragraph of MacArthur's reminiscences is a single sentence: "I got bread."

MacArthur had, almost immediately after moving his headquarters from Yokohama to Tokyo, set about creating a new Japan. Of the Emperor, he demanded that a new prime minister be immediately named. By October, the Emperor had replaced his uncle, the nominal prime minister at the time of surrender, with Baron Shidehara, to whom, on his first visit, MacArthur explained America's wishes for the new Japan.

MacArthur's directives were cut from the cloth of American good will. Japan (so ran his first directive) must completely emancipate Japanese women; must let workers organize in unions; ban abuse of child labor; abolish secret police. Further, Japan must reorganize its education system and "democratize" its industrial system. He left it to Shidehara to work out the details.

It was this broad grant of latitude that was most important. The Japanese could pick and chose their way through MacArthur's directives. The way they chose to implement them allowed their industry, their universities, their ingenuity to flourish. And the rebirth of Japan since its defeat is a parable of history. If one speeds up the interaction of ideas and drive, it becomes a drama.

IT IS IMPOSSIBLE to blame the Japanese for accepting American mercy and the MacArthur invitation to thrive. Neither Congress nor the United States War Department wanted to feed Japan indefinitely or pay for its recovery. It was up to the Japanese to work their own way back, to remove themselves from the backs of the American taxpayer.

A young lieutenant with the 27th Infantry Division was among the first to land in that week after the surrender; his company had fought in the battle of Okinawa; it had entered with 180 men and come out with only 20. That young combat lieutenant, Malcolm Baldrige, is now Secretary of Commerce, and he recalls the desolation in Japan. "We sent them," he recalls now, "blood-fractionating technology on humanitarian grounds. Today the company we gave the technology to competes with Americans around the world. We sent them technicians from the Underwriters Laboratory to certify that Japanese products were up to American standards, fit for export. Today U.S. companies fight to get their exports certified for entry into Japan." Baldrige is both wise and somber. The Japanese, as Government policy, are undermining one American industry after another. But Baldrige, as a senior Administration official, must restrain his forebodings in public.

To understand his bitterness one must again go back to the story of governing ideas. Early in 1947, as Japan was thawing from defeat, we sponsored something called GATT—the General Agreement on Tariffs and Trade, with headquarters in Geneva. GATT embodied an idea almost two centuries old, the idea of Adam Smith. Smith believed that history moves in stages, and, because he lived at the dawn of the Industrial Revolution, he denounced the outworn ideas of mercantilism—the world stage was now set for "free trade." An "invisible hand," Smith held, should and would shape the flow of goods from one nation to another, wherever "comparative advantage" in production would draw wares from one country to another.

By the mid-1940s, American thinking had made a holy cause of "free trade." Our conventional analysis of the Second World War held that both Hitler and the Japanese had violated the theology of "free trade," staking out spheres of economic dominance with bayonets, thus bringing war. Now, however, in 1947, GATT would enforce free trade in all the non-Marxist world, eliminating tariffs and barriers, and allowing goods to flow freely from country to country. We were at our peak in the history of commerce. Thus—onward and upward to the sunlit plateau of world prosperity and peace.

For the Japanese it must have seemed too good to be true, and it took them several years to learn that the Americans had rewarded them with a world market far larger than the Great East Asia Co-Prosperity Sphere. The Americans had given them an invitation to the world trading game in total ignorance of what Japanese genius and tactics might accomplish. As late as 1954, a haze of victory still clouded American thinking. Said John Foster Dulles, Secretary of State, at a National Security Council meeting in August of that year, I "told Premier Yoshida frankly that Japan should not expect to find a big American market because the Japanese don't make the things we want. Japan must find markets elsewhere for the goods they export." It would be at least 30 years before history proved Dulles wrong, before our trade deficit with Japan grew to the thunderhead of an estimated $45 billion for 1985.

There were, of course, several things wrong with the ideas that begot GATT. First was the belief that all the world would behave by the rules codified by GATT. We could not entertain the idea that some nations would race, like broken-field runners, through the new rules of tariffs and trade; that GATT would be riddled and pockholed by subsidies, regulations, quotas and barriers that made mockery of the idea of free trade.

But the more important thing that went wrong with GATT was almost too simple to consider. If all people of the world were entitled to equally free trade, then the cheapest producer would be those who paid their people least, yet mastered worldclass technology. In other words, nations whose workers were grateful for starvation wages could conquer the markets of countries like America, whose workers demanded the world's highest wages. The only way thus to compete was by efficiencies of production, in which the Japanese steadily strove to match the

Americans, or by wage standards with which American workers could not compete, or both. Asian standards of living would have to go up or our standards would go down until an equilibrium would be reached.

In the 40 years since defeat, Japan has grown to be a giant. Japan has passed the Soviet Union in industrial production and stands as world class No. 2 to our No. 1. If the present Japanese expansion of production continues, it will be, in 20 years, a greater industrial power than the United States.

WHEN THE Japanese looked out from their world of ruins in the months after defeat, disaster drew self-examination as tight as skin about every individual as well as the community. "Japan was smashed," says one American industrialist. "Its industry was shattered or obsolete. Every institution had failed them . . . There was no leadership, no model for creating a new Japan except that which America forced on it." So MacArthur and his staff became the leadership, America the model.

What the Japanese have done since in remodeling the American model is no less than spectacular. They have devised a system of government-industry partnership that is a paradigm for directing a modern industrial state for national purposes—and one designed for action in the new world of global commerce that the United States blueprinted.

The Japanese have a tangled bureaucracy that baffles foreign intruders, but one must recognize at least the two main players in the game to understand the dynamics of the Japanese trade thrust.

The Ministry of Finance comes first. In the words of one American Ambassador to Japan, "it has the ultimate call." Its policies set the exchange rate of the yen, keeping the currency undervalued in order to keep export prices low. It stimulates savings and investment, finances industry by directing the allocation of funds through the banks it controls. The Ministry of Finance provides the launching pad from which MITI directs the guided missiles of the trade offensive.

MITI—the Ministry of International Trade and Industry, the second major player in the game—is a totally new Japanese invention. MITI targets those Japanese industries that are to grow, targets the countries and markets to be penetrated. It can adjust depreciation rates for favored industries; coordinate research into arcane technologies—for example, into the fifth generation of computers. (Its only American rival in such research is the Pentagon, which can afford to match Japan Incorporated's budget.)

Sometimes MITI makes mistakes— as in the overbuilding of the Japanese steel and shipbuilding industries, now in surplus capacity because of competition from South Korea. More often it is wise enough to put to sleep industries that can no longer compete. The island of Kyushu once employed 200,000 coal miners; only 7,000 remain there because oil and coal come cheaper from abroad—and so Kyushu has become a

thriving center for electronics. MITI defines strategies; Japanese private enterprise follows through with zest. No better marriage of government planning and private enterprise has ever been seen.

The Japanese have caught the essence of Adam Smith—that history moves through its stages as opportunity and technology beckon. Nor is it alone in seeing the perspectives of the world America fostered. Although Jean Monnet designed Europe's Common Market, America was its godfather. Europe also presses to orient its industries to national purpose. West Germany, Europe's foremost industrial power, presses hardest. But the Germans expend much of their energies within the Common Market we sought to build. In American commerce, trade with West Germany is large, yet marginal. In 1971, when America first fell into the trade deficit that forced us off the gold standard, Germans exported $3.7 billion worth of goods to America, Japan $5.9 billion. Last year, the Germans shipped $16.9 billion—but the Japanese shipped $60.4 billion. The Germans, somehow, evoke little American bitterness because we understand their culture, establish American plants there without hindrance. The Japanese provoke American wrath because they are a locked and closed civilization that reciprocates our hushed fear with veiled contempt.

Few American businessmen abroad would qualify as Knights of the Round Table. American oil companies once, in the prime of their power, could make and unmake governments. But many American business have been welcomed overseas, if only because they usually pay higher wages than competitors. Most of all, they have been restrained by American antitrust laws from the kind of nationally coordinated trade offensive captained by MITI against all other countries.

American industry grew up in partnership with European industry. But Japan rouses different fears. Behind Japan ("the Big Dragon," some call it) march the "four little dragons" (Korea, Hong Kong, Taiwan, Singapore) following in its path. And behind loom China and India, desperate as they are to raise their standards of living—at the expense of American standards, if necessary.

THE JAPANESE are far ahead in the race for world trade markets, and they are moving now to yet another stage. Their export surplus gives them huge sums to invest—in the Middle East and America—so that Japanese capital is moving from penetration to control. Japanese are beginning to supply venture capital for the seedbeds of American technology, from Silicon Valley in California to Route 128 in Boston. They hover over the Draper Laboratories in Massachusetts—the national laboratories that devise the guidance system of our missiles—and acquire what patents security lets free to the public. In the Los Angeles area alone, the Japanese have installed or acquired 1,500 firms. Their acquisitions in our banking system have grown signifi-

cantly; contrariwise, Americans are all but excluded from Japanese capital markets. And, by the doctrine of GATT, all this is entirely legal.

Yet what is legal may also be unfair. While Japan's tariff rates are, in broad economic terms, roughly equal to those of other industrial nations, they are spiked with special tariffs in industries that are considered vulnerable to foreign competition. In addition, Japanese markets are protected by a maze of so-called nontariff barriers to trade—many of which fall outside the reach of GATT regulations. We cannot sell our exports freely in Japan, whether beef, tobacco, citrus fruits, or leather goods. Consumer markets, too, are closed by regulations that the Japanese attribute to "cultural differences."

What Japan does import from us are, chiefly, those raw materials always taken by master nations from colonial nations—grain, cotton, ores, fuel. We still ship to Japan a few remaining high technology items, like aircraft, and some telecommunications and high-powered computers in which we hold a narrowing lead. But the Japanese continue to squeeze that lead, because their infant-industry-protection laws are planned to give them time to catch up. They will not buy American satellites until they learn to make their own. Corning Glass Works has had a fiber-optics patent pending in Japan for 12 years; in this time, the Japanese have learned to make fiber optics of their own that they now sell in America. Crude oil may be sold to Japan; but the Japanese will not buy our refined oil. American products certified here must go through slow, tedious re-testing in Japan before entering the Japanese market, while Japanese technology catches up.

American markets for Japanese goods are not only open but come with an invitation. The United States Census makes its marketing information open to all; for a fee anyone can buy its tapes that define, area by area, country by country, income group by income group, where Toyota, Sony, Hitachi, Honda can best space their distributorships; and American advertising agencies will, for a fee, translate consumer appetite into market conquest. No nation that thinks of itself as an assembly of consumers can resist Japanese penetration. But a nation that thinks of itself as a community has reason for alarm.

Today not a single consumer radio is made in America, although Americans invented the modern radio; not a single black-and-white television set is made here, although America invented television. The few companies that assemble color television sets in the United States could not exist without import parts made in Asia, although color television was originally developed in America. Almost all our videocassette recorders are made in Japan; so are most hand-held calculators, watches, a huge share of our office machinery, and most high-fidelity audio equipment. Only one American motorcycle manufacturer remains (Harley-Davidson); the Japanese hold 95 percent of our market. Only one American piano manufacturer remains (Steinway).

The Brooklyn Navy Yard, where the conquering U.S.S. Missouri was launched in 1943, no longer exists.

The American automobile and steel industries were the first to be hit by Japan's trade offensive—they were vulnerable. Emerging from the war fat, stuffy and complacent, content largely with obsolescent equipment and practices, shortsighted American management let its technologies fall well behind those developing elsewhere. In 1966, the Japanese shipped only 63,000 automobiles to America; by 1970, MITI had stimulated the shipment of 415,000. Americans found Japanese cars to be good cars; they consumed little gasoline, they were cheaper; their fit-and-finish were splendid, and with the rise in gasoline prices, the American appetite for Japanese automobiles soared. But when the Reagan Administration this spring released Japan from negotiated voluntary quotas on car exports to the United States, Japan announced that it would raise its shipments to 2.3 million autos to America, as if we were a controlled colonial market. It was too much. By a vote of 92 to 0, the Senate declared Japanese trade practice unfair. But it was a belated revolt; this summer, American consumers are gobbling up Japanese automobiles faster than the Japanese can gear up to ship them.

This year, apparently, MITI's chief target is the American electronic industry. Last year, the trade deficit with Japan in electronics surpassed our trade deficit in automobiles—reaching $15.4 billion of our total adverse balance with

Japan of $37 billion. The American semiconductor industry is reeling from assault. The Japanese, without mercy, propose to wipe out our supremacy in this industry, based on our own research and invention. Hitachi, now an electronics exporter, was blasted to bits by our bombers in the last two weeks of the war as one of the leading Japanese arms-makers. But Hitachi is now on the counterattack, its tone martial again. Here, for example, is Hitachi's directive this year to its offices in Denver, where it is trying to take away the semiconductor market from America's Intel Corporation and Advanced Micro Devices. It reads: "Win with the 10 percent rule! Find AMD and Intel sockets. Quote 10 percent below their prices! If they requote, go 10 percent again. Don't quit till you win!"

A BENIGN PROSPERITY temporarily soothes the American economy. In the six years since 1979, America has added 6,000,000 jobs to its total work force. But these are mostly service jobs. In the skill-and-brawn base of American production, not only have real wages fallen, but the job base is shriveling. In machinery production, in these six years, the United States has lost 288,000 jobs; in primary metal-making (such as steel) we have lost 439,000 jobs; in fabricated metals, 241,000 jobs; in motor-vehicle production, 118,000 jobs; in textiles, 186,000 jobs. All in all, on the line, in the old shops, where Americans make things, we have lost 1,834,000 jobs.

No industry in America has been harder hit by Asian competition than the American garment industry, which has lost 155,000 jobs in the last six years alone. One should listen to Sol Chaikin, an air corps veteran of the China war theater against Japan.

Chaikin is now the president of the International Ladies Garment Workers Union. Once, in the early 1950s, his union counted 230,000 workers in New York City alone. Today he counts only 100,000 and they work at the lowest-paid union jobs in the city.

"Ours," says Chaikin, "is the most competitive industry in America. It's a cheap industry to get into and we have 15,000 ladies-garment manufacturers in the U.S.A. They all have the most modern machinery, but the Asians have the same machinery and they work for less and for longer hours. The Japanese once were our chief competitors, but Japanese wage rates have now risen to levels comparable to ours. The Japanese now buy American designs, open factories with new machinery in Singapore and Hong Kong, ship the fabrics from Japan, and export from offshore. In Korea and Taiwan, they pay 57 cents an hour; in Hong Kong, $1.08 an hour; and in Sri Lanka they pay $5.00 a week. In New York, our workers get only $175.00 a week take-home pay—and they pay almost $1 for a subway fare each way."

Chaikin knows that his workers in New York cannot compete with Asian standards of living. "It's as if we were being poured into a Mixmaster with China, India, Japan, Taiwan; they've homogenized the international labor market and are squeezing us out like toothpaste." Chaikin insists that some garment jobs, at least, must be preserved for American working people, that the American market should be shared with Americans. But there is no high-technology ladder to leap over cheap Asian wages when it comes to handwork. Of blue-collar jobs in America, one in seven is held by a textile-garment-apparel worker. The National Academy of Engineering estimated in 1983 that, of 2,000,000 jobs in the garment-textile industry, only 750,000 would be left in 10 years. Chaikin's back is up against the wall.

Less than a mile from Chaikin's union headquarters is the elegant executive suite of the Radio Corporation of America. Chairman of the Board Thornton F. Bradshaw is another combat veteran, whose destroyer was put out of action by the Japanese Navy in the last months of the war. Bradshaw, if anyone, is an authentic statesman of American industry. He is unworried about RCA, which is happy and prosperous. His view is entirely different from Chaikin's, for his company has adjusted to the world market. But RCA long ago gave up on penetrating Japan. Its creator, Gen. David Sarnoff, thought the American market was enough, and licensed to Japan and the rest of the world the technologies RCA has patented—technologies that underlie much of modern electronics production. RCA prospers from its lead in advanced electronics—from its satellites, from its arms contracts (like the Aegis guided missile cruiser) from its broadcast net, NBC, from its market-

ing of imported parts and products, from manufacturing television sets. But, despite RCA's prosperity, Bradshaw is deeply worried—about America as an industrial community where both work ethic and practice have decayed.

Bradshaw is concerned for America's economy as a whole, Chaikin for his working people—both equally honorable concerns. But neither believes that any reasonable persuasion can slow the Asian trade surge unless the American Government acts—sooner rather than later. What is needed is a structural change in American life and thinking, as sweeping as Japan's in 1945–1950—from factory floor to research labs and universities, from reduction of the Federal budget deficit, to a total review of our trading policies.

So the story moves to Washington.

WASHINGTON IS always in crisis—small crises, acute crises, lurking crises. But the trade crisis is quite extraordinary for the anarchy of ideas that prevails. Ideas clash in perception of a world that has totally changed since the days of victory. Trade, as we designed it, has become completely global, and America has become the last open gaming table for world adventurers. Within the confusion of Washington's thinking, however, at least three truths are taken as paramount.

The first truth, the starting point of all thoughtful conversations, is the overwhelming burden of the overvalued dollar.

"When I was dealing with Japan the

problem was different," says Robert S. Strauss, Jimmy Carter's trade representative from 1977 to 1979. "I talked in a universe of tariffs. . . of trade . . . non-trade . . . cultural barriers . . . political difficulties." Strauss, a very suave, but very tough man, is remembered as one of the few American trade representatives who have been able to out-negotiate the Japanese. For a brief period, his tenacity caused the impermeable membrane of Japanese resistance to yield. "Now," he says, "you're talking about a world where trade has reached $2 trillion a year, but capital flows have reached a magnitude of $20 trillion a year, swirling around the world like a jet stream. It drops off here because of safety and high interest rates, and pushes the dollar up. It makes the trade problem look like a pygmy problem. It distorts everything, and leaves the poor American exporter, no matter how good or efficient, like a runner doing a sprint with an anvil under his arm.

"The Japanese don't adjust the yen every day. But you don't have to be a genius to know that when the Bank of Japan coughs, everyone gets the sniffles. But we have no policy. Even if we started now, we couldn't work things out in a year, or five. We need a strategy."

There comes next the second truth: Japan's "unfair" trading practices, its regulations, rules, restrictions, quotas. Says Secretary of Commerce Baldrige: "Japanese export policy has as its objective not participation in, but dominance of, world markets. Japanese trade policies assume as a *right* protection of

their industries that are emerging, like satellites, depressed industries like paper and chemicals, politically important industries like agriculture, socially sensitive industries like leather. . . .

"In 1983, we took 30 percent of Japan's overseas exports, in 1984, 35 percent. In practical terms, this means that all the net increase in Japanese domestic employment in recent years is attributable to sale to the United States. . . . America's pursuit of free trade is like Sir Galahad's quest for the Holy Grail."

From the National Association of Manufacturers to the AFL-CIO, one catches the alarm in vivid language. "There are six to eight main interacting trade-and-production groups, or 'kei-retsu,'" says one association official, who asked not to be identified. "They buy and sell chiefly to their own subsidiaries, and they divide Japan's market up. When we squeeze, they'll allot, say, 11 percent of a particular market to all importers. They are opaque, insensitive people, who don't know that they have brought us to the edge."

Says Lane Kirkland, president of the AFL-CIO, the man most concerned for the fate of American workingmen, who last visited Japan this winter, "To hear the Japanese plead for free trade is like hearing the world 'love' on the lips of a harlot."

The last body of truths comes from the engineering community—it is the most serious, most somber, most challenging. It is that the Japanese are very, very good, better at some things than Americans. They are brilliant, efficient, aggressive people who prize education as much or more than Americans—and have learned to use it. John Gibbons is the head of Congress's Office of Technology Assessment—he is a physicist, who comes to Congress from the Oak Ridge Labs of the Atomic Energy Commission. He starts the story of Japan's renaissance with the occupation:

"The most important thing we did after the war was to reorganize it; we democratized it; we lifted the burden of arms from it, and they poured resources into education. We helped them. We gave free doctorates in nuclear science to their students and brought them to Oak Ridge. But you have to realize that the Japanese already had traditional skills and techniques; they were superb in alloying metals, in ceramics, in fermentation—out of the broths they knew how to brew came the fermentation know-how vital to biotechnologies.

"They are ahead of us in productivity in automobiles, in steel, in robotics. We are ahead in fundamental research, but they get all our science papers and research, and they add to that their mastery of 'process technology,' translating fundamental research into the making of things. They recruit their managers from the factory floor; we get ours out of law schools."

In Gibbons's view, the challenge lies, above all, to American technology and education. Unless we can translate our lead in fundamental research into practice, then others will be the chief beneficiaries of our science and laboratories.

IN A FEW days in Washington, one can trace a trail of irritations blistering under the bland rhetoric that still binds the Pacific alliance together.

Start at the State Department with middle-level officers who deal daily with the Japanese—and one hears language almost unheard elsewhere in that labyrinth of quiet diplomats. "Japan," said one, who asked not to be identified, "is a protectionist nation: They have no sense of moderation; they are aggressive. They are an island nation looking out on the rest of the world as plunder from a protected bastion. Negotiations are tedious, painful—oh, so painful—and, when they yield, they yield with no grace. It's not only quotas or beef, citrus fruits, leather, but even on our catsup and peanut butter.

"In 1981, they banned American metal baseball bats. We had the technology for making a safe cap for metal bats. The Japanese made a metal bat with a plastic plug top; a plug flew off at a baseball game and struck a spectator. So all metal bats, safe and dangerous; were banned. We negotiated for three years, we had to get them to change 18 laws and regulations; we had to get the consent of the Japanese Softball Association. Then, when the Japanese learned to make safe metal caps, they reopened the market. Last year, we finally managed to export 350 metal bats to Japan!"

This is the voice of a working diplomat in the State Department. The bureaucracy bows to political leadership. But it remains the national political scouting force abroad, and cannot help but observe politics at home. Its officers do not blink at the reality that Americans want to buy cheap quality goods; no one forces them to buy Japanese goods. Nor can they blink at the fact that no fewer than 30 states now have their own offices in Japan soliciting Japanese investment. But they cannot blink either at the fact that so much of American industry is being wiped out, and that the men and women discarded scream to Congress.

At the supreme level, President Reagan deals with Premier Yasuhiro Nakasone of Japan, who yields and, with exquisite courtesy, goes on television to urge his people to sample American and foreign imports. But at the working level, each negotiation is a tormented, ad hoc, item-by-item bargaining.

A shawl of self-restraint drapes over most official American spokesmen; to be accused of "Japan-bashing" is considered "protectionist" or, worse, "racist." Foremost among those who thus speak for the old free-trade tradition, one finds Secretary of State George P. Shultz. "There is a great sentiment for protection around the country," he told a gathering of the American Stock Exchange recently, "but in my opinion it's wrong . . . it's bad . . . this is a matter of deep conviction on my part." But no such restraint binds Congress, or the unions who influence so many constituencies. Congress is entertaining half-a-dozen bills right now sponsored by afflicted Congressmen; it is even considering a 25 percent tariff on all imported goods.

Congress is where one can best see the deadlock of ideas, as shoe workers, garment workers, steel workers, auto workers demand protection. But Senator Christopher Dodd of Connecticut is typical of a Congressman in the middle; he is a young, liberal, thoughtful Democrat, and knows that foreign trade is essential to America. He comes from that state in the Union that is most dependent on foreign trade—25 percent of Connecticut's gross state product goes into exports. But Dodd also sits on the Senate Foreign Relations Committee, which he describes as torn between "bumper sticker patriots" and those who believe that world peace rests on world trade.

Dodd is worried not about his state, but about the lack of an American strategy for dealing with the nature of the new trading world. He says: "We can't make a strategy by assembling a majority in the House to protect shoes, or automobiles, or tool-and-die makers. We need an overall trade policy and we need it now before the whole thing explodes."

And so Dodd comes down, as do Baldrige, Strauss, and the National Association of Manufacturers, to the conclusion that there must soon be a great international gathering that will create an orderly new system of trade to replace the present anarchy where the wolves pick off the laggards.

What such an international gathering will do, or can do, is still obscure. The Marshall Plan is remembered as an example of what may be won . . . but the Marshall Plan took five years to evolve, in interminable conferences from 1944 to 1949. Now the market that must be shared is not simply the

Atlantic basin; it is the whole globe. Korea makes steel and ships, Taiwan makes electronics, Brazil makes steel, arms, shoes, India and China creep up on every technological front. All seek to follow Japan's course, at whatever cost to American jobs. Conscience prevents Americans from spurning the poor and suffering of the world who seek to better themselves; but common sense forbids a course that permits their betterment by our impoverishment. Somehow a new way must be found to fairly share both world resources and markets. It will take a long time to work that way out, for America must restructure to live in this world as the Japanese have done. And time is short.

So ONE TRIES finally to penetrate the thinking of Executive policy—where an ailing President, plagued with budget deficits, tax reform, the Middle East and terrorism is too busy to reflect on trade policy, decide on his will, or impose it.

It is left for others to speak for him, and when they speak, they speak of peace:

"Who won the war?," an official State Department spokesman repeated my question and answered: "We won the war. What did we get from the victory? We expanded the area of freedom. We made a democratic Japan. Our bases in the Pacific and Japan are essential to our defense. There's peace in the Pacific now. Japan is our ally, it's stable. Peace is our reward."

Peace, of course, is primordial. But the Japanese share the same peace, and under our protection, paying little for it, reserve the right to press American livelihoods to the wall. How far or how deeply they can press their trade strategy before Congress explodes in anger is unknown. But it would be well for the Japanese to remember that if peace is paramount, they need us to keep the peace more than we need them. And if a ripple of depression forces Congress to act, a lockup of the open American market would wound Japan more than it would wound us. The superlative execution of their trade tactics may provoke an incalculable reaction—as the Japanese might well remember of the course that ran from Pearl Harbor to the deck of the U.S.S. Missouri in Tokyo Bay just 40 years ago.

THE NEW YORK TIMES MAGAZINE July 28, 1985

Chapter 17

The Labyrinthine World of the Pentagon

Nothing symbolizes the United States Department of Defense better than its own headquarters, the Pentagon. Both are mammoth; both have apparently simple and logical layouts which in fact are vastly complex structures that can confuse even insiders; and both sit slightly outside of Washington proper. To analyze DOD, a journalist must have more than a passing knowledge of both weaponry and the corporations that produce it; he must interview far more widely than usual; and he must above all keep himself out of the feuds, fights, and outright battles that swirl there. It is just the sort of challenge White loved.

It also brought him back to a field of interest he had reluctantly abandoned in 1954, when he had publicly criticized the government's lifting of Dr. J. Robert Oppenheimer's security clearance. This stance brought with it powerful enemies in the defense establishment, men who had been out to get Oppenheimer. Enemies don't give "access," and thus, as he ruefully recounted much later, for a decade he wrote nothing about national defense nor its dynamics with foreign policy.

In this chapter we meet two standout Secretaries of Defense—Robert Mc-Namara and Caspar Weinberger—separated in office by twenty years. White admired both men greatly, making objectivity that much tougher to achieve. That he succeeds is a mark of his talent.

REVOLUTION IN THE PENTAGON

A man with a steel grip and a diamond-hard mind has seized control of the Pentagon. How he is changing the odds on war and survival is examined in the following pages by a Pulitzer Prize-winning reporter.

No office in Washington receives a visitor more peacefully than the Office of the Secretary of Defense.

This tranquil chamber—white-walled, high-ceilinged, beige-carpeted—calms the visitor as much with its vast dimensions as with its hush. Certainly, it gives no hint that this is the most dangerous of all the ornate command posts of Washington leadership.

Yet it is. Eight Secretaries of Defense have occupied this post. One or two survived the ordeal with vigor and honor. But for the most part, here famous captains of industry have been stripped of magic and sent home, ham-fisted politicians defeated, great national heroes gutted of their vitality. And one, his reason cracking under the strain that pulses here, jumped from a window and killed himself.

This is, therefore, a room of peril. Yet no foreign enemy creates the peril—it is shaped by dedicated Americans whose imagination, will and passion clash at peak intensity in this room over the policies the Secretary of Defense must set. For more than 15 years, until now, no one has been able to say who was master of the forces gathered here.

There is little to tell the roving eye that today matters have changed in this room. The paint has been freshened; the battle paintings on the wall have been replaced by color blowups of the High Sierras. A cheap black-and-white Rouault print, crudely pasted to the glass of its frame, is a new touch at this level of American command. But the Rouault faces a man who sits, as all the Secretaries of Defense have sat, behind the same 8½-foot-long General Pershing desk. Beyond him is the traditional General Sherman table. The remorseless wall clock, with its sweep hand and its chart, marks the same globe-girdling problems that tormented his predecessors—problems ranging from CINCEUR in Paris (operating on ZULU time plus one, which is six hours later than Washington time) to CINCPAC in Hawaii (on ZULU time minus ten, five hours earlier than Washington time).

The change in this room can be measured neither in decor nor in charts, for this room disposes of power, and the nature of power is that it is felt—not seen. No sign announces here that the striking force of America's homeland reserve has tripled in two years, while abroad its political response has changed from 1961's nervous search for compromise in Laos to 1962's hammer blow poised to frustrate Khrushchev's Cuban attempt.

The man who has captained this change—Robert Strange McNamara, eighth Secretary of Defense—is already, after the President and his brother, the most important man in the American government. Power becomes him—gravely and easily. As you walk across the long Mussolini-sized room to visit Robert McNamara, you find the Secretary's eyes fixed on what he is reading, his left hand penciling the tiny cramped handwriting now famous in the Pentagon. He does not lift his eyes until you are right there standing before him. This, of course, is disconcerting. It will also be disconcerting when he silently dismisses you by dropping his eyes to the memorandum you interrupted. But this is McNamara, the man in white shirtsleeves, the IBM machine with legs, the man whose brown eyes behind the rimless, oval-cut eyeglasses are emotionless.

It is difficult to associate this Mc-Namara with the man who, pacing the large room late one night during his first few weeks in office, burst out, "I tell you this place is a jungle—a jungle." It is difficult also to associate the muscular quality of the tall body, the high, inflectionless voice, the slick black hair with the surgical quality of his thought. It is, lastly, difficult to associate this McNamara with the bubbling-charming evening McNamara,

one of the most completely engaging dinner companions on Washington's inner social circuit. But the evening McNamara must wait on the man behind this desk, for the daytime Mc-Namara is an artist of a particular kind who has, after two years, created news that should now be recorded.

First—the civilian authority in American government has won full control of the power of the Pentagon.

Second—American striking power is in a historic process of multiplication and change.

Third—the purpose and use of this power have been redefined.

These are developments of vast importance. Translated into simpler language, they mean that if America's leaders invite Americans to die in battle or under bombardment in the next few years, it will be by reasonable decision, rather than by accident or spastic reaction.

This may seem like a simple achievement. But to explain how it happened is a complicated story, reaching back through 15 years of merciless strife and chaos, as generals, admirals, scientists and statesmen—all seeking American security—set their hands, one against the other, in the corridors of this building.

The story starts in 1945 with the destruction of the United States Army in its hour of triumph. Americans did not demobilize their magnificent army, they destroyed it. So swift and chaotic was the dismantling of the nation's force around the world, as homesick GI's rioted from Marseilles to Manila, that all prospect of a reasonable and expectable balance of strength with the war-weary Russians evaporated in a few months. American ground power ceased to exist. So did the airlift and mobility that made this power global. Ten months after V-E day, the 3,500,000 Americans (68 combat divisions) in Europe had shrunk to 400,000. The 149 American air groups that had reduced Germany to rubble were sinking to their nadir of two combat wings; and in all the U.S.A., the combat backup of this force was 90 bombers, 460 fighter planes—and only 175 first-class pilots to man them.

Seized with the belief that the world was at peace, Americans cut their arms budget to a low of $9.7 billion (which, in 1948, maintained only one combat division in Europe). Within the confines of this ever contracting budget, America's generals and admirals swiftly learned to fight first over money, then over strategy.

The Korean War reversed matters momentarily. But once it was over, American ground power again shriveled. And since no reasoned strategy could rest on a ground force whose combat strength shot up and down like a Yo-Yo (from 12 divisions in 1950 to 23 in 1952 and 14 in 1960), American strategy, by default, began to tailor itself to a single new instrument, SAC—the Strategic Air Command, which sheltered all the Western world with its ability to wipe out Russia.

SAC was a reflection of the scientific, rather than political, "input" in Pentagon thinking. While the world abroad went from political explosion to more dramatic political explosion, American science went from technological breakthrough to more dramatic breakthrough, pouring the most dazzling developments into SAC. Nuclear physics leaped from fission to fusion bombs; new transistors invited ultra-swift new computers; these, wedding to rocketry development, ushered in the age of intercontinental missiles. The weapons they spawned created industries, then entire communities, dependent solely on weapons-systems decisions in Washington. Strategic decisions became live-or-die sentences for communities (from Suffolk County, N.Y., to San Diego, Calif.) whose political and industrial leaders intruded in the squabbles of the Pentagon.

The most experienced leadership would have had difficulty in absorbing such a torrent of "input." But the Pentagon from 1947 on was under new management. In 1947, Congress decided to make the Army, Navy, Air Force all equal and to place over them an instrument and a man entirely new to U.S. history—an Office and a Secretary of Defense—to "coordinate." What "coordinate" meant, Congress never defined. As if giving each nominee a "may-the-best-man-win" sendoff, it ratified seven successive Secretaries, and tossed each of them into the Pentagon ambuscades to explore what his true authority was.

THE GAME, AS it was played, could have been called: "Who's Boss Now?" Who really directed American military posture—civilian or military, amateur or professional? Who had the right to make what claim on America's total resources? For what defense purposes?

It was a lethal game. James Forrestal, a fragile man, was the first Secretary at bat. Neurotic, he thought of himself as being beaten by the uniforms and jumped to his death. Only in retrospect has he come to be recognized as a truly creative boss. After Forrestal, on the other hand, apparent victors in the game turned out to be Pentagon patsies. The toughest civilian team installed in the Pentagon was that of Charles E. (Engine Charlie) Wilson and Roger Kyes, both imported from General Motors. Pentagon generals still wince at the remembered rudeness of Wilson, and Kyes's treatment of one general is legendary. "I didn't come down here to shovel snow," said Kyes to the general. Then, bending over, he flicked the general's stars and continued, "I came down here to pluck stars." But such apparently "tough" civilians could be briefed, flattered, outwitted and finally absorbed by generals and admirals who systematically study all leadership patterns among men, from Red Square to Wall Street. By the end of the Eisenhower Administration, control of American strategy lay not in the hands of civilian leadership, but in the hands of the uniformed Chiefs of Staff.

This was tragedy. The duty of a Secretary of Defense is to get out of the Pentagon that kind of power which best advances the policies of America over the turbulent globe. If the Secretary fails to interpret to the Pentagon what kind of power his President wants, then power makes its own rules and strategy, like an inertially guided missile that moves only by interior technical reference.

This was tragedy, most of all for generals and admirals. The decay of civilian leadership should have made them happy. But it did not. They could no more agree among themselves as to what was a right and proper American military effort than could a college debating society. Year in, year out, in gross and detail, the Chiefs of Staff battled each other over disposition of American resources. Occasionally, their bitterness and anguish burst into the open—as when a general publicly denounced the admirals before Congress as "Fancy Dans." Occasionally, two services ganged up on a third—as happened in 1956, when the Air Force and Navy agreed to all but abolish the Army, reducing it to a Civil Defense police force at home and a number of atomic task forces abroad. (A calculated Army press leak exploded that plan before it got off the ground.) Occasionally, civilians, too, were destroyed—as when the Air Force shot down Robert Oppenheimer, the genius who tooled the first atom bomb, because it suspected him of forcing the Air Force to share its monopoly of atomic weapons with the Army and Navy.

Gradually, a pattern developed. Within the Air Force, the elite corps of SAC dominated thinking, and the Air Force thus spoke for the strategy of "massive retaliation," a strategy pleasing to both the most ferocious and most economy-minded American political thinkers. The Army spoke for a strategy of "flexible response," pleading, through spokesmen like Maxwell Taylor and James Gavin, for the manpower and equipment to face the changes of a changing world. The Navy was the cat that walked by itself, casting its vote, when it had to, for massive retaliation against flexible response.

Civilians controlled the feuding service chieftains mainly through budget recommendations. Gradually, strategy became the offspring of the budget. The Chiefs of Staff finally arrived at a bitter budgetary compromise, behind the blurred words of which lay this formula: Of any sum appropriated for defense, the Army would have 23 percent, the Navy 28 percent, the Air Force 46 percent. Under the compromise, each service planned its own future war against Russia; each had its own intelligence net and its own supply system; each had its own missile program. The plans might not fit, of course. The Army had plans for airlifting emergency reinforcements to meet a threat in Europe, but the Air Force had no plans for providing the matching lift. The Army planned for a long war and stockpiled two years of some combat consumables; the Air Force planned for a short war and stockpiled a few weeks of combat consumables. But all three services felt they were ready—more or less.

Thus, at the beginning of March, 1961, barely six weeks after his inauguration, John F. Kennedy gathered the Joint Chiefs of Staff to consider the Communist thrust in Laos. At this point, clarity struck. For, as the new President sat down in the long, gloomy Cabinet Room off the White House rose garden to inquire what he might do to meet the threat, he found this: The forces at his disposal were incredible— or else they were a joke. He might, if he chose, unleash the frightful power of SAC, which could wipe out any capital on earth with a spasm of its muscles. But, short of that, he was told, the armed forces could provide only a few combat teams for an operation in Laos—provided the emergency lasted no more than 30 days and there was no crisis in Berlin. Those present recall the President's disbelief. Unwilling to risk total war over Laos, the United States would have to settle for what it could get. Matters would grow worse in the next few months as Cuba followed Laos, and Berlin followed Cuba.

Yet, by this time, a superior if civilian intelligence had begun to examine the ailing American giant whose cramped muscles could respond to crisis in only one way—with a single cataclysmic spasm. Robert Strange McNamara had taken over at the Pentagon and was trying to find out how to restore flexibility to American power.

Robert McNamara, the new man in charge of the muscle-bound giant, was in 1961 no stranger to the Pentagon. During World War II, he had served an apprenticeship (as captain) in the building's 3C ring, where he could look out over an air well and get what is called a "bowel view" of Pentagon leadership.

McNamara, then 26 years old, was by all accounts a rather perplexing fellow, as he had been since school days. One of his earliest friends remembers him from high school (where he was president of the yearbook, president of the French club, a member of the glee club and a member of the board of student control). With the puzzlement that characterizes all memories of him, she says, "He was so painfully good; he was so neat, so clean; he was the kind of boy you'd trust with either your money or your sick kittens. But when I say that, I make him sound like a square. Yet he wasn't, he wasn't—a square is an object of ridicule, and Bob was a great talker, a good dancer; it was always fun to have him around. He was never left out of anything."

McNamara moved brilliantly from high school to college (the University of California), made Phi Beta Kappa in his junior year. After going on to Harvard Business School, he married Margaret Craig of San Francisco and later became an assistant professor at the school. "We were all broke," recalls Eugene Zuckert, a junior dean at the Business School, now Secretary of the Air Force. "We were all kids then, and the McNamaras lived at Morris Hall, and we would go out to parties just to sneak some punch. But, smack at 10:30, the McNamaras would go home to bed, because he had to be ready for work the next day."

It was McNamara's teaching speciality—statistical control—that brought him to the Pentagon in mid-war. (He had wanted to volunteer after Pearl Harbor, had instead been assigned to teach his speciality to Army Air Forces officers at Harvard.) The war, at this point, was giving Americans their first experience in dealing swiftly with waterfalls of data under emergency conditions. For the first time, men were groping for instantaneous decisions based on calculations involving thousands of miles, millions of human beings, billions of gallons of gasoline. After months of instructing air officers in such methods of calculation, McNamara, in February, 1943, decided simply to join them.

There is little romance to statistical control. Its purpose is to dump the drudgery of calculation on computers and machines. The supervising human is required only to think: first, to pose questions to the calculators; and finally, once questions have conscripted answering data, to make decisions on the basis of such data. It was in these statistical vineyards that McNamara first labored, then starred.

The ability to ask the proper questions governing oceans of data is rare today. It was even rarer in 1945. When the war ended, McNamara and a band of nine AAF companions were invited to move as a package (called the "Quiz Kids") from Pentagon desks to the ailing Ford Motor Co. McNamara was 29 when he arrived to probe Ford with his questions. The giant company, the outstanding invalid of the prewar automobile industry, was once again facing financial crisis with the end of military production. When McNamara left Ford as president, 14 years later, the company had an annual net profit of $427 million.

In Michigan, as everywhere else, there were always the two McNamaras. The Ford or daytime McNamara was a paragon of efficiency. Tough enough to recommend, as division chief, that Ford liquidate its Edsel venture and admit its $250,000,000 error, he foreshadowed the man who could later wipe out the half-billion-dollar Skybolt project with the same surgical precision.

The evening McNamara lived in a rambling, white-trimmed brick Tudor house at Ann Arbor, home of the University of Michigan, 30 miles from Detroit. The evening McNamara was a contributor to the NAACP and the American Civil Liberties Union, a recognized egghead in a university community. This McNamara, a vivid, rambling conversationalist, first joined a monthly discussion group of ten of Ann Arbor's leading businessmen-intellectuals. Then, his curiosity unslaked, he helped Professor Ralph Gerard, the university's distinguished neurophysiologist, organize another evening discussion group of out-and-out eggheads (an art historian, a sociologist, a physicist, several professors, two others business executives) to explore ideas in new books.

The evening McNamara was home folks. When discussion groups met at the McNamara home, Mrs. McNamara served; the house remained comfortable, not fancy—a place "where you found kids' boots and kid's' hockey sticks stacked in the entryway, not a picked-up house," says one friend. But the daytime McNamara was rising rapidly from division to division at Ford. As the salary of the once-broke professor climbed from Ford's $12,000 starting stipend to the $420,000 of 1960, the McNamaras became contributors—to civil improvement in Ann Arbor and Detroit, to an effort to establish an art

theater in Michigan and to politics. Now, high-minded, non-favor-seeking political contributors are as scarce in politics as albino candidates. And as McNamara contributed across the board to Republicans here, Democrats there, he began to appear on the radar screens of politicians. But it was difficult to label him: In 1960, he gave his dollars and support to Professor Paul Bagwell, Republican candidate for governor, and Sen. John F. Kennedy, Democratic candidate for President.

One cannot linger long over the dramatic timing that brought John F. Kennedy to the Presidency of the United States on Tuesday, November 8, 1960, and Robert S. McNamara to the presidency of the Ford Motor Co. the next day; or the frantic screening of the horizon by the Kennedy staff for a Secretary of Defense; or how McNamara's name was raised again and again during the hunt—by Wall Streeters, labor leaders, politicians, business leaders.

Two items of testimony stand out. The first is from the President's brother-in-law, Sargent Shriver, now chief of the Peace Corps, who on December 7, 1960, flew to Michigan to explore with Robert McNamara two jobs—Secretary of Defense and Secretary of the Treasury. Shriver recalls that he was impressed by several things: the matter-of-fact way that McNamara moved to a discussion of the posts—without surprise, or arrogance, or false modesty, or self-depreciation; the ease with which he could rattle off the three or four main problems of both the Treasury and Defense; his worry about deserting the Fords, who had just made him president, and his total indifference to money. According to Shriver, Mc-Namara leaned back in his chair at one point and remarked that, of course, he'd have to give up any stock or options in Ford; and that this would cost him several million dollars. "You know," Mc-Namara added, "I've got more money now than anybody in my family ever dreamed of having. I've got more money than I'm ever going to need or use." He straightened his chair, and that was that. ("Like that," says Shriver. "That was all there was to the matter.")

The second item comes from his friend Congressman Neil Staebler, then Democratic national committeeman in Michigan, with whom McNamara discussed the Defense post the night before his decision. "It was as if," says Staebler, "McNamara were asking the question: 'Why should I hire McNamara for the job?'—as if McNamara were trying to see McNamara as the President saw him. It was as if he were trying to write a report on himself to himself. Could the job be done? Could you get all the people involved at the Pentagon to agree? Could the thing truly be unified? McNamara had seen enough throat cutting at Ford to prepare anybody for the Pentagon—but did anybody have the power to unify the Pentagon? And then, finally—I can't remember the words, there was this phrase: that maybe nobody could do the job; that maybe he couldn't last six months; maybe nobody was qualified; but that after all, he had been asked, and therefore he would try."

About 10 days later, Bob McNamara visited the then Secretary of Defense,

Thomas Gates, for what was to be a short briefing on the duties he was about to assume. The session ran to six hours. When it was over, so the story is told at the White House, McNamara returned to the Ford Motor Co. suite at the Shoreham Hotel and telephoned President-elect Kennedy. "I've just been over talking with Tom Gates," said McNamara, "and you know—I think I can do that job."

Oh, Kennedy is said to have replied. Well, you know, I've been talking to Eisenhower this morning. And I think I can do that job too.

With this, the take-over of the Pentagon began.

TO TAKE OVER the military establishment of the United States is a stupefying task—rendered even more difficult than it might otherwise be by the stupefying character of the Pentagon itself. Squat and ugly, dank and drafty, the tawny building on the Potomac mud flats is one of the most bleakly depressing anthills in the world. The first of its qualities is that it is huge. An enormous labyrinth of 7,000 offices, 1,900 toilets, 150 staircases, 17½ miles of dingy corridors, it rouses in almost all its 25,000 working citizens, whether clerks or generals, the fear they may be lost and forgotten. The second of its qualities, for those who are not lost and forgotten, is tension. Though promising young officers, just in from healthy field duty, insist that their new ulcers, headaches, flu and colds are symptoms of a specific disease called

Pentagonitis, the medical staff of the Pentagon insists there is no such disease—it is simply nerves. And nervous tension increases at the Pentagon the higher one rises in the hierarchy. At the heights, the effects of an alternation between the humiliation of obedience and the ecstasy of command become more acute.

To understand the Pentagon, it is essential to grasp one fact—that only a handful of men in the building are important. Cut a wedge out of the huge perimeter between the fashionable Mall and River entrances; slice off this wedge the outer rim, the sunlit E ring; make the slice two layers thick, the 2nd and 3rd floors—and then, in this tiny sliver of the world's biggest office building, you have trapped the 20 or 30 men who shape the military policy and strategy of America.

A new Secretary of Defense has only two ways of imposing his authority on the 3,500,00 men and women of the American military establishment, all of whom get orders from this building: One is by power of the budget; the second, by power of appointment. And since men write budgets, not vice versa, one should look first at the 20 or 30 individuals who direct the nation's military effort—at the small team of civilians who man the Defense, Army, Navy and Air Force policy staffs, then at the team of generals and admirals they are supposed to select and supervise in running the services and commands. Rarely, indeed, have both civilians and military teams offered so romantic an intertwining of old and

new in American tradition as do McNamara's teams, which now, after two years, show the Secretary's emerging touch.

One is struck immediately, for example, by how top-heavy McNamara's choices have been in Ivy Leaguers. Deputy to McNamara, second man in the Department, is Roswell L. Gilpatric, Yale; followed by another Yale as Secretary of the Army, another Yale as Secretary of the Air Force, another Yale as Assistant Secretary of Defense for Manpower. A Harvard man and a Yale man serve as first and second in Defense's international security-affairs section, and a Princeton man serves as Assistant Secretary of Public Affairs. Yet it would be a narrow view to consider such a concentration of fashionable Ivy Leaguers as an expression of social connections. All through the Kennedy Administration runs the most intense, if unrecognized, desire to attach itself to the older traditions of American government. And the Gilpatric-Vance-Zuckert-Nitze team at the Pentagon can be seen as the direct descendant of the great Ivy League team of Stimson-Lovett-McCloy-Patterson-Forrestal (again predominantly Yale) that directed American effort in World War II for another President from Harvard, Franklin D. Roosevelt. Smooth, polished, tough under their good manners, the Pentagon's current leaders are men shaped by a tradition of public service almost as old as the uniformed forces they direct. They are part of the invisible web of government, gossip and private connections that links Pentagon with White House and State.

Yet one tradition can no longer stretch over the vast diversity of American life, and so, as a balance to his Ivy Leaguers, McNamara has developed another civilian team that can be called only the "Think Staff." Many journalists have tried to style the Think Staff: they are called by some, "Randsters" (for Rand Corporation, which so heavily nourished their thinking) or "technipols," or "Defense intellectuals," or the "Whiz Kids," or "the Wizards of ODD." What is common to these people is that almost all of them have been trained since the war either in science or in defense analysis at the direct expense of the armed services of the United States. They are as much children of the Pentagon as its uniformed personnel, and are hated by the leadership of the armed services because now they no longer serve, but apparently direct the generals. If the Ivy League crowd is predominantly East Coast-New York, then the Think Staff is predominantly West Coast-California. The Ivy Leaguers are older; the Think Staffers are, at first glance, rather academic, generally young, interested in war as a system of intellectual propositions, most at home with a piece of chalk and a blackboard.

It would be too much to inspect all of the top civilians to find the answer to the question: Who runs the Pentagon? Yet, certainly, the leaders of both civilian wings, as they jointly confront the military team, must be examined.

The leaders of the Ivy League team are almost all the kind of men, from the kind of families, who would have gone charging up San Juan Hill with Teddy Roosevelt. Chief among them is Roswell Gilpatric, tall, curly-haired, gray-eyed, Windsor knot to his necktie, an aficionado of Elizabethan poetry and yachting, extraordinarily able, closer to McNamara than anyone else. If ever Gilpatric were to leave his post to go back to his rich New York law practice, then the two chief rivals for the succession would be Paul Nitze (Harvard), silver-haired, graceful, the man chiefly responsible for the new, seemingly frictionless alliance of Pentagon and State Department; and Cyrus Vance (Yale), the capable, abrasive, thinly handsome Secretary of the Army. All three are of finest New York polish; all three have moved from good prep schools to good colleges to distinguished marriages; and all three have enough wealth and devotion to make America's welfare their primary concern in life.

The leaders of the Think Staff wing are more difficult to group and define, partly because there is no hard-and-fast cutoff between Ivy Leaguer administrator and Think Staffer. Adam Yarmolinsky, for example, McNamara's personal counsel and troubleshooter, bridges both groups. By education an Ivy Leaguer, he is by temperament and function a Think Staffer. So is the Defense Department's general counsel, the able John McNaughton. Senior among the pure Think Staffers, however, is probably Charles Hitch, 53, the department's comptroller, a mild-mannered, gentle Missourian, a onetime professor of economics. Clustered about Hitch are Alain Enthoven, a tall, darkly handsome Seattle-born economist of 32, and Henry S. Rowen, a professorial Bostonian, 37. These three were all research associates at the Air Force's Rand Corporation think factory in Santa Monica, Calif.; all three studied economics at Oxford. All helped transfer the British military doctrine of operations analysis to American military thinking.

To these must be added Dr. Harold Brown (New York, Bronx High School of Science and Columbia), a vastly impressive, if inscrutable man, who at 35 directs the expenditure of $5.5 billion in scientific research and engineering; and his deputy, John Rubel, 42, a lithe and graceful Chicago-born scientist, a thoroughly brilliant and charming man, who, like his chief, won his laurels in the West, in California.

Together, these are the top civilians who direct the top military team of the Pentagon. Actually, the point where brook meets river, where civilian meshes with military, can be made more precise.

Each Monday afternoon at 2:30, McNamara and Gilpatric (they are so close that their appearance anywhere is called the Rob-and-Ros Act) descend from the third to the second floor, where, off the barred and barricaded ninth corridor, a bay leads to the "tank," the "Gold Room," the meeting place of the Joint Chiefs of Staff. Here, around the huge table, scarred by cigarette and cigar butts abandoned in anger at past disputes, McNamara and Gilpatric discuss and decide the problems and plans of American strategy with the uniformed Chiefs of Staff.

Two of the Chiefs are relatively new and untested. The Army Chief of Staff is Gen. Earle G. Wheeler. Lean, dark, tense, a chain-smoker, Wheeler is the most important new military personality on the Washington scene. Clear and precise of speech, he is one of the most lucid thinkers in the Pentagon; all acknowledge this. The criticism of this attractive man comes chiefly from those who insist he is a staff man, not a man of combat-command experience. Traditionally, the military thinking of a new Administration shows itself in its choice of a new Army Chief of Staff, and Wheeler speaks the language of the new Administration. Philosophically a child of the Army's tradition of extreme mobility, Wheeler voices a doctrine that would have appealed to Nathan Bedford Forrest as much as John Fitzgerald Kennedy. Had Maxwell Taylor not been available, Wheeler might have won nomination as Chairman of the Joint Chiefs to succeed Gen. Lyman Lemnitzer (whose blandness discouraged the Administration, which sent him to Paris to soothe NATO). If Wheeler delivers as Army Chief of Staff, he should someday succeed to the Chairmanship of the Joint Chiefs.

ADM. GEORGE W. ANDERSON, Chief of Naval Operations—a husky, masculine sailor and the most perfectly type-cast of the four Chiefs—is also relatively untested in high combat command. The U.S. Navy is the closed service; it chooses its own leaders by its own promotion mechanisms, and civilians rarely dare interfere. (It took a near revolt by Congress to save Hyman Rickover when the Navy brotherhood wanted to dismiss the nuclear admiral.) Generally, the Navy offers for civilian ratification as CNO only its finest, and Anderson runs a superbly efficient Navy. Like all CNO's, Anderson feels his basic responsibility is to National Security—and only secondarily to any particular civilian administration installed over him. Traditionally, the Navy has been the most intellectual of the services. But the Think Staffers who rove the Pentagon have, finally, in this year's budget, also begun to close on the Navy, summoning it to account. And Anderson's resentment is as natural and bitter as that of any salt-sprayed sea dog against any land-bound civilian.

Wheeler and Anderson are the lesser Chiefs.

Then there are the greater Chiefs.

What separates the lesser from the greater Chiefs is "presence." America is running out of combat-tested leaders. Both Anderson and Wheeler belong to an untried generation of senior commanders. But the other two Chiefs, Gens. Maxwell Taylor and Curtis E. LeMay, are the last active personalities of America's military age of heroes. These two, when the world was troubled, commanded great forces in anger, and won. They are rivals, as they always have been. Only a respect for each other's achievements keeps them this side of outright clash. For if General LeMay is "Mr. Massive Retaliation" himself, then General Taylor is "Mr. Flexible Response."

General Taylor, 61, has begun to mellow but is still biting of phrase. As newly appointed Chairman of the Joint Chiefs, he has returned to the Pentagon from long exile, totally vindicated. Three years ago, as Chief of Staff, U.S. Army, he bade farewell to the armed services, crushed and dispirited by an Air Force strategy he despised. As a parting volley, he fired at his enemies a book called *The Uncertain Trumpet*. No military blast ever hit target more squarely than did his book, which became the military bible of the New Frontiersmen, from the new President to the new Secretary of Defense, on down the line. Invited back to the arena of his torment as master of the beasts, General Taylor is the first Chairman of the Joint Chiefs since Omar Bradley to regard civilians as intelligent partners in a joint venture of defense. A soldier loyal to the tradition of his cloth, Taylor indignantly opposes any civilian interference in the choice of military leaders. But he is himself, par excellence, the choice of civilians to command the apparatus of American power.

Contrast Taylor with his archrival, Gen. Curtis LeMay, Chief of Staff, U.S. Air Force: Where Taylor is thin and intellectual (he speaks French, Japanese, German, knows arts, music, science as well as airborne jump tactics), LeMay is burly, bluff, primeval. Taylor is eloquent in argument; LeMay normally grunts. Taylor likes to read classics (in Greek and Latin) or play tennis; LeMay likes to hunt. Now on the defensive, the great LeMay settles down in his chair, silver-haired and stout, his tunic unbuttoned, and regards civilian questioners warily, suspiciously, as if they were stalking him. LeMay created SAC. Dutiful, obedient to present strategy, he rumbles like a slumbering volcano. During the Cuban crisis, Taylor was for the escalated response, LeMay for the hard strike. Those who deal with both LeMay and McNamara report that no two men could be farther apart in the way they think; yet LeMay has earned McNamara's hard respect. It was LeMay's drive and prowess that for ten years made SAC the dominant chess piece on the board of world power; and it is behind SAC's shield that McNamara and Taylor have, finally, been able to redeploy the strength of America toward different ends.

The United States owes Curtis LeMay much. But if there is any thread to the story of two years of McNamara administration, it is the way in which the use of power has been brought back from LeMay's imagination and restored to civilian hands. In following this thread, we shall see not only how the Pentagon was taken over, but the particular art that distinguishes McNamara from other men.

At the heart of McNamara's art lie questions. The first tattoo rattled out of his office within four weeks of his arrival, as drafts of questions, seeking not answers but suggestions as to where and by what deadline answers could be had. Then, six weeks after taking office, McNamara fired the broadside known as "McNamara's 96 Trombones"—the famous 96 questions of March 1, 1961, each tagged with a deadline and the name of the man who must bring in the answer.

▶What of the missile gap? was a question McNamara had asked even before taking office.

All through 1960, the secret National Intelligence Estimates reported that Russia had an enormous margin of missile superiority; and appropriate leakage to the press by the armed services had made the gap a matter of clamorous political alarm. Now, on inquiry, it turned out that the separate intelligence services of the Army, Navy and Air Force each had different measures of the gap and peril, but none could offer hard evidence. The Pentagon, McNamara decided, could not afford three rival intelligence services, competing with each other and warping the flow of information in order to bolster particular missile programs. There followed the decision to unify the three intelligence services in a Defense Intelligence Agency, which would coordinate and cross-check all information.

Even before the new Defense Intelligence Agency took over, the use of new intelligence methods had led to periodic reductions in estimates of the size of the missile gap. By September, 1961, a major intelligence breakthrough of new sources established firmly that it was America, not Russia, that led in missile capacity—and by a wide margin. That margin has been maintained. The United States has today something more than 200 ICBM's ready to go, plus almost 200 target-ready Polaris missiles in submarines. It will have about 2,000 on-target missiles ready by the end of

1964, and approximately 2,000 on-target missiles by the end of 1967. Production capacity for the Minuteman is already beyond any current need. For the next two years, the United States Air Force will be adding on-target missiles at a rate of better than one every working day, to give us a total of 800 push-button-ready Minutemen by July 1, 1965. Russia's ready missile strength, in ICBM's that can hit the U.S., is probably under 100. But it is growing.

▶McNamara's 1961 questions on organization and procedure brought information that the Army, Navy and Air Force each maintained a division charged with examining its organization and procedure. But the Department of Defense, charged with supervising all three services, had none. Also, some 3,000 committees buzzed through the Pentagon, and McNamara could see little use in many of them. (Over 400 were abolished in his first six months in office.) McNamara had pulled Ford out of similar confusion, first by questioning, then by seizing the comptroller's reins. Now, at the Pentagon, he established in the Secretary of Defense's staff a brand-new Office of Organizational Management. Says an Assistant Secretary, "You must remember that, even in industry, McNamara is a new breed. Most industrial chiefs come up from the production or sales side. McNamara came up through the comptroller's side; in American industry, the comptroller's office is what the party secretary is in Russian government."

▶Other McNamara questions probed procurement and supply, budget and arms production. In the years since Korea, electronics, missile and other new weapons systems had jumped from 12 percent to 52 percent of the Pentagon's annual contract placement. How could competitive bidding be restored in this area of negotiated costs? How could the services be kept from bidding against each other for old-fashioned supplies? How could the missile race between services be controlled? A Defense Supply Agency for procuring all items of common use was set up, and space-missile development was concentrated under the Air Force.

▶Still other questions probed all international military commitments, from Morocco to Japan; the laboratories, procedures, perspectives of Defense science; installations and logistics; reserves and readiness; control and command. All answers were required to be "comprehensive and complete." Deputies, to spare McNamara from a torrent of paper, tried to boil the answers down. One recalls sending up a five-page answer. "Back it came in 20 minutes with his own little handwriting: 'This is not sufficiently comprehensive and complete.' So we upped the answer to nine pages. Back it came again. So I asked him what he wanted, and he looked at me and said, 'Just make it comprehensive and complete.' We finally gave him a White Paper of 16 pages, and it stayed. When you figure there were 96 questions in the first round—and 34 more later—you know what his reading must have been."

This lust for detail offended many officers on the Joint Staff as intrusive, juvenile and amateurish. But one must see McNamara's performance for what it really was: an athlete's feat. The mind is a large muscle, and its ability to grasp, sort and organize information can reach an artistry as perfect as an outfielder's leap for a backhand catch. This ability, like any muscular ability, withers apparently with age; but McNamara at 46 possesses it to an extraordinary degree. He can sit almost impervious to interruption and chatter as he concentrates. His staff knows that, for McNamara, the most important hours are the "alone hours" when he reads and thinks. What he reads, he compresses in notes, absorbs—and then files. Off his large office is a pantrylike vault lined with loose-leaf notebooks. These are his personal notebooks. Here are all the studies, reports and analyses on which he has penciled the marginal notations that tie the information into a whole.

All this makes Robert McNamara sound a very forbidding man—unless one enjoys the performance of a beautiful mind at work. Normally, McNamara talks in a dry, reedy voice; but when, in conversation, he begins to clarify a point, patterning new associations, his enthusiasm will begin to carry him away. His voice will rise several decibels, his head will wag back and forth, a huge smile will light his face— and, suddenly, he is your favorite professor, kindled by the excitement of talk. Whenever a problem becomes complicated, McNamara's zest rises— as when he finally devised the questions for a study of military dollar-and-gold

outflow. The questions were hunting tools. "Those figures are going to pop out, just pop out," he all but squealed to a friend, as if he had flushed a pheasant out of the bush.

OVER THE YEARS, the armed services have developed an information-delivery system for their masters that reaches its pinnacle in the Pentagon briefing. A truly great Pentagon briefing, complete with five-colored charts, flip cards, illuminations and slides, photo blowups the size of a wall, colonels dancing attendance and voices in the darkness, is an artistic production, like a ballet. "But briefings," says a close associate of McNamara's, "evaporate like the morning dew. When the briefers disappear with their charts and slides, you ask yourself: What did they say? McNamara wants it in writing first, so he can question it, and wants it in writing after they go, so other people can come in and argue with it. That's the way he gets to decision—by asking questions." For the armed services, which had entertained, befuddled and informed a long line of civilian secretaries with briefing performances over the years, the adjustment to McNamara was slow and painful. "To be questioned by McNamara," said one unhappy victim, "is like being picked over by bees."

Slowly, as 1961 turned the corner into 1962, the pace of questions slackened. It became apparent that McNamara hugely enjoyed not only his job, but Washington life in general. And Washington, like Detroit before it, began to recognize the different Mc-Namaras. There was a puckish Mc-Namara—who, when briefed for the umpteenth time on communications and reassured that this particular phone would reach Gen. Lauris Norstad anywhere in Europe within 30 seconds, simply lifted the phone, asked for Norstad and demonstrated conclusively that when Lauris Norstad was naked, taking a shower, at home in Marnes-la-Coquette, he could *not* be reached in 30 seconds. There was another McNamara, one of Washington's most earnest self-improvement characters and eggheads (he was a charter member of Robert Kennedy's Hickory Hill Study Group); there was McNamara the cold automaton, who treated his generals "like provincial branch managers of Ford factories." There was also the Mc-Namara who could laugh at both executives and eggheads, and enjoy being neither—as when a cherished professorial assistant struggled to close the door of his office, and McNamara strode over, closed it with a clap, then, with a twinkle and a laugh, said, "That's because I've met a payroll."

McNamara the bleak and McNamara the gay were both the same man. "He sits there at the table before a Cabinet meeting," recalls one watcher, "and he's cold business. Other Cabinet members come in, chat with each other, say hello, the way men do before a meeting begins. McNamara sits at his place, studies his papers, talks to no one. But, then, some night, there you are at a White House party, and you're supposed to be home at two o'clock in the morning, and who's still there twisting away? McNamara."

Like any man of size, McNamara can be seen from many angles. The best view offered this reporter was that of a scientist, John Rubel, deputy director of Defense Research, one of the prime architects of the destruction potential that overhangs the world.

"When he came in," says Rubel, "we were infinitely troubled people. Everyone is troubled—but we were *troubled* troubled people. We didn't see how we could get out of some of our problems—this endless escalation of the arms race, this needless multiplication of strategic weapons. We couldn't see how we were going to get a grip on the enormous programs we were supposed to supervise; we were worried about command control of nuclear weapons; we were worried about response. You don't know how worried we were right here in the Pentagon—much more than the public worriers who do it out loud.

"And you know what is the most significant observation I've made since McNamara came? Just the enormous difference one man can make, the tremendous changes in practice one can bring about with no effort at all to alter the laws. All of us live, in one way or another, by reacting to our environment; he's changed the environment."

LET US SEE how the environment has changed; and let us follow the change by examining the key words in the logic that has shaped American power and strategy to new ends.

"Quantify" is a favorite McNamara word, which means simply "to measure." On his entry into office, McNamara found that the last Eisenhower budget had asked Congress to give the Air Force one new wing of B-52's, the superdreadnaughts of the air. But one wing of B-52's, with the tankers, missiles and ground support necessary to maintain it for five years, would cost $1 billion. By McNamara's logic, such an expenditure had to be measured, "quantified," or "balanced" (another favorite word of his) against other possibilities. The Air Force already had 14 B-52 wings, 2 B-58 wings and obsolescing squadrons of B-47's. More money for the B-52's might increase our striking power by seven percent. But the same amount of money would buy and maintain 250 Minutemen missiles or six Polaris submarines. Which was the best way of doing what he wanted to do? Obviously, then, "quantification" required a corollary judgment, and this judgment depended on "functions" (another key McNamara word).

How did each exertion of the Army, Navy or Air Force fit the grand function or "functions" of our strategy? For a long time, scholars (as well as soldiers) had felt that the Defense effort was distorted by separate Army, Navy and Air Force submission of budget demands to Congress. Most persuasive among the scholars who argued for a new approach was Charles Hitch, coauthor of *The Economics of Defense*. Hitch advocated that all defense funds be allocated by function, by the purposes that animated them, not by the color of the uniform of the man who spent the money. McNamara read the book, then, immediately after he was nominated, recruited Hitch as comptroller of the Defense Department. Once installed, Hitch suggested to McNamara that they experiment by presenting a few programs to Congress as Defense requests, not Army, Air Force or Navy requests. McNamara's reply was no. There would be no experimental effort; instead, the entire Defense effort would be offered to Congress in terms of combined "programs" clarifying functions. Right then, and at that time.

Thus was born "program packaging." And program packaging brought clarity out of confusion, making plain, for the first time, to friend and foe alike, the new direction of American strategy.

Two Nuclear War Program packages governed direct interchange of death with Russia: a Strategic Retaliatory Forces Program (which considered the Titan, Atlas, Polaris, Minuteman and manned aircraft as a single family of weapons) and a complementary Continental Air and Missile Defense Program (against the Russian nuclear threat).

But two Conventional War Programs—one for General Purpose Forces and the other for complementary Sealift-Airlift Forces—directed attention back to the old-fashioned clash of men on battlefields.

It is significant that old-fashioned *battlefield war* is so much more expensive than new-fashioned *nuclear war* and growing more so. The Nuclear War Programs, now cut to $9.3 billion for 1964, can eliminate civilization from the globe and thus provide an all-time "biggest bang for the buck." The Conventional War Programs now cost more than twice as much—$20.5 billion in next year's proposed budget. War, by American strategy, is to be brought back to the battlefields where men can best defend the women and children of the cities.

This has been the decision and the change. The civilians who control the Pentagon now offer the White House an entirely new instrumentation of power—and a doctrine to manage it. They now offer the President "options." Since "options" is another key McNamara word that has colored all Washington thinking, we should examine what "options" means, and where the word has brought us.

"Options" means simply that civilized leadership should have at all times a variety of choices, an orchestration of forces, a range of responses that will permit instant dispatch of a company to quell a Southern riot, a battalion to beef up the Panama Canal defenses, a division to stabilize the Congo—or a total commitment in a clash over Berlin.

The Pentagon still retains, as it must, the fixed contingency plans for war, which the Joint Chiefs freshen regularly (there are 228 such contingency plans, according to the latest official report). These plans are necessary, but they no longer *control* American response. American power is no longer remorselessly locked in by them. McNamara's 1961 round of questions has been followed by another year of innovation. Underlying all the innovations

lies the same urge to unlock, unfreeze, make flexible the retaliation of the United States to challenge. The speedup of the hard-base Minutemen program, guaranteeing and multiplying America's second-strike capacity, reduces SAC's previously critical vulnerability—and takes nervous fingers off nuclear triggers. The elaboration and reelaboration of signals and command communications (there is now an airborne command of SAC in the air 24 hours a day) give new assurance that SAC will not act by button response alone. Military programs run forward on five-year plans; new procedures sensitively control, yet invite, changes in these programs.

Above all else, there is this achievement: The paper language of the laws that describe America's military leadership has finally become reality. The Army, Navy and Air Force are now service organizations—they train, equip, procure and make ready armed forces that they no longer command. The forces they make ready are handed over to nine great Unified and Specified Commands, which alone *operate* our military machine. These commands act only at the direct order of the civilian Secretary of Defense, who is advised by uniformed Chiefs of Staff beneath him and directed by the President above him.

Every turning in American strategy has been symbolized by a mighty new command. SAC in its day spoke American doctrine clearer than words. Today, no better symbol of the McNamara-Kennedy doctrine exists than the newest of the nine great Commands, the Administration's favorite and its own creation: Strike.

IT TAKES TIME for the imagination to grasp what Strike Command (STRICOM) is, what it means. A visitor may stand in a frost-covered meadow, at dawn, watching the sun glisten through the parachutes of 450 men as they soundlessly drop from the sky. Last night, these men were alerted 600 miles away at an Appalachian base. The two STRICOM combat teams from which today's unit was drawn are always ready for exactly such no-notice alerts—on call to fly, and jump, within an hour and a half. If this were war, two full airborne divisions would follow them to the airfields, where Strike's planes would be arriving to airlift them into combat. Across the country, six more divisions would, in days, be ready for air haul or sealift. Every combat-ready element in the continental reserve—eight divisions, three air forces, atomic artillery battalions, new transport fleets, new communications units—would act as part of one command: STRICOM.

STRICOM is not only a new system of using power, it is in fact also new power. Eighteen months ago, had there been such a command, it would have found only three divisions available in the U.S.; now it calls on eight. Eighteen months ago, Army would have negotiated with Air Force for airlift; now STRICOM commands its airlift, and that airlift has doubled, will shortly triple, in capacity. When Washington gives the word, STRICOM moves—anywhere in the world, in any strength, to cow riots or confront empires.

At MacDill Air Force base in Florida, STRICOM headquarters bubbles with the excitement of ideas in ferment. There is, for example, the ferment of rediscovery, as Army and Air Force once again find themselves joined organically in a single unified command. Gen. Paul D. Adams of the Army, a silver-haired, chunky field commander, is boss of STRICOM; his deputy is Lt. Gen. Bruce Holloway of the Air Force, a tall, soft-spoken wartime ace. They work together; they enjoy it. The officers under them have blended into a new, unified staff. New field tactics, new fire patterns, new air-support doctrines rise from conversations suspended too long by bureaucratic separation. In their offices or homes, STRICOM officers keep packed three kits—one for arctic war, one for tropical war, one for temperate-zone war. When STRICOM chooses the units that must move overnight to combat, it delivers also the leadership and plans to go with them. From its roster of 11 generals and 35 colonels (all combat veterans), STRICOM is prepared to peel off at once, without notice, a Task Force Alpha that commands anything up to regimental size; a Task Force Bravo that commands elements up to corps size. If more is required, STRICOM can lift itself and set up a headquarters for an entire Theater of Operations, ready to receive whatever the U.S. can mobilize.

———

STRICOM IS the best example of what McNamara, in another key phrase, calls "useful power."

"Everyone missed the point about Cuba," the Secretary reminisced recently. "It wasn't *just* power. It's true, a year and a half ago, we didn't have the combat-ready ground divisions, the combat consumables. We didn't have sufficient power to apply. But we also didn't have the theory of application of force, if we had had the power.

"Massive retaliation as a form of power just wasn't credible in response to a situation like the Berlin Wall, or to a situation like Vietnam, or Cuba. Massive retaliation had given us no *usable* power to prevent the U.S.S.R. from expanding its interests in Cuba. So we had to develop forms of *usable* power.

"Now, I'm not an engine engineer. But people who drive an automobile know almost as much about engines as an engineer—they know what they want the engine to *do*. Enough people know enough about driving an automobile to determine the form and characteristics of the engine. I never had to know the characteristics of metal stress when I was at Ford. I feel I don't have to be an expert in combat leadership of troops to lay down what we need in *useful power* in a situation like Cuba. We have an actual difference of physical force today. We had three ready divisions in the United States in 1961— now we have eight combat-ready divisions with their backup.

"But the application of power, *how* it should be applied, is even more difficult than any concern with the type or quantity of power. This was a major part of the Cuban question—the President knew the reasons for conceiving this delicate application of power, this sophisticated use of power. But this sophistication had to come from the top of the Government. A naval commander who blockades wants to blockade—period. He wants to stop all ships. That's his job. What complicates his decision is that the actions he takes during the blockade are also telegraphic messages to the Soviet Union, a way of signaling our intentions in a world where both sides have the military power to destroy a large part of civilization. This situation requires that the important signals come from the highest political power in the country. As a result, we've had a basic shift in the level where decisions on the application of power take place.

"At least until the world has developed a workable rule of law in international affairs, the foundation of foreign policy is power—but it has to be usable power, controlled to serve reasonable political ends. And that's the way we're moving—from unreason to reason."

Which is all any reasonable citizen can reasonably ask of his leadership.

LOOK April 23, 1963

WEINBERGER ON THE RAMPARTS

Caspar Willard Weinberger, age 65, a veteran of the Good War, 15th Secretary of Defense, is a man obsessed with his mission.

His mission, as he sees it, is twofold: First, to prepare the United States to defend itself immediately, in tomorrow's possible war; and, second, simultaneously, to commission and prepare the weapons for the wars of the 1990's. The cost of this dual purpose is absolutely staggering. But Weinberger, a man of unfailing courtesy and courtliness, is all but inflexible. "I may sound a bit paranoid to you," he says, "but people just don't understand the threat."

It is easy to see Weinberger as Washington's most controversial figure, for his problems are more than enormous and his solutions bewilder the nation. But his mission is to drive his overriding purpose—"readiness"—through a recalcitrant Congress, a divided White House, a hostile press and a major depression. In this struggle, the cheerful, ever humorous Caspar Weinberger has been transformed into a gaunt, somewhat lonely man, driving himself to the edge of exhaustion and frequently over that edge.

With a man so straightforward in a situation so complicated, it may be necessary to simplify his story, perhaps distorting it. For as one starts to probe the problems of an old college classmate, after decades of friendship and confidence, one is led on to more than a personality study. One is led, inevitably, to the problems that beset him. Here is a man demanding between a quarter and a third of the entire national budget; struggling to master the largest bureaucracy in the United States (2.1 million men and women at arms, almost a million civilian employees); confronted with bizarre techniques that prescribe the reflexes of slaughter but not its goals. Events overtake the personal story: the critical arms negotiations with the Russians have stalled; America's arms-control team is in turmoil; public relations people are rushed to defend a position that all too many Europeans find incomprehensible, and Russian rearmament, despite all Mr. Andropov says, goes on with no sign of slackening. Weinberger stands caught in the trap of history, squeezed by new forces reshaping politics abroad as well as at home.

So it is very important to start at the

beginnings, of the man and the problem.

ONE BEGINS, THUS, with a boy invited to Harvard on scholarship from San Francisco's Polytechnic High School, a stranger in a New England university. At Harvard, as he would always, Cap Weinberger "made" it—elected in his junior year (1937) to one of the highest honors his fellow undergraduates could give him—the presidency of the Harvard Crimson.

Franklin D. Roosevelt had once held that same honor; and Weinberger, always as much a Boy Scout as a scholar (he graduated magna cum laude), studied at the old Yard when Roosevelt launched the first "readiness" program for the Good War—the naval rearmament program of 1934. That program laid the keels of the flattops that won the battle of Midway eight years later and turned the tide of war. Weinberger, a major in government, was already a committed Anglophile, reading away in English history, in Siegfried Sassoon's war memoirs, enjoying Shakespeare, and above all: "I was a passionate believer in Winston Churchill," he says. "Civilization itself was at stake." Other undergraduates might chant, as so many of us did, "Scholarships not Battleships," but Weinberger was a true believer in the threat.

Cap Weinberger, son of a lawyer, went on to Harvard's Law School and, while there, tried to enlist in the Royal Canadian Air Force. Rejected for faulty depth perception ("They told me if I tried to land a plane I'd land it 50 feet above the runway"), he earned his law degree. Then he volunteered as a private in the United States infantry. "That," he says, in a homely phrase of another time, "seemed to me to be honorable service."

With basic training, his memories began to bite, reaching the intensity that now characterizes the once smiling young man. It was September 1941: "We did our basic with wooden rifles. Then Springfield rifles of World War I. No ammunition. They gave me a World War I helmet. We had no cadres, but we had time to form them. We were lucky that time; we had time to get ready. This time we may not be so lucky, we have to be ready *now.*" It is the recall of a man a full generation removed from the present generation, with its different vision of America.

Having passed through Officers Candidate School at Fort Benning, Ga., Weinberger put in to be sent to England to fight Hitler. Whereupon he was shipped to the Southwest Pacific—on a slow convoy where he met Jane Dalton, a nurse, and, on arriving in Australia, in August 1942, married her. As a second lieutenant in command of a platoon, and a crack shot, he was ordered with the 41st Infantry Division to New Guinea for the attack on Buna. Leading combat patrols, he made captain and was preparing to take his company on for the assault on Biak when it was discovered he had both a law degree and newspaper experience. Over his protest, he was shipped to the staff of Gen. Douglas MacArthur. Weinberger emerged from the war with both a Bronze Star and an everlasting admiration for MacArthur.

All this experience must be cranked into the world-view of the present Secretary of Defense: the view of an honors graduate in government, a platoon leader, a MacArthur intelligence-staff officer—and a man who believes in "projections of power." "I was defending California when I fought in New Guinea," he says. "It was better to defend California there than in Oregon."

But the young Weinberger had always been a Republican from student days. He had bet on Landon to beat Roosevelt in 1936. "Now we will hear from Weinberger, our Republican," his Harvard professor would say in a seminar overwhelmingly Democratic. Coming home from the war to San Francisco, he first practiced law, then led a revolt of liberal Republicans in the Bay area that brought him to the California Assembly, then to Gov. Ronald Reagan's notice and appointment as the state's Director of Finance. From Reagan's service he passed to Washington to serve Richard Nixon, first as chairman of the Federal Trade Commission, then as Director of the Office of Management and Budget, then as Secretary of Health, Education and Welfare—a skillful and charming politician, a fountain of quips and anecdotes.

There is a nostalgic perplexity in watching an old friend evolve into the grim chief of the United States armed forces embattled at home and abroad.

Caspar Weinberger believes today that the threat of the Soviet Union is as great as Hitler's, so great that every consideration of domestic politics must be subordinated to it. "If I have too little ready when the time comes," he said, "there won't be time to say 'too late.'"

Weinberger does not want American soldiers to train with wooden guns, with no ammunition. But, most importantly, Weinberger believes his mission is to spend and spend, whatever is necessary, to close the "window of vulnerability," the gap between our present strength and what we must have by the 90's.

Which brings us to another beginning.

THE OTHER BEGINNING must start with the development of the technology of mass slaughter.

Our weapons technology has usually been better than the Russians'—except that in one most important field of challenge, nuclear interchange, the accuracy of missiles, the Russians have recently overtaken and surpassed us. Always, during the long race, the Russians relied on the throw weight, the nuclear megatonnage, of their missiles—mass destruction delivered by heavy, clumsy, devastating nuclear warheads. They now outweigh us in such megatonnage by 5,000 to 3,000.

America has relied, up to now, on superior accuracy, rifleman accuracy. But we telemeter and watch Russian missile tests constantly—and in the last few years the Russians have brought their intercontinental missile target accuracy to a C.E.P. (Circular Error Probable) of 150 meters, or about 450 feet. That means that a Russian missile hurled from Siberia and aimed at New York's Central Park can probably hit it. This accuracy, coupled with their throw weight, undermines one of the underlying assumptions of American strategy. Given such accuracy and the superior megatonnage of their warheads, the Russians can "take out" America's 1,049 land-based missile launching sites at one strike. If you are Gen. Vladimir F. Tolubko, commander of the Russian Strategic Rocket Forces, and assign three warheads to each of the 1,049 American launching sites, and if—*an important if*—the Russian political leadership approves, then a single first-strike salvo permits the Russian Strategic Rocket Forces to wipe out one of the vital elements of American retaliatory strategy, an entire leg of the famous Triad.

This new accuracy of Russia's missile force rouses Weinberger's anger. He must live with it; and redress it; is not sure how; nor will Congress accept any of his solutions. Central to his thinking is the need to develop an American missile, more accurate than and as heavy as the Russian SS-18—the so-called American MX.

FROM THIS RACE for accuracy comes another train of his thinking: that there must be a shut-off of American technology to the Soviet Union. What exasperates Weinberger when accuracy is mentioned is the fact that the micro-

scopic ball-bearings, on which the gimbals of Russian missile-guidance systems turn, are stolen, or leached, from American technology. Most of these tiny ball-bearings (thousands of which can fit in one cup) are made in New England. The trick lies in the grinding tools that machine them to specification. Americans sold those grinding machines to the Russians, or let them slip out. And now the new Russian accuracy presumably holds all our bases in pawn. At this nightmare, Weinberger grows bitter; he insists there must be a shutdown as stringent as possible of American technological flow to Russia. But "people don't listen to me," he complains. "They don't want to listen."

It was this condition of Russian strategic development, as well as others almost as morbid, that Weinberger discovered shortly after he received his telephone call, on Dec. 1, 1980, from President-elect Reagan. ("I'm going to spoil it all for you," said Reagan. "I want you to be Secretary of Defense.") Several visits with Reagan followed, as Weinberger floundered between his comfortable life as a Bechtel Group executive and the call of the next President who wanted, above all, military buildup, and resolve.

Then, on to Washington, where, from Jan. 1, 1981, Weinberger was briefed daily. He had left Washington in 1975 as a cabinet member acquainted with Russian potential. But now, says he, "I was astounded. Their buildup had gone so far and so fast and all of it was in offensive, not defensive, weapons. . . . It was like running down a hill trying to catch up with a long, long runaway train. You come into this office and on your first day you find your in-basket full of decisions you have to make *today*. And, on top of this, you have to impose a new long-range policy, and people won't listen to you."

Out of his re-examination came, then, a figure or $1,600 billion (!) to be spent in five years to bring America into parity (*not*, says Weinberger, *superiority*) with the Soviet Union's arms capability. Whether the Russians, indeed, are superior in arms to America at the moment is a matter of intense debate among the Washington defense experts. But Weinberger's figure became the operational one. Such a figure had never before been heard in American politics; such a figure brings the Secretary of Defense up against the enduring question all previous Secretaries have had to face: How much is enough?

WITH THIS QUESTION we come to the last of the beginnings.

Between 1945 (when American armed forces dominated the world) and the stewardship of Robert S. McNamara in 1961, American armed power had dwindled year by year. But American policy still hoped to prevail, clinging to the John Foster Dulles doctrine of "massive retaliation," translated as "step on my toe and I'll bash in your skull." At that time we had both the throw weight and the delivery systems. But McNamara changed the savage doctrine of massive retaliation into the more civi-

lized one of "flexible response." By this doctrine McNamara and Kennedy played the 1962 Cuban missile crisis, knowing their hand held 400 intercontinental delivery systems as against what they believed to be a Russian total of 100. (Further intelligence has since told us that the Russians held probably only 10 operational ICBM's.) Khruschev backed down because he had to.

But Khruschev's backdown was also the beginning of another chapter, for the Russians set out on a military rearmament program matched in urgency only by that of Hitler in 1933–38, and much longer lasting and more shrewdly conceived. They would never again play from a bluff that could be called with impunity.

We face today the end result of that Russian decision. The Russians have 2,693 intercontinental delivery vehicles (chiefly in heavy-loaded ICBM's) as against America's 1,866 delivery vehicles. Their navy has launched its first two modern aircraft carriers and more are under way. Their military personnel numbers 4.3 million, backed by a conscription system that gives them 8.5 million ready reserves, while America has 2.1 million men and women under arms, backed only by a questionable 800,000 reserves. Of their weaponry, the most menacing are missiles—their progress in missiles has been spectacular. According to Richard N. Perle, Assistant Secretary of Defense for international security policy, in the 10 years of so-called détente, the Russians deployed seven new missile systems, while we deployed two. A bewildering array of Soviet missiles of all ages, ranges, weights now confronts American planners, with four new Russian systems coming on. Of all these, American policy is disturbed chiefly by two: the heavy SS-18 (300 or more, most with 10 warheads) that can reach anywhere in America, and the newly developed mobile SS-20 intermediate-range missile, with three warheads, targeted mainly on Western Europe.

Through all such figures on the equations of war one must run a divisor of unknowns. Russian strength in missilery or on the ground must be divided between their Asian and European borders. They have worries that do not burden us. Another divisor must be of the reliability both of their own troops and those of their allies. Will the Moslems of Central Asia, a growing element of their peoples, fight or flee when called on? Will the Warsaw Pact allies of Eastern Europe fight with, or rise against, the Russians when propelled into action? How will the Poles go? The East Germans? The Czechoslovaks? It is possible to believe that a Russian strike in Central Europe, if it can be stopped for 10 days, can be crushed like an eggshell. How does one weigh the tinder of politics against the SS-20?

Weinberger ignores such political questions. His job is to focus on Soviet capability, not what lies in the minds of their peoples. Therefore, by May 1982, the Weinberger Guidance Directive of the Pentagon to its armed structures: The policy is to achieve, first, a state of readiness sufficient to repel any Russian aggression against NATO; then to mod-

ernize and achieve a secure strategic nuclear capacity sufficient to fight a "protracted war"; then to fight in at least four major areas of contention, with a "projection of power" that will defend not chiefly our own American interests but those of our irritable and essential allies across the seas.

On the cost—$1,600 billion—Weinberger may give an inch—but no more. Somewhat proud of the nickname ("Cap the Knife") he earned as Nixon's budget director, he says: "I can cut this budget easily. I can decommission two divisions. I can wipe out two aircraft carriers. It's easy to cut the defense budget. But when the time comes when we need them, it will cost us a lot more."

This stubbornness has cost Weinberger the fragile margin of support for his critical strategic programs. His political base, until this year, has been the traditional national defense "consensus" in Congress; that has been chipped away now to the hard core. His base today lies at the White House, resting on two men—Ronald Reagan and William P. Clark of the National Security Council; and, even at the White House, Weinberger is under attack by several who see his inflexibility, at this time of political distress, as a gross liability—most notably James A. Baker 3d, chief of staff, and David A. Stockman, budget director. The divided Reagan White House has been debating the military budget for over a year and a half—since August 1981—and up until last month Weinberger, with the total support of President Reagan, has won hands down. Last month, Weinberger yielded slightly. Cutting $11.3 billion, or 4 percent from his next year's projections, he offered to settle for an appropriation of $273.4 billion for fiscal 1984— $41.9 billion *more* than the $231.5 billion Congress appropriated last year. In his State of the Union Message, Reagan obliquely but definitely backed Weinberger once again: There would be a 3.4 percent cut in the five-year program. But no more. The military budget must rise; as much else as possible would be frozen.

Weinberger's problem cannot be cut off from that of President Reagan. He can be called Mr. Straight Arrow. Snapped from the bow of the President, he cannot be deflected. Neither forbidding as was McNamara, nor hysterical as was James V. Forrestal, nor superbly deft as was Clark M. Clifford, nor technically dazzling as was Harold Brown among his predecessors, Weinberger is loyal; being loyal he has steamed on straight course directly into the hurricane that Reagan's politics and economics have brought about. The cost of this straight course—equivalence with the Russians in arms, now and in the 1990's—has brought him under such partisan scrutiny by a disturbed Congress as no other Secretary has faced before. Nor will 4 percent cut from his rising demand satisfy Congress. A depression of today's tragic dimensions has not been seen since the end of World War II; and the projected $200 billion-a-year deficit crushes planning of the future. The President has all but given up on the deficit; it stretches on in huge numbers to some date he cannot set.

But he will not give up on the cost of defense. Yet defense demands a rising budget at a time when most opposition Democrats, and many moderate Republicans, believe the American system, in this year of crisis, cannot satisfy both what the technologies of defense require and the requirements of the poor and the unemployed.

How much for guns, how much for butter?

The question pushes the story of Weinberger's struggle into the web of numbers.

THE NUMBERS headquarters of any administration is the Office of Management and Budget, once directed by Weinberger and now by David Stockman, both Reagan favorites. The fact that O.M.B. is so sharply critical of Weinberger and his Pentagon is of large significance.

An overview of O.M.B. figures gives a quicker look at the change in Federal responsibilities over the last 40 years than any other set of figures. And they define, quite simply, the historic trap of President Reagan and Weinberger.

Of all the O.M.B. sets of figures, the most enlightening, perhaps, are those that break down 40 years of the national budget. Back in 1945, when America was fighting World War II, 88 percent of the entire budget went to defense. In the aftermath of the Korean War, Eisenhower held the figure to an average of 56.5 percent during his eight years in office. Kennedy dropped it to an average of 46.2 percent; under Nixon that percentage dropped to 34.6. Under Carter the figure dropped to an average of 23.8 percent.

It is very difficult to make such figures leap and dance. But, when set in context, they give the flavor of change in American life. In the Eisenhower years, when defense demanded and received 56.5 percent of all the nation's expenses, the country's social programs consumed an average of 22.8 percent of the nation's budget. During the Nixon years (to pick a date, let us say fiscal 1971), the two sets of expenditures crossed—defense was down to 36.1 percent, while human welfare programs (chiefly entitlements and Social Security) took 42 percent. Since then the Federal expenditure on social programs has so far outrun the expenditures on defense as to startle. In the last year of the Carter Administration, social programs took 52 percent of all Federal expenditures while defense took 23.6 percent. In a generation the proportions had reversed themselves: from two to one, defense over social, in the Eisenhower years, to two to one, social over defense, in Carter's years.

These are the figures that illuminate the controversy. "They have to choose," said a general at the Strategic Air Command in Omaha, "between national security and Social Security." Some at the O.M.B. can make the clash even more poignant. "We have," said one spokesman, "three main components of the national budget—defense, human resources and interest on the national debt. That takes, this year, over 90 percent of our expenses. Which leaves only

7.2 percent for all the rest of the United States Government." All the rest consists of law and justice; of environment and the Coast Guard; of arts, medicine; farm price supports; shipbuilding subsidies; mass transit; aviation regulation—all those Federal commitments that make America still a pleasant country in which to live.

"Put it this way," the spokesman continued. "The clash over resources comes down to a choice between the armed services and the old folks, or between free school lunches and troops in Korea." Social Security retirement benefits and Medicare together consume today as much of the budget as the armed services. These are the programs that old people have come to depend on; they feel they have a contract with the Government and it must be honored. Somewhere, as one pokes through the quarrel between the "moralists" and the "realists," one comes to the grim truth facing a responsible government: Somehow defense expenditures *must* go up and swelling social entitlements *must* be restrained. But these realities have to be massaged through the world of politics.

REAGAN CAMPAIGNED on the promise that America would regain its military equivalence to Russia; he campaigned on other large themes—the cutting of taxes, the staying of inflation, the tantalizing theory that cutting taxes would provoke investment. But the horrors of an unbalanced budget overlay all promises. He has kept everyone of his promises, a rare event in

American politics—except that, so far, his governing theories simply have not worked and the nation is staggering through its worst depression in 50 years. There are now less than two years to make Reagan's theories work.

Well before the election of 1982, the military budget had become the favorite target of Congressional attack. With the election, however, not only did the military budget come under redoubled scrutiny but so did its personal sponsor, Caspar Weinberger. Was he smart and stubborn, or simply stubborn and insensitive?

To this question we must go now, but, first, one should describe the mentality of the Pentagon's leaders and explain their apparent inflexibility to all the calls of politics and compromise.

One quotes from random conversations:

The Secretary of Defense himself: "You're making a terrible mistake if you try to adjust your defense budget to food stamps, harbor dredging and highways. It's the threat that makes the budget. You've got to build your budget on the Russian budget."

From his recent Deputy Secretary, Frank C. Carlucci: "We are not responsible for the budget deficit. You shouldn't measure defense against social programs. The starting point is to measure it against the threat."

From his Under Secretary of Defense for Policy, Fred C. Iklé: "We're O.K. now on readiness. The critical things are the long-range programs. The trouble won't happen on Weinberger's watch, but in the next fellow's."

Those who oppose Weinberger are more discreet. Of three previous Secretaries of Defense to whom I spoke, none would permit attribution for direct quotation, sheltering behind the encoded gentleman's agreement that one does not knock a successor in public.

From ex-Secretary No. 1: "The trouble goes back to Reagan. His attitude to the Russians created this climate—he called them liars, cheats, thieves. Anybody can quarrel with the Soviets; a President's job is to find means of getting along with them. . . . I remember Churchill saying that if it comes to a second or third strike, all the bombs will do is bounce around in the rubble. Weinberger's done a good job on conventional forces. I support that. But he's been taken in by the Pentagon, the generals are in Beulah land—anything they want he gives them."

From ex-Secretary No. 2: "As a nation we can afford anything. Security is first priority. But you have to start with foreign policy and then you make defense strategy, and then you get down to force budgets, . . . Cappy's like a kid going into F.A.O. Schwarz and buying all the toys on the shelf. The services aren't being managed."

From ex-Secretary No. 3: "You can be Secretary of Defense in two ways. You can dig into the department and learn about weapons systems and management changes. Or you can rouse the public, educate the people. Cappy's done well on conventional forces. I give him credit for that. But all his energy has gone into this Churchillian rallying of the American people. He hasn't had the energy to learn about weapons systems or strategy."

From Senator Daniel P. Moynihan of New York, not too timid to be quoted, a member of the Senate Select Committee on Intelligence and one of the first to sound the alarm on the Russian buildup: "I've known Cap Weinberger for 14 years. He's a man of peace. You could hardly encounter a person with less aggression, less anger, less malevolence. But he is perfectly capable of having a wrong perspective on the enormity of nuclear weapons—and perfectly capable of a competitive view of who's ahead, who's behind and using what he's got. The Russian buildup is real. But the problem with the MX is it's a first-strike weapon. Cap inherited it—and he hasn't stopped to ask the military what they want to do with it. . . . His budget is plagued with implausibility."

Weinberger is, thus, pivotal in the debates that will engage the new 98th Congress. Torn by old politics: concerned by the rising number of jobless; certain that the sum of $231.5 billion voted for defense (in December) will rise even more sharply in the near future, or what the Pentagon calls the "out years"; and absolutely stunned by deficit projections that stupefy the imagination— Congress is in a state of disoriented rebellion against a military system that seems out of control.

Which leads us to the management of the Pentagon, and Weinberger's role.

THE PENTAGON—OVER-CROWDED, overstaffed, over-committed—must be seen as a continuum of ideas and programs so interwoven by esoteric technologies and career ambitions that it is difficult to discern where, in the passage of time, one Secretary's influence began and another Secretary's initiative changed its directions.

Programs have a life of their own and individual Secretaries of Defense can only nourish or slow them. In 1962, Robert McNamara introduced the idea of STRICOM, a rapidly moving strike command that could fight anywhere from the Arctic to the tropical jungle. By 1982, 20 years later, the same idea had been lifted to the concept of Rapid Deployment Joint Task Force. Then, finally, by Weinberger, to a new Central Command that can deploy strike forces over the troubled third world, and the blistering Middle East. But it is still based at the old STRICOM headquarters: MacDill Air Force Base in Florida.

In 1962, a young physicist at the Pentagon, Harold Brown, later to become a Secretary of Defense, was spending much of his thinking on a concept called Skybolt, an airborne strategic weapon that could be launched from a plane flying off the northern frontier of Russia. Skybolt was technically too soon for its time. In December 1982, finally, 20 years later, the concept became operational in an air-launching cruise missile squadron based at Griffiss Air Force Base in New York.

The Pentagon, a vast limestone and concrete fortress of bureaucrats on the south bank of the Potomac, sprawls over its 34 acres as if on an island of its own, detached from the politics and the intellectual flow of American life. Time was, in the Good War, that Roosevelt pumped his politics into it; and the senior minds of academia not only cooperated with defense but propelled the weapons systems with ideas like nuclear fission, radar, operational analysis. That cooperation came to an end with the Vietnam War, when academia distanced itself as if the Department of Defense was a colony of lepers. Even the august National Academy of Sciences separated itself, refusing to let defense scientists hold their conferences at the academy's summer retreat in Wood's Hole, Mass. The hostility of academia has, lately, changed—partly because universities, pinched for money, need defense research funds and partly because Russia's buildup frightens academics, too. But in the period of disassociation, the Pentagon came largely to incubate its own technical innovations in its own laboratories, and its chief outside source of ideas was the arms makers of the military-industrial complex. A new Secretary of Defense, thus, must choose from programs already on the shelf. And each choice involves billions of dollars, all taken from a national budget that must choose between programs for heart disease and kidney dialysis or a new Aegis cruiser ($896 million each).

In this continuum of shelf ideas, one must make a sharp distinction between administration and management, for the two are entirely different. Administration must make events march on time, have the right people in the right places, get maximum results at minimum cost. Management is different: It

must choose directions, decide on policies, set the targets, not for the day but for the decade.

The charge against Weinberger in the lobbies of Congress is that he does not manage. "That hurts," he says. His defense is best made by those who serve him at the Pentagon, for Weinberger is an expert administrator.

So, then, his credits must come first, and must start with the most important but unglamorous of his achievements, all of which flow from his fundamental concept of readiness.

"Weinberger," says the Chairman of the Joint Chiefs of Staff, Gen. John W. Vessey Jr., "has paid attention to people. The first and most important thing is people."

The United States armed forces as they stand are arguably ready today, which they were not three years ago. The hemorrhage of officers and noncommissioned personnel, the technicians who service the weird weapons of our times, has stopped. Re-enlistments are the highest in 19 years because pay is up by 14 percent a year and because the depression makes the service attractive. Quality has also gone up—86 percent of new recruits are high-school graduates, an educational level higher than that of the general population. This achievement soaks up a huge part of the Pentagon budget, of which half goes simply to pay people, including those retired. The Russians spend only 14 percent of their armed-forces budget on people—they conscript.

"We were a hollow army," says the Under Secretary Fred Iklé. Iklé is an unabashed hawk; an acknowledged first-rank member of Washington's college of cardinals of defense intellectuals, he concentrates on policy, while Weinberger and Carlucci have concentrated on administration. "Weinberger's priority when he came in was to spread money all over the place," says Iklé frankly. "Troops in Korea had only 20 days of ammunition to back them up, and it would take 53 days to resupply them if combat broke out. That's been corrected." American pilots were, by budget restraint and the cost of gasoline, reduced in 1978 to only 13 hours of air exercise a month; flight time is costly but crucial. The superiority of the Army Air Corps over the Luftwaffe in World War II became conclusive when Hitler ran out of gasoline to give his recruits enough air training to counter our veterans in combat. But the Israelis, whose lives depend on readiness, give their pilots 25 hours of air exercise a month. By 1984, the Weinberger budget hopes to give our pilots 20 hours of flight training monthly.

There are other credits.

One example: The Gulf of Sidra engagement, the only shooting action of the last two years. Two full weeks of diplomatic preparation preceded two minutes of action. All Arab countries adjacent to the domain of the Libyan fanatic, Muammar el-Qaddafi, were visited by Weinberger's alter-ego, Carlucci, to be told in advance that the Gulf of Sidra was no longer to be considered Qaddafi's pond; our Sixth Fleet would sail where it wanted in international waters. We planned not to provoke but to establish international law in the Mediterranean. And if, in turn, we were provoked in the Gulf of Sidra, our airmen would shoot back. So it happened: all the diplomatic niceties meticulously performed, all the legal rules of engagement neatly laid down for our pilots by the Pentagon's counsel. And in two minutes it was over, two Libyan planes destroyed and the presence of an American fleet in the Mediterranean confirmed as much by muscle as by law.

But such administrative achievements are at once accepted and ignored in Washington. Over the horizon gather clouds of the second war, the nuclear war of the future. Readiness for that war involves the modernization of our strategic arms, and the projection of power where it may be needed 10 years hence. Both the costs and the moral horror at preparing for the cataclysm have provoked the revolt against Weinberger.

THE LESSER QUARRELS in Defense turn on the instruments of conventional war.

All these can be resolved rationally, even if to Weinberger's distress. Do we or do we not need two more nuclear aircraft-carrier task forces? Is the new M-1 tank program (ultimate cost: $19.5 billion) sensible? Is the Bradley troop carrier worth so much more than the old six-by-sixes that carried American soldiers to the combat front in World War II? On such instruments Congress and civilians must listen to the men who use the tools; but they can argue. Stretchouts of time can be entertained, and the armed forces compelled to choose priorities.

BUT IT IS over the instruments of the "strategic war" that the debate about Weinberger rages most furiously. Many of the most ardent of Washington's patriots and defense experts question Weinberger's understanding of them. Altogether such instruments and the research on them today take only 15 percent of the Defense budget. But their cost will irresistibly soar . . . and they are the ones that torment conscience. These strategic instruments must fight the war that can reduce the world to rubble; yet, if they are not ready in time to retaliate, the only alternative may be to yield. It is the strategic system that involves policy, choices, projections.

And it is here, because "strategic programs" mean doom or survival, that the great debate sharpens on Weinberger. How reliable is his judgment? "At O.M.B.," said a friend who knew him there, "Cap knew enough to know that the economists didn't know. But in technology the scientists have got to know, have *got* to be right. The guys in here always tell you they can do it. But the results don't bear them out."

In dividing his time between his administrative duties, his Paul Revere role, and judgment on strategic technologies, Weinberger has let himself be swamped. The Pentagon has been his client; the public the jury, and, in defending his client, he has been overwhelmed. He rises at 5:30 in the morning, leaves his office at 7 in the

evening, his briefcase stuffed. Twelve to 14 routine appointments crowd his day. Meetings set by tradition demand his time each week, with the Joint Chiefs, the Secretary of State, the Vice President, the National Security Council. The White House is on him, daily. He must attend four NATO meetings a year, two meetings with Korea. Almost twice a month he must prepare for an appearance before one Congressional committee or another ("That's like cramming overnight for a doctoral exam," he says). He finds it difficult to say no to old friends, to erratic speech invitations across the country, to the exhortation role. He is left with not enough time to think forward.

Thus, Weinberger approached the climax of his strategic policies in early December with his long range programs all but won—all except the "dense pack"—MX basing scheme. But, in the previous three weeks, he had been on the exhortation rounds in Southeast Asia, in Australia, in New Zealand; the week before he had been in Brussels (for NATO) and in Yugoslavia.

All that year he had had one week of vacation in Maine and two weekends. Exhausted, he spent one day in the hospital with a touch of flu. And then approached Congress, pleading the case he had pleaded to monotony over the previous two years. But Congress had returned to Washington after an unsettling midterm election; it did not want to hear a lawyer's brief; it wanted to hear the decision of a judge who stood between what domestic politics required and the thrust of the Pentagon.

Now Congress was to be asked to accept a new MX basing program whose ultimate cost would be, by the President's guess, $26 billion. The resentment and confusion of Congress came to its point at the keystone of the strategic planning for the '90's—the MX, Missile Experimental. In the words of John Vessey, "MX stood up like a lightning rod. It took all the heat."

It also brought down the thunder of a Congress too confused to approve any course for an unthinkable war. And when Congress did, inevitably, break off from the dense-pack scheme, it broke the spearhead of the lance that Weinberger had been so long in preparing. And more: What was broken was the American politics of consensus on defense. What has been provoked is this generation's re-examination of the defense posture of the United States in a world where freedom depends on our muscle. What are to be the terms of nuclear engagement?

Is MX essential to those terms? Was dense pack?

MX IS A LONG-LIVED child of the continuum of technology that urges the Pentagon on with its weaponry. It was conceived as long ago as 1974 and molded over the years to its present design. It promises accuracy—twice as much as our present missiles, accuracy within 100 meters, or 300 feet, of target. It promises, with its 10 or more warheads, weight sufficient to crush the deep-hardened Russian silos whose missiles are targeted on us. But its final design—a 96-ton monster cannister—was set by the strictures of the SALT treaties that stipulated its upper limit and range. Smaller, equally effective, equally accurate weapons can be designed—but at substantially greater cost. One such design, the D-5, is already on the way, to be installed by 1989 in the new Trident II submarine.

There is a quality of insanity to all talk about missiles of the future. Does it matter who is left alive in the ruins, and whose ruins may still cradle civilization? Yet within this insanity responsible men must still think soberly about the calculus of destruction. American policy has long planned, if war comes, to hit Russian strategic bases—not to engage in "city-busting" or civilian holocaust. But if the Russian first strike can now wipe out our bases, then our response must provide a counterthreat of holocaust, inviting counter-holocaust.

To preserve the balance of terror, new, more accurate and heavier missiles are needed to catch up with the Russians; silos must be hardened; and missiles based.

Basing, then, is the first military political problem. And that touches nerves until now untwinged. So cumbersome and heavy a weapon as the MX cannot be carted around easily. It must have a launching site. Some 16, or 20, or 34 basing schemes have been proposed. The final scheme of the Carter Administration was the notorious "racetrack" idea, the mad shell game that would shuttle the MX around on flatbed rail wagons over thousands of miles of the western states. This scheme was rejected by the incoming Reagan Administration as silly and absurdly expensive; instead Reagan and Weinberger offered another rather sensible plan—an interim plan until a final one could be worked out. This was to unpack 30 or 40 old silos scattered through the western states, some of which still hold obsolete liquid-fueled Titans, and restock them with the new MX missiles until a final home could be found.

At which point politics intervened. "Congress didn't just say no," said Carlucci, the former Deputy Secretary. "They said, 'Hell, no!'" With Russian targeting capability, no state wanted a prime missile target in its backyard. Among the most reluctant to go along were several of Reagan's great loyalists in the Senate, particularly those of threatened western states where the slim Republican Senate majority rests. Utah (Jake Garn and Orrin G. Hatch), Nevada (Paul Laxalt), other states whose geography and sparse population invited sitings would not bear the responsibility of becoming the prime targets of a Russian first strike. Hell, no, thus, it was, and in August 1981 Congress demanded of the President that, before further funds for MX were appropriated, it must know where and how the new MX would find a home. Upon this rejection Congress hung a deadline: It must have a full-scheme basing plan before going further and must know by Dec. 1, 1982.

This deadline embitters both Weinberger and the President. Both had sought a deadline of October 1983 to let the scientists think through the intricate technical problems of combining the potent MX with its siting mode. But their hands were forced. If Congress insisted on a full-bodied plan by Dec. 1, it must have one—for Congress controls the money. Out of all the unpleasant options, the President and Weinberger chose the scheme called dense pack, based on a theory styled "fratricide." "Fratricide," said a Pentagon iconoclast, "is the military equivalent of supply-side economics." The thought was that, if one packed all the new MX missiles in one spot (Wyoming, where both Republican Senators and its one Republican Congressman were acquiescent to the choice), the Russians would have to clean out the entire pack, and their incoming missiles, as they exploded, would blow each other up—fratricide! Then we would strike back.

The theory has been explained to me over and over again and still makes no sense. Even its supporters make a weak defense, including Joint Chiefs Chairman Vessey. A veteran infantryman, Vessey is one of the rare ones in high command who has actually led troops in combat, actually trained troops. Of dense pack he says: "The first time I heard of it, I thought the thing was crazy. For guys like me, who'd been telling troops, spread out, don't bunch up, the idea of everyone bunching on the bull's-eye seemed crazy." Then, valiantly, supporting Weinberger, he adds that "they" convinced him the scheme would work—and he supported it.

Not so, however, with the other generals. Of the five commanders who make up the Joint Chiefs, three opposed the scheme.

Of this split opinion the President could have been in no possible doubt. The President met with Vessey and Weinberger at the White House in late fall and Vessey reported then that the Joint Chiefs all wanted the MX but were, in majority, opposed to dense pack—Army, Navy, Marines opposed, Air Force in favor (though SAC rumbled in opposition to its own chief) and he, Vessey, supportive. Weinberger gave his opinion: that no present American land-basing system could any longer be considered invulnerable to Russian first strike; that dense pack, on the advice of his scientists, would cause the Russians the most problems, diverting their resources; it would also be the least costly of plans. It was a gamble, and they were pressed by Congressional deadline. Thus, then, the President and Weinberger chose the gamble, hoping that the traditional "consensus" would bring a close battle in Congress to a victory.

But it could not, for MX, dense pack, aircraft carriers, B-1 bombers, all the rest, added up to a cost that a lame-duck Congress could not support without protest. Sensitized by the midterm elections, the freeze movement and the "fairness" issue, Congress was restless.

Said one of the most responsible men of the White House: "You simply have to recognize the political impact of the fairness issue—we can't cut benefits for poor people and increase military spending unless Cappy gives a little bit. We've got to get the economy going

again—everything rests on that, the election of 1984 rests on that. Any cuts we make in the budget must be balanced for fairness against some cuts in the military. And, anyway, dense pack wouldn't work. We knew within five days of the President's speech [on Nov. 22] that it wouldn't float. We tried to round up five eminent scientists who would testify to Congress that fratricide would work. We couldn't find one. So the consensus came apart."

American defense policy is thus wide open for re-examination—more so in definition of the wars of the 90's than it is in the field. Weinberger's call to arms has been accepted almost in its entirety—his readiness and stockpiling, his aircraft carriers, cruisers, submarines and new planes. But when Congress broke off the tip of his lance, giving him $231.5 billion for defense, all but the $1 billion for dense pack, and fenced off money for development of the MX and a basing scheme, it revolted against a future it could not understand whose bizarre technologies a representative democracy could not absorb.

Weinberger simply happens to be there at a time when exhortation has run its limits and the politics of America and its technologies require a total revision of thinking about war.

It has been a long time since any independent group has had the authority or courage to dig beyond the defense budget into the connection between American defense and the Russian threat, or between American defense and its home politics. This is a problem that philosophers call "cutting at the joints." But no one either in this Administration or the Carter Administration has known where the joints lie.

So, now, we await yet another panel's report, due 12 days hence—that of a new commission headed by former Air Force Lieut. Gen. Brent Scowcroft, a successor to Henry Kissinger as chief of the National Security Council. Its assignment is to re-examine the MX missile and the problem of its basing. The new commission includes as its participating consultant Harold Brown, ex-Secretary of Defense, Democrat, a preeminent technologist; as its leading personality Alexander M. Haig Jr., ex-Secretary of State, Republican, a veteran of White House and NATO politics. It includes at least one distinguished scientist, John Deutch of the Massachusetts Institute of Technology; several experienced administrators, and as many window-dressing names. It includes no experienced men of politics nor any historian.

The most important measure of the commission's considerable weight is that the Pentagon leadership is afraid of it and its impact on Congress. To govern is to choose; since Weinberger and Reagan could not force Congress to their choice, they have off-loaded the burden to a commission whose eminence may persuade Congress to make a choice.

The hope at the Pentagon is that this group can detach MX from dense pack, save the missile program and accuracy attainments and let them discard dense pack with honor. But their fears are clear, too—that the panel, whose authority runs beyond its arbitrary Feb. 18 deadline, may become a runaway grand jury: What if the new group urges that not only dense pack but the MX itself be discarded? Can its authority be overriden? Does the Administration dare oppose it?

So the commission is faced with conundrums that interlock with conundrums.

THE NEW YORK TIMES MAGAZINE February 6,
1983

Chapter 18

My Country

The four articles that make up this final chapter are not "standard" White. Rather, they are the reporter turned essayist. In "Second Time Around," written in 1961, he recalls a world of two decades earlier and reflects on America's new global responsibilities. The proper role of government is his underlying concern in "What America Means to Me," written during the Bicentennial Year. In "The American Idea" (the beginnings of an article that death kept him from finishing), White again demonstrates his great talent for bringing clarity to a complex subject in very few words. Finally, in his last completed article, White writes movingly of the tiny Connecticut town he came to call home.

SECOND TIME AROUND

Mr. White began his career as a foreign correspondent, serving overseas for fifteen years in China and Europe. This report is an account of a recent world trip to countries he had visited many years before.

The Political Topography of Today's World

No planes flew the Atlantic when I first set out around the world twenty-one years ago. It was a slow journey in time of trouble—but there was to be time for questions to shape and answers to come.

I sailed from New York, fresh out of college, in the old SS *President Roosevelt,* my chance cabin-mate a young Spanish anarchist named Serafin Aliaga. Aliaga might have lingered in New York, but since Franco's troops were closing on the Republic, he preferred to go home to Barcelona to face the end that was certain. It took eight days to cross the Atlantic and all the while he talked to me of European politics. It was very strange talk to a young American leaving a country that legally then bound the nation and its individuals by the Neutrality Act to absolute noninvolvement in any foreign strife. And then I was in Neville Chamberlain's London where the bitter taste of Munich was still fresh. In Hyde Park the newly cut air-raid trenches opened to the October sky and the government was distributing gas masks.

Then on to Paris, also waiting, also doomed, a somber city stagnant as it had been for decades, its velvet-gray heart paralyzed. In all its reaches, only one scaffold marked a new building rising; on the walls, the name of Daladier, the Premier, was smeared in contempt. In Paris, as in London, it seemed impossible that Americans could not be involved, despite all laws and hope to the contrary.

From Paris, a slow boat of the Messageries Maritimes carried me to the Middle East (disturbed then as now by an Arab-Jewish clash) and on into the placid imperial realms of Asia. It was there, in a colonial post office in Singapore, that I felt for the first time the crush of people in the crowded Orient, long files of Chinese and Malays waiting patiently to reach the stamp counter. "Go ahead," someone urged me as I looked for a way to the desk, "the line opens for you. White people go first; the natives really don't mind."

Then on to China to witness the wild flare of night bombings in Chungking, as the Japanese struck and the Chinese held, in the first chapter of the war that was to remake Asia. Here, finally, was the excitement of the clear answer-by-action, the thrill of challenge faced and response committed. And so, intrigued, I lingered in China for several years until I had become convinced that the challenge in Asia was a challenge to America, too, and it was time to come home.

By then, of course, after three years, the globe had begun to shrink and, reaching Hong Kong, facing home, I marveled: a fledgling airline was pioneering a flight across the Pacific and promised to fly from Hong Kong to San Francisco in only six days. The old Martin Flying Boat churned along just above the waters at 110 knots, and day after day the blue Pacific unfurled its distances and palm-tasseled islands, there was much time to wonder what the shriveling quality of distance and the sound of bombs in China all meant to America.

Finally, the plane came down over the new bridge across the Golden Gate, and I could see the tiny cars glistening like glass beads below—red and yellow, white and green, cream and black—bearing the familiar commuter procession from the suburbs of Marin County to work in San Francisco. The procession brought a lump to the throat, an irrational tear. For the automobile, in those days, was uniquely American—the imagined smell of gasoline fumes, the sound of horns, the heat of a traffic jam below were, all of them, the taste of homecoming. Automobiles existed nowhere else in the world in such numbers; they expressed plenty, and power.

Such power, it followed, would have to be used. For it was by then June of 1941: Asia and Europe were both locked in wars that only America's

power could resolve. America must act—the returning homecomer knew it in his bowels. The necessary response was clear. Yet would America act? Could it act?

A year later, of course, America *had* acted; and there were to be no more shining new cars available for three years.

THIS YEAR OF 1961, I needed only thirty-six days to round the globe again—a trip so leisurely and unhurried, yet so swift and unclarifying, that I have been brooding on it ever since.

From New York, flight swept us across the United States, then over the Pacific—Hawaii, Guam, Manila—in twenty-one hours of flying time. All the remembered distances of Asia—Manila-Hong Kong, Hong Kong-Formosa, Formosa-Bangkok, Bangkok-Delhi—all had, by this year of 1961, been gobbled by the jets that flew at speeds approaching sound, 40,00 feet in the air, a hundred or more people borne aloft in their cabins. Only the stars by which the pilots guided their planes were the same; beyond the stars, within the plane, all about us in the world, the clipper jet shared nothing, with the old Martin 120. Beneath, the world had shrunk apparently to one.

Shrunk though it was, however, so that we could girdle it in weeks, it seemed more difficult to grasp than in 1941; no cord of logic bound it together, no pattern of events marching to the strategy of any master plan, friendly or hostile, was at all apparent.

Now that I am home again in America, dependent on the report of events as they shape in our press, logic again begins to encase the world, clear patterns are once more visible. Only the memories of a recent trip resist the logic with the perplexity of reality.

None of the reporting I read now, for example, refreshes the overwhelming recent memory of what I can only call The Surge. Perhaps never before in history have men everywhere moved faster or more steadily toward well-being than in these years of postwar crisis while each day's headlines have called doom and prophesied woe. Wherever one goes, in Asia as in Europe, the hopes of 1941 are fact and deed to be seen by the visitor of 1961.

I woke in 1961 in a Manila remembered as war-torn and gutted from siege and liberation. But I woke to the sound of horns blaring and brakes screeching as, from the hotel window, I saw for the first time an Asian traffic jam. Where before the war a few automobiles forced their solitary ways through the crawl of horse-drawn charametas, I could in 1961 no longer find an animal-pulled vehicle. The trucks, the buses, the taxis, above all the "jeepnies"—the old jeeps, debris of war, reconditioned, chrome-plated, decorated with flags, painted in floral colors—now choked the streets. In the old city at night, once a huddle of dimlit alleys, electric lights glittered, radios crackled, and television glowed. The little middle-class enclave of Forbes Park had grown into a suburb of gardened elegance to match the most opulent stretch of Beverly Hills or Westchester. And, pulsing over new roads through the paddies of the countryside, The Surge was transforming the old nipa shack villages with square-cut mahogany cottages on stilts.

In Formosa, too, The Surge operated. Only the melancholy dirge of the bugler blowing the strains of "San Min Chu I" outside the red brick Defense Ministry of Chaing K'ai-shek recalled old China. For the rest, Formosa was something China might have been, had Chiang's government known fifteen years ago what it knows now. Most of the old familiar rascals were long departed from his government; the capital city was clean; the new bazaar in Taiwan, replacing the old tangle of peddlers' booths, swept in a mile-long arcade of square-gray concrete stalls. Public buildings stood fresh-painted, glistening with new gold and vermilion of Chinese traditional architecture. Above all, in the fields, where it counted most, the Chinese boasted most: today, Chinese farmers on Formosa command the highest agricultural productivity per acre of land in the entire civilized world; new seeds, crops, tools, land reform, extension programs have created a new agriculture.

IN HONG KONG, The Surge throbbed visibly. The sight of Hong Kong from the air was once as familiar to me as that of New York—when the Japanese held it during the war, it had been one of our favorite bombing targets and danger had printed on my memory the exact location of each landmark that fringed the docks. But from the air this summer Hong Kong was unrecognizable.

Where 700,000 people once lived, there now lived over 3,000,000. The bay was crusted with a new profile; the towers of the Gloucester Hotel and the Hong Kong-Shanghai Bank, those citadels of Empire, were lost in a forest of new buildings. It was a new Hong Kong. There were rickshaws still—but chiefly for tourists, because (like the horse-drawn carriages of Central Park) rickshaws were a luxury and taxis were cheaper than muscle-power. There were conspicuously fewer women in the shiny South China black silks, too many in modern clothes. And only in the back alleys off East Queens Road, in the depths of the Communist community, could one sniff the fragrances of spice and incense that made it part of old China—Hong Kong was now all but sanitized.

It was in Hong Kong, however, that we began to tune in on the perplexity.

In the evening, one could go, as we did, to visit friends whose villas on the green back-slope of the Peak faced the mainland. As one drank iced martinis in the sunset, the black and purple mountains of the Communist mainland across the narrow waters seemed close enough to touch. From beyond the mountains in the dusk came the flash of monsoon heat lightning as if enormous events were happening just beyond the hills about which we could only guess. The mountains glowered, then grew black with night, and we knew that beyond the mountains lay hunger, suffering, and all the relentless compulsions of Communism, while here, on this island, even the poorest Chinese lived in relative security and ate. It reminded

one of Berlin, how like an island of prosperity Hong Kong sat in the misery of Communism. Yet Hong Kong was not Berlin, which menaced a Communist empire more by the inflection of its ideas than by its manifest well-being. Hong Kong boomed—but its buildings were built to be rack-rented, the investment paid off in five years so the builders might flee. The boom was real—but made of clay, for no spirit moved it. No idea of any importance generated in Hong Kong to infest men's minds in the land of Communism as did the ideas that came from Berlin.

From Hong Kong a flight of two hours carried us down the South China Seas, over the white and coral islands, to Saigon and Vietnam, and here, in Vietnam, our perplexity grew. For here, in Vietnam, America herself was involved—Vietnam was our ward. In no Asian country (except China) had so much American effort been spent; already in the summer, while the monsoon rains still fell and the soldiers waited for the dry fall season to harden the ground for combat, our legates debated whether or not we should send American soldiers to die here in this country. This was the violent clash point of the Asian struggle—in desperate peril. Yet none of the facts would arrange themselves in a sequence that led to a clear conclusion.

There was, to begin with, the fact that no American in Vietnam had any reason for shame or embarrassment at the record of his government—Republican or Democratic—in South Vietnam. In the six years of existence of South Vietnam's government, American support had been its chief nourishment. We had spent more than $2 billion in aid and countless hours of care and thought and asked nothing for ourselves.

THERE WAS NEXT the fact that this American aid had mounted a Surge, the dimensions of which were all but unbelievable. Totally unreported in the reporting of the crisis were such staggering achievements as Vietnam's agricultural development: where in 1955 Vietnam had grown 2,000,000 tons of rice, it now grew 5,000,000 tons of rice annually; its exports had risen from a wartime low of 48,000 tons a year to 500,000 tons a year—and what was left the peasants ate. They no longer mixed their rice diet with potatoes and roots but ate unmixed rice and ate full. A combination of fertilizer, new seeds, and land reform (pushed as far as any reasonable man could ask) had created all this—and at every turn American advice or American aid had helped. Health had improved—the use of modern drugs had increased 50 per cent in six years. The peasants were beginning to move on wheels—bicycles had jumped from 200,000 to an estimated 1,000,000 in the same period. The number of students from primary grades to university had multiplied by four times; each year the number of children in primary grades was rising, so the ministry of education said, by 20 per cent; since 1954 they had risen from 400,000 to a total that had passed 1,520,000 by 1960.

To myself, who remembered Saigon

as the harsh and elegant capital of France's Indochina Empire, the city was a joy to see. Saigon was clean as ever, its streets swept, its tree-shaded avenues well tended, its flower stalls gay with tropical blossoms. The green and pleasant Botanical Gardens left by the French were thronged by people and, on Sundays, the citizens of the city and their children pressed like a subway mob into the dusty little museum seeking the roots of their past. French signs were now a rarity; all public directions were printed in Vietnamese. The majestic Avenue Norodom had become the Avenue of Independence; the graceful beige chateau that once housed France's Governors-General now housed a President of Indochina. Saigon was the capital of a free people, governed by its own leader who presided over an economy beginning to thrive in a manner undreamed of ten years ago.

Yet Saigon was a city under siege, a city of random assassinations and night bombings. Beyond the city, no white man would venture without armed escort or in military formation. At night, the black-pajamaed guerillas of the Communists prowled the countrysides, collected taxes, terrorizing the peasants or holding their loyalties by seduction.

America had created The Surge. It had also armed in Vietnam an army of 170,000 troops and supplied the guns of a Civil Guard of 50,000 more men. Yet for all their efforts a guerilla force estimated this summer at 12,000 (and now grown to 20,000) held 220,000 men at bay; the guerillas waxed in strength with no weapons more imposing than knife, mortar, rifle, and the ambuscades of roadblocks on highways or infected fish-hook spikes in the paddies.

There were heroes, to be sure, in the war against Communists—young government officials who went to sleep in their offices in the countryside not knowing whether they would wake safely in the morning, young army officers who itched and chafed to fight the Communists in open battle but could not find them. Yet there were the others who, rightly or wrongly, had given up—the government official who said he was exporting his art treasures and added, "I'm exporting myself along with them." And the others who didn't care—like the *"jeunesse cowboy,"* the young men and women we found dancing in the Saigon nightclub as the orchestra beat and the handsome Annamite girls swayed to the sounds. Fifteen miles away the Communist contemporaries of these young people prowled the countryside by night. The question repeated itself above the beat of the music; why were young Communists willing to die for what they believed in? What would make these young people willing to die, too?

In Saigon, one could not avoid reexamining afresh the whole theory of American aid—which now, it seemed, could more appropriately be called the Virgin Birth Theory of Aid. This theory was born in the early days of the Marshall Plan, in 1948. Hunger and poverty, so ran the theory then, were the enemies of democracy and thus of America. The program and cure were thus, we thought in those days, obvious from the diagnosis: America would

pump in billions of dollars of help; the economies of the recipient countries would slowly mend; food, housing, welfare would all slowly but perceptibly increase; as well-being grew, the people whom we helped would come to trust their governments which we aided; such governments would grow stronger and more democratic; being strong and democratic, they would become useful allies of America in preserving the peace. The sweet part of the theory was that it would all come about automatically—pour in aid at one end of the time sequence and five or ten years later Democracy and Friendship would come out the other end.

But in South Vietnam, the theory had not worked. The Communist guerillas seduced or terrorized an indifferent peasantry and propagandized the intellectuals by tagging the government of Ngo Dinh-Diem as the government of "Mei-Diem" (America's Diem), the puppet of the hated white man. And the most effective anti-Communist force in South Vietnam were not the peasants or the intellectuals or the government but the young army officers for whom democracy is as meaningless a word as for their Communist enemies.

An old discarded thought suddenly became fresh again: it is the spirit that moves men to fight and to organize; material well-being is important—but the spirit is more important. Fourteen years of experience had taught the administrators of our aid to stimulate almost any degree of material Surge. But it had given us no experience in providing a doctrine of politics which, in such countries as these, could match the doctrine and dynamic of the Communists. Except for the officer corps of the army, perhaps not one Vietnamese in a thousand made any connection between his own improved well-being and what America had tried to do. Indeed, we had not seriously tried to press this connection on them; we had left it to the government of the Vietnamese to provide the spirit of resistance; we had pressed it in every way to do so; but it could not; and now, what were we to do?

An hour and a quarter's flight carried us from Saigon to Bangkok.

In Bangkok, we landed at the new, glass-paneled, soon-to-be-air-conditioned terminal. Built with American aid, it is the finest in the Orient. Years ago, dispensers of Marshall Plan aid would have regarded such an airport as economic sin. A gaudy decoration for a nation's pride, the airport was of no remotely comparable economic value to dams, machine tools, fertilizer, deflationary financing. Yet the Thais loved their new airport—no more than one in twenty thousand would ever fly from this field; but it pleased them.

THE ROAD INTO Bangkok was rutty and dirty, but the driver with enormous pride told us of the new parallel split-lane concrete throughway being built from the capital to the new airport. Again, it was being done with American aid; again, it was an extravagance by the older sober theories of foreign aid; but the driver's pride was real, his friendship for America seemed genuine.

Bangkok, too, had changed. The palace of the king, the temple of the Emerald Buddha, the sound of bells tinkling as the wind teased them— these were all that were familiar from the remembered past. But the canals, the old picturesque water thoroughfares of the city, were being covered with concrete roads; new hotels marked the skyline; factories were being raised.

The American Embassy here in Bangkok was a trim, intelligent, well-directed operation. Its officers described the process of life in Bangkok clinically, as a transition from the old world of Asia into the new world of industry and technology; the Embassy was deeply concerned about the transition—but it did not try to change or advise this government. It did not meddle; we helped but we let the ruling dictator make his own way forward as he groped to move his people. No background of colonial race hate cramped the efforts of Americans to make friends with the Thais; nor did the American Embassy intrude where it was not invited. In Asia, Thailand looked solid.

It occurred to me only after I left Bangkok that neither there nor anywhere in the Orient did Americans in the field speak of "democracy" as our purpose, as we used to speak of our purposes in the early days of the Marshall Plan, or as we talked of "democracy" in China when we pressed Chiang K'ai-shek's dictatorship to those reforms which, half-heartedly tried, ended by weakening him.

Thus into Delhi.

I had first been sent to Delhi, as a

correspondent, in the summer of 1942 at one of those moments when the war might be won or lost. The Japanese had just seized Burma; Rommel camped outside Alexandria; and the Indians simmered. That summer nineteen years ago, I had visited Jawaharlal Nehru at his home in Allahabad where eloquently he told how the British must be made to quit India. Nehru had journeyed to Bombay the next day where he was jailed by the British; India had risen the following day in the greatest revolt since the Sepoy Mutiny of 1857; and on August 9, 1942, an insurrectionary earthquake had rocked Delhi.

The epicenter of the quake was in Chandni Chowk, the ancient market that bisects Old Delhi, and there on the street which sold copperware and jewelry, cloth and umbrellas, vegetables and fruits, the mob held control. It was absolutely essential, beyond any qualm of conscience, that this capital be held by the Allied Forces. So on mid-morning of August 9, I found myself with a column of British troops in Chandni Chowk surrounded by a mob throwing rocks and chanting *"Inqulab Zindabad"* (Independence Forever). Then the mob closed on the column and cut us off. A young Scottish wharf-worker handled the gun on our Bren gun-carrier. A member of the Labor party, he was really on the side of the rioters; he muttered how he hated to die on this side of the fence, a feeling I shared with him. But then as the rocks fell on us, and the mob tightened, the necessary response became clear and the column fired: I remember still the sight

of the first body that dropped from the roof, like a bundle of limp gray laundry flung down from above. There were several others killed in the British shooting—all unarmed civilians who had sought to kill us by hand. Then the mob cleared, the column withdrew from Chandni Chowk, and within twenty-four hours Delhi was militarily secure. Indians refer to it, still, as a massacre; yet had India been turned over to the uprising it is possible the war might have been lost right there—and India never been free.

THE AUGUST UPRISING is still a great memory in India, and when we arrived this year I read on the wall of the Mogul Red Fort a notice that on the anniversary of the uprising, Prime Minister Nehru himself—whose arrest along with Gandhi's had triggered the uprising of 1942—would address the Youth Rally of his party at Ram Lal Park, which stands at the head of Chandni Chowk. We went to hear him on a hot, muggy night and the park was crowded with thousands of young Indians. Nehru appeared on the rostrum on the hour scheduled and, since it was so long since I had seen him, I saddened as I saw how old his step had become, how he stooped slightly, how, when he folded his hands beneath his chin in welcome to the crowd, it was a gentle gesture, like a grandfather's. He spoke in Hindi; on the stream of Hindi discourse there floated such English words as "atomic energy" and "space travel" and "atom bomb" and "Major Titov" and "TVA" and "religion of spirituality." After perhaps half an hour of this, there came a gurgle of discontent on the edge of the crowd in the park. Nehru pulled the microphones closer to him as if they were yelling "louder, louder." He spoke more loudly—but the rumble increased. Then, suddenly, the realization came to him: they were booing him offstage. Not because of anything he was saying. They were urging offstage the hero of this anniversary because he was taking too much time. Following him there would come a movie star, an idol of the Indian screen, Dalip Kumar—it was Dalip Kumar they wanted to hear!

Nehru caught the meaning of the rumble quickly, finished his remarks abruptly but with dignity, and left. He arrived shortly thereafter for dinner with American Ambassador Kenneth Galbraith and Under Secretary of State Chester Bowles and, according to those present, could by then ruefully joke about it. But I could not help but wonder whether some of those youngsters might have had parents who nineteen years ago rioted for Independence, at however ill-timed a moment—and whether it might be better now for us to have such parents as allies in this world at this moment, or to have these youngsters.

Those I saw governing India were the rebels of twenty years ago—twenty years old. They were the same men, with the same ideas—but with the effervescence gone. Yet at least they had an idea, still. They held control of the country by the machinery of a civil service they had inherited from the British; but they could not adapt it to what they now wanted to do; they groped; with this machinery and by enormous effort they were attempting to inch forward the heat-drugged millions who lived in mud villages and worked the plains for food. In all their efforts, American aid was indispensable; but there could be no misreading their feeling: they resented it.

Between the old men who dominated the Indian parliament and the young people who wanted to hear Dalip Kumar, there stretched the uncertain gap in India's future. Could American aid hold the line of minimal well-being long enough for India to find its way with new ideas, long enough for new leadership to grow up between the very young who had forgotten the revolution and the very old who were frozen to its dead past? It is almost certain that if we withdrew our aid, India would spiral down in bitterness, ugliness, and chaos; or rest stagnant in its subcontinent outstripped in Asian imagination by the cruel yet spectacular industrial achievements of Communist China. Yet if we continued our aid or increased it, no responsible American official would guarantee anything—except that Indians would have a government of their own which then might denounce or befriend us as it chose.

FROM DELHI ACROSS Asia and Europe into Paris is only an overnight flight—and on such a night one can see the entire world, unimaginable twenty years ago, squeezed into one airplane's cabin, its dreams and hopes tangled impossibly together.

Boarding the plane after dinner in the sweltering heat of the Punjab summer we found: two cheerful Japanese businessmen, briefcases in hand, apparently happy in a world where their country, stripped of power, prospered as never under Imperial banners; several earnest and attractive American tourists, cameras slung over necks; several English families; one African student— slim, erect, and handsome, broadcasting his sensitivity as he watched where he was to be seated; numerous Indians of all kinds; and, across the aisle from us, an Indian peasant mother, gold ornament in her nose, watching two little girls dressed as for a party in red velvet dresses and what could be their first pair of shoes.

Through the night to the first stop: the unbelievable heat of Bahrein on the Persian Gulf, that dry, searing, windless heat which even at night parches the lungs. At Bahrein several Indians left; two Americans—oil engineers, their drawl echoing the Southwest— boarded; a swarthy, nondescript man in European clothes climbed in; the Indian mother, her children now asleep, peered about bewildered. At Bahrein I found an airmail edition of the *Times* of London and as the plane climbed toward Cairo, my eye picked up a story on Indian immigrants to England. There had been a race riot in one of England's midland industrial towns. Now, said the story, the Indian Commissioners in England were occupying themselves with the problem

of "integration." Most of the recent immigrants had been women and children, which was helpful because the moral standard of lone Indian males in England was unusually improved when their families came to join them. Nonetheless, Indian officials were urging the newcomers to adjust because "the habits . . . which may have been used at home are strange and sometimes obnoxious to Britons." I turned to the Indian family again, changing worlds, and winced at the adjustments in sound, in clothing, in cooking they would have to accomplish in the slums of English milltowns.

Shortly before Cairo, the swarthy, nondescript passenger from Bahrein retired to the lavatory at the rear of the plane. When he came out he had shed his European clothes and was robed in flowing Arab white, his head crowned with the white desert Khaffiyeh, ringed with the black braid circlet. It was for him, I found, that the little knot of Arabs were waiting in Nasser's Cairo, and for him they applauded. At the Cairo crossroads the African student left and another stream of passengers from Asia made coupling with this flight to Europe: half a dozen Australians transferring in flight; several more American tourists; three German girls, secretaries in a Cairene German firm, en route home for a summer vacation in Dusseldorf.

IN DÜSSELDORF, the next stop, it was dawn; a damp chill had swept down the Rhine from the moors so that all of us shivered after the heat of the desert countries. At Düsseldorf, the flight lost the happy German girls, homecomers; the two neat Japanese businessmen, exploring trade; several American tourists. But the Indian mother and her children stayed aboard the plane as the rest of us went to the coffee shop to stretch our legs. I had watched the mother as we left the plane—she had woken the restless children and led them to the door. Timidly all three had begun to descend the stairs—and stopped midway in their descent to the ground. Suddenly, the chill, astringent air of Europe had greeted them, the first taste of cold ever for three lives spent in the lands of heat, the first sight of the West for which no one had prepared them. She had thrown her arms protectively about the two little girls, turned them about, and tugged them back up to the plane—their last link with Asia.

At Düsseldorf we picked up the last new contingent—German students en route to the United States; it was only an hour on to London where the Indian father shyly greeted his family at the gates and the company of flight dissolved, the Englishmen and Australians passing through customs, the Americans transshipping across the Atlantic to New York, a few of us going on to Paris where we arrived before lunch.

Always before, I had come to Europe across the Atlantic. To approach it now out of Asia was to see it entirely fresh in all its solid grandeur—and without the wrappings of postwar political cliché.

———

FOR YEARS SINCE the war, too many Europeans and Americans had relished the phrase "Little Europe." Europe had, indeed, seemed little when the war ended and it lay powerless between the giants of Russia and America. Yet now, coming in on Europe from Asia, I could see Europe as it really was—a giant in herself, a healthy giant at last. I had first seen Düsseldorf shortly after the war when fighter planes still fringed its airfields; from the field one could then see the chimneys on the ridges of the Ruhr, racked against the sky like pencils, three out of four of them smokeless. In those days Düsseldorf and its satellite cities—Essen, Mulheim, Duisberg, Solingen, Dortmund—were storm patches in an ocean of tumbled concrete, the waves of rubble frozen in a convulsion of violence. I had first come to Düsseldorf to be driven down the Rhine to visit a solemn old man whom American officials thought might just possibly make a decent guide for the civilian German government they wanted to form. His name was Konrad Adenauer. His flag in 1961 now flew above the airport; the new air terminal was more comfortable and efficient than the old terminal at LaGuardia Field; the food even at dawn in the restaurant was excellent and plentiful; and the plane lighting above the Rhine could show us a Ruhr below, whose healthy pulse recorded itself in smoke over an entire valley.

And Paris glowed. It was in Paris, where I lingered, that it slowly came to me that Europe was recovering not simply from the last war—but from two wars and perhaps from the wars of centuries. All the way in from Orly airport, I could see the new emblem of the French skyline—the traveling crane, forked across new buildings rising. Housing goes up in France now at the rate of over 300,000 lodgings a year, more rapidly than in America; for France is trying to catch up not with a twenty-year but a fifty-year lag. And Paris, its beds of fall geraniums blooming in every public place, was resplendent. By city ordinance, the city was scrubbing its buildings. Nor were the buildings being scrubbed simply of the grime accumulated since 1939 but of the grime that has frosted their beauty since 1914. As the buildings emerge from two generations of dark gray soot into the pastel beige and cream colors of French sandstone, one can see it as Frenchmen must have seen it in 1914 when France was great, and Europe, too.

Proudly, some French economists insisted that, since 1952, French industry had built plant and equipment equivalent to the entire previous investment in plant and equipment in all French history. I had lived in Paris through the Marshall Plan years of 1948 to 1952 and could tell myself that America's contribution to all this was still there like bedrock under foundation—the dams America had financed to make electricity, the steel for railways and bridges, the first rolling mills to stimulate the steel expansion of Lorraine, the food that had brought France through domestic crisis in tranquility. But all had passed in the flow of time and made no echo in anyone's conversation in 1961.

What we had purchased with the $5 billion sent to France, it was clear in 1961, was not friendship, and certainly not docility from the present government of France or any government of Europe. We had purchased Power; and Europe, its energies meshing and uniting for the first time as a result of American initiative, was a new power fact of primordial importance, of a power which by its nature must be on our side. If Communism had won China, then we had won Western Europe with its 200,000,000 people; and Europe with its skills, energies, genius, and numbers more than balanced China.

This was a victory; and it struck me now that it was characteristic of the kind of victories America has won and will win that they are entirely different from the kind of victories that Communism wins. No Communists were ever voted to power—they seize, orchestrate the public report of their work, announce each new success in a clap of thunder and stun the world. All victories of democracies—except those won in war—are won slowly, by the daily accumulation of achievement on achievement, by the slow clearing of the path of opportunity, and so, by their nature, are unrecognized. Yet it was essential, it seemed to me, that America as well as the Communists recognize the nature and appearance of its victories; for only then can America's limitations be measured and its vulnerability be curtailed.

It was six hours by jet back from Europe to America this fall of 1961—

lunch in Paris and (with the time differential) cocktails in New York. The transoceanic clipper of 1961 was, however, no longer received by the tower at Idlewild as the old Martin Flying Boat was received at the Golden Gate in 1941. At Idlewild, the plane was no longer an adventurer returning from the hazard of ocean flight; the chief hazard now was whether this blip on the radar-scope in the tower could be efficiently strained from all the other blips hurtling through the crowded sky into New York. The trip was routine, only the terminal traffic hazardous.

Yet the scrutiny of the flight from the tower of Idlewild involved far more than the routine of safety—and reached far beyond Idlewild. Long before this plane passed the mid-Atlantic, invisible webs of radar had been reaching for it in the air, caught it, checked, screened it as friendly or hostile, followed it down the long North Atlantic air lanes; and at Goose Bay Field in Labrador, the fighter planes had been ready to scramble and challenge it at any suspicious deviation.

Nothing now passes through the high air or any frontier of America that is not thus checked, instantly and with the utmost precision. For America is vulnerable now as it was not twenty years ago, and the world it has sought to make one has become frighteningly tight—to be girdled at leisure in a month, or by a missile in anger in an hour.

The homecoming traveler returns in 1961 from a world that waits and presses on America for responses just as impatiently as it waited in 1941. Only today, the impatience of the outer world is surpassed by that of Americans at home who demand of their leadership that single stroke of action, that one clear response which will settle all as it did in 1941, when a declaration of war, the exertion of force and power, could do it.

But this, ultimately, is the chief learning the returning traveler brings back from the second time around: that America and her friends, just as her Communist enemies, will never again be able to enjoy the luxury of the clear response, can never anticipate the broad clean stroke that settles all as it cleaves.

Whatever business there is to transact in making an orderly world will indeed wait on American leadership—but the business will stretch over decades and generations. And not simply because America is vulnerable—it is because of the manner in which, without recognizing it, we have helped change the world.

FOR WE HAVE carried with us for twenty years the same set of ideas that took us into The Great War and gave us victory. That war was, fundamentally, a civil war in the Atlantic civilization coupled with a raid by the Japanese into empires of Asia that lived in thrall to the Atlantic civilization. It seemed only natural that once Atlantic civilization had settled its violent differences and crushed the Japanese, order would automatically be re-established, the world become one, framed in a United Nations. And yet the war, creating and fostering the technologies to bind the world into one, freed its many communities to go their separate ways ungoverned by the traditions of the Atlantic World which, in 1941, seemed to promise to dominate it.

For there is in 1961 not One World. Nor even Two Worlds. There are a diverse medley of communities gathered together in a spurious unity by debate and technologies. These communities do not move in an orderly flow of history from one level to another, from each predictable stage to the next to a final common standard of civilization—rather, they exist in a common convulsion where old systems and myths die at differing rates, where men hunger for new faiths as much as they hunger for material well-being, where pent-up racial hatreds surge out of the past beyond the control of reason, where the impulses of science and technology speed men's hopes but never as fast as these hopes speed forward on their own.

To this kind of convulsion there can be no one clear response, no definite solution in the life of any man who lives in the twentieth century—and, above all, no final victory. The convulsion is too vast for any single strategy to master—either the democratic or the Communist.

What obscures the problem most is the dialogue in which for years it has been couched, ever since Woodrow Wilson cast the great phrase "making the world safe for democracy." In implementing the phrase we have ourselves confused two aspects of American life and thus confused others, too. We have

equated the spectacular material mastery of Americans over technology and industry with the more spectacular American mastery of a set of political principles that gives all men private dignity with liberty and order. We have learned, in the years of our aid programs, to be able to export our material skills. But where growing material well-being brings neither effective government (as in Vietnam) nor friendship (as in India) we have accepted these developments as failures of our political principles, too, and thus as defeat.

Rather than seeing our own political systems as the ultimate sophistication in the art of government, we have tried to export it to peoples unable to master even the more primitive forms of authoritarian government. We have extended aid to many peoples whether they were ready for it or not, whether or not (as in some cases) our aid weakened rather than strengthened the governments we were trying to help. We have committed ourselves to a theory which holds that political neuroses can in all cases be cured by material help.

A newer theory and newer strategy for 1961 and the years that follow require a more realistic appreciation of the many worlds that inhabit one globe.

For America, the world presents a series of gambles and each of a different kind. Some we will win and some we will lose—and, unless it comes to war, whether we win or lose depends essentially on how other people go about solving their own problems, on how they grope their way to govern themselves. The Surge that we have financed and launched all around the globe will continue now, in Japan as in Europe, in Asia as in Africa, at a rate that may be speeded or slowed by American participation—but it will continue in any event. The politics that flow from this surge will, however, be of other people's making. And only as other peoples clarify their politics will Americans have a chance to choose their own role. There will be victories for Atlantic civilization in the decades ahead—but such victories, as in the making of Europe's union, will be deceptively slow in appearance and the credit will be claimed primarily by others than Americans. So, too, there will be defeats—nor can Americans accept for themselves the blame of such defeats.

In such a world, it is essential for America to discriminate in strategy— to decide what we defend because liberty and our political principles are at stake; to decide what we defend because military security requires it; and to decide which areas of the globe must be left to grope their own way forward without either aid or intervention until they find governments that meet our standards either of decency or effectiveness.

Above all, it will be necessary not merely to defend. What we have lost by trying to defend all is the freedom of creative initiative. Bound by old formulas of lavish aid and timid intervention, we have attempted to administer a set of commitments around the globe in which material things have come first and the doctrines of democratic subversion have come last. Counterinitiative requires discrimination, the choice of where we concentrate our energies, the beginning of elaboration of a political doctrine flexible enough and infectious enough to make our material efforts in the communities we choose produce the political end-results we seek.

Somewhere between the exasperation of total withdrawal and the rigid overcommitment of too many burdens, American statecraft will have to find its middle way. Then only, and if we hold firm long enough, with our power ready but never used, will it be conceivable that, after generations, our political ideas will take root in alien cultures and explode, as liberty always does, when the condition of man is ripe.

SATURDAY REVIEW December 23, 1961

WHAT AMERICA MEANS TO ME

I am home in New England after many weeks on the campaign trail. From Boston's Faneuil Hall, through the hives of Florida's sun-washed condominiums, to the fashionable parlors of Manhattan, I have been listening again to the men who want to be President. This year more than ever they perplex me—for there must be some thread, some common concern that binds Americans together beneath the crackling overgrowth of party politics and clashing visions.

The only clue to an answer comes through a window as I sit looking down over a valley in my Connecticut town of Bridgewater. Beyond, a low gray ridge hides the cleft through which runs the Housatonic River. And beyond rises the hazy blue line of the Berkshires, and beyond that flows the Hudson. Still farther away lift the unseen Appalachians; and yet farther come the Great Plains, the Rockies, the tawny slopes that run down to the far edge of California.

I have crisscrossed this America for many years, looking for meaning. But it started here in New England. When I clear brush, I come across the overgrown stone walls of abandoned farms.

How other men's backs must have ached as they cleared fields, pulled the stumps, piled the stones! Then up over the ridge and down into the next valley rolled their wagons, over the next river, over the next range. On and on for 200 years—questing. Seeking opportunity for themselves and a promise for their children. They were followed by millions and millions more from Europe, and are followed today by what is the largest wave of immigrants in our history, legal and illegal alike, seeking the same opportunities, demanding the same promises for their children.

Only it is harder now. Not harder physically, to be sure. The men and women who pushed their plows with horses or oxen through unturned bottomland died young. But if they persisted, and they did, they could raise their own church, choose their own schoolmaster, and pass on their farms to their children—with no interference from a distant government. And if opportunity ran out, it was off and over the next ridge, all the way to the Wilamette Valley in Oregon.

But to get that far, government had to help—with the Cumberland trail over the Alleghenies, with subsidies to the railroads, with irrigation works to water the parched West. Government knew its role was to help.

It is harder now to think clearly about government in this year of the Bicentennial. It strikes me now that we are crossing some vast invisible ridge of the mind, that an era is ending. We are locked into a crush of big organizations that squeeze us all—Big Government, Big Business, Big Unions. From the candidates of the Right to the candidates of the Left, all are trying to pry open or keep open the opportunity which once lay only over the next ridge.

But it is far more complicated today. There will be no opportunity for black children in the ghettoes unless the government reorganizes our big cities; yet the cities will become all-black ghettoes if the government forces policies that drive white families away. If the government mangles American industry with controls, it can halt the engines of prosperity; yet if it does not restrain Big Business, there will be no little busi-

nessmen seeding the future with new enterprise.

This valley I see from my window needs government to keep its water clean and its air clear. This vast country needs government to save its cities and defend its shores and skies. But if government crushes opportunity—what then?

All these months I have been listening to men, one of whom will certainly be our next President, making their promises and seeking to keep opportunity open. None have real answers, as yet. All their discourse reduces to questions.

Perhaps that is the meaning of America: the unending question of how to enlarge opportunity while yet maintaining an orderly, balanced government of free men. That was the question with which America began. And the enduring vitality of the question is as important to the spirit of America as the answer any new President can give.

READER'S DIGEST August 1976

THE AMERICAN IDEA

When he died seven weeks ago, Theodore H. White, the Pulitzer Prize-winning author and journalist was working on an article for this magazine to commemorate the Fourth of July. Below is an excerpt from the unfinished piece.

The idea was there at the very beginning, well before Thomas Jefferson put it into words—and the idea rang the call.

Jefferson himself could not have imagined the reach of his call across the world in time to come when he wrote:

"We hold these truths to be self-evident, that all men are created equal, that they are endowed by their Creator with certain unalienable rights, that among these are life, liberty and the pursuit of happiness."

But over the next two centuries the call would reach the potato patches of Ireland, the ghettoes of Europe, the paddyfields of China, stirring farmers to leave their lands and townsmen their trades and thus unsettling all traditional civilization.

It is the call from Thomas Jefferson, embodied in the great statue that looks down the Narrows of New York Harbor, and in the immigrants who answered the call, that we now celebrate.

SOME OF THE first European Americans had come to the new continent to worship God in their own way, others to seek their fortunes. But, over a century-and-a-half, the new world changed those Europeans, above all the Englishmen who had come to North America. Neither King nor Court nor Church could stretch over the ocean to the wild continent. To survive, the first emigrants had to learn to govern themselves. But the freedom of the wilderness whetted their appetites for more freedoms. By the time Jefferson drafted his call, men were in the field fighting for those new-learned freedoms, killing and being killed by English soldiers, the best-trained troops in the world, supplied by the world's greatest navy. Only something worth dying for could unite American volunteers and keep them in the field—a stated cause, a flag, a nation they could call their own.

When, on the Fourth of July, 1776, the colonial leaders who had been meeting as a Continental Congress in Philadelphia voted to approve Jefferson's Declaration of Independence, it was not puffed-up rhetoric for them to pledge to each other "our lives, our fortunes and our sacred honor." Unless their new "United States of America" won the war, the Congressmen would be judged

659

traitors as relentlessly as would the irregulars-under-arms in the field. And all knew what English law allowed in the case of a traitor. The victim could be partly strangled; drawn, or disemboweled, while still alive, his entrails then burned and his body quartered.

The new Americans were tough men fighting for a very tough idea. How they won their battle is a story for the schoolbooks, studied by scholars, wrapped in myths by historians and poets. But what is important is the story of the idea that made them into a nation, the idea that had an explosive power undreamed of in 1776.

All other nations had come into being among people whose families had lived for time out of mind on the same land where they were born. Englishmen are English, Frenchmen are French, Chinese are Chinese, while their governments come and go; their national states can be torn apart and remade without losing their nationhood. But Americans are a nation born of an idea; not the place, but the idea, created the United States Government.

The story we celebrate this weekend is the story of how this idea worked itself out, how it stretched and changed and how the call for "life, liberty and the pursuit of happiness" does still, as it did in the beginning, mean different things to different people.

THE DEBATE BEGAN with the drafting of the Declaration of Independence. That task was left to Jefferson of Virginia, who spent two weeks in an up-stairs room in a Philadelphia boarding house penning a draft, while John Adams and Benjamin Franklin questioned, edited, hardened his phrases. By the end of that hot and muggy June, the three had reached agreement: the Declaration contained the ringing universal theme Jefferson strove for and, at the same time, voiced American grievances toughly enough to please the feisty Adams and the pragmatic Franklin. After brief debate, Congress passed it.

As the years wore on, the great debate expanded between Jefferson and Adams. The young nation flourished and Jefferson chose to think of America's promise as a call to all the world, its promises universal. A few weeks before he died, he wrote, "May it be to the world, what I believe it will be (to some parts sooner, to others later, but finally to all), the signal of arousing men to burst their chains." To Adams, the call meant something else—it was the call for *American* independence, the cornerstone of an *American* state.

Their argument ran through their successive Administrations. Adams, the second President, suspected the French Revolutionaries; Alien and Sedition Acts were passed during his term of office to protect the American state and its liberties against French subversion. But Jefferson, the third President, welcomed the French. The two men, once close friends, became archrivals. Still, as they grew old, their rivalry faded; there was glory enough to share in what they had made; in 1812, they began a correspondence that has since become classic, remembering and taking comfort in the triumphs of their youth.

Adams and Jefferson lived long lives and died on the same day—the Fourth of July, 1826, 50 years to the day from the Continental Congress's approval of the Declaration. Legend has it that Adams breathed on his death bed, "Thomas Jefferson still survives." As couriers set out from Braintree carrying the news of Adam's death, couriers were riding north from Virginia with the news of Jefferson's death. The couriers met in Philadelphia. Horace Greeley, then a youth in Vermont, later remembered: ". . . When we learned . . . that Thomas Jefferson and John Adams, the author and the great champion, respectively, of the Declaration, had both died on that day, and that the messengers bearing South and North, respectively, the tidings of their decease, had met in Philadelphia, under the shadow of that Hall in which our independence was declared, it seemed that a Divine attestation had solemnly hallowed and sanctified the great anniversary by the impressive ministration of Death."

THE NEW YORK TIMES MAGAZINE July 6, 1986

OUR TOWN, BRIDGEWATER, CONNECTICUT

I turn off Route 7 and there I am on [Connecticut] Route 133. I twist under the overpass, jounce through Brookfield and then cross the big bridge. And I'm home. I was born in New England seventy years ago, left Boston for the wars, traveled the world, criss-crossed the country in the presidential campaigns.

But when I cross the bridge on the Housatonic, the world lies behind. There's the winding drive along the creek—a bumpy road. But there's treeland on either side of me, bare in winter, a blaze of color in autumn; then I pass the cow pasture to the right, the slope of hills to the left, and I'm coming in. The firehouse first, the school, then the library, the town hall, then the village green. When guests are along, they ask, "Are we getting there now?" And I say, "You've just passed through town, that's all there is."

People who come with me want to know more. Most of them want to talk politics. What's the town like? they ask. That stumps me. They want the feel of the "grassroots," but grass grows quietly, I tell them. Visitors press. So I reel off figures. We have, more or less, 1600 people in our town—about the

same number who live in the apartment houses on the single block in New York where I keep my office. Bridgewater usually produces about sixteen babies a year. They grow up to be good kids—a little tom-foolery on Halloween, of course; some go off to college; some join the Marines; but mostly even the children like it here; they like to see their birthdays posted on the door of the village store. Those who can, stay on, but the cost of housing is squeezing the kids out. We'll have to do something about that. We take care of our old folks—but mostly that's a volunteer service, rushing the ailing to a hospital at night. Fire Department—that's volunteers, too. Taxes—we all groan at the taxes, but they can't be helped; you pay for what you get and we get peace in the streets here. Crime?—not much, if at all, and what there is is unpredictable.

But how about politics? visitors press on. To those out there beyond Route 7 I am supposed to be an expert on politics—on polling, tactics, plottings, delegate hunts; on Star Wars, the Japanese export push, the rise and fall of the international dollar, on immigration and its impact. But I am no expert on the politics of Bridgewater where I live. Our Congressional district had Democrats in Congress for twelve years—then it switched and elected a Republican woman, a good woman. Our first selectman was Republican from time out of mind—then the town switched and elected a Democrat as first selectman, a cattleman, good man. The town is still Republican but slowly going Democratic. No telling how it will vote in 1988.

But how about issues? they ask. Well, the issues here aren't the issues on television. War and Peace, for example. I guess the town is evenly divided on whether to press on with rearmament or to stop it. But we don't argue about that here in Bridgewater. Bridgewater has sent its men off to war ever since the Revolution; revolutionary veterans sleep in the graveyard just beyond the road crossing; the others who gave their lives in the wars that came later are memorialized on the village green, just under the Christmas tree. Race problems? None. The village is preponderantly Protestant, but Catholics and Jews live here happily, too. No frictions. I tell visitors of coming back here in 1976 from a visit in Plains, Georgia with Jimmy Carter. Plains is just about our size but it has a main street that divides white from black. The whites live in good homes, not as good as ours but more than respectable. On the other side of Main Street are black shanties and there's no contact between white and black. On our town we have no Main Street to divide us. We can argue about whether it's nicer to live down by the river bank or up on Skyline Ridge But it's nice to live here, anywhere.

Conversation with visitors runs out at this point because they don't want to hear about the issues that cut in Bridgewater. We put 75 percent of our tax money into the schools, and our parents argue furiously about the schools. We put another ten or twelve percent of our taxes into roads and we gripe, as I do, when the road to my house is rutted, pot-holed and getting worse. No one argues about the library; it's a fine library; we're proud of it—but it gets less than 1 percent and needs more money.

We do argue, though, about one thing: how to keep Bridgewater as it is and yet make room for growth and jobs and homes for our young people. We want to have the Christmas carols sung every year when the lights are lit on our big tree; we want to keep our Memorial Day parades; we like our big summer fair. And yet the world keeps crunching in on us. We have resistance lines—foremost the Conservation-Inland Wetlands Commission. I know something about that because my wife is involved in those politics. She is a writer of American history; she sits on the Commission with an engineer, a farmer, a screen writer, a journalist, trying to protect our brooks, our ponds, our maples and mosses from being overrun by outsiders who would transform us into another suburb of the Northeast megalopolis.

I stand with her, and the Commission, and the Selectmen. Bridgewater wants to remain Bridgewater. That's the binding force of politics here—to keep it a place where old ladies can walk in the streets and youngsters can ride their bikes.

Outside, I'm all for progress. But once across the big bridge, progress wears a different face. It means preserving our tranquility against distant forces which press against us. We like it here; we mean to keep it this way. That's basic politics in Bridgewater.

OUR TOWN May 1986

INDEX

Abner, Willoughby, 504
Abramovitz, Moses, 403
Acheson, Dean, 54, 57, 59, 63–64, 334
Ackley, Gardner, 397
Action-intellectuals, 387–431
Adams, Henry, 406, 408
Adams, John, 660
Adams, Gen. Paul D., 621
Adams, Sherman, 261
Adenauer, Konrad, 176, 178, 185, 188,
     190, 200, 202, 204–7, 209, 652
Afghanistan, 61
Africa, 211–26
Agency for International Development
     (AID), 55
Agnew, Spiro, 443–44, 456–58
Agriculture Department, U.S., 56
Ahmanson, Howard, 364–65
Air Force, U.S., 605–6, 614–15, 619–21,
     638
Alderedge, H. R., 351–52
Algeria, 215, 217–18, 223, 226
Aliaga, Serafin, 642
Alinsky, Saul, 525
Alioto, Mayor, 445
Allied High Commission, 190
Alsop, Steward, 536
America in Search of Itself (White), 444
American Automobile Association, 249,
     257, 260
American Legion, 348
American Revolution, 405
American Trucking Associations (ATA), 258
Anderson, Adm. George W., 613–14
Annamites, 560, 565–67
Arab-Israeli War (1967), 433–42
Arab League, 218
Argenlieu, Adm. Thierry d', 565

Army, Chinese, 111–13
Army, Jápanese, 5–7, 82, 94–95
Army, U.S., 61, 94, 122, 604–7, 613,
     615–16, 619–21, 638
Army, West German, 186–88, 196–201
Army Air Forces (AAF), U.S., 608–10
Arnold, William J., 549
Arvey, Jake, 234, 236, 360
Ascoli, Max, xxix–xx, 227
Ashcraft, E. P., 90
Asia. *See also specific countries.* Communists in,
     559–72, 576–79, 607, 645–48
     hatred of whites in, 23–25
     Japanese plans for, 82, 586
     U.S. foreign policy failure in, 4, 23–27
Atomic energy, action-intellectuals and,
     400, 416–17
Atomic Energy Commission (AEC), 56,
     421–22
August Uprising (1942), 649
Auschwitz, 168–69
Automobiles, 643–44

Back, Julian, xx
Backer, George, 236
Backlash, 534–45
Bagwell, Paul, 609
Bahrein, 651
Bailey, Joe, 353
Bailey, John, 234–36, 267, 297
Baker, James A., III, 628
Baker, John Earl, 77
Baker, Newton D., 408
Baldrige, Malcolm, 590, 597
Bali, George, 16, 60–61
Banfield, Edward C., 391
Bangkok, 648
Bank of Japan, 597

THEODORE H. WHITE was born in Boston in 1915. He attended the Boston Public Latin School, then went on to Harvard College, where he studied history. He first won wide attention as a war correspondent in China during World War II and, after the war, as coauthor of *Thunder Out of China*. He spent the postwar years reporting the recovery of Europe, where he wrote *Fire in the Ashes*. He returned to America in 1953.

Starting in the mid-1950s, Theodore White reported American politics, chiefly in his *The Making of the President* series, the first volume of which won a Pulitzer Prize in 1962. *America in Search of Itself* (1982) was the climax of that series, the story of the revolutionary transformation of contemporary American politics. He also wrote *Breach of Faith: The Fall of Richard Nixon* and *In Search of History: A Personal Adventure*, two novels, one play, and several prizewinning television documentaries.

Teddy White, as he was universally known, died in 1986.

EDWARD T. THOMPSON, former Editor-in-Chief of *Reader's Digest,* has been a magazine journalist for forty years. A graduate of The Lawrenceville School and The Massachusetts Institute of Technology (1949), he briefly pursued a career in chemical engineering before becoming a writer for McGraw-Hill's *Chemical Engineering* magazine. From there he went to *Fortune* and then in 1960 to *The Digest*. He lives with his wife, Susan, in Waccabuc, New York, where he consults for various publications and continues his own writing and editing.